TRAINERS

JUMPS STATISTICS 2017-2018

Published in 2018 by Raceform Ltd
27 Kingfisher Court, Hambridge Road, Newbury, Berkshire RG14 5SJ

A catalogue record for this book is available from the British Library

ISBN 978-1-910497-62-3

Printed in Great Britain by Page Bros Print, Norwich

CONTENTS

WINNING TRAINERS

Jumps statistics for the 2017-18 season for winning British-based trainers. Trainers with less than ten winners are shown with abbreviated statistics.

Winning horses preceded by an asterisk joined the stable during the course of the season.

An asterisk following the horse's name denotes a switch to another trainer during the season.

Course and Month tables are for the last five seasons starting on 28 April 2013 and ending on 28 April 2018.

N W ALEXANDER

KINNESTON, PERTH & KINROSS

	No. of Hrs	Races Run	1st	2nd	3rd	Unpl	Per cent	£1 Level Stake
NH Flat	6	12	0	0	1	11	0.0	-12.00
Hurdles	29	94	5	12	5	72	5.3	-40.75
Chases	25	79	7	12	9	51	8.9	-24.17
Totals	50	185	12	24	15	134	6.5	-76.92
16-17	45	192	20	12	23	137	10.4	-69.37
15-16	48	226	31	24	25	145	13.7	-64.08

BY MONTH

NH Flat	W-R	Per cent	£1 Level Stake	Hurdles	W-R	Per cent	£1 Level Stake
May	0-1	0.0	-1.00	May	0-9	0.0	-9.00
June	0-0	0.0	0.00	June	0-3	0.0	-3.00
July	0-0	0.0	0.00	July	0-2	0.0	-2.00
August	0-0	0.0	0.00	August	0-2	0.0	-2.00
September	0-0	0.0	0.00	September	1-2	50.0	+1.25
October	0-0	0.0	0.00	October	1-8	12.5	+26.00
November	0-2	0.0	-2.00	November	2-11	18.2	0.00
December	0-2	0.0	-2.00	December	0-10	0.0	-10.00
January	0-3	0.0	-3.00	January	1-13	7.7	-8.00
February	0-0	0.0	0.00	February	0-11	0.0	-11.00
March	0-3	0.0	-3.00	March	0-6	0.0	-6.00
April	0-1	0.0	-1.00	April	0-17	0.0	-17.00

Chases	W-R	Per cent	£1 Level Stake	Totals	W-R	Per cent	£1 Level Stake
May	0-6	0.0	-6.00	May	0-16	0.0	-16.00
June	0-3	0.0	-3.00	June	0-6	0.0	-6.00
July	0-0	0.0	0.00	July	0-2	0.0	-2.00
August	0-0	0.0	0.00	August	0-2	0.0	-2.00
September	0-0	0.0	0.00	September	1-2	50.0	+1.25
October	0-3	0.0	-3.00	October	1-11	9.1	+23.00
November	0-9	0.0	-9.00	November	2-22	9.1	-11.00
December	2-7	28.6	+7.50	December	2-19	10.5	-4.50
January	0-16	0.0	-16.00	January	1-32	3.1	-27.00
February	2-11	18.2	-4.17	February	2-22	9.1	-15.17
March	0-9	0.0	-9.00	March	0-18	0.0	-18.00
April	3-15	20.0	+18.50	April	3-33	9.1	+0.50

DISTANCE

Hurdles	W-R	Per cent	£1 Level Stake	Chases	W-R	Per cent	£1 Level Stake
2m-2m3f	2-45	4.4	-36.25	2m-2m3f	0-8	0.0	-8.00
2m4f-2m7f	2-25	8.0	+14.50	2m4f-2m7f	7-45	15.6	+9.83
3m+	1-24	4.2	-19.00	3m+	0-26	0.0	-26.00

TYPE OF RACE

Non-Handicaps	W-R	Per cent	£1 Level Stake	Handicaps	W-R	Per cent	£1 Level Stake
Nov Hrdls	0-18	0.0	-18.00	Nov Hrdls	0-5	0.0	-5.00
Hrdls	0-7	0.0	-7.00	Hrdls	5-64	7.8	-10.75
Nov Chs	0-3	0.0	-3.00	Nov Chs	1-5	20.0	-0.67
Chases	0-8	0.0	-8.00	Chases	4-56	7.1	-14.00
Sell/Claim	0-0	0.0	0.00	Sell/Claim	0-0	0.0	0.00

RACE CLASS

	W-R	Per cent	£1 Level Stake
Class 1	0-1	0.0	-1.00
Class 2	0-11	0.0	-11.00
Class 3	4-27	14.8	-5.00
Class 4	7-90	7.8	-13.92
Class 5	1-52	1.9	-42.00
Class 6	0-4	0.0	-4.00

FIRST TIME OUT

	W-R	Per cent	£1 Level Stake
Bumpers	0-6	0.0	-6.00
Hurdles	1-25	4.0	-19.50
Chases	0-19	0.0	-19.00
Totals	1-50	2.0	-44.50

JOCKEYS

	W-R	Per cent	£1 Level Stake
Lucy Alexander	7-72	9.7	+6.58
Stephen Mulqueen	2-13	15.4	-4.50
Grant Cockburn	2-49	4.1	-33.50
Mr Kit Alexander	1-29	3.4	-23.50

COURSE RECORD

	Total W-R	Non-Hndcps Hurdles	Chases	Hndcps Hurdles	Chases	NH Flat	Per cent	£1 Level Stake
Kelso	4-35	0-6	0-2	3-15	1-7	0-5	11.4	+24.50
Newcastle	3-17	0-1	0-0	0-2	3-13	0-1	17.6	+7.50
Haydock	2-11	0-1	0-1	0-3	2-6	0-0	18.2	0.00
Wetherby	1-5	0-0	0-0	0-2	1-3	0-0	20.0	-0.67
Hexham	1-17	0-3	0-1	1-7	0-6	0-0	5.9	-11.50
Perth	1-27	0-6	0-2	1-13	0-5	0-1	3.7	-23.75

WINNING HORSES

Horse	Races Run	1st	2nd	3rd	£
Lake View Lad	7	2	2	3	17318
Clan Legend	5	2	1	0	13776
Gold Opera	6	1	0	0	7408
Landecker	9	1	2	0	6243
*Massini's Lady	5	1	2	0	4809
*Always Tipsy	2	1	0	0	4614
Bertalus	5	1	0	1	4159
Benny's Secret	5	2	0	0	6498
Jet Master	7	1	0	1	3165
Total winning prize-money					£67990
Favourites	1-6	16.7%			-3.50

R J ALFORD

COLLOMPTON, DEVON

	No. of Hrs	Races Run	1st	2nd	3rd	Unpl	Per cent	£1 Level Stake
NH Flat	0	0	0	0	0	0	0.0	0.00
Hurdles	0	0	0	0	0	0	0.0	0.00
Chases	1	1	1	0	0	0	100.0	+2.00
Totals	1	1	1	0	0	0	100.0	+2.00
15-16	1	1	0	0	0	1	0.0	-1.00

JOCKEYS

	W-R	Per cent	£1 Level Stake
Rex Dingle	1-1	100.0	+2.00

COURSE RECORD

	Total W-R	Non-Hndcps Hurdles	Chases	Hndcps Hurdles	Chases	NH Flat	Per cent	£1 Level Stake
Exeter	1-1	0-0	1-1	0-0	0-0	0-0	100.0	+2.00

WINNING HORSES

Horse	Races Run	1st	2nd	3rd	£
*Herbert Park	1	1	0	0	2089
Total winning prize-money					£2089
Favourites	0-0		0.0%		0.00

JOCKEYS

	W-R	Per cent	£1 Level Stake
Mr Sam Jukes	1-2	50.0	+3.00

COURSE RECORD

	Total W-R	Non-Hndcps Hurdles	Chases	Hndcps Hurdles	Chases	NH Flat	Per cent	£1 Level Stake
Worcester	1-1	0-0	1-1	0-0	0-0	0-0	100.0	+4.00

WINNING HORSES

Horse	Races Run	1st	2nd	3rd	£
Rye Cross	2	1	0	0	1248
Total winning prize-money					£1248
Favourites	0-0		0.0%		0.00

S ALLWOOD
WHITCHURCH, SHROPSHIRE

	No. of Hrs	Races Run	1st	2nd	3rd	Unpl	Per cent	£1 Level Stake
NH Flat	0	0	0	0	0	0	0.0	0.00
Hurdles	0	0	0	0	0	0	0.0	0.00
Chases	1	2	1	0	0	1	50.0	+15.00
Totals	1	2	1	0	0	1	50.0	+15.00
16-17	1	1	0	0	0	1	0.0	-1.00
15-16	2	2	0	0	0	2	0.0	-2.00

JOCKEYS

	W-R	Per cent	£1 Level Stake
Mr Edward Glassonbury	1-2	50.0	+15.00

COURSE RECORD

	Total W-R	Non-Hndcps Hurdles	Chases	Hndcps Hurdles	Chases	NH Flat	Per cent	£1 Level Stake
Sedgefield	1-1	0-0	1-1	0-0	0-0	0-0	100.0	+16.00

WINNING HORSES

Horse	Races Run	1st	2nd	3rd	£
*Mantou	2	1	0	0	1872
Total winning prize-money					£1872
Favourites	0-0		0.0%		0.00

MICHAEL APPLEBY
OAKHAM, RUTLAND

	No. of Hrs	Races Run	1st	2nd	3rd	Unpl	Per cent	£1 Level Stake
NH Flat	5	7	0	0	1	6	0.0	-7.00
Hurdles	7	17	1	0	1	15	5.9	-11.50
Chases	2	3	0	0	0	3	0.0	-3.00
Totals	11	27	1	0	2	24	3.7	-21.50
16-17	12	32	5	3	5	19	15.6	+9.50
15-16	13	44	1	2	6	35	2.3	-33.00

JOCKEYS

	W-R	Per cent	£1 Level Stake
Jack Sherwood	1-7	14.3	-1.50

COURSE RECORD

	Total W-R	Non-Hndcps Hurdles	Chases	Hndcps Hurdles	Chases	NH Flat	Per cent	£1 Level Stake
Fakenham	1-4	0-0	0-0	1-3	0-0	0-1	25.0	+1.50

WINNING HORSES

Horse	Races Run	1st	2nd	3rd	£
Beyeh	8	1	0	0	4159
Total winning prize-money					£4159
Favourites	0-0		0.0%		0.00

MISS E ALVIS
DYMOCK, GLOUCES

	No. of Hrs	Races Run	1st	2nd	3rd	Unpl	Per cent	£1 Level Stake
NH Flat	0	0	0	0	0	0	0.0	0.00
Hurdles	0	0	0	0	0	0	0.0	0.00
Chases	1	2	1	0	0	1	50.0	+3.00
Totals	1	2	1	0	0	1	50.0	+3.00

PETER ATKINSON
YAFFORTH, N YORKS

	No. of Hrs	Races Run	1st	2nd	3rd	Unpl	Per cent	£1 Level Stake
NH Flat	1	1	0	0	0	1	0.0	-1.00
Hurdles	3	17	5	5	0	7	29.4	-0.19
Chases	0	0	0	0	0	0	0.0	0.00
Totals	3	18	5	5	0	8	27.8	-1.19

16-17	2	12	4	1	3	4	33.3	+9.50
15-16	1	2	0	0	0	2	0.0	-2.00

JOCKEYS

	W-R	Per cent	£1 Level Stake
Henry Brooke	4-8	50.0	+3.32
Finian O'Toole	1-9	11.1	-3.50

COURSE RECORD

	Total W-R	Non-Hndcps Hurdles	Chases	Hndcps Hurdles	Chases	NH Flat	Per cent	£1 Level Stake
Doncaster	2-3	0-1	0-0	2-2	0-0	0-0	66.7	+4.50
Cartmel	1-1	1-1	0-0	0-0	0-0	0-0	100.0	+0.61
Catterick	1-1	0-0	0-0	1-1	0-0	0-0	100.0	+4.50
Southwell	1-1	1-1	0-0	0-0	0-0	0-0	100.0	+1.20

WINNING HORSES

Horse	Races Run	1st	2nd	3rd	£
Irish Roe	8	4	2	0	28418
Reverant Cust	8	1	3	0	4484
Total winning prize-money					**£32902**
Favourites	**4-4**		**100.0%**		**7.31**

KIM BAILEY

ANDOVERSFORD, GLOUCS

	No. of Hrs	Races Run	1st	2nd	3rd	Unpl	Per cent	£1 Level Stake
NH Flat	20	38	9	3	5	21	23.7	+14.73
Hurdles	52	148	29	23	12	84	19.6	-22.61
Chases	31	105	9	21	14	61	8.6	-78.97
Totals	**83**	**291**	**47**	**47**	**31**	**166**	**16.2**	**-86.85**
16-17	86	323	41	58	43	181	12.7	-81.01
15-16	76	276	44	37	34	161	15.9	-77.21

BY MONTH

NH Flat	W-R	Per cent	£1 Level Stake	Hurdles	W-R	Per cent	£1 Level Stake
May	2-7	28.6	-1.63	May	2-13	15.4	-4.50
June	0-1	0.0	-1.00	June	1-3	33.3	-1.20
July	0-0	0.0	0.00	July	0-3	0.0	-3.00
August	0-0	0.0	0.00	August	0-1	0.0	-1.00
September	0-0	0.0	0.00	September	0-2	0.0	-2.00
October	0-1	0.0	-1.00	October	4-20	20.0	+7.67
November	2-3	66.7	+21.00	November	6-30	20.0	-4.38
December	1-7	14.3	+4.00	December	5-19	26.3	+3.11
January	1-3	33.3	+2.00	January	4-14	28.6	-0.75
February	1-6	16.7	-2.75	February	3-13	23.1	-4.06
March	1-5	20.0	-2.80	March	2-12	16.7	-4.88
April	1-5	20.0	-3.09	April	2-18	11.1	-7.63

Chases	W-R	Per cent	£1 Level Stake	Totals	W-R	Per cent	£1 Level Stake
May	0-4	0.0	-4.00	May	4-24	16.7	-10.13
June	1-3	33.3	-0.13	June	2-7	28.6	-2.33
July	1-1	100.0	+2.25	July	1-4	25.0	-0.75

August	1-3	33.3	-0.13	August	1-4	25.0	-1.13
September	0-2	0.0	-2.00	September	0-4	0.0	-4.00
October	0-12	0.0	-12.00	October	4-33	12.1	-5.33
November	1-16	6.3	-12.25	November	9-49	18.4	+4.37
December	2-20	10.0	-14.06	December	8-46	17.4	-6.95
January	2-12	16.7	-6.50	January	7-29	24.1	-5.25
February	0-11	0.0	-11.00	February	4-30	13.3	-17.81
March	1-11	9.1	-9.17	March	4-28	14.3	-16.85
April	0-10	0.0	-10.00	April	3-33	9.1	-20.72

DISTANCE

Hurdles	W-R	Per cent	£1 Level Stake	Chases	W-R	Per cent	£1 Level Stake
2m-2m3f	4-36	11.1	-17.55	2m-2m3f	2-12	16.7	-6.06
2m4f-2m7f	16-77	20.8	-8.59	2m4f-2m7f	3-35	8.6	-26.00
3m+	9-35	25.7	+3.53	3m+	4-58	6.9	-46.92

TYPE OF RACE

Non-Handicaps	W-R	Per cent	£1 Level Stake	Handicaps	W-R	Per cent	£1 Level Stake
Nov Hrdls	22-67	32.8	+18.94	Nov Hrdls	0-5	0.0	-5.00
Hrdls	4-15	26.7	+8.20	Hrdls	3-58	5.2	-41.75
Nov Chs	2-10	20.0	-4.42	Nov Chs	0-5	0.0	-5.00
Chases	0-8	0.0	-8.00	Chases	5-63	7.9	-46.63
Sell/Claim	0-0	0.0	0.00	Sell/Claim	0-0	0.0	0.00

RACE CLASS / FIRST TIME OUT

Race Class	W-R	Per cent	£1 Level Stake	First Time Out	W-R	Per cent	£1 Level Stake
Class 1	2-21	9.5	-14.25	Bumpers	5-20	25.0	+20.38
Class 2	1-18	5.6	-14.00	Hurdles	4-39	10.3	-18.75
Class 3	11-63	17.5	-24.92	Chases	2-24	8.3	-17.38
Class 4	27-145	18.6	-27.63				
Class 5	4-35	11.4	-13.55	Totals	11-83	13.3	-15.75
Class 6	2-9	22.2	+8.50				

JOCKEYS

	W-R	Per cent	£1 Level Stake
David Bass	29-184	15.8	-63.83
Mikey Hamill	10-54	18.5	-7.14
Sean Bowen	3-4	75.0	+4.58
Dave Crosse	2-5	40.0	+2.38
Richard Condon	2-5	40.0	+15.00
Tom Bellamy	1-23	4.3	-21.83

COURSE RECORD

	Total W-R	Non-Hndcps Hurdles	Chases	Hndcps Hurdles	Chases	NH Flat	Per cent	£1 Level Stake
Ludlow	10-31	6-10	0-1	0-5	0-8	4-7	32.3	+9.53
Huntingdon	4-25	3-7	0-0	1-6	0-7	0-5	16.0	-0.50
Chepstow	3-12	2-4	0-0	0-3	1-4	0-1	25.0	-3.97
Warwick	3-15	1-4	0-0	0-6	0-1	2-4	20.0	+8.00
Worcester	3-17	1-7	0-2	0-4	2-3	0-1	17.6	-9.71
Catterick	2-3	0-0	0-0	0-0	1-2	1-1	66.7	+0.64
Newbury	2-4	1-1	0-0	0-0	1-3	0-0	50.0	+2.70
Musselbgh	2-5	1-1	0-1	1-2	0-1	0-0	40.0	+2.25

Course	Total						Per cent	£1 Level Stake
Leicester	2-6	2-4	0-0	0-0	0-2	0-0	33.3	+6.75
Southwell	2-10	1-4	0-0	0-3	0-1	1-2	20.0	+5.50
Wetherby	2-10	1-3	1-1	0-3	0-3	0-0	20.0	-6.72
Uttoxeter	2-16	1-5	1-1	0-3	0-6	0-1	12.5	-10.45
Fontwell	1-3	0-1	0-0	0-1	1-1	0-0	33.3	-0.13
Haydock	1-4	1-1	0-1	0-0	0-2	0-0	25.0	-0.75
Hereford	1-4	0-1	0-0	0-1	1-1	0-1	25.0	-1.13
Ffos Las	1-5	1-2	0-0	0-0	0-3	0-0	20.0	0.00
Doncaster	1-6	0-2	0-0	0-1	0-2	1-1	16.7	-2.75
Lingfield	1-6	1-1	0-0	0-1	0-4	0-0	16.7	+1.50
Ascot	1-8	1-3	0-0	0-1	0-2	0-2	12.5	-5.00
Wincanton	1-8	1-3	0-0	0-2	0-3	0-0	12.5	0.00
Kempton	1-9	1-3	0-0	0-2	0-3	0-1	11.1	-6.13
Towcester	1-13	0-3	0-2	1-4	0-1	0-3	7.7	-5.50

WINNING HORSES

Horse	Races Run	1st	2nd	3rd	£
Vinndication	4	4	0	0	33590
First Flow	5	3	0	0	26832
Another Venture	7	2	1	1	25970
Red River	3	2	0	1	16457
Cresswell Legend	6	3	1	0	11956
Sainte Ladylime	6	2	3	0	13738
Lake Field	6	2	1	1	11498
Sonneofpresenting	7	3	1	1	17036
Robin The Raven	5	3	0	1	13841
Rosmuc Relay	3	2	0	1	10267
Bandon Roc	6	1	1	0	5269
Silver Kayf	6	2	0	1	9097
*Station Master	5	2	0	1	9097
Kilfilum Cross	4	2	1	0	8288
Dandy Dan	5	2	1	1	7148
Laval Noir	4	1	0	0	3899
Imperial Aura	2	1	0	1	3899
Sea Story	5	2	0	0	7018
El Presente	5	1	0	3	3249
Mon Palois	6	2	0	0	5848
Two For Gold	3	2	0	0	5198
Rhaegar	6	2	1	1	1949
Diamond Gait	4	1	1	0	1949
Total winning prize-money					**£253093**
Favourites	20-59		33.9%		-10.00

G T H BAILEY

HOLDENBY, NORTHANTS

	No. of Hrs	Races Run	1st	2nd	3rd	Unpl	Per cent	£1 Level Stake
NH Flat	0	0	0	0	0	0	0.0	0.00
Hurdles	0	0	0	0	0	0	0.0	0.00
Chases	1	3	3	0	0	0	100.0	+5.14
Totals	1	3	3	0	0	0	100.0	+5.14
16-17	3	4	0	1	2	1	0.0	-4.00
15-16	4	6	2	2	1	1	33.3	-1.70

JOCKEYS

	W-R	Per cent	£1 Level Stake
Mr Thomas Mcclorey	3-3	100.0	+5.14

COURSE RECORD

	Total W-R	Non-Hndcps Hurdles	Chases	Hndcps Hurdles	Chases	NH Flat	Per cent	£1 Level Stake
Southwell	1-1	0-0	1-1	0-0	0-0	0-0	100.0	+2.25
Warwick	1-1	0-0	1-1	0-0	0-0	0-0	100.0	+2.75
Wetherby	1-1	0-0	1-1	0-0	0-0	0-0	100.0	+0.14

WINNING HORSES

Horse	Races Run	1st	2nd	3rd	£
*Galway Jack	3	3	0	0	5636
Total winning prize-money					**£5636**
Favourites	1-1		100.0%		0.14

CAROLINE BAILEY

HOLDENBY, NORTHANTS

	No. of Hrs	Races Run	1st	2nd	3rd	Unpl	Per cent	£1 Level Stake
NH Flat	1	1	0	0	0	1	0.0	-1.00
Hurdles	13	46	5	5	5	31	10.9	-20.47
Chases	12	47	5	8	9	25	10.6	-24.25
Totals	22	94	10	13	14	57	10.6	-45.72
16-17	30	129	18	18	15	78	14.0	-40.33
15-16	26	92	16	19	10	47	17.4	+14.21

BY MONTH

NH Flat	W-R	Per cent	£1 Level Stake	Hurdles	W-R	Per cent	£1 Level Stake
May	0-0	0.0	0.00	May	0-2	0.0	-2.00
June	0-0	0.0	0.00	June	0-1	0.0	-1.00
July	0-0	0.0	0.00	July	0-4	0.0	-4.00
August	0-0	0.0	0.00	August	0-2	0.0	-2.00
September	0-0	0.0	0.00	September	0-3	0.0	-3.00
October	0-0	0.0	0.00	October	1-4	25.0	+1.50
November	0-0	0.0	0.00	November	0-6	0.0	-6.00
December	0-0	0.0	0.00	December	1-4	25.0	+0.33
January	0-0	0.0	0.00	January	2-4	50.0	+2.70
February	0-0	0.0	0.00	February	0-8	0.0	-8.00
March	0-1	0.0	-1.00	March	0-4	0.0	-4.00
April	0-0	0.0	0.00	April	1-4	25.0	+5.00

Chases	W-R	Per cent	£1 Level Stake	Totals	W-R	Per cent	£1 Level Stake
May	1-8	12.5	-5.25	May	1-10	10.0	-7.25
June	1-4	25.0	+4.50	June	1-5	20.0	+3.50
July	0-4	0.0	-4.00	July	0-8	0.0	-8.00
August	0-2	0.0	-2.00	August	0-4	0.0	-4.00
September	0-3	0.0	-3.00	September	0-6	0.0	-6.00
October	1-3	33.3	+3.00	October	2-7	28.6	+4.50
November	0-8	0.0	-8.00	November	0-14	0.0	-14.00

December	0-5	0.0	-5.00	December	1-9	11.1	-4.67
January	0-3	0.0	-3.00	January	2-7	28.6	-0.30
February	0-3	0.0	-3.00	February	0-11	0.0	-11.00
March	0-1	0.0	-1.00	March	0-6	0.0	-6.00
April	2-3	66.7	+2.50	April	3-7	42.9	+7.50

DISTANCE

Hurdles	W-R	Per cent	£1 Level Stake	Chases	W-R	Per cent	£1 Level Stake
2m-2m3f	0-20	0.0	-20.00	2m-2m3f	1-11	9.1	-5.00
2m4f-2m7f	5-18	27.8	+7.53	2m4f-2m7f	4-25	16.0	-8.25
3m+	0-8	0.0	-8.00	3m+	0-11	0.0	-11.00

TYPE OF RACE

Non-Handicaps	W-R	Per cent	£1 Level Stake	Handicaps	W-R	Per cent	£1 Level Stake
Nov Hrdls	0-9	0.0	-9.00	Nov Hrdls	0-1	0.0	-1.00
Hrdls	0-4	0.0	-4.00	Hrdls	4-29	13.8	-5.67
Nov Chs	1-4	25.0	-1.38	Nov Chs	0-3	0.0	-3.00
Chases	1-1	100.0	+1.75	Chases	2-36	5.6	-24.63
Sell/Claim	1-1	100.0	+1.20	Sell/Claim	0-0	0.0	0.00

RACE CLASS / FIRST TIME OUT

	W-R	Per cent	£1 Level Stake		W-R	Per cent	£1 Level Stake
Class 1	0-1	0.0	-1.00	Bumpers	0-1	0.0	-1.00
Class 2	0-5	0.0	-5.00	Hurdles	1-11	9.1	-5.50
Class 3	1-17	5.9	-12.50	Chases	1-10	10.0	-7.25
Class 4	7-41	17.1	-2.17				
Class 5	1-29	3.4	-26.80	Totals	2-22	9.1	-13.75
Class 6	1-1	100.0	+1.75				

JOCKEYS

	W-R	Per cent	£1 Level Stake
Sean Bowen	7-47	14.9	-10.09
Mr Thomas Mcclorey	2-7	28.6	+1.63
Miss Gina Andrews	1-2	50.0	+0.75

COURSE RECORD

	Total W-R	Non-Hndcps Hurdles	Non-Hndcps Chases	Hndcps Hurdles	Hndcps Chases	NH Flat	Per cent	£1 Level Stake
Southwell	3-22	0-6	1-1	1-4	1-11	0-0	13.6	-5.25
Leicester	2-4	1-1	0-0	1-1	0-2	0-0	50.0	+2.70
Fakenham	1-4	0-0	0-0	0-0	1-4	0-0	25.0	-1.13
Towcester	1-6	0-0	1-2	0-1	0-3	0-0	16.7	-3.38
Mrket Rsn	1-10	0-1	0-0	1-3	0-6	0-0	10.0	-1.00
Uttoxeter	1-11	0-0	0-0	1-6	0-5	0-0	9.1	-6.67
Huntingdon	1-12	0-3	0-0	0-4	1-4	0-1	8.3	-6.00

WINNING HORSES

Horse	Races Run	1st	2nd	3rd	£
Malapie	10	3	0	2	18573
McCabe Creek	7	1	3	0	7473
Global Domination	6	1	2	2	5458
Reckless Behavior	8	1	2	1	4874

Early Retirement	4	1	1	0	3899
Gold Ingot	6	1	0	1	3899
Robin Of Locksley	5	1	1	1	3834
Galway Jack	1	1	0	0	1872
Total winning prize-money					**£49882**
Favourites	3-15		20.0%		-5.59

ANDREW BALDING

KINGSCLERE, HANTS

	No. of Hrs	Races Run	1st	2nd	3rd	Unpl	Per cent	£1 Level Stake
NH Flat	0	0	0	0	0	0	0.0	0.00
Hurdles	1	3	1	0	2	0	33.3	-1.00
Chases	0	0	0	0	0	0	0.0	0.00
Totals	1	3	1	0	2	0	33.3	-1.00
16-17	1	2	0	0	0	2	0.0	-2.00

JOCKEYS

	W-R	Per cent	£1 Level Stake
Paddy Brennan	1-3	33.3	-1.00

COURSE RECORD

	Total W-R	Non-Hndcps Hurdles	Non-Hndcps Chases	Hndcps Hurdles	Hndcps Chases	NH Flat	Per cent	£1 Level Stake
Fontwell	1-1	1-1	0-0	0-0	0-0	0-0	100.0	+1.00

WINNING HORSES

Horse	Races Run	1st	2nd	3rd	£
*Night Of Glory	3	1	0	2	4094
Total winning prize-money					**£4094**
Favourites	653-654		99.8%		652.00

RICHARD J BANDEY

TADLEY, HANTS

	No. of Hrs	Races Run	1st	2nd	3rd	Unpl	Per cent	£1 Level Stake
NH Flat	1	1	0	0	1	0	0.0	-1.00
Hurdles	0	0	0	0	0	0	0.0	0.00
Chases	4	4	1	0	0	3	25.0	+9.00
Totals	5	5	1	0	1	3	20.0	+8.00
16-17	1	1	0	0	1	0	0.0	-1.00
15-16	2	2	0	0	0	2	0.0	-2.00

JOCKEYS

	W-R	Per cent	£1 Level Stake
Mr Martin McIntyre	1-3	33.3	+10.00

COURSE RECORD

	Total W-R	Non-Hndcps Hurdles	Non-Hndcps Chases	Hndcps Hurdles	Hndcps Chases	NH Flat	Per cent	£1 Level Stake
Cheltenham	1-2	0-0	1-2	0-0	0-0	0-0	50.0	+11.00

WINNING HORSES

Horse	Races Run	1st	2nd	3rd	£
Woodfleet	1	1	0	0	4367
Total winning prize-money					**£4367**
Favourites	**0-0**		**0.0%**		**0.00**

JACK R BARBER

CREWKERNE, SOMERSET

	No. of Hrs	Races Run	1st	2nd	3rd	Unpl	Per cent	£1 Level Stake
NH Flat	3	5	0	0	1	4	0.0	-5.00
Hurdles	12	30	5	6	2	17	16.7	+7.00
Chases	4	11	3	1	2	5	27.3	-0.17
Totals	**16**	**46**	**8**	**7**	**5**	**26**	**17.4**	**+1.83**
16-17	2	3	1	0	1	1	33.3	-1.56
15-16	3	3	1	0	0	2	33.3	-1.17

JOCKEYS

	W-R	Per cent	£1 Level Stake
Nick Scholfield	5-30	16.7	+2.83
Noel Fehily	1-1	100.0	+4.00
Bryony Frost	1-1	100.0	+2.00
Ian Popham	1-5	20.0	+2.00

COURSE RECORD

	Total W-R	Non-Hndcps Hurdles	Chases	Hndcps Hurdles	Chases	NH Flat	Per cent	£1 Level Stake
Taunton	2-9	1-5	0-0	1-2	0-2	0-0	22.2	+9.00
Warwick	1-1	0-0	0-0	0-0	1-1	0-0	100.0	+2.00
Plumpton	1-2	0-0	0-0	1-2	0-0	0-0	50.0	+5.00
Fontwell	1-3	0-0	0-0	0-1	1-1	0-1	33.3	+0.50
Southwell	1-4	1-2	0-0	0-0	0-1	0-1	25.0	+1.00
Wincanton	1-4	1-4	0-0	0-0	0-0	0-0	25.0	+3.00
Exeter	1-5	0-4	0-0	0-0	1-1	0-0	20.0	-0.67

WINNING HORSES

Horse	Races Run	1st	2nd	3rd	£
Ask The Weatherman	4	1	0	0	9495
*Smart Boy	5	2	2	1	8707
*Darcy Ward	3	1	1	0	5458
Redmond	4	1	1	2	4614
Ballyknock Cloud	3	1	0	0	3574
*Posh Totty	3	1	2	0	3314
King Calvin	3	1	1	0	3249
Total winning prize-money					**£38411**
Favourites	**3-7**		**42.9%**		**2.50**

J R BARLOW

CROPWELL BISHOP, NOTTINGHAMSHIRE

	No. of Hrs	Races Run	1st	2nd	3rd	Unpl	Per cent	£1 Level Stake
NH Flat	0	0	0	0	0	0	0.0	0.00
Hurdles	0	0	0	0	0	0	0.0	0.00
Chases	1	3	1	0	0	2	33.3	+31.00
Totals	**1**	**3**	**1**	**0**	**0**	**2**	**33.3**	**+31.00**

JOCKEYS

	W-R	Per cent	£1 Level Stake
Mr Rory Bevin	1-2	50.0	+32.00

COURSE RECORD

	Total W-R	Non-Hndcps Hurdles	Chases	Hndcps Hurdles	Chases	NH Flat	Per cent	£1 Level Stake
Leicester	1-1	0-0	1-1	0-0	0-0	0-0	100.0	+33.00

WINNING HORSES

Horse	Races Run	1st	2nd	3rd	£
*Argot	3	1	0	0	2496
Total winning prize-money					**£2496**
Favourites	**0-0**		**0.0%**		**0.00**

MAURICE BARNES

FARLAM, CUMBRIA

	No. of Hrs	Races Run	1st	2nd	3rd	Unpl	Per cent	£1 Level Stake
NH Flat	4	7	0	0	1	6	0.0	-7.00
Hurdles	13	57	3	5	6	43	5.3	+4.38
Chases	11	60	7	3	7	43	11.7	+3.75
Totals	**25**	**124**	**10**	**8**	**14**	**92**	**8.1**	**+1.13**
16-17	25	124	13	12	11	88	10.5	-8.00
15-16	26	118	11	14	10	83	9.3	-38.50

BY MONTH

NH Flat	W-R	Per cent	£1 Level Stake	Hurdles	W-R	Per cent	£1 Level Stake
May	0-0	0.0	0.00	May	0-8	0.0	-8.00
June	0-1	0.0	-1.00	June	1-7	14.3	-4.13
July	0-1	0.0	-1.00	July	0-3	0.0	-3.00
August	0-2	0.0	-2.00	August	1-8	12.5	-0.50
September	0-0	0.0	0.00	September	1-5	20.0	+46.00
October	0-0	0.0	0.00	October	0-8	0.0	-8.00
November	0-1	0.0	-1.00	November	0-6	0.0	-6.00
December	0-0	0.0	0.00	December	0-1	0.0	-1.00
January	0-0	0.0	0.00	January	0-1	0.0	-1.00
February	0-0	0.0	0.00	February	0-1	0.0	-1.00
March	0-2	0.0	-2.00	March	0-4	0.0	-4.00
April	0-0	0.0	0.00	April	0-5	0.0	-5.00

Chases

Chases	W-R	Per cent	£1 Level Stake
May	3-10	30.0	+28.00
June	2-8	25.0	-2.25
July	0-5	0.0	-5.00
August	0-7	0.0	-7.00
September	1-6	16.7	+2.00
October	1-8	12.5	+4.00
November	0-10	0.0	-10.00
December	0-2	0.0	-2.00
January	0-0	0.0	0.00
February	0-0	0.0	0.00
March	0-2	0.0	-2.00
April	0-2	0.0	-2.00

Totals

Totals	W-R	Per cent	£1 Level Stake
May	3-18	16.7	+20.00
June	3-16	18.8	-7.38
July	0-9	0.0	-9.00
August	1-17	5.9	-9.50
September	2-11	18.2	+48.00
October	1-16	6.3	-4.00
November	0-17	0.0	-17.00
December	0-3	0.0	-3.00
January	0-1	0.0	-1.00
February	0-1	0.0	-1.00
March	0-8	0.0	-8.00
April	0-7	0.0	-7.00

DISTANCE

Hurdles	W-R	Per cent	£1 Level Stake
2m-2m3f	2-30	6.7	+23.88
2m4f-2m7f	1-27	3.7	-19.50
3m+	0-0	0.0	0.00

Chases	W-R	Per cent	£1 Level Stake
2m-2m3f	2-24	8.3	+10.00
2m4f-2m7f	5-22	22.7	+7.75
3m+	0-14	0.0	-14.00

TYPE OF RACE

Non-Handicaps

	W-R	Per cent	£1 Level Stake
Nov Hrdls	1-21	4.8	+30.00
Hrdls	0-10	0.0	-10.00
Nov Chs	0-4	0.0	-4.00
Chases	0-1	0.0	-1.00
Sell/Claim	0-3	0.0	-3.00

Handicaps

	W-R	Per cent	£1 Level Stake
Nov Hrdls	0-0	0.0	0.00
Hrdls	2-23	8.7	-12.63
Nov Chs	2-6	33.3	0.00
Chases	5-48	10.4	+9.75
Sell/Claim	0-0	0.0	0.00

RACE CLASS

	W-R	Per cent	£1 Level Stake
Class 1	0-0	0.0	0.00
Class 2	0-2	0.0	-2.00
Class 3	1-14	7.1	-11.13
Class 4	4-69	5.8	+5.50
Class 5	5-36	13.9	+11.75
Class 6	0-3	0.0	-3.00

FIRST TIME OUT

	W-R	Per cent	£1 Level Stake
Bumpers	0-4	0.0	-4.00
Hurdles	0-11	0.0	-11.00
Chases	2-10	20.0	+25.50
Totals	2-25	8.0	+10.50

JOCKEYS

	W-R	Per cent	£1 Level Stake
Dale Irving	7-87	8.0	-3.38
Thomas Dowson	1-6	16.7	+2.00
Stephen Mulqueen	1-6	16.7	+20.00
Daragh Bourke	1-24	4.2	-16.50

COURSE RECORD

	Total W-R	Non-Hndcps Hurdles	Chases	Hndcps Hurdles	Chases	NH Flat	Per cent	£1 Level Stake
Hexham	6-33	0-7	0-1	2-7	4-17	0-1	18.2	-0.38
Sedgefield	2-26	0-10	0-2	0-6	2-8	0-0	7.7	+12.00
Uttoxeter	1-3	0-1	0-0	0-0	1-1	0-1	33.3	+0.50
Perth	1-18	1-5	0-0	0-2	0-9	0-2	5.6	+33.00

WINNING HORSES

Horse	Races Run	1st	2nd	3rd	£
Desert Island Dusk	9	1	1	2	6279
No Such Number	8	4	0	2	14219
My Idea	10	1	0	1	4431
Indian Voyage	13	1	0	1	3899
Hope For Glory	1	1	0	0	3249
Sir Tommy	7	1	0	0	3249
Flying Jack	9	1	1	0	2849
Total winning prize-money					£38175
Favourites	3-8		37.5%		-0.38

BRIAN BARR

LONGBURTON, DORSET

	No. of Hrs	Races Run	1st	2nd	3rd	Unpl	Per cent	£1 Level Stake
NH Flat	4	5	0	0	0	5	0.0	-5.00
Hurdles	13	56	3	7	5	41	5.4	-34.50
Chases	1	4	0	0	1	3	0.0	-4.00
Totals	17	65	3	7	6	49	4.6	-43.50
16-17	27	96	5	10	12	69	5.2	-64.25
15-16	12	50	0	5	9	36	0.0	-50.00

JOCKEYS

	W-R	Per cent	£1 Level Stake
Richard Johnson	2-9	22.2	+4.50
Dave Crosse	1-15	6.7	-7.00

COURSE RECORD

	Total W-R	Non-Hndcps Hurdles	Chases	Hndcps Hurdles	Chases	NH Flat	Per cent	£1 Level Stake
Nton Abbot	2-10	0-4	0-0	2-6	0-0	0-0	20.0	+3.50
Southwell	1-4	0-0	0-0	1-4	0-0	0-0	25.0	+4.00

WINNING HORSES

Horse	Races Run	1st	2nd	3rd	£
Clearly Capable	6	2	0	1	7798
Byron Blue	5	1	2	0	2924
Total winning prize-money					£10722
Favourites	0-2		0.0%		-2.00

JOHN BERRY

NEWMARKET, SUFFOLK

	No. of Hrs	Races Run	1st	2nd	3rd	Unpl	Per cent	£1 Level Stake
NH Flat	2	3	1	1	0	1	33.3	+10.00
Hurdles	1	1	0	0	0	1	0.0	-1.00
Chases	0	0	0	0	0	0	0.0	0.00
Totals	2	4	1	1	0	2	25.0	+9.00
16-17	3	7	2	1	0	4	28.6	+78.00
15-16	3	7	0	0	0	7	0.0	-7.00

12 TRAINERS JUMPS STATISTICS

JOCKEYS

	W-R	Per cent	£1 Level Stake
Will Kennedy	1-1	100.0	+12.00

COURSE RECORD

	Total W-R	Non-Hndcps Hurdles Chases	Hndcps Hurdles Chases	NH Flat	Per cent	£1 Level Stake
Sedgefield	1-1	0-0 0-0	0-0 0-0	1-1	100.0	+12.00

WINNING HORSES

Horse	Races Run	1st	2nd	3rd	£
Delatite	2	1	0	0	1560
Total winning prize-money					£1560
Favourites	0-0		0.0%		0.00

SUZI BEST
LEWES, EAST SUSSEX

	No. of Hrs	Races Run	1st	2nd	3rd	Unpl	Per cent	£1 Level Stake
NH Flat	1	1	0	0	0	1	0.0	-1.00
Hurdles	5	11	2	0	1	8	18.2	+19.00
Chases	0	0	0	0	0	0	0.0	0.00
Totals	5	12	2	0	1	9	16.7	+18.00

JOCKEYS

	W-R	Per cent	£1 Level Stake
Bryony Frost	1-1	100.0	+25.00
Brendan Powell	1-4	25.0	0.00

COURSE RECORD

	Total W-R	Non-Hndcps Hurdles Chases	Hndcps Hurdles Chases	NH Flat	Per cent	£1 Level Stake
Kempton	1-2	0-0 0-0	1-2 0-0	0-0	50.0	+24.00
Plumpton	1-4	1-2 0-0	0-2 0-0	0-0	25.0	0.00

WINNING HORSES

Horse	Races Run	1st	2nd	3rd	£
Six Gun Serenade	3	1	0	0	4094
Alberta	4	1	0	1	4094
Total winning prize-money					£8188
Favourites	0-0		0.0%		0.00

JAMES BETHELL
MIDDLEHAM MOOR, N YORKS

	No. of Hrs	Races Run	1st	2nd	3rd	Unpl	Per cent	£1 Level Stake
NH Flat	2	4	2	0	1	1	50.0	+15.75
Hurdles	2	2	0	0	0	2	0.0	-2.00
Chases	1	4	0	1	0	3	0.0	-4.00
Totals	4	10	2	1	1	6	20.0	+9.75
16-17	3	11	2	3	2	4	18.2	-7.00
15-16	3	9	0	1	0	8	0.0	-9.00

JOCKEYS

	W-R	Per cent	£1 Level Stake
Brian Hughes	2-6	33.3	+13.75

COURSE RECORD

	Total W-R	Non-Hndcps Hurdles Chases	Hndcps Hurdles Chases	NH Flat	Per cent	£1 Level Stake
Carlisle	1-1	0-0 0-0	0-0 0-0	1-1	100.0	+1.75
Huntingdon	1-1	0-0 0-0	0-0 0-0	1-1	100.0	+16.00

WINNING HORSES

Horse	Races Run	1st	2nd	3rd	£
Cuckoo's Calling	3	2	0	1	4224
Total winning prize-money					£4224
Favourites	1-3		33.3%		-0.25

HARRIET BETHELL
ARNOLD, E YORKS

	No. of Hrs	Races Run	1st	2nd	3rd	Unpl	Per cent	£1 Level Stake
NH Flat	0	0	0	0	0	0	0.0	0.00
Hurdles	4	9	0	0	1	8	0.0	-9.00
Chases	3	15	5	3	5	2	33.3	+5.75
Totals	7	24	5	3	6	10	20.8	-3.25
16-17	7	31	2	3	3	23	6.5	-8.25
15-16	11	49	4	8	7	30	8.2	-14.00

JOCKEYS

	W-R	Per cent	£1 Level Stake
Aidan Coleman	3-9	33.3	+4.50
Richard Johnson	1-1	100.0	+2.75
Sean Bowen	1-2	50.0	+1.50

COURSE RECORD

	Total W-R	Non-Hndcps Hurdles Chases	Hndcps Hurdles Chases	NH Flat	Per cent	£1 Level Stake
Southwell	2-3	0-0 0-0	0-1 2-2	0-0	66.7	+3.25
Mrket Rsn	1-1	0-0 0-0	0-0 1-1	0-0	100.0	+1.75
Wetherby	1-2	0-0 0-0	0-0 1-2	0-0	50.0	+1.75
Uttoxeter	1-6	0-0 0-0	0-3 1-3	0-0	16.7	+2.00

WINNING HORSES

Horse	Races Run	1st	2nd	3rd	£
Newberry New	7	2	1	4	8577
Miami Present	7	3	2	1	12365
Total winning prize-money					£20942
Favourites	3-3		100.0%		6.25

GEORGE BEWLEY

COLBY, CUMBRIA

	No. of Hrs	Races Run	1st	2nd	3rd	Unpl	Per cent	£1 Level Stake
NH Flat	8	11	0	0	0	11	0.0	-11.00
Hurdles	12	34	0	2	2	30	0.0	-34.00
Chases	9	21	1	1	3	16	4.8	-13.00
Totals	**24**	**66**	**1**	**3**	**5**	**57**	**1.5**	**-58.00**
16-17	24	111	14	11	10	76	12.6	-16.13
15-16	21	94	11	12	10	61	11.7	-16.75

JOCKEYS

	W-R	Per cent	£1 Level Stake
Jonathon Bewley	1-56	1.8	-48.00

COURSE RECORD

	Total W-R	Non-Hndcps Hurdles	Chases	Hndcps Hurdles	Chases	NH Flat	Per cent	£1 Level Stake
Carlisle	1-7	0-0	0-0	0-2	1-3	0-2	14.3	+1.00

WINNING HORSES

Horse	Races Run	1st	2nd	3rd	£
Onderun	6	1	0	1	6498
Total winning prize-money					**£6498**
Favourites	0-1	0.0%			-1.00

KEVIN BISHOP

SPAXTON, SOMERSET

	No. of Hrs	Races Run	1st	2nd	3rd	Unpl	Per cent	£1 Level Stake
NH Flat	1	1	0	0	1	0	0.0	-1.00
Hurdles	12	37	2	3	3	29	5.4	-27.25
Chases	2	4	0	0	0	4	0.0	-4.00
Totals	**14**	**42**	**2**	**3**	**4**	**33**	**4.8**	**-32.25**
16-17	11	52	4	3	6	39	7.7	-27.30
15-16	14	68	9	6	6	47	13.2	+24.00

JOCKEYS

	W-R	Per cent	£1 Level Stake
Conor Smith	2-10	20.0	-0.25

COURSE RECORD

	Total W-R	Non-Hndcps Hurdles	Chases	Hndcps Hurdles	Chases	NH Flat	Per cent	£1 Level Stake
Aintree	1-2	0-0	0-0	1-2	0-0	0-0	50.0	+1.25
Wincanton	1-4	0-0	0-0	1-4	0-0	0-0	25.0	+2.50

WINNING HORSES

Horse	Races Run	1st	2nd	3rd	£
Just Spot	6	1	1	1	4549

Lets Go Dutchess	4	1	1	0	3899
Total winning prize-money					**£8448**
Favourites	1-2	50.0%			1.25

EMMA-JANE BISHOP

NAUNTON, GLOUCS

	No. of Hrs	Races Run	1st	2nd	3rd	Unpl	Per cent	£1 Level Stake
NH Flat	0	0	0	0	0	0	0.0	0.00
Hurdles	2	2	0	0	0	2	0.0	-2.00
Chases	7	22	3	1	5	13	13.6	-1.63
Totals	**7**	**24**	**3**	**1**	**5**	**15**	**12.5**	**-3.63**
16-17	9	43	4	2	6	31	9.3	-7.00
15-16	12	48	3	6	7	32	6.3	-26.50

JOCKEYS

	W-R	Per cent	£1 Level Stake
James Banks	2-13	15.4	+4.50
Jamie Bargary	1-9	11.1	-6.13

COURSE RECORD

	Total W-R	Non-Hndcps Hurdles	Chases	Hndcps Hurdles	Chases	NH Flat	Per cent	£1 Level Stake
Fakenham	1-1	0-0	0-0	0-0	1-1	0-0	100.0	+5.50
Lingfield	1-2	0-0	0-0	0-0	1-2	0-0	50.0	+9.00
Leicester	1-4	0-0	0-0	0-0	1-4	0-0	25.0	-1.13

WINNING HORSES

Horse	Races Run	1st	2nd	3rd	£
Church Hall	4	1	0	0	6963
Glance Back	4	1	0	1	6238
Bajardo	5	1	0	2	4549
Total winning prize-money					**£17750**
Favourites	1-3	33.3%			-0.13

ALAN BLACKMORE

LITTLE BERKHAMSTED, HERTS

	No. of Hrs	Races Run	1st	2nd	3rd	Unpl	Per cent	£1 Level Stake
NH Flat	0	0	0	0	0	0	0.0	0.00
Hurdles	2	11	2	0	0	9	18.2	+15.25
Chases	0	0	0	0	0	0	0.0	0.00
Totals	**2**	**11**	**2**	**0**	**0**	**9**	**18.2**	**+15.25**
16-17	2	7	1	0	1	5	14.3	+3.00
15-16	4	18	3	0	3	12	16.7	+7.00

JOCKEYS

	W-R	Per cent	£1 Level Stake
Jack Quinlan	1-2	50.0	+1.25
Miss Tabitha Worsley	1-4	25.0	+19.00

COURSE RECORD

	Total W-R	Non-Hndcps Hurdles	Non-Hndcps Chases	Hndcps Hurdles	Chases	NH Flat	Per cent	£1 Level Stake
Fakenham	1-4	0-0	0-0	1-4	0-0	0-0	25.0	-0.75
Huntingdon	1-4	0-1	0-0	1-3	0-0	0-0	25.0	+19.00

WINNING HORSES

Horse	Races Run	1st	2nd	3rd	£
Occasionally Yours	7	2	0	0	7798
Total winning prize-money					**£7798**
Favourites	0-0		0.0%		0.00

MICHAEL BLAKE

TROWBRIDGE, WILTS

	No. of Hrs	Races Run	1st	2nd	3rd	Unpl	Per cent	£1 Level Stake
NH Flat	1	1	0	0	0	1	0.0	-1.00
Hurdles	11	40	6	8	3	23	15.0	+16.91
Chases	3	9	0	0	1	8	0.0	-9.00
Totals	13	50	6	8	4	32	12.0	+6.91
16-17	13	53	2	8	4	39	3.8	-25.50
15-16	13	44	10	5	4	25	22.7	-3.82

JOCKEYS

	W-R	Per cent	£1 Level Stake
Harry Cobden	4-12	33.3	+6.91
Brendan Powell	1-1	100.0	+25.00
Philip Donovan	1-8	12.5	+4.00

COURSE RECORD

	Total W-R	Non-Hndcps Hurdles	Chases	Hndcps Hurdles	Chases	NH Flat	Per cent	£1 Level Stake
Nton Abbot	3-9	2-2	0-0	1-6	0-1	0-0	33.3	+2.91
Cheltenham	1-2	0-0	0-0	1-1	0-1	0-0	50.0	+24.00
Wincanton	1-4	0-3	0-0	1-1	0-0	0-0	25.0	+8.00
Worcester	1-5	0-0	0-0	1-5	0-0	0-0	20.0	+2.00

WINNING HORSES

Horse	Races Run	1st	2nd	3rd	£
Coole Cody	4	3	0	0	22909
Doubly Clever	5	2	1	1	12597
Barney From Tyanee	6	1	0	1	3184
Total winning prize-money					**£38690**
Favourites	1-3		33.3%		-1.09

GILLIAN BOANAS

LINGDALE, REDCAR & CLEVELAND

	No. of Hrs	Races Run	1st	2nd	3rd	Unpl	Per cent	£1 Level Stake
NH Flat	7	8	0	1	1	6	0.0	-8.00
Hurdles	14	54	3	6	9	36	5.6	-39.50

Chases	3	15	1	2	3	9	6.7	-9.00
Totals	18	77	4	9	13	51	5.2	-56.50
16-17	11	23	1	9	1	12	4.3	-12.00

JOCKEYS

	W-R	Per cent	£1 Level Stake
Brian Hughes	3-7	42.9	+11.00
Miss Emma Todd	1-38	2.6	-35.50

COURSE RECORD

	Total W-R	Non-Hndcps Hurdles	Chases	Hndcps Hurdles	Chases	NH Flat	Per cent	£1 Level Stake
Hexham	2-12	2-5	0-1	0-2	0-1	0-3	16.7	0.00
Cartmel	1-3	0-0	0-0	0-1	1-2	0-0	33.3	+3.00
Catterick	1-6	1-3	0-0	0-2	0-0	0-1	16.7	-3.50

WINNING HORSES

Horse	Races Run	1st	2nd	3rd	£
Brave Spartacus	8	1	2	1	6256
Crixss's Escape	2	2	0	0	8058
Teescomponents Lad	7	1	2	3	0
Total winning prize-money					**£14314**
Favourites	0-1		0.0%		-1.00

PETER BOWEN

LITTLE NEWCASTLE, PEMBROKES

	No. of Hrs	Races Run	1st	2nd	3rd	Unpl	Per cent	£1 Level Stake
NH Flat	10	16	0	2	3	11	0.0	-16.00
Hurdles	39	136	20	13	16	86	14.7	-27.12
Chases	31	141	32	22	17	70	22.7	+24.47
Totals	59	293	52	37	36	167	17.7	-18.65
16-17	55	297	39	51	25	182	13.1	-99.11
15-16	61	236	33	34	28	141	14.0	-84.96

BY MONTH

NH Flat	W-R	Per cent	£1 Level Stake	Hurdles	W-R	Per cent	£1 Level Stake
May	0-0	0.0	0.00	May	2-13	15.4	+1.50
June	0-0	0.0	0.00	June	4-13	30.8	+5.85
July	0-0	0.0	0.00	July	2-15	13.3	-6.25
August	0-0	0.0	0.00	August	3-12	25.0	+3.50
September	0-1	0.0	-1.00	September	2-7	28.6	+2.25
October	0-5	0.0	-5.00	October	1-16	6.3	-11.67
November	0-2	0.0	-2.00	November	0-10	0.0	-10.00
December	0-1	0.0	-1.00	December	1-14	7.1	-10.75
January	0-1	0.0	-1.00	January	0-9	0.0	-9.00
February	0-1	0.0	-1.00	February	3-8	37.5	+20.00
March	0-1	0.0	-1.00	March	1-8	12.5	-6.56
April	0-4	0.0	-4.00	April	1-11	9.1	-6.00

Chases	W-R	Per cent	£1 Level Stake	Totals	W-R	Per cent	£1 Level Stake
May	1-12	8.3	-8.25	May	3-25	12.0	-6.75
June	5-13	38.5	+16.10	June	9-26	34.6	+21.95

	W-R	Per cent	£1 Level Stake		W-R	Per cent	£1 Level Stake
July	5-14	35.7	+15.50	July	7-29	24.1	+9.25
August	2-12	16.7	-0.50	August	5-24	20.8	+3.00
September	3-15	20.0	-3.38	September	5-23	21.7	-2.13
October	0-8	0.0	-8.00	October	1-29	3.4	-24.67
November	5-14	35.7	+20.00	November	5-26	19.2	+8.00
December	2-9	22.2	+3.50	December	3-24	12.5	-8.25
January	0-11	0.0	-11.00	January	0-21	0.0	-21.00
February	1-8	12.5	-6.43	February	4-17	23.5	+12.57
March	2-11	18.2	-1.50	March	3-20	15.0	-9.06
April	6-14	42.9	+8.43	April	7-29	24.1	-1.57

Aintree	2-13	0-0	0-0	1-6	1-6	0-1	15.4	-2.25
Chepstow	2-21	0-7	0-2	0-3	2-7	0-2	9.5	-12.70
Hereford	1-2	0-0	0-0	0-0	1-2	0-0	50.0	+3.00
Kelso	1-2	0-1	1-1	0-0	0-0	0-0	50.0	-0.43
Ludlow	1-3	1-1	0-0	0-2	0-0	0-0	33.3	+3.00
Haydock	1-4	0-0	0-0	0-1	1-3	0-0	25.0	+0.50
Wincanton	1-4	0-0	0-0	0-1	1-3	0-0	25.0	+1.50
Kempton	1-5	0-1	0-0	0-1	1-2	0-1	20.0	+2.00
Fontwell	1-9	0-0	0-0	1-6	0-2	0-1	11.1	-4.50
Bangor	1-16	0-2	0-1	0-4	1-7	0-2	6.3	-13.13

DISTANCE

Hurdles	W-R	Per cent	£1 Level Stake	Chases	W-R	Per cent	£1 Level Stake
2m-2m3f	5-29	17.2	-5.50	2m-2m3f	6-15	40.0	+19.43
2m4f-2m7f	11-71	15.5	-8.37	2m4f-2m7f	20-61	32.8	+31.57
3m+	4-36	11.1	-13.25	3m+	6-65	9.2	-26.52

TYPE OF RACE

Non-Handicaps	W-R	Per cent	£1 Level Stake	Handicaps	W-R	Per cent	£1 Level Stake
Nov Hrdls	1-14	7.1	-12.56	Nov Hrdls	2-5	40.0	+2.10
Hrdls	1-7	14.3	-1.00	Hrdls	16-109	14.7	-14.67
Nov Chs	3-9	33.3	-1.93	Nov Chs	1-9	11.1	-6.90
Chases	2-3	66.7	+1.75	Chases	22-107	20.6	+21.92
Sell/Claim	1-3	33.3	-0.63	Sell/Claim	0-0	0.0	0.00

RACE CLASS / FIRST TIME OUT

	W-R	Per cent	£1 Level Stake		W-R	Per cent	£1 Level Stake
Class 1	1-21	4.8	-18.63	Bumpers	0-10	0.0	-10.00
Class 2	3-27	11.1	-13.50	Hurdles	4-28	14.3	-5.40
Class 3	15-82	18.3	+0.58	Chases	2-21	9.5	-2.00
Class 4	26-127	20.5	+9.17				
Class 5	7-30	23.3	+9.73	Totals	6-59	10.2	-17.40
Class 6	0-6	0.0	-6.00				

JOCKEYS

	W-R	Per cent	£1 Level Stake
Sean Bowen	35-187	18.7	+2.30
James Bowen	16-90	17.8	-7.75
Robert Dunne	1-2	50.0	+0.80

COURSE RECORD

	Total W-R	Non-Hndcps Hurdles	Non-Hndcps Chases	Hndcps Hurdles	Hndcps Chases	NH Flat	Per cent	£1 Level Stake
Stratford	6-15	0-1	0-0	1-6	5-8	0-0	40.0	+19.58
Ffos Las	6-38	0-4	1-4	3-14	2-13	0-3	15.8	-6.63
Cartmel	5-15	0-0	2-2	3-5	0-8	0-0	33.3	+7.75
Southwell	4-13	0-1	0-0	1-5	3-6	0-1	30.8	+15.60
Mrket Rsn	4-21	0-1	0-0	2-9	2-10	0-1	19.0	-1.88
Uttoxeter	4-24	0-2	0-0	2-10	2-12	0-0	16.7	-3.90
Worcester	4-24	0-0	0-1	2-13	2-8	0-2	16.7	-2.00
Perth	3-4	0-0	1-1	1-1	1-2	0-0	75.0	+8.38
Sedgefield	2-6	1-1	0-0	0-1	1-4	0-0	33.3	+6.44
Nton Abbot	2-9	0-0	0-0	1-6	1-3	0-0	22.2	+6.00

WINNING HORSES

Horse	Races Run	1st	2nd	3rd	£
Rons Dream	11	3	4	0	59164
Wadswick Court	9	2	4	0	34408
Henri Parry Morgan	6	1	1	0	15890
Earthmoves	8	2	1	0	18194
Play The Ace	12	6	1	2	44285
Beggar's Wishes	5	2	1	0	13646
Potters Story	3	1	0	0	9747
Curious Carlos	7	1	2	0	9384
Lord Bryan	9	3	0	2	18649
Forever My Friend	5	1	0	2	6498
Souriyan	8	2	1	0	9579
Jeannot De Nonant	4	1	0	0	6077
Oscartea	7	1	1	0	5848
Awaywiththegreys	4	1	0	1	5523
Strumble Head	7	2	1	1	9796
*Deadly Move	5	1	1	2	5198
Kinari	3	1	0	0	5064
Get Home Now	7	3	1	1	11761
Mont Choisy	7	1	0	2	4711
*Lord Napier	5	3	0	0	12908
*Dotties Dilema	8	3	0	1	10929
Land Of Vic	4	1	0	1	4224
Dr Robin	5	1	0	0	4159
*Flying Eagle	7	2	0	1	7993
Court King	9	2	2	2	7893
Sam Noir	11	1	0	2	3574
Hillary View	5	1	0	0	3509
Alf 'N' Dor	10	1	1	4	3509
Cougar's Gold	8	1	1	0	2599
*Lime Street	7	1	3	0	2599
Total winning prize-money					£357318
Favourites	17-53		32.1%		-1.65

MICKEY BOWEN

HAVERFORDWEST, PEMBROKES

	No. of Hrs	Races Run	1st	2nd	3rd	Unpl	Per cent	£1 Level Stake
NH Flat	0	0	0	0	0	0	0.0	0.00
Hurdles	0	0	0	0	0	0	0.0	0.00
Chases	4	9	3	1	0	5	33.3	+10.07
Totals	4	9	3	1	0	5	33.3	+10.07
16-17	4	8	2	1	0	5	25.0	+10.25

15-16	4	10	2	4	0	4	20.0	-1.50

JOCKEYS

	W-R	Per cent	£1 Level Stake
Mr Peter Bryan	3-9	33.3	+10.07

COURSE RECORD

	Total W-R	Non-Hndcps Hurdles	Chases	Hndcps Hurdles	Chases	NH Flat	Per cent	£1 Level Stake
Nton Abbot	1-1	0-0	1-1	0-0	0-0	0-0	100.0	+9.00
Ffos Las	1-1	0-0	1-1	0-0	0-0	0-0	100.0	+0.57
Kelso	1-2	0-0	1-2	0-0	0-0	0-0	50.0	+5.50

WINNING HORSES

Horse	Races Run	1st	2nd	3rd	£
Wells De Lune	4	1	1	0	4180
*Al Co	3	1	0	0	2496
*Strumble Head	1	1	0	0	1317
Total winning prize-money					£7993
Favourites	1-1	100.0%			0.57

MARK BRADSTOCK

LETCOMBE BASSETT, OXON

	No. of Hrs	Races Run	1st	2nd	3rd	Unpl	Per cent	£1 Level Stake
NH Flat	1	1	0	0	0	1	0.0	-1.00
Hurdles	9	28	3	2	1	22	10.7	-16.67
Chases	3	9	2	3	1	3	22.2	+0.62
Totals	12	38	5	5	2	26	13.2	-17.05
16-17	14	36	2	6	2	26	5.6	-23.00
15-16	10	17	3	1	0	13	17.6	+0.25

JOCKEYS

	W-R	Per cent	£1 Level Stake
Nico de Boinville	3-24	12.5	-15.39
Jamie Moore	1-2	50.0	+6.00
David Bass	1-5	20.0	-0.67

COURSE RECORD

	Total W-R	Non-Hndcps Hurdles	Chases	Hndcps Hurdles	Chases	NH Flat	Per cent	£1 Level Stake
Fakenham	1-1	0-0	1-1	0-0	0-0	0-0	100.0	+0.61
Exeter	1-3	0-1	0-1	1-1	0-0	0-0	33.3	+1.33
Sandown	1-3	0-0	0-0	0-1	1-2	0-0	33.3	+5.00
Fontwell	1-4	1-3	0-0	0-1	0-0	0-0	25.0	-1.00
Plumpton	1-4	1-3	0-0.	0-1	0-0	0-0	25.0	0.00

WINNING HORSES

Horse	Races Run	1st	2nd	3rd	£
Step Back	4	2	1	1	89997
Jaisalmer	6	2	0	0	9487
Robert's Star	6	1	1	1	4549

Total winning prize-money		£104033
Favourites	2-5	40.0%	0.95

BARRY BRENNAN

UPPER LAMBOURN, BERKS

	No. of Hrs	Races Run	1st	2nd	3rd	Unpl	Per cent	£1 Level Stake
NH Flat	0	0	0	0	0	0	0.0	0.00
Hurdles	8	29	1	5	3	20	3.4	-16.00
Chases	6	18	1	3	2	12	5.6	-1.00
Totals	10	47	2	8	5	32	4.3	-17.00
16-17	14	50	0	2	8	40	0.0	-50.00
15-16	15	61	11	8	6	36	18.0	+12.50

JOCKEYS

	W-R	Per cent	£1 Level Stake
James Banks	1-5	20.0	+8.00
Dave Crosse	1-10	10.0	+7.00

COURSE RECORD

	Total W-R	Non-Hndcps Hurdles	Chases	Hndcps Hurdles	Chases	NH Flat	Per cent	£1 Level Stake
Lingfield	1-3	0-1	0-0	0-0	1-2	0-0	33.3	+14.00
Uttoxeter	1-4	0-0	0-0	1-4	0-0	0-0	25.0	+9.00

WINNING HORSES

Horse	Races Run	1st	2nd	3rd	£
Lightentertainment	11	1	2	2	3509
Mrsrobin	4	1	1	0	3249
Total winning prize-money					£6758
Favourites	0-0	0.0%			0.00

G C BREWER

HOVINGHAM, N YORKS

	No. of Hrs	Races Run	1st	2nd	3rd	Unpl	Per cent	£1 Level Stake
NH Flat	0	0	0	0	0	0	0.0	0.00
Hurdles	0	0	0	0	0	0	0.0	0.00
Chases	1	3	2	0	0	1	66.7	+17.75
Totals	1	3	2	0	0	1	66.7	+17.75
16-17	1	2	0	1	0	1	0.0	-2.00
15-16	1	1	0	0	1	0	0.0	-1.00

JOCKEYS

	W-R	Per cent	£1 Level Stake
Mr John Dawson	2-3	66.7	+17.75

COURSE RECORD

	Total W-R	Non-Hndcps Hurdles	Chases	Hndcps Hurdles	Chases	NH Flat	Per cent	£1 Level Stake
Kelso	1-1	0-0	1-1	0-0	0-0	0-0	100.0	+2.75
Stratford	1-1	0-0	1-1	0-0	0-0	0-0	100.0	+16.00

WINNING HORSES

Horse	Races Run	1st	2nd	3rd	£
Young Hurricane	3	2	0	0	19357
Total winning prize-money					£19357
Favourites	0-0		0.0%		0.00

DAVID BRIDGWATER

ICOMB, GLOUCS

	No. of Hrs	Races Run	1st	2nd	3rd	Unpl	Per cent	£1 Level Stake
NH Flat	6	9	0	0	0	9	0.0	-9.00
Hurdles	15	53	3	8	5	37	5.7	-44.15
Chases	12	51	8	7	8	28	15.7	-6.92
Totals	28	113	11	15	13	74	9.7	-60.07
16-17	35	151	14	18	16	103	9.3	-43.88
15-16	45	137	16	16	20	85	11.7	-63.14

BY MONTH

NH Flat	W-R	Per cent	£1 Level Stake	Hurdles	W-R	Per cent	£1 Level Stake
May	0-1	0.0	-1.00	May	1-7	14.3	-4.75
June	0-1	0.0	-1.00	June	0-3	0.0	-3.00
July	0-1	0.0	-1.00	July	1-7	14.3	-4.90
August	0-1	0.0	-1.00	August	1-2	50.0	+2.50
September	0-0	0.0	0.00	September	0-3	0.0	-3.00
October	0-0	0.0	0.00	October	0-5	0.0	-5.00
November	0-0	0.0	0.00	November	0-5	0.0	-5.00
December	0-0	0.0	0.00	December	0-2	0.0	-2.00
January	0-2	0.0	-2.00	January	0-4	0.0	-4.00
February	0-2	0.0	-2.00	February	0-6	0.0	-6.00
March	0-0	0.0	0.00	March	0-6	0.0	-6.00
April	0-1	0.0	-1.00	April	0-3	0.0	-3.00

Chases	W-R	Per cent	£1 Level Stake	Totals	W-R	Per cent	£1 Level Stake
May	0-7	0.0	-7.00	May	1-15	6.7	-12.75
June	2-6	33.3	+1.25	June	2-10	20.0	-2.75
July	2-9	22.2	-2.17	July	3-17	17.6	-8.07
August	0-4	0.0	-4.00	August	1-7	14.3	-2.50
September	0-5	0.0	-5.00	September	0-8	0.0	-8.00
October	4-10	40.0	+20.00	October	4-15	26.7	+15.00
November	0-5	0.0	-5.00	November	0-10	0.0	-10.00
December	0-3	0.0	-3.00	December	0-5	0.0	-5.00
January	0-1	0.0	-1.00	January	0-7	0.0	-7.00
February	0-0	0.0	0.00	February	0-8	0.0	-8.00
March	0-0	0.0	0.00	March	0-6	0.0	-6.00
April	0-1	0.0	-1.00	April	0-5	0.0	-5.00

DISTANCE

Hurdles	W-R	Per cent	£1 Level Stake	Chases	W-R	Per cent	£1 Level Stake
2m-2m3f	0-38	0.0	-38.00	2m-2m3f	4-23	17.4	+3.33
2m4f-2m7f	3-11	27.3	-2.15	2m4f-2m7f	1-15	6.7	-7.00
3m+	0-4	0.0	-4.00	3m+	3-13	23.1	-3.25

TYPE OF RACE

Non-Handicaps	W-R	Per cent	£1 Level Stake	Handicaps	W-R	Per cent	£1 Level Stake
Nov Hrdls	0-15	0.0	-15.00	Nov Hrdls	0-3	0.0	-3.00
Hrdls	1-22	4.5	-19.90	Hrdls	0-9	0.0	-9.00
Nov Chs	0-1	0.0	-1.00	Nov Chs	2-13	15.4	+4.00
Chases	0-0	0.0	0.00	Chases	5-34	14.7	-11.92
Sell/Claim	2-5	40.0	+1.75	Sell/Claim	0-0	0.0	0.00

RACE CLASS

	W-R	Per cent	£1 Level Stake
Class 1	0-1	0.0	-1.00
Class 2	0-2	0.0	-2.00
Class 3	0-8	0.0	-8.00
Class 4	6-62	9.7	-30.25
Class 5	5-37	13.5	-15.82
Class 6	0-3	0.0	-3.00

FIRST TIME OUT

	W-R	Per cent	£1 Level Stake
Bumpers	0-6	0.0	-6.00
Hurdles	1-12	8.3	-9.75
Chases	2-10	20.0	-1.00
Totals	3-28	10.7	-16.75

JOCKEYS

	W-R	Per cent	£1 Level Stake
Tom Scudamore	4-41	9.8	-28.15
Callum McKinnes	3-20	15.0	-3.50
Daniel Hiskett	2-19	10.5	-10.67
Alain Cawley	1-2	50.0	+11.00
Mitchell Bastyan	1-5	20.0	-2.75

COURSE RECORD

	Total W-R	Non-Hndcps Hurdles	Chases	Hndcps Hurdles	Chases	NH Flat	Per cent	£1 Level Stake
Fontwell	3-9	0-0	0-0	0-0	3-8	0-1	33.3	+8.00
Nton Abbot	3-10	1-2	0-0	0-0	2-7	0-1	30.0	-1.07
Worcester	2-6	2-2	0-0	0-0	0-3	0-1	33.3	+0.75
Ffos Las	1-1	0-0	0-0	0-0	1-1	0-0	100.0	+2.25
Southwell	1-10	0-5	0-0	0-1	1-4	0-0	10.0	+3.00
Plumpton	1-16	0-6	0-0	0-2	1-7	0-1	6.3	-12.00

WINNING HORSES

Horse	Races Run	1st	2nd	3rd	£
*Fort Gabriel	7	3	1	1	13321
Saffron Prince	9	2	2	1	4386
Fair Frank	6	1	0	1	3899
Buble	6	2	1	1	6498
Accord	5	1	0	0	3899
Orchestrated	5	1	1	0	2599
Lakeshore Lady	1	1	0	0	2397

Total winning prize-money			£36999
Favourites	4-9	44.4%	3.85

JULIA BROOKE

MIDDLEHAM, N YORKS

	No. of Hrs	Races Run	1st	2nd	3rd	Unpl	Per cent	£1 Level Stake
NH Flat	2	2	0	0	0	2	0.0	-2.00
Hurdles	13	49	1	4	2	42	2.0	-15.00
Chases	2	13	0	2	2	9	0.0	-13.00
Totals	15	64	1	6	4	53	1.6	-30.00
16-17	13	36	6	1	5	24	16.7	+21.00
15-16	11	23	3	2	1	17	13.0	-6.17

JOCKEYS

	W-R	Per cent	£1 Level Stake
John Kington	1-17	5.9	+17.00

COURSE RECORD

	Total W-R	Non-Hndcps Hurdles	Chases	Hndcps Hurdles	Chases	NH Flat	Per cent	£1 Level Stake
Perth	1-5	1-1	0-0	0-3	0-0	0-1	20.0	+29.00

WINNING HORSES

Horse	Races Run	1st	2nd	3rd	£
*Asylo	1	1	0	0	4431
Total winning prize-money					£4431
Favourites	0-0	0.0%			0.00

LADY SUSAN BROOKE

DOLAU, POWYS

	No. of Hrs	Races Run	1st	2nd	3rd	Unpl	Per cent	£1 Level Stake
NH Flat	0	0	0	0	0	0	0.0	0.00
Hurdles	2	5	0	0	0	5	0.0	-5.00
Chases	6	35	3	2	5	25	8.6	+22.00
Totals	6	40	3	2	5	30	7.5	+17.00
16-17	8	40	2	2	4	32	5.0	-1.50
15-16	8	31	0	1	4	26	0.0	-31.00

JOCKEYS

	W-R	Per cent	£1 Level Stake
Miss Lorna Brooke	3-38	7.9	+19.00

COURSE RECORD

	Total W-R	Non-Hndcps Hurdles	Chases	Hndcps Hurdles	Chases	NH Flat	Per cent	£1 Level Stake
Chepstow	1-2	0-0	0-0	0-0	1-2	0-0	50.0	+15.00
Fontwell	1-3	0-0	0-0	0-0	1-3	0-0	33.3	+18.00
Hereford	1-4	0-1	0-0	0-1	1-2	0-0	25.0	+15.00

WINNING HORSES

Horse	Races Run	1st	2nd	3rd	£
Spock	14	2	1	1	8053
Astigos	10	1	1	2	3314
Total winning prize-money					£11367
Favourites	0-0	0.0%			0.00

MISS H BROOKSHAW

WHITCHURCH, SHROPSHIRE

	No. of Hrs	Races Run	1st	2nd	3rd	Unpl	Per cent	£1 Level Stake
NH Flat	0	0	0	0	0	0	0.0	0.00
Hurdles	0	0	0	0	0	0	0.0	0.00
Chases	3	9	2	4	0	3	22.2	+4.75
Totals	3	9	2	4	0	3	22.2	+4.75
16-17	3	6	0	0	1	5	0.0	-6.00
15-16	2	4	1	0	0	3	25.0	+6.00

JOCKEYS

	W-R	Per cent	£1 Level Stake
Max Kendrick	1-3	33.3	-0.25
Mr Hugh Nugent	1-4	25.0	+7.00

COURSE RECORD

	Total W-R	Non-Hndcps Hurdles	Chases	Hndcps Hurdles	Chases	NH Flat	Per cent	£1 Level Stake
Hereford	1-1	0-0	1-1	0-0	0-0	0-0	100.0	+10.00
Stratford	1-2	0-0	1-1	0-0	0-1	0-0	50.0	+0.75

WINNING HORSES

Horse	Races Run	1st	2nd	3rd	£
*Bay Sly	3	1	0	0	6239
Shotavodka	4	1	2	0	3120
Total winning prize-money					£9359
Favourites	1-1	100.0%			1.75

ROY BROTHERTON

ELMLEY CASTLE, WORCS

	No. of Hrs	Races Run	1st	2nd	3rd	Unpl	Per cent	£1 Level Stake
NH Flat	3	5	0	0	0	5	0.0	-5.00
Hurdles	2	4	0	0	0	4	0.0	-4.00
Chases	2	8	1	0	2	5	12.5	+4.00
Totals	6	17	1	0	2	14	5.9	-5.00
16-17	11	36	1	5	8	22	2.8	-29.00
15-16	7	20	1	2	1	16	5.0	-7.00

JOCKEYS

	W-R	Per cent	£1 Level Stake
Jamie Moore	1-8	12.5	+4.00

COURSE RECORD

	Total W-R	Non-Hndcps Hurdles	Chases	Hndcps Hurdles	Chases	NH Flat	Per cent	£1 Level Stake
Southwell	1-1	0-0	0-0	0-0	1-1	0-0	100.0	+11.00

WINNING HORSES

Horse	Races Run	1st	2nd	3rd	£
Deise Vu	7	1	0	2	3249
Total winning prize-money					**£3249**
Favourites	0-0		0.0%		0.00

BOB BUCKLER

COURTWAY, SOMERSET

	No. of Hrs	Races Run	1st	2nd	3rd	Unpl	Per cent	£1 Level Stake
NH Flat	3	5	2	0	0	3	40.0	+6.75
Hurdles	4	7	1	0	1	5	14.3	+4.00
Chases	7	25	4	3	2	16	16.0	+13.00
Totals	12	37	7	3	3	24	18.9	+23.75
16-17	10	45	2	8	4	31	4.4	-35.00
15-16	9	43	4	9	3	27	9.3	-11.75

JOCKEYS

	W-R	Per cent	£1 Level Stake
Sean Houlihan	7-23	30.4	+37.75

COURSE RECORD

	Total W-R	Non-Hndcps Hurdles	Chases	Hndcps Hurdles	Chases	NH Flat	Per cent	£1 Level Stake
Wincanton	2-3	0-0	0-0	0-0	1-1	1-2	66.7	+8.25
Taunton	2-7	0-0	0-0	1-1	1-4	0-2	28.6	+9.00
Uttoxeter	1-1	0-0	0-0	0-0	1-1	0-0	100.0	+16.00
Towcester	1-4	0-0	0-0	0-1	1-3	0-0	25.0	+4.00
Exeter	1-5	0-0	0-0	0-2	0-2	1-1	20.0	+3.50

WINNING HORSES

Horse	Races Run	1st	2nd	3rd	£
Regal Flow	7	3	1	1	92472
Hoo Bally Diva	1	1	0	0	4159
Ballyegan	6	1	0	1	3249
Unwin VC	2	2	0	0	4549
Total winning prize-money					**£104429**
Favourites	1-2		50.0%		3.00

DAI BURCHELL

BRIERY HILL, BLAENAU GWENT

	No. of Hrs	Races Run	1st	2nd	3rd	Unpl	Per cent	£1 Level Stake
NH Flat	0	0	0	0	0	0	0.0	0.00
Hurdles	9	26	0	1	4	21	0.0	-26.00
Chases	6	14	2	1	4	7	14.3	+2.25
Totals	12	40	2	2	8	28	5.0	-23.75
16-17	21	85	10	9	12	54	11.8	+6.50
15-16	21	89	9	9	12	59	10.1	-24.88

JOCKEYS

	W-R	Per cent	£1 Level Stake
Tom Scudamore	1-5	20.0	+8.00
Robert Dunne	1-27	3.7	-23.75

COURSE RECORD

	Total W-R	Non-Hndcps Hurdles	Chases	Hndcps Hurdles	Chases	NH Flat	Per cent	£1 Level Stake
Ffos Las	1-4	0-1	0-0	0-1	1-2	0-0	25.0	-0.75
Worcester	1-7	0-0	1-1	0-2	0-4	0-0	14.3	+6.00

WINNING HORSES

Horse	Races Run	1st	2nd	3rd	£
King Alfonso	7	1	0	3	4289
Butlergrove King	3	1	1	1	3249
Total winning prize-money					**£7538**
Favourites	1-2		50.0%		1.25

KEIRAN BURKE

SUTTON VENY, WILTS

	No. of Hrs	Races Run	1st	2nd	3rd	Unpl	Per cent	£1 Level Stake
NH Flat	0	0	0	0	0	0	0.0	0.00
Hurdles	2	2	1	0	0	1	50.0	+11.00
Chases	0	0	0	0	0	0	0.0	0.00
Totals	2	2	1	0	0	1	50.0	+11.00

JOCKEYS

	W-R	Per cent	£1 Level Stake
Wayne Hutchinson	1-1	100.0	+12.00

COURSE RECORD

	Total W-R	Non-Hndcps Hurdles	Chases	Hndcps Hurdles	Chases	NH Flat	Per cent	£1 Level Stake
Exeter	1-2	0-1	0-0	1-1	0-0	0-0	50.0	+11.00

WINNING HORSES

Horse	Races Run	1st	2nd	3rd	£
*Jully Les Buxy	1	1	0	0	6498
Total winning prize-money					**£6498**
Favourites	0-0		0.0%		0.00

BARBARA BUTTERWORTH

BOLTON, CUMBRIA

	No. of Hrs	Races Run	1st	2nd	3rd	Unpl	Per cent	£1 Level Stake
NH Flat	0	0	0	0	0	0	0.0	0.00
Hurdles	6	32	3	1	2	26	9.4	+14.00
Chases	2	8	0	3	0	5	0.0	-8.00
Totals	7	40	3	4	2	31	7.5	+6.00
16-17	6	26	1	1	2	22	3.8	-22.75
15-16	3	13	0	0	2	11	0.0	-13.00

JOCKEYS

	W-R	Per cent	£1 Level Stake
Sean Quinlan	2-28	7.1	-5.00
Mr Liam Quinlan	1-3	33.3	+20.00

COURSE RECORD

	Total W-R	Non-Hndcps Hurdles	Chases	Hndcps Hurdles	Chases	NH Flat	Per cent	£1 Level Stake
Wetherby	1-2	0-0	0-0	1-2	0-0	0-0	50.0	+13.00
Catterick	1-3	0-0	0-0	1-3	0-0	0-0	33.3	+5.00
Hexham	1-3	0-0	0-0	1-3	0-0	0-0	33.3	+20.00

WINNING HORSES

Horse	Races Run	1st	2nd	3rd	£
Snowed In	12	1	1	2	4809
Age Of Glory	2	1	0	0	3509
Cherry Princess	4	1	0	0	2732
Total winning prize-money					**£11050**
Favourites	0-0		0.0%		0.00

JENNIE CANDLISH

BASFORD GREEN, STAFFS

	No. of Hrs	Races Run	1st	2nd	3rd	Unpl	Per cent	£1 Level Stake
NH Flat	5	6	0	0	2	4	0.0	-6.00
Hurdles	28	120	8	16	21	75	6.7	-49.22
Chases	16	72	9	1	11	51	12.5	-15.17
Totals	41	198	17	17	34	130	8.6	-70.39
16-17	39	174	23	22	17	112	13.2	-64.79
15-16	35	143	14	16	15	98	9.8	-49.15

BY MONTH

NH Flat	W-R	Per cent	£1 Level Stake	Hurdles	W-R	Per cent	£1 Level Stake
May	0-2	0.0	-2.00	May	0-7	0.0	-7.00
June	0-0	0.0	0.00	June	3-8	37.5	+9.88
July	0-0	0.0	0.00	July	2-9	22.2	+33.00
August	0-0	0.0	0.00	August	0-8	0.0	-8.00
September	0-0	0.0	0.00	September	0-4	0.0	-4.00
October	0-0	0.0	0.00	October	0-11	0.0	-11.00
November	0-1	0.0	-1.00	November	0-13	0.0	-13.00
December	0-0	0.0	0.00	December	1-16	6.3	-13.50
January	0-1	0.0	-1.00	January	1-14	7.1	-12.09
February	0-0	0.0	0.00	February	0-11	0.0	-11.00
March	0-0	0.0	0.00	March	1-10	10.0	-3.50
April	0-2	0.0	-2.00	April	0-9	0.0	-9.00

Chases	W-R	Per cent	£1 Level Stake	Totals	W-R	Per cent	£1 Level Stake
May	0-4	0.0	-4.00	May	0-13	0.0	-13.00
June	2-7	28.6	+16.00	June	5-15	33.3	+25.88
July	0-4	0.0	-4.00	July	2-13	15.4	+29.00
August	0-1	0.0	-1.00	August	0-9	0.0	-9.00
September	1-2	50.0	+0.20	September	1-6	16.7	-3.80
October	0-4	0.0	-4.00	October	0-15	0.0	-15.00
November	0-9	0.0	-9.00	November	0-23	0.0	-23.00
December	1-13	7.7	-7.00	December	2-29	6.9	-20.50
January	1-9	11.1	-2.00	January	2-24	8.3	-15.09
February	1-8	12.5	-1.50	February	1-19	5.3	-12.50
March	3-5	60.0	+7.13	March	4-15	26.7	+3.63
April	0-6	0.0	-6.00	April	0-17	0.0	-17.00

DISTANCE

Hurdles	W-R	Per cent	£1 Level Stake	Chases	W-R	Per cent	£1 Level Stake
2m-2m3f	3-57	5.3	-8.00	2m-2m3f	1-15	6.7	-5.00
2m4f-2m7f	5-44	11.4	-22.22	2m4f-2m7f	5-24	20.8	-1.18
3m+	0-19	0.0	-19.00	3m+	3-33	9.1	-9.00

TYPE OF RACE

Non-Handicaps	W-R	Per cent	£1 Level Stake	Handicaps	W-R	Per cent	£1 Level Stake
Nov Hrdls	3-19	15.8	+19.41	Nov Hrdls	0-7		-7.00
Hrdls	2-24	8.3	-9.00	Hrdls	3-70	4.3	-52.63
Nov Chs	0-1	0.0	-1.00	Nov Chs	0-10	0.0	-10.00
Chases	0-1	0.0	-1.00	Chases	9-57	15.8	-0.17
Sell/Claim	0-0	0.0	0.00	Sell/Claim	0-0	0.0	0.00

RACE CLASS

	W-R	Per cent	£1 Level Stake
Class 1	0-2	0.0	-2.00
Class 2	1-19	5.3	-6.00
Class 3	2-27	7.4	-12.50
Class 4	13-108	12.0	-13.89
Class 5	1-41	2.4	-35.00
Class 6	0-1	0.0	-1.00

FIRST TIME OUT

	W-R	Per cent	£1 Level Stake
Bumpers	0-5	0.0	-5.00
Hurdles	1-23	4.3	-14.00
Chases	1-13	7.7	0.00
Totals	2-41	4.9	-19.00

JOCKEYS

	W-R	Per cent	£1 Level Stake
Sean Quinlan	14-154	9.1	-72.89
David Noonan	2-23	8.7	+17.50
Richie McLernon	1-2	50.0	+4.00

COURSE RECORD

	Total W-R	Non-Hndcps Hurdles	Chases	Hndcps Hurdles	Chases	NH Flat	Per cent	£1 Level Stake
Uttoxeter	3-33	1-10	0-0	1-11	1-12	0-0	9.1	+10.88
Mrket Rsn	2-9	1-3	0-0	1-3	0-3	0-0	22.2	+3.50

Sedgefield	2-10	2-3	0-1	0-4	0-2	0-0	20.0	-5.59
Carlisle	2-16	0-1	0-0	0-8	2-5	0-2	12.5	-6.88
Aintree	1-3	0-1	0-0	0-0	1-2	0-0	33.3	+7.00
Hexham	1-4	1-3	0-0	0-0	0-0	0-1	25.0	+5.00
Kelso	1-4	0-0	0-0	0-2	1-2	0-0	25.0	-1.80
Southwell	1-4	0-0	0-0	1-1	0-3	0-0	25.0	+4.00
Leicester	1-6	0-1	0-0	0-1	1-4	0-0	16.7	-1.50
Perth	1-7	0-0	0-0	0-5	1-2	0-0	14.3	+6.00
Huntingdon	1-8	0-1	0-0	0-5	1-2	0-0	12.5	-2.00
Bangor	1-18	0-2	0-0	0-7	1-7	0-2	5.6	-13.00

WINNING HORSES

Horse	Races Run	1st	2nd	3rd	£
Beeves	3	1	0	0	18768
Granville Island	7	3	0	1	19494
Theflyingportrait	7	1	0	1	6882
Grove Silver	7	1	0	1	6498
Bridane Rebel	12	2	1	2	8577
Spirit Of Hale	6	1	1	1	4614
*Costa Percy	4	2	1	1	8413
Quick Pick	8	2	1	2	7993
Red Giant	7	1	0	0	3899
Restraint Of Trade	4	2	1	1	7148
Basford Ben	9	1	0	0	3574
Total winning prize-money					**£95860**
Favourites	**4-12**		**33.3%**		**-2.39**

GRANT CANN
BATH, GLOUCESTERSHIRE

	No. of Hrs	Races Run	1st	2nd	3rd	Unpl	Per cent	£1 Level Stake
NH Flat	1	1	0	0	1	0	0.0	-1.00
Hurdles	3	3	0	0	1	2	0.0	-3.00
Chases	3	17	5	2	3	7	29.4	+33.50
Totals	6	21	5	2	5	9	23.8	+29.50
16-17	8	25	3	3	0	19	12.0	+14.00
15-16	4	14	1	3	1	9	7.1	-5.50

JOCKEYS

	W-R	Per cent	£1 Level Stake
Nick Scholfield	3-11	27.3	+26.50
James Bowen	1-2	50.0	+4.00
Tom O'Brien	1-4	25.0	+3.00

COURSE RECORD

	Total W-R	Non-Hndcps Hurdles	Chases	Hndcps Hurdles	Chases	NH Flat	Per cent	£1 Level Stake
Towcester	4-5	0-0	1-1	0-1	3-3	0-0	80.0	+38.50
Warwick	1-3	0-0	0-0	0-0	1-3	0-0	33.3	+4.00

WINNING HORSES

Horse	Races Run	1st	2nd	3rd	£
Cadeau Du Bresil	4	1	0	1	5588
How's My Friend	7	3	2	0	14023
Goosen Maverick	7	1	0	2	3249
Total winning prize-money					**£22860**
Favourites		1-3		33.3%	3.00

DON CANTILLON
NEWMARKET, SUFFOLK

	No. of Hrs	Races Run	1st	2nd	3rd	Unpl	Per cent	£1 Level Stake
NH Flat	0	0	0	0	0	0	0.0	0.00
Hurdles	3	7	1	1	0	5	14.3	-5.75
Chases	0	0	0	0	0	0	0.0	0.00
Totals	3	7	1	1	0	5	14.3	-5.75
16-17	7	15	4	5	2	4	26.7	+0.28
15-16	7	25	4	3	4	14	16.0	-3.13

JOCKEYS

	W-R	Per cent	£1 Level Stake
Conor Shoemark	1-1	100.0	+0.25

COURSE RECORD

	Total W-R	Non-Hndcps Hurdles	Chases	Hndcps Hurdles	Chases	NH Flat	Per cent	£1 Level Stake
Hexham	1-1	1-1	0-0	0-0	0-0	0-0	100.0	+0.25

WINNING HORSES

Horse	Races Run	1st	2nd	3rd	£
Hint Of Grey	5	1	1	0	3249
Total winning prize-money					**£3249**
Favourites		1-2		50.0%	-0.75

TONY CARROLL
CROPTHORNE, WORCS

	No. of Hrs	Races Run	1st	2nd	3rd	Unpl	Per cent	£1 Level Stake
NH Flat	3	3	0	0	0	3	0.0	-3.00
Hurdles	11	32	5	6	3	18	15.6	-0.88
Chases	10	41	1	7	3	30	2.4	-36.00
Totals	20	76	6	13	6	51	7.9	-39.88
16-17	24	97	5	11	13	68	5.2	-18.00
15-16	28	103	8	17	9	69	7.8	-8.00

JOCKEYS

	W-R	Per cent	£1 Level Stake
Lee Edwards	5-43	11.6	-19.88
James Nixon	1-17	5.9	-4.00

COURSE RECORD

	Total W-R	Non-Hndcps Hurdles	Chases	Hndcps Hurdles	Chases	NH Flat	Per cent	£1 Level Stake
Bangor	2-5	0-1	0-0	2-2	0-1	0-1	40.0	+3.63
Sedgefield	1-1	0-0	0-0	0-0	1-1	0-0	100.0	+4.00
Aintree	1-2	0-0	0-0	1-1	0-1	0-0	50.0	+11.00
Huntingdon	1-4	1-1	0-0	0-1	0-1	0-1	25.0	+1.00
Stratford	1-6	0-2	0-0	1-3	0-1	0-0	16.7	-1.50

WINNING HORSES

Horse	Races Run	1st	2nd	3rd	£
Havana Beat	5	2	2	1	34199
Prairie Town	7	1	1	2	7343
Be My Sea	2	1	1	0	3899
Black Buble	4	1	0	1	3509
Mr Mafia	11	1	2	0	3249
Total winning prize-money					£52199
Favourites	1-1		100.0%		1.63

BEN CASE

EDGCOTE, NORTHANTS

	No. of Hrs	Races Run	1st	2nd	3rd	Unpl	Per cent	£1 Level Stake
NH Flat	13	26	1	1	4	20	3.8	-11.00
Hurdles	25	103	8	11	13	71	7.8	-41.50
Chases	7	29	3	3	3	20	10.3	-11.00
Totals	37	158	12	15	20	111	7.6	-63.50
16-17	36	138	16	16	15	91	11.6	-28.93
15-16	38	159	7	24	21	107	4.4	-107.50

BY MONTH

NH Flat	W-R	Per cent	£1 Level Stake	Hurdles	W-R	Per cent	£1 Level Stake
May	0-3	0.0	-3.00	May	1-12	8.3	-7.50
June	0-1	0.0	-1.00	June	1-5	20.0	+3.50
July	0-2	0.0	-2.00	July	0-1	0.0	-1.00
August	0-0	0.0	0.00	August	1-2	50.0	+5.00
September	0-0	0.0	0.00	September	0-5	0.0	-5.00
October	0-1	0.0	-1.00	October	1-8	12.5	+4.00
November	0-2	0.0	-2.00	November	1-17	5.9	-5.00
December	0-2	0.0	-2.00	December	1-16	6.3	-8.50
January	1-1	100.0	+14.00	January	0-10	0.0	-10.00
February	0-4	0.0	-4.00	February	1-10	10.0	-2.50
March	0-4	0.0	-4.00	March	1-12	8.3	-9.50
April	0-6	0.0	-6.00	April	0-5	0.0	-5.00

Chases	W-R	Per cent	£1 Level Stake	Totals	W-R	Per cent	£1 Level Stake
May	1-5	20.0	+0.50	May	2-20	10.0	-10.00
June	0-1	0.0	-1.00	June	1-7	14.3	+1.50
July	0-0	0.0	0.00	July	0-3	0.0	-3.00
August	0-0	0.0	0.00	August	1-2	50.0	+5.00
September	0-0	0.0	0.00	September	0-5	0.0	-5.00
October	0-1	0.0	-1.00	October	1-10	10.0	+2.00
November	0-4	0.0	-4.00	November	1-23	4.3	-11.00

December	1-6	16.7	+1.00	December	2-24	8.3	-9.50
January	1-3	33.3	+2.50	January	2-14	14.3	+6.50
February	0-3	0.0	-3.00	February	1-17	5.9	-9.50
March	0-2	0.0	-2.00	March	1-18	5.6	-15.50
April	0-4	0.0	-4.00	April	0-15	0.0	-15.00

DISTANCE

Hurdles	W-R	Per cent	£1 Level Stake	Chases	W-R	Per cent	£1 Level Stake
2m-2m3f	5-51	9.8	-21.00	2m-2m3f	1-2	50.0	+3.50
2m4f-2m7f	2-42	4.8	-18.00	2m4f-2m7f	0-11	0.0	-11.00
3m+	1-10	10.0	-2.50	3m+	2-16	12.5	-3.50

TYPE OF RACE

Non-Handicaps	W-R	Per cent	£1 Level Stake	Handicaps	W-R	Per cent	£1 Level Stake
Nov Hrdls	3-28	10.7	-10.50	Nov Hrdls	0-5	0.0	-5.00
Hrdls	2-19	10.5	-2.50	Hrdls	3-49	6.1	-21.50
Nov Chs	0-0	0.0	0.00	Nov Chs	0-3	0.0	-3.00
Chases	0-0	0.0	0.00	Chases	3-26	11.5	-8.00
Sell/Claim	0-0	0.0	0.00	Sell/Claim	0-0	0.0	0.00

RACE CLASS

	W-R	Per cent	£1 Level Stake
Class 1	0-12	0.0	-12.00
Class 2	0-5	0.0	-5.00
Class 3	3-19	15.8	+4.00
Class 4	7-61	11.5	-16.50
Class 5	2-53	3.8	-26.00
Class 6	0-8	0.0	-8.00

FIRST TIME OUT

	W-R	Per cent	£1 Level Stake
Bumpers	1-13	7.7	+2.00
Hurdles	0-19	0.0	-19.00
Chases	1-5	20.0	+0.50
Totals	2-37	5.4	-16.50

JOCKEYS

	W-R	Per cent	£1 Level Stake
Max Kendrick	7-62	11.3	-8.00
Daryl Jacob	4-44	9.1	-18.50
Kielan Woods	1-21	4.8	-6.00

COURSE RECORD

	Total W-R	Non-Hndcps Hurdles	Chases	Hndcps Hurdles	Chases	NH Flat	Per cent	£1 Level Stake
Doncaster	3-9	2-4	0-0	0-2	0-1	1-2	33.3	+21.00
Haydock	1-2	0-0	0-0	0-1	1-1	0-0	50.0	+3.50
Wincanton	1-2	0-0	0-0	0-0	1-2	0-0	50.0	+3.50
Ascot	1-3	0-1	0-0	1-2	0-0	0-0	33.3	+9.00
Fontwell	1-4	0-1	0-0	1-1	0-2	0-0	25.0	+4.50
Mrket Rsn	1-11	1-4	0-0	0-3	0-3	0-1	9.1	-8.50
Uttoxeter	1-11	1-3	0-0	0-5	0-1	0-2	9.1	+1.00
Worcester	1-12	0-3	0-0	1-6	0-1	0-2	8.3	-5.00
Warwick	1-15	0-7	0-0	0-2	1-1	0-5	6.7	-8.00
Towcester	1-16	1-7	0-0	0-3	0-3	0-3	6.3	-11.50

WINNING HORSES

Horse	Races Run	1st	2nd	3rd	£
Themanfrom Minella	8	2	1	0	22244
Crookstown	9	1	0	0	9747
Graceful Legend	6	1	0	3	6498
First Drift	5	2	1	0	8642
Oski	4	2	0	1	6563
Ginger Fizz	8	2	0	1	6628
Monar Rose	7	1	0	0	3249
Princess Roxy	3	1	0	0	2274
Total winning prize-money					**£65845**
Favourites	0-5	0.0%			-5.00

MICK CHANNON

WEST ILSLEY, BERKS

	No. of Hrs	Races Run	1st	2nd	3rd	Unpl	Per cent	£1 Level Stake
NH Flat	5	11	2	1	0	8	18.2	0.00
Hurdles	3	8	0	0	0	8	0.0	-8.00
Chases	1	5	3	1	1	0	60.0	+17.50
Totals	6	24	5	2	1	16	20.8	+9.50
16-17	6	23	1	3	4	15	4.3	-19.00
15-16	14	43	4	6	4	29	9.3	-18.50

JOCKEYS

	W-R	Per cent	£1 Level Stake
Brian Hughes	2-2	100.0	+11.50
A P Heskin	2-8	25.0	+7.00
Graham Lee	1-5	20.0	0.00

COURSE RECORD

	Total W-R	Non-Hndcps Hurdles	Chases	Hndcps Hurdles	Chases	NH Flat	Per cent	£1 Level Stake
Cheltenham	2-2	0-0	0-0	0-0	2-2	0-0	100.0	+12.50
Ascot	1-1	0-0	0-0	0-0	0-0	1-1	100.0	+5.00
Carlisle	1-2	0-0	0-0	0-0	1-1	0-1	50.0	+6.00
Warwick	1-2	0-1	0-0	0-0	0-0	1-1	50.0	+3.00

WINNING HORSES

Horse	Races Run	1st	2nd	3rd	£
Mister Whitaker	5	3	1	1	64867
Buildmeupbuttercup	3	2	0	0	4549
Total winning prize-money					**£69416**
Favourites	0-2	0.0%			-2.00

PAUL COLLINS

SALTBURN, CLEVELAND

	No. of Hrs	Races Run	1st	2nd	3rd	Unpl	Per cent	£1 Level Stake
NH Flat	0	0	0	0	0	0	0.0	0.00

							Per cent	£1 Level Stake
Hurdles	0	0	0	0	0	0	0.0	0.00
Chases	2	16	5	3	4	4	31.3	+33.50
Totals	2	16	5	3	4	4	31.3	+33.50
16-17	2	2	0	0	0	2	0.0	-2.00
15-16	2	2	0	0	0	2	0.0	-2.00

JOCKEYS

	W-R	Per cent	£1 Level Stake
Ross Chapman	5-15	33.3	+34.50

COURSE RECORD

	Total W-R	Non-Hndcps Hurdles	Chases	Hndcps Hurdles	Chases	NH Flat	Per cent	£1 Level Stake
Sedgefield	2-2	0-0	0-0	0-0	2-2	0-0	100.0	+14.50
Hexham	2-5	0-0	0-0	0-0	2-5	0-0	40.0	+24.50
Catterick	1-2	0-0	0-1	0-0	1-1	0-0	50.0	+1.50

WINNING HORSES

Horse	Races Run	1st	2nd	3rd	£
Dica	12	5	3	2	21703
Total winning prize-money					**£21703**
Favourites	0-1	0.0%			-1.00

MISS V COLLINS

BASINGSTOKE, HANTS

	No. of Hrs	Races Run	1st	2nd	3rd	Unpl	Per cent	£1 Level Stake
NH Flat	0	0	0	0	0	0	0.0	0.00
Hurdles	0	0	0	0	0	0	0.0	0.00
Chases	3	7	1	3	0	3	14.3	-3.50
Totals	3	7	1	3	0	3	14.3	-3.50
16-17	4	5	1	1	2	1	20.0	+3.00
15-16	2	2	0	0	0	2	0.0	-2.00

JOCKEYS

	W-R	Per cent	£1 Level Stake
Mr Samuel Davies-Thomas	1-2	50.0	+1.50

COURSE RECORD

	Total W-R	Non-Hndcps Hurdles	Chases	Hndcps Hurdles	Chases	NH Flat	Per cent	£1 Level Stake
Fontwell	1-3	0-0	1-3	0-0	0-0	0-0	33.3	+0.50

WINNING HORSES

Horse	Races Run	1st	2nd	3rd	£
Queen Olivia	3	1	2	0	1280
Total winning prize-money					**£1280**
Favourites	0-0	0.0%			0.00

STUART COLTHERD

SELKIRK, BORDERS

	No. of Hrs	Races Run	1st	2nd	3rd	Unpl	Per cent	£1 Level Stake
NH Flat	1	1	0	0	0	1	0.0	-1.00
Hurdles	19	67	2	4	8	53	3.0	-48.50
Chases	12	37	2	4	8	23	5.4	-16.50
Totals	26	105	4	8	16	77	3.8	-66.00
16-17	22	117	18	17	13	69	15.4	+1.00
15-16	24	130	10	13	14	93	7.7	-23.00

JOCKEYS

	W-R	Per cent	£1 Level Stake
Sam Coltherd	3-89	3.4	-55.50
Conor O'Farrell	1-1	100.0	+4.50

COURSE RECORD

	Total W-R	Non-Hndcps Hurdles	Chases	Hndcps Hurdles	Chases	NH Flat	Per cent	£1 Level Stake
Wetherby	1-5	0-0	0-0	1-4	0-1	0-0	20.0	+7.00
Haydock	1-9	0-2	0-0	0-3	1-4	0-0	11.1	+6.00
Ayr	1-17	0-7	0-0	1-5	0-5	0-0	5.9	-10.50
Carlisle	1-19	0-4	0-0	0-11	1-4	0-0	5.3	-13.50

WINNING HORSES

Horse	Races Run	1st	2nd	3rd	£
Captain Redbeard	6	2	1	1	26355
Achill Road Boy	11	1	2	1	6498
Pookie Pekan	5	1	0	0	4809
Total winning prize-money					£37662
Favourites	0-3		0.0%		-3.00

MRS H CONNORS

MELTON MOWBRAY, LEICESTERSHIRE

	No. of Hrs	Races Run	1st	2nd	3rd	Unpl	Per cent	£1 Level Stake
NH Flat	0	0	0	0	0	0	0.0	0.00
Hurdles	0	0	0	0	0	0	0.0	0.00
Chases	1	4	1	0	1	2	25.0	-1.00
Totals	1	4	1	0	1	2	25.0	-1.00
16-17	1	2	0	1	0	1	0.0	-2.00
15-16	1	1	0	0	0	1	0.0	-1.00

JOCKEYS

	W-R	Per cent	£1 Level Stake
Mr Tom Chatfeild-Roberts	1-4	25.0	-1.00

COURSE RECORD

	Total W-R	Non-Hndcps Hurdles	Chases	Hndcps Hurdles	Chases	NH Flat	Per cent	£1 Level Stake
Doncaster	1-1	0-0	1-1	0-0	0-0	0-0	100.0	+2.00

WINNING HORSES

Horse	Races Run	1st	2nd	3rd	£
*Warden Hill	4	1	0	1	2496
Total winning prize-money					£2496
Favourites	0-0		0.0%		0.00

SUSAN CORBETT

OTTERBURN, NORTHUMBERLAND

	No. of Hrs	Races Run	1st	2nd	3rd	Unpl	Per cent	£1 Level Stake
NH Flat	12	26	2	1	7	16	7.7	-14.50
Hurdles	25	117	11	17	17	72	9.4	-37.75
Chases	2	3	0	0	0	3	0.0	-3.00
Totals	31	146	13	18	24	91	8.9	-55.25
16-17	21	81	6	6	9	60	7.4	-6.17
15-16	14	82	5	11	4	62	6.1	-49.50

BY MONTH

NH Flat	W-R	Per cent	£1 Level Stake	Hurdles	W-R	Per cent	£1 Level Stake
May	1-2	50.0	+3.50	May	0-7	0.0	-7.00
June	0-2	0.0	-2.00	June	0-5	0.0	-5.00
July	0-2	0.0	-2.00	July	1-10	10.0	-7.75
August	0-5	0.0	-5.00	August	2-10	20.0	+7.00
September	0-0	0.0	0.00	September	1-9	11.1	-0.50
October	0-1	0.0	-1.00	October	1-12	8.3	-3.00
November	1-7	14.3	0.00	November	1-18	5.6	-6.00
December	0-0	0.0	0.00	December	2-13	15.4	+3.50
January	0-3	0.0	-3.00	January	0-8	0.0	-8.00
February	0-2	0.0	-2.00	February	1-7	14.3	-1.50
March	0-1	0.0	-1.00	March	1-10	10.0	-4.50
April	0-1	0.0	-1.00	April	1-8	12.5	-5.00

Chases	W-R	Per cent	£1 Level Stake	Totals	W-R	Per cent	£1 Level Stake
May	0-0	0.0	0.00	May	1-9	11.1	-3.50
June	0-0	0.0	0.00	June	0-7	0.0	-7.00
July	0-0	0.0	0.00	July	1-12	8.3	-9.75
August	0-0	0.0	0.00	August	2-15	13.3	+2.00
September	0-0	0.0	0.00	September	1-9	11.1	-0.50
October	0-1	0.0	-1.00	October	1-14	7.1	-5.00
November	0-0	0.0	0.00	November	2-25	8.0	-7.00
December	0-1	0.0	-1.00	December	2-14	14.3	+2.50
January	0-0	0.0	0.00	January	0-11	0.0	-11.00
February	0-0	0.0	0.00	February	1-9	11.1	-3.50
March	0-0	0.0	0.00	March	1-11	9.1	-5.50
April	0-1	0.0	-1.00	April	1-10	10.0	-7.00

DISTANCE

Hurdles	W-R	Per cent	£1 Level Stake	Chases	W-R	Per cent	£1 Level Stake
2m-2m3f	5-65	7.7	-33.50	2m-2m3f	0-1	0.0	-1.00
2m4f-2m7f	4-39	10.3	-10.75	2m4f-2m7f	0-2	0.0	-2.00
3m+	2-13	15.4	+6.50	3m+	0-0	0.0	0.00

TYPE OF RACE

Non-Handicaps

	W-R	Per cent	£1 Level Stake
Nov Hrdls	0-30	0.0	-30.00
Hrdls	2-18	11.1	-2.75
Nov Chs	0-0	0.0	0.00
Chases	0-0	0.0	0.00
Sell/Claim	0-3	0.0	-3.00

Handicaps

	W-R	Per cent	£1 Level Stake
Nov Hrdls	0-5	0.0	-5.00
Hrdls	9-61	14.8	+3.00
Nov Chs	0-0	0.0	0.00
Chases	0-3	0.0	-3.00
Sell/Claim	0-0	0.0	0.00

RACE CLASS

	W-R	Per cent	£1 Level Stake
Class 1	0-2	0.0	-2.00
Class 2	1-4	25.0	+7.00
Class 3	2-15	13.3	-8.00
Class 4	5-78	6.4	-36.50
Class 5	4-34	11.8	-8.75
Class 6	1-13	7.7	-7.00

FIRST TIME OUT

	W-R	Per cent	£1 Level Stake
Bumpers	1-12	8.3	-6.50
Hurdles	1-18	5.6	-6.00
Chases	0-1	0.0	-1.00
Totals	2-31	6.5	-13.50

JOCKEYS

	W-R	Per cent	£1 Level Stake
James Corbett	11-131	8.4	-54.25
Thomas Dowson	1-2	50.0	+1.00
Sam Coltherd	1-6	16.7	+5.00

COURSE RECORD

	Total W-R	Non-Hndcps Hurdles	Chases	Hndcps Hurdles	Chases	NH Flat	Per cent	£1 Level Stake
Perth	4-20	1-6	0-0	3-10	0-0	0-4	20.0	+8.50
Kelso	2-14	0-5	0-0	1-5	0-1	1-3	14.3	+0.50
Catterick	1-2	0-0	0-0	1-2	0-0	0-0	50.0	+3.50
Uttoxeter	1-2	1-2	0-0	0-0	0-0	0-0	50.0	+0.25
Newcastle	1-8	0-3	0-0	1-3	0-1	0-1	12.5	-2.50
Carlisle	1-11	0-3	0-0	1-5	0-1	0-2	9.1	0.00
Wetherby	1-14	0-7	0-0	0-4	0-0	1-3	7.1	-8.00
Mrket Rsn	1-17	0-6	0-0	1-6	0-0	0-5	5.9	-5.00
Musselbgh	1-20	0-3	0-0	1-14	0-0	0-3	5.0	-14.50

WINNING HORSES

Horse	Races Run	1st	2nd	3rd	£
Ebony Rose	7	3	1	1	22522
Morning With Ivan	6	4	1	1	17220
Ahead Of The Curve	10	2	3	1	9481
Toarmandowithlove	7	1	1	0	3509
Heartasia	4	1	1	2	3249
Reivers Lodge	15	1	3	2	3249
Harrisons Promise	3	1	0	1	2209
Total winning prize-money					**£61439**
Favourites	2-6	33.3%			-0.75

JOHN CORNWALL

LONG CLAWSON, LEICS

	No. of Hrs	Races Run	1st	2nd	3rd	Unpl	Per cent	£1 Level Stake
NH Flat	0	0	0	0	0	0	0.0	0.00
Hurdles	1	1	0	0	0	1	0.0	-1.00
Chases	4	30	3	2	2	23	10.0	+22.00
Totals	5	31	3	2	2	24	9.7	+21.00
16-17	5	56	3	7	15	31	5.4	-13.00
15-16	6	28	0	1	5	22	0.0	-28.00

JOCKEYS

	W-R	Per cent	£1 Level Stake
Lee Edwards	2-20	10.0	+6.00
Ben Poste	1-9	11.1	+17.00

COURSE RECORD

	Total W-R	Non-Hndcps Hurdles	Chases	Hndcps Hurdles	Chases	NH Flat	Per cent	£1 Level Stake
Fakenham	2-4	0-0	0-0	0-0	2-4	0-0	50.0	+22.00
Huntingdon	1-7	0-0	0-0	0-0	1-7	0-0	14.3	+19.00

WINNING HORSES

Horse	Races Run	1st	2nd	3rd	£
That's The Deal	15	3	2	2	18433
Total winning prize-money					**£18433**
Favourites	0-0		0.0%		0.00

MRS SHEILA CROW

SHREWSBURY, SHROPSHIRE

	No. of Hrs	Races Run	1st	2nd	3rd	Unpl	Per cent	£1 Level Stake
NH Flat	0	0	0	0	0	0	0.0	0.00
Hurdles	0	0	0	0	0	0	0.0	0.00
Chases	3	7	3	0	0	4	42.9	+5.80
Totals	3	7	3	0	0	4	42.9	+5.80
16-17	4	9	2	1	0	6	22.2	0.00
15-16	4	10	0	1	3	6	0.0	-10.00

JOCKEYS

	W-R	Per cent	£1 Level Stake
Mr Henry Crow	2-3	66.7	+2.80
Mr Jack Andrews	1-3	33.3	+4.00

COURSE RECORD

	Total W-R	Non-Hndcps Hurdles	Chases	Hndcps Hurdles	Chases	NH Flat	Per cent	£1 Level Stake
Ludlow	2-2	0-0	2-2	0-0	0-0	0-0	100.0	+3.80
Towcester	1-1	0-0	1-1	0-0	0-0	0-0	100.0	+6.00

WINNING HORSES

Horse	Races Run	1st	2nd	3rd	£
Mr Mercurial	3	2	0	0	7105
Abbeyview	2	1	0	0	1872
Total winning prize-money					£8977
Favourites	1-1		100.0%		0.80

REBECCA CURTIS

NEWPORT, PEMBROKESHIRE

	No. of Hrs	Races Run	1st	2nd	3rd	Unpl	Per cent	£1 Level Stake
NH Flat	5	5	0	0	0	5	0.0	-5.00
Hurdles	12	32	0	9	3	20	0.0	-32.00
Chases	15	52	9	3	6	34	17.3	+16.00
Totals	27	89	9	12	9	59	10.1	-21.00
16-17	57	212	30	16	29	137	14.2	-9.77
15-16	56	194	24	16	25	129	12.4	-34.31

JOCKEYS

	W-R	Per cent	£1 Level Stake
Adam Wedge	3-21	14.3	+22.50
Jonathan Moore	3-31	9.7	-20.00
Niall P Madden	2-3	66.7	+4.50
James Bowen	1-6	16.7	0.00

COURSE RECORD

	Total W-R	Non-Hndcps Hurdles	Chases	Hndcps Hurdles	Chases	NH Flat	Per cent	£1 Level Stake
Worcester	2-6	0-1	0-0	0-1	2-4	0-0	33.3	+5.00
Ayr	1-1	0-0	0-0	0-0	1-1	0-0	100.0	+33.00
Nton Abbot	1-3	0-0	0-0	0-0	1-3	0-0	33.3	-0.25
Hereford	1-6	0-4	1-1	0-0	0-0	0-1	16.7	-3.50
Aintree	1-6	0-1	0-1	0-1	1-3	0-0	16.7	-3.25
Taunton	1-7	0-2	0-0	0-1	1-4	0-0	14.3	-2.00
Ludlow	1-8	0-2	0-0	0-0	1-6	0-0	12.5	-2.00
Newbury	1-9	0-1	0-0	0-2	1-5	0-1	11.1	-5.00

WINNING HORSES

Horse	Races Run	1st	2nd	3rd	£
Joe Farrell	6	2	1	1	129785
Relentless Dreamer	8	1	1	1	15640
Geordie Des Champs	4	2	0	1	14395
Vintage Vinnie	2	1	0	0	6882
One Term	5	1	0	1	6330
Going For Broke	6	2	0	0	9162
Total winning prize-money					£182194
Favourites	4-10		40.0%		2.00

KEITH DALGLEISH

CARLUKE, S LANARKS

	No. of Hrs	Races Run	1st	2nd	3rd	Unpl	Per cent	£1 Level Stake
NH Flat	5	13	6	3	2	2	46.2	+8.00
Hurdles	21	63	16	7	5	35	25.4	+23.40
Chases	4	9	2	1	2	4	22.2	+0.50
Totals	27	85	24	11	9	41	28.2	+31.90
16-17	14	40	11	2	3	24	27.5	-6.89
15-16	16	46	10	11	2	23	21.7	+4.23

BY MONTH

NH Flat	W-R	Per cent	£1 Level Stake	Hurdles	W-R	Per cent	£1 Level Stake
May	0-0	0.0	0.00	May	0-0	0.0	0.00
June	0-0	0.0	0.00	June	0-0	0.0	0.00
July	0-0	0.0	0.00	July	1-1	100.0	+5.00
August	0-0	0.0	0.00	August	1-7	14.3	-4.25
September	1-2	50.0	+4.00	September	3-3	100.0	+7.25
October	1-1	100.0	+1.25	October	2-6	33.3	+1.00
November	2-4	50.0	+3.75	November	3-9	33.3	-4.37
December	0-0	0.0	0.00	December	1-5	20.0	-3.90
January	1-2	50.0	0.00	January	2-12	16.7	+31.00
February	0-1	0.0	-1.00	February	3-9	33.3	+2.67
March	1-1	100.0	+2.00	March	0-4	0.0	-4.00
April	0-2	0.0	-2.00	April	0-7	0.0	-7.00

Chases	W-R	Per cent	£1 Level Stake	Totals	W-R	Per cent	£1 Level Stake
May	0-2	0.0	-2.00	May	0-2	0.0	-2.00
June	0-0	0.0	0.00	June	0-0	0.0	0.00
July	0-0	0.0	0.00	July	1-1	100.0	+5.00
August	0-0	0.0	0.00	August	1-7	14.3	-4.25
September	0-0	0.0	0.00	September	4-5	80.0	+11.25
October	0-0	0.0	0.00	October	3-7	42.9	+2.25
November	0-2	0.0	-2.00	November	5-15	33.3	-2.62
December	0-1	0.0	-1.00	December	1-6	16.7	-4.90
January	1-1	100.0	+1.00	January	4-15	26.7	+32.00
February	1-1	100.0	+6.50	February	4-11	36.4	+8.17
March	0-0	0.0	0.00	March	1-5	20.0	-2.00
April	0-2	0.0	-2.00	April	0-11	0.0	-11.00

DISTANCE

Hurdles	W-R	Per cent	£1 Level Stake	Chases	W-R	Per cent	£1 Level Stake
2m-2m3f	11-46	23.9	+27.34	2m-2m3f	1-4	25.0	-2.00
2m4f-2m7f	4-12	33.3	-1.69	2m4f-2m7f	1-3	33.3	+4.50
3m+	1-5	20.0	-2.25	3m+	0-2	0.0	-2.00

TYPE OF RACE

Non-Handicaps	W-R	Per cent	£1 Level Stake	Handicaps	W-R	Per cent	£1 Level Stake
Nov Hrdls	5-14	35.7	-2.17	Nov Hrdls	0-0	0.0	0.00
Hrdls	4-14	28.6	+0.32	Hrdls	6-33	18.2	+18.25
Nov Chs	1-2	50.0	+5.50	Nov Chs	0-0	0.0	0.00

Chases	0-0	0.0	0.00	Chases	1-4	25.0	-2.00
Sell/Claim	0-0	0.0	0.00	Sell/Claim	0-0	0.0	0.00

HENRY DALY

STANTON LACY, SHROPSHIRE

	No. of Hrs	Races Run	1st	2nd	3rd	Unpl	Per cent	£1 Level Stake
NH Flat	14	20	4	1	1	14	20.0	+15.75
Hurdles	19	89	18	14	6	51	20.2	+17.63
Chases	15	53	11	6	6	30	20.8	-2.67
Totals	**37**	**162**	**33**	**21**	**13**	**95**	**20.4**	**+30.71**
16-17	42	146	20	14	15	97	13.7	+7.50
15-16	43	167	18	21	19	109	10.8	-85.43

RACE CLASS

	W-R	Per cent	£1 Level Stake
Class 1	0-6	0.0	-6.00
Class 2	2-10	20.0	+28.00
Class 3	3-15	20.0	-6.25
Class 4	11-37	29.7	+6.15
Class 5	5-12	41.7	+5.00
Class 6	3-5	60.0	+5.00

FIRST TIME OUT

	W-R	Per cent	£1 Level Stake
Bumpers	2-5	40.0	+4.75
Hurdles	8-19	42.1	+13.57
Chases	1-3	33.3	-1.00
Totals	11-27	40.7	+17.32

JOCKEYS

	W-R	Per cent	£1 Level Stake
Brian Hughes	13-41	31.7	+1.82
Craig Nichol	5-13	38.5	+1.83
Callum Bewley	5-26	19.2	+27.25
Finian O'Toole	1-2	50.0	+4.00

COURSE RECORD

	Total W-R	Non-Hndcps Hurdles	Chases	Hndcps Hurdles	Chases	NH Flat	Per cent	£1 Level Stake
Musselbgh	8-18	4-6	1-1	0-7	1-1	2-3	44.4	+9.34
Kelso	6-12	2-3	0-0	4-8	0-0	0-1	50.0	+41.98
Perth	4-7	1-2	0-0	2-3	0-1	1-1	57.1	+8.00
Hexham	3-6	2-4	0-0	0-0	0-1	1-1	50.0	+0.83
Stratford	1-1	1-1	0-0	0-0	0-0	0-0	100.0	+5.00
Catterick	1-4	0-1	0-0	0-2	0-0	1-1	25.0	-0.25
Newcastle	1-5	0-2	0-0	0-1	0-1	1-1	20.0	-1.00

WINNING HORSES

Horse	Races Run	1st	2nd	3rd	£
Mirsaale	10	3	0	2	32922
Mixboy	2	1	1	0	10007
Mac N Cheese	5	2	0	1	10137
Delegate	4	1	0	1	4614
*Picture Painter	2	1	0	0	4549
Taxmeifyoucan	5	2	0	1	8772
Niceandeasy	5	2	1	0	7473
Silver Concorde	5	3	1	0	10701
*Uptown Funk	3	1	0	0	4094
Senor Lombardy	4	2	2	0	5458
Eneko	4	1	1	0	3249
I'm To Blame	2	2	0	0	4549
*Chanceanotherfive	4	2	1	0	4092
Sporting Press	3	1	0	1	2274
Total winning prize-money					**£112891**
Favourites	12-30		40.0%		-5.10

BY MONTH

NH Flat	W-R	Per cent	£1 Level Stake	Hurdles	W-R	Per cent	£1 Level Stake
May	2-3	66.7	+25.00	May	4-10	40.0	+15.75
June	0-1	0.0	-1.00	June	0-2	0.0	-2.00
July	0-0	0.0	0.00	July	1-3	33.3	+4.00
August	0-0	0.0	0.00	August	0-2	0.0	-2.00
September	0-1	0.0	-1.00	September	1-2	50.0	+7.00
October	0-3	0.0	-3.00	October	1-5	20.0	+2.50
November	0-3	0.0	-3.00	November	1-12	8.3	-6.50
December	0-2	0.0	-2.00	December	3-12	25.0	+5.50
January	1-1	100.0	+2.75	January	3-15	20.0	+2.50
February	0-1	0.0	-1.00	February	2-6	33.3	+2.50
March	0-2	0.0	-2.00	March	2-9	22.2	-0.63
April	1-3	33.3	+1.00	April	0-11	0.0	-11.00

Chases	W-R	Per cent	£1 Level Stake	Totals	W-R	Per cent	£1 Level Stake
May	1-5	20.0	-1.00	May	7-18	38.9	+39.75
June	0-1	0.0	-1.00	June	0-4	0.0	-4.00
July	0-0	0.0	0.00	July	1-3	33.3	+4.00
August	0-0	0.0	0.00	August	0-2	0.0	-2.00
September	0-0	0.0	0.00	September	1-3	33.3	+6.00
October	0-5	0.0	-5.00	October	1-13	7.7	-5.50
November	3-10	30.0	+2.25	November	4-25	16.0	-7.25
December	0-8	0.0	-8.00	December	3-22	13.6	-4.50
January	3-7	42.9	+7.50	January	7-23	30.4	+12.75
February	3-6	50.0	+9.25	February	5-13	38.5	+10.75
March	0-5	0.0	-5.00	March	2-16	12.5	-7.63
April	1-6	16.7	-1.67	April	2-20	10.0	-11.67

DISTANCE

Hurdles	W-R	Per cent	£1 Level Stake	Chases	W-R	Per cent	£1 Level Stake
2m-2m3f	5-26	19.2	-0.88	2m-2m3f	0-1	0.0	-1.00
2m4f-2m7f	6-46	13.0	+0.50	2m4f-2m7f	2-20	10.0	-11.25
3m+	7-17	41.2	+18.00	3m+	9-32	28.1	+9.58

TYPE OF RACE

Non-Handicaps	W-R	Per cent	£1 Level Stake	Handicaps	W-R	Per cent	£1 Level Stake
Nov Hrdls	6-32	18.8	-1.38	Nov Hrdls	0-3	0.0	-3.00
Hrdls	2-9	22.2	+1.50	Hrdls	10-44	22.7	+21.50
Nov Chs	0-3	0.0	-3.00	Nov Chs	1-5	20.0	-0.50

| Chases | 0-1 | 0.0 | -1.00 | Chases | 10-36 | 27.8 | +9.83 |
| Sell/Claim | 0-0 | 0.0 | 0.00 | Sell/Claim | 0-0 | 0.0 | 0.00 |

RACE CLASS | ## FIRST TIME OUT

	W-R	Per cent	£1 Level Stake		W-R	Per cent	£1 Level Stake
Class 1	0-13	0.0	-13.00	Bumpers	2-14	14.3	+14.00
Class 2	0-10	0.0	-10.00	Hurdles	3-10	30.0	+8.75
Class 3	6-32	18.8	+3.75	Chases	3-13	23.1	-1.92
Class 4	18-77	23.4	+6.21				
Class 5	9-24	37.5	+50.75	Totals	8-37	21.6	+20.83
Class 6	0-6	0.0	-6.00				

JOCKEYS

	W-R	Per cent	£1 Level Stake
Richard Johnson	13-41	31.7	+18.46
Andrew Tinkler	10-65	15.4	+16.50
Paddy Brennan	4-6	66.7	+13.25
Mr M A Galligan	3-5	60.0	+5.50
Nico de Boinville	1-2	50.0	+6.00
Jack Sherwood	1-7	14.3	-2.00
Mr Hugh Nugent	1-12	8.3	-3.00

COURSE RECORD

	Total W-R	Non-Hndcps Hurdles	Chases	Hndcps Hurdles	Chases	NH Flat	Per cent	£1 Level Stake
Warwick	6-14	2-4	0-0	2-5	1-3	1-2	42.9	+13.88
Ludlow	6-24	2-12	0-0	2-4	2-6	0-2	25.0	+1.00
Bangor	4-9	1-3	0-0	0-1	1-2	2-3	44.4	+28.50
Towcester	3-7	1-2	0-0	0-0	1-4	1-1	42.9	+13.00
Stratford	3-8	1-1	0-0	2-5	0-2	0-0	37.5	+13.50
Uttoxeter	2-12	0-1	0-0	1-4	1-6	0-1	16.7	+2.00
Lingfield	1-1	0-0	0-0	0-0	1-1	0-0	100.0	+6.50
Wincanton	1-1	0-0	0-0	1-1	0-0	0-0	100.0	+8.00
Chepstow	1-2	0-1	0-0	0-0	1-1	0-0	50.0	+1.75
Fakenham	1-2	0-0	0-0	0-0	1-2	0-0	50.0	+0.75
Southwell	1-2	0-0	0-0	1-1	0-0	0-1	50.0	+0.75
Leicester	1-3	0-0	0-0	0-1	1-2	0-0	33.3	+0.75
Hereford	1-4	0-2	0-0	1-2	0-0	0-0	25.0	+2.00
Aintree	1-4	1-2	0-0	0-1	0-0	0-1	25.0	-1.25
Mrket Rsn	1-7	0-1	0-1	0-2	1-2	0-1	14.3	-2.67

WINNING HORSES

Horse	Races Run	1st	2nd	3rd	£
The Artful Cobbler	5	3	0	1	23605
Head To The Stars	7	1	3	0	9495
Goohar	5	1	1	1	9109
Tara Mist	6	2	0	1	12606
Crucial Role	8	2	3	0	10462
*Thedrinkymeister	1	1	0	0	6498
Honest Vic	5	2	0	0	9097
Kayfleur	3	1	2	0	5771
Chilli Filli	6	2	0	1	8123
Spider's Bite	5	1	0	2	4809
Flashjack	6	4	0	0	13256
Back To The Thatch	6	1	1	1	4614
Vice Et Vertu	5	2	0	1	9162
Black Tulip	8	2	1	1	4549
Whatmore	6	3	0	0	11566
Pearlita	7	3	1	0	9422
Stoney Mountain	4	2	0	0	4874
Total winning prize-money					**£157018**
Favourites	2-11		18.2%		-4.50

PHILLIP DANDO
PETERSTON-SUPER-ELY, S GLAMORG

	No. of Hrs	Races Run	1st	2nd	3rd	Unpl	Per cent	£1 Level Stake
NH Flat	2	4	0	0	1	3	0.0	-4.00
Hurdles	5	30	3	2	1	24	10.0	-1.50
Chases	1	3	0	0	0	3	0.0	-3.00
Totals	6	37	3	2	2	30	8.1	-8.50
16-17	5	21	0	4	3	14	0.0	-21.00
15-16	6	32	4	2	5	21	12.5	-3.50

JOCKEYS

	W-R	Per cent	£1 Level Stake
Mr Conor Orr	2-9	22.2	+8.50
Mr Ben Jones	1-25	4.0	-14.00

COURSE RECORD

	Total W-R	Non-Hndcps Hurdles	Chases	Hndcps Hurdles	Chases	NH Flat	Per cent	£1 Level Stake
Warwick	1-1	0-0	0-0	1-1	0-0	0-0	100.0	+10.00
Nton Abbot	1-6	0-1	0-0	1-4	0-0	0-1	16.7	+0.50
Worcester	1-6	0-1	0-0	1-4	0-0	0-1	16.7	+5.00

WINNING HORSES

Horse	Races Run	1st	2nd	3rd	£
Rainbow Haze	3	2	0	0	7538
Sahara Haze	9	1	1	1	3249
Total winning prize-money					**£10787**
Favourites	0-0		0.0%		0.00

VICTOR DARTNALL
BRAYFORD, DEVON

	No. of Hrs	Races Run	1st	2nd	3rd	Unpl	Per cent	£1 Level Stake
NH Flat	5	6	1	1	0	4	16.7	+1.00
Hurdles	11	42	3	7	2	30	7.1	-23.38
Chases	7	25	3	3	1	18	12.0	-10.13
Totals	19	73	7	11	3	52	9.6	-32.51
16-17	27	85	6	9	8	61	7.1	-54.25
15-16	22	85	11	11	13	50	12.9	-14.25

JOCKEYS

	W-R	Per cent	£1 Level Stake
Conor Shoemark	2-5	40.0	+7.00
Ciaran Gethings	2-15	13.3	-2.00

Nick Scholfield	2-30	6.7	-17.38
James Best	1-4	25.0	-1.13

COURSE RECORD

	Total W-R	Non-Hndcps Hurdles	Chases	Hndcps Hurdles	Chases	NH Flat	Per cent	£1 Level Stake
Exeter	2-18	2-7	0-0	0-8	0-3	0-0	11.1	-5.38
Bangor	1-1	0-0	0-0	0-0	1-1	0-0	100.0	+3.50
Ludlow	1-2	0-0	0-0	0-0	1-2	0-0	50.0	+5.50
Southwell	1-2	0-1	0-0	0-0	0-0	1-1	50.0	+5.00
Taunton	1-7	0-2	0-0	0-1	1-4	0-0	14.3	-4.13
Chepstow	1-9	0-3	0-0	1-4	0-1	0-1	11.1	-3.00

WINNING HORSES

Horse	Races Run	1st	2nd	3rd	£
Exmoor Mist	5	1	1	0	6583
Admiral's Secret	5	2	0	0	10722
Dancing Shadow	5	1	0	1	5523
Run To Milan	5	1	3	0	4549
Heluvagood	6	1	1	0	4094
Sweet Adare	2	1	0	0	0
Total winning prize-money					£31471
Favourites	2-6	33.3%			-0.50

TRISTAN DAVIDSON

IRTHINGTON, CUMBRIA

	No. of Hrs	Races Run	1st	2nd	3rd	Unpl	Per cent	£1 Level Stake
NH Flat	0	0	0	0	0	0	0.0	0.00
Hurdles	3	11	2	1	1	7	18.2	-3.25
Chases	1	5	0	1	0	4	0.0	-5.00
Totals	4	16	2	2	1	11	12.5	-8.25
16-17	7	20	0	4	1	15	0.0	-20.00
15-16	3	15	2	2	5	6	13.3	-7.25

JOCKEYS

	W-R	Per cent	£1 Level Stake
Harry Reed	2-5	40.0	+2.75

COURSE RECORD

	Total W-R	Non-Hndcps Hurdles	Chases	Hndcps Hurdles	Chases	NH Flat	Per cent	£1 Level Stake
Kelso	1-2	0-0	0-0	1-1	0-1	0-0	50.0	+1.75
Ayr	1-3	0-0	0-0	1-3	0-0	0-0	33.3	+1.00

WINNING HORSES

Horse	Races Run	1st	2nd	3rd	£
Chicoria	6	2	1	0	9292
Total winning prize-money					£9292
Favourites	0-0	0.0%			0.00

SARAH-JAYNE DAVIES

LEOMINSTER, H'FORDS

	No. of Hrs	Races Run	1st	2nd	3rd	Unpl	Per cent	£1 Level Stake
NH Flat	3	4	0	0	0	4	0.0	-4.00
Hurdles	13	32	1	1	2	28	3.1	-27.50
Chases	12	51	4	10	7	30	7.8	-29.17
Totals	21	87	5	11	9	62	5.7	-60.67
16-17	24	95	2	12	16	65	2.1	-78.50
15-16	18	93	7	12	8	66	7.5	-25.50

JOCKEYS

	W-R	Per cent	£1 Level Stake
David Bass	1-2	50.0	+2.50
Tommy Phelan	1-3	33.3	+1.33
Richard Johnson	1-6	16.7	-2.00
Robert Dunne	1-18	5.6	-13.50
Charlie Hammond	1-30	3.3	-21.00

COURSE RECORD

	Total W-R	Non-Hndcps Hurdles	Chases	Hndcps Hurdles	Chases	NH Flat	Per cent	£1 Level Stake
Nton Abbot	2-4	1-1	0-0	0-1	1-2	0-0	50.0	+9.50
Taunton	2-5	0-0	0-0	0-0	2-5	0-0	40.0	+3.33
Bangor	1-14	0-3	0-0	0-5	1-5	0-1	7.1	-9.50

WINNING HORSES

Horse	Races Run	1st	2nd	3rd	£
*Royal Act	8	2	1	1	11566
Whos De Baby	6	1	2	1	5198
Higgs	4	1	1	0	5003
Accessallareas	12	1	1	1	4874
Total winning prize-money					£26641
Favourites	0-1	0.0%			-1.00

JO DAVIS

EAST GARSTON, BERKS

	No. of Hrs	Races Run	1st	2nd	3rd	Unpl	Per cent	£1 Level Stake
NH Flat	4	6	0	0	1	5	0.0	-6.00
Hurdles	10	40	4	5	5	26	10.0	-20.50
Chases	4	12	1	1	0	10	8.3	-9.13
Totals	15	58	5	6	6	41	8.6	-35.63
16-17	12	35	2	6	2	25	5.7	-4.00
15-16	12	44	4	3	6	31	9.1	-8.63

JOCKEYS

	W-R	Per cent	£1 Level Stake
Tom O'Brien	2-6	33.3	+2.25
Page Fuller	1-4	25.0	+4.00
Jeremiah McGrath	1-5	20.0	-2.13
Richard Johnson	1-6	16.7	-2.75

16-17	15	61	4	3	6	48	6.6	+0.50
15-16	18	58	4	3	4	47	6.9	+4.00

COURSE RECORD

	Total W-R	Non-Hndcps Hurdles	Chases	Hndcps Hurdles	Chases	NH Flat	Per cent	£1 Level Stake
Mrket Rsn	2-4	0-1	0-0	2-3	0-0	0-0	50.0	+4.25
Huntingdon	2-9	0-1	0-0	2-6	0-0	0-2	22.2	+2.25
Worcester	1-4	0-0	0-0	0-2	1-2	0-0	25.0	-1.13

WINNING HORSES

Horse	Races Run	1st	2nd	3rd	£
Star Foot	8	3	0	1	6498
Heroes Or Ghosts	8	1	1	0	4061
Marmont	10	1	3	2	3899
Total winning prize-money					£14458
Favourites	2-2		100.0%		4.13

DOMINIC FFRENCH DAVIS

LAMBOURN, BERKS

	No. of Hrs	Races Run	1st	2nd	3rd	Unpl	Per cent	£1 Level Stake
NH Flat	3	4	0	0	0	4	0.0	-4.00
Hurdles	5	10	1	0	1	8	10.0	-4.00
Chases	1	2	1	0	0	1	50.0	+24.00
Totals	9	16	2	0	1	13	12.5	+16.00
16-17	12	33	3	2	6	22	9.1	-8.00
15-16	8	26	0	3	5	18	0.0	-26.00

JOCKEYS

	W-R	Per cent	£1 Level Stake
Mark Grant	2-14	14.3	+18.00

COURSE RECORD

	Total W-R	Non-Hndcps Hurdles	Chases	Hndcps Hurdles	Chases	NH Flat	Per cent	£1 Level Stake
Huntingdon	1-1	0-0	0-0	0-0	1-1	0-0	100.0	+25.00
Ludlow	1-3	0-0	0-0	1-1	0-0	0-2	33.3	+3.00

WINNING HORSES

Horse	Races Run	1st	2nd	3rd	£
Whatthebutlersaw	1	1	0	0	5848
Chill In The Wood	2	1	0	0	3899
Total winning prize-money					£9747
Favourites	0-0		0.0%		0.00

ZOE DAVISON

HAMMERWOOD, E SUSSEX

	No. of Hrs	Races Run	1st	2nd	3rd	Unpl	Per cent	£1 Level Stake
NH Flat	0	0	0	0	0	0	0.0	0.00
Hurdles	6	20	6	0	4	10	30.0	+42.00
Chases	8	40	9	7	8	16	22.5	+11.50
Totals	11	60	15	7	12	26	25.0	+53.50

BY MONTH

NH Flat	W-R	Per cent	£1 Level Stake	Hurdles	W-R	Per cent	£1 Level Stake
May	0-0	0.0	0.00	May	0-1	0.0	-1.00
June	0-0	0.0	0.00	June	0-0	0.0	0.00
July	0-0	0.0	0.00	July	0-0	0.0	0.00
August	0-0	0.0	0.00	August	0-0	0.0	0.00
September	0-0	0.0	0.00	September	0-0	0.0	0.00
October	0-0	0.0	0.00	October	0-0	0.0	0.00
November	0-0	0.0	0.00	November	2-3	66.7	+21.25
December	0-0	0.0	0.00	December	1-5	20.0	-1.25
January	0-0	0.0	0.00	January	1-4	25.0	0.00
February	0-0	0.0	0.00	February	2-3	66.7	+27.00
March	0-0	0.0	0.00	March	0-3	0.0	-3.00
April	0-0	0.0	0.00	April	0-1	0.0	-1.00

Chases	W-R	Per cent	£1 Level Stake	Totals	W-R	Per cent	£1 Level Stake
May	0-2	0.0	-2.00	May	0-3	0.0	-3.00
June	0-0	0.0	0.00	June	0-0	0.0	0.00
July	0-0	0.0	0.00	July	0-0	0.0	0.00
August	0-0	0.0	0.00	August	0-0	0.0	0.00
September	0-0	0.0	0.00	September	0-0	0.0	0.00
October	0-0	0.0	0.00	October	0-0	0.0	0.00
November	0-4	0.0	-4.00	November	2-7	28.6	+17.25
December	3-6	50.0	+19.75	December	4-11	36.4	+18.50
January	0-8	0.0	-8.00	January	1-12	8.3	-8.00
February	0-3	0.0	-3.00	February	2-6	33.3	+24.00
March	2-7	28.6	+1.50	March	2-10	20.0	-1.50
April	4-10	40.0	+7.25	April	4-11	36.4	+6.25

DISTANCE

Hurdles	W-R	Per cent	£1 Level Stake	Chases	W-R	Per cent	£1 Level Stake
2m-2m3f	3-11	27.3	+9.25	2m-2m3f	4-16	25.0	+0.75
2m4f-2m7f	1-5	20.0	+16.00	2m4f-2m7f	2-14	14.3	-8.75
3m+	1-3	33.3	+14.00	3m+	3-10	30.0	+19.50

TYPE OF RACE

Non-Handicaps	W-R	Per cent	£1 Level Stake	Handicaps	W-R	Per cent	£1 Level Stake
Nov Hrdls	0-0	0.0	0.00	Nov Hrdls	0-1	0.0	-1.00
Hrdls	0-2	0.0	-2.00	Hrdls	6-17	35.3	+45.00
Nov Chs	0-1	0.0	-1.00	Nov Chs	0-4	0.0	-4.00
Chases	0-0	0.0	0.00	Chases	9-33	27.3	+18.50
Sell/Claim	0-0	0.0	0.00	Sell/Claim	0-0	0.0	0.00

RACE CLASS

	W-R	Per cent	£1 Level Stake
Class 1	0-0	0.0	0.00
Class 2	0-0	0.0	0.00
Class 3	1-2	50.0	+11.00
Class 4	8-33	24.2	+27.00
Class 5	6-25	24.0	+15.50

FIRST TIME OUT

	W-R	Per cent	£1 Level Stake
Bumpers	0-0	0.0	0.00
Hurdles	0-4	0.0	-4.00
Chases	0-7	0.0	-7.00
Totals	0-11	0.0	-11.00

JOCKEYS

	W-R	Per cent	£1 Level Stake
Tommy Dowling	7-26	26.9	+38.75
Page Fuller	2-3	66.7	+8.00
James Bowen	2-6	33.3	+1.25
Rob Hornby	1-1	100.0	+2.25
Noel Fehily	1-1	100.0	+2.00
Nick Scholfield	1-1	100.0	+2.25
William Featherstone	1-4	25.0	+17.00

COURSE RECORD

	Total W-R	Non-Hndcps Hurdles	Chases	Hndcps Hurdles	Chases	NH Flat	Per cent	£1 Level Stake
Plumpton	7-16	0-1	0-0	2-3	5-12	0-0	43.8	+55.75
Lingfield	3-8	0-0	0-1	2-3	1-4	0-0	37.5	+2.50
Leicester	2-12	0-0	0-0	1-5	1-7	0-0	16.7	-3.00
Exeter	1-1	0-0	0-0	0-0	1-1	0-0	100.0	+2.25
Stratford	1-1	0-0	0-0	0-0	1-1	0-0	100.0	+5.00
Towcester	1-2	0-0	0-0	1-2	0-0	0-0	50.0	+11.00

WINNING HORSES

Horse	Races Run	1st	2nd	3rd	£
The Game Is A Foot	6	4	0	0	22350
Kilinakin	4	1	0	0	6758
Georgieshore	7	1	1	1	5509
Dylanseoghan	7	1	2	2	4809
Finnegan's Garden	10	3	2	2	12807
Frank N Fair	9	2	2	1	8772
The Golden Hour	4	1	0	2	4354
Gustav	3	1	0	2	3899
Brother Bennett	6	1	0	2	3314
Total winning prize-money					£72572
Favourites	19-22	86.4%			39.00

N J DAWE

KILVE, SOMERSET

	No. of Hrs	Races Run	1st	2nd	3rd	Unpl	Per cent	£1 Level Stake
NH Flat	0	0	0	0	0	0	0.0	0.00
Hurdles	0	0	0	0	0	0	0.0	0.00
Chases	1	3	1	0	1	1	33.3	+1.50
Totals	1	3	1	0	1	1	33.3	+1.50

JOCKEYS

	W-R	Per cent	£1 Level Stake
Mr Darren Andrews	1-3	33.3	+1.50

COURSE RECORD

	Total W-R	Non-Hndcps Hurdles	Chases	Hndcps Hurdles	Chases	NH Flat	Per cent	£1 Level Stake
Exeter	1-1	0-0	1-1	0-0	0-0	0-0	100.0	+3.50

WINNING HORSES

Horse	Races Run	1st	2nd	3rd	£
*Mountain Cliche	3	1	0	1	2184
Total winning prize-money					£2184
Favourites	0-0	0.0%			0.00

GEOFFREY DEACON

COMPTON, BERKS

	No. of Hrs	Races Run	1st	2nd	3rd	Unpl	Per cent	£1 Level Stake
NH Flat	2	2	0	0	0	2	0.0	-2.00
Hurdles	2	4	1	0	1	2	25.0	+17.00
Chases	1	2	0	1	0	1	0.0	-2.00
Totals	5	8	1	1	1	5	12.5	+13.00
16-17	4	7	0	0	0	7	0.0	-7.00
15-16	6	18	0	2	2	14	0.0	-18.00

JOCKEYS

	W-R	Per cent	£1 Level Stake
Dave Crosse	1-3	33.3	+18.00

COURSE RECORD

	Total W-R	Non-Hndcps Hurdles	Chases	Hndcps Hurdles	Chases	NH Flat	Per cent	£1 Level Stake
Fontwell	1-2	0-0	0-0	1-2	0-0	0-0	50.0	+19.00

WINNING HORSES

Horse	Races Run	1st	2nd	3rd	£
Moon Trip	2	1	0	0	2599
Total winning prize-money					£2599
Favourites	0-0	0.0%			0.00

DAVID DENNIS

HANLEY SWAN, WORCESTERSHIRE

	No. of Hrs	Races Run	1st	2nd	3rd	Unpl	Per cent	£1 Level Stake
NH Flat	6	12	0	1	3	8	0.0	-12.00
Hurdles	33	103	10	8	14	71	9.7	-41.34
Chases	20	91	15	16	9	51	16.5	+11.83
Totals	43	206	25	25	26	130	12.1	-41.51
16-17	54	268	20	37	37	173	7.5	-106.80
15-16	55	220	27	32	32	129	12.3	-81.39

BY MONTH

NH Flat	W-R	Per cent	£1 Level Stake	Hurdles	W-R	Per cent	£1 Level Stake
May	0-1	0.0	-1.00	May	1-10	10.0	-2.00
June	0-1	0.0	-1.00	June	1-11	9.1	-7.00
July	0-0	0.0	0.00	July	0-4	0.0	-4.00
August	0-0	0.0	0.00	August	0-9	0.0	-9.00
September	0-0	0.0	0.00	September	0-6	0.0	-6.00

October	0-0	0.0	0.00	October	0-6	0.0	-6.00
November	0-1	0.0	-1.00	November	1-9	11.1	-3.00
December	0-3	0.0	-3.00	December	2-13	15.4	-3.09
January	0-1	0.0	-1.00	January	2-11	18.2	+7.00
February	0-1	0.0	-1.00	February	2-9	22.2	-1.25
March	0-2	0.0	-2.00	March	1-8	12.5	0.00
April	0-2	0.0	-2.00	April	0-7	0.0	-7.00

Kieron Edgar	2-4	50.0	+6.91
Sean Houlihan	1-6	16.7	-3.75
Leighton Aspell	1-6	16.7	-3.75
Tommy Dowling	1-10	10.0	-6.00

Chases	W-R	Per cent	£1 Level Stake	Totals	W-R	Per cent	£1 Level Stake
May	1-7	14.3	-2.67	May	2-18	11.1	-5.67
June	3-7	42.9	+11.50	June	4-19	21.1	+3.50
July	0-7	0.0	-7.00	July	0-11	0.0	-11.00
August	0-7	0.0	-7.00	August	0-16	0.0	-16.00
September	1-3	33.3	-0.25	September	1-9	11.1	-6.25
October	1-7	14.3	+4.00	October	1-13	7.7	-2.00
November	1-7	14.3	+4.00	November	2-17	11.8	0.00
December	4-8	50.0	+15.25	December	6-24	25.0	+9.16
January	1-10	10.0	-2.00	January	3-22	13.6	+4.00
February	1-6	16.7	+2.00	February	3-16	18.8	-0.25
March	2-12	16.7	+4.00	March	3-22	13.6	+2.00
April	0-10	0.0	-10.00	April	0-19	0.0	-19.00

COURSE RECORD

	Total W-R	Non-Hndcps Hurdles	Non-Hndcps Chases	Hndcps Hurdles	Chases	NH Flat	Per cent	£1 Level Stake
Huntingdon	5-10	0-0	0-0	2-6	3-4	0-0	50.0	+28.33
Mrket Rsn	3-10	0-0	0-0	1-3	2-6	0-1	30.0	+13.00
Uttoxeter	2-13	0-2	0-0	1-5	1-6	0-0	15.4	+4.00
Plumpton	1-1	0-0	0-0	0-0	1-1	0-0	100.0	+1.75
Newbury	1-2	0-0	0-0	0-0	1-2	0-0	50.0	+6.00
Fakenham	1-3	0-0	0-0	0-0	1-3	0-0	33.3	+8.00
Ffos Las	1-3	0-1	0-0	0-1	1-1	0-0	33.3	+2.50
Sandown	1-4	0-0	0-0	1-2	0-2	0-0	25.0	-1.75
Nton Abbot	1-5	0-1	0-0	0-0	1-4	0-0	20.0	-3.00
Taunton	1-5	0-2	0-0	0-2	1-1	0-0	20.0	+3.00
Kempton	1-7	0-0	0-0	1-4	0-2	0-1	14.3	-1.50
Doncaster	1-8	0-3	0-0	0-3	1-2	0-0	12.5	-5.75
Ludlow	1-9	0-3	0-0	1-2	0-2	0-2	11.1	-7.09
Southwell	1-10	0-0	0-0	0-6	1-4	0-0	10.0	+1.00
Stratford	1-10	0-2	0-0	1-2	0-6	0-0	10.0	-2.00
Wincanton	1-12	0-0	0-0	0-5	1-6	0-1	8.3	-4.00
Exeter	1-13	0-6	0-0	1-4	0-3	0-0	7.7	-7.00
Worcester	1-30	1-11	0-0	0-9	0-9	0-1	3.3	-26.00

DISTANCE

Hurdles	W-R	Per cent	£1 Level Stake	Chases	W-R	Per cent	£1 Level Stake
2m-2m3f	3-41	7.3	-23.00	2m-2m3f	5-22	22.7	+3.08
2m4f-2m7f	7-51	13.7	-7.34	2m4f-2m7f	6-31	19.4	+17.00
3m+	0-11	0.0	-11.00	3m+	4-38	10.5	-8.25

TYPE OF RACE

Non-Handicaps	W-R	Per cent	£1 Level Stake	Handicaps	W-R	Per cent	£1 Level Stake
Nov Hrdls	1-22	4.5	-18.00	Nov Hrdls	3-17	17.6	-3.84
Hrdls	0-10	0.0	-10.00	Hrdls	6-50	12.0	-5.50
Nov Chs	0-0	0.0	0.00	Nov Chs	2-18	11.1	-2.00
Chases	0-1	0.0	-1.00	Chases	11-60	18.3	+16.58
Sell/Claim	0-0	0.0	0.00	Sell/Claim	0-0	0.0	0.00

RACE CLASS / FIRST TIME OUT

	W-R	Per cent	£1 Level Stake		W-R	Per cent	£1 Level Stake
Class 1	0-7	0.0	-7.00	Bumpers	0-6	0.0	-6.00
Class 2	0-3	0.0	-3.00	Hurdles	2-26	7.7	-9.00
Class 3	4-34	11.8	-4.75	Chases	0-11	0.0	-11.00
Class 4	15-112	13.4	-22.76				
Class 5	6-46	13.0	0.00	Totals	2-43	4.7	-26.00
Class 6	0-4	0.0	-4.00				

JOCKEYS

	W-R	Per cent	£1 Level Stake
Sam Twiston-Davies	4-23	17.4	+5.50
Aidan Coleman	4-42	9.5	-14.00
David Bass	3-7	42.9	+14.00
Trevor Whelan	3-12	25.0	+12.00
Brian Hughes	3-27	11.1	+4.00
Noel Fehily	3-29	10.3	-16.42

WINNING HORSES

Horse	Races Run	1st	2nd	3rd	£
Cyclop	7	1	1	0	12512
Deauville Dancer	14	5	2	0	33955
Indy Five	6	2	1	0	14388
Jaune Et Bleue	4	1	0	1	6506
Shanty Town	6	1	2	1	5848
Marquis Of Carabas	9	1	2	1	5198
Crank Em Up	8	1	1	1	4614
Just So Cool	3	1	0	0	4549
Broken Quest	8	3	0	1	13191
Doitforjoe	8	1	0	3	3994
Schnabel	5	1	1	1	3899
Included	3	1	0	2	3639
Norse Light	13	3	2	2	10072
King's Song	4	1	0	2	3249
Bitter Virtue	7	1	0	0	3249
Innisfree Lad	8	1	1	2	2469
Total winning prize-money					**£131332**
Favourites	**5-24**		**20.8%**		**-12.84**

ROBIN DICKIN

ALCESTER, WARKS

	No. of Hrs	Races Run	1st	2nd	3rd	Unpl	Per cent	£1 Level Stake
NH Flat	3	4	0	1	0	3	0.0	-4.00
Hurdles	16	68	5	4	7	52	7.4	-22.38
Chases	13	58	10	12	7	29	17.2	+7.50

Totals	30	130	15	17	14	84	11.5	-18.88
16-17	31	155	17	15	17	106	11.0	-23.50
15-16	30	143	7	15	19	102	4.9	-110.75

BY MONTH

NH Flat	W-R	Per cent	£1 Level Stake	Hurdles	W-R	Per cent	£1 Level Stake
May	0-0	0.0	0.00	May	0-6	0.0	-6.00
June	0-0	0.0	0.00	June	0-2	0.0	-2.00
July	0-0	0.0	0.00	July	0-1	0.0	-1.00
August	0-0	0.0	0.00	August	0-1	0.0	-1.00
September	0-0	0.0	0.00	September	0-2	0.0	-2.00
October	0-1	0.0	-1.00	October	0-5	0.0	-5.00
November	0-1	0.0	-1.00	November	1-8	12.5	-3.50
December	0-1	0.0	-1.00	December	0-8	0.0	-8.00
January	0-0	0.0	0.00	January	2-8	25.0	-1.88
February	0-0	0.0	0.00	February	1-8	12.5	+1.00
March	0-0	0.0	0.00	March	1-9	11.1	+17.00
April	0-1	0.0	-1.00	April	0-10	0.0	-10.00

Chases	W-R	Per cent	£1 Level Stake	Totals	W-R	Per cent	£1 Level Stake
May	0-6	0.0	-6.00	May	0-12	0.0	-12.00
June	1-5	20.0	+12.00	June	1-7	14.3	+10.00
July	0-0	0.0	0.00	July	0-1	0.0	-1.00
August	0-0	0.0	0.00	August	0-1	0.0	-1.00
September	0-2	0.0	-2.00	September	0-4	0.0	-4.00
October	0-4	0.0	-4.00	October	0-10	0.0	-10.00
November	1-5	20.0	-1.75	November	2-14	14.3	-6.25
December	2-7	28.6	+14.00	December	2-16	12.5	+5.00
January	2-5	40.0	+0.25	January	4-13	30.8	-1.63
February	2-11	18.2	-3.75	February	3-19	15.8	-2.75
March	2-7	28.6	+4.75	March	3-16	18.8	+21.75
April	0-6	0.0	-6.00	April	0-17	0.0	-17.00

DISTANCE

Hurdles	W-R	Per cent	£1 Level Stake	Chases	W-R	Per cent	£1 Level Stake
2m-2m3f	1-29	3.4	-26.13	2m-2m3f	4-12	33.3	+18.13
2m4f-2m7f	3-30	10.0	-13.25	2m4f-2m7f	4-29	13.8	-1.88
3m+	1-9	11.1	+17.00	3m+	2-17	11.8	-8.75

TYPE OF RACE

Non-Handicaps	W-R	Per cent	£1 Level Stake	Handicaps	W-R	Per cent	£1 Level Stake
Nov Hrdls	0-8	0.0	-8.00	Nov Hrdls	1-12	8.3	-9.13
Hrdls	0-9	0.0	-9.00	Hrdls	4-38	10.5	+4.75
Nov Chs	0-0	0.0	0.00	Nov Chs	2-8	25.0	+0.50
Chases	0-0	0.0	0.00	Chases	5-41	12.2	+2.88
Sell/Claim	0-0	0.0	0.00	Sell/Claim	0-0	0.0	0.00

RACE CLASS

	W-R	Per cent	£1 Level Stake
Class 1	0-0	0.0	0.00
Class 2	0-3	0.0	-3.00
Class 3	1-10	10.0	-2.00
Class 4	11-70	15.7	+22.88

FIRST TIME OUT

	W-R	Per cent	£1 Level Stake
Bumpers	0-3	0.0	-3.00
Hurdles	0-15	0.0	-15.00
Chases	1-12	8.3	+5.00

Class 5	3-46	6.5	-35.75	Totals	1-30	3.3	-13.00
Class 6	0-1	0.0	-1.00				

JOCKEYS

	W-R	Per cent	£1 Level Stake
Jack Quinlan	6-48	12.5	-8.13
Charlie Poste	5-42	11.9	-9.00
Tom O'Brien	1-1	100.0	+3.50
A P Heskin	1-6	16.7	-1.50
Miss Tabitha Worsley	1-11	9.1	+15.00
James Nixon	1-17	5.9	-13.75

COURSE RECORD

	Total W-R	Non-Hndcps Hurdles	Chases	Hndcps Hurdles	Chases	NH Flat	Per cent	£1 Level Stake
Leicester	4-9	0-0	0-0	1-1	3-8	0-0	44.4	+18.13
Towcester	3-20	0-3	0-0	0-4	3-11	0-2	15.0	-8.50
Taunton	2-4	0-0	0-0	0-1	2-3	0-0	50.0	+1.13
Ludlow	2-18	0-5	0-0	2-10	0-3	0-0	11.1	-4.50
Hereford	1-3	0-0	0-0	1-2	0-1	0-0	33.3	-0.13
Kempton	1-5	0-0	0-0	0-1	1-4	0-0	20.0	+3.00
Worcester	1-5	0-1	0-0	0-3	1-1	0-0	20.0	+12.00
Warwick	1-18	0-4	0-0	1-4	0-9	0-1	5.6	+8.00

WINNING HORSES

Horse	Races Run	1st	2nd	3rd	£
Vocaliser	9	4	2	1	28627
Galactic Power	8	2	1	2	11761
Dontminddboys	10	3	4	2	17340
Oneida Tribe	5	1	1	0	5588
Young Lou	4	1	0	0	4419
Get Involved	2	1	0	0	4289
Tara Well	10	1	3	1	4159
All Is Good	5	1	0	0	4159
Some Finish	7	1	0	1	3899
Total winning prize-money					**£84241**
Favourites	**5-13**		**38.5%**		**4.13**

JOHN DIXON

THURSBY, CUMBRIA

	No. of Hrs	Races Run	1st	2nd	3rd	Unpl	Per cent	£1 Level Stake
NH Flat	1	1	0	0	0	1	0.0	-1.00
Hurdles	2	10	1	1	2	6	10.0	+3.00
Chases	0	0	0	0	0	0	0.0	0.00
Totals	3	11	1	1	2	7	9.1	+2.00
16-17	3	11	1	0	2	8	9.1	+6.00
15-16	2	14	2	1	1	10	14.3	+4.75

JOCKEYS

	W-R	Per cent	£1 Level Stake
Mr John Dixon	1-11	9.1	+2.00

COURSE RECORD

	Total W-R	Non-Hndcps Hurdles	Chases	Hndcps Hurdles	Chases	NH Flat	Per cent	£1 Level Stake
Carlisle	1-4	0-0	0-0	1-4	0-0	0-0	25.0	+9.00

WINNING HORSES

Horse	Races Run	1st	2nd	3rd	£
Pistol	9	1	1	2	4549
Total winning prize-money					£4549
Favourites	0-0		0.0%		0.00

ROSE DOBBIN

SOUTH HAZELRIGG, NORTHUMBRIA

	No. of Hrs	Races Run	1st	2nd	3rd	Unpl	Per cent	£1 Level Stake
NH Flat	6	8	0	1	0	7	0.0	-8.00
Hurdles	27	102	15	12	11	64	14.7	-18.89
Chases	16	64	10	10	8	36	15.6	-19.25
Totals	39	174	25	23	19	107	14.4	-46.14
16-17	37	143	16	18	15	94	11.2	-43.38
15-16	41	154	16	14	26	97	10.4	-53.91

BY MONTH

NH Flat	W-R	Per cent	£1 Level Stake	Hurdles	W-R	Per cent	£1 Level Stake
May	0-0	0.0	0.00	May	0-2	0.0	-2.00
June	0-0	0.0	0.00	June	0-1	0.0	-1.00
July	0-0	0.0	0.00	July	0-2	0.0	-2.00
August	0-0	0.0	0.00	August	1-5	20.0	-0.67
September	0-0	0.0	0.00	September	0-2	0.0	-2.00
October	0-1	0.0	-1.00	October	3-17	17.6	-8.75
November	0-1	0.0	-1.00	November	2-15	13.3	+2.50
December	0-1	0.0	-1.00	December	3-15	20.0	+10.75
January	0-1	0.0	-1.00	January	4-17	23.5	-0.22
February	0-2	0.0	-2.00	February	2-9	22.2	+1.50
March	0-1	0.0	-1.00	March	0-8	0.0	-8.00
April	0-1	0.0	-1.00	April	0-9	0.0	-9.00

Chases	W-R	Per cent	£1 Level Stake	Totals	W-R	Per cent	£1 Level Stake
May	0-2	0.0	-2.00	May	0-4	0.0	-4.00
June	0-1	0.0	-1.00	June	0-2	0.0	-2.00
July	0-0	0.0	0.00	July	0-2	0.0	-2.00
August	0-2	0.0	-2.00	August	1-7	14.3	-2.67
September	0-1	0.0	-1.00	September	0-3	0.0	-3.00
October	2-13	15.4	-6.00	October	5-31	16.1	-15.75
November	0-9	0.0	-9.00	November	2-25	8.0	-7.50
December	3-10	30.0	+8.50	December	6-26	23.1	+18.25
January	1-8	12.5	-3.50	January	5-26	19.2	-4.72
February	2-6	33.3	+1.00	February	4-17	23.5	+0.50
March	1-6	16.7	-3.25	March	1-15	6.7	-12.25
April	1-6	16.7	-1.00	April	1-16	6.3	-11.00

DISTANCE

Hurdles	W-R	Per cent	£1 Level Stake	Chases	W-R	Per cent	£1 Level Stake
2m-2m3f	5-48	10.4	-18.00	2m-2m3f	2-6	33.3	+2.25
2m4f-2m7f	6-34	17.6	-12.72	2m4f-2m7f	2-16	12.5	-7.75
3m+	4-20	20.0	+11.83	3m+	6-42	14.3	-13.75

TYPE OF RACE

Non-Handicaps	W-R	Per cent	£1 Level Stake	Handicaps	W-R	Per cent	£1 Level Stake
Nov Hrdls	5-29	17.2	-13.06	Nov Hrdls	0-6	0.0	-6.00
Hrdls	2-6	33.3	+0.50	Hrdls	8-61	13.1	-0.33
Nov Chs	1-2	50.0	+1.75	Nov Chs	1-9	11.1	-4.50
Chases	0-0	0.0	0.00	Chases	7-47	14.9	-13.75
Sell/Claim	0-0	0.0	0.00	Sell/Claim	0-1	0.0	-1.00

RACE CLASS

	W-R	Per cent	£1 Level Stake
Class 1	0-1	0.0	-1.00
Class 2	2-9	22.2	+5.75
Class 3	4-22	18.2	-1.25
Class 4	12-97	12.4	-47.72
Class 5	7-43	16.3	+0.08
Class 6	0-2	0.0	-2.00

FIRST TIME OUT

	W-R	Per cent	£1 Level Stake
Bumpers	0-6	0.0	-6.00
Hurdles	2-20	10.0	-13.25
Chases	2-13	15.4	-6.00
Totals	4-39	10.3	-25.25

JOCKEYS

	W-R	Per cent	£1 Level Stake
Craig Nichol	11-89	12.4	-36.31
Ryan Day	5-16	31.3	+5.75
Adam Nicol	3-8	37.5	+11.67
Conor O'Farrell	3-13	23.1	+3.75
Lorcan Murtagh	2-17	11.8	-7.50
Daniel Sansom	1-3	33.3	+4.50

COURSE RECORD

	Total W-R	Non-Hndcps Hurdles	Chases	Hndcps Hurdles	Chases	NH Flat	Per cent	£1 Level Stake
Doncaster	4-9	0-0	0-0	1-3	3-6	0-0	44.4	+15.00
Carlisle	4-21	1-3	1-1	1-5	1-10	0-2	19.0	+2.75
Ayr	3-8	1-2	0-0	0-2	2-3	0-1	37.5	+2.75
Catterick	3-16	0-4	0-0	2-8	1-4	0-0	18.8	+3.00
Kelso	3-32	3-8	0-0	0-15	0-6	0-3	9.4	-26.31
Newcastle	2-8	2-5	0-0	0-0	0-2	0-1	25.0	-0.25
Hexham	2-15	0-1	0-0	1-5	1-9	0-0	13.3	-7.42
Musselbgh	2-17	0-3	0-0	1-8	1-6	0-0	11.8	-3.00
Wetherby	2-17	0-3	0-0	2-9	0-5	0-0	11.8	-1.67

WINNING HORSES

Horse	Races Run	1st	2nd	3rd	£
Monfass	7	1	1	3	15475
Coole Hall	5	3	1	0	17801
Mister Don	8	1	3	1	9136
Attention Please	8	3	0	1	16612

Doktor Glaz	6	2	1	1	12086
Planet Nine	6	2	0	1	12996
Jonniesofa	2	1	1	0	6498
Bigirononhiship	2	1	0	0	5198
Slanelough	7	2	2	1	8317
Romulus Du Donjon	10	1	1	2	3899
Final Fling	9	3	1	1	10239
Sweet As Candy	4	1	0	1	3509
Smuggler's Stash	9	2	2	2	6628
Lady London	6	1	1	1	3249
Some Reign	5	1	1	2	3249
Total winning prize-money					**£134892**
Favourites	**8-28**		**28.6%**		**-3.72**

CONOR DORE

HUBBERT'S BRIDGE, LINCS

	No. of Hrs	Races Run	1st	2nd	3rd	Unpl	Per cent	£1 Level Stake
NH Flat	0	0	0	0	0	0	0.0	0.00
Hurdles	9	39	3	3	4	29	7.7	+42.00
Chases	0	0	0	0	0	0	0.0	0.00
Totals	9	39	3	3	4	29	7.7	+42.00
16-17	6	18	1	1	1	15	5.6	-12.00
15-16	5	22	2	2	3	15	9.1	-8.50

JOCKEYS

	W-R	Per cent	£1 Level Stake
Paddy Brennan	2-13	15.4	+34.00
Niall P Madden	1-8	12.5	+26.00

COURSE RECORD

	Total W-R	Non-Hndcps Hurdles	Chases	Hndcps Hurdles	Chases	NH Flat	Per cent	£1 Level Stake
Uttoxeter	2-6	0-0	0-0	2-6	0-0	0-0	33.3	+54.00
Mrket Rsn	1-9	0-1	0-0	1-8	0-0	0-0	11.1	+12.00

WINNING HORSES

Horse	Races Run	1st	2nd	3rd	£
*Towering	11	2	1	0	8837
Yasir	5	1	2	0	2469
Total winning prize-money					**£11306**
Favourites	0-0		0.0%		0.00

CHRIS DOWN

MUTTERTON, DEVON

	No. of Hrs	Races Run	1st	2nd	3rd	Unpl	Per cent	£1 Level Stake
NH Flat	1	2	0	0	0	2	0.0	-2.00
Hurdles	14	61	7	7	4	43	11.5	-0.90
Chases	6	14	1	2	0	11	7.1	-5.00
Totals	16	77	8	9	4	56	10.4	-7.90
16-17	21	105	8	9	10	78	7.6	-49.00

| 15-16 | 27 | 113 | 9 | 12 | 13 | 79 | 8.0 | -48.42 |

JOCKEYS

	W-R	Per cent	£1 Level Stake
Page Fuller	7-26	26.9	+34.10
Ciaran Gethings	1-9	11.1	0.00

COURSE RECORD

	Total W-R	Non-Hndcps Hurdles	Chases	Hndcps Hurdles	Chases	NH Flat	Per cent	£1 Level Stake
Nton Abbot	4-18	2-3	0-1	1-11	1-3	0-0	22.2	+8.10
Stratford	2-4	0-0	0-0	2-4	0-0	0-0	50.0	+10.00
Taunton	1-11	0-0	0-0	1-10	0-1	0-0	9.1	-3.00
Exeter	1-12	1-1	0-0	0-8	0-2	0-1	8.3	+9.00

WINNING HORSES

Horse	Races Run	1st	2nd	3rd	£
Foxy Act	8	3	1	0	13321
Culm Counsellor	11	2	2	0	6882
Ice Tres	3	1	0	0	4159
Ladies Dancing	8	1	0	2	3899
Starlit Night	7	1	2	0	3249
Total winning prize-money					**£31510**
Favourites	1-4		25.0%		-2.90

SAMUEL DRINKWATER

STRENSHAM, WORCS

	No. of Hrs	Races Run	1st	2nd	3rd	Unpl	Per cent	£1 Level Stake
NH Flat	6	8	0	1	0	7	0.0	-8.00
Hurdles	12	47	4	6	6	31	8.5	-16.50
Chases	2	4	0	0	2	2	0.0	-4.00
Totals	16	59	4	7	8	40	6.8	-28.50
16-17	9	20	4	0	0	16	20.0	+47.25

JOCKEYS

	W-R	Per cent	£1 Level Stake
Robert Dunne	2-32	6.3	-22.50
Bryony Frost	1-2	50.0	+4.00
Mr Joseph Drinkwater	1-5	20.0	+10.00

COURSE RECORD

	Total W-R	Non-Hndcps Hurdles	Chases	Hndcps Hurdles	Chases	NH Flat	Per cent	£1 Level Stake
Lingfield	2-2	0-0	0-0	2-2	0-0	0-0	100.0	+8.00
Southwell	1-4	0-1	0-0	1-3	0-0	0-0	25.0	+1.50
Warwick	1-8	1-3	0-0	0-5	0-0	0-0	12.5	+7.00

WINNING HORSES

Horse	Races Run	1st	2nd	3rd	£
*Northandsouth	6	1	0	1	4484
General Consensus	2	1	0	0	4419
Rif Raftou	7	1	1	2	3899

Pray For A Rainbow	3	1	0	1	3509
Total winning prize-money					£16311
Favourites	0-4		0.0%		-4.00

IAN DUNCAN

COYLTON, AYRSHIRE

	No. of Hrs	Races Run	1st	2nd	3rd	Unpl	Per cent	£1 Level Stake
NH Flat	3	6	0	0	1	5	0.0	-6.00
Hurdles	7	17	0	0	1	16	0.0	-17.00
Chases	6	26	3	5	1	17	11.5	-2.50
Totals	11	49	3	5	3	38	6.1	-25.50
16-17	8	35	7	9	5	14	20.0	+4.69
15-16	11	39	2	3	6	28	5.1	-20.00

JOCKEYS

	W-R	Per cent	£1 Level Stake
Henry Brooke	2-13	15.4	+1.50
Derek Fox	1-21	4.8	-12.00

COURSE RECORD

	Total W-R	Non-Hndcps Hurdles	Chases	Hndcps Hurdles	Chases	NH Flat	Per cent	£1 Level Stake
Ayr	2-26	0-5	0-0	0-5	2-12	0-4	7.7	-11.50
Carlisle	1-5	0-2	0-0	0-0	1-2	0-1	20.0	+4.00

WINNING HORSES

Horse	Races Run	1st	2nd	3rd	£
Finaghy Ayr	6	1	3	0	15475
Lochnell	8	2	2	0	9162
Total winning prize-money					£24637
Favourites	0-2		0.0%		-2.00

ALEXANDRA DUNN

WEST BUCKLAND, SOMERSET

	No. of Hrs	Races Run	1st	2nd	3rd	Unpl	Per cent	£1 Level Stake
NH Flat	4	5	0	0	0	5	0.0	-5.00
Hurdles	37	104	9	7	9	79	8.7	-39.63
Chases	20	53	3	10	8	32	5.7	-36.50
Totals	49	162	12	17	17	116	7.4	-81.13
16-17	47	199	14	19	27	139	7.0	-64.30
15-16	45	156	20	10	17	109	12.8	-27.63

BY MONTH

NH Flat	W-R	Per cent	£1 Level Stake	Hurdles	W-R	Per cent	£1 Level Stake
May	0-1	0.0	-1.00	May	2-14	14.3	-6.13
June	0-0	0.0	0.00	June	2-12	16.7	-2.00
July	0-1	0.0	-1.00	July	1-13	7.7	+10.00
August	0-1	0.0	-1.00	August	1-11	9.1	-6.50
September	0-0	0.0	0.00	September	1-7	14.3	-1.50
October	0-1	0.0	-1.00	October	0-9	0.0	-9.00
November	0-0	0.0	0.00	November	0-14	0.0	-14.00
December	0-0	0.0	0.00	December	0-5	0.0	-5.00
January	0-0	0.0	0.00	January	0-1	0.0	-1.00
February	0-0	0.0	0.00	February	2-8	25.0	+5.50
March	0-1	0.0	-1.00	March	0-5	0.0	-5.00
April	0-0	0.0	0.00	April	0-5	0.0	-5.00

Chases	W-R	Per cent	£1 Level Stake	Totals	W-R	Per cent	£1 Level Stake
May	1-7	14.3	0.00	May	3-22	13.6	-7.13
June	0-3	0.0	-3.00	June	2-15	13.3	-5.00
July	0-7	0.0	-7.00	July	1-21	4.8	+2.00
August	0-0	0.0	0.00	August	1-12	8.3	-7.50
September	0-0	0.0	0.00	September	1-7	14.3	-1.50
October	0-6	0.0	-6.00	October	0-16	0.0	-16.00
November	0-7	0.0	-7.00	November	0-21	0.0	-21.00
December	0-4	0.0	-4.00	December	0-9	0.0	-9.00
January	0-1	0.0	-1.00	January	0-2	0.0	-2.00
February	0-1	0.0	-1.00	February	2-9	22.2	+4.50
March	2-9	22.2	+0.50	March	2-15	13.3	-5.50
April	0-8	0.0	-8.00	April	0-13	0.0	-13.00

DISTANCE

Hurdles	W-R	Per cent	£1 Level Stake	Chases	W-R	Per cent	£1 Level Stake
2m-2m3f	7-67	10.4	-32.13	2m-2m3f	1-24	4.2	-20.00
2m4f-2m7f	2-28	7.1	+1.50	2m4f-2m7f	1-17	5.9	-10.00
3m+	0-9	0.0	-9.00	3m+	1-12	8.3	-6.50

TYPE OF RACE

Non-Handicaps	W-R	Per cent	£1 Level Stake	Handicaps	W-R	Per cent	£1 Level Stake
Nov Hrdls	3-25	12.0	-12.63	Nov Hrdls	0-4	0.0	-4.00
Hrdls	0-9	0.0	-9.00	Hrdls	5-52	9.6	-3.50
Nov Chs	0-1	0.0	-1.00	Nov Chs	1-7	14.3	-3.00
Chases	0-3	0.0	-3.00	Chases	2-42	4.8	-29.50
Sell/Claim	2-6	33.3	-0.13	Sell/Claim	0-6	0.0	-6.00

RACE CLASS / FIRST TIME OUT

	W-R	Per cent	£1 Level Stake		W-R	Per cent	£1 Level Stake
Class 1	0-0	0.0	0.00	Bumpers	0-4	0.0	-4.00
Class 2	0-0	0.0	0.00	Hurdles	6-32	18.8	+14.38
Class 3	0-5	0.0	-5.00	Chases	0-13	0.0	-13.00
Class 4	6-74	8.1	-25.00				
Class 5	6-79	7.6	-47.13	Totals	6-49	12.2	-2.62
Class 6	0-4	0.0	-4.00				

JOCKEYS

	W-R	Per cent	£1 Level Stake
Richie McLernon	7-53	13.2	-2.13
Adam Wedge	2-43	4.7	-33.50
Mr Lorcan Williams	1-4	25.0	+2.50
James Bowen	1-7	14.3	-1.50
Thomas Cheesman	1-8	12.5	+0.50

COURSE RECORD

	Total W-R	Non-Hndcps Hurdles	Chases	Hndcps Hurdles	Chases	NH Flat	Per cent	£1 Level Stake
Uttoxeter	2-9	0-2	0-0	1-4	1-3	0-0	22.2	+21.00
Stratford	2-12	2-5	0-0	0-3	0-3	0-1	16.7	-5.13
Hexham	1-2	1-2	0-0	0-0	0-0	0-0	50.0	+1.50
Sedgefield	1-2	0-0	0-0	0-0	1-2	0-0	50.0	+3.50
Warwick	1-3	1-1	0-0	0-1	0-1	0-0	33.3	+2.50
Southwell	1-5	0-0	0-0	0-2	1-3	0-0	20.0	-1.00
Towcester	1-5	0-0	0-0	1-3	0-1	0-1	20.0	0.00
Ffos Las	1-7	0-2	0-0	1-2	0-3	0-0	14.3	-0.50
Taunton	1-13	0-3	0-0	1-5	0-5	0-0	7.7	-4.50
Worcester	1-17	0-6	0-0	1-7	0-4	0-0	5.9	-11.50

WINNING HORSES

Horse	Races Run	1st	2nd	3rd	£
Argus	2	1	0	0	5198
Black Narcissus	9	1	1	1	4614
Minella Voucher	10	2	0	1	8512
Tactical Manoeuvre	6	1	1	2	4159
Deebaj	2	1	1	0	3899
Thahab Ifraj	3	1	1	0	3899
Tsundoku	2	1	0	0	3379
Towering	4	1	1	0	2924
The Kid	4	1	0	2	2859
Triptico	5	1	0	1	2859
Marienstar	1	1	0	0	2599
Total winning prize-money					**£44901**
Favourites	**1-4**		**25.0%**		**-1.63**

SEAMUS DURACK

UPPER LAMBOURN, BERKSHIRE

	No. of Hrs	Races Run	1st	2nd	3rd	Unpl	Per cent	£1 Level Stake
NH Flat	2	4	0	1	0	3	0.0	-4.00
Hurdles	7	29	3	3	5	18	10.3	-9.63
Chases	3	7	0	2	1	4	0.0	-7.00
Totals	10	40	3	6	6	25	7.5	-20.63
16-17	12	48	9	9	3	27	18.8	-4.00
15-16	11	36	9	7	5	15	25.0	+0.31

JOCKEYS

	W-R	Per cent	£1 Level Stake
Conor O'Farrell	3-26	11.5	-6.63

COURSE RECORD

	Total W-R	Non-Hndcps Hurdles	Chases	Hndcps Hurdles	Chases	NH Flat	Per cent	£1 Level Stake
Mrket Rsn	1-1	1-1	0-0	0-0	0-0	0-0	100.0	+7.00
Worcester	1-3	1-2	0-0	0-0	0-0	0-1	33.3	-0.63
Plumpton	1-5	0-1	0-0	1-4	0-0	0-0	20.0	+4.00

WINNING HORSES

Horse	Races Run	1st	2nd	3rd	£
Plato's Kode	5	2	1	1	6628
Kenyan	7	1	1	1	3249
Total winning prize-money					**£9877**
Favourites	**1-5**		**20.0%**		**-2.63**

CLAIRE DYSON

CLEEVE PRIOR, WORCS

	No. of Hrs	Races Run	1st	2nd	3rd	Unpl	Per cent	£1 Level Stake
NH Flat	5	5	1	0	0	4	20.0	+4.00
Hurdles	9	31	0	0	4	27	0.0	-31.00
Chases	5	12	1	1	0	10	8.3	+9.00
Totals	12	48	2	1	4	41	4.2	-18.00
16-17	16	52	1	3	5	43	1.9	+15.00
15-16	19	100	5	5	8	82	5.0	-42.50

JOCKEYS

	W-R	Per cent	£1 Level Stake
Ian Popham	1-2	50.0	+7.00
Brendan Powell	1-15	6.7	+6.00

COURSE RECORD

	Total W-R	Non-Hndcps Hurdles	Chases	Hndcps Hurdles	Chases	NH Flat	Per cent	£1 Level Stake
Bangor	1-4	0-0	0-0	0-2	0-0	1-2	25.0	+5.00
Ludlow	1-5	0-3	1-1	0-1	0-0	0-0	20.0	+16.00

WINNING HORSES

Horse	Races Run	1st	2nd	3rd	£
*Cap'N	5	1	0	1	10184
Passam	6	1	0	2	1949
Total winning prize-money					**£12133**
Favourites	**0-0**		**0.0%**		**0.00**

SIMON EARLE

TYTHERINGTON, WILTS

	No. of Hrs	Races Run	1st	2nd	3rd	Unpl	Per cent	£1 Level Stake
NH Flat	0	0	0	0	0	0	0.0	0.00
Hurdles	0	0	0	0	0	0	0.0	0.00
Chases	2	8	1	2	0	5	12.5	-5.00
Totals	2	8	1	2	0	5	12.5	-5.00
16-17	3	8	0	0	1	7	0.0	-8.00
15-16	4	10	0	0	2	8	0.0	-10.00

JOCKEYS

	W-R	Per cent	£1 Level Stake
Conor Shoemark	1-6	16.7	-3.00

COURSE RECORD

	Total W-R	Non-Hndcps Hurdles	Chases	Hndcps Hurdles	Chases	NH Flat	Per cent	£1 Level Stake
Exeter	1-1	0-0	0-0	0-0	1-1	0-0	100.0	+2.00

WINNING HORSES

Horse	Races Run	1st	2nd	3rd	£
Kavanaghs Corner	6	1	2	0	3994
Total winning prize-money					**£3994**
Favourites	**0-0**		**0.0%**		**0.00**

TIM EASTERBY

GREAT HABTON, N YORKS

	No. of Hrs	Races Run	1st	2nd	3rd	Unpl	Per cent	£1 Level Stake
NH Flat	7	9	0	0	0	9	0.0	-9.00
Hurdles	17	44	5	2	4	33	11.4	0.00
Chases	6	24	3	6	3	12	12.5	-17.99
Totals	25	77	8	8	7	54	10.4	-26.99
16-17	18	86	6	8	12	60	7.0	-57.00
15-16	20	86	6	16	14	50	7.0	-50.75

JOCKEYS

	W-R	Per cent	£1 Level Stake
Brian Hughes	3-13	23.1	-2.89
Mr William Easterby	3-22	13.6	+8.50
Mr Kaine Wood	1-5	20.0	+3.00
Henry Brooke	1-8	12.5	-6.60

COURSE RECORD

	Total W-R	Non-Hndcps Hurdles	Chases	Hndcps Hurdles	Chases	NH Flat	Per cent	£1 Level Stake
Hexham	2-4	0-1	1-1	1-1	0-1	0-0	50.0	+1.61
Ayr	1-1	0-0	0-0	1-1	0-0	0-0	100.0	+4.50
Leicester	1-1	0-0	1-1	0-0	0-0	0-0	100.0	+0.40
Haydock	1-3	0-0	0-0	1-1	0-2	0-0	33.3	+12.00
Newcastle	1-4	0-0	0-1	0-2	1-1	0-0	25.0	-0.50
Cartmel	1-5	0-1	0-0	1-3	0-1	0-0	20.0	+6.00
Mrket Rsn	1-6	0-3	0-0	1-2	0-1	0-0	16.7	+2.00

WINNING HORSES

Horse	Races Run	1st	2nd	3rd	£
Randy Pike	9	3	0	1	17480
Bollin Ace	7	1	3	0	7733
Very First Time	6	2	1	0	10515
Attention Seeker	2	1	0	0	4874

What A Game			3	1	1	0	2599
Total winning prize-money							**£43201**
Favourites		2-6		33.3%			-3.49

MICHAEL EASTERBY

SHERIFF HUTTON, N YORKS

	No. of Hrs	Races Run	1st	2nd	3rd	Unpl	Per cent	£1 Level Stake
NH Flat	4	6	1	1	1	3	16.7	-3.63
Hurdles	8	18	5	2	1	10	27.8	+25.38
Chases	6	12	4	1	3	4	33.3	+14.50
Totals	14	36	10	4	5	17	27.8	+36.25
16-17	17	71	7	9	7	48	9.9	-23.75
15-16	20	59	7	6	13	33	11.9	-17.25

BY MONTH

NH Flat	W-R	Per cent	£1 Level Stake	Hurdles	W-R	Per cent	£1 Level Stake
May	0-1	0.0	-1.00	May	0-0	0.0	0.00
June	0-0	0.0	0.00	June	0-0	0.0	0.00
July	0-0	0.0	0.00	July	0-0	0.0	0.00
August	0-0	0.0	0.00	August	0-0	0.0	0.00
September	0-0	0.0	0.00	September	0-0	0.0	0.00
October	0-0	0.0	0.00	October	0-0	0.0	0.00
November	1-1	100.0	+1.38	November	1-1	100.0	+18.00
December	0-0	0.0	0.00	December	1-3	33.3	-0.75
January	0-0	0.0	0.00	January	1-3	33.3	+3.00
February	0-1	0.0	-1.00	February	1-4	25.0	-0.88
March	0-1	0.0	-1.00	March	1-4	25.0	+9.00
April	0-2	0.0	-2.00	April	0-3	0.0	-3.00

Chases	W-R	Per cent	£1 Level Stake	Totals	W-R	Per cent	£1 Level Stake
May	1-1	100.0	+2.00	May	1-2	50.0	+1.00
June	0-1	0.0	-1.00	June	0-1	0.0	-1.00
July	0-0	0.0	0.00	July	0-0	0.0	0.00
August	0-0	0.0	0.00	August	0-0	0.0	0.00
September	0-0	0.0	0.00	September	0-0	0.0	0.00
October	0-0	0.0	0.00	October	0-0	0.0	0.00
November	2-2	100.0	+12.00	November	4-4	100.0	+31.38
December	1-1	100.0	+8.50	December	2-4	50.0	+7.75
January	0-3	0.0	-3.00	January	1-6	16.7	0.00
February	0-2	0.0	-2.00	February	1-7	14.3	-3.88
March	0-1	0.0	-1.00	March	1-6	16.7	+7.00
April	0-1	0.0	-1.00	April	0-6	0.0	-6.00

DISTANCE

Hurdles	W-R	Per cent	£1 Level Stake	Chases	W-R	Per cent	£1 Level Stake
2m-2m3f	4-9	44.4	+21.38	2m-2m3f	1-5	20.0	-2.00
2m4f-2m7f	1-4	25.0	+9.00	2m4f-2m7f	3-4	75.0	+19.50
3m+	0-5	0.0	-5.00	3m+	0-3	0.0	-3.00

TYPE OF RACE

Non-Handicaps	W-R	Per cent	£1 Level Stake	Handicaps	W-R	Per cent	£1 Level Stake
Nov Hrdls	1-4	25.0	-0.88	Nov Hrdls	1-1	100.0	+12.00
Hrdls	2-3	66.7	+18.25	Hrdls	1-10	10.0	-4.00
Nov Chs	0-0	0.0	0.00	Nov Chs	0-0	0.0	0.00
Chases	0-0	0.0	0.00	Chases	4-12	33.3	+14.50
Sell/Claim	0-0	0.0	0.00	Sell/Claim	0-0	0.0	0.00

RACE CLASS

	W-R	Per cent	£1 Level Stake
Class 1	1-2	50.0	+11.00
Class 2	0-1	0.0	-1.00
Class 3	2-8	25.0	+8.50
Class 4	6-21	28.6	+19.38
Class 5	0-2	0.0	-2.00
Class 6	1-2	50.0	+0.38

FIRST TIME OUT

	W-R	Per cent	£1 Level Stake
Bumpers	1-4	25.0	-1.63
Hurdles	2-5	40.0	+20.00
Chases	4-5	80.0	+21.50
Totals	7-14	50.0	+39.87

JOCKEYS

	W-R	Per cent	£1 Level Stake
Harry Bannister	5-22	22.7	+6.88
Brian Hughes	2-2	100.0	+19.25
Will Kennedy	2-5	40.0	+14.00
Sean Quinlan	1-3	33.3	+0.13

COURSE RECORD

	Total W-R	Non-Hndcps Hurdles	Chases	Hndcps Hurdles	Chases	NH Flat	Per cent	£1 Level Stake
Newcastle	2-2	0-0	0-0	0-0	2-2	0-0	100.0	+14.50
Catterick	2-4	1-2	0-0	1-1	0-1	0-0	50.0	+5.13
Wetherby	2-5	2-2	0-0	0-1	0-1	0-1	40.0	+16.25
Sandown	1-1	0-0	0-0	1-1	0-0	0-0	100.0	+12.00
Musselbgh	1-3	0-0	0-0	0-0	0-1	1-2	33.3	-0.63
Sedgefield	1-4	0-1	0-0	0-1	1-2	0-0	25.0	-1.00
Southwell	1-4	0-0	0-0	0-2	1-1	0-1	25.0	+3.00

WINNING HORSES

Horse	Races Run	1st	2nd	3rd	£
Sam's Gunner	5	2	2	0	46686
Saints And Sinners	1	1	0	0	6498
Rear Admiral	2	1	0	1	6498
*Steel City	3	1	0	0	4809
Banny's Lad	5	1	0	1	4549
Chasma	3	1	0	1	3899
Albert's Back	2	2	0	0	6823
Town Head	1	1	0	0	1949
Total winning prize-money					**£81711**
Favourites	**2-4**		**50.0%**		**0.63**

STUART EDMUNDS
NEWPORT PAGNELL, BUCKS

	No. of Hrs	Races Run	1st	2nd	3rd	Unpl	Per cent	£1 Level Stake
NH Flat	11	16	3	4	1	8	18.8	+3.50
Hurdles	24	82	19	16	11	36	23.2	-10.26
Chases	7	20	1	1	2	16	5.0	-15.50
Totals	**33**	**118**	**23**	**21**	**14**	**60**	**19.5**	**-22.26**
16-17	26	76	9	13	6	48	11.8	+2.95
15-16	23	93	16	15	16	46	17.2	+24.85

BY MONTH

NH Flat	W-R	Per cent	£1 Level Stake	Hurdles	W-R	Per cent	£1 Level Stake
May	0-0	0.0	0.00	May	0-5	0.0	-5.00
June	0-1	0.0	-1.00	June	0-0	0.0	0.00
July	0-0	0.0	0.00	July	0-0	0.0	0.00
August	0-0	0.0	0.00	August	0-1	0.0	-1.00
September	0-1	0.0	-1.00	September	1-6	16.7	-2.25
October	0-3	0.0	-3.00	October	2-6	33.3	-0.50
November	1-7	14.3	+1.00	November	4-12	33.3	+0.25
December	1-2	50.0	+4.00	December	5-13	38.5	+8.71
January	0-0	0.0	0.00	January	2-10	20.0	-4.09
February	0-1	0.0	-1.00	February	0-8	0.0	-8.00
March	1-1	100.0	+4.50	March	3-10	30.0	+3.13
April	0-0	0.0	0.00	April	2-11	18.2	-1.50

Chases	W-R	Per cent	£1 Level Stake	Totals	W-R	Per cent	£1 Level Stake
May	0-0	0.0	0.00	May	0-5	0.0	-5.00
June	0-0	0.0	0.00	June	0-1	0.0	-1.00
July	0-2	0.0	-2.00	July	0-2	0.0	-2.00
August	0-0	0.0	0.00	August	0-1	0.0	-1.00
September	0-1	0.0	-1.00	September	1-8	12.5	-4.25
October	0-5	0.0	-5.00	October	2-14	14.3	-8.50
November	1-4	25.0	+0.50	November	6-23	26.1	+1.75
December	0-4	0.0	-4.00	December	6-19	31.6	+8.71
January	0-1	0.0	-1.00	January	2-11	18.2	-5.09
February	0-1	0.0	-1.00	February	0-10	0.0	-10.00
March	0-1	0.0	-1.00	March	4-12	33.3	+6.63
April	0-1	0.0	-1.00	April	2-12	16.7	-2.50

DISTANCE

Hurdles	W-R	Per cent	£1 Level Stake	Chases	W-R	Per cent	£1 Level Stake
2m-2m3f	11-39	28.2	-6.59	2m-2m3f	0-5	0.0	-5.00
2m4f-2m7f	8-31	25.8	+8.33	2m4f-2m7f	0-6	0.0	-6.00
3m+	0-11	0.0	-11.00	3m+	1-9	11.1	-4.50

TYPE OF RACE

Non-Handicaps	W-R	Per cent	£1 Level Stake	Handicaps	W-R	Per cent	£1 Level Stake
Nov Hrdls	7-23	30.4	+1.58	Nov Hrdls	0-5	0.0	-5.00
Hrdls	6-13	46.2	+11.66	Hrdls	6-38	15.8	-15.50
Nov Chs	0-2	0.0	-2.00	Nov Chs	0-4	0.0	-4.00

Chases	0-0	0.0	0.00	Chases	1-10	10.0	-5.50
Sell/Claim	0-1	0.0	-1.00	Sell/Claim	0-0	0.0	0.00

RACE CLASS | FIRST TIME OUT

	W-R	Per cent	£1 Level Stake		W-R	Per cent	£1 Level Stake
Class 1	3-14	21.4	-4.22	Bumpers	1-11	9.1	-3.00
Class 2	1-9	11.1	-7.00	Hurdles	3-18	16.7	-5.75
Class 3	4-14	28.6	+4.50	Chases	0-4	0.0	-4.00
Class 4	12-61	19.7	-13.29				
Class 5	2-12	16.7	-2.25	Totals	4-33	12.1	-12.75
Class 6	1-8	12.5	0.00				

JOCKEYS

	W-R	Per cent	£1 Level Stake
Ciaran Gethings	17-68	25.0	+2.37
Tom O'Brien	2-6	33.3	+2.63
Joshua Moore	2-13	15.4	-4.50
Brendan Powell	2-17	11.8	-8.75

COURSE RECORD

	Total W-R	Non-Hndcps Hurdles	Non-Hndcps Chases	Hndcps Hurdles	Hndcps Chases	NH Flat	Per cent	£1 Level Stake
Fakenham	3-6	2-3	0-0	0-1	0-1	1-1	50.0	+7.08
Warwick	3-6	1-1	0-0	2-4	0-0	0-1	50.0	+9.13
Huntingdon	3-9	2-4	0-0	1-2	0-1	0-2	33.3	+6.38
Sandown	2-5	0-0	0-0	1-2	0-1	1-2	40.0	+5.50
Leicester	2-6	2-3	0-0	0-3	0-0	0-0	33.3	0.00
Mrket Rsn	2-13	0-1	0-0	1-8	1-3	0-1	15.4	-6.13
Nton Abbot	1-1	1-1	0-0	0-0	0-0	0-0	100.0	+1.25
Plumpton	1-2	1-2	0-0	0-0	0-0	0-0	50.0	+1.00
Taunton	1-2	1-1	0-0	0-1	0-0	0-0	50.0	+0.38
Bangor	1-3	1-1	0-0	0-0	0-2	0-0	33.3	+0.75
Ascot	1-4	1-2	0-0	0-1	0-0	0-1	25.0	+3.50
Doncaster	1-5	1-2	0-0	0-3	0-0	0-0	20.0	-3.09
Ludlow	1-6	0-1	0-0	1-3	0-2	0-0	16.7	-4.00
Towcester	1-10	0-4	0-1	0-3	0-1	1-1	10.0	-4.00

WINNING HORSES

Horse	Races Run	1st	2nd	3rd	£
Maria's Benefit	7	5	1	0	69586
Queenohearts	3	2	0	0	17406
*Kaloci	6	2	2	1	10267
Clondaw Native	7	1	1	2	7798
Hillcrest Fire	4	1	0	2	6330
Chandos Belle	6	1	0	1	6173
Vinegar Hill	4	1	0	0	5198
Molly Childers	6	1	1	2	4874
Theclockisticking	6	2	2	2	4549
Classic Ben	7	2	3	0	8447
Now McGinty	8	2	1	2	8967
*Earlshill	1	1	0	0	4224
Pull Together	7	1	3	0	4094
Land League	5	1	0	0	2599
Total winning prize-money					**£160512**
Favourites	9-21	42.9%			0.87

LUCINDA EGERTON

MALTON, N YORKS

	No. of Hrs	Races Run	1st	2nd	3rd	Unpl	Per cent	£1 Level Stake
NH Flat	2	2	0	0	0	2	0.0	-2.00
Hurdles	8	21	4	1	4	12	19.0	+26.00
Chases	6	13	1	1	1	10	7.7	-4.50
Totals	15	36	5	2	5	24	13.9	+19.50
16-17	12	49	3	5	2	39	6.1	+36.00
15-16	8	35	2	3	6	24	5.7	-23.67

JOCKEYS

	W-R	Per cent	£1 Level Stake
Mr Aaron Anderson	3-13	23.1	+13.00
Tony Kelly	1-2	50.0	+19.00
Lee Edwards	1-13	7.7	-4.50

COURSE RECORD

	Total W-R	Non-Hndcps Hurdles	Non-Hndcps Chases	Hndcps Hurdles	Hndcps Chases	NH Flat	Per cent	£1 Level Stake
Ludlow	2-2	0-0	0-0	2-2	0-0	0-0	100.0	+15.00
Catterick	1-4	0-1	0-0	0-1	1-1	0-1	25.0	+4.50
Mrket Rsn	1-7	1-3	0-1	0-0	0-2	0-1	14.3	+2.00
Sedgefield	1-8	0-3	0-0	1-2	0-3	0-0	12.5	+13.00

WINNING HORSES

Horse	Races Run	1st	2nd	3rd	£
Bollin Line	12	5	0	1	16739
Total winning prize-money					**£16739**
Favourites	0-1	0.0%			-1.00

CLARE ELLAM

MARKET DRAYTON, SHROPSHIRE

	No. of Hrs	Races Run	1st	2nd	3rd	Unpl	Per cent	£1 Level Stake
NH Flat	0	0	0	0	0	0	0.0	0.00
Hurdles	3	6	1	0	0	5	16.7	+61.00
Chases	1	2	0	0	0	2	0.0	-2.00
Totals	4	8	1	0	0	7	12.5	+59.00
16-17	9	38	2	1	2	33	5.3	-13.00
15-16	5	28	2	1	3	22	7.1	+4.00

JOCKEYS

	W-R	Per cent	£1 Level Stake
Leighton Aspell	1-2	50.0	+65.00

COURSE RECORD

	Total W-R	Non-Hndcps Hurdles	Non-Hndcps Chases	Hndcps Hurdles	Hndcps Chases	NH Flat	Per cent	£1 Level Stake
Worcester	1-3	0-0	0-0	1-2	0-1	0-0	33.3	+64.00

WINNING HORSES

Horse	Races Run	1st	2nd	3rd	£
Amber Flush	4	1	0	0	2599
Total winning prize-money					£2599
Favourites	0-0		0.0%		0.00

BRIAN ELLISON

NORTON, N YORKS

	No. of Hrs	Races Run	1st	2nd	3rd	Unpl	Per cent	£1 Level Stake
NH Flat	10	16	4	0	1	11	25.0	-9.33
Hurdles	43	143	10	16	23	94	7.0	-109.36
Chases	22	77	15	8	10	44	19.5	-15.46
Totals	65	236	29	24	34	149	12.3	-134.15
16-17	62	228	45	33	34	116	19.7	-63.17
15-16	70	252	48	36	34	133	19.0	-13.23

BY MONTH

NH Flat	W-R	Per cent	£1 Level Stake	Hurdles	W-R	Per cent	£1 Level Stake
May	0-1	0.0	-1.00	May	0-8	0.0	-8.00
June	1-1	100.0	+1.38	June	1-7	14.3	-5.00
July	1-1	100.0	+0.61	July	1-3	33.3	-1.43
August	0-0	0.0	0.00	August	0-6	0.0	-6.00
September	0-1	0.0	-1.00	September	1-6	16.7	+0.50
October	0-2	0.0	-2.00	October	5-25	20.0	-10.43
November	0-0	0.0	0.00	November	0-18	0.0	-18.00
December	0-1	0.0	-1.00	December	0-18	0.0	-18.00
January	1-2	50.0	-0.43	January	1-13	7.7	-8.00
February	1-3	33.3	-1.89	February	1-14	7.1	-10.00
March	0-2	0.0	-2.00	March	0-11	0.0	-11.00
April	0-2	0.0	-2.00	April	0-14	0.0	-14.00

Chases	W-R	Per cent	£1 Level Stake	Totals	W-R	Per cent	£1 Level Stake
May	1-3	33.3	-1.33	May	1-12	8.3	-10.33
June	1-4	25.0	-2.00	June	3-12	25.0	-5.62
July	0-3	0.0	-3.00	July	2-7	28.6	-3.82
August	0-1	0.0	-1.00	August	0-7	0.0	-7.00
September	1-1	100.0	+1.00	September	2-8	25.0	+0.50
October	2-9	22.2	-2.30	October	7-36	19.4	-14.73
November	1-8	12.5	-1.00	November	1-26	3.8	-19.00
December	3-15	20.0	+3.05	December	3-34	8.8	-15.95
January	3-9	33.3	+6.25	January	5-24	20.8	-2.18
February	1-9	11.1	-6.75	February	3-26	11.5	-18.64
March	1-9	11.1	-5.00	March	1-22	4.5	-18.00
April	1-6	16.7	-3.38	April	1-22	4.5	-19.38

DISTANCE

Hurdles	W-R	Per cent	£1 Level Stake	Chases	W-R	Per cent	£1 Level Stake
2m-2m3f	9-91	9.9	-59.36	2m-2m3f	9-38	23.7	+3.04
2m4f-2m7f	1-43	2.3	-41.00	2m4f-2m7f	3-18	16.7	-10.55
3m+	0-9	0.0	-9.00	3m+	3-21	14.3	-7.95

TYPE OF RACE

Non-Handicaps	W-R	Per cent	£1 Level Stake	Handicaps	W-R	Per cent	£1 Level Stake
Nov Hrdls	1-31	3.2	-27.00	Nov Hrdls	0-3	0.0	-3.00
Hrdls	3-22	13.6	-16.93	Hrdls	6-81	7.4	-56.43
Nov Chs	5-12	41.7	+0.42	Nov Chs	3-4	75.0	+3.50
Chases	2-7	28.6	+4.25	Chases	4-41	9.8	-12.88
Sell/Claim	0-4	0.0	-4.00	Sell/Claim	0-1	0.0	-1.00

RACE CLASS

	W-R	Per cent	£1 Level Stake
Class 1	2-20	10.0	-8.75
Class 2	1-22	4.5	-16.50
Class 3	7-66	10.6	-37.80
Class 4	14-102	13.7	-53.65
Class 5	4-20	20.0	-13.82
Class 6	1-6	16.7	-3.63

FIRST TIME OUT

	W-R	Per cent	£1 Level Stake
Bumpers	2-10	20.0	-6.05
Hurdles	3-40	7.5	-30.43
Chases	5-15	33.3	+4.12
Totals	10-65	15.4	-32.36

JOCKEYS

	W-R	Per cent	£1 Level Stake
Danny Cook	8-58	13.8	-30.83
Brian Hughes	6-21	28.6	-6.82
Mr Kaine Wood	5-31	16.1	-11.43
Henry Brooke	5-51	9.8	-32.25
Tom Scudamore	3-10	30.0	-4.81
Nico de Boinville	1-1	100.0	+3.00
Conor O'Farrell	1-7	14.3	+6.00

COURSE RECORD

	Total W-R	Non-Hndcps Hurdles	Chases	Hndcps Hurdles	Chases	NH Flat	Per cent	£1 Level Stake
Sedgefield	7-40	1-11	1-4	2-13	2-6	1-6	17.5	-18.51
Carlisle	5-23	0-4	1-1	2-9	1-6	1-3	21.7	-10.69
Perth	3-6	1-1	0-0	0-2	1-2	1-1	50.0	-0.81
Kelso	3-11	0-3	1-1	1-5	1-2	0-0	27.3	-0.30
Catterick	2-8	0-1	1-2	1-4	0-1	0-0	25.0	+0.75
Mrket Rsn	2-26	0-5	0-3	0-9	1-6	1-3	7.7	-10.63
Aintree	1-3	0-0	1-2	0-0	0-1	0-0	33.3	+0.25
Southwell	1-3	1-2	0-0	0-1	0-0	0-0	33.3	+1.00
Cartmel	1-4	1-3	0-0	0-0	0-1	0-0	25.0	-2.00
Fakenham	1-4	0-0	0-0	0-2	1-2	0-0	25.0	-2.00
Cheltenham	1-6	0-0	1-2	0-4	0-0	0-0	16.7	+2.00
Ayr	1-15	0-0	0-0	0-8	1-6	0-1	6.7	-8.00
Wetherby	1-19	0-3	1-2	0-8	0-6	0-0	5.3	-17.20

WINNING HORSES

Horse	Races Run	1st	2nd	3rd	£
Definitly Red	5	2	0	1	85085
Forest Bihan	5	1	0	1	18582
Archive	4	1	0	1	11696
Eyes Of A Tiger	5	2	0	1	12346
Pistol Park	7	1	2	1	8123

Ballycrystal	4	1	1	1	7473
Barrys Jack	12	3	1	0	14195
Fair Loch	5	1	0	0	6498
Totalize	1	1	0	0	5592
Our Kylie	5	2	0	0	10904
Bordeaux Bill	5	1	1	0	5198
Crackdeloust	8	1	0	2	4809
Instant Replay	7	2	1	0	4614
Newstart	6	1	2	1	4549
Point The Way	6	1	0	2	4224
Contre Tous	4	1	0	2	4094
Ballyvic Boru	4	1	0	1	3798
Ravenhill Road	3	1	0	1	3249
Scottsdale	2	2	0	0	4725
Its Pandorama	8	1	2	1	2599
Windsor Avenue	2	2	0	0	2599
Total winning prize-money					**£224952**
Favourites	**16-31**		**51.6%**		**0.36**

DAVID ELSWORTH

NEWMARKET, SUFFOLK

	No. of Hrs	Races Run	1st	2nd	3rd	Unpl	Per cent	£1 Level Stake
NH Flat	2	4	1	1	0	2	25.0	+2.00
Hurdles	0	0	0	0	0	0	0.0	0.00
Chases	0	0	0	0	0	0	0.0	0.00
Totals	**2**	**4**	**1**	**1**	**0**	**2**	**25.0**	**+2.00**
16-17	2	2	0	0	0	2	0.0	-2.00
15-16	1	1	1	0	0	0	100.0	+2.00

JOCKEYS

	W-R	Per cent	£1 Level Stake
Jack Quinlan	1-2	50.0	+4.00

COURSE RECORD

	Total W-R	Non-Hndcps Hurdles	Hndcps Chases	Hndcps Hurdles	Chases	NH Flat	Per cent	£1 Level Stake
Taunton	1-1	0-0	0-0	0-0	0-0	1-1	100.0	+5.00

WINNING HORSES

Horse	Races Run	1st	2nd	3rd	£
Miss Heritage	2	1	1	0	2924
Total winning prize-money					**£2924**
Favourites	**0-180**		**0.0%**		**-180.00**

SAM ENGLAND

GUISELEY, WEST YORKSHIRE

	No. of Hrs	Races Run	1st	2nd	3rd	Unpl	Per cent	£1 Level Stake
NH Flat	0	0	0	0	0	0	0.0	0.00
Hurdles	14	47	5	6	0	36	10.6	-13.13
Chases	17	40	5	7	7	21	12.5	-15.92
Totals	**25**	**87**	**10**	**13**	**7**	**57**	**11.5**	**-29.05**

16-17	21	100	11	10	9	70	11.0	-21.22
15-16	10	25	6	1	4	14	24.0	+3.25

BY MONTH

NH Flat	W-R	Per cent	£1 Level Stake	Hurdles	W-R	Per cent	£1 Level Stake
May	0-0	0.0	0.00	May	1-10	10.0	-0.50
June	0-0	0.0	0.00	June	0-2	0.0	-2.00
July	0-0	0.0	0.00	July	1-5	20.0	+8.00
August	0-0	0.0	0.00	August	0-1	0.0	-1.00
September	0-0	0.0	0.00	September	0-3	0.0	-3.00
October	0-0	0.0	0.00	October	0-6	0.0	-6.00
November	0-0	0.0	0.00	November	0-3	0.0	-3.00
December	0-0	0.0	0.00	December	1-5	20.0	-0.50
January	0-0	0.0	0.00	January	1-2	50.0	+0.88
February	0-0	0.0	0.00	February	1-5	20.0	-1.00
March	0-0	0.0	0.00	March	0-3	0.0	-3.00
April	0-0	0.0	0.00	April	0-2	0.0	-2.00

Chases	W-R	Per cent	£1 Level Stake	Totals	W-R	Per cent	£1 Level Stake
May	0-3	0.0	-3.00	May	1-13	7.7	-3.50
June	0-0	0.0	0.00	June	0-2	0.0	-2.00
July	0-0	0.0	0.00	July	1-5	20.0	+8.00
August	0-2	0.0	-2.00	August	0-3	0.0	-3.00
September	1-2	50.0	+2.00	September	1-5	20.0	-1.00
October	1-7	14.3	-2.67	October	1-13	7.7	-8.67
November	1-9	11.1	-5.75	November	1-12	8.3	-8.75
December	1-5	20.0	+1.50	December	2-10	20.0	+1.00
January	0-1	0.0	-1.00	January	1-3	33.3	-0.12
February	1-3	33.3	+3.00	February	2-8	25.0	+2.00
March	0-5	0.0	-5.00	March	0-8	0.0	-8.00
April	0-3	0.0	-3.00	April	0-5	0.0	-5.00

DISTANCE

Hurdles	W-R	Per cent	£1 Level Stake	Chases	W-R	Per cent	£1 Level Stake
2m-2m3f	4-29	13.8	-8.13	2m-2m3f	1-15	6.7	-11.00
2m4f-2m7f	0-14	0.0	-14.00	2m4f-2m7f	2-11	18.2	-0.67
3m+	1-4	25.0	+9.00	3m+	2-14	14.3	-4.25

TYPE OF RACE

Non-Handicaps	W-R	Per cent	£1 Level Stake	Handicaps	W-R	Per cent	£1 Level Stake
Nov Hrdls	1-13	7.7	-9.00	Nov Hrdls	0-3	0.0	-3.00
Hrdls	1-2	50.0	+0.88	Hrdls	2-28	7.1	-5.50
Nov Chs	1-7	14.3	-0.50	Nov Chs	3-10	30.0	+1.58
Chases	0-0	0.0	0.00	Chases	1-22	4.5	-16.00
Sell/Claim	0-0	0.0	0.00	Sell/Claim	1-1	100.0	+3.50

RACE CLASS   FIRST TIME OUT

	W-R	Per cent	£1 Level Stake		W-R	Per cent	£1 Level Stake
Class 1	0-1	0.0	-1.00	Bumpers	0-0	0.0	0.00
Class 2	0-0	0.0	0.00	Hurdles	1-13	7.7	-3.50
Class 3	1-7	14.3	-0.50	Chases	0-12	0.0	-12.00
Class 4	5-51	9.8	-23.54				
Class 5	4-28	14.3	-4.00	**Totals**	**1-25**	**4.0**	**-15.50**

Class 6   0-0   0.0   0.00

JOCKEYS

	W-R	Per cent	£1 Level Stake
Jonathan England	10-67	14.9	-9.04

COURSE RECORD

	Total W-R	Non-Hndcps Hurdles	Chases	Hndcps Hurdles	Chases	NH Flat	Per cent	£1 Level Stake
Cartmel	2-7	0-0	0-0	2-7	0-0	0-0	28.6	+15.50
Hexham	2-14	0-4	0-0	0-5	2-5	0-0	14.3	-6.42
Newcastle	1-1	0-0	0-0	0-0	1-1	0-0	100.0	+5.00
Fakenham	1-3	1-1	0-0	0-0	0-2	0-0	33.3	-0.13
Bangor	1-5	1-3	0-0	0-0	0-2	0-0	20.0	-1.00
Mrket Rsn	1-5	0-1	0-0	1-3	0-1	0-0	20.0	-0.50
Catterick	1-6	0-1	1-2	0-0	0-3	0-0	16.7	+0.50
Sedgefield	1-16	0-0	0-1	0-6	1-9	0-0	6.3	-12.00

WINNING HORSES

Horse	Races Run	1st	2nd	3rd	£
Alzammaar	6	1	3	0	10834
The Linksman	7	2	1	0	8902
*Western Jo	5	2	1	1	8980
*Brown Trix	8	1	0	1	3314
My Renaissance	6	2	1	0	3249
Ninepointsixthree	8	1	2	1	3249
Nicki's Nipper	8	1	0	0	3249
Total winning prize-money					£41777
Favourites	2-5		40.0%		2.25

JAMES EUSTACE

NEWMARKET, SUFFOLK

	No. of Hrs	Races Run	1st	2nd	3rd	Unpl	Per cent	£1 Level Stake
NH Flat	1	3	0	0	0	3	0.0	-3.00
Hurdles	10	31	3	3	2	23	9.7	-4.00
Chases	0	0	0	0	0	0	0.0	0.00
Totals	11	34	3	3	2	26	8.8	-7.00
16-17	10	26	4	7	6	9	15.4	-5.75
15-16	7	27	6	6	2	13	22.2	-3.00

JOCKEYS

	W-R	Per cent	£1 Level Stake
Jack Quinlan	2-26	7.7	-10.00
Trevor Whelan	1-5	20.0	+6.00

COURSE RECORD

	Total W-R	Non-Hndcps Hurdles	Chases	Hndcps Hurdles	Chases	NH Flat	Per cent	£1 Level Stake
Wincanton	1-1	0-0	0-0	1-1	0-0	0-0	100.0	+10.00
Mrket Rsn	1-5	1-2	0-0	0-3	0-0	0-0	20.0	+1.00
Huntingdon	1-7	0-4	0-0	1-2	0-0	0-1	14.3	+3.00

WINNING HORSES

Horse	Races Run	1st	2nd	3rd	£
Apache Song	6	2	1	0	10722
Captain Felix	4	1	0	1	3899
Total winning prize-money					£14621
Favourites	0-0		0.0%		0.00

DAVID EVANS

PANDY, MONMOUTHS

	No. of Hrs	Races Run	1st	2nd	3rd	Unpl	Per cent	£1 Level Stake
NH Flat	0	0	0	0	0	0	0.0	0.00
Hurdles	2	2	0	0	0	2	0.0	-2.00
Chases	1	1	1	0	0	0	100.0	+3.50
Totals	2	3	1	0	0	2	33.3	+1.50
16-17	4	5	0	0	1	4	0.0	-5.00
15-16	8	13	0	3	2	8	0.0	-13.00

JOCKEYS

	W-R	Per cent	£1 Level Stake
Robert Dunne	1-1	100.0	+3.50

COURSE RECORD

	Total W-R	Non-Hndcps Hurdles	Chases	Hndcps Hurdles	Chases	NH Flat	Per cent	£1 Level Stake
Southwell	1-1	0-0	0-0	0-0	1-1	0-0	100.0	+3.50

WINNING HORSES

Horse	Races Run	1st	2nd	3rd	£
John Reel	2	1	0	0	3899
Total winning prize-money					£3899
Favourites	0-0		0.0%		0.00

JAMES EVANS

KINNERSLEY, WORCS

	No. of Hrs	Races Run	1st	2nd	3rd	Unpl	Per cent	£1 Level Stake
NH Flat	2	3	1	0	0	2	33.3	+1.00
Hurdles	8	32	0	1	2	29	0.0	-32.00
Chases	5	14	3	2	1	8	21.4	-0.25
Totals	11	49	4	3	3	39	8.2	-31.25
16-17	20	60	3	3	6	48	5.0	-27.50
15-16	17	73	9	6	10	48	12.3	+5.46

JOCKEYS

	W-R	Per cent	£1 Level Stake
Liam Treadwell	4-18	22.2	-0.25

COURSE RECORD

	Total W-R	Non-Hndcps Hurdles	Non-Hndcps Chases	Hndcps Hurdles	Hndcps Chases	NH Flat	Per cent	£1 Level Stake
Fontwell	1-3	0-0	0-0	0-2	0-0	1-1	33.3	+1.00
Uttoxeter	1-3	0-0	0-0	0-1	1-2	0-0	33.3	+0.50
Fakenham	1-4	0-0	0-0	0-1	1-3	0-0	25.0	+3.00
Stratford	1-4	0-0	0-0	0-2	1-1	0-1	25.0	-0.75

WINNING HORSES

Horse	Races Run	1st	2nd	3rd	£
Amiral Collonges	6	1	2	0	16245
Optimistic Bias	4	2	0	0	10359
Malindi Bay	3	1	0	0	1560
Total winning prize-money					**£28164**
Favourites	**2-4**		**50.0%**		**2.75**

JAMES EWART

LANGHOLM, DUMFRIES & G'WAY

	No. of Hrs	Races Run	1st	2nd	3rd	Unpl	Per cent	£1 Level Stake
NH Flat	*15*	*22*	*5*	*3*	*1*	*13*	*22.7*	*+32.20*
Hurdles	*24*	*72*	*11*	*8*	*10*	*43*	*15.3*	*+17.35*
Chases	*10*	*30*	*4*	*6*	*5*	*14*	*13.3*	*+9.25*
Totals	**41**	**124**	**20**	**17**	**16**	**70**	**16.1**	**+58.80**
16-17	*34*	*169*	*18*	*19*	*32*	*100*	*10.7*	*-49.13*
15-16	*26*	*101*	*14*	*5*	*13*	*69*	*13.9*	*-0.50*

BY MONTH

NH Flat	W-R	Per cent	£1 Level Stake	Hurdles	W-R	Per cent	£1 Level Stake
May	0-1	0.0	-1.00	May	1-2	50.0	+5.00
June	0-0	0.0	0.00	June	0-3	0.0	-3.00
July	0-1	0.0	-1.00	July	1-3	33.3	+10.00
August	0-0	0.0	0.00	August	1-3	33.3	+31.00
September	0-0	0.0	0.00	September	0-2	0.0	-2.00
October	0-0	0.0	0.00	October	2-4	50.0	+9.00
November	1-3	33.3	+23.00	November	2-14	14.3	-5.50
December	2-6	33.3	+15.50	December	3-12	25.0	-3.65
January	0-7	0.0	-7.00	January	0-14	0.0	-14.00
February	2-2	100.0	+4.70	February	0-8	0.0	-8.00
March	0-0	0.0	0.00	March	0-5	0.0	-5.00
April	0-2	0.0	-2.00	April	1-2	50.0	+3.50

Chases	W-R	Per cent	£1 Level Stake	Totals	W-R	Per cent	£1 Level Stake
May	0-4	0.0	-4.00	May	1-7	14.3	0.00
June	0-4	0.0	-4.00	June	0-7	0.0	-7.00
July	0-1	0.0	-1.00	July	1-5	20.0	+8.00
August	0-2	0.0	-2.00	August	1-5	20.0	+29.00
September	0-0	0.0	0.00	September	0-2	0.0	-2.00
October	0-0	0.0	0.00	October	2-4	50.0	+9.00
November	1-5	20.0	+7.00	November	4-22	18.2	+24.50
December	0-3	0.0	-3.00	December	5-21	23.8	+8.85
January	2-4	50.0	+19.50	January	2-25	8.0	-1.50
February	0-1	0.0	-1.00	February	2-11	18.2	-4.30
March	0-1	0.0	-1.00	March	0-6	0.0	-6.00
April	1-5	20.0	-1.25	April	2-9	22.2	+0.25

DISTANCE

Hurdles	W-R	Per cent	£1 Level Stake	Chases	W-R	Per cent	£1 Level Stake
2m-2m3f	10-45	22.2	+39.85	2m-2m3f	1-15	6.7	-8.50
2m4f-2m7f	1-14	7.1	-9.50	2m4f-2m7f	3-12	25.0	+20.75
3m+	0-13	0.0	-13.00	3m+	0-3	0.0	-3.00

TYPE OF RACE

Non-Handicaps	W-R	Per cent	£1 Level Stake	Handicaps	W-R	Per cent	£1 Level Stake
Nov Hrdls	2-7	28.6	+3.00	Nov Hrdls	1-4	25.0	-0.25
Hrdls	0-7	0.0	-7.00	Hrdls	8-54	14.8	+21.60
Nov Chs	0-0	0.0	0.00	Nov Chs	0-6	0.0	-6.00
Chases	0-0	0.0	0.00	Chases	4-24	16.7	+15.25
Sell/Claim	0-0	0.0	0.00	Sell/Claim	0-1	0.0	-1.00

RACE CLASS / FIRST TIME OUT

Race Class	W-R	Per cent	£1 Level Stake	First Time Out	W-R	Per cent	£1 Level Stake
Class 1	0-1	0.0	-1.00	Bumpers	4-15	26.7	+38.00
Class 2	1-3	33.3	+14.00	Hurdles	5-20	25.0	+7.75
Class 3	3-15	20.0	-1.50	Chases	2-6	33.3	+9.75
Class 4	7-48	14.6	+22.35				
Class 5	7-50	14.0	+10.45	Totals	11-41	26.8	+55.50
Class 6	2-7	28.6	+14.50				

JOCKEYS

	W-R	Per cent	£1 Level Stake
Steven Fox	7-56	12.5	+13.80
Conor O'Farrell	4-17	23.5	+27.00
Henry Brooke	3-16	18.8	+3.50
Brian Hughes	2-8	25.0	+1.50
Rachael McDonald	1-1	100.0	+25.00
Craig Nichol	1-2	50.0	+0.50
Richard Johnson	1-2	50.0	+2.50
Lucy Alexander	1-9	11.1	-2.00

COURSE RECORD

	Total W-R	Non-Hndcps Hurdles	Non-Hndcps Chases	Hndcps Hurdles	Hndcps Chases	NH Flat	Per cent	£1 Level Stake
Ayr	4-19	0-4	0-0	1-5	1-2	2-8	21.1	+3.80
Kelso	4-21	1-1	0-0	1-9	1-6	1-5	19.0	+34.50
Wetherby	3-7	0-3	0-0	2-3	0-0	1-1	42.9	+5.00
Carlisle	2-7	0-0	0-0	1-3	1-4	0-0	28.6	+13.50
Sedgefield	2-11	0-0	0-0	2-9	0-2	0-0	18.2	-2.75
Newcastle	2-12	1-3	0-0	0-4	1-4	0-1	16.7	-3.75
Bangor	1-2	0-0	0-0	1-1	0-1	0-0	50.0	+32.00
Cartmel	1-2	0-0	0-0	1-2	0-0	0-0	50.0	+11.00
Doncaster	1-6	0-0	0-0	0-4	0-0	1-2	16.7	+2.50

WINNING HORSES

Horse	Races Run	1st	2nd	3rd	£
Un Guet Apens	8	2	2	0	20514
Lycidas	2	1	0	1	7596
Aristo Du Plessis	2	2	0	0	12346
Ascot De Bruyere	1	1	0	0	4614
Calix Delafayette	2	1	0	0	4549
Charmant	5	2	1	0	6498
Durbanville	5	1	0	2	3899
Civil Unrest	7	1	2	0	3249
Jassas	3	1	0	0	3249
Sky Full Of Stars	9	1	3	1	2924
Betancourt	5	1	0	0	2599
Strike The Pose	3	1	0	0	2599
Black Pirate	3	2	1	0	4874
Ange Des Malberaux	11	1	1	3	2599
Ettila De Sivola	1	1	0	0	1949
Sao Maxence	2	1	1	0	1949
Total winning prize-money					**£86007**
Favourites	**6-16**		**37.5%**		**1.80**

RICHARD FAHEY

MUSLEY BANK, N YORKS

	No. of Hrs	Races Run	1st	2nd	3rd	Unpl	Per cent	£1 Level Stake
NH Flat	1	1	1	0	0	0	100.0	+3.50
Hurdles	3	11	0	1	1	9	0.0	-11.00
Chases	0	0	0	0	0	0	0.0	0.00
Totals	**3**	**12**	**1**	**1**	**1**	**9**	**8.3**	**-7.50**
16-17	5	15	1	0	3	11	6.7	-7.50
15-16	5	13	2	2	2	7	15.4	-6.75

JOCKEYS

	W-R	Per cent	£1 Level Stake
Craig Nichol	1-2	50.0	+2.50

COURSE RECORD

	Total W-R	Non-Hndcps Hurdles	Chases	Hndcps Hurdles	Chases	NH Flat	Per cent	£1 Level Stake
Sedgefield	1-4	0-1	0-0	0-2	0-0	1-1	25.0	+0.50

WINNING HORSES

Horse	Races Run	1st	2nd	3rd	£
Judge Earle	7	1	1	1	1560
Total winning prize-money					**£1560**
Favourites	**0-0**		**0.0%**		**0.00**

JOHNNY FARRELLY

ENMORE, SOMERSET

	No. of Hrs	Races Run	1st	2nd	3rd	Unpl	Per cent	£1 Level Stake
NH Flat	5	9	2	1	2	4	22.2	+1.00
Hurdles	37	116	14	14	12	76	12.1	-60.61
Chases	13	39	5	4	5	25	12.8	+11.00
Totals	**46**	**164**	**21**	**19**	**19**	**105**	**12.8**	**-48.61**
16-17	45	166	25	14	24	103	15.1	-0.17
15-16	35	177	17	12	24	124	9.6	-88.96

BY MONTH

NH Flat	W-R	Per cent	£1 Level Stake	Hurdles	W-R	Per cent	£1 Level Stake
May	0-1	0.0	-1.00	May	2-11	18.2	-4.04
June	0-0	0.0	0.00	June	3-14	21.4	-2.42
July	1-2	50.0	+2.00	July	0-13	0.0	-13.00
August	0-2	0.0	-2.00	August	1-10	10.0	-4.00
September	0-0	0.0	0.00	September	2-9	22.2	-3.83
October	0-0	0.0	0.00	October	0-8	0.0	-8.00
November	0-0	0.0	0.00	November	1-13	7.7	-11.09
December	0-2	0.0	-2.00	December	0-10	0.0	-10.00
January	0-0	0.0	0.00	January	3-8	37.5	+11.16
February	1-1	100.0	+5.00	February	0-6	0.0	-6.00
March	0-0	0.0	0.00	March	2-5	40.0	-0.39
April	0-1	0.0	-1.00	April	0-9	0.0	-9.00

Chases	W-R	Per cent	£1 Level Stake	Totals	W-R	Per cent	£1 Level Stake
May	0-3	0.0	-3.00	May	2-15	13.3	-8.04
June	0-1	0.0	-1.00	June	3-15	20.0	-3.42
July	1-3	33.3	+2.50	July	2-18	11.1	-8.50
August	1-6	16.7	-2.50	August	2-18	11.1	-8.50
September	0-2	0.0	-2.00	September	2-11	18.2	-5.83
October	2-6	33.3	+22.00	October	2-14	14.3	+14.00
November	0-3	0.0	-3.00	November	1-16	6.3	-14.09
December	0-1	0.0	-1.00	December	0-13	0.0	-13.00
January	0-4	0.0	-4.00	January	3-12	25.0	+7.16
February	0-3	0.0	-3.00	February	1-10	10.0	-4.00
March	0-4	0.0	-4.00	March	2-9	22.2	-4.39
April	1-3	33.3	+10.00	April	1-13	7.7	0.00

DISTANCE

Hurdles	W-R	Per cent	£1 Level Stake	Chases	W-R	Per cent	£1 Level Stake
2m-2m3f	6-51	11.8	-19.98	2m-2m3f	1-10	10.0	-4.50
2m4f-2m7f	7-50	14.0	-29.96	2m4f-2m7f	1-14	7.1	-1.00
3m+	1-14	7.1	-9.67	3m+	3-15	20.0	+16.50

TYPE OF RACE

Non-Handicaps	W-R	Per cent	£1 Level Stake	Handicaps	W-R	Per cent	£1 Level Stake
Nov Hrdls	1-5	20.0	+10.00	Nov Hrdls	1-10	10.0	-5.67
Hrdls	0-0	0.0	0.00	Hrdls	6-95	6.3	-74.71
Nov Chs	0-0	0.0	0.00	Nov Chs	0-4	0.0	-4.00

Chases	0-0	0.0	0.00	Chases	5-35	14.3	+15.00
Sell/Claim	6-6	100.0	+9.77	Sell/Claim	0-0	0.0	0.00

RACE CLASS   FIRST TIME OUT

	W-R	Per cent	£1 Level Stake		W-R	Per cent	£1 Level Stake
Class 1	0-2	0.0	-2.00	Bumpers	2-5	40.0	+5.00
Class 2	0-1	0.0	-1.00	Hurdles	4-34	11.8	-17.04
Class 3	3-25	12.0	+8.50	Chases	1-7	14.3	+6.00
Class 4	5-62	8.1	-23.75				
Class 5	12-71	16.9	-31.36	Totals	7-46	15.2	-6.04
Class 6	1-3	33.3	+1.00				

JOCKEYS

	W-R	Per cent	£1 Level Stake
Noel Fehily	7-16	43.8	+29.17
Brendan Powell	6-75	8.0	-37.71
Patrick Cowley	3-4	75.0	+1.52
Sean Houlihan	1-2	50.0	-0.09
Sean Bowen	1-7	14.3	-3.75
James Best	1-9	11.1	+4.00
Mr Garry Lavery	1-10	10.0	-6.75
Tom Cannon	1-12	8.3	-6.00

COURSE RECORD

	Total W-R	Non-Hndcps Hurdles	Chases	Hndcps Hurdles	Chases	NH Flat	Per cent	£1 Level Stake
Worcester	4-18	1-1	0-0	2-14	0-2	1-1	22.2	-2.92
Fakenham	2-3	2-2	0-0	0-0	0-1	0-0	66.7	+1.24
Huntingdon	2-6	1-1	0-0	0-3	0-0	1-2	33.3	+1.91
Sedgefield	1-2	1-1	0-0	0-0	0-1	0-0	50.0	-0.71
Hexham	1-3	0-0	0-0	1-2	0-1	0-0	33.3	-0.38
Kempton	1-3	0-1	0-0	0-1	1-1	0-0	33.3	+10.00
Bangor	1-4	0-0	0-0	1-4	0-0	0-0	25.0	-2.33
Doncaster	1-4	1-2	0-0	0-1	0-1	0-0	25.0	+11.00
Ffos Las	1-4	1-1	0-0	0-3	0-0	0-0	25.0	0.00
Mrket Rsn	1-5	0-0	0-0	0-4	1-1	0-0	20.0	+2.00
Exeter	1-7	0-0	0-0	0-6	1-1	0-0	14.3	+14.00
Plumpton	1-8	0-0	0-0	1-3	0-5	0-0	12.5	-4.75
Fontwell	1-9	0-0	0-0	0-3	1-5	0-1	11.1	-5.50
Stratford	1-9	0-1	0-0	0-4	1-2	0-2	11.1	-3.50
Southwell	1-11	0-0	0-0	1-10	0-1	0-0	9.1	-6.67
Nton Abbot	1-13	0-0	0-0	1-9	0-3	0-1	7.7	-7.00

WINNING HORSES

Horse	Races Run	1st	2nd	3rd	£
Gingili	6	3	2	0	16400
Sporting Boy	6	1	2	0	6498
Degooch	7	1	0	1	6330
Conna Cross	1	1	0	0	5588
Ascendant	7	6	0	1	18621
And The New	3	1	0	2	4094
Ambre Des Marais	5	3	1	0	10397
Mr Lando	6	1	2	0	3119
Lake Shore Drive	2	1	1	0	2924
Shouting Hill	1	1	0	0	2599

Sparkling Dawn	2	1	0	0	2274
Blue N Yellow	1	1	0	0	1560
Total winning prize-money					£80404
Favourites	9-19		47.4%		4.43

DEBORAH FAULKNER

NEWPORT, NEWPORT

	No. of Hrs	Races Run	1st	2nd	3rd	Unpl	Per cent	£1 Level Stake
NH Flat	0	0	0	0	0	0	0.0	0.00
Hurdles	8	15	0	0	0	15	0.0	-15.00
Chases	4	12	2	3	1	6	16.7	0.00
Totals	9	27	2	3	1	21	7.4	-15.00
16-17	6	19	1	0	4	14	5.3	-2.00

JOCKEYS

	W-R	Per cent	£1 Level Stake
Nick Scholfield	2-10	20.0	+2.00

COURSE RECORD

	Total W-R	Non-Hndcps Hurdles	Chases	Hndcps Hurdles	Chases	NH Flat	Per cent	£1 Level Stake
Chepstow	2-10	0-2	0-0	0-2	2-6	0-0	20.0	+2.00

WINNING HORSES

Horse	Races Run	1st	2nd	3rd	£
Beallandendall	9	2	3	0	6628
Total winning prize-money					£6628
Favourites	0-0		0.0%		0.00

MARJORIE FIFE

STILLINGTON, N YORKS

	No. of Hrs	Races Run	1st	2nd	3rd	Unpl	Per cent	£1 Level Stake
NH Flat	0	0	0	0	0	0	0.0	0.00
Hurdles	2	2	1	0	0	1	50.0	+9.00
Chases	0	0	0	0	0	0	0.0	0.00
Totals	2	2	1	0	0	1	50.0	+9.00
16-17	4	16	1	3	1	11	6.3	-12.00
15-16	4	10	1	2	0	7	10.0	+5.00

JOCKEYS

	W-R	Per cent	£1 Level Stake
Jeremiah McGrath	1-1	100.0	+10.00

COURSE RECORD

	Total W-R	Non-Hndcps Hurdles	Chases	Hndcps Hurdles	Chases	NH Flat	Per cent	£1 Level Stake
Kelso	1-1	0-0	0-0	1-1	0-0	0-0	100.0	+10.00

WINNING HORSES

Horse	Races Run	1st	2nd	3rd	£
Notnow Seamus	1	1	0	0	4549
Total winning prize-money					£4549
Favourites	0-0		0.0%		0.00

JOHN FLINT
KENFIG HILL, BRIDGEND

	No. of Hrs	Races Run	1st	2nd	3rd	Unpl	Per cent	£1 Level Stake
NH Flat	4	6	0	1	0	5	0.0	-6.00
Hurdles	19	75	5	9	8	53	6.7	-41.13
Chases	3	12	0	4	1	7	0.0	-12.00
Totals	21	93	5	14	9	65	5.4	-59.13
16-17	19	87	12	11	11	53	13.8	-0.25
15-16	16	63	3	6	9	45	4.8	-30.00

JOCKEYS

	W-R	Per cent	£1 Level Stake
Robert Dunne	2-12	16.7	-6.50
Jamie Moore	1-8	12.5	+3.00
Ian Popham	1-18	5.6	-3.00
Mitchell Bastyan	1-18	5.6	-15.63

COURSE RECORD

	Total W-R	Non-Hndcps Hurdles	Chases	Hndcps Hurdles	Chases	NH Flat	Per cent	£1 Level Stake
Stratford	1-2	0-0	0-0	1-2	0-0	0-0	50.0	+0.50
Uttoxeter	1-5	0-1	0-0	1-4	0-0	0-0	20.0	+6.00
Nton Abbot	1-8	0-0	0-0	1-8	0-0	0-0	12.5	-5.63
Chepstow	1-17	1-6	0-0	0-6	0-2	0-3	5.9	-14.00
Ffos Las	1-17	0-5	0-1	1-7	0-4	0-0	5.9	-2.00

WINNING HORSES

Horse	Races Run	1st	2nd	3rd	£
Cillian's Well	9	2	2	1	7310
Kayf Moss	4	1	0	0	4094
Ayla's Emperor	6	1	0	2	3249
Arian	4	1	3	0	3119
Total winning prize-money					£17772
Favourites	121-125		96.8%		236.88

STEVE FLOOK
LEOMINSTER, HEREFORDSHIRE

	No. of Hrs	Races Run	1st	2nd	3rd	Unpl	Per cent	£1 Level Stake
NH Flat	3	5	0	0	1	4	0.0	-5.00
Hurdles	9	23	1	0	1	21	4.3	-14.00
Chases	5	14	1	0	1	12	7.1	-2.00
Totals	13	42	2	0	3	37	4.8	-21.00

16-17	14	38	3	1	5	29	7.9	-22.90
15-16	15	44	1	3	6	34	2.3	-37.00

JOCKEYS

	W-R	Per cent	£1 Level Stake
Ben Poste	2-13	15.4	+8.00

COURSE RECORD

	Total W-R	Non-Hndcps Hurdles	Chases	Hndcps Hurdles	Chases	NH Flat	Per cent	£1 Level Stake
Bangor	1-2	0-0	0-0	1-1	0-1	0-0	50.0	+7.00
Worcester	1-9	0-4	0-1	0-1	1-2	0-1	11.1	+3.00

WINNING HORSES

Horse	Races Run	1st	2nd	3rd	£
*Vikekhal	7	1	0	1	6882
*Centreofexcellence	7	1	0	1	3509
Total winning prize-money					£10391
Favourites	0-0		0.0%		0.00

RICHARD FORD
GARSTANG, LANCS

	No. of Hrs	Races Run	1st	2nd	3rd	Unpl	Per cent	£1 Level Stake
NH Flat	0	0	0	0	0	0	0.0	0.00
Hurdles	2	7	2	0	0	5	28.6	+4.00
Chases	2	4	3	0	0	1	75.0	+9.67
Totals	3	11	5	0	0	6	45.5	+13.67
16-17	13	47	4	5	4	34	8.5	-9.50
15-16	10	32	3	4	3	22	9.4	-6.50

JOCKEYS

	W-R	Per cent	£1 Level Stake
Miss Becky Smith	4-7	57.1	+13.33
Craig Nichol	1-1	100.0	+3.33

COURSE RECORD

	Total W-R	Non-Hndcps Hurdles	Chases	Hndcps Hurdles	Chases	NH Flat	Per cent	£1 Level Stake
Cartmel	3-4	0-0	0-0	0-0	3-4	0-0	75.0	+9.67
Uttoxeter	1-1	0-0	0-0	1-1	0-0	0-0	100.0	+4.50
Fakenham	1-2	0-0	0-0	1-2	0-0	0-0	50.0	+3.50

WINNING HORSES

Horse	Races Run	1st	2nd	3rd	£
Camillas Wish	6	4	0	0	16122
Shake It Up	1	1	0	0	4419
Total winning prize-money					£20541
Favourites	0-1		0.0%		-1.00

RICHENDA FORD
BROCKHAMPTON GREEN, DORSET

	No. of Hrs	Races Run	1st	2nd	3rd	Unpl	Per cent	£1 Level Stake
NH Flat	3	3	0	0	0	3	0.0	-3.00
Hurdles	5	38	2	0	3	33	5.3	-6.50
Chases	2	8	0	0	1	7	0.0	-8.00
Totals	7	49	2	0	4	43	4.1	-17.50
16-17	5	27	1	3	5	18	3.7	-20.00
15-16	5	16	3	1	4	8	18.8	+2.50

JOCKEYS

	W-R	Per cent	£1 Level Stake
David Noonan	1-5	20.0	+0.50
Conor Shoemark	1-5	20.0	+21.00

COURSE RECORD

	Total W-R	Non-Hndcps Hurdles	Chases	Hndcps Hurdles	Chases	NH Flat	Per cent	£1 Level Stake
Exeter	1-5	0-1	0-0	1-3	0-1	0-0	20.0	+0.50
Wincanton	1-10	0-4	0-0	1-4	0-1	0-1	10.0	+16.00

WINNING HORSES

Horse	Races Run	1st	2nd	3rd	£
Breaking Ground	15	2	0	1	7408
Total winning prize-money					**£7408**
Favourites	0-1		0.0%		**-1.00**

SANDY FORSTER
KIRK YETHOLM, ROXBURGHSHIRE

	No. of Hrs	Races Run	1st	2nd	3rd	Unpl	Per cent	£1 Level Stake
NH Flat	1	1	0	0	0	1	0.0	-1.00
Hurdles	4	11	0	2	0	9	0.0	-11.00
Chases	2	15	4	1	4	6	26.7	+13.33
Totals	6	27	4	3	4	16	14.8	+1.33
16-17	8	34	0	2	3	29	0.0	-34.00
15-16	5	22	2	2	2	16	9.1	-15.38

JOCKEYS

	W-R	Per cent	£1 Level Stake
Jamie Hamilton	2-9	22.2	+6.33
Thomas Willmott	2-10	20.0	+3.00

COURSE RECORD

	Total W-R	Non-Hndcps Hurdles	Chases	Hndcps Hurdles	Chases	NH Flat	Per cent	£1 Level Stake
Kelso	2-9	0-1	0-1	0-2	2-4	0-1	22.2	+1.33
Newcastle	1-2	0-0	0-0	0-1	1-1	0-0	50.0	+9.00
Hexham	1-4	0-1	0-0	0-1	1-2	0-0	25.0	+3.00

WINNING HORSES

Horse	Races Run	1st	2nd	3rd	£
Lowanbehold	8	2	0	3	13180
*Charlie Snow Angel	7	2	1	1	9552
Total winning prize-money					**£22732**
Favourites	0-1		0.0%		**-1.00**

JOANNE FOSTER
MENSTON, W YORKS

	No. of Hrs	Races Run	1st	2nd	3rd	Unpl	Per cent	£1 Level Stake
NH Flat	0	0	0	0	0	0	0.0	0.00
Hurdles	11	20	1	0	1	18	5.0	-11.00
Chases	6	18	3	3	0	12	16.7	-5.40
Totals	13	38	4	3	1	30	10.5	-16.40
16-17	17	64	5	5	7	47	7.8	-13.25
15-16	16	70	5	6	9	50	7.1	-27.50

JOCKEYS

	W-R	Per cent	£1 Level Stake
Danny Cook	2-9	22.2	+7.00
Sean Quinlan	1-5	20.0	-2.90
Henry Brooke	1-8	12.5	-4.50

COURSE RECORD

	Total W-R	Non-Hndcps Hurdles	Chases	Hndcps Hurdles	Chases	NH Flat	Per cent	£1 Level Stake
Sedgefield	3-11	0-3	0-0	0-1	3-7	0-0	27.3	+1.60
Southwell	1-1	0-0	0-0	1-1	0-0	0-0	100.0	+8.00

WINNING HORSES

Horse	Races Run	1st	2nd	3rd	£
Frankie Ballou	7	3	2	0	11242
Houndscourt	5	1	0	0	3119
Total winning prize-money					**£14361**
Favourites	1-1		100.0%		**1.10**

JIMMY FROST
BUCKFAST, DEVON

	No. of Hrs	Races Run	1st	2nd	3rd	Unpl	Per cent	£1 Level Stake
NH Flat	0	0	0	0	0	0	0.0	0.00
Hurdles	18	56	2	3	6	45	3.6	-40.00
Chases	8	19	2	4	1	12	10.5	-9.50
Totals	23	75	4	7	7	57	5.3	-49.50
16-17	27	111	5	12	12	82	4.5	-54.00
15-16	25	97	6	7	7	77	6.2	-50.00

JOCKEYS

	W-R	Per cent	£1 Level Stake
Bryony Frost	4-53	7.5	-27.50

COURSE RECORD

	Total W-R	Non-Hndcps Hurdles	Chases	Hndcps Hurdles	Chases	NH Flat	Per cent	£1 Level Stake
Taunton	2-10	0-0	0-0	1-9	1-1	0-0	20.0	+6.00
Fontwell	1-3	0-0	0-0	1-2	0-1	0-0	33.3	+3.00
Nton Abbot	1-32	0-6	0-0	0-18	1-8	0-0	3.1	-28.50

WINNING HORSES

Horse	Races Run	1st	2nd	3rd	£
*Triple Chief	7	2	2	0	10657
Bogoss Du Perret	3	1	1	0	4549
*Findusatgorcombe	6	1	0	1	3249
Total winning prize-money					£18455
Favourites	0-1	0.0%			-1.00

KEVIN FROST

MARKET DRAYTON, SHROPSHIRE

	No. of Hrs	Races Run	1st	2nd	3rd	Unpl	Per cent	£1 Level Stake
NH Flat	1	3	0	0	0	3	0.0	-3.00
Hurdles	7	18	2	3	4	9	11.1	-14.40
Chases	2	6	0	3	1	2	0.0	-6.00
Totals	9	27	2	6	5	14	7.4	-23.40
16-17	12	39	3	4	3	29	7.7	-27.75
15-16	11	34	2	2	3	27	5.9	-22.00

JOCKEYS

	W-R	Per cent	£1 Level Stake
Aidan Coleman	1-3	33.3	-1.20
Brian Hughes	1-8	12.5	-6.20

COURSE RECORD

	Total W-R	Non-Hndcps Hurdles	Chases	Hndcps Hurdles	Chases	NH Flat	Per cent	£1 Level Stake
Sedgefield	1-1	1-1	0-0	0-0	0-0	0-0	100.0	+0.80
Mrket Rsn	1-2	1-2	0-0	0-0	0-0	0-0	50.0	-0.20

WINNING HORSES

Horse	Races Run	1st	2nd	3rd	£
Redemption Song	4	1	0	2	3249
Hurricane Dylan	4	1	1	1	3119
Total winning prize-money					£6368
Favourites	2-4	50.0%			-0.40

HARRY FRY

SEABOROUGH, DORSET

	No. of Hrs	Races Run	1st	2nd	3rd	Unpl	Per cent	£1 Level Stake
NH Flat	17	23	5	5	2	11	21.7	-5.42
Hurdles	41	130	30	17	20	63	23.1	-22.26
Chases	22	87	15	12	12	48	17.2	-27.57
Totals	71	240	50	34	34	122	20.8	-55.25
16-17	87	283	67	42	33	140	23.7	+4.52
15-16	77	239	54	53	30	102	22.6	-11.36

BY MONTH

NH Flat	W-R	Per cent	£1 Level Stake	Hurdles	W-R	Per cent	£1 Level Stake
May	0-1	0.0	-1.00	May	5-11	45.5	+4.83
June	0-0	0.0	0.00	June	0-3	0.0	-3.00
July	0-0	0.0	0.00	July	1-4	25.0	-0.50
August	0-0	0.0	0.00	August	0-2	0.0	-2.00
September	0-0	0.0	0.00	September	1-2	50.0	+4.00
October	0-2	0.0	-2.00	October	6-20	30.0	+4.00
November	1-2	50.0	+0.75	November	9-24	37.5	+3.42
December	0-4	0.0	-4.00	December	2-17	11.8	-10.00
January	0-3	0.0	-3.00	January	2-12	16.7	+0.10
February	0-1	0.0	-1.00	February	0-10	0.0	-10.00
March	3-5	60.0	+3.83	March	1-12	8.3	-9.90
April	1-5	20.0	+1.00	April	3-13	23.1	-3.22

Chases	W-R	Per cent	£1 Level Stake	Totals	W-R	Per cent	£1 Level Stake
May	3-6	50.0	+3.10	May	8-18	44.4	+6.93
June	0-0	0.0	0.00	June	0-3	0.0	-3.00
July	0-2	0.0	-2.00	July	1-6	16.7	-2.50
August	1-4	25.0	-1.25	August	1-6	16.7	-3.25
September	0-2	0.0	-2.00	September	1-4	25.0	+2.00
October	1-8	12.5	-3.00	October	7-30	23.3	-1.00
November	3-14	21.4	-0.67	November	13-40	32.5	+3.50
December	2-12	16.7	+1.00	December	4-33	12.1	-13.00
January	4-13	30.8	-0.75	January	6-28	21.4	-3.65
February	0-10	0.0	-10.00	February	0-21	0.0	-21.00
March	1-7	14.3	-3.00	March	5-24	20.8	-9.07
April	0-9	0.0	-9.00	April	4-27	14.8	-11.22

DISTANCE

Hurdles	W-R	Per cent	£1 Level Stake	Chases	W-R	Per cent	£1 Level Stake
2m-2m3f	17-60	28.3	+5.35	2m-2m3f	4-23	17.4	-5.32
2m4f-2m7f	12-53	22.6	-12.72	2m4f-2m7f	7-32	21.9	-7.25
3m+	1-17	5.9	-14.90	3m+	4-32	12.5	-15.00

TYPE OF RACE

Non-Handicaps	W-R	Per cent	£1 Level Stake	Handicaps	W-R	Per cent	£1 Level Stake
Nov Hrdls	7-35	20.0	-16.63	Nov Hrdls	0-2	0.0	-2.00
Hrdls	6-16	37.5	+0.45	Hrdls	15-75	20.0	-5.25
Nov Chs	3-14	21.4	-5.90	Nov Chs	1-3	33.3	+1.00

50 TRAINERS JUMPS STATISTICS

Chases	0-10	0.0	-10.00	Chases	5-49	10.2	-28.25
Sell/Claim	1-1	100.0	+0.33	Sell/Claim	0-0	0.0	0.00

RACE CLASS / FIRST TIME OUT

	W-R	Per cent	£1 Level Stake		W-R	Per cent	£1 Level Stake
Class 1	0-45	0.0	-45.00	Bumpers	4-17	23.5	-2.92
Class 2	15-67	22.4	-6.77	Hurdles	14-35	40.0	+24.19
Class 3	15-53	28.3	+11.68	Chases	6-19	31.6	+2.35
Class 4	13-50	26.0	-9.50				
Class 5	6-18	33.3	-1.40	Totals	24-71	33.8	+23.62
Class 6	1-7	14.3	-4.25				

JOCKEYS

	W-R	Per cent	£1 Level Stake
Noel Fehily	32-115	27.8	-7.52
Niall P Madden	8-53	15.1	-17.70
Miss A B O'Connor	4-7	57.1	+9.50
Barry Geraghty	3-14	21.4	-2.77
Aidan Coleman	1-2	50.0	+5.00
Mr Michael Legg	1-15	6.7	-11.50
Kieron Edgar	1-21	4.8	-17.25

COURSE RECORD

	Total W-R	Non-Hndcps Hurdles	Chases	Hndcps Hurdles	Chases	NH Flat	Per cent	£1 Level Stake
Kempton	5-16	2-6	0-1	2-5	1-4	0-0	31.3	+1.50
Wincanton	4-17	0-4	0-0	1-6	1-3	2-4	23.5	+3.08
Fontwell	3-9	1-4	0-2	2-3	0-0	0-0	33.3	-2.15
Exeter	3-11	2-4	0-3	0-1	1-2	0-1	27.3	+5.50
Uttoxeter	3-11	0-1	1-3	0-2	2-6	0-0	27.3	+0.10
Nton Abbot	3-12	0-1	0-1	2-8	1-2	0-0	25.0	+1.50
Ascot	3-16	1-5	0-1	0-3	2-6	0-1	18.8	-5.50
Bangor	2-3	1-2	0-0	1-1	0-0	0-0	66.7	+1.36
Leicester	2-3	1-1	0-0	0-1	1-1	0-0	66.7	+1.08
Stratford	2-5	1-1	0-0	1-3	0-1	0-0	40.0	+2.50
Aintree	2-6	1-2	0-0	1-1	0-3	0-0	33.3	-0.27
Warwick	2-7	1-2	0-1	1-1	0-2	0-1	28.6	+0.88
Worcester	2-9	2-5	0-1	0-2	0-0	0-1	22.2	-4.79
Mrket Rsn	2-10	0-0	0-1	0-3	1-4	1-2	20.0	-6.17
Taunton	2-13	1-3	0-1	1-6	0-1	0-2	15.4	-0.47
Newbury	2-15	0-3	0-1	0-5	1-5	1-1	13.3	-4.00
Towcester	1-1	0-0	0-0	0-0	0-0	1-1	100.0	+2.50
Doncaster	1-2	0-0	1-1	0-0	0-0	0-1	50.0	+1.00
Southwell	1-4	0-0	0-0	0-1	1-3	0-0	25.0	-1.25
Ffos Las	1-4	0-0	1-1	0-0	0-2	0-1	25.0	-1.00
Chepstow	1-8	0-1	0-0	1-4	0-2	0-1	12.5	-3.00
Huntingdon	1-9	1-3	0-1	0-2	0-0	0-3	11.1	-6.90
Ludlow	1-11	0-2	0-1	1-2	0-5	0-1	9.1	-6.50
Cheltenham	1-23	0-3	0-2	1-10	0-6	0-2	4.3	-19.25

WINNING HORSES

Horse	Races Run	1st	2nd	3rd	£
Acting Lass	4	3	0	0	63854
Caribert	3	2	1	0	31454
Unowhatimeanharry	4	1	1	1	28152
Overtown Express	7	1	1	1	25024
Golden Birthday	4	3	0	1	35843
Behind Time	8	1	1	2	18768
Bags Groove	4	2	0	0	29090
Lamanver Odyssey	6	1	2	0	15640
Art Of Payroll	3	1	1	0	14076
Dashing Oscar	4	2	0	0	23571
Henryville	7	1	0	1	13826
Hell's Kitchen	3	1	1	0	13814
Misterton	3	1	1	0	12996
Wotzizname	6	2	1	1	17610
If The Cap Fits	3	3	0	0	19660
Drumcliff	5	2	0	0	18705
Canelie	2	1	0	0	8058
Mr One More	4	2	0	0	12346
Melrose Boy	5	2	0	2	11701
Litterale Ci	5	2	0	1	12997
Black Mischief	6	2	0	2	6498
Sir Ivan	6	2	0	1	10229
Space Oddity	8	1	2	0	6330
Cockney Wren	3	1	0	1	5458
Lady Of Lamanver	3	1	1	0	5393
Onefortheroadtom	4	1	0	1	3899
Steel Bob	3	1	1	0	3574
As I See It	6	1	1	1	3574
Old Harry Rocks	6	2	2	0	6173
Little Acorn	1	1	0	0	3249
Captain Drake	1	1	0	0	3119
Samarquand	1	1	0	0	2274
*Definitelyanoscar	2	1	1	0	2274
Total winning prize-money					**£489229**
Favourites	26-64		40.6%		2.57

CAROLINE FRYER

WYMONDHAM, NORFOLK

	No. of Hrs	Races Run	1st	2nd	3rd	Unpl	Per cent	£1 Level Stake
NH Flat	0	0	0	0	0	0	0.0	0.00
Hurdles	7	26	4	2	1	19	15.4	+1.00
Chases	2	10	1	1	3	5	10.0	-7.13
Totals	7	36	5	3	4	24	13.9	-6.13
16-17	7	36	4	2	6	24	11.1	-8.13
15-16	7	33	5	5	6	17	15.2	+1.40

JOCKEYS

	W-R	Per cent	£1 Level Stake
Mr Jack Andrews	2-11	18.2	-1.13
Mr Samuel Davies-Thomas	1-1	100.0	+2.00
Bridget Andrews	1-7	14.3	+4.00
Fergus Gregory	1-10	10.0	-4.00

COURSE RECORD

	Total W-R	Non-Hndcps Hurdles	Chases	Hndcps Hurdles	Chases	NH Flat	Per cent	£1 Level Stake
Towcester	3-11	0-2	0-0	2-5	1-4	0-0	27.3	+1.88
Mrket Rsn	1-2	0-0	0-0	1-1	0-1	0-0	50.0	+4.00

Warwick	1-4	0-1	0-0	1-2	0-1	0-0	25.0	+7.00

WINNING HORSES

Horse	Races Run	1st	2nd	3rd	£
Riddlestown	9	2	0	3	8447
The Blue Bomber	9	1	2	0	4094
Goodnight Charlie	7	2	1	0	7018
Total winning prize-money					**£19559**
Favourites	**0-0**		**0.0%**		**0.00**

T GALLAGHER
ST ALBANS, HERTFORDSHIRE

	No. of Hrs	Races Run	1st	2nd	3rd	Unpl	Per cent	£1 Level Stake
NH Flat	0	0	0	0	0	0	0.0	0.00
Hurdles	0	0	0	0	0	0	0.0	0.00
Chases	1	1	1	0	0	0	100.0	+0.80
Totals	**1**	**1**	**1**	**0**	**0**	**0**	**100.0**	**+0.80**
16-17	*1*	*2*	*1*	*0*	*1*	*0*	*50.0*	*+5.00*

JOCKEYS

	W-R	Per cent	£1 Level Stake
Mr Samuel Davies-Thomas	1-1	100.0	+0.80

COURSE RECORD

	Total W-R	Non-Hndcps Hurdles	Chases	Hndcps Hurdles	Chases	NH Flat	Per cent	£1 Level Stake
Sedgefield	1-1	0-0	1-1	0-0	0-0	0-0	100.0	+0.80

WINNING HORSES

Horse	Races Run	1st	2nd	3rd	£
Mr Raj	1	1	0	0	1872
Total winning prize-money					**£1872**
Favourites	**1-1**		**100.0%**		**0.80**

SUE GARDNER
LONGDOWN, DEVON

	No. of Hrs	Races Run	1st	2nd	3rd	Unpl	Per cent	£1 Level Stake
NH Flat	9	19	0	2	3	14	0.0	-19.00
Hurdles	19	79	8	4	7	60	10.1	-34.75
Chases	5	19	2	4	2	11	10.5	-10.17
Totals	**28**	**117**	**10**	**10**	**12**	**85**	**8.5**	**-63.92**
16-17	*24*	*93*	*9*	*9*	*7*	*68*	*9.7*	*-34.63*
15-16	*18*	*95*	*9*	*14*	*11*	*61*	*9.5*	*-34.42*

BY MONTH

NH Flat	W-R	Per cent	£1 Level Stake	Hurdles	W-R	Per cent	£1 Level Stake
May	0-4	0.0	-4.00	May	3-11	27.3	+7.00
June	0-0	0.0	0.00	June	1-2	50.0	+2.50
July	0-0	0.0	0.00	July	0-1	0.0	-1.00
August	0-0	0.0	0.00	August	0-2	0.0	-2.00
September	0-0	0.0	0.00	September	0-4	0.0	-4.00
October	0-1	0.0	-1.00	October	2-9	22.2	+6.00
November	0-2	0.0	-2.00	November	0-13	0.0	-13.00
December	0-2	0.0	-2.00	December	2-7	28.6	-0.25
January	0-2	0.0	-2.00	January	0-8	0.0	-8.00
February	0-5	0.0	-5.00	February	0-7	0.0	-7.00
March	0-2	0.0	-2.00	March	0-5	0.0	-5.00
April	0-1	0.0	-1.00	April	0-10	0.0	-10.00

Chases	W-R	Per cent	£1 Level Stake	Totals	W-R	Per cent	£1 Level Stake
May	0-1	0.0	-1.00	May	3-16	18.8	+2.00
June	0-1	0.0	-1.00	June	1-3	33.3	+1.50
July	0-0	0.0	0.00	July	0-1	0.0	-1.00
August	0-3	0.0	-3.00	August	0-5	0.0	-5.00
September	0-3	0.0	-3.00	September	0-7	0.0	-7.00
October	0-1	0.0	-1.00	October	2-11	18.2	+4.00
November	1-4	25.0	+0.33	November	1-19	5.3	-14.67
December	1-3	33.3	+1.50	December	3-12	25.0	-0.75
January	0-0	0.0	0.00	January	0-10	0.0	-10.00
February	0-1	0.0	-1.00	February	0-13	0.0	-13.00
March	0-1	0.0	-1.00	March	0-8	0.0	-8.00
April	0-1	0.0	-1.00	April	0-12	0.0	-12.00

DISTANCE

Hurdles	W-R	Per cent	£1 Level Stake	Chases	W-R	Per cent	£1 Level Stake
2m-2m3f	4-40	10.0	-17.25	2m-2m3f	2-7	28.6	+1.83
2m4f-2m7f	4-30	13.3	-8.50	2m4f-2m7f	0-2	0.0	-2.00
3m+	0-8	0.0	-8.00	3m+	0-10	0.0	-10.00

TYPE OF RACE

Non-Handicaps	W-R	Per cent	£1 Level Stake	Handicaps	W-R	Per cent	£1 Level Stake
Nov Hrdls	0-16	0.0	-16.00	Nov Hrdls	1-9	11.1	-2.00
Hrdls	0-6	0.0	-6.00	Hrdls	7-47	14.9	-9.75
Nov Chs	0-1	0.0	-1.00	Nov Chs	0-1	0.0	-1.00
Chases	0-0	0.0	0.00	Chases	2-16	12.5	-7.17
Sell/Claim	0-0	0.0	0.00	Sell/Claim	0-0	0.0	0.00

RACE CLASS / FIRST TIME OUT

RACE CLASS	W-R	Per cent	£1 Level Stake	FIRST TIME OUT	W-R	Per cent	£1 Level Stake
Class 1	0-6	0.0	-6.00	Bumpers	0-9	0.0	-9.00
Class 2	0-2	0.0	-2.00	Hurdles	3-16	18.8	+2.00
Class 3	3-23	13.0	-10.25	Chases	1-3	33.3	+1.33
Class 4	5-54	9.3	-22.17				
Class 5	2-29	6.9	-20.50	Totals	4-28	14.3	-5.67
Class 6	0-3	0.0	-3.00				

JOCKEYS

	W-R	Per cent	£1 Level Stake
Lucy Gardner	8-95	8.4	-52.92
Sean Houlihan	2-17	11.8	-6.00

COURSE RECORD

	Total W-R	Non-Hndcps Hurdles	Chases	Hndcps Hurdles	Chases	NH Flat	Per cent	£1 Level Stake
Exeter	4-31	0-9	0-0	4-14	0-4	0-4	12.9	-5.50
Uttoxeter	2-8	0-1	0-0	2-4	0-2	0-1	25.0	+0.50
Towcester	1-2	0-0	0-0	1-2	0-0	0-0	50.0	+6.00
Wincanton	1-5	0-1	0-0	1-4	0-0	0-0	20.0	-2.75
Ffos Las	1-6	0-2	0-0	0-1	1-2	0-1	16.7	-1.67
Fontwell	1-7	0-0	0-0	0-4	1-2	0-1	14.3	-2.50

WINNING HORSES

Horse	Races Run	1st	2nd	3rd	£
Trans Express	7	2	1	0	11696
Coeur Blimey	6	1	0	0	6330
Doctor Look Here	2	1	0	0	6173
While You Wait	5	1	0	0	4549
Bredon Hill Lad	5	2	0	2	7798
Eddy	10	3	2	0	9357
Total winning prize-money					**£45903**
Favourites	**2-7**		**28.6%**		**-0.75**

ROSEMARY GASSON

BALSCOTE, OXON

	No. of Hrs	Races Run	1st	2nd	3rd	Unpl	Per cent	£1 Level Stake
NH Flat	1	1	0	0	0	1	0.0	-1.00
Hurdles	3	17	2	4	2	9	11.8	+5.50
Chases	3	10	3	0	0	7	30.0	+15.00
Totals	**6**	**28**	**5**	**4**	**2**	**17**	**17.9**	**+19.50**
16-17	8	36	2	1	6	27	5.6	-14.00
15-16	9	43	3	3	12	25	7.0	-17.00

JOCKEYS

	W-R	Per cent	£1 Level Stake
Ben Poste	5-27	18.5	+20.50

COURSE RECORD

	Total W-R	Non-Hndcps Hurdles	Chases	Hndcps Hurdles	Chases	NH Flat	Per cent	£1 Level Stake
Worcester	3-6	0-0	0-0	2-5	1-1	0-0	50.0	+33.50
Uttoxeter	2-6	0-0	0-0	0-3	2-3	0-0	33.3	+2.00

WINNING HORSES

Horse	Races Run	1st	2nd	3rd	£
Mr McGuiness	8	2	1	0	16958
Irish Octave	5	3	0	0	9629

Total winning prize-money			£26587
Favourites	0-1	0.0%	-1.00

TOM GEORGE

SLAD, GLOUCS

	No. of Hrs	Races Run	1st	2nd	3rd	Unpl	Per cent	£1 Level Stake
NH Flat	21	30	3	5	4	18	10.0	-17.25
Hurdles	40	142	23	25	21	73	16.2	-42.68
Chases	54	184	21	36	19	108	11.4	-75.88
Totals	**105**	**356**	**47**	**66**	**44**	**199**	**13.2**	**-135.81**
16-17	77	339	69	50	53	167	20.4	+40.84
15-16	62	226	39	32	28	127	17.3	-24.06

BY MONTH

NH Flat	W-R	Per cent	£1 Level Stake		Hurdles	W-R	Per cent	£1 Level Stake
May	0-0	0.0	0.00		May	3-12	25.0	+7.87
June	0-0	0.0	0.00		June	3-11	27.3	-4.79
July	0-0	0.0	0.00		July	2-6	33.3	-0.85
August	0-0	0.0	0.00		August	0-1	0.0	-1.00
September	0-0	0.0	0.00		September	1-3	33.3	-1.17
October	0-3	0.0	-3.00		October	1-13	7.7	-8.50
November	0-3	0.0	-3.00		November	3-15	20.0	-0.93
December	2-6	33.3	+3.00		December	3-22	13.6	-10.25
January	0-3	0.0	-3.00		January	4-22	18.2	-3.07
February	1-4	25.0	-0.25		February	0-11	0.0	-11.00
March	0-4	0.0	-4.00		March	1-12	8.3	-2.00
April	0-7	0.0	-7.00		April	2-14	14.3	-7.00

Chases	W-R	Per cent	£1 Level Stake		Totals	W-R	Per cent	£1 Level Stake
May	2-14	14.3	-6.25		May	5-26	19.2	+1.62
June	1-12	8.3	-8.50		June	4-23	17.4	-13.29
July	2-6	33.3	+3.75		July	4-12	33.3	+2.90
August	1-4	25.0	+1.50		August	1-5	20.0	+0.50
September	1-2	50.0	+2.50		September	2-5	40.0	+1.33
October	2-21	9.5	-13.00		October	3-37	8.1	-24.50
November	3-17	17.6	+6.50		November	6-35	17.1	+2.57
December	3-28	10.7	-15.38		December	8-56	14.3	-22.63
January	2-18	11.1	-3.50		January	6-43	14.0	-9.57
February	1-18	5.6	-14.00		February	2-33	6.1	-25.25
March	0-17	0.0	-17.00		March	1-33	3.0	-23.00
April	3-27	11.1	-12.50		April	5-48	10.4	-26.50

DISTANCE

Hurdles	W-R	Per cent	£1 Level Stake		Chases	W-R	Per cent	£1 Level Stake
2m-2m3f	12-72	16.7	-25.92		2m-2m3f	7-47	14.9	-6.25
2m4f-2m7f	6-45	13.3	-14.47		2m4f-2m7f	8-64	12.5	-27.13
3m+	4-24	16.7	-4.17		3m+	6-73	8.2	-42.50

TYPE OF RACE

Non-Handicaps		Per cent	£1 Level Stake		Handicaps		Per cent	£1 Level Stake
	W-R					W-R		
Nov Hrdls	8-43	18.6	-11.33		Nov Hrdls	1-5	20.0	-2.00

Hrdls	7-32	21.9	-12.98	Hrdls	7-62	11.3	-16.38
Nov Chs	1-5	20.0	-3.00	Nov Chs	3-13	23.1	-1.25
Chases	0-17	0.0	-17.00	Chases	13-136	9.6	-56.38
Sell/Claim	0-0	0.0	0.00	Sell/Claim	0-0	0.0	0.00

RACE CLASS

	W-R	Per cent	£1 Level Stake
Class 1	3-50	6.0	-27.00
Class 2	7-56	12.5	-8.38
Class 3	13-95	13.7	-29.88
Class 4	20-118	16.9	-49.59
Class 5	3-27	11.1	-18.47
Class 6	1-10	10.0	-2.50

FIRST TIME OUT

	W-R	Per cent	£1 Level Stake
Bumpers	2-21	9.5	-9.75
Hurdles	7-35	20.0	+7.77
Chases	6-49	12.2	-21.25
Totals	15-105	14.3	-23.23

JOCKEYS

	W-R	Per cent	£1 Level Stake
A P Heskin	24-185	13.0	-88.02
Paddy Brennan	6-32	18.8	-7.17
Ciaran Gethings	6-49	12.2	-18.20
Noel Fehily	5-13	38.5	+17.33
Mr Noel George	4-45	8.9	-28.00
Niall P Madden	1-2	50.0	+1.25
Jonathan Burke	1-8	12.5	+9.00

COURSE RECORD

	Total W-R	Non-Hndcps Hurdles	Non-Hndcps Chases	Hndcps Hurdles	Hndcps Chases	NH Flat	Per cent	£1 Level Stake
Perth	5-21	2-5	0-1	0-1	3-13	0-1	23.8	-3.30
Mrket Rsn	4-11	0-2	0-0	2-4	2-5	0-0	36.4	+23.00
Southwell	4-20	2-7	0-0	1-5	1-5	0-3	20.0	-6.42
Bangor	3-10	1-1	0-1	0-0	2-7	0-1	30.0	+0.38
Stratford	3-18	2-4	0-1	1-2	0-11	0-0	16.7	-10.43
Aintree	3-20	1-4	0-1	0-2	2-12	0-1	15.0	-6.50
Kelso	2-5	2-2	0-0	0-1	0-2	0-0	40.0	-1.23
Leicester	2-9	0-1	0-0	0-2	2-6	0-0	22.2	-1.63
Huntingdon	2-14	1-3	0-0	0-2	0-6	1-3	14.3	-4.30
Ludlow	2-18	0-5	1-1	0-3	1-8	0-1	11.1	-10.50
Chepstow	2-19	0-3	0-0	1-5	1-9	0-2	10.5	-3.00
Cheltenham	2-33	1-9	0-4	1-9	0-8	0-3	6.1	-16.50
Ffos Las	1-2	0-0	0-0	0-0	1-2	0-0	50.0	+1.50
Lingfield	1-3	0-0	0-0	1-1	0-2	0-0	33.3	-0.13
Nton Abbot	1-6	0-3	0-0	0-2	1-1	0-0	16.7	0.00
Ascot	1-7	0-1	0-1	0-0	1-5	0-0	14.3	+10.00
Hereford	1-7	0-1	0-1	1-4	0-1	0-0	14.3	-3.75
Sandown	1-7	1-1	0-4	0-1	0-1	0-0	14.3	+2.00
Musselbgh	1-8	0-1	0-0	0-2	0-4	1-1	12.5	-4.25
Haydock	1-9	0-1	0-0	0-4	0-3	1-1	11.1	-7.50
Uttoxeter	1-10	1-4	0-1	0-2	0-2	0-1	10.0	-8.33
Worcester	1-10	0-2	0-0	0-1	1-5	0-2	10.0	-4.50
Newbury	1-11	0-3	0-0	0-1	1-7	0-0	9.1	-8.25
Kempton	1-14	0-0	0-3	0-1	1-10	0-0	7.1	-9.50
Doncaster	1-19	1-4	0-2	0-3	0-7	0-3	5.3	-17.67

WINNING HORSES

Horse	Races Run	1st	2nd	3rd	£
Summerville Boy	5	2	2	1	99663
Sir Valentino	3	1	0	0	62560
Black Op	5	2	2	0	59260
The Romford Pele	2	2	0	0	37536
Stamp Your Feet	7	1	2	0	15640
Boyhood	3	2	0	0	22603
Baby King	7	2	1	0	27726
Sandymount	3	1	1	0	12996
Wild West Wind	5	1	0	0	12660
Some Buckle	1	1	0	0	11819
Kilbree Kid	5	1	0	0	9384
Noche De Reyes	5	1	2	0	8791
Roc D'Apsis	2	1	0	0	8447
Valseur Du Granval	5	1	1	0	8187
Some Are Lucky	7	1	2	1	8058
Miss Night Owl	3	1	0	0	7596
Rocklander	5	2	0	1	13871
Bigpipenotobacee	3	1	0	0	6498
Minella Aris	3	1	0	0	6330
Otter Moon	7	2	1	3	6238
Until Winning	5	1	1	0	5848
Champagne City	7	3	0	2	14296
Cernunnos	7	1	0	1	5198
Get Rhythm	7	2	2	1	7798
Cuirassier Dempire	4	2	2	0	8447
Clondaw Castle	4	2	0	1	7408
Dandy Duke	3	2	0	0	7642
Bomber Command	3	1	2	0	3751
Air Squadron	6	1	3	0	3329
Air Navigator	6	1	1	1	3249
Seddon	2	1	0	0	3249
Just Before Dawn	1	1	0	0	3249
Super Sid	5	1	0	0	2599
The Big Bite	2	1	0	0	1949
Total winning prize-money					**£523875**
Favourites	20-65		30.8%		**-17.43**

D C GIBBS

PONTYPRIDD, RHONDDA C TAFF

	No. of Hrs	Races Run	1st	2nd	3rd	Unpl	Per cent	£1 Level Stake
NH Flat	0	0	0	0	0	0	0.0	0.00
Hurdles	0	0	0	0	0	0	0.0	0.00
Chases	2	3	1	1	0	1	33.3	+7.00
Totals	**2**	**3**	**1**	**1**	**0**	**1**	**33.3**	**+7.00**
16-17	1	1	1	0	0	0	100.0	+1.10
15-16	1	1	1	0	0	0	100.0	+2.00

JOCKEYS

	W-R	Per cent	£1 Level Stake
Mr Bradley Gibbs	1-3	33.3	+7.00

COURSE RECORD

	Total W-R	Non-Hndcps Hurdles Chases	Hndcps Hurdles Chases NH Flat	Per cent	£1 Level Stake
Cheltenham 1-1	0-0	1-1	0-0 0-0 0-0	100.0	+9.00

WINNING HORSES

Horse	Races Run	1st	2nd	3rd	£
Frelia	2	1	1	0	3840
Total winning prize-money					£3840
Favourites	0-1		0.0%		-1.00

NICK GIFFORD

FINDON, W SUSSEX

	No. of Hrs	Races Run	1st	2nd	3rd	Unpl	Per cent	£1 Level Stake
NH Flat	4	7	1	1	2	3	14.3	+4.00
Hurdles	18	80	4	16	7	53	5.0	-47.25
Chases	6	14	1	2	2	9	7.1	-10.50
Totals	22	101	6	19	11	65	5.9	-53.75
16-17	15	64	5	10	10	39	7.8	-34.50
15-16	19	66	5	3	6	52	7.6	-32.34

JOCKEYS

	W-R	Per cent	£1 Level Stake
Leighton Aspell	4-37	10.8	-4.00
Barry Geraghty	1-1	100.0	+10.00
Tom Cannon	1-27	3.7	-23.75

COURSE RECORD

	Total W-R	Non-Hndcps Hurdles Chases	Hndcps Hurdles Chases NH Flat	Per cent	£1 Level Stake
Ascot	2-7	0-3 0-0	1-2 0-1 1-1	28.6	+21.00
Fontwell	2-28	0-6 0-0	1-15 1-7 0-0	7.1	-17.50
Kempton	1-4	1-2 0-0	0-2 0-0 0-0	25.0	-0.75
Sandown	1-5	1-1 0-0	0-3 0-1 0-0	20.0	+0.50

WINNING HORSES

Horse	Races Run	1st	2nd	3rd	£
Didtheyleaveuoutto	2	1	0	0	17085
Brown Bear	7	3	0	0	12346
Notre Ami	9	2	2	0	8642
Total winning prize-money					£38073
Favourites	1-7		14.3%		-3.50

MARK GILLARD

HOLWELL, DORSET

	No. of Hrs	Races Run	1st	2nd	3rd	Unpl	Per cent	£1 Level Stake
NH Flat	2	4	0	0	0	4	0.0	-4.00
Hurdles	11	42	1	3	4	34	2.4	-33.00
Chases	3	20	2	2	3	13	10.0	+2.00
Totals	14	66	3	5	7	51	4.5	-35.00
16-17	16	98	4	8	15	71	4.1	-35.50
15-16	18	105	2	8	8	87	1.9	-89.50

JOCKEYS

	W-R	Per cent	£1 Level Stake
Tommy Dowling	2-16	12.5	+6.00
Dave Crosse	1-12	8.3	-3.00

COURSE RECORD

	Total W-R	Non-Hndcps Hurdles Chases	Hndcps Hurdles Chases NH Flat	Per cent	£1 Level Stake
Lingfield	1-4	0-1 0-0	0-0 1-3 0-0	25.0	+9.00
Taunton	1-6	0-2 0-0	1-4 0-0 0-0	16.7	+3.00
Nton Abbot	1-16	0-6 0-0	0-8 1-2 0-0	6.3	-7.00

WINNING HORSES

Horse	Races Run	1st	2nd	3rd	£
No No Cardinal	7	1	2	0	4874
Touch Screen	10	1	0	3	4549
Karl Marx	8	1	2	2	4159
Total winning prize-money					£13582
Favourites	0-0		0.0%		0.00

JIM GOLDIE

UPLAWMOOR, E RENFREWS

	No. of Hrs	Races Run	1st	2nd	3rd	Unpl	Per cent	£1 Level Stake
NH Flat	3	4	0	0	0	4	0.0	-4.00
Hurdles	11	32	1	1	2	28	3.1	-28.50
Chases	0	0	0	0	0	0	0.0	0.00
Totals	14	36	1	1	2	32	2.8	-32.50
16-17	12	36	3	3	3	27	8.3	-16.63
15-16	23	90	8	12	6	64	8.9	-39.22

JOCKEYS

	W-R	Per cent	£1 Level Stake
Callum Bewley	1-25	4.0	-21.50

COURSE RECORD

	Total W-R	Non-Hndcps Hurdles Chases	Hndcps Hurdles Chases NH Flat	Per cent	£1 Level Stake
Musselbgh 1-16	0-3	0-0	1-11 0-0 0-2	6.3	-12.50

WINNING HORSES

Horse	Races Run	1st	2nd	3rd	£
Sir Chauvelin	3	1	0	0	19494
Total winning prize-money					**£19494**
Favourites	**0-1**		**0.0%**		**-1.00**

STEVE GOLLINGS

SCAMBLESBY, LINCS

	No. of Hrs	Races Run	1st	2nd	3rd	Unpl	Per cent	£1 Level Stake
NH Flat	2	5	1	0	1	3	20.0	-2.50
Hurdles	5	12	2	0	0	10	16.7	+12.25
Chases	0	0	0	0	0	0	0.0	0.00
Totals	**7**	**17**	**3**	**0**	**1**	**13**	**17.6**	**+9.75**
16-17	5	18	0	1	4	13	0.0	-18.00
15-16	4	12	0	1	3	8	0.0	-12.00

JOCKEYS

	W-R	Per cent	£1 Level Stake
Jamie Moore	2-3	66.7	+21.25
Richard Johnson	1-2	50.0	+0.50

COURSE RECORD

	Total W-R	Non-Hndcps Hurdles	Chases	Hndcps Hurdles	Chases	NH Flat	Per cent	£1 Level Stake
Southwell	3-4	0-0	0-0	2-3	0-0	1-1	75.0	+22.75

WINNING HORSES

Horse	Races Run	1st	2nd	3rd	£
Zamoyski	3	2	0	0	6498
Rococo Style	4	1	0	0	1949
Total winning prize-money					**£8447**
Favourites	**2-3**		**66.7%**		**2.75**

CHRIS GORDON

MORESTEAD, HAMPSHIRE

	No. of Hrs	Races Run	1st	2nd	3rd	Unpl	Per cent	£1 Level Stake
NH Flat	9	16	3	1	4	8	18.8	+10.88
Hurdles	33	137	19	29	18	71	13.9	-2.77
Chases	12	41	7	10	5	19	17.1	-18.52
Totals	**39**	**194**	**29**	**40**	**27**	**98**	**14.9**	**-10.41**
16-17	39	170	23	19	27	101	13.5	-18.07
15-16	44	192	21	17	20	134	10.9	-7.59

BY MONTH

NH Flat	W-R	Per cent	£1 Level Stake		Hurdles	W-R	Per cent	£1 Level Stake
May	0-1	0.0	-1.00		May	1-6	16.7	-1.50
June	0-1	0.0	-1.00		June	1-4	25.0	+1.50
July	0-0	0.0	0.00		July	0-4	0.0	-4.00
August	0-1	0.0	-1.00		August	1-5	20.0	-2.25
September	1-2	50.0	+10.00		September	1-4	25.0	+5.00
October	0-2	0.0	-2.00		October	1-14	7.1	-9.50
November	0-3	0.0	-3.00		November	2-22	9.1	-8.50
December	0-1	0.0	-1.00		December	1-20	5.0	-18.27
January	0-1	0.0	-1.00		January	4-14	28.6	+36.50
February	1-1	100.0	+11.00		February	1-14	7.1	-3.00
March	0-0	0.0	0.00		March	1-14	7.1	-12.00
April	1-3	33.3	-0.13		April	5-16	31.3	+13.25

Chases	W-R	Per cent	£1 Level Stake		Totals	W-R	Per cent	£1 Level Stake
May	1-1	100.0	+3.50		May	2-8	25.0	+1.00
June	0-0	0.0	0.00		June	1-5	20.0	+0.50
July	0-0	0.0	0.00		July	0-4	0.0	-4.00
August	0-0	0.0	0.00		August	1-6	16.7	-3.25
September	1-2	50.0	+1.00		September	3-8	37.5	+16.00
October	0-3	0.0	-3.00		October	1-19	5.3	-14.50
November	0-4	0.0	-4.00		November	2-29	6.9	-15.50
December	0-6	0.0	-6.00		December	1-27	3.7	-25.27
January	2-7	28.6	-2.40		January	6-22	27.3	+33.10
February	2-7	28.6	-0.13		February	4-22	18.2	+7.87
March	0-5	0.0	-5.00		March	1-19	5.3	-17.00
April	1-6	16.7	-2.50		April	7-25	28.0	+10.62

DISTANCE

Hurdles	W-R	Per cent	£1 Level Stake		Chases	W-R	Per cent	£1 Level Stake
2m-2m3f	9-73	12.3	-5.02		2m-2m3f	5-18	27.8	-2.03
2m4f-2m7f	4-37	10.8	-15.75		2m4f-2m7f	1-12	8.3	-9.00
3m+	6-24	25.0	+21.00		3m+	1-11	9.1	-7.50

TYPE OF RACE

Non-Handicaps	W-R	Per cent	£1 Level Stake		Handicaps	W-R	Per cent	£1 Level Stake
Nov Hrdls	2-14	14.3	-9.52		Nov Hrdls	0-1	0.0	-1.00
Hrdls	1-17	5.9	-12.50		Hrdls	16-103	15.5	+22.25
Nov Chs	0-0	0.0	0.00		Nov Chs	1-8	12.5	-5.00
Chases	0-1	0.0	-1.00		Chases	6-31	19.4	-11.53
Sell/Claim	0-1	0.0	-1.00		Sell/Claim	0-0	0.0	0.00

RACE CLASS / FIRST TIME OUT

Race Class	W-R	Per cent	£1 Level Stake		First Time Out	W-R	Per cent	£1 Level Stake
Class 1	0-5	0.0	-5.00		Bumpers	1-9	11.1	+3.00
Class 2	2-15	13.3	+10.50		Hurdles	0-26	0.0	-26.00
Class 3	7-48	14.6	+11.38		Chases	1-4	25.0	+0.50
Class 4	10-81	12.3	-40.17					
Class 5	9-35	25.7	+10.88		**Totals**	**2-39**	**5.1**	**-22.50**
Class 6	1-10	10.0	+2.00					

JOCKEYS

	W-R	Per cent	£1 Level Stake
Tom Cannon	13-80	16.3	+18.85
Harry Reed	8-29	27.6	+20.25

James Bowen	3-8	37.5	+7.23
David Noonan	3-45	6.7	-33.75
Marc Goldstein	2-12	16.7	-3.00

COURSE RECORD

	Total W-R	Non-Hndcps Hurdles	Chases	Hndcps Hurdles	Chases	NH Flat	Per cent	£1 Level Stake
Plumpton	7-40	1-7	0-0	4-24	1-7	1-2	17.5	+5.88
Fontwell	7-57	1-13	0-0	4-27	2-12	0-5	12.3	-30.02
Kempton	4-20	1-5	0-0	1-8	1-6	1-1	20.0	+0.25
Nton Abbot	2-3	0-0	0-0	1-2	0-0	1-1	66.7	+14.50
Huntingdon	2-7	0-2	0-0	2-3	0-0	0-2	28.6	+5.50
Wincanton	2-9	0-0	0-0	1-5	1-4	0-0	22.2	+6.50
Warwick	1-3	0-1	0-0	1-1	0-0	0-1	33.3	+5.50
Ascot	1-5	0-1	0-0	1-4	0-0	0-0	20.0	+6.00
Cheltenham	1-5	0-0	0-0	1-4	0-1	0-0	20.0	+16.00
Lingfield	1-8	0-1	0-0	0-4	1-3	0-0	12.5	-5.90
Sandown	1-8	0-0	0-0	0-5	1-3	0-0	12.5	-5.63

WINNING HORSES

Horse	Races Run	1st	2nd	3rd	£
Remiluc	11	1	5	1	17204
Sea Wall	6	2	3	0	22908
Ballyheigue Bay	8	2	2	2	16245
King Uther	5	1	1	2	9747
Bugsie Malone	6	1	1	0	8447
Tara Bridge	4	2	1	0	12641
Rothman	10	1	5	1	6953
Lake Chapala	6	3	0	0	12168
Atlantic Roller	4	1	3	0	4614
Mellow Ben	7	1	0	1	4094
Highway One O One	8	4	3	0	12628
Ramore Will	12	4	1	4	14326
Night Generation	4	1	0	2	3899
Rob Robin	5	1	0	1	3249
Fizzlestix	4	1	2	1	3119
Commanche Red	3	1	0	1	2859
Baddesley Knight	3	1	1	1	2274
*Roparta Avenue	3	1	0	0	2274
Total winning prize-money					£159649
Favourites	12-29		41.4%		3.08

HARRIET GRAHAM

PHILIP LAW, BORDERS

	No. of Hrs	Races Run	1st	2nd	3rd	Unpl	Per cent	£1 Level Stake
NH Flat	4	6	1	0	1	4	16.7	+15.00
Hurdles	5	13	2	2	0	9	15.4	+2.00
Chases	2	4	2	0	1	1	50.0	+12.50
Totals	8	23	5	2	2	14	21.7	+29.50
16-17	7	32	6	3	7	16	18.8	+3.33
15-16	7	28	1	4	2	21	3.6	-16.00

JOCKEYS

	W-R	Per cent	£1 Level Stake
Callum Bewley	3-12	25.0	+20.00
Thomas Dowson	2-7	28.6	+13.50

COURSE RECORD

	Total W-R	Non-Hndcps Hurdles	Chases	Hndcps Hurdles	Chases	NH Flat	Per cent	£1 Level Stake
Carlisle	3-6	0-1	0-0	1-2	1-1	1-2	50.0	+37.00
Kelso	2-12	0-1	0-0	1-6	1-3	0-2	16.7	-2.50

WINNING HORSES

Horse	Races Run	1st	2nd	3rd	£
Sudski Star	6	3	0	1	19039
Rhymers Stone	4	1	0	0	3899
Aye Right	4	1	2	1	2274
Total winning prize-money					£25212
Favourites	1-2		50.0%		0.00

CHRIS GRANT

NEWTON BEWLEY, CO DURHAM

	No. of Hrs	Races Run	1st	2nd	3rd	Unpl	Per cent	£1 Level Stake
NH Flat	11	23	2	1	4	16	8.7	+5.75
Hurdles	25	86	8	11	8	59	9.3	-15.75
Chases	10	31	3	8	4	16	9.7	-20.02
Totals	36	140	13	20	16	91	9.3	-30.02
16-17	51	147	11	15	19	102	7.5	-67.67
15-16	45	168	10	12	15	131	6.0	-77.15

BY MONTH

NH Flat	W-R	Per cent	£1 Level Stake	Hurdles	W-R	Per cent	£1 Level Stake
May	0-5	0.0	-5.00	May	1-10	10.0	-3.00
June	0-0	0.0	0.00	June	0-6	0.0	-6.00
July	0-1	0.0	-1.00	July	0-2	0.0	-2.00
August	0-1	0.0	-1.00	August	1-5	20.0	+2.00
September	0-0	0.0	0.00	September	0-1	0.0	-1.00
October	1-2	50.0	+24.00	October	0-5	0.0	-5.00
November	0-3	0.0	-3.00	November	1-10	10.0	0.00
December	1-1	100.0	+1.75	December	0-10	0.0	-10.00
January	0-4	0.0	-4.00	January	1-10	10.0	+11.00
February	0-1	0.0	-1.00	February	1-7	14.3	+1.00
March	0-3	0.0	-3.00	March	3-12	25.0	+5.25
April	0-2	0.0	-2.00	April	0-8	0.0	-8.00

Chases	W-R	Per cent	£1 Level Stake	Totals	W-R	Per cent	£1 Level Stake
May	0-2	0.0	-2.00	May	1-17	5.9	-10.00
June	0-4	0.0	-4.00	June	0-10	0.0	-10.00
July	0-2	0.0	-2.00	July	0-5	0.0	-5.00
August	0-0	0.0	0.00	August	1-6	16.7	+1.00
September	0-0	0.0	0.00	September	0-1	0.0	-1.00

October	0-5	0.0	-5.00	October	1-12	8.3	+14.00
November	1-4	25.0	+0.50	November	2-17	11.8	-2.50
December	0-2	0.0	-2.00	December	1-13	7.7	-10.25
January	1-3	33.3	-0.13	January	2-17	11.8	+6.87
February	0-2	0.0	-2.00	February	1-10	10.0	-2.00
March	0-4	0.0	-4.00	March	3-19	15.8	-1.75
April	1-3	33.3	+0.60	April	1-13	7.7	-9.40

DISTANCE

Hurdles	W-R	Per cent	£1 Level Stake	Chases	W-R	Per cent	£1 Level Stake
2m-2m3f	3-41	7.3	-17.00	2m-2m3f	0-4	0.0	-4.00
2m4f-2m7f	3-36	8.3	0.00	2m4f-2m7f	2-16	12.5	-9.53
3m+	2-9	22.2	+1.25	3m+	1-11	9.1	-6.50

TYPE OF RACE

Non-Handicaps	W-R	Per cent	£1 Level Stake	Handicaps	W-R	Per cent	£1 Level Stake
Nov Hrdls	0-23	0.0	-23.00	Nov Hrdls	1-8	12.5	-2.00
Hrdls	1-15	6.7	-7.00	Hrdls	6-39	15.4	+17.25
Nov Chs	1-6	16.7	-3.13	Nov Chs	0-2	0.0	-2.00
Chases	0-1	0.0	-1.00	Chases	1-15	6.7	-10.50
Sell/Claim	0-1	0.0	-1.00	Sell/Claim	0-1	0.0	-1.00

RACE CLASS

	W-R	Per cent	£1 Level Stake	FIRST TIME OUT	W-R	Per cent	£1 Level Stake
Class 1	1-3	33.3	+5.00	Bumpers	1-11	9.1	+15.00
Class 2	1-6	16.7	+1.00	Hurdles	2-17	11.8	+11.00
Class 3	4-14	28.6	+25.60	Chases	0-8	0.0	-8.00
Class 4	3-61	4.9	-47.63				
Class 5	2-45	4.4	-31.75	Totals	3-36	8.3	+18.00
Class 6	2-11	18.2	+17.75				

JOCKEYS

	W-R	Per cent	£1 Level Stake
Brian Hughes	5-40	12.5	+4.50
Callum Bewley	4-58	6.9	-13.00
Mr Liam Quinlan	2-4	50.0	+2.47
Paddy Brennan	2-5	40.0	+9.00

COURSE RECORD

	Total W-R	Non-Hndcps Hurdles	Non-Hndcps Chases	Hndcps Hurdles	Hndcps Chases	NH Flat	Per cent	£1 Level Stake
Sedgefield	4-40	0-19	0-1	2-10	0-3	2-7	10.0	-2.00
Haydock	2-3	1-1	0-0	1-2	0-0	0-0	66.7	+26.00
Southwell	2-5	0-0	0-0	2-4	0-0	0-1	40.0	+12.00
Kelso	2-16	0-4	1-4	0-4	1-2	0-2	12.5	-9.53
Aintree	1-3	0-0	0-0	1-2	0-0	0-1	33.3	+4.00
Ayr	1-9	0-2	0-0	0-2	1-4	0-1	11.1	-4.50
Musselbgh	1-12	0-1	0-0	1-3	0-4	0-4	8.3	-4.00

WINNING HORSES

Horse	Races Run	1st	2nd	3rd	£
Donna's Diamond	4	2	1	0	31171
Jacks Last Hope	5	2	1	0	17422
Acdc	9	3	2	1	17891
Blunder Buss	4	1	1	2	6238
Drums Of War	7	1	1	1	4094
Hey Bob	9	1	1	1	3249
Broadway Belle	9	1	3	1	3119
Theatre Legend	4	2	0	0	3249
Total winning prize-money					**£86433**
Favourites	3-11		27.3%		-0.50

WARREN GREATREX
UPPER LAMBOURN, BERKS

	No. of Hrs	Races Run	1st	2nd	3rd	Unpl	Per cent	£1 Level Stake
NH Flat	23	37	10	4	6	17	27.0	+23.01
Hurdles	62	195	36	33	20	106	18.5	+9.64
Chases	11	43	6	9	8	20	14.0	-13.42
Totals	75	275	52	46	34	143	18.9	+19.23
16-17	91	317	58	48	52	159	18.3	-77.47
15-16	93	254	53	45	40	116	20.9	-58.89

BY MONTH

NH Flat	W-R	Per cent	£1 Level Stake	Hurdles	W-R	Per cent	£1 Level Stake
May	1-2	50.0	+0.10	May	1-10	10.0	+11.00
June	2-2	100.0	+5.25	June	2-4	50.0	+5.33
July	0-3	0.0	-3.00	July	0-2	0.0	-2.00
August	1-2	50.0	+3.50	August	1-1	100.0	+3.00
September	1-1	100.0	+1.88	September	0-1	0.0	-1.00
October	0-2	0.0	-2.00	October	0-11	0.0	-11.00
November	2-8	25.0	-0.59	November	7-29	24.1	+9.77
December	1-6	16.7	-3.63	December	6-32	18.8	+0.88
January	0-3	0.0	-3.00	January	7-33	21.2	-5.24
February	0-3	0.0	-3.00	February	4-22	18.2	+4.35
March	0-2	0.0	-2.00	March	4-23	17.4	+5.92
April	2-3	66.7	+29.50	April	4-27	14.8	-11.37

Chases	W-R	Per cent	£1 Level Stake	Totals	W-R	Per cent	£1 Level Stake
May	0-1	0.0	-1.00	May	2-13	15.4	+10.10
June	0-2	0.0	-2.00	June	4-8	50.0	+8.58
July	0-2	0.0	-2.00	July	0-7	0.0	-7.00
August	0-2	0.0	-2.00	August	2-5	40.0	+4.50
September	0-1	0.0	-1.00	September	1-3	33.3	-0.12
October	0-0	0.0	0.00	October	0-13	0.0	-13.00
November	1-8	12.5	-6.92	November	10-45	22.2	+2.26
December	2-6	33.3	+2.50	December	9-44	20.5	-0.25
January	1-4	25.0	-1.50	January	8-40	20.0	-9.74
February	1-7	14.3	+1.50	February	5-32	15.6	+2.85
March	1-6	16.7	+3.00	March	5-31	16.1	+6.92
April	0-4	0.0	-4.00	April	6-34	17.6	+14.13

DISTANCE

Hurdles	W-R	Per cent	£1 Level Stake	Chases	W-R	Per cent	£1 Level Stake
2m-2m3f	16-74	21.6	+23.32	2m-2m3f	1-7	14.3	-2.00
2m4f-2m7f	11-82	13.4	-15.49	2m4f-2m7f	2-17	11.8	-13.42
3m+	9-37	24.3	+3.82	3m+	3-19	15.8	+2.00

TYPE OF RACE

Non-Handicaps	W-R	Per cent	£1 Level Stake	Handicaps	W-R	Per cent	£1 Level Stake
Nov Hrdls	11-70	15.7	-41.70	Nov Hrdls	0-4	0.0	-4.00
Hrdls	9-34	26.5	+9.26	Hrdls	16-87	18.4	+46.08
Nov Chs	3-15	20.0	-5.42	Nov Chs	0-5	0.0	-5.00
Chases	0-0	0.0	0.00	Chases	3-21	14.3	-1.00
Sell/Claim	0-0	0.0	0.00	Sell/Claim	0-0	0.0	0.00

RACE CLASS

	W-R	Per cent	£1 Level Stake
Class 1	5-37	13.5	-0.11
Class 2	4-23	17.4	+7.50
Class 3	9-53	17.0	+11.75
Class 4	22-117	18.8	-6.71
Class 5	7-33	21.2	-1.82
Class 6	5-12	41.7	+8.63

FIRST TIME OUT

	W-R	Per cent	£1 Level Stake
Bumpers	7-23	30.4	+3.13
Hurdles	7-46	15.2	+12.71
Chases	1-6	16.7	-4.92
Totals	15-75	20.0	+10.92

JOCKEYS

	W-R	Per cent	£1 Level Stake
Richard Johnson	22-94	23.4	-1.38
Gavin Sheehan	13-60	21.7	+17.38
Harry Bannister	5-18	27.8	+23.42
Thomas Greatrex	3-34	8.8	-8.50
Ben Hicks	2-12	16.7	-2.50
A P Heskin	2-17	11.8	-10.42
Andrew Tinkler	2-17	11.8	+0.50
Noel Fehily	1-1	100.0	+0.73
Mr Adam Elias	1-2	50.0	+11.00
Mr N McParlan	1-2	50.0	+7.00

COURSE RECORD

	Total W-R	Non-Hndcps Hurdles	Chases	Hndcps Hurdles	Chases	NH Flat	Per cent	£1 Level Stake
Uttoxeter	7-19	1-3	0-0	1-7	1-4	4-5	36.8	+19.63
Chepstow	5-16	3-10	0-0	2-6	0-0	0-0	31.3	+9.29
Taunton	4-10	2-3	0-0	2-7	0-0	0-0	40.0	-0.29
Wetherby	4-14	3-7	0-1	1-4	0-1	0-1	28.6	-2.80
Stratford	4-15	1-6	1-2	0-3	0-1	2-3	26.7	-4.94
Hereford	3-9	1-4	0-0	1-2	0-1	1-2	33.3	+0.71
Ffos Las	3-9	2-5	0-1	1-3	0-0	0-0	33.3	+4.33
Wincanton	3-14	0-4	0-1	2-7	1-1	0-1	21.4	+8.00
Perth	2-3	0-0	0-0	2-2	0-1	0-0	66.7	+6.33
Exeter	2-5	0-2	1-1	1-2	0-0	0-0	40.0	+3.75
Warwick	2-9	0-1	0-0	1-4	0-2	1-2	22.2	+18.50
Cheltenham	2-21	1-5	0-1	0-7	1-4	0-4	9.5	-8.50
Newcastle	1-2	1-2	0-0	0-0	0-0	0-0	50.0	0.00
Doncaster	1-3	0-1	1-1	0-0	0-0	0-1	33.3	+0.50
Nton Abbot	1-4	0-1	0-0	0-0	0-0	1-3	25.0	+1.50
Southwell	1-4	1-3	0-0	0-1	0-0	0-0	25.0	+9.00
Fontwell	1-6	0-2	0-0	1-2	0-0	0-2	16.7	+15.00
Kempton	1-6	1-1	0-0	0-3	0-1	0-1	16.7	-2.25
Aintree	1-6	0-3	0-0	0-1	0-1	1-1	16.7	+20.00
Ascot	1-7	1-3	0-0	0-2	0-0	0-2	14.3	-5.27
Sandown	1-8	1-3	0-0	0-1	0-3	0-1	12.5	-6.75
Bangor	1-9	1-3	0-2	0-2	0-0	0-2	11.1	-3.50
Plumpton	1-11	0-3	0-1	1-6	0-0	0-1	9.1	+2.00

WINNING HORSES

Horse	Races Run	1st	2nd	3rd	£
Missed Approach	6	1	1	1	41972
La Bague Au Roi	4	3	0	0	55577
Portrush Ted	4	1	2	0	25322
Keeper Hill	6	2	1	0	24985
Carnspindle	7	1	0	2	11711
The Nipper	8	2	1	1	18891
Lovenormoney	5	2	0	0	17465
Boite	5	1	1	0	11574
Western Ryder	7	2	1	0	11047
Savoy Court	4	1	0	1	7408
Attest	7	3	1	0	14343
Groundunderrepair	5	1	2	2	6238
Jammin Masters	4	2	1	0	10432
Dicosimo	4	1	0	0	6238
Brianstorm	7	2	1	2	10118
Don't Ask	5	2	1	2	8707
Another Emotion	2	1	1	0	4809
Fly Du Charmil	4	1	0	0	4809
Ceann Sibheal	6	1	1	2	4614
Mahlervous	6	1	2	0	4549
Final Choice	4	1	0	1	4484
Bob Mahler	6	1	3	1	4484
The Caller	2	1	0	0	4224
Petticoat Tails	5	2	0	1	7668
Rock My Style	2	2	0	0	7733
Mulcahys Hill	5	2	1	0	6498
Pennywell	8	1	1	1	3639
Gvs Irportensa	1	1	0	0	3249
Sandhurst Lad	6	1	2	0	3120
Peculiar Places	3	1	0	0	3119
The Black Squirrel	6	1	1	1	2599
Emitom	1	1	0	0	2599
Indian Hercules	5	1	0	2	2469
Rose Of Cimarron	5	1	0	0	1949
Dory	4	1	1	0	1689
*Article Fifty	4	1	1	1	1689
Thelunarschooner	3	1	1	0	1625
Don Des Fosses	2	1	0	0	1560
Total winning prize-money					**£365206**
Favourites	21-49		42.9%		-1.56

OLIVER GREENALL

OLDCASTLE HEATH, CHESHIRE

	No. of Hrs	Races Run	1st	2nd	3rd	Unpl	Per cent	£1 Level Stake
NH Flat	8	11	0	2	1	8	0.0	-11.00
Hurdles	28	112	8	14	10	80	7.1	-54.38
Chases	8	21	3	2	2	14	14.3	-10.00
Totals	**40**	**144**	**11**	**18**	**13**	**102**	**7.6**	**-75.38**
16-17	21	70	6	7	10	47	8.6	-32.75
15-16	5	6	0	0	3	3	0.0	-6.00

BY MONTH

NH Flat	W-R	Per cent	£1 Level Stake	Hurdles	W-R	Per cent	£1 Level Stake
May	0-0	0.0	0.00	May	0-3	0.0	-3.00
June	0-0	0.0	0.00	June	0-0	0.0	0.00
July	0-0	0.0	0.00	July	0-2	0.0	-2.00
August	0-0	0.0	0.00	August	0-1	0.0	-1.00
September	0-0	0.0	0.00	September	0-2	0.0	-2.00
October	0-1	0.0	-1.00	October	1-14	7.1	-6.00
November	0-0	0.0	0.00	November	2-13	15.4	+6.75
December	0-0	0.0	0.00	December	1-16	6.3	-13.63
January	0-1	0.0	-1.00	January	3-20	15.0	-3.50
February	0-1	0.0	-1.00	February	0-12	0.0	-12.00
March	0-3	0.0	-3.00	March	0-13	0.0	-13.00
April	0-5	0.0	-5.00	April	1-16	6.3	-5.00

Chases	W-R	Per cent	£1 Level Stake	Totals	W-R	Per cent	£1 Level Stake
May	1-4	25.0	-0.50	May	1-7	14.3	-3.50
June	0-4	0.0	-4.00	June	0-4	0.0	-4.00
July	0-0	0.0	0.00	July	0-2	0.0	-2.00
August	0-2	0.0	-2.00	August	0-3	0.0	-3.00
September	0-0	0.0	0.00	September	0-2	0.0	-2.00
October	0-0	0.0	0.00	October	1-15	6.7	-7.00
November	0-1	0.0	-1.00	November	2-14	14.3	+5.75
December	0-1	0.0	-1.00	December	1-17	5.9	-14.63
January	0-1	0.0	-1.00	January	3-22	13.6	-5.50
February	0-3	0.0	-3.00	February	0-16	0.0	-16.00
March	1-2	50.0	+2.00	March	1-18	5.6	-14.00
April	1-3	33.3	+0.50	April	2-24	8.3	-9.50

DISTANCE

Hurdles	W-R	Per cent	£1 Level Stake	Chases	W-R	Per cent	£1 Level Stake
2m-2m3f	4-67	6.0	-42.50	2m-2m3f	0-4	0.0	-4.00
2m4f-2m7f	3-38	7.9	-21.88	2m4f-2m7f	3-11	27.3	0.00
3m+	1-7	14.3	+10.00	3m+	0-6	0.0	-6.00

TYPE OF RACE

Non-Handicaps	W-R	Per cent	£1 Level Stake	Handicaps	W-R	Per cent	£1 Level Stake
Nov Hrdls	0-26	0.0	-26.00	Nov Hrdls	1-9	11.1	+4.00
Hrdls	1-17	5.9	-15.33	Hrdls	6-58	10.3	-15.04
Nov Chs	0-0	0.0	0.00	Nov Chs	3-7	42.9	+4.00
Chases	0-0	0.0	0.00	Chases	0-14	0.0	-14.00

| | Sell/Claim | 0-0 | 0.0 | 0.00 | Sell/Claim | 0-0 | 0.0 | 0.00 |

RACE CLASS

	W-R	Per cent	£1 Level Stake
Class 1	0-2	0.0	-2.00
Class 2	0-4	0.0	-4.00
Class 3	1-8	12.5	-5.63
Class 4	7-81	8.6	-48.25
Class 5	3-48	6.3	-14.50
Class 6	0-1	0.0	-1.00

FIRST TIME OUT

	W-R	Per cent	£1 Level Stake
Bumpers	0-8	0.0	-8.00
Hurdles	1-25	4.0	-17.00
Chases	1-7	14.3	-3.50
Totals	2-40	5.0	-28.50

JOCKEYS

	W-R	Per cent	£1 Level Stake
Ross Turner	3-34	8.8	-27.04
Ian Popham	3-47	6.4	-24.83
Harry Skelton	2-11	18.2	-3.50
Mr William Biddick	1-1	100.0	+7.00
Mr Edward Glassonbury	1-2	50.0	+9.00
David England	1-22	4.5	-9.00

COURSE RECORD

	Total W-R	Non-Hndcps Hurdles	Chases	Hndcps Hurdles	Chases	NH Flat	Per cent	£1 Level Stake
Uttoxeter	3-25	0-8	0-0	3-12	0-4	0-1	12.0	-8.88
Carlisle	2-7	0-2	0-0	0-1	2-2	0-2	28.6	+0.50
Exeter	1-1	0-0	0-0	1-1	0-0	0-0	100.0	+7.00
Taunton	1-1	0-0	0-0	1-1	0-0	0-0	100.0	+16.00
Doncaster	1-3	0-0	0-0	1-1	0-0	0-0	33.3	+10.00
Newcastle	1-4	0-0	0-0	1-2	0-2	0-0	25.0	-2.17
Stratford	1-4	0-0	0-0	0-2	1-2	0-0	25.0	-0.50
Ludlow	1-14	1-9	0-0	0-4	0-0	0-1	7.1	-12.33

WINNING HORSES

Horse	Races Run	1st	2nd	3rd	£
Asking Questions	10	2	2	1	12996
Cave Top	8	3	2	0	12841
Zalvados	7	1	3	0	4809
Lord County	7	3	0	2	11307
Quarry Lami	2	1	0	0	3899
Desert Sting	4	1	0	1	3249
Total winning prize-money					**£49101**
Favourites	5-14		35.7%		-1.88

TOM GRETTON

HOLBERROW GREEN, WORCS

	No. of Hrs	Races Run	1st	2nd	3rd	Unpl	Per cent	£1 Level Stake
NH Flat	1	2	0	0	0	2	0.0	-2.00
Hurdles	12	25	0	1	4	20	0.0	-25.00
Chases	9	41	5	8	6	22	12.2	-22.00
Totals	**14**	**68**	**5**	**9**	**10**	**44**	**7.4**	**-49.00**
16-17	19	87	5	12	11	59	5.7	-40.63
15-16	16	59	5	3	7	44	8.5	-11.33

JOCKEYS

	W-R	Per cent	£1 Level Stake
Brian Hughes	2-5	40.0	+1.00
Robert Dunne	2-13	15.4	-6.00
James Davies	1-9	11.1	-3.00

COURSE RECORD

	Total W-R	Non-Hndcps Hurdles	Chases	Hndcps Hurdles	Chases	NH Flat	Per cent	£1 Level Stake
Newcastle	1-3	0-0	0-0	0-1	1-2	0-0	33.3	+0.25
Plumpton	1-3	0-0	0-0	0-1	1-2	0-0	33.3	+1.00
Ffos Las	1-3	0-0	0-0	0-0	1-3	0-0	33.3	0.00
Taunton	1-4	0-0	0-0	0-1	1-3	0-0	25.0	-1.25
Huntingdon	1-8	0-0	0-0	0-2	1-6	0-0	12.5	-2.00

WINNING HORSES

Horse	Races Run	1st	2nd	3rd	£
Kauto Riko	4	2	1	0	9357
Lickpenny Larry	9	2	0	1	10787
Jackthejourneyman	9	1	1	1	3314
Total winning prize-money					**£23458**
Favourites	1-2	50.0%			0.75

DIANA GRISSELL

BRIGHTLING, E SUSSEX

	No. of Hrs	Races Run	1st	2nd	3rd	Unpl	Per cent	£1 Level Stake
NH Flat	2	2	0	0	0	2	0.0	-2.00
Hurdles	4	12	1	0	0	11	8.3	-7.00
Chases	5	14	1	2	0	11	7.1	+1.00
Totals	10	28	2	2	0	24	7.1	-8.00
16-17	16	58	0	2	5	51	0.0	-58.00
15-16	18	57	6	1	11	39	10.5	-0.30

JOCKEYS

	W-R	Per cent	£1 Level Stake
Jack Sherwood	1-3	33.3	+2.00
Marc Goldstein	1-21	4.8	-6.00

COURSE RECORD

	Total W-R	Non-Hndcps Hurdles	Chases	Hndcps Hurdles	Chases	NH Flat	Per cent	£1 Level Stake
Fontwell	1-6	0-1	0-1	0-0	1-4	0-0	16.7	+9.00
Plumpton	1-10	0-5	0-0	1-1	0-3	0-1	10.0	-5.00

WINNING HORSES

Horse	Races Run	1st	2nd	3rd	£
Canyouhearmenow	8	1	0	0	3679
Mickieblueeyes	4	1	0	0	3119
Total winning prize-money					**£6798**
Favourites	0-0	0.0%			0.00

JOHN GROUCOTT

BOURTON, SHROPSHIRE

	No. of Hrs	Races Run	1st	2nd	3rd	Unpl	Per cent	£1 Level Stake
NH Flat	4	8	0	0	0	8	0.0	-8.00
Hurdles	6	14	0	1	1	12	0.0	-14.00
Chases	5	28	4	5	4	15	14.3	+19.00
Totals	11	50	4	6	5	35	8.0	-3.00
16-17	13	47	5	2	5	35	10.6	-8.67
15-16	9	35	6	3	5	21	17.1	-1.38

JOCKEYS

	W-R	Per cent	£1 Level Stake
Lee Edwards	4-39	10.3	+8.00

COURSE RECORD

	Total W-R	Non-Hndcps Hurdles	Chases	Hndcps Hurdles	Chases	NH Flat	Per cent	£1 Level Stake
Cheltenham	1-1	0-0	0-0	0-0	1-1	0-0	100.0	+3.50
Worcester	1-1	0-0	0-0	0-0	1-1	0-0	100.0	+33.00
Huntingdon	1-5	0-1	0-0	0-0	1-3	0-1	20.0	-1.00
Bangor	1-16	0-3	0-1	0-3	1-7	0-2	6.3	-11.50

WINNING HORSES

Horse	Races Run	1st	2nd	3rd	£
Midnight Target	7	2	3	0	29278
Heavenly Promise	8	1	1	1	4614
Truckers Highway	9	1	1	1	4549
Total winning prize-money					**£38441**
Favourites	0-0	0.0%			0.00

RICHARD GUEST

INGMANTHORPE, W YORKS

	No. of Hrs	Races Run	1st	2nd	3rd	Unpl	Per cent	£1 Level Stake
NH Flat	0	0	0	0	0	0	0.0	0.00
Hurdles	2	6	1	2	0	3	16.7	+0.50
Chases	0	0	0	0	0	0	0.0	0.00
Totals	2	6	1	2	0	3	16.7	+0.50
16-17	2	2	0	0	0	2	0.0	-2.00
15-16	5	7	0	0	0	7	0.0	-7.00

JOCKEYS

	W-R	Per cent	£1 Level Stake
Leighton Aspell	1-3	33.3	+3.50

COURSE RECORD

	Total W-R	Non-Hndcps Hurdles	Chases	Hndcps Hurdles	Chases	NH Flat	Per cent	£1 Level Stake
Wetherby	1-3	0-0	0-0	1-3	0-0	0-0	33.3	+3.50

WINNING HORSES

Horse	Races Run	1st	2nd	3rd	£
Lough Salt	4	1	1	0	5523
Total winning prize-money					£5523
Favourites	0-0		0.0%		0.00

POLLY GUNDRY

OTTERY ST MARY, DEVON

	No. of Hrs	Races Run	1st	2nd	3rd	Unpl	Per cent	£1 Level Stake
NH Flat	1	1	0	1	0	0	0.0	-1.00
Hurdles	10	22	0	2	1	19	0.0	-22.00
Chases	5	19	1	3	3	12	5.3	-10.00
Totals	13	42	1	6	4	31	2.4	-33.00
16-17	14	56	6	7	2	41	10.7	-16.25
15-16	16	46	5	7	5	29	10.9	+25.00

JOCKEYS

	W-R	Per cent	£1 Level Stake
Andrew Thornton	1-8	12.5	+1.00

COURSE RECORD

	Total W-R	Non-Hndcps Hurdles	Chases	Hndcps Hurdles	Chases	NH Flat	Per cent	£1 Level Stake
Exeter	1-8	0-3	0-0	0-1	1-4	0-0	12.5	+1.00

WINNING HORSES

Horse	Races Run	1st	2nd	3rd	£
Dawson City	6	1	1	1	15640
Total winning prize-money					£15640
Favourites	0-0		0.0%		0.00

BEN DE HAAN

LAMBOURN, BERKS

	No. of Hrs	Races Run	1st	2nd	3rd	Unpl	Per cent	£1 Level Stake
NH Flat	1	1	1	0	0	0	100.0	+0.40
Hurdles	0	0	0	0	0	0	0.0	0.00
Chases	0	0	0	0	0	0	0.0	0.00
Totals	1	1	1	0	0	0	100.0	+0.40
16-17	2	7	2	1	0	4	28.6	+2.00
15-16	3	5	1	1	0	3	20.0	-2.25

JOCKEYS

	W-R	Per cent	£1 Level Stake
Harry Cobden	1-1	100.0	+0.40

COURSE RECORD

	Total W-R	Non-Hndcps Hurdles	Chases	Hndcps Hurdles	Chases	NH Flat	Per cent	£1 Level Stake
Warwick	1-1	0-0	0-0	0-0	0-0	1-1	100.0	+0.40

WINNING HORSES

Horse	Races Run	1st	2nd	3rd	£
Mon Port	1	1	0	0	3249
Total winning prize-money					£3249
Favourites	14-14		100.0%		5.60

ALEX HALES

EDGCOTE, NORTHAMPTONSHIRE

	No. of Hrs	Races Run	1st	2nd	3rd	Unpl	Per cent	£1 Level Stake
NH Flat	2	4	0	0	0	4	0.0	-4.00
Hurdles	16	48	6	5	7	30	12.5	-18.13
Chases	9	38	4	10	4	20	10.5	-21.25
Totals	23	90	10	15	11	54	11.1	-43.38
16-17	27	105	12	11	12	70	11.4	-6.25
15-16	27	118	11	13	20	74	9.3	-28.84

BY MONTH

NH Flat	W-R	Per cent	£1 Level Stake		Hurdles	W-R	Per cent	£1 Level Stake
May	0-0	0.0	0.00		May	0-3	0.0	-3.00
June	0-0	0.0	0.00		June	1-3	33.3	+7.00
July	0-0	0.0	0.00		July	0-2	0.0	-2.00
August	0-0	0.0	0.00		August	0-0	0.0	0.00
September	0-0	0.0	0.00		September	0-1	0.0	-1.00
October	0-1	0.0	-1.00		October	0-2	0.0	-2.00
November	0-1	0.0	-1.00		November	1-6	16.7	-2.00
December	0-1	0.0	-1.00		December	2-10	20.0	-4.50
January	0-0	0.0	0.00		January	0-6	0.0	-6.00
February	0-0	0.0	0.00		February	0-2	0.0	-2.00
March	0-0	0.0	0.00		March	1-5	20.0	-2.63
April	0-1	0.0	-1.00		April	1-8	12.5	-2.00

Chases	W-R	Per cent	£1 Level Stake		Totals	W-R	Per cent	£1 Level Stake
May	1-2	50.0	+4.00		May	1-5	20.0	+1.00
June	0-1	0.0	-1.00		June	1-4	25.0	+6.00
July	0-0	0.0	0.00		July	0-2	0.0	-2.00
August	0-0	0.0	0.00		August	0-0	0.0	0.00
September	0-0	0.0	0.00		September	0-1	0.0	-1.00
October	0-3	0.0	-3.00		October	0-6	0.0	-6.00
November	2-11	18.2	-3.75		November	3-18	16.7	-6.75
December	0-5	0.0	-5.00		December	2-16	12.5	-10.50
January	1-6	16.7	-2.50		January	1-12	8.3	-8.50
February	0-2	0.0	-2.00		February	0-4	0.0	-4.00
March	0-5	0.0	-5.00		March	1-10	10.0	-7.63
April	0-3	0.0	-3.00		April	1-12	8.3	-4.00

DISTANCE

Hurdles	W-R	Per cent	£1 Level Stake	Chases	W-R	Per cent	£1 Level Stake
2m-2m3f	4-24	16.7	+0.50	2m-2m3f	1-10	10.0	-6.50
2m4f-2m7f	2-22	9.1	-16.63	2m4f-2m7f	2-13	15.4	-2.50
3m+	0-2	0.0	-2.00	3m+	1-15	6.7	-12.25

TYPE OF RACE

Non-Handicaps	W-R	Per cent	£1 Level Stake	Handicaps	W-R	Per cent	£1 Level Stake
Nov Hrdls	1-13	7.7	-10.63	Nov Hrdls	1-4	25.0	-1.50
Hrdls	1-2	50.0	+6.00	Hrdls	3-29	10.3	-12.00
Nov Chs	1-5	20.0	-2.25	Nov Chs	1-7	14.3	-1.00
Chases	0-0	0.0	0.00	Chases	2-23	8.7	-15.00
Sell/Claim	0-0	0.0	0.00	Sell/Claim	0-0	0.0	0.00

RACE CLASS

	W-R	Per cent	£1 Level Stake
Class 1	0-5	0.0	-5.00
Class 2	0-10	0.0	-10.00
Class 3	3-16	18.8	-5.75
Class 4	5-42	11.9	-23.63
Class 5	2-16	12.5	+2.00
Class 6	0-1	0.0	-1.00

FIRST TIME OUT

	W-R	Per cent	£1 Level Stake
Bumpers	0-2	0.0	-2.00
Hurdles	1-13	7.7	-5.00
Chases	1-8	12.5	-2.00
Totals	2-23	8.7	-9.00

JOCKEYS

	W-R	Per cent	£1 Level Stake
Kielan Woods	4-40	10.0	-20.75
Harry Bannister	3-19	15.8	-10.13
Trevor Whelan	2-7	28.6	+9.00
James Bowen	1-4	25.0	-1.50

COURSE RECORD

	Total W-R	Non-Hndcps Hurdles	Chases	Hndcps Hurdles	Chases	NH Flat	Per cent	£1 Level Stake
Mrket Rsn	3-11	1-1	0-0	1-4	1-6	0-0	27.3	+0.38
Hereford	2-3	1-1	0-0	1-1	0-1	0-0	66.7	+9.00
Exeter	1-2	0-0	1-1	0-0	0-1	0-0	50.0	+0.75
Doncaster	1-3	0-1	0-0	1-2	0-0	0-0	33.3	-0.50
Warwick	1-6	0-0	0-1	0-1	1-3	0-1	16.7	-2.50
Leicester	1-7	0-1	0-0	0-2	1-4	0-0	14.3	-2.50
Southwell	1-7	0-1	0-0	1-5	0-1	0-0	14.3	+3.00

WINNING HORSES

Horse	Races Run	1st	2nd	3rd	£
Duel At Dawn	5	1	3	0	12660
Big Jim	5	1	1	0	9747
Stepover	5	2	2	0	10431
Running Wolf	5	2	1	0	9858
Huntsman Son	6	2	2	0	8447
Florrie Knox	6	1	1	3	4549
*Royal Sunday	2	1	0	0	3119

Total winning prize-money			£58811
Favourites	2-6	33.3%	-0.50

DEBRA HAMER

NANTYCAWS, CARMARTHENS

	No. of Hrs	Races Run	1st	2nd	3rd	Unpl	Per cent	£1 Level Stake
NH Flat	2	4	0	0	0	4	0.0	-4.00
Hurdles	12	30	3	3	4	20	10.0	-15.05
Chases	8	27	5	2	2	18	18.5	+11.50
Totals	16	61	8	5	6	42	13.1	-7.55
16-17	16	62	9	2	5	46	14.5	+5.38
15-16	16	56	10	6	4	36	17.9	+14.25

JOCKEYS

	W-R	Per cent	£1 Level Stake
Tom Bellamy	3-6	50.0	+14.00
Richard Patrick	3-10	30.0	+4.95
Stan Sheppard	1-1	100.0	+6.50
Trevor Whelan	1-33	3.0	-22.00

COURSE RECORD

	Total W-R	Non-Hndcps Hurdles	Chases	Hndcps Hurdles	Chases	NH Flat	Per cent	£1 Level Stake
Worcester	3-13	0-2	0-0	3-7	0-4	0-0	23.1	+1.95
Ffos Las	3-16	0-4	0-2	0-3	3-7	0-0	18.8	+4.00
Chepstow	2-7	0-1	0-0	0-1	2-5	0-0	28.6	+11.50

WINNING HORSES

Horse	Races Run	1st	2nd	3rd	£
Super Scorpion	6	2	0	1	11696
Looks Like Power	7	2	2	1	9227
Shanksforamillion	5	3	1	0	8577
Magical Man	5	1	0	0	3249
Total winning prize-money				£32749
Favourites	1-3	33.3%		-0.80

ANN HAMILTON

GREAT BAVINGTON, NORTHUMBLAND

	No. of Hrs	Races Run	1st	2nd	3rd	Unpl	Per cent	£1 Level Stake
NH Flat	0	0	0	0	0	0	0.0	0.00
Hurdles	3	8	0	0	0	8	0.0	-8.00
Chases	4	18	6	3	3	6	33.3	+6.50
Totals	6	26	6	3	3	14	23.1	-1.50
16-17	7	48	4	7	8	29	8.3	-31.25
15-16	9	38	10	6	4	18	26.3	+35.19

JOCKEYS

	W-R	Per cent	£1 Level Stake
Ross Chapman	4-10	40.0	+5.00
Brian Hughes	1-5	20.0	-3.00
Jamie Hamilton	1-7	14.3	+0.50

COURSE RECORD

	Total W-R	Non-Hndcps Hurdles	Chases	Hndcps Hurdles	Chases	NH Flat	Per cent	£1 Level Stake
Sedgefield	2-5	0-0	0-0	0-0	2-5	0-0	40.0	+2.25
Musselbgh	1-1	0-0	0-0	0-0	1-1	0-0	100.0	+6.50
Catterick	1-3	0-0	0-0	0-0	1-3	0-0	33.3	-0.25
Kelso	1-4	0-0	0-0	0-0	1-4	0-0	25.0	+1.00
Carlisle	1-6	0-0	1-2	0-3	0-1	0-0	16.7	-4.00

WINNING HORSES

Horse	Races Run	1st	2nd	3rd	£
Nuts Well	2	1	1	0	12820
Trust Thomas	7	1	0	2	6498
Oak Vintage	9	4	2	1	18584
Total winning prize-money					**£37902**
Favourites	2-6		33.3%		-1.25

ALISON HAMILTON

DENHOLM, BORDERS

	No. of Hrs	Races Run	1st	2nd	3rd	Unpl	Per cent	£1 Level Stake
NH Flat	1	1	0	0	0	1	0.0	-1.00
Hurdles	10	19	1	0	1	17	5.3	-7.00
Chases	7	11	0	0	4	7	0.0	-11.00
Totals	13	31	1	0	5	25	3.2	-19.00
16-17	14	55	1	4	5	45	1.8	-47.00
15-16	11	37	3	3	3	27	8.1	-5.00

JOCKEYS

	W-R	Per cent	£1 Level Stake
Jamie Hamilton	1-21	4.8	-9.00

COURSE RECORD

	Total W-R	Non-Hndcps Hurdles	Chases	Hndcps Hurdles	Chases	NH Flat	Per cent	£1 Level Stake
Ayr	1-3	0-1	0-0	1-2	0-0	0-0	33.3	+9.00

WINNING HORSES

Horse	Races Run	1st	2nd	3rd	£
What A Dream	5	1	0	1	3509
Total winning prize-money					**£3509**
Favourites	0-0		0.0%		0.00

ANDREW HAMILTON

CARLUKE, SOUTH LANARKSHIRE

	No. of Hrs	Races Run	1st	2nd	3rd	Unpl	Per cent	£1 Level Stake
NH Flat	0	0	0	0	0	0	0.0	0.00
Hurdles	4	20	3	0	3	14	15.0	-5.25
Chases	3	8	1	1	0	6	12.5	-4.25
Totals	6	28	4	1	3	20	14.3	-9.50
16-17	8	26	0	0	0	26	0.0	-26.00
15-16	7	28	0	0	0	28	0.0	-28.00

JOCKEYS

	W-R	Per cent	£1 Level Stake
Mr Bruce Lynn	2-3	66.7	+8.75
Ross Chapman	2-14	14.3	-7.25

COURSE RECORD

	Total W-R	Non-Hndcps Hurdles	Chases	Hndcps Hurdles	Chases	NH Flat	Per cent	£1 Level Stake
Ayr	2-9	0-0	1-2	1-6	0-1	0-0	22.2	-1.50
Carlisle	1-3	0-1	0-0	1-2	0-0	0-0	33.3	0.00
Kelso	1-4	0-0	0-0	1-2	0-2	0-0	25.0	+4.00

WINNING HORSES

Horse	Races Run	1st	2nd	3rd	£
Bobbie's Diamond	5	1	1	0	5162
Letemgo	15	3	0	3	10852
Total winning prize-money					**£16014**
Favourites	1-1		100.0%		2.00

MRS WENDY HAMILTON

HAWICK, BORDERS

	No. of Hrs	Races Run	1st	2nd	3rd	Unpl	Per cent	£1 Level Stake
NH Flat	0	0	0	0	0	0	0.0	0.00
Hurdles	0	0	0	0	0	0	0.0	0.00
Chases	2	2	1	0	0	1	50.0	+0.25
Totals	2	2	1	0	0	1	50.0	+0.25
16-17	1	3	1	0	0	2	33.3	0.00
15-16	1	5	2	0	2	1	40.0	+6.83

JOCKEYS

	W-R	Per cent	£1 Level Stake
Mr T Hamilton	1-2	50.0	+0.25

COURSE RECORD

	Total W-R	Non-Hndcps Hurdles	Chases	Hndcps Hurdles	Chases	NH Flat	Per cent	£1 Level Stake
Kelso	1-2	0-0	1-2	0-0	0-0	0-0	50.0	+0.25

WINNING HORSES

Horse	Races Run	1st	2nd	3rd	£
*Diamond Brig	1	1	0	0	4367
Total winning prize-money					**£4367**
Favourites	1-2	50.0%			0.25

MIKE HAMMOND

GARSTANG, LANCS

	No. of Hrs	Races Run	1st	2nd	3rd	Unpl	Per cent	£1 Level Stake
NH Flat	1	2	0	0	0	2	0.0	-2.00
Hurdles	8	22	0	0	1	21	0.0	-22.00
Chases	2	10	2	1	2	5	20.0	+7.50
Totals	10	34	2	1	3	28	5.9	-16.50
16-17	7	36	0	3	6	27	0.0	-36.00
15-16	6	12	0	1	0	11	0.0	-12.00

JOCKEYS

	W-R	Per cent	£1 Level Stake
Charlie Hammond	2-31	6.5	-13.50

COURSE RECORD

	Total W-R	Non-Hndcps Hurdles	Chases	Hndcps Hurdles	Chases	NH Flat	Per cent	£1 Level Stake
Huntingdon	1-1	0-0	0-0	0-0	1-1	0-0	100.0	+10.00
Nton Abbot	1-1	0-0	0-0	0-0	1-1	0-0	100.0	+5.50

WINNING HORSES

Horse	Races Run	1st	2nd	3rd	£
Charlie Mon	9	2	1	2	7668
Total winning prize-money					**£7668**
Favourites	0-0	0.0%			0.00

MICKY HAMMOND

MIDDLEHAM, N YORKS

	No. of Hrs	Races Run	1st	2nd	3rd	Unpl	Per cent	£1 Level Stake
NH Flat	10	12	1	1	1	9	8.3	-6.00
Hurdles	54	181	28	16	19	118	15.5	+62.93
Chases	35	150	17	17	21	95	11.3	-41.80
Totals	85	343	46	34	41	222	13.4	+15.13
16-17	80	352	24	34	33	261	6.8	-169.30
15-16	74	348	43	39	45	221	12.4	-120.97

BY MONTH

NH Flat	W-R	Per cent	£1 Level Stake	Hurdles	W-R	Per cent	£1 Level Stake
May	0-0	0.0	0.00	May	5-12	41.7	+17.75
June	0-0	0.0	0.00	June	0-3	0.0	-3.00
July	0-0	0.0	0.00	July	1-8	12.5	-3.00
August	0-0	0.0	0.00	August	0-7	0.0	-7.00
September	1-1	100.0	+5.00	September	0-3	0.0	-3.00
October	0-2	0.0	-2.00	October	0-10	0.0	-10.00
November	0-3	0.0	-3.00	November	4-27	14.8	+18.38
December	0-1	0.0	-1.00	December	3-27	11.1	-2.17
January	0-1	0.0	-1.00	January	1-23	4.3	-15.00
February	0-2	0.0	-2.00	February	5-17	29.4	+45.38
March	0-1	0.0	-1.00	March	2-21	9.5	+11.00
April	0-1	0.0	-1.00	April	7-23	30.4	+13.60

Chases	W-R	Per cent	£1 Level Stake	Totals	W-R	Per cent	£1 Level Stake
May	0-17	0.0	-17.00	May	5-29	17.2	+0.75
June	0-9	0.0	-9.00	June	0-12	0.0	-12.00
July	1-5	20.0	0.00	July	2-13	15.4	-3.00
August	0-4	0.0	-4.00	August	0-11	0.0	-11.00
September	1-2	50.0	+1.50	September	2-6	33.3	+3.50
October	0-16	0.0	-16.00	October	0-28	0.0	-28.00
November	4-20	20.0	+18.50	November	8-50	16.0	+33.88
December	5-22	22.7	+7.07	December	8-50	16.0	+3.90
January	1-16	6.3	-12.00	January	2-40	5.0	-28.00
February	0-8	0.0	-8.00	February	5-27	18.5	+35.38
March	3-16	18.8	+4.00	March	5-38	13.2	+14.00
April	2-15	13.3	-6.88	April	9-39	23.1	+5.72

DISTANCE

Hurdles	W-R	Per cent	£1 Level Stake	Chases	W-R	Per cent	£1 Level Stake
2m-2m3f	17-105	16.2	+29.60	2m-2m3f	11-59	18.6	+10.13
2m4f-2m7f	9-58	15.5	+40.33	2m4f-2m7f	3-42	7.1	-27.43
3m+	2-18	11.1	-7.00	3m+	3-49	6.1	-24.50

TYPE OF RACE

Non-Handicaps	W-R	Per cent	£1 Level Stake	Handicaps	W-R	Per cent	£1 Level Stake
Nov Hrdls	4-31	12.9	-20.93	Nov Hrdls	2-11	18.2	-1.50
Hrdls	2-14	14.3	-3.00	Hrdls	19-117	16.2	+83.36
Nov Chs	0-7	0.0	-7.00	Nov Chs	0-16	0.0	-16.00
Chases	0-1	0.0	-1.00	Chases	15-114	13.2	-13.80
Sell/Claim	0-3	0.0	-3.00	Sell/Claim	1-5	20.0	+8.00

RACE CLASS / FIRST TIME OUT

	W-R	Per cent	£1 Level Stake		W-R	Per cent	£1 Level Stake
Class 1	0-4	0.0	-4.00	Bumpers	1-10	10.0	-4.00
Class 2	2-17	11.8	-1.00	Hurdles	6-44	13.6	+19.50
Class 3	2-43	4.7	-28.50	Chases	0-31	0.0	-31.00
Class 4	27-182	14.8	+26.88				
Class 5	14-91	15.4	+21.75	Totals	7-85	8.2	-15.50
Class 6	1-6	16.7	0.00				

JOCKEYS

	W-R	Per cent	£1 Level Stake
Finian O'Toole	10-106	9.4	-14.75
Joe Colliver	9-70	12.9	+26.13
Miss Becky Smith	7-26	26.9	+9.07
Alain Cawley	5-32	15.6	-9.60

Hugo Thompson Brown	4-17	23.5	+2.28
Jamie Hamilton	3-5	60.0	+34.00
Henry Brooke	3-46	6.5	-31.50
Harry Reed	1-1	100.0	+12.00
Richard Johnson	1-2	50.0	+4.00
James Bowen	1-3	33.3	+2.00
Miss Catherine Walton	1-3	33.3	+1.50
Sean Quinlan	1-5	20.0	+7.00

COURSE RECORD

	Total W-R	Non-Hndcps Hurdles	Chases	Hndcps Hurdles	Chases	NH Flat	Per cent	£1 Level Stake
Sedgefield	10-69	4-12	0-1	2-28	4-26	0-2	14.5	-22.30
Wetherby	8-53	0-8	0-2	5-24	3-17	0-2	15.1	+63.50
Hexham	6-47	1-7	0-0	3-14	2-24	0-2	12.8	-5.50
Carlisle	5-26	0-3	0-2	5-12	0-8	0-1	19.2	+4.77
Catterick	4-32	1-7	0-2	2-11	1-10	0-2	12.5	+17.00
Leicester	2-2	0-0	0-0	1-1	1-1	0-0	100.0	+11.33
Perth	2-12	0-3	0-0	2-8	0-1	0-0	16.7	-3.75
Mrket Rsn	2-17	0-1	0-0	1-6	1-10	0-0	11.8	-7.00
Kelso	2-18	0-2	0-0	0-4	1-11	1-1	11.1	-6.50
Bangor	1-2	0-0	0-0	0-0	1-2	0-0	50.0	-0.43
Uttoxeter	1-2	0-0	0-0	0-0	1-2	0-0	50.0	+6.00
Musselbgh	1-7	0-1	0-0	1-3	0-2	0-1	14.3	+5.00
Ayr	1-13	0-1	0-0	0-7	1-5	0-0	7.7	-9.00
Cartmel	1-14	0-2	0-0	0-4	1-8	0-0	7.1	-9.00

WINNING HORSES

Horse	Races Run	1st	2nd	3rd	£
Just Cameron	6	1	1	0	14945
Alderbrook Lad	8	1	2	0	12512
Caraline	7	2	2	2	11112
Knocknamona	10	4	0	0	19976
Waterclock	1	1	0	0	5848
Roxyfet	14	2	3	3	8447
Only Orsenfoolsies	5	1	1	1	5523
Skywards Reward	8	3	1	0	12931
Dakota Grey	8	1	0	1	4874
Cornerstone Lad	7	2	3	2	8058
Applaus	6	1	1	2	4809
Justforjames	7	2	0	2	9227
Strike West	7	1	0	1	4549
Allfredandnobell	5	1	0	1	4484
*Tyrell	6	1	0	0	4484
Bulkov	8	3	3	0	11436
Strait Run	5	1	0	1	4094
Just Bobby	5	1	1	1	4094
Tickenwolf	7	1	0	0	3956
Becky The Thatcher	4	1	0	0	3899
Onlyfoolsownhorses	5	3	1	0	10946
Frank The Slink	4	1	0	1	3899
Rhythm Of Sound	10	2	0	0	6498
Witness	5	1	0	1	3509
Rockliffe	5	2	0	0	6368
Paddling	8	1	2	3	3249
Swinton Diamond	2	1	1	0	3249

Wig Wam Wiggle	5	1	0	0	2924
The Pine Martin	2	1	1	0	2808
Shalamzar	4	1	0	0	2599
Ey Up Rocky	1	1	0	0	1949
Total winning prize-money					**£207256**
Favourites	8-172		4.7%		**-152.00**

GARY HANMER

NANTWICH, CHESHIRE

	No. of Hrs	Races Run	1st	2nd	3rd	Unpl	Per cent	£1 Level Stake
NH Flat	1	1	0	0	0	1	0.0	-1.00
Hurdles	5	10	0	1	0	9	0.0	-10.00
Chases	5	15	3	2	1	9	20.0	+12.33
Totals	11	26	3	3	1	19	11.5	+1.33
16-17	17	56	2	5	3	46	3.6	-3.00
15-16	12	20	4	3	3	10	20.0	+27.00

JOCKEYS

	W-R	Per cent	£1 Level Stake
Mr Alex Edwards	2-4	50.0	+6.33
Tom O'Brien	1-3	33.3	+14.00

COURSE RECORD

	Total W-R	Non-Hndcps Hurdles	Chases	Hndcps Hurdles	Chases	NH Flat	Per cent	£1 Level Stake
Bangor	2-6	0-0	0-0	0-1	2-4	0-1	33.3	+17.00
Hereford	1-1	0-0	0-0	0-0	1-1	0-0	100.0	+3.33

WINNING HORSES

Horse	Races Run	1st	2nd	3rd	£
*Packettotherafters	5	1	1	0	5198
*High Counsel	3	1	1	0	5064
Cruising Bye	3	1	0	1	2996
Total winning prize-money					**£13258**
Favourites	0-0		0.0%		**0.00**

GEOFFREY HARKER

THIRKLEBY, N YORKS

	No. of Hrs	Races Run	1st	2nd	3rd	Unpl	Per cent	£1 Level Stake
NH Flat	1	3	1	1	1	0	33.3	-0.63
Hurdles	0	0	0	0	0	0	0.0	0.00
Chases	0	0	0	0	0	0	0.0	0.00
Totals	1	3	1	1	1	0	33.3	-0.63
16-17	3	4	0	0	1	3	0.0	-4.00
15-16	1	1	0	0	0	1	0.0	-1.00

JOCKEYS

	W-R	Per cent	£1 Level Stake
Lorcan Murtagh	1-3	33.3	-0.63

COURSE RECORD

	Total W-R	Non-Hndcps Hurdles Chases	Hndcps Hurdles Chases	NH Flat	Per cent	£1 Level Stake
Hexham	1-1	0-0 0-0	0-0 0-0	1-1	100.0	+1.38

WINNING HORSES

Horse	Races Run	1st	2nd	3rd	£
Buy Mistake	3	1	1	1	1884
Total winning prize-money					**£1884**
Favourites	1-1		100.0%		1.38

GRACE HARRIS

SHIRENEWTON, MONMOUTHSHIRE

	No. of Hrs	Races Run	1st	2nd	3rd	Unpl	Per cent	£1 Level Stake
NH Flat	2	4	0	0	0	4	0.0	-4.00
Hurdles	10	41	2	6	4	29	4.9	-15.67
Chases	3	15	3	4	2	6	20.0	+7.25
Totals	12	60	5	10	6	39	8.3	-12.42
16-17	16	88	3	9	17	59	3.4	-62.00
15-16	7	41	3	8	1	29	7.3	-11.25

JOCKEYS

	W-R	Per cent	£1 Level Stake
Conor Ring	2-11	18.2	+8.00
Mikey Hamill	2-20	10.0	-12.42
Miss Catherine Walton	1-2	50.0	+19.00

COURSE RECORD

	Total W-R	Non-Hndcps Hurdles Chases	Hndcps Hurdles Chases	NH Flat	Per cent	£1 Level Stake
Chepstow	2-14	0-1 0-0	0-5 2-7	0-1	14.3	+5.00
Stratford	1-2	0-0 0-0	1-2 0-0	0-0	50.0	+19.00
Ffos Las	1-2	0-1 0-0	0-0 1-1	0-0	50.0	+1.25
Nton Abbot	1-5	0-0 0-0	1-3 0-2	0-0	20.0	-0.67

WINNING HORSES

Horse	Races Run	1st	2nd	3rd	£
Maguire's Glen	11	2	2	1	9357
Paddy The Oscar	9	2	4	1	8512
Berry De Carjac	7	1	1	0	3120
Total winning prize-money					**£20989**
Favourites	0-2		0.0%		-2.00

SHAUN HARRIS

CARBURTON, NOTTS

	No. of Hrs	Races Run	1st	2nd	3rd	Unpl	Per cent	£1 Level Stake
NH Flat	1	1	0	0	0	1	0.0	-1.00
Hurdles	8	27	1	1	3	22	3.7	-12.00
Chases	2	2	0	0	0	2	0.0	-2.00
Totals	9	30	1	1	3	25	3.3	-15.00
16-17	14	36	1	1	4	30	2.8	-31.00
15-16	11	37	2	1	3	31	5.4	-20.50

JOCKEYS

	W-R	Per cent	£1 Level Stake
Jack Quinlan	1-8	12.5	+7.00

COURSE RECORD

	Total W-R	Non-Hndcps Hurdles Chases	Hndcps Hurdles Chases	NH Flat	Per cent	£1 Level Stake
Uttoxeter	1-5	0-1 0-0	1-4 0-0	0-0	20.0	+10.00

WINNING HORSES

Horse	Races Run	1st	2nd	3rd	£
Aza Run	6	1	0	1	2599
Total winning prize-money					**£2599**
Favourites	0-0		0.0%		0.00

RONALD HARRIS

EARLSWOOD, MONMOUTHS

	No. of Hrs	Races Run	1st	2nd	3rd	Unpl	Per cent	£1 Level Stake
NH Flat	1	3	0	0	0	3	0.0	-3.00
Hurdles	1	5	0	0	0	5	0.0	-5.00
Chases	2	5	1	2	1	1	20.0	+21.00
Totals	4	13	1	2	1	9	7.7	+13.00
16-17	1	3	0	0	0	3	0.0	-3.00
15-16	3	5	0	0	0	5	0.0	-5.00

JOCKEYS

	W-R	Per cent	£1 Level Stake
Mr Conor Orr	1-9	11.1	+17.00

COURSE RECORD

	Total W-R	Non-Hndcps Hurdles Chases	Hndcps Hurdles Chases	NH Flat	Per cent	£1 Level Stake
Worcester	1-8	0-1 0-0	0-1 1-4	0-2	12.5	+18.00

WINNING HORSES

Horse	Races Run	1st	2nd	3rd	£
Romeo Is Bleeding	4	1	2	0	2859
Total winning prize-money					**£2859**
Favourites	0-0		0.0%		0.00

LISA HARRISON

ALDOTH, CUMBRIA

	No. of Hrs	Races Run	1st	2nd	3rd	Unpl	Per cent	£1 Level Stake
NH Flat	5	8	0	1	1	6	0.0	-8.00
Hurdles	13	51	7	3	5	36	13.7	-16.42
Chases	5	43	3	12	8	20	7.0	-14.00
Totals	**17**	**102**	**10**	**16**	**14**	**62**	**9.8**	**-38.42**
16-17	21	93	6	4	9	74	6.5	-27.75
15-16	20	152	13	24	21	94	8.6	-65.25

BY MONTH

NH Flat	W-R	Per cent	£1 Level Stake	Hurdles	W-R	Per cent	£1 Level Stake
May	0-0	0.0	0.00	May	0-5	0.0	-5.00
June	0-1	0.0	-1.00	June	0-5	0.0	-5.00
July	0-4	0.0	-4.00	July	4-8	50.0	+11.00
August	0-2	0.0	-2.00	August	1-12	8.3	-7.67
September	0-1	0.0	-1.00	September	0-3	0.0	-3.00
October	0-0	0.0	0.00	October	0-8	0.0	-8.00
November	0-0	0.0	0.00	November	0-3	0.0	-3.00
December	0-0	0.0	0.00	December	0-1	0.0	-1.00
January	0-0	0.0	0.00	January	0-1	0.0	-1.00
February	0-0	0.0	0.00	February	1-2	50.0	+6.00
March	0-0	0.0	0.00	March	1-2	50.0	+1.25
April	0-0	0.0	0.00	April	0-1	0.0	-1.00

Chases	W-R	Per cent	£1 Level Stake	Totals	W-R	Per cent	£1 Level Stake
May	1-5	20.0	+12.00	May	1-10	10.0	+7.00
June	0-3	0.0	-3.00	June	0-9	0.0	-9.00
July	1-7	14.3	-3.00	July	5-19	26.3	+4.00
August	0-6	0.0	-6.00	August	1-20	5.0	-15.67
September	0-6	0.0	-6.00	September	0-10	0.0	-10.00
October	0-5	0.0	-5.00	October	0-13	0.0	-13.00
November	0-5	0.0	-5.00	November	0-8	0.0	-8.00
December	0-2	0.0	-2.00	December	0-3	0.0	-3.00
January	0-2	0.0	-2.00	January	0-3	0.0	-3.00
February	1-2	50.0	+6.00	February	2-4	50.0	+12.00
March	0-0	0.0	0.00	March	1-2	50.0	+1.25
April	0-0	0.0	0.00	April	0-1	0.0	-1.00

DISTANCE

Hurdles	W-R	Per cent	£1 Level Stake	Chases	W-R	Per cent	£1 Level Stake
2m-2m3f	3-12	25.0	+2.25	2m-2m3f	2-15	13.3	+6.00
2m4f-2m7f	2-20	10.0	-9.50	2m4f-2m7f	0-6	0.0	-6.00
3m+	2-19	10.5	-9.17	3m+	1-22	4.5	-14.00

TYPE OF RACE

Non-Handicaps	W-R	Per cent	£1 Level Stake	Handicaps	W-R	Per cent	£1 Level Stake
Nov Hrdls	0-5	0.0	-5.00	Nov Hrdls	1-5	20.0	-1.75
Hrdls	0-2	0.0	-2.00	Hrdls	6-39	15.4	-7.67
Nov Chs	0-1	0.0	-1.00	Nov Chs	0-5	0.0	-5.00

	W-R	Per cent	£1 Level Stake		W-R	Per cent	£1 Level Stake
Chases	0-0	0.0	0.00	Chases	3-37	8.1	-8.00
Sell/Claim	0-0	0.0	0.00	Sell/Claim	0-0	0.0	0.00

RACE CLASS

	W-R	Per cent	£1 Level Stake
Class 1	0-0	0.0	0.00
Class 2	0-3	0.0	-3.00
Class 3	0-15	0.0	-15.00
Class 4	7-57	12.3	-11.67
Class 5	3-26	11.5	-7.75
Class 6	0-1	0.0	-1.00

FIRST TIME OUT

	W-R	Per cent	£1 Level Stake
Bumpers	0-5	0.0	-5.00
Hurdles	0-11	0.0	-11.00
Chases	1-1	100.0	+16.00
Totals	**1-17**	**5.9**	**0.00**

JOCKEYS

	W-R	Per cent	£1 Level Stake
Callum Bewley	4-48	8.3	-18.50
Ross Chapman	3-24	12.5	-4.75
Henry Brooke	2-11	18.2	-0.50
Miss Catherine Walton	1-1	100.0	+3.33

COURSE RECORD

	Total W-R	Non-Hndcps Hurdles	Chases	Hndcps Hurdles	Chases	NH Flat	Per cent	£1 Level Stake
Perth	4-42	0-5	0-1	4-20	0-9	0-7	9.5	-22.17
Ayr	2-8	0-0	0-0	1-3	1-5	0-0	25.0	+8.00
Mrket Rsn	1-3	0-0	0-0	0-1	1-2	0-0	33.3	+1.00
Sedgefield	1-6	0-0	0-0	0-3	1-3	0-0	16.7	+11.00
Carlisle	1-7	0-0	0-0	1-4	0-3	0-0	14.3	-3.75
Uttoxeter	1-9	0-0	0-0	1-4	0-4	0-1	11.1	-5.50

WINNING HORSES

Horse	Races Run	1st	2nd	3rd	£
Solway Prince	3	1	0	0	6256
Muwalla	18	2	6	3	9747
Presented	18	1	3	3	4874
Johnny Go	8	1	2	2	4249
Instinctive	12	2	0	1	7538
Green Zone	9	3	0	0	10613
Total winning prize-money					**£43277**
Favourites	2-3		66.7%		3.25

BEN HASLAM

MIDDLEHAM MOOR, N YORKS

	No. of Hrs	Races Run	1st	2nd	3rd	Unpl	Per cent	£1 Level Stake
NH Flat	0	0	0	0	0	0	0.0	0.00
Hurdles	6	18	3	1	4	10	16.7	-4.88
Chases	7	29	2	3	4	20	6.9	-8.50
Totals	**9**	**47**	**5**	**4**	**8**	**30**	**10.6**	**-13.38**
16-17	15	58	6	5	5	42	10.3	-14.70
15-16	10	33	1	2	3	27	3.0	-28.50

JOCKEYS

	W-R	Per cent	£1 Level Stake
Richie McLernon	5-43	11.6	-9.38

COURSE RECORD

	Total W-R	Non-Hndcps Hurdles	Chases	Hndcps Hurdles	Chases	NH Flat	Per cent	£1 Level Stake
Sedgefield	4-13	1-1	0-1	1-6	2-5	0-0	30.8	+17.88
Carlisle	1-2	1-1	0-0	0-0	0-1	0-0	50.0	+0.75

WINNING HORSES

Horse	Races Run	1st	2nd	3rd	£
Cash Again	7	1	0	1	7343
Ever So Much	6	1	0	1	4094
The Doorman	11	3	0	2	11047
Total winning prize-money					**£22484**
Favourites		1-4	25.0%		-1.25

NIGEL HAWKE

STOODLEIGH, DEVON

	No. of Hrs	Races Run	1st	2nd	3rd	Unpl	Per cent	£1 Level Stake
NH Flat	7	7	0	1	0	6	0.0	-7.00
Hurdles	43	135	12	11	14	98	8.9	-52.53
Chases	20	47	5	3	8	31	10.6	-10.22
Totals	50	189	17	15	22	135	9.0	-69.75
16-17	46	227	28	24	27	148	12.3	-55.68
15-16	38	128	11	9	14	94	8.6	-58.14

BY MONTH

NH Flat	W-R	Per cent	£1 Level Stake	Hurdles	W-R	Per cent	£1 Level Stake
May	0-2	0.0	-2.00	May	0-9	0.0	-9.00
June	0-0	0.0	0.00	June	0-4	0.0	-4.00
July	0-0	0.0	0.00	July	1-6	16.7	-3.13
August	0-0	0.0	0.00	August	0-4	0.0	-4.00
September	0-0	0.0	0.00	September	2-6	33.3	+6.00
October	0-1	0.0	-1.00	October	3-14	21.4	+12.60
November	0-0	0.0	0.00	November	1-20	5.0	-16.25
December	0-0	0.0	0.00	December	1-9	11.1	-5.00
January	0-1	0.0	-1.00	January	1-14	7.1	-10.00
February	0-0	0.0	0.00	February	0-19	0.0	-19.00
March	0-1	0.0	-1.00	March	1-13	7.7	-7.00
April	0-2	0.0	-2.00	April	2-17	11.8	+6.25

Chases	W-R	Per cent	£1 Level Stake	Totals	W-R	Per cent	£1 Level Stake
May	1-2	50.0	+2.50	May	1-13	7.7	-8.50
June	1-3	33.3	-0.63	June	1-7	14.3	-4.63
July	0-2	0.0	-2.00	July	1-8	12.5	-5.13
August	1-5	20.0	+16.00	August	1-9	11.1	+12.00
September	0-3	0.0	-3.00	September	2-9	22.2	+3.00
October	0-8	0.0	-8.00	October	3-23	13.0	+3.60
November	0-10	0.0	-10.00	November	1-30	3.3	-26.25

December	1-4	25.0	+3.00	December	2-13	15.4	-2.00
January	1-3	33.3	-1.09	January	2-18	11.1	-12.09
February	0-3	0.0	-3.00	February	0-22	0.0	-22.00
March	0-0	0.0	0.00	March	1-14	7.1	-8.00
April	0-4	0.0	-4.00	April	2-23	8.7	+0.25

DISTANCE

Hurdles	W-R	Per cent	£1 Level Stake	Chases	W-R	Per cent	£1 Level Stake
2m-2m3f	5-67	7.5	-40.25	2m-2m3f	1-10	10.0	-8.09
2m4f-2m7f	7-52	13.5	+3.73	2m4f-2m7f	2-19	10.5	+9.00
3m+	0-16	0.0	-16.00	3m+	2-18	11.1	-11.13

TYPE OF RACE

Non-Handicaps	W-R	Per cent	£1 Level Stake	Handicaps	W-R	Per cent	£1 Level Stake
Nov Hrdls	2-38	5.3	-33.02	Nov Hrdls	0-5	0.0	-5.00
Hrdls	3-30	10.0	-10.00	Hrdls	7-58	12.1	-0.50
Nov Chs	2-10	20.0	+18.00	Nov Chs	1-13	7.7	-8.50
Chases	0-2	0.0	-2.00	Chases	2-20	10.0	-15.72
Sell/Claim	0-2	0.0	-2.00	Sell/Claim	0-2	0.0	-2.00

RACE CLASS / FIRST TIME OUT

	W-R	Per cent	£1 Level Stake		W-R	Per cent	£1 Level Stake
Class 1	1-6	16.7	+15.00	Bumpers	0-7	0.0	-7.00
Class 2	1-8	12.5	-6.09	Hurdles	5-31	16.1	+9.25
Class 3	2-22	9.1	-11.25	Chases	1-12	8.3	-5.00
Class 4	11-105	10.5	-28.15				
Class 5	2-45	4.4	-36.25	Totals	6-50	12.0	-2.75
Class 6	0-3	0.0	-3.00				

JOCKEYS

	W-R	Per cent	£1 Level Stake
Sean Bowen	6-28	21.4	+16.51
Sean Houlihan	2-7	28.6	+1.00
James Bowen	2-8	25.0	+12.75
Tom Cannon	2-16	12.5	+11.00
Ciaran Gethings	2-47	4.3	-40.13
Gavin Sheehan	1-1	100.0	+6.00
Aidan Coleman	1-5	20.0	-2.13
Tom Buckley	1-11	9.1	-8.75

COURSE RECORD

	Total W-R	Non-Hndcps Hurdles	Chases	Hndcps Hurdles	Chases	NH Flat	Per cent	£1 Level Stake
Hexham	3-7	2-4	0-0	1-2	0-1	0-0	42.9	+7.10
Exeter	3-23	0-7	0-1	3-13	0-2	0-0	13.0	0.00
Sedgefield	2-5	1-2	0-1	1-2	0-0	0-0	40.0	+6.50
Nton Abbot	2-23	0-11	0-0	0-4	2-6	0-2	8.7	-16.13
Taunton	2-26	1-10	0-0	1-13	0-0	0-3	7.7	-16.00
Mrket Rsn	1-4	1-3	0-1	0-0	0-0	0-0	25.0	-1.13
Sandown	1-4	0-1	0-0	0-0	1-3	0-0	25.0	-2.09
Cheltenham	1-6	0-1	0-0	1-3	0-2	0-0	16.7	+15.00
Worcester	1-7	0-1	1-1	0-4	0-1	0-0	14.3	+14.00
Wincanton	1-8	0-4	1-1	0-2	0-1	0-0	12.5	-1.00

WINNING HORSES

Horse	Races Run	1st	2nd	3rd	£
Speredek	5	2	2	0	26566
Rejaah	3	1	0	0	14238
Pearl Royale	2	1	0	0	7798
Calin Du Brizais	7	2	1	1	10199
Camron De Chaillac	8	2	0	2	9292
Le Musee	4	1	2	0	4159
Midnight Request	7	1	0	0	3899
Nachi Falls	5	1	1	1	3899
Heart Of Kernow	2	2	0	0	6455
Pomme	4	1	1	0	3574
Take A Break	9	1	1	1	3482
Level Of Intensity	4	1	0	1	3379
Point N Shoot	8	1	2	1	3249
Total winning prize-money					**£100189**
Favourites	5-10		50.0%		2.38

RICHARD HAWKER

RODE, SOMERSET

	No. of Hrs	Races Run	1st	2nd	3rd	Unpl	Per cent	£1 Level Stake
NH Flat	1	1	0	0	0	1	0.0	-1.00
Hurdles	6	14	1	1	0	12	7.1	+7.00
Chases	1	1	0	0	0	1	0.0	-1.00
Totals	7	16	1	1	0	14	6.3	+5.00
16-17	5	9	0	0	0	9	0.0	-9.00
15-16	4	18	1	1	1	15	5.6	-13.50

JOCKEYS

	W-R	Per cent	£1 Level Stake
Mr Robert Hawker	1-13	7.7	+8.00

COURSE RECORD

	Total W-R	Non-Hndcps Hurdles	Chases	Hndcps Hurdles	Chases	NH Flat	Per cent	£1 Level Stake
Towcester	1-2	0-0	0-0	1-2	0-0	0-0	50.0	+19.00

WINNING HORSES

Horse	Races Run	1st	2nd	3rd	£
Parlour Maid	5	1	1	0	2599
Total winning prize-money					**£2599**
Favourites	0-0		0.0%		0.00

SALLY HAYNES

MELSONBY, N YORKS

	No. of Hrs	Races Run	1st	2nd	3rd	Unpl	Per cent	£1 Level Stake
NH Flat	4	7	2	0	2	3	28.6	+10.10
Hurdles	7	10	0	0	3	7	0.0	-10.00
Chases	1	2	0	0	0	2	0.0	-2.00

| **Totals** | 11 | 19 | 2 | 0 | 5 | 12 | 10.5 | -1.90 |

JOCKEYS

	W-R	Per cent	£1 Level Stake
Leighton Aspell	1-4	25.0	-1.90
Nathan Moscrop	1-6	16.7	+9.00

COURSE RECORD

	Total W-R	Non-Hndcps Hurdles	Chases	Hndcps Hurdles	Chases	NH Flat	Per cent	£1 Level Stake
Newcastle	1-1	0-0	0-0	0-0	0-0	1-1	100.0	+14.00
Mrket Rsn	1-4	0-1	0-0	0-1	0-0	1-2	25.0	-1.90

WINNING HORSES

Horse	Races Run	1st	2nd	3rd	£
*Brecon Hill	1	1	0	0	1949
Star Of Lanka	3	1	0	2	1560
Total winning prize-money					**£3509**
Favourites	1-1		100.0%		1.10

JONATHAN HAYNES

LOW ROW, CUMBRIA

	No. of Hrs	Races Run	1st	2nd	3rd	Unpl	Per cent	£1 Level Stake
NH Flat	1	2	0	0	0	2	0.0	-2.00
Hurdles	5	39	4	1	3	31	10.3	-2.50
Chases	0	0	0	0	0	0	0.0	0.00
Totals	6	41	4	1	3	33	9.8	-4.50
16-17	6	60	5	6	3	46	8.3	-25.38
15-16	5	49	5	6	2	36	10.2	-9.59

JOCKEYS

	W-R	Per cent	£1 Level Stake
Thomas Dowson	3-31	9.7	+1.00
Sean Quinlan	1-2	50.0	+2.50

COURSE RECORD

	Total W-R	Non-Hndcps Hurdles	Chases	Hndcps Hurdles	Chases	NH Flat	Per cent	£1 Level Stake
Newcastle	2-3	0-0	0-0	2-3	0-0	0-0	66.7	+16.50
Hexham	2-22	0-8	0-0	2-12	0-0	0-2	9.1	-5.00

WINNING HORSES

Horse	Races Run	1st	2nd	3rd	£
Beyondtemptation	16	3	0	3	11566
Mrs Grass	7	1	1	0	3899
Total winning prize-money					**£15465**
Favourites	0-0		0.0%		0.00

J H HENDERSON

FARINGDON, OXFORDSHIRE

	No. of Hrs	Races Run	1st	2nd	3rd	Unpl	Per cent	£1 Level Stake
NH Flat	0	0	0	0	0	0	0.0	0.00
Hurdles	0	0	0	0	0	0	0.0	0.00
Chases	3	3	1	0	0	2	33.3	-0.38
Totals	3	3	1	0	0	2	33.3	-0.38
15-16	1	1	0	0	0	1	0.0	-1.00

JOCKEYS

	W-R	Per cent	£1 Level Stake
Mr Frederick Henderson	1-3	33.3	-0.38

COURSE RECORD

	Total W-R	Non-Hndcps Hurdles	Chases	Hndcps Hurdles	Chases	NH Flat	Per cent	£1 Level Stake
Stratford	1-1	0-0	1-1	0-0	0-0	0-0	100.0	+1.63

WINNING HORSES

Horse	Races Run	1st	2nd	3rd	£
*Abricot De L'Oasis	1	1	0	0	2496
Total winning prize-money					**£2496**
Favourites	**0-0**		**0.0%**		**0.00**

PAUL HENDERSON

WHITSBURY, HANTS

	No. of Hrs	Races Run	1st	2nd	3rd	Unpl	Per cent	£1 Level Stake
NH Flat	1	3	0	1	0	2	0.0	-3.00
Hurdles	19	81	4	7	13	57	4.9	-67.00
Chases	13	56	6	8	10	32	10.7	-30.00
Totals	24	140	10	16	23	91	7.1	-100.00
16-17	18	115	16	16	15	68	13.9	-3.24
15-16	31	146	7	16	13	110	4.8	-87.50

BY MONTH

NH Flat	W-R	Per cent	£1 Level Stake	Hurdles	W-R	Per cent	£1 Level Stake
May	0-0	0.0	0.00	May	2-6	33.3	+0.25
June	0-1	0.0	-1.00	June	1-6	16.7	-2.25
July	0-2	0.0	-2.00	July	0-2	0.0	-2.00
August	0-0	0.0	0.00	August	0-1	0.0	-1.00
September	0-0	0.0	0.00	September	0-0	0.0	0.00
October	0-0	0.0	0.00	October	0-12	0.0	-12.00
November	0-0	0.0	0.00	November	0-12	0.0	-12.00
December	0-0	0.0	0.00	December	1-10	10.0	-6.00
January	0-0	0.0	0.00	January	0-11	0.0	-11.00
February	0-0	0.0	0.00	February	0-9	0.0	-9.00
March	0-0	0.0	0.00	March	0-5	0.0	-5.00
April	0-0	0.0	0.00	April	0-7	0.0	-7.00

Chases	W-R	Per cent	£1 Level Stake	Totals	W-R	Per cent	£1 Level Stake
May	2-6	33.3	+2.25	May	4-12	33.3	+2.50
June	0-3	0.0	-3.00	June	1-10	10.0	-6.25
July	0-1	0.0	-1.00	July	0-5	0.0	-5.00
August	0-1	0.0	-1.00	August	0-2	0.0	-2.00
September	0-0	0.0	0.00	September	0-0	0.0	0.00
October	0-6	0.0	-6.00	October	0-18	0.0	-18.00
November	1-8	12.5	-0.50	November	1-20	5.0	-12.50
December	0-5	0.0	-5.00	December	1-15	6.7	-11.00
January	0-6	0.0	-6.00	January	0-17	0.0	-17.00
February	1-7	14.3	-4.00	February	1-16	6.3	-13.00
March	1-5	20.0	-2.25	March	1-10	10.0	-7.25
April	1-8	12.5	-3.50	April	1-15	6.7	-10.50

DISTANCE

Hurdles	W-R	Per cent	£1 Level Stake	Chases	W-R	Per cent	£1 Level Stake
2m-2m3f	0-21	0.0	-21.00	2m-2m3f	1-17	5.9	-9.50
2m4f-2m7f	4-39	10.3	-25.00	2m4f-2m7f	3-18	16.7	-5.25
3m+	0-20	0.0	-20.00	3m+	2-21	9.5	-15.25

TYPE OF RACE

Non-Handicaps	W-R	Per cent	£1 Level Stake	Handicaps	W-R	Per cent	£1 Level Stake
Nov Hrdls	0-11	0.0	-11.00	Nov Hrdls	0-8	0.0	-8.00
Hrdls	0-10	0.0	-10.00	Hrdls	4-51	7.8	-37.00
Nov Chs	0-0	0.0	0.00	Nov Chs	0-6	0.0	-6.00
Chases	0-0	0.0	0.00	Chases	6-45	13.3	-19.00
Sell/Claim	0-0	0.0	0.00	Sell/Claim	0-1	0.0	-1.00

RACE CLASS

	W-R	Per cent	£1 Level Stake
Class 1	0-2	0.0	-2.00
Class 2	1-6	16.7	+1.50
Class 3	2-22	9.1	-16.00
Class 4	5-75	6.7	-56.75
Class 5	2-32	6.3	-23.75
Class 6	0-3	0.0	-3.00

FIRST TIME OUT

	W-R	Per cent	£1 Level Stake
Bumpers	0-1	0.0	-1.00
Hurdles	1-18	5.6	-15.50
Chases	1-5	20.0	0.00
Totals	2-24	8.3	-16.50

JOCKEYS

	W-R	Per cent	£1 Level Stake
Paddy Brennan	7-44	15.9	-14.00
Nick Scholfield	3-34	8.8	-24.00

COURSE RECORD

	Total W-R	Non-Hndcps Hurdles	Chases	Hndcps Hurdles	Chases	NH Flat	Per cent	£1 Level Stake
Fakenham	2-6	0-0	0-0	2-4	0-2	0-0	33.3	+0.50
Warwick	2-9	0-2	0-0	0-4	2-3	0-0	22.2	-3.25
Nton Abbot	2-14	0-1	0-0	1-5	1-5	0-3	14.3	-5.75
Worcester	1-1	0-0	0-0	1-1	0-0	0-0	100.0	+2.75
Southwell	1-4	0-0	0-0	0-2	1-2	0-0	25.0	-0.75
Cheltenham	1-5	0-0	0-0	0-0	1-5	0-0	20.0	+2.50

Fontwell   1-20   0-3   0-0   0-8   1-9   0-0   5.0   -15.00

WINNING HORSES

Horse	Races Run	1st	2nd	3rd	£
Doitforthevillage	7	1	1	0	28152
Talk Of The South	10	2	1	3	20578
Minella Tweet	9	2	0	3	10229
Minella Gathering	8	1	2	1	5198
Amron Kali	9	2	0	1	8772
For Carmel	8	1	3	1	4809
Raising Hope	7	1	1	1	3899
Total winning prize-money					£81637
Favourites	6-20		30.0%		0.50

NICKY HENDERSON
UPPER LAMBOURN, BERKS

	No. of Hrs	Races Run	1st	2nd	3rd	Unpl	Per cent	£1 Level Stake
NH Flat	36	51	11	8	9	23	21.6	-20.20
Hurdles	103	327	93	44	28	161	28.4	-17.50
Chases	48	141	36	29	12	64	25.5	-38.79
Totals	154	519	140	81	49	248	27.0	-76.49
16-17	170	595	149	94	67	283	25.0	-107.37
15-16	151	412	81	53	49	229	19.7	-99.03

BY MONTH

NH Flat	W-R	Per cent	£1 Level Stake	Hurdles	W-R	Per cent	£1 Level Stake
May	2-5	40.0	+1.50	May	4-16	25.0	-3.49
June	3-5	60.0	+3.60	June	5-9	55.6	+1.15
July	0-1	0.0	-1.00	July	3-7	42.9	-0.13
August	0-0	0.0	0.00	August	1-2	50.0	+2.33
September	0-0	0.0	0.00	September	1-3	33.3	-1.09
October	0-3	0.0	-3.00	October	3-17	17.6	-7.75
November	2-7	28.6	-3.17	November	13-47	27.7	-4.16
December	0-4	0.0	-4.00	December	19-51	37.3	+21.08
January	2-7	28.6	+1.00	January	14-38	36.8	+11.70
February	0-8	0.0	-8.00	February	10-44	22.7	-17.15
March	1-3	33.3	-0.75	March	8-43	18.6	-22.90
April	1-8	12.5	-6.38	April	12-50	24.0	+2.93

Chases	W-R	Per cent	£1 Level Stake	Totals	W-R	Per cent	£1 Level Stake
May	3-13	23.1	0.00	May	9-34	26.5	-1.99
June	3-7	42.9	-1.17	June	11-21	52.4	+3.58
July	0-5	0.0	-5.00	July	3-13	23.1	-6.13
August	1-3	33.3	+2.50	August	2-5	40.0	+4.83
September	0-0	0.0	0.00	September	1-3	33.3	-1.09
October	0-5	0.0	-5.00	October	3-25	12.0	-15.75
November	7-27	25.9	-13.53	November	22-81	27.2	-20.86
December	7-27	25.9	+2.05	December	26-82	31.7	+19.13
January	4-13	30.8	-4.31	January	20-58	34.5	+8.39
February	3-8	37.5	-2.51	February	13-60	21.7	-27.66
March	3-16	18.8	-7.60	March	12-62	19.4	-31.25
April	5-17	29.4	-4.22	April	18-75	24.0	-7.67

DISTANCE

Hurdles	W-R	Per cent	£1 Level Stake	Chases	W-R	Per cent	£1 Level Stake
2m-2m3f	44-153	28.8	-26.87	2m-2m3f	13-32	40.6	-6.11
2m4f-2m7f	41-130	31.5	+22.34	2m4f-2m7f	16-70	22.9	-20.80
3m+	7-42	16.7	-12.50	3m+	7-39	17.9	-11.88

TYPE OF RACE

Non-Handicaps	W-R	Per cent	£1 Level Stake	Handicaps	W-R	Per cent	£1 Level Stake
Nov Hrdls	40-113	35.4	+0.17	Nov Hrdls	1-12	8.3	-5.00
Hrdls	30-63	47.6	+21.32	Hrdls	18-132	13.6	-35.04
Nov Chs	14-46	30.4	-15.41	Nov Chs	1-10	10.0	-7.38
Chases	11-19	57.9	+4.67	Chases	9-57	15.8	-14.17
Sell/Claim	0-0	0.0	0.00	Sell/Claim	0-0	0.0	0.00

RACE CLASS

	W-R	Per cent	£1 Level Stake
Class 1	38-146	26.0	-32.31
Class 2	14-79	17.7	-4.61
Class 3	20-98	20.4	-40.13
Class 4	54-152	35.5	+5.11
Class 5	8-30	26.7	-7.48
Class 6	6-14	42.9	+2.93

FIRST TIME OUT

	W-R	Per cent	£1 Level Stake
Bumpers	9-36	25.0	-8.92
Hurdles	25-79	31.6	+17.85
Chases	13-39	33.3	-3.94
Totals	47-154	30.5	+4.99

JOCKEYS

	W-R	Per cent	£1 Level Stake
Nico de Boinville	59-213	27.7	-21.53
Daryl Jacob	16-40	40.0	+0.75
Jeremiah McGrath	14-85	16.5	-36.59
Barry Geraghty	12-26	46.2	-2.78
James Bowen	10-37	27.0	+14.50
Ned Curtis	8-33	24.2	-4.16
Noel Fehily	6-17	35.3	+1.44
Mr Hugo Hunt	3-8	37.5	+0.13
David Bass	2-7	28.6	-0.93
Alan Doyle	2-7	28.6	-2.42
Brian Hughes	1-1	100.0	+0.73
Richard Johnson	1-1	100.0	+3.00
Mr Billy Aprahamian	1-1	100.0	+4.00
Mr Sam Waley-Cohen	1-3	33.3	-0.90
Sean Bowen	1-4	25.0	-0.25
Davy Russell	1-6	16.7	-4.33
David Mullins	1-7	14.3	-5.50
Aidan Coleman	1-19	5.3	-17.67

COURSE RECORD

	Total W-R	Non-Hndcps Hurdles	Non-Hndcps Chases	Hndcps Hurdles	Hndcps Chases	NH Flat	Per cent	£1 Level Stake
Cheltenham	14-71	9-22	1-9	3-23	1-16	0-1	19.7	-14.47
Newbury	13-49	8-18	1-2	2-15	1-8	1-6	26.5	+4.25
Kempton	13-52	6-16	3-6	3-18	0-7	1-5	25.0	-12.72
Sandown	12-33	4-6	5-7	3-17	0-3	0-0	36.4	+0.40

Course							
Huntingdon	8-21	3-7	2-3	0-4	2-2	1-5	38.1	-0.63
Worcester	7-17	3-6	1-3	1-3	0-1	2-4	41.2	+2.53
Aintree	7-25	4-12	2-3	0-4	0-3	1-3	28.0	-2.70
Ascot	7-46	2-15	1-4	2-12	2-11	0-4	15.2	-13.88
Uttoxeter	6-12	4-5	1-3	0-0	1-3	0-1	50.0	+1.17
Taunton	5-11	2-5	1-2	2-4	0-0	0-0	45.5	+9.39
Mrket Rsn	5-12	4-4	1-1	0-4	0-3	0-0	41.7	-1.44
Southwell	5-13	3-6	0-2	0-2	0-0	2-3	38.5	-1.17
Ludlow	4-22	4-11	0-2	0-2	0-2	0-5	18.2	-3.30
Warwick	3-8	3-4	0-0	0-1	0-0	0-3	37.5	-0.95
Fakenham	3-9	1-4	1-1	0-3	0-0	1-1	33.3	-3.72
Haydock	3-10	1-2	0-0	1-4	1-4	0-0	30.0	+0.38
Towcester	3-10	1-4	1-3	1-1	0-0	0-2	30.0	-3.61
Newcastle	2-2	1-1	0-0	0-0	1-1	0-0	100.0	+2.92
Lingfield	2-3	1-2	1-1	0-0	0-0	0-0	66.7	-0.07
Ffos Las	2-4	1-2	0-0	0-1	0-0	1-1	50.0	+0.75
Nton Abbot	2-6	2-3	0-0	0-2	0-1	0-0	33.3	+1.00
Stratford	2-6	0-0	1-1	0-2	1-2	0-1	33.3	+3.50
Doncaster	2-18	2-10	0-2	0-3	0-2	0-1	11.1	-14.50
Carlisle	1-1	1-1	0-0	0-0	0-0	0-0	100.0	+0.91
Catterick	1-1	0-0	1-1	0-0	0-0	0-0	100.0	+0.73
Hereford	1-1	1-1	0-0	0-0	0-0	0-0	100.0	+0.13
Hexham	1-2	0-0	1-1	0-1	0-0	0-0	50.0	-0.80
Musselbgh	1-4	1-3	0-1	0-0	0-0	0-0	25.0	-2.80
Fontwell	1-4	1-3	0-1	0-0	0-0	0-0	25.0	-0.50
Chepstow	1-5	1-2	0-0	0-2	0-1	0-0	20.0	-3.27
Wincanton	1-5	0-2	0-0	1-3	0-0	0-0	20.0	+6.00
Bangor	1-7	0-2	0-1	0-2	0-0	1-2	14.3	-5.00
Ayr	1-12	0-0	0-0	0-7	1-4	0-1	8.3	-8.00

WINNING HORSES

Horse	Races Run	1st	2nd	3rd	£
Buveur D'Air	4	4	0	0	413706
Altior	3	3	0	0	331730
L'Ami Serge	5	1	2	1	140525
Might Bite	4	3	1	0	251967
My Tent Or Yours	2	1	0	0	74035
Gold Present	4	2	0	0	81974
Terrefort	4	3	1	0	95457
Santini	4	3	0	1	80946
We Have A Dream	5	5	0	0	129653
Beware The Bear	4	1	0	0	40053
Top Notch	5	3	0	1	99810
Call Me Lord	5	2	1	2	46963
Jenkins	7	2	0	0	34713
William Henry	4	1	0	0	25628
Days Of Heaven	6	2	0	0	29338
Theinval	8	1	1	1	22780
Soul Emotion	2	2	0	0	31280
Claimantakinforgan	5	2	1	1	24481
Mr Whipped	5	3	1	0	28380
Verdana Blue	5	1	0	1	18768
Hammersly Lake	1	1	0	0	18768
Apple's Shakira	5	3	0	1	47821
On The Blind Side	4	3	0	0	39255
Thomas Campbell	6	2	0	0	32725

Chef Des Obeaux	6	3	1	0	25679
Vyta Du Roc	3	1	0	0	15784
Champagne Express	1	1	0	0	15640
Dame De Compagnie	4	2	1	0	17487
Kayf Grace	4	1	0	0	12512
Diese Des Bieffes	6	3	1	0	20310
Whisper	3	1	1	0	12512
Protek Des Flos	4	1	0	1	11574
Brave Eagle	4	1	1	0	11303
Pougne Bobbi	4	1	0	0	9747
Divine Spear	3	2	1	0	14296
Barman	7	1	1	1	8229
Baden	5	1	2	0	7736
Tales Of The Tweed	1	1	0	0	7656
Rather Be	4	2	1	0	13738
Whatswrongwithyou	4	2	1	1	11307
Countister	4	2	1	0	12021
Burrows Edge	6	2	2	0	11307
Cool Macavity	3	1	0	0	6498
River Wylde	2	1	1	0	6330
Big Robin	3	1	0	1	5458
Colonial Dreams	5	2	1	1	9552
Maestro Royal	5	2	0	0	10360
Casablanca Mix	4	1	1	1	5198
Whoshotwho	3	2	0	1	7034
With Discretion	2	2	0	0	9812
War Creation	4	1	0	0	4874
Melangerie	6	2	0	1	8707
*Indian Hawk	6	2	1	0	9227
Pacific De Baune	4	2	1	0	9357
Brain Power	5	1	1	0	4660
Duke Debarry	5	1	1	0	4549
Peace And Co	3	1	0	1	4549
The Vocalist	3	1	2	0	4549
Turtle Wars	4	1	0	1	4549
Ballinure	5	2	0	0	8447
Style De Garde	4	1	1	0	4549
Darius Des Bois	5	1	1	0	4549
Comely	3	1	0	1	4549
Forever Field	6	1	3	0	4289
Kupatana	3	1	1	0	4159
Ok Corral	5	2	2	0	7343
Take To Heart	6	2	1	0	7538
Malachite	5	1	0	1	3899
Polly's Pursuit	8	1	2	1	3899
Sunshade	4	2	0	1	7148
Turn Turk	3	2	1	0	7278
Follow The Bear	6	1	1	1	3899
Monbeg Legend	5	3	1	0	10397
Malton Rose	2	2	0	0	5278
*The Bottom Bar	2	1	1	0	3249
Kings Ryde	4	1	1	2	3249
Welsby	1	1	0	0	3128
Mister Fisher	2	1	0	0	3119
Morning Vicar	3	1	1	0	2274
Before Midnight	3	2	0	1	4549
Storm Of Intrigue	2	1	0	0	1949

Drumlynn	2	1	0	1	1949
French Crusader	3	1	1	0	1949
Tell It To Me	3	1	0	1	1949
Total winning prize-money					**£2609442**
Favourites	**94-189**		**49.7%**		**12.38**

ALAN HILL

ASTON ROWANT, OXFORDSHIRE

	No. of Hrs	Races Run	1st	2nd	3rd	Unpl	Per cent	£1 Level Stake
NH Flat	0	0	0	0	0	0	0.0	0.00
Hurdles	0	0	0	0	0	0	0.0	0.00
Chases	6	14	4	0	4	6	28.6	+6.50
Totals	**6**	**14**	**4**	**0**	**4**	**6**	**28.6**	**+6.50**
16-17	6	14	4	0	3	7	28.6	-1.84
15-16	7	12	1	2	2	7	8.3	-8.25

JOCKEYS

	W-R	Per cent	£1 Level Stake
Mr Joe Hill	4-11	36.4	+9.50

COURSE RECORD

	Total W-R	Non-Hndcps Hurdles	Chases	Hndcps Hurdles	Chases	NH Flat	Per cent	£1 Level Stake
Fontwell	2-2	0-0	2-2	0-0	0-0	0-0	100.0	+13.00
Cartmel	1-1	0-0	1-1	0-0	0-0	0-0	100.0	+1.25
Huntingdon	1-1	0-0	1-1	0-0	0-0	0-0	100.0	+2.25

WINNING HORSES

Horse	Races Run	1st	2nd	3rd	£
*Man Of Steel	4	2	0	1	4367
Broken Eagle	3	1	0	0	1560
Supreme Danehill	3	1	0	2	1248
Total winning prize-money					**£7175**
Favourites	1-1		100.0%		1.25

MARTIN HILL

LITTLEHEMPSTON, DEVON

	No. of Hrs	Races Run	1st	2nd	3rd	Unpl	Per cent	£1 Level Stake
NH Flat	3	5	0	0	0	5	0.0	-5.00
Hurdles	10	38	3	4	3	28	7.9	-26.90
Chases	5	12	0	1	4	7	0.0	-12.00
Totals	**14**	**55**	**3**	**5**	**7**	**40**	**5.5**	**-43.90**
16-17	19	64	3	4	7	49	4.7	-23.50
15-16	18	55	4	6	8	37	7.3	-32.75

JOCKEYS

	W-R	Per cent	£1 Level Stake
Jeremiah McGrath	2-21	9.5	-13.90
Charlie Deutsch	1-14	7.1	-10.00

COURSE RECORD

	Total W-R	Non-Hndcps Hurdles	Chases	Hndcps Hurdles	Chases	NH Flat	Per cent	£1 Level Stake
Nton Abbot	3-25	1-5	0-0	2-14	0-6	0-0	12.0	-13.90

WINNING HORSES

Horse	Races Run	1st	2nd	3rd	£
Cleni Wells	9	1	1	2	12686
Watcombe Heights	5	1	2	1	4711
Treasure The Ridge	7	1	1	0	4711
Total winning prize-money					**£22108**
Favourites	2-4		50.0%		3.10

LAWNEY HILL

ASTON ROWANT, OXON

	No. of Hrs	Races Run	1st	2nd	3rd	Unpl	Per cent	£1 Level Stake
NH Flat	1	1	0	0	0	1	0.0	-1.00
Hurdles	5	18	1	2	3	12	5.6	-11.50
Chases	4	20	6	2	1	11	30.0	+11.60
Totals	**9**	**39**	**7**	**4**	**4**	**24**	**17.9**	**-0.90**
16-17	11	51	6	8	7	30	11.8	-22.75
15-16	24	56	5	7	5	39	8.9	-10.00

JOCKEYS

	W-R	Per cent	£1 Level Stake
Aidan Coleman	6-16	37.5	+19.60
David Bass	1-1	100.0	+1.50

COURSE RECORD

	Total W-R	Non-Hndcps Hurdles	Chases	Hndcps Hurdles	Chases	NH Flat	Per cent	£1 Level Stake
Fontwell	3-10	0-1	0-1	0-2	3-6	0-0	30.0	+0.10
Leicester	1-2	0-1	0-0	0-0	1-1	0-0	50.0	+3.50
Huntingdon	1-3	0-0	0-0	0-2	1-1	0-0	33.3	+6.00
Kempton	1-3	0-0	0-0	0-1	1-1	0-1	33.3	+4.00
Plumpton	1-7	0-1	0-0	1-4	0-2	0-0	14.3	-0.50

WINNING HORSES

Horse	Races Run	1st	2nd	3rd	£
Oliver's Hill	6	2	1	0	14463
Clondaw Westie	7	4	0	1	21002
Miss Mayfair	5	1	2	0	3249
Total winning prize-money					**£38714**
Favourites	2-3		66.7%		1.60

MARK HOAD

LEWES, E SUSSEX

	No. of Hrs	Races Run	1st	2nd	3rd	Unpl	Per cent	£1 Level Stake
NH Flat	1	2	0	0	0	2	0.0	-2.00
Hurdles	4	10	1	0	0	9	10.0	+1.00
Chases	0	0	0	0	0	0	0.0	0.00
Totals	5	12	1	0	0	11	8.3	-1.00
16-17	11	22	2	1	1	18	9.1	-7.50
15-16	8	28	0	2	3	23	0.0	-28.00

JOCKEYS

	W-R	Per cent	£1 Level Stake
James Bowen	1-4	25.0	+7.00

COURSE RECORD

	Total W-R	Non-Hndcps Hurdles	Chases	Hndcps Hurdles	Chases	NH Flat	Per cent	£1 Level Stake
Fontwell	1-6	0-0	0-0	1-5	0-0	0-1	16.7	+5.00

WINNING HORSES

Horse	Races Run	1st	2nd	3rd	£
Willshebetrying	5	1	0	0	2274
Total winning prize-money					**£2274**
Favourites	0-0		0.0%		0.00

PHILIP HOBBS

WITHYCOMBE, SOMERSET

	No. of Hrs	Races Run	1st	2nd	3rd	Unpl	Per cent	£1 Level Stake
NH Flat	29	47	13	4	5	25	27.7	+34.45
Hurdles	94	265	36	34	39	156	13.6	-100.88
Chases	51	148	14	32	22	80	9.5	-95.51
Totals	143	460	63	70	66	261	13.7	-161.94
16-17	157	587	107	92	66	322	18.2	-101.41
15-16	144	523	113	82	81	247	21.6	-59.98

BY MONTH

NH Flat	W-R	Per cent	£1 Level Stake	Hurdles	W-R	Per cent	£1 Level Stake
May	1-2	50.0	0.00	May	4-16	25.0	-4.37
June	1-3	33.3	+0.50	June	0-7	0.0	-7.00
July	1-1	100.0	+0.36	July	0-11	0.0	-11.00
August	0-0	0.0	0.00	August	2-6	33.3	+5.00
September	0-0	0.0	0.00	September	3-13	23.1	+4.33
October	1-2	50.0	+4.00	October	6-38	15.8	-16.82
November	2-4	50.0	+10.00	November	7-46	15.2	+21.75
December	0-5	0.0	-5.00	December	1-20	5.0	-18.00
January	1-2	50.0	+5.00	January	4-17	23.5	-7.84
February	1-6	16.7	-4.17	February	0-18	0.0	-18.00
March	2-8	25.0	+1.25	March	3-30	10.0	-21.25
April	3-14	21.4	+22.50	April	6-43	14.0	-27.69

Chases	W-R	Per cent	£1 Level Stake	Totals	W-R	Per cent	£1 Level Stake
May	1-9	11.1	-7.09	May	6-27	22.2	-11.46
June	1-6	16.7	-3.90	June	2-16	12.5	-10.40
July	0-1	0.0	-1.00	July	1-13	7.7	-11.64
August	0-5	0.0	-5.00	August	2-11	18.2	0.00
September	1-4	25.0	-2.27	September	4-17	23.5	+2.06
October	3-25	12.0	-11.88	October	10-65	15.4	-24.70
November	3-30	10.0	-15.50	November	12-80	15.0	+16.25
December	0-16	0.0	-16.00	December	1-41	2.4	-39.00
January	2-14	14.3	-3.13	January	7-33	21.2	-5.97
February	1-12	8.3	-9.25	February	2-36	5.6	-31.42
March	0-13	0.0	-13.00	March	5-51	9.8	-33.00
April	2-13	15.4	-7.50	April	11-70	15.7	-12.69

DISTANCE

Hurdles	W-R	Per cent	£1 Level Stake	Chases	W-R	Per cent	£1 Level Stake
2m-2m3f	12-138	8.7	-48.79	2m-2m3f	4-41	9.8	-23.40
2m4f-2m7f	21-99	21.2	-36.93	2m4f-2m7f	7-61	11.5	-33.86
3m+	3-28	10.7	-15.17	3m+	3-46	6.5	-38.25

TYPE OF RACE

Non-Handicaps	W-R	Per cent	£1 Level Stake	Handicaps	W-R	Per cent	£1 Level Stake
Nov Hrdls	17-80	21.3	+6.97	Nov Hrdls	0-2	0.0	-2.00
Hrdls	5-44	11.4	-33.44	Hrdls	14-135	10.4	-68.42
Nov Chs	6-32	18.8	-13.49	Nov Chs	1-12	8.3	-8.50
Chases	1-7	14.3	-5.00	Chases	6-78	7.7	-49.52
Sell/Claim	0-1	0.0	-1.00	Sell/Claim	0-0	0.0	0.00

RACE CLASS

	W-R	Per cent	£1 Level Stake
Class 1	2-43	4.7	-35.13
Class 2	4-47	8.5	-34.13
Class 3	19-140	13.6	-66.08
Class 4	23-169	13.6	-48.64
Class 5	11-48	22.9	+26.15
Class 6	4-13	30.8	-4.14

FIRST TIME OUT

	W-R	Per cent	£1 Level Stake
Bumpers	8-29	27.6	+11.75
Hurdles	9-77	11.7	-40.10
Chases	5-37	13.5	-16.97
Totals	22-143	15.4	-45.32

JOCKEYS

	W-R	Per cent	£1 Level Stake
Richard Johnson	38-240	15.8	-90.15
Micheal Nolan	8-53	15.1	+26.70
Tom O'Brien	7-60	11.7	-36.75
Mr David Maxwell	3-16	18.8	+1.50
Ciaran Gethings	2-3	66.7	+6.50
Sean Houlihan	2-23	8.7	-17.50
Noel Fehily	1-1	100.0	+2.25
Barry Geraghty	1-4	25.0	-2.00
Liam Heard	1-15	6.7	-7.50

COURSE RECORD

	Total W-R	Non-Hndcps Hurdles	Non-Hndcps Chases	Hndcps Hurdles	Hndcps Chases	NH Flat	Per cent	£1 Level Stake
Worcester	11-33	4-8	1-3	3-11	2-9	1-2	33.3	+37.78
Nton Abbot	6-22	1-5	1-1	1-8	0-4	3-4	27.3	+5.49
Exeter	5-34	4-15	0-3	1-6	0-9	0-1	14.7	-10.68
Uttoxeter	4-18	2-5	1-3	1-7	0-2	0-1	22.2	-5.84
Warwick	4-23	0-5	1-2	1-6	1-5	1-5	17.4	-6.67
Chepstow	4-27	1-9	1-3	1-6	1-8	0-1	14.8	-14.58
Hexham	3-3	1-1	1-1	0-0	0-0	1-1	100.0	+4.41
Newbury	3-17	0-2	1-2	1-5	0-7	1-1	17.6	+0.50
Wincanton	3-42	0-16	0-0	1-10	1-10	1-6	7.1	-3.13
Sedgefield	2-4	2-2	0-1	0-1	0-0	0-0	50.0	0.00
Wetherby	2-5	0-0	0-1	1-2	1-2	0-0	40.0	+5.50
Hereford	2-7	1-1	0-2	0-1	0-1	1-2	28.6	+2.25
Sandown	2-14	1-4	0-1	0-4	1-5	0-0	14.3	-3.13
Ludlow	2-23	1-9	0-4	1-6	0-1	0-3	8.7	-18.35
Fakenham	1-1	0-0	0-0	0-0	0-0	1-1	100.0	+0.83
Leicester	1-1	1-1	0-0	0-0	0-0	0-0	100.0	+0.08
Southwell	1-4	0-0	0-0	1-2	0-0	0-2	25.0	-0.75
Aintree	1-11	0-2	0-0	1-4	0-3	0-2	9.1	-7.50
Stratford	1-11	1-1	0-1	0-5	0-4	0-0	9.1	-9.56
Huntingdon	1-12	0-4	0-0	0-2	0-3	1-3	8.3	-8.75
Fontwell	1-14	1-2	0-0	0-7	0-4	0-1	7.1	-9.50
Kempton	1-21	1-5	0-2	0-4	0-6	0-4	4.8	-18.38
Taunton	1-29	0-15	0-0	0-7	0-5	1-2	3.4	-23.00
Cheltenham	1-32	0-6	0-2	0-11	0-10	1-3	3.1	-27.00

WINNING HORSES

Horse	Races Run	1st	2nd	3rd	£
Rock The Kasbah	3	1	1	0	19494
Ozzie The Oscar	5	2	1	1	25135
Show On The Road	8	2	3	1	17545
Kayf Adventure	8	2	2	2	17147
Poppy Kay	6	2	0	1	19027
Louis' Vac Pouch	4	1	0	0	12512
Crooks Peak	3	2	0	0	13785
Scoop The Pot	4	2	0	0	14954
Chef D'Equipe	5	1	0	1	9384
Springtown Lake	6	2	1	1	11215
I'm A Game Changer	4	1	0	0	8187
Rolling Dylan	7	2	2	1	15389
Big Easy	3	1	0	1	7798
Ink Master	4	1	1	0	6882
Westend Story	4	2	1	0	12216
Strong Pursuit	1	1	0	0	6657
Brother Tedd	2	1	1	0	6569
Quadriller	2	1	0	0	6498
Ice Cool Champs	5	1	1	2	6256
Ballotin	3	1	1	0	6256
Braavos	6	1	1	1	5697
Steely Addition	4	2	0	0	9422
Gumball	7	3	3	0	13971
Pointed And Sharp	6	1	1	0	5064
Wait For Me	6	1	1	0	5064

Katy P	4	2	1	0	8220
Waiheke	5	1	1	0	4224
Pineapple Rush	4	2	1	1	8187
Who's My Jockey	5	2	1	2	7343
Vodka All The Way	5	1	2	0	4094
Reikers Island	3	1	0	0	4094
Master Work	4	1	0	0	3899
Royal Village	2	1	0	0	3639
Robbin'hannon	4	1	1	0	3509
Melekhov	3	2	1	0	5696
Contented	5	1	1	1	3249
Majestic Touch	1	1	0	0	2729
Umndeni	1	1	0	0	2599
Arthur Mac	2	1	0	0	2599
Tidal Flow	2	1	0	0	2599
Cedar Valley	2	1	0	0	2395
Ebony Gale	2	1	0	0	2274
That's A Given	1	1	0	0	2274
Mendip Express	3	1	0	0	2240
Mcnamaras Band	1	1	0	0	1949
*Horse Force One	3	2	0	1	1625
Total winning prize-money					**£361561**
Favourites	33-95		34.7%		-15.82

RICHARD HOBSON

STOW-ON-THE-WOLD, GLOUCS

	No. of Hrs	Races Run	1st	2nd	3rd	Unpl	Per cent	£1 Level Stake
NH Flat	4	5	1	1	0	3	20.0	+12.00
Hurdles	13	35	5	3	3	24	14.3	-8.65
Chases	9	31	4	5	4	18	12.9	-9.00
Totals	20	71	10	9	7	45	14.1	-5.65
16-17	15	55	12	2	7	34	21.8	+46.29
15-16	10	47	6	11	7	23	12.8	-18.59

BY MONTH

NH Flat	W-R	Per cent	£1 Level Stake	Hurdles	W-R	Per cent	£1 Level Stake
May	0-0	0.0	0.00	May	0-5	0.0	-5.00
June	0-0	0.0	0.00	June	2-3	66.7	+13.57
July	0-0	0.0	0.00	July	0-0	0.0	0.00
August	0-0	0.0	0.00	August	0-1	0.0	-1.00
September	0-0	0.0	0.00	September	0-0	0.0	0.00
October	0-0	0.0	0.00	October	1-3	33.3	-1.60
November	0-1	0.0	-1.00	November	0-2	0.0	-2.00
December	1-1	100.0	+16.00	December	1-4	25.0	+2.00
January	0-0	0.0	0.00	January	0-5	0.0	-5.00
February	0-0	0.0	0.00	February	0-4	0.0	-4.00
March	0-1	0.0	-1.00	March	1-4	25.0	-1.63
April	0-2	0.0	-2.00	April	0-4	0.0	-4.00

Chases	W-R	Per cent	£1 Level Stake	Totals	W-R	Per cent	£1 Level Stake
May	0-3	0.0	-3.00	May	0-8	0.0	-8.00
June	0-2	0.0	-2.00	June	2-5	40.0	+11.57
July	0-0	0.0	0.00	July	0-0	0.0	0.00

	W-R	Per cent	£1 Level Stake		W-R	Per cent	£1 Level Stake
August	0-1	0.0	-1.00	August	0-2	0.0	-2.00
September	0-1	0.0	-1.00	September	0-1	0.0	-1.00
October	0-1	0.0	-1.00	October	1-4	25.0	-2.60
November	0-5	0.0	-5.00	November	0-8	0.0	-8.00
December	0-1	0.0	-1.00	December	2-6	33.3	+17.00
January	1-4	25.0	+0.50	January	1-9	11.1	-4.50
February	1-3	33.3	+1.00	February	1-7	14.3	-3.00
March	0-3	0.0	-3.00	March	1-8	12.5	-5.63
April	2-7	28.6	+6.50	April	2-13	15.4	+0.50

DISTANCE

Hurdles	W-R	Per cent	£1 Level Stake	Chases	W-R	Per cent	£1 Level Stake
2m-2m3f	3-21	14.3	-11.23	2m-2m3f	2-5	40.0	+3.50
2m4f-2m7f	2-11	18.2	+5.57	2m4f-2m7f	0-9	0.0	-9.00
3m+	0-3	0.0	-3.00	3m+	2-17	11.8	-3.50

TYPE OF RACE

Non-Handicaps	W-R	Per cent	£1 Level Stake	Handicaps	W-R	Per cent	£1 Level Stake
Nov Hrdls	4-13	30.8	-1.65	Nov Hrdls	0-0	0.0	0.00
Hrdls	0-7	0.0	-7.00	Hrdls	1-12	8.3	+3.00
Nov Chs	1-4	25.0	0.00	Nov Chs	0-1	0.0	-1.00
Chases	0-5	0.0	-5.00	Chases	3-19	15.8	-1.00
Sell/Claim	0-1	0.0	-1.00	Sell/Claim	0-0	0.0	0.00

RACE CLASS

	W-R	Per cent	£1 Level Stake	FIRST TIME OUT	W-R	Per cent	£1 Level Stake
Class 1	1-14	7.1	-8.00	Bumpers	1-4	25.0	+13.00
Class 2	0-17	0.0	-17.00	Hurdles	2-10	20.0	+6.40
Class 3	5-15	33.3	+19.07	Chases	1-6	16.7	-2.00
Class 4	3-16	18.8	-7.72				
Class 5	0-7	0.0	-7.00	Totals	4-20	20.0	+17.40
Class 6	1-2	50.0	+15.00				

JOCKEYS

	W-R	Per cent	£1 Level Stake
Danny Cook	2-8	25.0	-2.10
Jamie Bargary	2-11	18.2	+5.57
James Bowen	2-12	16.7	-5.63
Tom Broughton	1-2	50.0	+7.50
Richard Johnson	1-2	50.0	+4.00
Charlie Hammond	1-4	25.0	+13.00
Jonathan Burke	1-13	7.7	-9.00

COURSE RECORD

	Total W-R	Non-Hndcps Hurdles	Chases	Hndcps Hurdles	Chases	NH Flat	Per cent	£1 Level Stake
Hexham	3-3	2-2	0-0	1-1	0-0	0-0	100.0	+14.97
Perth	2-4	0-0	0-0	0-0	2-3	0-1	50.0	+9.50
Carlisle	1-1	1-1	0-0	0-0	0-0	0-0	100.0	+1.38
Ffos Las	1-1	0-0	0-0	0-0	0-0	1-1	100.0	+16.00
Exeter	1-2	0-0	1-2	0-0	0-0	0-0	50.0	+2.00
Catterick	1-3	0-0	0-1	0-0	1-1	0-1	33.3	+1.50
Newbury	1-3	1-3	0-0	0-0	0-0	0-0	33.3	+3.00

WINNING HORSES

Horse	Races Run	1st	2nd	3rd	£
Chic Name	4	1	0	1	15335
Dame Rose	7	2	0	1	18759
Allysson Monterg	4	2	0	1	19494
Ramonex	7	1	2	1	6758
Surf And Turf	5	1	0	0	5848
Petiville	3	1	1	1	5393
Going Gold	7	1	1	1	4549
Echo Watt	5	1	0	0	1949
Total winning prize-money					**£78085**
Favourites	3-7		42.9%		-0.03

RON HODGES

CHARLTON MACKRELL, SOMERSET

	No. of Hrs	Races Run	1st	2nd	3rd	Unpl	Per cent	£1 Level Stake
NH Flat	2	3	0	0	0	3	0.0	-3.00
Hurdles	5	22	2	2	3	15	9.1	-10.50
Chases	2	10	1	2	2	5	10.0	+11.00
Totals	7	35	3	4	5	23	8.6	-2.50
16-17	6	29	2	3	4	20	6.9	-3.00
15-16	4	16	1	4	2	9	6.3	-9.00

JOCKEYS

	W-R	Per cent	£1 Level Stake
Nick Scholfield	2-8	25.0	+3.50
Harry Cobden	1-11	9.1	+10.00

COURSE RECORD

	Total W-R	Non-Hndcps Hurdles	Chases	Hndcps Hurdles	Chases	NH Flat	Per cent	£1 Level Stake
Wincanton	2-11	0-2	0-0	2-4	0-4	0-1	18.2	+0.50
Lingfield	1-1	0-0	0-0	0-0	1-1	0-0	100.0	+20.00

WINNING HORSES

Horse	Races Run	1st	2nd	3rd	£
Daytime Ahead	9	2	2	1	4224
General Girling	9	1	2	2	3509
Total winning prize-money					**£7733**
Favourites	0-1		0.0%		-1.00

HENRY HOGARTH

STILLINGTON, N YORKS

	No. of Hrs	Races Run	1st	2nd	3rd	Unpl	Per cent	£1 Level Stake
NH Flat	0	0	0	0	0	0	0.0	0.00
Hurdles	5	13	0	0	1	12	0.0	-13.00
Chases	7	29	3	2	4	20	10.3	-18.75
Totals	10	42	3	2	5	32	7.1	-31.75

16-17	11	46	4	6	4	32	8.7	-15.75
15-16	10	43	4	3	6	30	9.3	-22.30

JOCKEYS

	W-R	Per cent	£1 Level Stake
Jamie Hamilton	3-36	8.3	-25.75

COURSE RECORD

	Total W-R	Non-Hndcps Hurdles Chases	Hndcps Hurdles Chases	NH Flat	Per cent	£1 Level Stake
Hexham	3-12	0-2 0-0	0-2 3-8	0-0	25.0	-1.75

WINNING HORSES

Horse	Races Run	1st	2nd	3rd	£
Hattons Hill	6	3	0	0	10917
Total winning prize-money					**£10917**
Favourites	3-5		60.0%		5.25

SARAH HOLLINSHEAD
UPPER LONGDON, STAFFS

	No. of Hrs	Races Run	1st	2nd	3rd	Unpl	Per cent	£1 Level Stake
NH Flat	1	3	0	0	1	2	0.0	-3.00
Hurdles	7	14	1	1	1	11	7.1	-10.25
Chases	1	1	0	0	0	1	0.0	-1.00
Totals	7	18	1	1	2	14	5.6	-14.25
16-17	7	25	1	3	3	18	4.0	-17.50
15-16	5	9	1	0	1	7	11.1	-5.25

JOCKEYS

	W-R	Per cent	£1 Level Stake
Niall P Madden	1-5	20.0	-1.25

COURSE RECORD

	Total W-R	Non-Hndcps Hurdles Chases	Hndcps Hurdles Chases	NH Flat	Per cent	£1 Level Stake
Bangor	1-4	0-1 0-0	1-3 0-0	0-0	25.0	-0.25

WINNING HORSES

Horse	Races Run	1st	2nd	3rd	£
Zenafire	2	1	0	0	3899
Total winning prize-money					**£3899**
Favourites	0-0		0.0%		0.00

D HOLMES
MORPETH, NORTHUMBERLAND

	No. of Hrs	Races Run	1st	2nd	3rd	Unpl	Per cent	£1 Level Stake
NH Flat	0	0	0	0	0	0	0.0	0.00
Hurdles	0	0	0	0	0	0	0.0	0.00
Chases	2	2	1	0	0	1	50.0	+7.00

Totals	2	2	1	0	0	1	50.0	+7.00
16-17	4	4	0	1	1	2	0.0	-4.00
15-16	2	4	1	2	0	1	25.0	+0.33

JOCKEYS

	W-R	Per cent	£1 Level Stake
Mr Joe Wright	1-1	100.0	+8.00

COURSE RECORD

	Total W-R	Non-Hndcps Hurdles Chases	Hndcps Hurdles Chases	NH Flat	Per cent	£1 Level Stake
Kelso	1-1	0-0 1-1	0-0 0-0	0-0	100.0	+8.00

WINNING HORSES

Horse	Races Run	1st	2nd	3rd	£
Five Piers	1	1	0	0	3120
Total winning prize-money					**£3120**
Favourites	0-0		0.0%		0.00

PATRICK HOLMES
MIDDLEHAM, N YORKS

	No. of Hrs	Races Run	1st	2nd	3rd	Unpl	Per cent	£1 Level Stake
NH Flat	2	2	1	0	0	1	50.0	+11.00
Hurdles	12	31	0	1	1	29	0.0	-31.00
Chases	2	9	1	1	0	7	11.1	0.00
Totals	15	42	2	2	1	37	4.8	-20.00
16-17	14	38	1	1	4	32	2.6	-31.50
15-16	10	22	3	2	2	14	13.6	+24.00

JOCKEYS

	W-R	Per cent	£1 Level Stake
Finian O'Toole	1-1	100.0	+12.00
Adam Nicol	1-9	11.1	0.00

COURSE RECORD

	Total W-R	Non-Hndcps Hurdles Chases	Hndcps Hurdles Chases	NH Flat	Per cent	£1 Level Stake
Sedgefield	1-1	0-0 0-0	0-0 0-0	1-1	100.0	+12.00
Southwell	1-4	0-1 0-0	0-0 1-3	0-0	25.0	+5.00

WINNING HORSES

Horse	Races Run	1st	2nd	3rd	£
Stormbay Bomber	6	1	0	0	3249
*Jaxlight	1	1	0	0	2274
Total winning prize-money					**£5523**
Favourites	0-0		0.0%		0.00

ANTHONY HONEYBALL

MOSTERTON, DORSET

	No. of Hrs	Races Run	1st	2nd	3rd	Unpl	Per cent	£1 Level Stake
NH Flat	17	35	10	5	3	17	28.6	+10.86
Hurdles	22	69	13	9	11	36	18.8	-26.57
Chases	15	57	11	14	4	28	19.3	-3.84
Totals	44	161	34	28	18	81	21.1	-19.55
16-17	37	141	32	19	23	67	22.7	+15.24
15-16	43	170	28	27	20	95	16.5	-29.53

BY MONTH

NH Flat	W-R	Per cent	£1 Level Stake	Hurdles	W-R	Per cent	£1 Level Stake
May	0-2	0.0	-2.00	May	0-7	0.0	-7.00
June	0-1	0.0	-1.00	June	0-2	0.0	-2.00
July	0-0	0.0	0.00	July	0-3	0.0	-3.00
August	0-0	0.0	0.00	August	2-3	66.7	+0.52
September	0-0	0.0	0.00	September	1-2	50.0	+2.00
October	0-1	0.0	-1.00	October	0-5	0.0	-5.00
November	3-10	30.0	+3.25	November	2-12	16.7	-5.20
December	4-7	57.1	+8.61	December	4-11	36.4	+3.13
January	2-2	100.0	+8.50	January	2-5	40.0	+0.73
February	1-5	20.0	+1.50	February	1-10	10.0	-5.00
March	0-4	0.0	-4.00	March	0-4	0.0	-4.00
April	0-3	0.0	-3.00	April	1-5	20.0	-1.75

Chases	W-R	Per cent	£1 Level Stake	Totals	W-R	Per cent	£1 Level Stake
May	0-3	0.0	-3.00	May	0-12	0.0	-12.00
June	0-0	0.0	0.00	June	0-3	0.0	-3.00
July	0-0	0.0	0.00	July	0-3	0.0	-3.00
August	0-0	0.0	0.00	August	2-3	66.7	+0.52
September	0-0	0.0	0.00	September	1-2	50.0	+2.00
October	0-1	0.0	-1.00	October	0-7	0.0	-7.00
November	4-13	30.8	+12.38	November	9-35	25.7	+10.43
December	2-16	12.5	-7.25	December	10-34	29.4	+4.49
January	3-7	42.9	+2.16	January	7-14	50.0	+11.39
February	2-8	25.0	+1.88	February	4-23	17.4	-1.62
March	0-3	0.0	-3.00	March	0-11	0.0	-11.00
April	0-6	0.0	-6.00	April	1-14	7.1	-10.75

DISTANCE

Hurdles	W-R	Per cent	£1 Level Stake	Chases	W-R	Per cent	£1 Level Stake
2m-2m3f	7-26	26.9	-1.68	2m-2m3f	1-9	11.1	-5.00
2m4f-2m7f	5-30	16.7	-14.90	2m4f-2m7f	6-19	31.6	+10.00
3m+	1-13	7.7	-10.00	3m+	4-29	13.8	-8.84

TYPE OF RACE

Non-Handicaps	W-R	Per cent	£1 Level Stake	Handicaps	W-R	Per cent	£1 Level Stake
Nov Hrdls	4-18	22.2	-2.52	Nov Hrdls	0-2	0.0	-2.00
Hrdls	3-11	27.3	-2.83	Hrdls	5-34	14.7	-19.23
Nov Chs	4-12	33.3	+8.13	Nov Chs	1-5	20.0	-1.00
Chases	0-1	0.0	-1.00	Chases	5-33	15.2	-7.72
Sell/Claim	0-1	0.0	-1.00	Sell/Claim	0-1	0.0	-1.00

RACE CLASS

	W-R	Per cent	£1 Level Stake
Class 1	7-27	25.9	+7.50
Class 2	2-9	22.2	-4.09
Class 3	6-29	20.7	-6.48
Class 4	10-47	21.3	-3.60
Class 5	4-35	11.4	-18.75
Class 6	5-14	35.7	+5.86

FIRST TIME OUT

	W-R	Per cent	£1 Level Stake
Bumpers	6-17	35.3	+13.75
Hurdles	2-16	12.5	-12.29
Chases	3-11	27.3	+10.88
Totals	11-44	25.0	+12.34

JOCKEYS

	W-R	Per cent	£1 Level Stake
Aidan Coleman	16-58	27.6	-7.33
Noel Fehily	6-21	28.6	+10.48
David Noonan	5-33	15.2	-13.95
Sean Bowen	2-5	40.0	+6.25
Richie McLernon	2-8	25.0	+4.50
Brian Hughes	1-1	100.0	+5.50
Andrew Tinkler	1-1	100.0	+5.50
Richard Johnson	1-2	50.0	+1.50

COURSE RECORD

	Total W-R	Non-Hndcps Hurdles	Chases	Hndcps Hurdles	Chases	NH Flat	Per cent	£1 Level Stake
Fontwell	7-15	2-4	1-1	2-5	1-4	1-1	46.7	+20.80
Plumpton	4-20	2-5	0-0	0-4	1-7	1-4	20.0	-10.16
Wincanton	3-18	1-6	0-1	0-1	0-5	2-5	16.7	-6.88
Kempton	2-3	0-0	0-1	1-1	1-1	0-0	66.7	+1.91
Southwell	2-4	0-1	1-1	0-0	0-1	1-1	50.0	+5.63
Nton Abbot	2-5	0-0	0-0	2-5	0-0	0-0	40.0	-1.48
Cheltenham	2-6	0-0	0-1	0-0	1-3	1-2	33.3	+3.50
Newbury	2-8	0-0	1-3	0-1	0-1	1-3	25.0	+1.75
Taunton	2-10	0-2	0-0	0-3	1-4	1-1	20.0	-3.63
Ludlow	1-1	0-0	0-0	0-0	0-0	1-1	100.0	+5.50
Huntingdon	1-3	0-0	0-0	0-0	0-1	1-2	33.3	+2.50
Warwick	1-3	0-0	1-1	0-0	0-1	0-1	33.3	+0.25
Ffos Las	1-3	0-0	0-0	0-1	1-1	0-1	33.3	+0.75
Ascot	1-5	0-1	0-1	0-0	1-3	0-0	20.0	+2.00
Worcester	1-5	1-4	0-0	0-1	0-0	0-0	20.0	-1.00
Sandown	1-6	1-2	0-0	0-1	0-2	0-1	16.7	-1.00
Exeter	1-12	1-4	0-0	0-2	0-5	0-1	8.3	-6.00

WINNING HORSES

Horse	Races Run	1st	2nd	3rd	£
Regal Encore	5	1	0	1	42713
Midnight Tune	6	3	1	0	33669
Ms Parfois	7	3	3	1	36273
Acey Milan	5	3	1	0	27577
Cresswell Breeze	4	1	0	1	12660
Fountains Windfall	5	2	0	0	18461
Duhallow Gesture	2	1	0	1	11390
*Cloudy Bob	3	1	0	1	9357
Coeur Tantre	7	2	3	1	13469
Drops Of Jupitor	7	1	1	0	5198
Pure Vision	5	1	1	0	5198

Le Coeur Net	10	1	3	0	4874
Tacenda	4	1	2	0	4549
My Dance	5	2	0	0	7798
Rebound	1	1	0	0	3899
Jukebox Jive	2	1	0	0	3574
Soulsaver	6	2	1	2	6368
Sam Brown	2	1	0	0	3249
Represented	1	1	0	0	3249
G For Ginger	4	1	1	0	2859
Everlanes	3	1	0	0	1949
Lechlade Magician	3	1	0	1	1949
Hideaway Vic	3	1	2	0	1625
Don Lami	4	1	1	1	1560
Total winning prize-money					**£263467**
Favourites	**15-47**		**31.9%**		**-7.43**

MISS L V HORNER
LOW WORSALL, NORTH YORKSHIRE

	No. of Hrs	Races Run	1st	2nd	3rd	Unpl	Per cent	£1 Level Stake
NH Flat	0	0	0	0	0	0	0.0	0.00
Hurdles	0	0	0	0	0	0	0.0	0.00
Chases	2	4	1	0	0	3	25.0	+1.50
Totals	2	4	1	0	0	3	25.0	+1.50
16-17	2	2	0	0	1	1	0.0	-2.00

JOCKEYS

	W-R	Per cent	£1 Level Stake
Mr Sam Lee	1-1	100.0	+4.50

COURSE RECORD

	Total W-R	Non-Hndcps Hurdles	Chases	Hndcps Hurdles	Chases	NH Flat	Per cent	£1 Level Stake
Hexham	1-1	0-0	1-1	0-0	0-0	0-0	100.0	+4.50

WINNING HORSES

Horse	Races Run	1st	2nd	3rd	£
Tallow Fair	3	1	0	0	3120
Total winning prize-money					**£3120**
Favourites	0-0		0.0%		0.00

JO HUGHES
LAMBOURN, BERKS

	No. of Hrs	Races Run	1st	2nd	3rd	Unpl	Per cent	£1 Level Stake
NH Flat	2	3	0	0	0	3	0.0	-3.00
Hurdles	1	4	1	1	0	2	25.0	+30.00
Chases	1	3	1	0	0	2	33.3	+1.00
Totals	3	10	2	1	0	7	20.0	+28.00
16-17	1	7	0	1	3	3	0.0	-7.00
15-16	6	13	3	3	1	6	23.1	+6.75

JOCKEYS

	W-R	Per cent	£1 Level Stake
Richard Johnson	1-1	100.0	+3.00
Mark Grant	1-5	20.0	+29.00

COURSE RECORD

	Total W-R	Non-Hndcps Hurdles	Chases	Hndcps Hurdles	Chases	NH Flat	Per cent	£1 Level Stake
Cartmel	1-1	0-0	0-0	0-0	1-1	0-0	100.0	+3.00
Chepstow	1-2	1-1	0-0	0-0	0-0	0-1	50.0	+32.00

WINNING HORSES

Horse	Races Run	1st	2nd	3rd	£
Silver Man	3	1	0	0	8758
Diablo De Rouhet	6	1	1	0	4159
Total winning prize-money					**£12917**
Favourites	1-1		100.0%		3.00

MS N M HUGO
EDGE GREEN, CHESHIRE

	No. of Hrs	Races Run	1st	2nd	3rd	Unpl	Per cent	£1 Level Stake
NH Flat	1	1	1	0	0	0	100.0	+9.00
Hurdles	0	0	0	0	0	0	0.0	0.00
Chases	0	0	0	0	0	0	0.0	0.00
Totals	1	1	1	0	0	0	100.0	+9.00
15-16	2	2	0	0	0	2	0.0	-2.00

JOCKEYS

	W-R	Per cent	£1 Level Stake
Jack Quinlan	1-1	100.0	+9.00

COURSE RECORD

	Total W-R	Non-Hndcps Hurdles	Chases	Hndcps Hurdles	Chases	NH Flat	Per cent	£1 Level Stake
Bangor	1-1	0-0	0-0	0-0	0-0	1-1	100.0	+9.00

WINNING HORSES

Horse	Races Run	1st	2nd	3rd	£
Captain Zebo	1	1	0	0	1949
Total winning prize-money					**£1949**
Favourites	0-0		0.0%		0.00

SARAH HUMPHREY
WEST WRATTING, CAMBS

	No. of Hrs	Races Run	1st	2nd	3rd	Unpl	Per cent	£1 Level Stake
NH Flat	4	4	0	0	0	4	0.0	-4.00
Hurdles	10	28	1	2	4	21	3.6	-11.00
Chases	5	16	2	1	0	13	12.5	-2.13

Totals	14	48	3	3	4	38	6.3	-17.13
16-17	18	43	0	1	5	37	0.0	-43.00
15-16	16	58	5	5	3	45	8.6	+7.00

JOCKEYS

	W-R	Per cent	£1 Level Stake
Nick Scholfield	2-4	50.0	+24.00
Aidan Coleman	1-2	50.0	+0.88

COURSE RECORD

	Total W-R	Non-Hndcps Hurdles	Chases	Hndcps Hurdles	Chases	NH Flat	Per cent	£1 Level Stake
Ludlow	1-3	0-0	0-0	0-0	1-3	0-0	33.3	+8.00
Sedgefield	1-4	0-1	0-0	0-2	1-1	0-0	25.0	-1.13
Huntingdon	1-8	0-2	0-1	1-5	0-0	0-0	12.5	+9.00

WINNING HORSES

Horse	Races Run	1st	2nd	3rd	£
The Happy Chappy	6	3	1	0	20303
Total winning prize-money					**£20303**
Favourites	0-1		**0.0%**		**-1.00**

IAIN JARDINE

CARRUTHERSTOWN, D'FRIES & G'WAY

	No. of Hrs	Races Run	1st	2nd	3rd	Unpl	Per cent	£1 Level Stake
NH Flat	4	6	1	3	0	2	16.7	-3.25
Hurdles	30	99	14	10	13	62	14.1	-27.65
Chases	11	28	6	4	0	18	21.4	+14.75
Totals	35	133	21	17	13	82	15.8	-16.15
16-17	31	142	17	18	27	80	12.0	-38.17
15-16	16	56	11	7	7	31	19.6	-5.62

BY MONTH

NH Flat	W-R	Per cent	£1 Level Stake	Hurdles	W-R	Per cent	£1 Level Stake
May	1-2	50.0	+0.75	May	1-5	20.0	-1.50
June	0-0	0.0	0.00	June	1-8	12.5	-4.50
July	0-0	0.0	0.00	July	0-5	0.0	-5.00
August	0-0	0.0	0.00	August	3-11	27.3	+10.50
September	0-0	0.0	0.00	September	1-4	25.0	-1.13
October	0-0	0.0	0.00	October	0-12	0.0	-12.00
November	0-0	0.0	0.00	November	0-7	0.0	-7.00
December	0-0	0.0	0.00	December	0-10	0.0	-10.00
January	0-1	0.0	-1.00	January	2-12	16.7	-0.70
February	0-1	0.0	-1.00	February	2-5	40.0	+3.73
March	0-2	0.0	-2.00	March	2-9	22.2	+3.44
April	0-0	0.0	0.00	April	2-11	18.2	-3.50

Chases	W-R	Per cent	£1 Level Stake	Totals	W-R	Per cent	£1 Level Stake
May	2-5	40.0	+5.75	May	4-12	33.3	+5.00
June	0-2	0.0	-2.00	June	1-10	10.0	-6.50

BY MONTH (right continuation)

	W-R	Per cent	£1 Level Stake		W-R	Per cent	£1 Level Stake
July	0-4	0.0	-4.00	July	0-9	0.0	-9.00
August	0-0	0.0	0.00	August	3-11	27.3	+10.50
September	0-0	0.0	0.00	September	1-4	25.0	-1.13
October	0-0	0.0	0.00	October	0-12	0.0	-12.00
November	0-2	0.0	-2.00	November	0-9	0.0	-9.00
December	1-1	100.0	+7.50	December	1-11	9.1	-2.50
January	1-4	25.0	+2.50	January	3-17	17.6	+0.80
February	1-3	33.3	+10.00	February	3-9	33.3	+12.73
March	0-4	0.0	-4.00	March	2-15	13.3	-2.56
April	1-3	33.3	+1.00	April	3-14	21.4	-2.50

DISTANCE

Hurdles	W-R	Per cent	£1 Level Stake	Chases	W-R	Per cent	£1 Level Stake
2m-2m3f	8-53	15.1	-5.38	2m-2m3f	0-2	0.0	-2.00
2m4f-2m7f	4-31	12.9	-16.00	2m4f-2m7f	2-13	15.4	+8.50
3m+	1-14	7.1	-7.00	3m+	4-13	30.8	+8.25

TYPE OF RACE

Non-Handicaps	W-R	Per cent	£1 Level Stake	Handicaps	W-R	Per cent	£1 Level Stake
Nov Hrdls	4-23	17.4	-14.38	Nov Hrdls	0-3	0.0	-3.00
Hrdls	3-20	15.0	+1.50	Hrdls	7-52	13.5	-10.77
Nov Chs	0-3	0.0	-3.00	Nov Chs	0-1	0.0	-1.00
Chases	0-0	0.0	0.00	Chases	5-19	26.3	+19.75
Sell/Claim	0-1		-1.00	Sell/Claim	0-0	0.0	0.00

RACE CLASS / FIRST TIME OUT

Race Class	W-R	Per cent	£1 Level Stake	First Time Out	W-R	Per cent	£1 Level Stake
Class 1	0-5	0.0	-5.00	Bumpers	1-4	25.0	-1.25
Class 2	1-6	16.7	+5.00	Hurdles	3-24	12.5	-4.06
Class 3	4-23	17.4	+5.50	Chases	3-7	42.9	+12.25
Class 4	11-69	15.9	-17.40				
Class 5	5-29	17.2	-3.25	Totals	7-35	20.0	+6.94
Class 6	0-1	0.0	-1.00				

JOCKEYS

	W-R	Per cent	£1 Level Stake
Ross Chapman	15-82	18.3	-13.45
Mr Bruce Lynn	2-8	25.0	+16.00
Mr Liam Quinlan	1-1	100.0	+3.50
Brian Hughes	1-3	33.3	-1.70
Dale Irving	1-6	16.7	-2.50
Henry Brooke	1-22	4.5	-7.00

COURSE RECORD

	Total W-R	Non-Hndcps Hurdles	Chases	Hndcps Hurdles	Chases	NH Flat	Per cent	£1 Level Stake
Kelso	4-12	1-4	0-0	0-3	2-4	1-1	33.3	+2.80
Ayr	4-13	0-3	0-0	4-8	0-1	0-1	30.8	+10.23
Cartmel	3-6	2-3	0-0	1-2	0-1	0-0	50.0	+4.00
Newcastle	2-9	0-5	0-0	0-1	2-3	0-0	22.2	+12.50
Hexham	2-11	1-3	0-1	1-5	0-2	0-0	18.2	+7.50
Perth	2-23	1-5	0-1	0-13	1-4	0-0	8.7	-16.13
Mrket Rsn	1-2	1-2	0-0	0-0	0-0	0-0	50.0	+1.00

	Total W-R						Per cent	£1 Level Stake
Catterick	1-3	0-0	0-1	0-0	1-1	0-1	33.3	+3.50
Haydock	1-3	0-0	0-0	1-3	0-0	0-0	33.3	+8.00
Musselbgh	1-22	1-6	0-0	0-9	0-6	0-1	4.5	-20.56

WINNING HORSES

Horse	Races Run	1st	2nd	3rd	£
The Delray Munky	9	4	0	1	43556
Double Whammy	1	1	0	0	12660
Cool Mix	6	2	2	1	14296
*Rainy City	7	1	2	0	7538
Plus Jamais	5	2	0	0	11242
Heart O Annandale	5	1	0	0	6498
*Vercingetorix	5	1	2	1	4419
So Satisfied	7	1	1	0	4159
*Bedrock	2	1	0	1	4094
River Icon	5	2	2	0	6498
Golden Jeffrey	11	3	1	0	9971
Something Brewing	3	1	0	0	3165
L'Inganno Felice	2	1	0	1	3119
Total winning prize-money					**£131215**
Favourites	**7-19**		**36.8%**		**-0.03**

RUTH JEFFERSON

NORTON, N YORKS

	No. of Hrs	Races Run	1st	2nd	3rd	Unpl	Per cent	£1 Level Stake
NH Flat	1	1	1	0	0	0	100.0	+14.00
Hurdles	18	26	1	2	6	17	3.8	-22.50
Chases	10	14	1	1	4	8	7.1	-11.00
Totals	25	41	3	3	10	25	7.3	-19.50

JOCKEYS

	W-R	Per cent	£1 Level Stake
Brian Hughes	3-22	13.6	-0.50

COURSE RECORD

	Total W-R	Non-Hndcps Hurdles	Chases	Hndcps Hurdles	Chases	NH Flat	Per cent	£1 Level Stake
Ascot	1-2	0-0	1-2	0-0	0-0	0-0	50.0	+1.00
Kelso	1-4	1-1	0-0	0-3	0-0	0-0	25.0	-0.50
Mrket Rsn	1-6	0-2	0-0	0-3	0-0	1-1	16.7	+9.00

WINNING HORSES

Horse	Races Run	1st	2nd	3rd	£
*Waiting Patiently	1	1	0	0	85827
*Cyrus Darius	2	1	0	0	16245
*Northern Soul	1	1	0	0	2274
Total winning prize-money					**£104346**
Favourites	**1-3**		**33.3%**		**0.00**

MALCOLM JEFFERSON

NORTON, N YORKS

	No. of Hrs	Races Run	1st	2nd	3rd	Unpl	Per cent	£1 Level Stake
NH Flat	13	20	2	1	3	14	10.0	-14.00
Hurdles	26	61	9	10	5	37	14.8	-14.38
Chases	18	35	6	8	5	16	17.1	-18.40
Totals	48	116	17	19	13	67	14.7	-46.78
16-17	51	201	40	48	22	91	19.9	-59.38
15-16	45	168	37	32	37	62	22.0	+15.72

BY MONTH

NH Flat	W-R	Per cent	£1 Level Stake	Hurdles	W-R	Per cent	£1 Level Stake
May	0-5	0.0	-5.00	May	0-6	0.0	-6.00
June	0-2	0.0	-2.00	June	1-2	50.0	+3.50
July	1-1	100.0	+2.75	July	0-1	0.0	-1.00
August	0-0	0.0	0.00	August	1-2	50.0	+5.00
September	0-1	0.0	-1.00	September	2-6	33.3	+2.00
October	0-2	0.0	-2.00	October	1-13	7.7	-2.00
November	0-4	0.0	-4.00	November	2-13	15.4	-6.50
December	1-4	25.0	-1.75	December	1-11	9.1	-8.38
January	0-1	0.0	-1.00	January	1-7	14.3	-1.00
February	0-0	0.0	0.00	February	0-0	0.0	0.00
March	0-0	0.0	0.00	March	0-0	0.0	0.00
April	0-0	0.0	0.00	April	0-0	0.0	0.00

Chases	W-R	Per cent	£1 Level Stake	Totals	W-R	Per cent	£1 Level Stake
May	0-4	0.0	-4.00	May	0-15	0.0	-15.00
June	0-1	0.0	-1.00	June	1-5	20.0	+0.50
July	0-1	0.0	-1.00	July	1-3	33.3	+0.75
August	0-0	0.0	0.00	August	1-2	50.0	+5.00
September	1-2	50.0	+2.50	September	3-9	33.3	+3.50
October	0-7	0.0	-7.00	October	1-22	4.5	-11.00
November	3-9	33.3	-0.83	November	5-26	19.2	-11.33
December	0-5	0.0	-5.00	December	2-20	10.0	-15.13
January	2-6	33.3	-2.08	January	3-14	21.4	-4.08
February	0-0	0.0	0.00	February	0-0	0.0	0.00
March	0-0	0.0	0.00	March	0-0	0.0	0.00
April	0-0	0.0	0.00	April	0-0	0.0	0.00

DISTANCE

Hurdles	W-R	Per cent	£1 Level Stake	Chases	W-R	Per cent	£1 Level Stake
2m-2m3f	3-30	10.0	-10.00	2m-2m3f	2-13	15.4	-8.82
2m4f-2m7f	3-26	11.5	-14.88	2m4f-2m7f	3-12	25.0	-4.08
3m+	3-5	60.0	+10.50	3m+	1-10	10.0	-5.50

TYPE OF RACE

Non-Handicaps	W-R	Per cent	£1 Level Stake	Handicaps	W-R	Per cent	£1 Level Stake
Nov Hrdls	2-21	9.5	-16.00	Nov Hrdls	0-1	0.0	-1.00
Hrdls	1-4	25.0	+7.00	Hrdls	6-35	17.1	-4.38
Nov Chs	1-6	16.7	-4.70	Nov Chs	0-3	0.0	-3.00

	W-R	Per cent	£1 Level Stake		W-R	Per cent	£1 Level Stake
Chases	2-5	40.0	-0.58	Chases	2-15	13.3	-7.00
Sell/Claim	0-0	0.0	0.00	Sell/Claim	0-0	0.0	0.00

RACE CLASS

	W-R	Per cent	£1 Level Stake
Class 1	2-6	33.3	-1.58
Class 2	2-11	18.2	-2.38
Class 3	5-23	21.7	-2.63
Class 4	6-54	11.1	-24.20
Class 5	0-6	0.0	-6.00
Class 6	2-16	12.5	-10.00

FIRST TIME OUT

	W-R	Per cent	£1 Level Stake
Bumpers	0-13	0.0	-13.00
Hurdles	0-19	0.0	-19.00
Chases	3-16	18.8	-6.20
Totals	3-48	6.3	-38.20

JOCKEYS

	W-R	Per cent	£1 Level Stake
Brian Hughes	12-81	14.8	-44.27
Jamie Hamilton	5-28	17.9	+4.50

COURSE RECORD

	Total W-R	Non-Hndcps Hurdles	Chases	Hndcps Hurdles	Chases	NH Flat	Per cent	£1 Level Stake
Perth	2-4	0-1	0-1	1-1	1-1	0-0	50.0	+5.50
Southwell	2-11	0-1	0-0	1-7	0-1	1-2	18.2	-1.75
Kelso	2-12	2-6	0-0	0-2	0-2	0-2	16.7	+2.00
Sedgefield	2-14	0-3	0-0	1-6	1-2	0-3	14.3	-6.63
Kempton	1-1	0-0	1-1	0-0	0-0	0-0	100.0	+1.63
Warwick	1-1	0-0	0-0	1-1	0-0	0-0	100.0	+5.00
Carlisle	1-5	0-1	1-1	0-0	0-3	0-0	20.0	-3.20
Aintree	1-5	0-0	0-1	1-2	0-1	0-1	20.0	-2.38
Ayr	1-6	0-1	0-0	0-1	1-2	0-2	16.7	-2.50
Mrket Rsn	1-6	0-2	0-0	1-2	0-1	0-1	16.7	+1.00
Doncaster	1-7	0-1	1-2	0-2	0-1	0-1	14.3	-5.70
Catterick	1-8	0-3	0-1	0-1	0-1	1-2	12.5	-5.75
Wetherby	1-12	1-5	0-1	0-3	0-2	0-1	8.3	-10.00

WINNING HORSES

Horse	Races Run	1st	2nd	3rd	£
Waiting Patiently	2	2	0	0	39865
Black Ivory	3	2	1	0	28613
Cyrus Darius	3	1	0	1	11696
Ballyben	2	1	0	0	8133
Robbing The Prey	2	1	1	0	6657
Sun Cloud	4	2	0	0	11637
Mount Mews	4	1	1	1	4614
Sweet Holly	5	3	0	1	11047
Schiaparannie	4	1	1	1	3574
Temple Man	3	1	0	0	3249
Return Ticket	2	1	0	1	1949
Fingareeta	2	1	1	0	1949
Total winning prize-money					**£132983**
Favourites	8-21		38.1%		-0.77

MRS L J JEFFORD

KENTISBEARE, DEVON

	No. of Hrs	Races Run	1st	2nd	3rd	Unpl	Per cent	£1 Level Stake
NH Flat	0	0	0	0	0	0	0.0	0.00
Hurdles	0	0	0	0	0	0	0.0	0.00
Chases	1	2	1	1	0	0	50.0	+0.88
Totals	1	2	1	1	0	0	50.0	+0.88
15-16	1	1	0	0	0	1	0.0	-1.00

JOCKEYS

	W-R	Per cent	£1 Level Stake
Mrs Jo Supple	1-2	50.0	+0.88

COURSE RECORD

	Total W-R	Non-Hndcps Hurdles	Chases	Hndcps Hurdles	Chases	NH Flat	Per cent	£1 Level Stake
Taunton	1-1	0-0	1-1	0-0	0-0	0-0	100.0	+1.88

WINNING HORSES

Horse	Races Run	1st	2nd	3rd	£
*Master Baker	2	1	1	0	3369
Total winning prize-money					**£3369**
Favourites	1-2		50.0%		0.88

J R JENKINS

ROYSTON, HERTS

	No. of Hrs	Races Run	1st	2nd	3rd	Unpl	Per cent	£1 Level Stake
NH Flat	0	0	0	0	0	0	0.0	0.00
Hurdles	10	24	1	0	4	19	4.2	-7.00
Chases	1	3	0	0	1	2	0.0	-3.00
Totals	10	27	1	0	5	21	3.7	-10.00
16-17	7	39	3	4	5	27	7.7	-18.50
15-16	12	49	3	3	10	33	6.1	-36.00

JOCKEYS

	W-R	Per cent	£1 Level Stake
Jack Quinlan	1-5	20.0	+12.00

COURSE RECORD

	Total W-R	Non-Hndcps Hurdles	Chases	Hndcps Hurdles	Chases	NH Flat	Per cent	£1 Level Stake
Mrket Rsn	1-2	0-0	0-0	1-2	0-0	0-0	50.0	+15.00

WINNING HORSES

Horse	Races Run	1st	2nd	3rd	£
Tiradia	5	1	0	1	3249
Total winning prize-money					**£3249**
Favourites	0-0		0.0%		0.00

LINDA JEWELL
SUTTON VALENCE, KENT

	No. of Hrs	Races Run	1st	2nd	3rd	Unpl	Per cent	£1 Level Stake
NH Flat	4	7	1	0	0	6	14.3	+2.00
Hurdles	9	23	2	3	2	16	8.7	-10.50
Chases	3	10	0	2	0	8	0.0	-10.00
Totals	12	40	3	5	2	30	7.5	-18.50
16-17	12	43	3	7	6	27	7.0	-5.00
15-16	14	55	1	4	8	42	1.8	-46.00

JOCKEYS

	W-R	Per cent	£1 Level Stake
Jack Sherwood	2-14	14.3	-0.50
Tom Cannon	1-9	11.1	-1.00

COURSE RECORD

	Total W-R	Non-Hndcps Hurdles	Chases	Hndcps Hurdles	Chases	NH Flat	Per cent	£1 Level Stake
Fontwell	2-15	0-6	0-0	2-3	0-4	0-2	13.3	-2.50
Plumpton	1-16	0-6	0-0	0-3	0-4	1-3	6.3	-7.00

WINNING HORSES

Horse	Races Run	1st	2nd	3rd	£
Mab Dab	5	1	2	1	3119
Kayflin	3	1	1	0	2599
Madam Anna	2	1	0	0	1625
Total winning prize-money					£7343
Favourites	0-1	0.0%			-1.00

BRETT JOHNSON
EPSOM, SURREY

	No. of Hrs	Races Run	1st	2nd	3rd	Unpl	Per cent	£1 Level Stake
NH Flat	1	1	0	0	0	1	0.0	-1.00
Hurdles	1	5	2	0	2	1	40.0	+8.00
Chases	0	0	0	0	0	0	0.0	0.00
Totals	2	6	2	0	2	2	33.3	+7.00
16-17	1	2	0	0	2	0	0.0	-2.00
15-16	1	1	0	0	0	1	0.0	-1.00

JOCKEYS

	W-R	Per cent	£1 Level Stake
Tom Cannon	2-2	100.0	+11.00

COURSE RECORD

	Total W-R	Non-Hndcps Hurdles	Chases	Hndcps Hurdles	Chases	NH Flat	Per cent	£1 Level Stake
Fontwell	2-2	2-2	0-0	0-0	0-0	0-0	100.0	+11.00

WINNING HORSES

Horse	Races Run	1st	2nd	3rd	£
Jackblack	5	2	0	2	7148
Total winning prize-money					£7148
Favourites	0-0	0.0%			0.00

KENNY JOHNSON
NEWBURN, TYNE & WEAR

	No. of Hrs	Races Run	1st	2nd	3rd	Unpl	Per cent	£1 Level Stake
NH Flat	1	2	0	0	0	2	0.0	-2.00
Hurdles	9	34	0	2	3	29	0.0	-34.00
Chases	10	68	4	5	10	49	5.9	-16.00
Totals	12	104	4	7	13	80	3.8	-52.00
16-17	16	90	2	10	11	67	2.2	-65.00
15-16	13	57	2	5	5	45	3.5	-21.00

JOCKEYS

	W-R	Per cent	£1 Level Stake
Harry Reed	1-3	33.3	+7.00
Henry Brooke	1-4	25.0	0.00
Callum Bewley	1-10	10.0	+5.00
Thomas Dowson	1-25	4.0	-2.00

COURSE RECORD

	Total W-R	Non-Hndcps Hurdles	Chases	Hndcps Hurdles	Chases	NH Flat	Per cent	£1 Level Stake
Hexham	3-20	0-1	0-1	0-3	3-14	0-1	15.0	+22.00
Ayr	1-1	0-0	0-0	0-0	1-1	0-0	100.0	+9.00

WINNING HORSES

Horse	Races Run	1st	2nd	3rd	£
Rosquero	7	1	0	0	4614
Mr Witmore	14	1	1	4	4159
Captain Sharpe	11	1	1	1	3249
Notonebuttwo	14	1	0	2	3249
Total winning prize-money					£15271
Favourites	0-0	0.0%			0.00

SUSAN JOHNSON
MADLEY, H'FORDS

	No. of Hrs	Races Run	1st	2nd	3rd	Unpl	Per cent	£1 Level Stake
NH Flat	0	0	0	0	0	0	0.0	0.00
Hurdles	0	0	0	0	0	0	0.0	0.00
Chases	1	7	3	0	1	2	42.9	+15.50
Totals	1	7	3	0	1	2	42.9	+15.50
16-17	2	15	1	2	5	7	6.7	+11.00
15-16	4	11	0	1	2	8	0.0	-11.00

JOCKEYS

	W-R	Per cent	£1 Level Stake
Charlie Deutsch	2-2	100.0	+12.50
Richard Johnson	1-4	25.0	+4.00

COURSE RECORD

	Total W-R	Non-Hndcps Hurdles	Chases	Hndcps Hurdles	Chases	NH Flat	Per cent	£1 Level Stake
Mrket Rsn	2-2	0-0	0-0	0-0	2-2	0-0	100.0	+13.00
Warwick	1-2	0-0	0-0	0-0	1-2	0-0	50.0	+5.50

WINNING HORSES

Horse	Races Run	1st	2nd	3rd	£
The Last Bridge	7	3	0	1	11696
Total winning prize-money					**£11696**
Favourites	0-1		0.0%		**-1.00**

ALAN JONES

BICKHAM, SOMERSET

	No. of Hrs	Races Run	1st	2nd	3rd	Unpl	Per cent	£1 Level Stake
NH Flat	1	1	0	0	0	1	0.0	-1.00
Hurdles	7	16	0	1	1	14	0.0	-16.00
Chases	4	9	2	2	1	4	22.2	+5.00
Totals	10	26	2	3	2	19	7.7	-12.00
16-17	11	18	6	4	1	7	33.3	+33.00
15-16	14	46	0	8	7	31	0.0	-46.00

JOCKEYS

	W-R	Per cent	£1 Level Stake
Tom O'Brien	2-8	25.0	+6.00

COURSE RECORD

	Total W-R	Non-Hndcps Hurdles	Chases	Hndcps Hurdles	Chases	NH Flat	Per cent	£1 Level Stake
Plumpton	1-1	0-0	0-0	0-0	1-1	0-0	100.0	+3.00
Newbury	1-2	0-0	0-0	0-1	1-1	0-0	50.0	+8.00

WINNING HORSES

Horse	Races Run	1st	2nd	3rd	£
Tiquer	3	1	0	0	12660
Duhallow Lad	7	1	2	1	5122
Total winning prize-money					**£17782**
Favourites	1-3		33.3%		**1.00**

CAROLINE KEEVIL

MOTCOMBE, DORSET

	No. of Hrs	Races Run	1st	2nd	3rd	Unpl	Per cent	£1 Level Stake
NH Flat	0	0	0	0	0	0	0.0	0.00

							Per cent	£1 Level Stake
Hurdles	0	0	0	0	0	0	0.0	0.00
Chases	1	1	1	0	0	0	100.0	+2.50
Totals	1	1	1	0	0	0	100.0	+2.50
16-17	3	12	1	0	0	11	8.3	+1.00
15-16	22	74	5	5	4	60	6.8	-40.77

JOCKEYS

	W-R	Per cent	£1 Level Stake
Mr William Biddick	1-1	100.0	+2.50

COURSE RECORD

	Total W-R	Non-Hndcps Hurdles	Chases	Hndcps Hurdles	Chases	NH Flat	Per cent	£1 Level Stake
Exeter	1-1	0-0	1-1	0-0	0-0	0-0	100.0	+2.50

WINNING HORSES

Horse	Races Run	1st	2nd	3rd	£
*Palmaria	1	1	0	0	2888
Total winning prize-money					**£2888**
Favourites	0-0		0.0%		**0.00**

MARTIN KEIGHLEY

CONDICOTE, GLOUCS

	No. of Hrs	Races Run	1st	2nd	3rd	Unpl	Per cent	£1 Level Stake
NH Flat	17	30	4	2	3	21	13.3	-11.00
Hurdles	35	121	13	10	12	86	10.7	-36.25
Chases	8	26	4	3	3	16	15.4	+4.25
Totals	43	177	21	15	18	123	11.9	-43.00
16-17	43	177	16	25	21	114	9.0	-72.83
15-16	42	179	25	11	19	124	14.0	+15.04

BY MONTH

NH Flat	W-R	Per cent	£1 Level Stake	Hurdles	W-R	Per cent	£1 Level Stake
May	0-3	0.0	-3.00	May	2-14	14.3	-5.50
June	1-5	20.0	0.00	June	1-9	11.1	-5.50
July	2-4	50.0	+5.50	July	0-7	0.0	-7.00
August	0-0	0.0	0.00	August	0-7	0.0	-7.00
September	0-1	0.0	-1.00	September	1-6	16.7	-2.25
October	1-3	33.3	+1.50	October	3-13	23.1	+30.00
November	0-2	0.0	-2.00	November	1-13	7.7	-9.50
December	0-5	0.0	-5.00	December	2-11	18.2	-1.50
January	0-3	0.0	-3.00	January	0-13	0.0	-13.00
February	0-3	0.0	-3.00	February	3-10	30.0	+3.00
March	0-0	0.0	0.00	March	0-9	0.0	-9.00
April	0-1	0.0	-1.00	April	0-9	0.0	-9.00

Chases	W-R	Per cent	£1 Level Stake	Totals	W-R	Per cent	£1 Level Stake
May	0-2	0.0	-2.00	May	2-19	10.5	-10.50
June	0-0	0.0	0.00	June	2-14	14.3	-5.50
July	1-1	100.0	+5.00	July	3-12	25.0	+3.50
August	0-3	0.0	-3.00	August	0-10	0.0	-10.00
September	0-2	0.0	-2.00	September	1-9	11.1	-5.25

October	0-3	0.0	-3.00	October	4-19	21.1	+28.50
November	1-3	33.3	+12.00	November	2-18	11.1	+0.50
December	1-6	16.7	0.00	December	3-22	13.6	-6.50
January	1-4	25.0	-0.75	January	1-20	5.0	-16.75
February	0-1	0.0	-1.00	February	3-14	21.4	-1.00
March	0-1	0.0	-1.00	March	0-10	0.0	-10.00
April	0-0	0.0	0.00	April	0-10	0.0	-10.00

DISTANCE

Hurdles	W-R	Per cent	£1 Level Stake	Chases	W-R	Per cent	£1 Level Stake
2m-2m3f	5-54	9.3	-4.00	2m-2m3f	1-8	12.5	-4.75
2m4f-2m7f	6-52	11.5	-27.25	2m4f-2m7f	3-16	18.8	+11.00
3m+	2-14	14.3	-4.00	3m+	0-2	0.0	-2.00

TYPE OF RACE

Non-Handicaps	W-R	Per cent	£1 Level Stake	Handicaps	W-R	Per cent	£1 Level Stake
Nov Hrdls	4-26	15.4	-11.75	Nov Hrdls	0-6	0.0	-6.00
Hrdls	1-16	6.3	-12.50	Hrdls	8-70	11.4	-3.00
Nov Chs	0-1	0.0	-1.00	Nov Chs	1-4	25.0	+11.00
Chases	0-0	0.0	0.00	Chases	2-18	11.1	-6.00
Sell/Claim	0-2	0.0	-2.00	Sell/Claim	0-0	0.0	0.00

RACE CLASS / FIRST TIME OUT

Class	W-R	Per cent	£1 Level Stake		W-R	Per cent	£1 Level Stake
Class 1	0-5	0.0	-5.00	Bumpers	2-17	11.8	-7.50
Class 2	1-11	9.1	-9.00	Hurdles	2-23	8.7	-14.50
Class 3	4-32	12.5	+14.25	Chases	0-3	0.0	-3.00
Class 4	10-69	14.5	-12.75				
Class 5	4-44	9.1	-24.00	Totals	4-43	9.3	-25.00
Class 6	2-16	12.5	-6.50				

JOCKEYS

	W-R	Per cent	£1 Level Stake
Harry Stock	9-55	16.4	+14.50
Andrew Tinkler	6-62	9.7	-30.75
Richard Johnson	3-15	20.0	-2.00
Aidan Coleman	2-12	16.7	-6.75
Leighton Aspell	1-1	100.0	+14.00

COURSE RECORD

	Total W-R	Non-Hndcps Hurdles	Chases	Hndcps Hurdles	Chases	NH Flat	Per cent	£1 Level Stake
Towcester	4-14	2-8	0-0	1-3	0-1	1-2	28.6	+2.00
Southwell	3-11	0-0	0-0	2-6	1-2	0-3	27.3	+5.50
Worcester	3-24	0-1	0-0	1-13	1-7	1-3	12.5	-8.00
Catterick	2-6	0-0	0-0	1-1	1-4	0-1	33.3	+2.25
Uttoxeter	2-16	1-4	0-1	0-6	0-1	1-4	12.5	-8.25
Cheltenham	2-22	1-6	0-0	1-11	0-3	0-2	9.1	+14.00
Doncaster	1-3	0-1	0-0	1-2	0-0	0-0	33.3	+2.00
Ffos Las	1-3	1-1	0-0	0-1	0-0	0-1	33.3	+1.50
Kempton	1-5	0-0	0-0	1-4	0-0	0-0	20.0	-1.00
Lingfield	1-6	0-2	0-0	0-1	1-3	0-0	16.7	+9.00
Stratford	1-13	0-3	0-0	0-6	0-1	1-3	7.7	-8.00

WINNING HORSES

Horse	Races Run	1st	2nd	3rd	£
Brillare Momento	7	2	1	0	18750
Somewhere To Be	6	2	0	0	9357
Bobble Emerald	4	2	0	1	9830
Buckle Street	9	2	1	2	9326
Spice Girl	8	5	0	0	14556
Ballymountain Boy	5	2	0	1	8963
Weyburn	5	1	0	2	3899
Fairmount	5	1	0	1	3899
Viking Mistress	7	2	2	0	6498
Thady Quil	9	1	0	0	3119
Raving Bonkers	2	1	0	0	2599
Total winning prize-money					£90796
Favourites	6-11		54.5%		11.50

DAVID KEMP
THETFORD, NORFOLK

	No. of Hrs	Races Run	1st	2nd	3rd	Unpl	Per cent	£1 Level Stake
NH Flat	0	0	0	0	0	0	0.0	0.00
Hurdles	0	0	0	0	0	0	0.0	0.00
Chases	3	7	3	0	0	4	42.9	+2.16
Totals	3	7	3	0	0	4	42.9	+2.16
16-17	3	6	3	0	1	2	50.0	+18.33
15-16	6	7	1	3	0	3	14.3	+10.00

JOCKEYS

	W-R	Per cent	£1 Level Stake
Mr Samuel Davies-Thomas	2-3	66.7	+2.41
Mr Shane Roche	1-2	50.0	+1.75

COURSE RECORD

	Total W-R	Non-Hndcps Hurdles	Chases	Hndcps Hurdles	Chases	NH Flat	Per cent	£1 Level Stake
Fontwell	1-1	0-0	1-1	0-0	0-0	0-0	100.0	+0.91
Fakenham	1-2	0-0	1-2	0-0	0-0	0-0	50.0	+1.50
Stratford	1-2	0-0	0-1	0-0	1-1	0-0	50.0	+1.75

WINNING HORSES

Horse	Races Run	1st	2nd	3rd	£
Curraigflemens	4	2	0	0	6239
Master Workman	2	1	0	0	2184
Total winning prize-money					£8423
Favourites	2-2		100.0%		3.66

NICK KENT
BRIGG, LINCS

	No. of Hrs	Races Run	1st	2nd	3rd	Unpl	Per cent	£1 Level Stake
NH Flat	4	4	0	0	0	4	0.0	-4.00

Hurdles	13	35	0	3	2	30	0.0	-35.00
Chases	4	8	1	2	1	4	12.5	+7.00
Totals	15	47	1	5	3	38	2.1	-32.00
16-17	15	45	2	6	6	31	4.4	-31.50
15-16	19	70	4	6	12	47	5.7	-49.38

JOCKEYS

	W-R	Per cent	£1 Level Stake
Adam Wedge	1-3	33.3	+12.00

COURSE RECORD

	Total W-R	Non-Hndcps Hurdles	Chases	Hndcps Hurdles	Chases	NH Flat	Per cent	£1 Level Stake
Wetherby	1-3	0-1	0-0	0-1	1-1	0-0	33.3	+12.00

WINNING HORSES

Horse	Races Run	1st	2nd	3rd	£
Gonalston Cloud	5	1	1	0	7408
Total winning prize-money					**£7408**
Favourites	0-0		0.0%		0.00

LEONARD KERR

IRVINE, NORTH AYRSHIRE

	No. of Hrs	Races Run	1st	2nd	3rd	Unpl	Per cent	£1 Level Stake
NH Flat	0	0	0	0	0	0	0.0	0.00
Hurdles	2	2	0	0	0	2	0.0	-2.00
Chases	3	15	2	1	1	11	13.3	+36.00
Totals	3	17	2	1	1	13	11.8	+34.00
16-17	3	11	1	0	1	9	9.1	-3.50
15-16	2	8	0	0	0	8	0.0	-8.00

JOCKEYS

	W-R	Per cent	£1 Level Stake
Jonathon Bewley	1-1	100.0	+40.00
Danny Cook	1-4	25.0	+6.00

COURSE RECORD

	Total W-R	Non-Hndcps Hurdles	Chases	Hndcps Hurdles	Chases	NH Flat	Per cent	£1 Level Stake
Hexham	1-2	0-0	0-1	0-0	1-1	0-0	50.0	+39.00
Kelso	1-4	0-0	0-2	0-0	1-2	0-0	25.0	+6.00

WINNING HORSES

Horse	Races Run	1st	2nd	3rd	£
Chicago Outfit	5	1	0	0	4809
Havana Jack	9	1	1	1	3899
Total winning prize-money					**£8708**
Favourites	0-1		0.0%		-1.00

KIERAN PRICE

YNYSYBWLN, PONTYPRIDD

	No. of Hrs	Races Run	1st	2nd	3rd	Unpl	Per cent	£1 Level Stake
NH Flat	0	0	0	0	0	0	0.0	0.00
Hurdles	0	0	0	0	0	0	0.0	0.00
Chases	1	2	1	0	0	1	50.0	+0.25
Totals	1	2	1	0	0	1	50.0	+0.25
16-17	2	2	0	0	1	1	0.0	-2.00

JOCKEYS

	W-R	Per cent	£1 Level Stake
Mr Byron Moorcroft	1-2	50.0	+0.25

COURSE RECORD

	Total W-R	Non-Hndcps Hurdles	Chases	Hndcps Hurdles	Chases	NH Flat	Per cent	£1 Level Stake
Fontwell	1-1	0-0	1-1	0-0	0-0	0-0	100.0	+1.25

WINNING HORSES

Horse	Races Run	1st	2nd	3rd	£
*Spencer Moon	2	1	0	0	1248
Total winning prize-money					**£1248**
Favourites	1-1		100.0%		1.25

NEIL KING

BARBURY CASTLE, WILTS

	No. of Hrs	Races Run	1st	2nd	3rd	Unpl	Per cent	£1 Level Stake
NH Flat	6	14	0	0	4	10	0.0	-14.00
Hurdles	27	110	11	18	14	67	10.0	-24.63
Chases	11	56	7	9	9	31	12.5	-13.25
Totals	36	180	18	27	27	108	10.0	-51.88
16-17	44	178	16	34	17	111	9.0	-90.76
15-16	44	214	33	30	30	121	15.4	-40.19

BY MONTH

NH Flat	W-R	Per cent	£1 Level Stake	Hurdles	W-R	Per cent	£1 Level Stake
May	0-1	0.0	-1.00	May	1-12	8.3	-2.00
June	0-0	0.0	0.00	June	1-5	20.0	-1.00
July	0-0	0.0	0.00	July	0-1	0.0	-1.00
August	0-0	0.0	0.00	August	1-6	16.7	-0.50
September	0-0	0.0	0.00	September	0-10	0.0	-10.00
October	0-1	0.0	-1.00	October	2-7	28.6	+3.50
November	0-3	0.0	-3.00	November	3-20	15.0	+11.25
December	0-2	0.0	-2.00	December	1-11	9.1	-4.50
January	0-1	0.0	-1.00	January	0-9	0.0	-9.00
February	0-2	0.0	-2.00	February	0-5	0.0	-5.00
March	0-0	0.0	0.00	March	1-9	11.1	-6.38
April	0-4	0.0	-4.00	April	1-15	6.7	0.00
Chases	W-R	Per cent	£1 Level Stake	**Totals**	W-R	Per cent	£1 Level Stake

	Total W-R	Non-Hndcps Hurdles	Chases	Hndcps Hurdles	Chases	NH Flat	Per cent	£1 Level Stake
Hereford	1-4	0-0	0-0	1-3	0-1	0-0	25.0	-1.38
Ffos Las	1-4	0-0	0-0	1-1	0-2	0-1	25.0	+6.00
Kempton	1-5	0-1	0-0	1-2	0-0	0-2	20.0	+10.00
Warwick	1-11	0-2	0-0	0-4	1-4	0-1	9.1	+2.00
Huntingdon	1-15	1-3	0-0	0-8	0-3	0-1	6.7	-11.50
Uttoxeter	1-16	0-1	0-0	0-10	1-5	0-0	6.3	-12.00

	W-R				W-R		
May	0-3	0.0	-3.00	May	1-16	6.3	-6.00
June	0-0	0.0	0.00	June	1-5	20.0	-1.00
July	0-0	0.0	0.00	July	0-1	0.0	-1.00
August	0-0	0.0	0.00	August	1-6	16.7	-0.50
September	0-2	0.0	-2.00	September	0-12	0.0	-12.00
October	0-2	0.0	-2.00	October	2-10	20.0	+0.50
November	1-6	16.7	-3.25	November	4-29	13.8	+5.00
December	0-7	0.0	-7.00	December	1-20	5.0	-13.50
January	3-10	30.0	+16.00	January	3-20	15.0	+6.00
February	1-9	11.1	-7.50	February	1-16	6.3	-14.50
March	0-6	0.0	-6.00	March	1-15	6.7	-12.38
April	2-11	18.2	+1.50	April	3-30	10.0	-2.50

DISTANCE

Hurdles	W-R	Per cent	£1 Level Stake	Chases	W-R	Per cent	£1 Level Stake
2m-2m3f	8-47	17.0	+22.25	2m-2m3f	1-4	25.0	+0.50
2m4f-2m7f	2-41	4.9	-31.88	2m4f-2m7f	2-22	9.1	-11.50
3m+	1-22	4.5	-15.00	3m+	4-30	13.3	-2.25

TYPE OF RACE

Non-Handicaps	W-R	Per cent	£1 Level Stake	Handicaps	W-R	Per cent	£1 Level Stake
Nov Hrdls	2-14	14.3	-6.50	Nov Hrdls	0-7	0.0	-7.00
Hrdls	2-13	15.4	-2.75	Hrdls	7-73	9.6	-5.38
Nov Chs	2-2	100.0	+2.25	Nov Chs	1-2	50.0	+2.00
Chases	0-0	0.0	0.00	Chases	4-44	9.1	-9.50
Sell/Claim	0-3	0.0	-3.00	Sell/Claim	0-0	0.0	0.00

RACE CLASS / FIRST TIME OUT

	W-R	Per cent	£1 Level Stake		W-R	Per cent	£1 Level Stake
Class 1	2-11	18.2	+5.25	Bumpers	0-6	0.0	-6.00
Class 2	0-11	0.0	-11.00	Hurdles	2-23	8.7	-6.00
Class 3	4-47	8.5	-27.25	Chases	1-7	14.3	-4.25
Class 4	10-84	11.9	-3.50				
Class 5	2-22	9.1	-10.38	Totals	3-36	8.3	-16.25
Class 6	0-5	0.0	-5.00				

JOCKEYS

	W-R	Per cent	£1 Level Stake
Trevor Whelan	7-98	7.1	-50.00
Harry Teal	5-51	9.8	-27.38
Richard Condon	2-3	66.7	+6.50
Bryony Frost	2-5	40.0	+23.00
Mr Jack Andrews	1-5	20.0	+4.00
Jamie Moore	1-6	16.7	+4.00

COURSE RECORD

	Total W-R	Non-Hndcps Hurdles	Chases	Hndcps Hurdles	Chases	NH Flat	Per cent	£1 Level Stake
Fakenham	5-27	1-3	1-1	2-11	1-10	0-2	18.5	+19.25
Stratford	3-9	1-2	0-0	1-3	1-4	0-0	33.3	+5.00
Plumpton	3-15	0-1	1-1	1-6	1-7	0-0	20.0	+1.50
Ascot	1-2	1-2	0-0	0-0	0-0	0-0	50.0	+1.25

WINNING HORSES

Horse	Races Run	1st	2nd	3rd	£
Lil Rockerfeller	7	1	2	1	56950
Milansbar	7	1	1	1	42713
Princeton Royale	6	1	3	1	9748
Holbrook Park	8	3	1	0	17710
Oh Land Abloom	6	1	1	0	6498
Comanche Chieftain	7	3	2	1	13971
*Cubswin	6	1	2	1	5198
Big Meadow	9	1	1	1	4726
Little Windmill	12	1	2	3	4617
Mamoo	8	1	1	2	4549
*Dizzey Heights	7	1	0	0	4549
*Sackett	7	1	2	2	4159
Regulation	5	1	0	0	4094
Canyon City	5	1	0	2	3899
Total winning prize-money					£183381
Favourites	2-14		14.3%		-9.88

ALAN KING
BARBURY CASTLE, WILTS

	No. of Hrs	Races Run	1st	2nd	3rd	Unpl	Per cent	£1 Level Stake
NH Flat	28	45	7	8	7	23	15.6	-3.33
Hurdles	88	274	35	49	47	142	12.8	-126.57
Chases	22	66	15	10	16	25	22.7	-4.97
Totals	124	385	57	67	70	190	14.8	-134.87
16-17	127	485	103	90	77	215	21.2	-67.25
15-16	122	401	68	59	53	221	17.0	-118.54

BY MONTH

NH Flat	W-R	Per cent	£1 Level Stake	Hurdles	W-R	Per cent	£1 Level Stake
May	4-4	100.0	+15.18	May	5-19	26.3	+1.97
June	0-0	0.0	0.00	June	1-7	14.3	-5.67
July	0-0	0.0	0.00	July	1-3	33.3	+6.00
August	0-0	0.0	0.00	August	1-4	25.0	+3.00
September	0-0	0.0	0.00	September	3-8	37.5	+6.75
October	0-5	0.0	-5.00	October	2-27	7.4	-17.27
November	0-5	0.0	-5.00	November	4-51	7.8	-24.63
December	1-5	20.0	+10.00	December	4-41	9.8	-29.09
January	1-4	25.0	-0.50	January	3-22	13.6	-17.49
February	1-7	14.3	-3.00	February	7-34	20.6	-1.87
March	0-6	0.0	-6.00	March	2-28	7.1	-24.50
April	0-9	0.0	-9.00	April	2-30	6.7	-23.77

Chases	W-R	Per cent	£1 Level Stake	Totals	W-R	Per cent	£1 Level Stake
May	2-4	50.0	+2.50	May	11-27	40.7	+19.65
June	0-3	0.0	-3.00	June	1-10	10.0	-8.67
July	0-3	0.0	-3.00	July	1-6	16.7	+3.00
August	2-2	100.0	+4.50	August	3-6	50.0	+7.50
September	0-1	0.0	-1.00	September	3-9	33.3	+5.75
October	4-15	26.7	+6.12	October	6-47	12.8	-16.15
November	2-12	16.7	-7.69	November	6-68	8.8	-37.32
December	2-9	22.2	+7.50	December	7-55	12.7	-11.59
January	2-5	40.0	-0.63	January	6-31	19.4	-18.62
February	1-5	20.0	-3.27	February	9-46	19.6	-8.14
March	0-2	0.0	-2.00	March	2-36	5.6	-32.50
April	0-5	0.0	-5.00	April	2-44	4.5	-37.77

DISTANCE

Hurdles	W-R	Per cent	£1 Level Stake	Chases	W-R	Per cent	£1 Level Stake
2m-2m3f	24-156	15.4	-65.44	2m-2m3f	7-22	31.8	+1.68
2m4f-2m7f	9-82	11.0	-38.96	2m4f-2m7f	5-25	20.0	+1.88
3m+	2-35	5.7	-21.17	3m+	3-19	15.8	-8.52

TYPE OF RACE

Non-Handicaps	W-R	Per cent	£1 Level Stake	Handicaps	W-R	Per cent	£1 Level Stake
Nov Hrdls	14-76	18.4	-40.83	Nov Hrdls	0-5	0.0	-5.00
Hrdls	9-65	13.8	-37.47	Hrdls	11-127	8.7	-44.00
Nov Chs	8-23	34.8	+4.28	Nov Chs	2-3	66.7	+3.50
Chases	1-5	20.0	-1.75	Chases	3-25	12.0	-5.50
Sell/Claim	0-0	0.0	0.00	Sell/Claim	0-0	0.0	0.00

RACE CLASS

	W-R	Per cent	£1 Level Stake
Class 1	9-67	13.4	-8.47
Class 2	6-60	10.0	-17.38
Class 3	12-70	17.1	-29.02
Class 4	23-147	15.6	-68.55
Class 5	3-29	10.3	-18.63
Class 6	4-12	33.3	+7.18

FIRST TIME OUT

	W-R	Per cent	£1 Level Stake
Bumpers	6-28	21.4	+9.68
Hurdles	8-78	10.3	-41.91
Chases	3-18	16.7	-2.38
Totals	17-124	13.7	-34.61

JOCKEYS

	W-R	Per cent	£1 Level Stake
Wayne Hutchinson	37-241	15.4	-76.90
Tom Bellamy	5-24	20.8	+1.43
Tom Cannon	4-50	8.0	-32.52
Daryl Jacob	3-6	50.0	+8.40
Barry Geraghty	3-14	21.4	-8.11
Noel Fehily	2-5	40.0	-1.66
Kevin Dowling	2-19	10.5	-4.00
A P Heskin	1-6	16.7	-1.50

COURSE RECORD

	Total W-R	Non-Hndcps Hurdles	Chases	Hndcps Hurdles	Chases	NH Flat	Per cent	£1 Level Stake
Warwick	9-34	4-14	2-2	0-8	1-2	2-8	26.5	-11.40
Fontwell	5-11	4-8	0-1	0-1	0-0	1-1	45.5	+4.57
Mrket Rsn	5-15	1-6	1-1	1-3	1-3	1-2	33.3	+16.50
Kempton	5-41	4-17	0-5	0-12	1-4	0-3	12.2	-30.43
Stratford	3-8	2-4	0-0	0-3	1-1	0-0	37.5	-1.47
Doncaster	3-21	1-8	2-2	0-5	0-4	0-2	14.3	-15.15
Newbury	3-26	1-7	0-2	1-10	1-3	0-4	11.5	-7.59
Plumpton	2-9	2-5	0-0	0-3	0-1	0-0	22.2	-1.38
Bangor	2-12	1-4	0-2	1-3	0-0	0-3	16.7	-2.00
Sandown	2-14	0-2	1-2	1-10	0-0	0-0	14.3	+3.00
Ascot	2-16	1-6	0-1	1-7	0-1	0-1	12.5	-7.27
Huntingdon	2-21	0-7	0-2	1-6	0-3	1-3	9.5	-13.88
Cheltenham	2-23	0-5	1-2	1-13	0-1	0-2	8.7	-9.13
Haydock	1-6	0-1	0-0	1-5	0-0	0-0	16.7	+5.00
Uttoxeter	1-6	1-4	0-0	0-1	0-1	0-0	16.7	-4.86
Southwell	1-7	1-2	0-0	0-2	0-3	0-0	14.3	-5.17
Towcester	1-7	0-3	0-0	1-1	0-0	0-3	14.3	-1.00
Wincanton	1-8	1-4	0-0	0-4	0-0	0-0	12.5	-2.00
Ludlow	1-9	0-3	0-0	0-3	0-1	1-2	11.1	+6.00
Worcester	1-9	0-2	0-1	1-3	0-0	0-0	11.1	-3.00
Aintree	1-10	0-4	0-0	0-3	1-1	0-2	10.0	+3.00
Ayr	1-12	0-1	0-1	1-6	0-3	0-1	8.3	-7.50
Taunton	1-12	0-4	0-0	0-5	0-0	1-3	8.3	-8.50
Exeter	1-13	0-4	1-2	0-4	0-2	0-1	7.7	-11.71
Chepstow	1-14	0-3	1-1	0-7	0-1	0-2	7.1	-8.50

WINNING HORSES

Horse	Races Run	1st	2nd	3rd	£
Elgin	6	3	0	0	125451
Smad Place	3	1	0	0	39389
Sceau Royal	5	4	1	0	64325
Yanworth	5	2	1	0	27640
Mia's Storm	5	3	0	0	42585
*Redicean	4	3	0	0	33756
Azzerti	6	1	1	1	15640
Talkischeap	5	3	0	0	20310
The Tourard Man	4	1	0	0	11696
Dino Velvet	5	1	0	0	10007
City Dreamer	8	2	3	1	12996
Midnight Cowboy	6	3	0	2	20542
Awesome Rosie	4	1	0	1	9384
Nayati	3	2	0	0	12447
Bastien	5	1	0	1	6498
Dingo Dollar	5	2	1	0	10992
Good Man Pat	7	2	2	1	10332
Mille Nautique	4	1	1	1	5198
Lord Huntingdon	5	1	0	1	4874
Harefield	5	1	1	0	4549
*Doctor Bartolo	3	1	2	0	4419
Chosen Path	5	2	0	1	7733
Canelo	6	2	2	0	8187
*Lisp	5	2	1	1	7343

Inn The Bull	5	1	0	2	3899
Herewego Herewego	3	1	2	0	3899
Passmore	2	1	0	1	3899
Harambe	3	1	1	1	3899
Zipple Back	2	2	0	0	6628
Smith's Bay	2	1	0	0	3217
Midnightreferendum	3	1	1	1	2599
Paddy Boss	1	1	0	0	1949
Potterman	4	1	1	2	1819
Second Time Around	5	1	0	0	1560
Canford Chimes	1	1	0	0	1560
Total winning prize-money					**£551221**
Favourites	29-87		33.3%		-25.11

PAUL KING

CHIPPING CAMPDEN, GLOUCS

	No. of Hrs	Races Run	1st	2nd	3rd	Unpl	Per cent	£1 Level Stake
NH Flat	0	0	0	0	0	0	0.0	0.00
Hurdles	0	0	0	0	0	0	0.0	0.00
Chases	1	1	1	0	0	0	100.0	+25.00
Totals	1	1	1	0	0	0	100.0	+25.00

JOCKEYS

	W-R	Per cent	£1 Level Stake
Miss Lilly Pinchin	1-1	100.0	+25.00

COURSE RECORD

	Total W-R	Non-Hndcps Hurdles	Chases	Hndcps Hurdles	Chases	NH Flat	Per cent	£1 Level Stake
Cheltenham	1-1	0-0	1-1	0-0	0-0	0-0	100.0	+25.00

WINNING HORSES

Horse	Races Run	1st	2nd	3rd	£
Knockaderry Flyer	1	1	0	0	3743
Total winning prize-money					**£3743**
Favourites	0-0		0.0%		0.00

PHILIP KIRBY

EAST APPLETON, N YORKS

	No. of Hrs	Races Run	1st	2nd	3rd	Unpl	Per cent	£1 Level Stake
NH Flat	12	18	1	0	1	16	5.6	-7.00
Hurdles	38	159	16	17	19	107	10.1	-63.67
Chases	7	16	6	1	2	7	37.5	+11.67
Totals	50	193	23	18	22	130	11.9	-59.00
16-17	40	173	21	21	16	115	12.1	-33.13
15-16	38	134	19	19	14	82	14.2	-5.62

BY MONTH

NH Flat	W-R	Per cent	£1 Level Stake	Hurdles	W-R	Per cent	£1 Level Stake
May	0-1	0.0	-1.00	May	0-1	0.0	-1.00
June	0-3	0.0	-3.00	June	0-3	0.0	-3.00
July	0-1	0.0	-1.00	July	0-3	0.0	-3.00
August	0-0	0.0	0.00	August	1-7	14.3	-1.50
September	0-0	0.0	0.00	September	0-6	0.0	-6.00
October	1-3	33.3	+8.00	October	1-18	5.6	-8.00
November	0-2	0.0	-2.00	November	2-31	6.5	-19.00
December	0-1	0.0	-1.00	December	2-25	8.0	-8.50
January	0-4	0.0	-4.00	January	2-16	12.5	-5.75
February	0-0	0.0	0.00	February	1-11	9.1	0.00
March	0-2	0.0	-2.00	March	5-21	23.8	+2.08
April	0-1	0.0	-1.00	April	2-17	11.8	-10.00

Chases	W-R	Per cent	£1 Level Stake	Totals	W-R	Per cent	£1 Level Stake
May	0-2	0.0	-2.00	May	0-4	0.0	-4.00
June	0-0	0.0	0.00	June	0-6	0.0	-6.00
July	0-0	0.0	0.00	July	0-4	0.0	-4.00
August	0-0	0.0	0.00	August	1-7	14.3	-1.50
September	0-0	0.0	0.00	September	0-6	0.0	-6.00
October	2-2	100.0	+10.50	October	4-23	17.4	+10.50
November	1-4	25.0	+1.00	November	3-37	8.1	-20.00
December	0-0	0.0	0.00	December	2-26	7.7	-9.50
January	0-0	0.0	0.00	January	2-20	10.0	-9.75
February	1-3	33.3	-1.33	February	2-14	14.3	-1.33
March	2-4	50.0	+4.50	March	7-27	25.9	+4.58
April	0-1	0.0	-1.00	April	2-19	10.5	-12.00

DISTANCE

Hurdles	W-R	Per cent	£1 Level Stake	Chases	W-R	Per cent	£1 Level Stake
2m-2m3f	5-70	7.1	-39.42	2m-2m3f	2-3	66.7	+3.67
2m4f-2m7f	7-63	11.1	-20.50	2m4f-2m7f	1-2	50.0	+1.50
3m+	4-26	15.4	-3.75	3m+	3-11	27.3	+6.50

TYPE OF RACE

Non-Handicaps	W-R	Per cent	£1 Level Stake	Handicaps	W-R	Per cent	£1 Level Stake
Nov Hrdls	4-33	12.1	-2.50	Nov Hrdls	0-6	0.0	-6.00
Hrdls	0-16	0.0	-16.00	Hrdls	10-96	10.4	-38.42
Nov Chs	2-3	66.7	+3.67	Nov Chs	0-1	0.0	-1.00
Chases	0-1	0.0	-1.00	Chases	4-9	44.4	+12.00
Sell/Claim	2-6	33.3	+1.25	Sell/Claim	0-2	0.0	-2.00

RACE CLASS

	W-R	Per cent	£1 Level Stake
Class 1	1-5	20.0	0.00
Class 2	1-14	7.1	-12.33
Class 3	5-33	15.2	-2.75
Class 4	14-96	14.6	-14.92
Class 5	1-33	3.0	-28.00
Class 6	1-12	8.3	-1.00

FIRST TIME OUT

	W-R	Per cent	£1 Level Stake
Bumpers	1-12	8.3	-1.00
Hurdles	3-33	9.1	-14.17
Chases	2-5	40.0	+7.50
Totals	6-50	12.0	-7.67

JOCKEYS

	W-R	Per cent	£1 Level Stake
Adam Nicol	12-83	14.5	-12.08
Thomas Dowson	9-84	10.7	-35.92
James Bowen	1-2	50.0	+8.00
Nathan Moscrop	1-14	7.1	-9.00

COURSE RECORD

	Total W-R	Non-Hndcps Hurdles	Chases	Hndcps Hurdles	Chases	NH Flat	Per cent	£1 Level Stake
Wetherby	6-41	3-17	0-0	2-18	1-1	0-5	14.6	-9.25
Newcastle	4-8	0-3	1-1	3-4	0-0	0-0	50.0	+4.42
Catterick	2-10	1-5	0-0	1-4	0-1	0-0	20.0	+3.50
Carlisle	2-11	0-1	0-0	1-7	1-2	0-1	18.2	+1.50
Hexham	2-11	0-5	0-0	0-4	2-2	0-0	18.2	-1.50
Sedgefield	2-17	1-7	0-0	1-9	0-1	0-0	11.8	-7.17
Bangor	1-2	0-1	1-1	0-0	0-0	0-0	50.0	+3.00
Haydock	1-7	0-1	0-0	1-4	0-2	0-0	14.3	+0.50
Southwell	1-9	1-2	0-0	0-5	0-0	0-2	11.1	+1.00
Uttoxeter	1-10	0-1	0-0	1-7	0-1	0-1	10.0	+1.00
Ayr	1-16	0-3	0-0	0-9	0-1	1-3	6.3	-5.00

WINNING HORSES

Horse	Races Run	1st	2nd	3rd	£
Lady Buttons	4	2	1	0	25948
Courtown Oscar	2	1	1	0	8123
Skipthescales	9	3	0	3	15465
Kilcullen Flem	4	2	0	1	7148
Sakhee's City	7	2	1	0	12996
Top Ville Ben	8	1	1	1	6498
Eastview Boy	2	2	0	0	10202
Allmyown	8	1	0	2	4809
Shine Baby Shine	5	1	0	1	4484
Transient Bay	5	1	0	0	4094
*Asum	2	1	1	0	3574
Wemyss Point	3	1	0	1	3574
Nemean Lion	7	2	1	0	6823
Rock Of Leon	7	1	2	1	3509
Little Bruce	7	1	0	2	3249
Hangard	6	1	0	1	1689
Total winning prize-money					**£122185**
Favourites	2-11	18.2%			-7.08

STUART KITTOW

BLACKBOROUGH, DEVON

	No. of Hrs	Races Run	1st	2nd	3rd	Unpl	Per cent	£1 Level Stake
NH Flat	3	5	3	0	1	1	60.0	+18.83
Hurdles	5	27	4	1	3	19	14.8	+10.50
Chases	1	2	0	0	0	2	0.0	-2.00
Totals	**7**	**34**	**7**	**1**	**4**	**22**	**20.6**	**+27.33**
16-17	*11*	*29*	*2*	*4*	*6*	*17*	*6.9*	*-13.50*

| 15-16 | 7 | 21 | 2 | 6 | 2 | 11 | 9.5 | -13.00 |

JOCKEYS

	W-R	Per cent	£1 Level Stake
Tom Scudamore	3-7	42.9	+26.83
Alexander Thorne	2-3	66.7	+16.00
Richard Johnson	1-1	100.0	+4.00
Nick Scholfield	1-10	10.0	-6.50

COURSE RECORD

	Total W-R	Non-Hndcps Hurdles	Chases	Hndcps Hurdles	Chases	NH Flat	Per cent	£1 Level Stake
Nton Abbot	4-10	0-2	0-0	2-5	0-0	2-3	40.0	+30.50
Taunton	2-4	0-0	0-0	2-4	0-0	0-0	50.0	+15.00
Fontwell	1-2	0-0	0-0	0-0	0-1	1-1	50.0	-0.17

WINNING HORSES

Horse	Races Run	1st	2nd	3rd	£
Our Folly	6	1	0	0	4711
Midnight Gypsy	9	2	0	2	9097
Pengo's Boy	7	1	1	1	3899
King Vince	2	2	0	0	3184
Rosie Lea	2	1	0	0	1625
Total winning prize-money					**£22516**
Favourites	2-5	40.0%			0.83

TOM LACEY

LEDBURY, H'FORDS

	No. of Hrs	Races Run	1st	2nd	3rd	Unpl	Per cent	£1 Level Stake
NH Flat	20	31	6	5	2	18	19.4	+10.25
Hurdles	25	102	23	16	11	52	22.5	+53.72
Chases	7	25	10	3	5	7	40.0	+15.82
Totals	**41**	**158**	**39**	**24**	**18**	**77**	**24.7**	**+79.79**
16-17	*34*	*100*	*20*	*4*	*19*	*57*	*20.0*	*+74.32*
15-16	*27*	*82*	*9*	*13*	*8*	*52*	*11.0*	*-25.00*

BY MONTH

NH Flat	W-R	Per cent	£1 Level Stake	Hurdles	W-R	Per cent	£1 Level Stake
May	1-1	100.0	+2.50	May	1-4	25.0	+1.00
June	0-2	0.0	-2.00	June	0-5	0.0	-5.00
July	0-1	0.0	-1.00	July	0-0	0.0	0.00
August	0-2	0.0	-2.00	August	0-2	0.0	-2.00
September	0-2	0.0	-2.00	September	2-8	25.0	-0.75
October	1-4	25.0	+13.00	October	3-13	23.1	+15.72
November	1-5	20.0	+4.50	November	4-18	22.2	+6.13
December	0-2	0.0	-2.00	December	5-18	27.8	+0.63
January	0-1	0.0	-1.00	January	2-9	22.2	+14.50
February	0-2	0.0	-2.00	February	0-9	0.0	-9.00
March	1-3	33.3	+0.50	March	4-8	50.0	+14.50
April	2-6	33.3	+1.75	April	2-8	25.0	+18.00
Chases	W-R	Per cent	£1 Level Stake	**Totals**	W-R	Per cent	£1 Level Stake

May	0-0	0.0	0.00	May	2-5	40.0	+3.50
June	1-1	100.0	+2.25	June	1-8	12.5	-4.75
July	0-1	0.0	-1.00	July	0-2	0.0	-2.00
August	0-2	0.0	-2.00	August	0-6	0.0	-6.00
September	0-1	0.0	-1.00	September	2-11	18.2	-3.75
October	0-2	0.0	-2.00	October	4-19	21.1	+26.72
November	0-1	0.0	-1.00	November	5-24	20.8	+9.63
December	1-2	50.0	+5.50	December	6-22	27.3	+4.13
January	0-3	0.0	-3.00	January	2-13	15.4	+10.50
February	1-4	25.0	+3.00	February	1-15	6.7	-8.00
March	5-5	100.0	+10.32	March	10-16	62.5	+25.32
April	2-3	66.7	+4.75	April	6-17	35.3	+24.50

DISTANCE

Hurdles	W-R	Per cent	£1 Level Stake	Chases	W-R	Per cent	£1 Level Stake
2m-2m3f	10-61	16.4	+16.22	2m-2m3f	1-3	33.3	+0.25
2m4f-2m7f	8-27	29.6	+29.25	2m4f-2m7f	3-11	27.3	+0.74
3m+	5-14	35.7	+8.25	3m+	6-11	54.5	+14.83

TYPE OF RACE

Non-Handicaps	W-R	Per cent	£1 Level Stake	Handicaps	W-R	Per cent	£1 Level Stake
Nov Hrdls	4-32	12.5	-21.78	Nov Hrdls	2-10	20.0	+13.50
Hrdls	3-12	25.0	+20.38	Hrdls	14-44	31.8	+45.63
Nov Chs	1-4	25.0	+3.00	Nov Chs	1-1	100.0	+2.25
Chases	0-0	0.0	0.00	Chases	6-16	37.5	+3.32
Sell/Claim	0-0	0.0	0.00	Sell/Claim	0-0	0.0	0.00

RACE CLASS

	W-R	Per cent	£1 Level Stake	FIRST TIME OUT	W-R	Per cent	£1 Level Stake
Class 1	2-8	25.0	+17.00	Bumpers	6-20	30.0	+21.25
Class 2	1-9	11.1	-4.00	Hurdles	2-17	11.8	+14.00
Class 3	6-23	26.1	+10.25	Chases	2-4	50.0	+1.88
Class 4	18-77	23.4	+50.47				
Class 5	10-29	34.5	+5.07	Totals	10-41	24.4	+37.13
Class 6	2-12	16.7	+1.00				

JOCKEYS

	W-R	Per cent	£1 Level Stake
Richard Johnson	10-36	27.8	+14.35
Robert Dunne	9-36	25.0	+39.75
Mr Tommie M O'Brien	6-32	18.8	-3.29
Alan Johns	4-13	30.8	+3.74
Aidan Coleman	3-13	23.1	-1.50
Ciaran Gethings	2-3	66.7	+5.00
Tom Scudamore	2-8	25.0	+4.00
Niall P Madden	1-2	50.0	+1.75
Nico de Boinville	1-2	50.0	+24.00
Sean Bowen	1-3	33.3	+2.00

COURSE RECORD

	Total W-R	Non-Hndcps Hurdles	Non-Hndcps Chases	Hndcps Hurdles	Chases	NH Flat	Per cent	£1 Level Stake
Chepstow	6-12	1-4	1-1	1-2	1-1	2-4	50.0	+50.25
Worcester	4-15	2-6	0-0	1-3	1-2	0-4	26.7	-1.53
Mrket Rsn	3-7	0-2	0-0	1-2	1-1	1-2	42.9	+6.63
Exeter	3-12	1-5	0-0	1-3	0-3	1-1	25.0	+4.50
Plumpton	2-2	0-0	0-0	2-2	0-0	0-0	100.0	+9.50
Taunton	2-3	0-1	0-0	2-2	0-0	0-0	66.7	+9.00
Hereford	2-4	0-0	0-0	2-3	0-0	0-1	50.0	+9.50
Towcester	2-4	0-1	0-0	1-2	0-0	1-1	50.0	+8.25
Aintree	2-5	0-0	0-0	1-2	1-1	0-2	40.0	+20.00
Warwick	2-10	0-2	0-0	1-7	1-1	0-0	20.0	+8.75
Lingfield	1-1	0-0	0-0	0-0	1-1	0-0	100.0	+1.63
Stratford	1-1	1-1	0-0	0-0	0-0	0-0	100.0	+2.50
Ayr	1-2	0-0	0-0	0-1	0-0	1-1	50.0	+2.00
Catterick	1-2	0-0	0-0	1-1	0-0	0-1	50.0	+1.00
Huntingdon	1-4	0-0	0-0	0-2	1-2	0-0	25.0	-2.67
Leicester	1-4	0-2	0-0	0-1	1-1	0-0	25.0	-2.38
Newbury	1-4	0-0	0-0	0-0	1-2	0-2	25.0	+2.00
Perth	1-4	0-0	0-0	1-2	0-1	0-1	25.0	+1.00
Ludlow	1-5	0-3	0-0	1-1	0-0	0-1	20.0	+0.50
Newcastle	1-5	1-2	0-0	0-1	0-1	0-1	20.0	-2.38
Uttoxeter	1-6	1-3	0-1	0-2	0-0	0-0	16.7	-2.25

WINNING HORSES

Horse	Races Run	1st	2nd	3rd	£
Thomas Patrick	10	4	2	0	63802
Jester Jet	9	3	2	2	57231
Vado Forte	8	3	2	2	42053
Flashing Glance	6	2	1	1	11761
Kimberlite Candy	8	2	0	2	15140
*Sebastopol	1	1	0	0	6498
Sir Egbert	6	1	0	2	5458
Polydora	4	2	0	0	9097
*Alberto's Dream	5	4	1	0	17407
*Colt Lightning	7	2	0	0	8447
David's Phoebe	5	1	1	0	4549
Sword Of Fate	6	2	1	0	8330
David John	6	1	1	2	4159
Triopas	10	4	0	3	12996
Equus Amadeus	6	2	1	1	5198
Kateson	5	1	3	0	3249
Meep Meep	2	1	0	0	2274
Dorking Boy	1	1	0	0	2274
Mary Eleanor	2	1	1	0	2216
Thistle Do Nicely	1	1	0	0	1949
Total winning prize-money					£284088
Favourites	11-29		37.9%		0.92

EMMA LAVELLE

OGBOURNE MAIZEY, WILTS

	No. of Hrs	Races Run	1st	2nd	3rd	Unpl	Per cent	£1 Level Stake
NH Flat	19	27	2	3	1	21	7.4	-13.50

92 TRAINERS JUMPS STATISTICS

Hurdles	28	95	20	12	12	51	21.1	+3.54
Chases	20	77	6	8	8	55	7.8	-42.75
Totals	**62**	**199**	**28**	**23**	**21**	**127**	**14.1**	**-52.71**
16-17	55	181	34	25	24	98	18.8	+26.60
15-16	54	161	19	17	20	105	11.8	-38.42

Class 2	2-28	7.1	-16.00		Hurdles	5-24	20.8	-0.83
Class 3	9-45	20.0	-6.50		Chases	3-19	15.8	+1.50
Class 4	11-70	15.7	-8.71					
Class 5	3-27	11.1	-13.00		Totals	10-62	16.1	-4.83
Class 6	0-6	0.0	-6.00					

BY MONTH

NH Flat	W-R	Per cent	£1 Level Stake	Hurdles	W-R	Per cent	£1 Level Stake
May	0-0	0.0	0.00	May	1-5	20.0	-0.50
June	0-0	0.0	0.00	June	1-3	33.3	+1.50
July	0-0	0.0	0.00	July	0-0	0.0	0.00
August	0-0	0.0	0.00	August	0-1	0.0	-1.00
September	0-1	0.0	-1.00	September	0-2	0.0	-2.00
October	0-4	0.0	-4.00	October	1-14	7.1	-10.00
November	0-3	0.0	-3.00	November	2-12	16.7	-4.83
December	0-3	0.0	-3.00	December	5-14	35.7	+8.13
January	2-7	28.6	+6.50	January	4-14	28.6	+13.75
February	0-4	0.0	-4.00	February	3-11	27.3	+3.00
March	0-2	0.0	-2.00	March	2-8	25.0	+1.50
April	0-3	0.0	-3.00	April	1-11	9.1	-6.00

Chases	W-R	Per cent	£1 Level Stake	Totals	W-R	Per cent	£1 Level Stake
May	1-7	14.3	-3.50	May	2-12	16.7	-4.00
June	0-2	0.0	-2.00	June	1-5	20.0	-0.50
July	0-2	0.0	-2.00	July	0-2	0.0	-2.00
August	0-1	0.0	-1.00	August	0-2	0.0	-2.00
September	0-2	0.0	-2.00	September	0-5	0.0	-5.00
October	0-8	0.0	-8.00	October	1-26	3.8	-22.00
November	4-15	26.7	+12.50	November	6-30	20.0	+4.67
December	0-14	0.0	-14.00	December	5-31	16.1	-8.87
January	0-7	0.0	-7.00	January	6-28	21.4	+13.25
February	0-6	0.0	-6.00	February	3-21	14.3	-7.00
March	0-4	0.0	-4.00	March	2-14	14.3	-4.50
April	1-9	11.1	-5.75	April	2-23	8.7	-14.75

DISTANCE

Hurdles	W-R	Per cent	£1 Level Stake	Chases	W-R	Per cent	£1 Level Stake
2m-2m3f	7-28	25.0	+6.17	2m-2m3f	1-4	25.0	+1.00
2m4f-2m7f	10-51	19.6	-1.63	2m4f-2m7f	3-35	8.6	-21.25
3m+	3-14	21.4	+1.00	3m+	2-38	5.3	-22.50

TYPE OF RACE

Non-Handicaps	W-R	Per cent	£1 Level Stake	Handicaps	W-R	Per cent	£1 Level Stake
Nov Hrdls	7-45	15.6	-13.88	Nov Hrdls	1-3	33.3	+2.50
Hrdls	4-13	30.8	+3.67	Hrdls	8-34	23.5	+11.25
Nov Chs	0-4	0.0	-4.00	Nov Chs	1-4	25.0	+1.00
Chases	0-0	0.0	0.00	Chases	5-63	7.9	-33.75
Sell/Claim	0-0	0.0	0.00	Sell/Claim	0-0	0.0	0.00

RACE CLASS / FIRST TIME OUT

	W-R	Per cent	£1 Level Stake		W-R	Per cent	£1 Level Stake
Class 1	3-23	13.0	-2.50	Bumpers	2-19	10.5	-5.50

JOCKEYS

	W-R	Per cent	£1 Level Stake
Nick Scholfield	8-49	16.3	-5.00
Leighton Aspell	6-44	13.6	-21.08
Patrick Cowley	4-29	13.8	-6.50
Gavin Sheehan	3-13	23.1	+14.00
Daryl Jacob	2-9	22.2	-1.00
Richard Johnson	2-9	22.2	-0.50
Jonathan Burke	1-3	33.3	+2.50
Adam Wedge	1-10	10.0	-5.00
Aidan Coleman	1-21	4.8	-18.13

COURSE RECORD

	Total W-R	Non-Hndcps Hurdles	Non-Hndcps Chases	Hndcps Hurdles	Hndcps Chases	NH Flat	Per cent	£1 Level Stake
Doncaster	5-19	3-6	0-0	2-5	0-5	0-3	26.3	+7.25
Fontwell	3-13	1-4	0-1	1-1	0-6	1-1	23.1	-0.25
Wincanton	3-18	0-5	0-0	2-5	1-7	0-1	16.7	-4.75
Mrket Rsn	2-6	0-0	0-0	0-0	1-3	1-3	33.3	+6.50
Warwick	2-8	1-2	0-1	0-0	1-3	0-2	25.0	+10.00
Worcester	2-8	0-1	0-0	2-4	0-2	0-1	25.0	+2.00
Chepstow	2-15	1-6	0-0	1-3	0-3	0-3	13.3	-3.50
Ffos Las	1-2	1-1	0-0	0-0	0-1	0-0	50.0	+2.00
Hereford	1-3	1-1	0-0	0-0	0-0	0-2	33.3	+5.00
Lingfield	1-3	0-2	0-0	0-0	1-1	0-0	33.3	+2.00
Southwell	1-4	1-1	0-0	0-1	0-2	0-0	25.0	-1.13
Ascot	1-5	0-0	0-0	0-0	1-5	0-0	20.0	+0.50
Sandown	1-7	1-1	0-0	0-4	0-2	0-0	14.3	-5.33
Exeter	1-8	0-3	0-0	1-1	0-3	0-1	12.5	-2.50
Ludlow	1-8	0-1	0-0	0-2	1-5	0-0	12.5	-3.00
Nton Abbot	1-8	1-2	0-0	0-1	0-4	0-1	12.5	-3.50

WINNING HORSES

Horse	Races Run	1st	2nd	3rd	£
Fortunate George	8	2	0	2	28134
Enniscoffey Oscar	7	2	0	1	21634
*Woolstone One	4	3	1	0	23205
Buster Thomas	5	1	0	1	13256
Full Irish	5	1	0	0	12777
Talent To Amuse	2	1	0	0	11995
Flemcara	6	3	0	0	21791
Dissavril	2	1	0	0	11390
Pawn Star	1	1	0	0	7798
The Sweeney	6	1	0	2	7733
Gunfleet	4	2	1	0	11242
Dark Mahler	2	1	0	0	7148
De Rasher Counter	7	1	2	1	6238
Water Wagtail	4	1	0	1	5198
Irish Prophecy	4	1	1	0	4549
Paisley Park	4	1	2	0	4549

Belle Empress	3	1	0	1	4094
Majestic Moll	4	1	1	0	3899
Reelingintheyears	2	1	0	0	3119
Vendredi Trois	5	1	0	2	2599
Fontsanta	2	1	0	0	2274
Total winning prize-money					£214622
Favourites		10-21		47.6%	14.54

KERRY LEE

BYTON, H'FORDS

	No. of Hrs	Races Run	1st	2nd	3rd	Unpl	Per cent	£1 Level Stake
NH Flat	2	2	0	1	0	1	0.0	-2.00
Hurdles	22	73	9	6	10	48	12.3	-18.67
Chases	24	105	19	18	8	60	18.1	-25.38
Totals	39	180	28	25	18	109	15.6	-46.05
16-17	39	159	22	31	19	87	13.8	-15.84
15-16	26	110	23	19	9	59	20.9	+39.06

BY MONTH

NH Flat	W-R	Per cent	£1 Level Stake	Hurdles	W-R	Per cent	£1 Level Stake
May	0-0	0.0	0.00	May	0-5	0.0	-5.00
June	0-0	0.0	0.00	June	0-2	0.0	-2.00
July	0-0	0.0	0.00	July	0-1	0.0	-1.00
August	0-0	0.0	0.00	August	0-1	0.0	-1.00
September	0-0	0.0	0.00	September	0-1	0.0	-1.00
October	0-0	0.0	0.00	October	1-6	16.7	-2.00
November	0-0	0.0	0.00	November	3-13	23.1	+3.83
December	0-0	0.0	0.00	December	1-6	16.7	+1.00
January	0-2	0.0	-2.00	January	0-7	0.0	-7.00
February	0-0	0.0	0.00	February	0-9	0.0	-9.00
March	0-0	0.0	0.00	March	2-12	16.7	+2.50
April	0-0	0.0	0.00	April	2-10	20.0	+2.00

Chases	W-R	Per cent	£1 Level Stake	Totals	W-R	Per cent	£1 Level Stake
May	2-3	66.7	+9.38	May	2-8	25.0	+4.38
June	2-5	40.0	+5.00	June	2-7	28.6	+3.00
July	0-3	0.0	-3.00	July	0-4	0.0	-4.00
August	1-4	25.0	0.00	August	1-5	20.0	-1.00
September	1-5	20.0	+0.50	September	1-6	16.7	-0.50
October	1-9	11.1	-7.20	October	2-15	13.3	-9.20
November	3-15	20.0	-3.40	November	6-28	21.4	+0.43
December	2-13	15.4	-0.50	December	3-19	15.8	+0.50
January	3-17	17.6	-5.65	January	3-26	11.5	-14.65
February	3-12	25.0	-4.25	February	3-21	14.3	-13.25
March	1-12	8.3	-9.25	March	3-24	12.5	-6.75
April	0-7	0.0	-7.00	April	2-17	11.8	-5.00

DISTANCE

Hurdles	W-R	Per cent	£1 Level Stake	Chases	W-R	Per cent	£1 Level Stake
2m-2m3f	4-40	10.0	-21.17	2m-2m3f	11-49	22.4	-6.98
2m4f-2m7f	1-22	4.5	-15.00	2m4f-2m7f	7-28	25.0	+7.10
3m+	4-11	36.4	+17.50	3m+	1-28	3.6	-25.50

TYPE OF RACE

Non-Handicaps		Per cent	£1 Level Stake	Handicaps		Per cent	£1 Level Stake
	W-R				W-R		
Nov Hrdls	0-11	0.0	-11.00	Nov Hrdls	1-4	25.0	+0.33
Hrdls	1-11	9.1	-4.00	Hrdls	6-44	13.6	-5.00
Nov Chs	3-11	27.3	-4.15	Nov Chs	2-6	33.3	+1.00
Chases	1-3	33.3	-1.20	Chases	8-75	10.7	-36.52
Sell/Claim	1-1	100.0	+0.80	Sell/Claim	1-1	100.0	+3.00

RACE CLASS

	W-R	Per cent	£1 Level Stake
Class 1	0-25	0.0	-25.00
Class 2	3-20	15.0	-5.50
Class 3	15-59	25.4	+23.78
Class 4	7-52	13.5	-27.82
Class 5	3-24	12.5	-11.50
Class 6	0-0	0.0	0.00

FIRST TIME OUT

	W-R	Per cent	£1 Level Stake
Bumpers	0-2	0.0	-2.00
Hurdles	0-17	0.0	-17.00
Chases	5-20	25.0	+2.68
Totals	5-39	12.8	-16.32

JOCKEYS

	W-R	Per cent	£1 Level Stake
Richard Patrick	14-65	21.5	+7.06
Jamie Moore	8-67	11.9	-33.10
Richard Johnson	4-17	23.5	+1.00
Mitchell Bastyan	1-1	100.0	+4.50
Harry Skelton	1-3	33.3	+1.50

COURSE RECORD

	Total W-R	Non-Hndcps Hurdles	Non-Hndcps Chases	Hndcps Hurdles	Hndcps Chases	NH Flat	Per cent	£1 Level Stake
Cheltenham	3-9	0-0	0-0	2-4	1-5	0-0	33.3	+6.33
Worcester	3-11	0-0	0-0	0-3	3-8	0-0	27.3	+4.50
Uttoxeter	3-15	1-4	0-1	0-2	2-8	0-0	20.0	+2.50
Ascot	2-7	0-2	1-2	1-3	0-0	0-0	28.6	+4.75
Ludlow	2-10	0-2	1-3	0-3	1-2	0-0	20.0	-2.40
Bangor	2-11	0-1	1-2	0-2	1-6	0-0	18.2	-5.00
Fontwell	1-1	0-0	0-0	1-1	0-0	0-0	100.0	+4.50
Kempton	1-1	0-0	0-0	1-1	0-0	0-0	100.0	+3.00
Leicester	1-1	0-0	0-0	0-0	1-1	0-0	100.0	+0.25
Nton Abbot	1-1	0-0	0-0	1-1	0-0	0-0	100.0	+3.00
Kelso	1-2	0-0	0-0	1-2	0-0	0-0	50.0	+3.50
Ayr	1-4	0-0	0-0	1-4	0-0	0-0	25.0	+4.50
Ffos Las	1-4	0-0	1-1	0-1	0-2	0-0	25.0	-2.20
Aintree	1-6	0-1	0-0	1-1	0-4	0-0	16.7	+3.50
Wetherby	1-7	0-1	0-0	0-0	1-6	0-0	14.3	-4.90
Stratford	1-8	0-0	0-0	0-3	1-5	0-0	12.5	-5.13
Sandown	1-9	0-0	0-0	0-5	1-4	0-0	11.1	-4.50
Chepstow	1-11	0-4	0-0	0-1	1-6	0-0	9.1	-4.00
Hereford	1-15	0-2	0-2	0-2	1-8	0-1	6.7	-11.25

WINNING HORSES

Horse	Races Run	1st	2nd	3rd	£
Kris Spin	7	3	1	0	42946
Gino Trail	7	3	2	2	44034

Town Parks	7	2	0	0	16685
Happy Diva	7	3	3	1	23187
*Magic Dancer	5	3	1	0	21153
Tree Of Liberty	5	2	2	0	16375
Itshard To No	3	1	0	1	7798
Definite Future	5	2	0	0	14414
Grey Gold	6	1	0	1	6498
Sir Will	6	2	0	1	9682
Altiepix	5	1	0	1	6330
Sage Monkey	9	1	2	2	4874
Krackatoa King	6	1	2	0	4118
Scales	8	1	2	0	3249
Desertmore Hill	4	2	0	0	6108
Total winning prize-money					**£227451**
Favourites	**11-26**		**42.3%**		**3.96**

SOPHIE LEECH

ELTON, GLOUCS

	No. of Hrs	Races Run	1st	2nd	3rd	Unpl	Per cent	£1 Level Stake
NH Flat	1	1	0	0	0	1	0.0	-1.00
Hurdles	16	85	7	10	7	61	8.2	-7.00
Chases	7	28	0	3	5	20	0.0	-28.00
Totals	**20**	**114**	**7**	**13**	**12**	**82**	**6.1**	**-36.00**
16-17	45	196	12	21	21	142	6.1	-122.91
15-16	40	172	9	12	23	128	5.2	-81.13

JOCKEYS

	W-R	Per cent	£1 Level Stake
James Best	3-20	15.0	+10.00
Paddy Brennan	2-32	6.3	-11.00
Richard Johnson	1-1	100.0	+16.00
Sean Houlihan	1-18	5.6	-8.00

COURSE RECORD

	Total W-R	Non-Hndcps Hurdles	Chases	Hndcps Hurdles	Chases	NH Flat	Per cent	£1 Level Stake
Uttoxeter	2-9	0-0	0-0	2-6	0-3	0-0	22.2	+12.50
Nton Abbot	2-10	1-1	0-0	1-8	0-1	0-0	20.0	+7.50
Huntingdon	1-1	0-0	0-0	1-1	0-0	0-0	100.0	+16.00
Stratford	1-4	0-0	0-0	1-4	0-0	0-0	25.0	+8.00
Southwell	1-6	0-0	0-1	1-4	0-1	0-0	16.7	+4.00

WINNING HORSES

Horse	Races Run	1st	2nd	3rd	£
Saxo Jack	8	1	2	1	6498
Soiesauvage	7	1	1	0	6330
Samson	10	2	0	2	9579
Birch Hill	5	1	0	0	5198
Tamarillo Grove	7	1	1	0	4711
Stuccodor	8	1	0	1	3119
Total winning prize-money					**£35435**
Favourites	**0-4**		**0.0%**		**-4.00**

DR CHARLES LEVINSON

ANDOVERSFORD, GLOUCS

	No. of Hrs	Races Run	1st	2nd	3rd	Unpl	Per cent	£1 Level Stake
NH Flat	0	0	0	0	0	0	0.0	0.00
Hurdles	0	0	0	0	0	0	0.0	0.00
Chases	1	3	1	0	0	2	33.3	+8.00
Totals	**1**	**3**	**1**	**0**	**0**	**2**	**33.3**	**+8.00**
16-17	2	5	1	0	0	4	20.0	+8.00

JOCKEYS

	W-R	Per cent	£1 Level Stake
Mr Gus Levinson	1-3	33.3	+8.00

COURSE RECORD

	Total W-R	Non-Hndcps Hurdles	Chases	Hndcps Hurdles	Chases	NH Flat	Per cent	£1 Level Stake
Taunton	1-1	0-0	1-1	0-0	0-0	0-0	100.0	+10.00

WINNING HORSES

Horse	Races Run	1st	2nd	3rd	£
*Premier Portrait	3	1	0	0	2470
Total winning prize-money					**£2470**
Favourites	**0-1**		**0.0%**		**-1.00**

BERNARD LLEWELLYN

FOCHRIW, CAERPHILLY

	No. of Hrs	Races Run	1st	2nd	3rd	Unpl	Per cent	£1 Level Stake
NH Flat	2	4	0	0	1	3	0.0	-4.00
Hurdles	18	70	8	7	16	39	11.4	-21.29
Chases	1	10	1	1	1	7	10.0	-5.00
Totals	**19**	**84**	**9**	**8**	**18**	**49**	**10.7**	**-30.29**
16-17	23	104	6	10	14	74	5.8	-47.50
15-16	23	111	9	16	17	69	8.1	-50.36

JOCKEYS

	W-R	Per cent	£1 Level Stake
Robert Williams	3-35	8.6	-17.50
Mitchell Bastyan	2-2	100.0	+12.33
Page Fuller	1-1	100.0	+4.00
George Blackwell	1-2	50.0	+7.00
Sean Bowen	1-3	33.3	+2.00
Sean Houlihan	1-7	14.3	-4.13

COURSE RECORD

	Total W-R	Non-Hndcps Hurdles	Chases	Hndcps Hurdles	Chases	NH Flat	Per cent	£1 Level Stake
Stratford	2-2	0-0	0-0	2-2	0-0	0-0	100.0	+12.00
Wincanton	2-8	0-1	0-0	2-6	0-1	0-0	25.0	+3.33

Kempton	1-1	0-0	0-0	1-1	0-0	0-0	100.0	+9.00
Fontwell	1-5	1-1	0-0	0-4	0-0	0-0	20.0	-0.50
Uttoxeter	1-10	0-0	0-0	0-6	1-4	0-0	10.0	-5.00
Nton Abbot	1-13	0-2	0-0	1-10	0-0	0-1	7.7	-7.00
Ffos Las	1-13	0-2	0-0	1-10	0-1	0-0	7.7	-10.13

WINNING HORSES

Horse	Races Run	1st	2nd	3rd	£
Never Equalled	5	1	0	1	6923
Global Thrill	8	3	0	2	12346
Shadow's Boy	5	1	1	3	3994
Taste The Wine	5	1	1	0	3899
Arty Campbell	5	1	1	1	3899
Hansupfordetroit	11	1	2	1	3769
Norab	3	1	0	1	3509
Total winning prize-money					**£38339**
Favourites	1-2		50.0%		0.88

JOHN E LONG
ROYSTON, HERTS

	No. of Hrs	Races Run	1st	2nd	3rd	Unpl	Per cent	£1 Level Stake
NH Flat	0	0	0	0	0	0	0.0	0.00
Hurdles	1	2	1	0	0	1	50.0	+5.00
Chases	0	0	0	0	0	0	0.0	0.00
Totals	1	2	1	0	0	1	50.0	+5.00

JOCKEYS

	W-R	Per cent	£1 Level Stake
Mattie Batchelor	1-2	50.0	+5.00

COURSE RECORD

	Total W-R	Non-Hndcps Hurdles	Chases	Hndcps Hurdles	Chases	NH Flat	Per cent	£1 Level Stake
Fontwell	1-2	0-1	0-0	1-1	0-0	0-0	50.0	+5.00

WINNING HORSES

Horse	Races Run	1st	2nd	3rd	£
Norman The Red	2	1	0	0	4094
Total winning prize-money					**£4094**
Favourites	0-0		0.0%		0.00

CHARLIE LONGSDON
OVER NORTON, OXON

	No. of Hrs	Races Run	1st	2nd	3rd	Unpl	Per cent	£1 Level Stake
NH Flat	18	21	0	1	4	16	0.0	-21.00
Hurdles	60	165	15	16	19	115	9.1	-91.55
Chases	45	199	29	28	23	119	14.6	+3.22
Totals	95	385	44	45	46	250	11.4	-109.33
16-17	101	405	51	65	52	237	12.6	-98.30
15-16	93	416	62	59	34	261	14.9	-105.15

BY MONTH

NH Flat	W-R	Per cent	£1 Level Stake	Hurdles	W-R	Per cent	£1 Level Stake
May	0-0	0.0	0.00	May	0-13	0.0	-13.00
June	0-0	0.0	0.00	June	1-4	25.0	+1.00
July	0-0	0.0	0.00	July	2-8	25.0	-2.00
August	0-0	0.0	0.00	August	1-6	16.7	+9.00
September	0-1	0.0	-1.00	September	2-10	20.0	-2.00
October	0-8	0.0	-8.00	October	0-15	0.0	-15.00
November	0-4	0.0	-4.00	November	0-21	0.0	-21.00
December	0-3	0.0	-3.00	December	2-19	10.5	-2.00
January	0-1	0.0	-1.00	January	0-20	0.0	-20.00
February	0-2	0.0	-2.00	February	3-14	21.4	+0.10
March	0-0	0.0	0.00	March	3-14	21.4	-8.40
April	0-2	0.0	-2.00	April	1-21	4.8	-18.25

Chases	W-R	Per cent	£1 Level Stake	Totals	W-R	Per cent	£1 Level Stake
May	5-16	31.3	+3.50	May	5-29	17.2	-9.50
June	1-6	16.7	-3.75	June	2-10	20.0	-2.75
July	2-7	28.6	+4.25	July	4-15	26.7	+2.25
August	0-3	0.0	-3.00	August	1-9	11.1	+6.00
September	5-14	35.7	+12.73	September	7-25	28.0	+9.73
October	4-30	13.3	-3.00	October	4-53	7.5	-26.00
November	1-23	4.3	-19.25	November	1-48	2.1	-44.25
December	3-27	11.1	+26.50	December	5-49	10.2	+21.50
January	2-21	9.5	-7.50	January	2-42	4.8	-28.50
February	1-14	7.1	-9.00	February	4-30	13.3	-10.90
March	1-12	8.3	-2.00	March	4-26	15.4	-10.40
April	4-26	15.4	+3.75	April	5-49	10.2	-16.50

DISTANCE

Hurdles	W-R	Per cent	£1 Level Stake	Chases	W-R	Per cent	£1 Level Stake
2m-2m3f	5-75	6.7	-37.88	2m-2m3f	5-32	15.6	+11.85
2m4f-2m7f	9-74	12.2	-39.40	2m4f-2m7f	12-83	14.5	-21.50
3m+	1-16	6.3	-14.27	3m+	12-84	14.3	+12.88

TYPE OF RACE

Non-Handicaps	W-R	Per cent	£1 Level Stake	Handicaps	W-R	Per cent	£1 Level Stake
Nov Hrdls	7-47	14.9	-17.65	Nov Hrdls	0-7	0.0	-7.00
Hrdls	2-37	5.4	-33.40	Hrdls	5-70	7.1	-44.50
Nov Chs	4-18	22.2	-8.65	Nov Chs	3-21	14.3	-2.00
Chases	0-1	0.0	-1.00	Chases	18-131	13.7	+3.13
Sell/Claim	0-1	0.0	-1.00	Sell/Claim	0-0	0.0	0.00

RACE CLASS

	W-R	Per cent	£1 Level Stake
Class 1	1-26	3.8	-15.00
Class 2	2-47	4.3	-35.00
Class 3	7-77	9.1	+0.38
Class 4	29-179	16.2	-37.05
Class 5	5-49	10.2	-15.65
Class 6	0-7	0.0	-7.00

FIRST TIME OUT

	W-R	Per cent	£1 Level Stake
Bumpers	0-18	0.0	-18.00
Hurdles	3-38	7.9	-21.00
Chases	3-39	7.7	-27.63
Totals	6-95	6.3	-66.63

JOCKEYS

	W-R	Per cent	£1 Level Stake
Paul O'Brien	13-65	20.0	+7.88
Jonathan Burke	10-190	5.3	-115.28
Brian Hughes	5-19	26.3	+6.35
Aidan Coleman	5-21	23.8	+2.00
Mr Jordan Nailor	4-13	30.8	+4.00
Richard Johnson	2-16	12.5	-8.50
Andrew Tinkler	1-1	100.0	+0.73
Mr D Skehan	1-2	50.0	+24.00
Tom O'Brien	1-2	50.0	+5.50
Charlie Poste	1-6	16.7	+9.00
Sean Bowen	1-11	9.1	-6.00

COURSE RECORD

	Total W-R	Non-Hndcps Hurdles	Chases	Hndcps Hurdles	Chases	NH Flat	Per cent	£1 Level Stake
Uttoxeter	7-23	2-8	0-0	2-4	3-11	0-0	30.4	+13.75
Huntingdon	4-21	1-7	0-0	0-2	3-11	0-1	19.0	-0.75
Towcester	3-13	0-6	2-2	0-0	1-4	0-1	23.1	-2.00
Sandown	3-17	0-0	0-0	0-3	3-14	0-0	17.6	+24.00
Worcester	3-29	2-10	0-2	0-6	1-9	0-2	10.3	-4.00
Kempton	2-17	0-1	0-0	0-6	2-10	0-0	11.8	-5.75
Stratford	2-17	0-5	1-1	0-4	1-6	0-1	11.8	-11.15
Doncaster	2-23	0-5	0-0	1-6	1-10	0-2	8.7	-9.50
Ludlow	2-23	0-6	0-2	0-3	2-11	0-1	8.7	-13.25
Carlisle	1-1	1-1	0-0	0-0	0-0	0-0	100.0	+0.13
Perth	1-1	0-0	0-0	0-0	1-1	0-0	100.0	+6.00
Hexham	1-2	0-0	1-1	0-0	0-1.	0-0	50.0	+0.25
Nton Abbot	1-2	0-0	0-0	0-0	1-2	0-0	50.0	+0.63
Ayr	1-3	1-1	0-0	0-1	0-1	0-0	33.3	-1.90
Hereford	1-3	1-1	0-0	0-1	0-0	0-1	33.3	-1.27
Wetherby	1-4	1-3	0-1	0-0	0-0	0-0	25.0	+5.00
Exeter	1-5	0-0	0-0	0-1	1-4	0-0	20.0	+2.50
Wincanton	1-5	0-1	0-0	0-1	1-3	0-0	20.0	0.00
Bangor	1-9	0-2	0-0	1-3	0-3	0-1	11.1	-4.00
Aintree	1-9	0-2	0-0	0-0	1-6	0-1	11.1	+2.00
Chepstow	1-10	0-1	0-0	0-1	1-7	0-1	10.0	-1.00
Fontwell	1-13	0-1	0-1	0-4	1-7	0-0	7.7	-7.50
Warwick	1-18	1-8	0-1	0-2	0-6	0-1	5.6	-9.00
Mrket Rsn	1-22	0-6	0-1	1-5	0-8	0-2	4.5	-18.50
Southwell	1-22	0-3	0-2	0-9	1-7	0-1	4.5	-1.00

WINNING HORSES

Horse	Races Run	1st	2nd	3rd	£
Bentelimar	6	1	2	1	50517
Ballydine	3	1	1	1	31280
*Hammersly Lake	4	1	2	0	15784
Midnight Shot	10	4	0	1	29611
Pete The Feat	5	2	1	0	21680
Nightfly	5	1	3	0	10635
Azure Fly	4	1	0	0	7187
Leith Hill Lad	6	2	0	1	11761
Wilberdragon	6	1	0	2	7148
Fly Home Harry	6	2	1	0	11577

Horse					
Monbeg Charmer	5	1	0	1	6498
Vivas	7	1	1	3	6330
Kilfinichen Bay	6	1	0	0	6330
Bestwork	11	5	0	0	9874
Western Miller	12	3	3	0	13646
Just Don't Ask	4	2	1	1	8004
Just Your Type	3	1	1	0	4809
Shanroe In Milan	6	1	0	1	4614
Louse Talk	3	2	0	0	9097
Aunty Ann	7	1	1	3	4289
Jet Set	6	1	2	1	4224
Castafiore	7	2	1	1	8058
Definitly Grey	8	1	1	0	3899
Hepijeu	8	1	4	1	3899
Barton Rose	6	1	2	1	3769
Treackle Tart	6	1	1	0	3769
Lisdoonvarna Lad	5	1	1	1	3574
Burrows Lane	7	1	2	3	3509
Jacobite Rising	3	1	0	0	2469
Total winning prize-money					**£307841**
Favourites	**13-30**		**43.3%**		**7.68**

SHAUN LYCETT

LEAFIELD, OXON

	No. of Hrs	Races Run	1st	2nd	3rd	Unpl	Per cent	£1 Level Stake
NH Flat	3	3	0	0	1	2	0.0	-3.00
Hurdles	6	20	4	2	0	14	20.0	+11.50
Chases	1	1	0	0	0	1	0.0	-1.00
Totals	**10**	**24**	**4**	**2**	**1**	**17**	**16.7**	**+7.50**
16-17	*10*	*30*	*0*	*1*	*0*	*29*	*0.0*	*-30.00*
15-16	*12*	*31*	*1*	*3*	*6*	*21*	*3.2*	*-18.00*

JOCKEYS

	W-R	Per cent	£1 Level Stake
Marc Goldstein	4-11	36.4	+20.50

COURSE RECORD

	Total W-R	Non-Hndcps Hurdles	Chases	Hndcps Hurdles	Chases	NH Flat	Per cent	£1 Level Stake
Worcester	4-15	0-5	0-0	4-8	0-1	0-1	26.7	+16.50

WINNING HORSES

Horse	Races Run	1st	2nd	3rd	£
Hallings Comet	7	4	2	0	17004
Total winning prize-money					**£17004**
Favourites	**0-33**		**0.0%**		**-33.00**

JOHN MACKIE

CHURCH BROUGHTON, DERBYS

	No. of Hrs	Races Run	1st	2nd	3rd	Unpl	Per cent	£1 Level Stake
NH Flat	5	8	0	1	1	6	0.0	-8.00

Hurdles	5	17	1	4	3	9	5.9	-13.50
Chases	0	0	0	0	0	0	0.0	0.00
Totals	10	25	1	5	4	15	4.0	-21.50
16-17	9	26	2	3	4	17	7.7	+2.00
15-16	10	45	3	4	3	35	6.7	-19.50

JOCKEYS

	W-R	Per cent	£1 Level Stake
A P Heskin	1-2	50.0	+1.50

COURSE RECORD

	Total W-R	Non-Hndcps Hurdles	Chases	Hndcps Hurdles	Chases	NH Flat	Per cent	£1 Level Stake
Wetherby	1-2	1-1	0-0	0-1	0-0	0-0	50.0	+1.50

WINNING HORSES

Horse	Races Run	1st	2nd	3rd	£
Barton Knoll	4	1	1	0	3249
Total winning prize-money					£3249
Favourites	0-0	0.0%			0.00

CHARLIE MANN

UPPER LAMBOURN, BERKS

	No. of Hrs	Races Run	1st	2nd	3rd	Unpl	Per cent	£1 Level Stake
NH Flat	1	1	0	0	0	1	0.0	-1.00
Hurdles	20	64	9	6	9	40	14.1	+16.48
Chases	10	47	8	4	8	27	17.0	-0.44
Totals	26	112	17	10	17	68	15.2	+15.04
16-17	31	118	23	18	11	66	19.5	+16.19
15-16	31	140	13	13	15	99	9.3	-33.13

BY MONTH

NH Flat	W-R	Per cent	£1 Level Stake	Hurdles	W-R	Per cent	£1 Level Stake
May	0-0	0.0	0.00	May	3-5	60.0	+6.48
June	0-0	0.0	0.00	June	0-1	0.0	-1.00
July	0-0	0.0	0.00	July	0-1	0.0	-1.00
August	0-0	0.0	0.00	August	1-2	50.0	+10.00
September	0-0	0.0	0.00	September	0-1	0.0	-1.00
October	0-0	0.0	0.00	October	3-9	33.3	+10.00
November	0-0	0.0	0.00	November	0-11	0.0	-11.00
December	0-0	0.0	0.00	December	1-9	11.1	+17.00
January	0-0	0.0	0.00	January	0-8	0.0	-8.00
February	0-0	0.0	0.00	February	0-7	0.0	-7.00
March	0-0	0.0	0.00	March	0-4	0.0	-4.00
April	0-1	0.0	-1.00	April	1-6	16.7	+6.00

Chases	W-R	Per cent	£1 Level Stake	Totals	W-R	Per cent	£1 Level Stake
May	1-3	33.3	-0.38	May	4-8	50.0	+6.10
June	0-0	0.0	0.00	June	0-1	0.0	-1.00
July	0-2	0.0	-2.00	July	0-3	0.0	-3.00
August	0-0	0.0	0.00	August	1-2	50.0	+10.00
September	0-1	0.0	-1.00	September	0-2	0.0	-2.00

October	1-9	11.1	-3.00	October	4-18	22.2	+7.00
November	0-6	0.0	-6.00	November	0-17	0.0	-17.00
December	1-5	20.0	+0.50	December	2-14	14.3	+17.50
January	1-3	33.3	+7.00	January	1-11	9.1	-1.00
February	0-6	0.0	-6.00	February	0-13	0.0	-13.00
March	2-5	40.0	+9.33	March	2-9	22.2	+5.33
April	2-7	28.6	+1.10	April	3-14	21.4	+6.10

DISTANCE

Hurdles	W-R	Per cent	£1 Level Stake	Chases	W-R	Per cent	£1 Level Stake
2m-2m3f	5-31	16.1	+15.98	2m-2m3f	1-3	33.3	+7.00
2m4f-2m7f	3-23	13.0	-1.50	2m4f-2m7f	1-16	6.3	-10.50
3m+	1-10	10.0	+2.00	3m+	6-28	21.4	+3.06

TYPE OF RACE

Non-Handicaps	W-R	Per cent	£1 Level Stake	Handicaps	W-R	Per cent	£1 Level Stake
Nov Hrdls	1-18	5.6	-16.27	Nov Hrdls	0-1	0.0	-1.00
Hrdls	3-10	30.0	+9.25	Hrdls	5-34	14.7	+25.50
Nov Chs	0-4	0.0	-4.00	Nov Chs	1-2	50.0	+0.10
Chases	0-2	0.0	-2.00	Chases	6-34	17.6	+4.46
Sell/Claim	0-0	0.0	0.00	Sell/Claim	0-0	0.0	0.00

RACE CLASS

	W-R	Per cent	£1 Level Stake
Class 1	0-0	0.0	0.00
Class 2	0-6	0.0	-6.00
Class 3	3-30	10.0	+12.00
Class 4	9-68	13.2	-11.67
Class 5	5-8	62.5	+20.71
Class 6	0-0	0.0	0.00

FIRST TIME OUT

	W-R	Per cent	£1 Level Stake
Bumpers	0-1	0.0	-1.00
Hurdles	4-17	23.5	+6.48
Chases	2-8	25.0	+0.63
Totals	6-26	23.1	+6.11

JOCKEYS

	W-R	Per cent	£1 Level Stake
Harry Bannister	7-44	15.9	+16.75
Gavin Sheehan	4-13	30.8	+3.46
Noel Fehily	2-9	22.2	-5.17
Joshua Moore	1-1	100.0	+9.00
Capt Charlie O'Shea	1-1	100.0	+11.00
Brian Hughes	1-2	50.0	+10.00
Jamie Moore	1-4	25.0	+8.00

COURSE RECORD

	Total W-R	Non-Hndcps Hurdles	Chases	Hndcps Hurdles	Chases	NH Flat	Per cent	£1 Level Stake
Plumpton	3-7	0-1	0-0	0-3	3-3	0-0	42.9	+2.06
Fakenham	3-13	0-0	0-1	1-4	2-8	0-0	23.1	+6.00
Mrket Rsn	2-6	1-2	0-0	1-2	0-2	0-0	33.3	+3.50
Fontwell	2-11	0-2	0-1	1-2	1-6	0-0	18.2	+11.00
Cartmel	1-1	1-1	0-0	0-0	0-0	0-0	100.0	+11.00
Ffos Las	1-3	0-1	0-0	0-0	1-2	0-0	33.3	+3.00
Huntingdon	1-4	1-1	0-0	0-2	0-1	0-0	25.0	-0.25
Wincanton	1-4	0-1	0-0	1-2	0-1	0-0	25.0	+8.00
Doncaster	1-5	0-3	0-0	1-2	0-0	0-0	20.0	+21.00

Nton Abbot	1-5	0-0	0-0	0-2	1-3	0-0	20.0	+1.00
Kempton	1-6	1-5	0-0	0-0	0-1	0-0	16.7	-4.27

WINNING HORSES

Horse	Races Run	1st	2nd	3rd	£
Fixed Rate	9	2	1	1	15256
Morney Wing	9	1	1	2	8255
Pickamix	6	1	2	1	7798
Lex Talionis	5	1	1	1	6489
Cody Wyoming	7	2	1	0	10462
The Lion Dancer	9	3	0	1	13036
Maid Of Milan	3	1	0	1	4874
*Glorvina	7	1	1	2	3994
Royals And Rebels	8	1	0	2	3994
Zen Master	7	1	1	1	3899
American Gigolo	1	1	0	0	3899
Ilewindelilah	4	1	1	0	3574
Ocean Jive	1	1	0	0	2924
Total winning prize-money					**£88454**
Favourites	4-13		30.8%		-3.05

MRS F J MARRIOTT

CHIPPING NORTON, OXON

	No. of Hrs	Races Run	1st	2nd	3rd	Unpl	Per cent	£1 Level Stake
NH Flat	0	0	0	0	0	0	0.0	0.00
Hurdles	0	0	0	0	0	0	0.0	0.00
Chases	1	4	1	2	0	1	25.0	+2.50
Totals	1	4	1	2	0	1	25.0	+2.50

JOCKEYS

	W-R	Per cent	£1 Level Stake
Mrs Claire Hardwick	1-4	25.0	+2.50

COURSE RECORD

	Total W-R	Non-Hndcps Hurdles	Chases	Hndcps Hurdles	Chases	NH Flat	Per cent	£1 Level Stake
Stratford	1-1	0-0	1-1	0-0	0-0	0-0	100.0	+5.50

WINNING HORSES

Horse	Races Run	1st	2nd	3rd	£
Dabinett Moon	4	1	2	0	6239
Total winning prize-money					**£6239**
Favourites	0-0		0.0%		0.00

MRS F MARSHALL

BRIGHTLING, E.SUSSEX

	No. of Hrs	Races Run	1st	2nd	3rd	Unpl	Per cent	£1 Level Stake
NH Flat	0	0	0	0	0	0	0.0	0.00
Hurdles	0	0	0	0	0	0	0.0	0.00

Chases	1	4	1	0	1	2	25.0	-0.25
Totals	1	4	1	0	1	2	25.0	-0.25
16-17	1	2	0	1	0	1	0.0	-2.00
15-16	1	1	0	0	0	1	0.0	-1.00

JOCKEYS

	W-R	Per cent	£1 Level Stake
Miss Tabitha Worsley	1-1	100.0	+2.75

COURSE RECORD

	Total W-R	Non-Hndcps Hurdles	Chases	Hndcps Hurdles	Chases	NH Flat	Per cent	£1 Level Stake
Fontwell	1-1	0-0	1-1	0-0	0-0	0-0	100.0	+2.75

WINNING HORSES

Horse	Races Run	1st	2nd	3rd	£
*Never Complain	4	1	0	1	1248
Total winning prize-money					**£1248**
Favourites	0-0		0.0%		0.00

NICKY MARTIN

MINEHEAD, SOMERSET

	No. of Hrs	Races Run	1st	2nd	3rd	Unpl	Per cent	£1 Level Stake
NH Flat	3	6	1	0	1	4	16.7	+2.00
Hurdles	9	26	2	3	1	20	7.7	+14.00
Chases	6	19	1	2	1	15	5.3	+4.00
Totals	13	51	4	5	3	39	7.8	+20.00
16-17	6	16	4	3	2	7	25.0	+10.00
15-16	2	3	0	1	0	2	0.0	-3.00

JOCKEYS

	W-R	Per cent	£1 Level Stake
Matt Griffiths	3-37	8.1	+26.00
Mr Darren Edwards	1-5	20.0	+3.00

COURSE RECORD

	Total W-R	Non-Hndcps Hurdles	Chases	Hndcps Hurdles	Chases	NH Flat	Per cent	£1 Level Stake
Stratford	1-1	0-0	0-0	0-0	0-0	1-1	100.0	+7.00
Bangor	1-2	1-1	0-0	0-0	0-1	0-0	50.0	+27.00
Ffos Las	1-2	0-0	0-0	1-1	0-1	0-0	50.0	+9.00
Exeter	1-7	0-3	0-2	0-1	1-1	0-0	14.3	+16.00

WINNING HORSES

Horse	Races Run	1st	2nd	3rd	£
Sonoftheking	5	1	1	0	7656
Sykes	6	1	2	0	6882
*Pistol Shoot	8	1	1	0	4431
Merry Milan	2	1	0	0	3444
Total winning prize-money					**£22413**
Favourites	0-0		0.0%		0.00

JENNIFER MASON

ABLINGTON, GLOUCS

	No. of Hrs	Races Run	1st	2nd	3rd	Unpl	Per cent	£1 Level Stake
NH Flat	0	0	0	0	0	0	0.0	0.00
Hurdles	3	11	3	0	1	7	27.3	+98.00
Chases	0	0	0	0	0	0	0.0	0.00
Totals	3	11	3	0	1	7	27.3	+98.00
16-17	9	23	0	2	2	19	0.0	-23.00
15-16	5	16	0	0	0	16	0.0	-16.00

JOCKEYS

	W-R	Per cent	£1 Level Stake
Ben Hicks	1-1	100.0	+1.50
David Bass	1-1	100.0	+100.00
Mr James King	1-1	100.0	+4.50

COURSE RECORD

	Total W-R	Non-Hndcps Hurdles	Chases	Hndcps Hurdles	Chases	NH Flat	Per cent	£1 Level Stake
Catterick	1-1	0-0	0-0	1-1	0-0	0-0	100.0	+4.50
Ludlow	1-1	1-1	0-0	0-0	0-0	0-0	100.0	+100.00
Fontwell	1-2	0-1	0-0	1-1	0-0	0-0	50.0	+0.50

WINNING HORSES

Horse	Races Run	1st	2nd	3rd	£
Call Me Sid	4	1	0	0	4809
Oskar Denarius	5	2	0	0	5095
Total winning prize-money					£9904
Favourites	1-1		100.0%		1.50

JANE MATHIAS

LLANCARFAN, VALE OF GLAMORGAN

	No. of Hrs	Races Run	1st	2nd	3rd	Unpl	Per cent	£1 Level Stake
NH Flat	0	0	0	0	0	0	0.0	0.00
Hurdles	2	9	1	1	2	5	11.1	+17.00
Chases	0	0	0	0	0	0	0.0	0.00
Totals	2	9	1	1	2	5	11.1	+17.00
16-17	2	11	0	0	1	10	0.0	-11.00
15-16	2	11	0	0	0	11	0.0	-11.00

JOCKEYS

	W-R	Per cent	£1 Level Stake
Conor Ring	1-6	16.7	+20.00

COURSE RECORD

	Total W-R	Non-Hndcps Hurdles	Chases	Hndcps Hurdles	Chases	NH Flat	Per cent	£1 Level Stake
Hereford	1-3	1-2	0-0	0-1	0-0	0-0	33.3	+23.00

WINNING HORSES

Horse	Races Run	1st	2nd	3rd	£
Definately Vinnie	7	1	1	2	3639
Total winning prize-money					£3639
Favourites	0-0		0.0%		0.00

G C MAUNDRELL

OGBOURNE ST ANDREW, WILTS

	No. of Hrs	Races Run	1st	2nd	3rd	Unpl	Per cent	£1 Level Stake
NH Flat	2	4	0	1	3	0	0.0	-4.00
Hurdles	2	11	2	0	0	9	18.2	+1.50
Chases	0	0	0	0	0	0	0.0	0.00
Totals	3	15	2	0	1	12	13.3	-2.50
16-17	2	8	1	1	1	5	12.5	-4.75
15-16	1	9	1	2	3	3	11.1	-5.25

JOCKEYS

	W-R	Per cent	£1 Level Stake
Mr Zac Baker	2-9	22.2	+3.50

COURSE RECORD

	Total W-R	Non-Hndcps Hurdles	Chases	Hndcps Hurdles	Chases	NH Flat	Per cent	£1 Level Stake
Towcester	1-2	0-0	0-0	1-1	0-0	0-1	50.0	+2.50
Plumpton	1-3	0-0	0-0	1-3	0-0	0-0	33.3	+5.00

WINNING HORSES

Horse	Races Run	1st	2nd	3rd	£
Tambura	7	2	0	0	14036
Total winning prize-money					£14036
Favourites	0-0		0.0%		0.00

DONALD MCCAIN

CHOLMONDELEY, CHESHIRE

	No. of Hrs	Races Run	1st	2nd	3rd	Unpl	Per cent	£1 Level Stake
NH Flat	20	30	5	7	6	12	16.7	-8.18
Hurdles	79	334	54	47	47	186	16.2	-23.02
Chases	41	168	36	27	21	83	21.4	+14.03
Totals	113	532	95	81	74	281	17.9	-17.17
16-17	114	570	79	89	95	307	13.9	-129.20
15-16	126	498	54	60	73	311	10.8	-133.27

BY MONTH

NH Flat	W-R	Per cent	£1 Level Stake	Hurdles	W-R	Per cent	£1 Level Stake
May	1-2	50.0	+0.88	May	2-27	7.4	-21.18
June	0-1	0.0	-1.00	June	0-16	0.0	-16.00
July	1-3	33.3	+6.00	July	3-15	20.0	-4.51
August	1-2	50.0	+2.00	August	10-20	50.0	+45.64
September	0-0	0.0	0.00	September	4-13	30.8	+6.75
October	0-2	0.0	-2.00	October	3-35	8.6	-13.00
November	0-6	0.0	-6.00	November	5-39	12.8	+14.50
December	0-4	0.0	-4.00	December	10-39	25.6	+14.33
January	1-2	50.0	+0.20	January	7-39	17.9	-7.25
February	1-1	100.0	+2.75	February	2-26	7.7	-12.50
March	0-1	0.0	-1.00	March	6-33	18.2	-6.81
April	0-6	0.0	-6.00	April	2-32	6.3	-23.00

Chases	W-R	Per cent	£1 Level Stake	Totals	W-R	Per cent	£1 Level Stake
May	4-19	21.1	-7.38	May	7-48	14.6	-27.68
June	1-10	10.0	-7.50	June	1-27	3.7	-24.50
July	2-8	25.0	+14.00	July	6-26	23.1	+15.49
August	2-7	28.6	+7.50	August	13-29	44.8	+55.14
September	1-7	14.3	-3.00	September	5-20	25.0	+3.75
October	2-12	16.7	+7.00	October	5-49	10.2	-8.00
November	4-13	30.8	+13.00	November	9-58	15.5	+21.50
December	8-25	32.0	+7.75	December	18-68	26.5	+18.08
January	8-22	36.4	+4.03	January	16-63	25.4	-3.02
February	2-12	16.7	-0.13	February	5-39	12.8	-9.88
March	2-17	11.8	-5.25	March	8-51	15.7	-13.06
April	0-16	0.0	-16.00	April	2-54	3.7	-45.00

DISTANCE

Hurdles	W-R	Per cent	£1 Level Stake	Chases	W-R	Per cent	£1 Level Stake
2m-2m3f	27-191	14.1	-77.16	2m-2m3f	12-47	25.5	+2.75
2m4f-2m7f	21-106	19.8	+50.64	2m4f-2m7f	15-61	24.6	+15.41
3m+	6-37	16.2	+3.50	3m+	9-60	15.0	-4.13

TYPE OF RACE

Non-Handicaps	W-R	Per cent	£1 Level Stake	Handicaps	W-R	Per cent	£1 Level Stake
Nov Hrdls	19-82	23.2	-8.80	Nov Hrdls	0-11	0.0	-11.00
Hrdls	3-30	10.0	-16.47	Hrdls	32-209	15.3	+15.25
Nov Chs	5-16	31.3	-1.22	Nov Chs	2-15	13.3	-7.75
Chases	0-6	0.0	-6.00	Chases	23-108	21.3	+21.88
Sell/Claim	0-0	0.0	0.00	Sell/Claim	0-0	0.0	0.00

RACE CLASS

	W-R	Per cent	£1 Level Stake
Class 1	1-24	4.2	-22.47
Class 2	7-35	20.0	+51.50
Class 3	18-92	19.6	-2.63
Class 4	50-291	17.2	-35.67
Class 5	18-79	22.8	+0.23
Class 6	1-11	9.1	-8.13

FIRST TIME OUT

	W-R	Per cent	£1 Level Stake
Bumpers	4-20	20.0	-2.18
Hurdles	6-65	9.2	+4.70
Chases	6-28	21.4	+3.13
Totals	16-113	14.2	+5.65

JOCKEYS

	W-R	Per cent	£1 Level Stake
Will Kennedy	44-270	16.3	+0.88
Brian Hughes	22-89	24.7	+0.63
Lorcan Murtagh	14-85	16.5	-2.63
Miss Abbie McCain	7-21	33.3	+6.88
A P Heskin	4-8	50.0	+1.58
Mr Derek O'Connor	1-2	50.0	+7.00
Wayne Hutchinson	1-3	33.3	-0.50
Mr Aaron McGlinchey	1-4	25.0	+2.00
Mr Theo Gillard	1-18	5.6	-1.00

COURSE RECORD

	Total W-R	Non-Hndcps Hurdles	Chases	Hndcps Hurdles	Chases	NH Flat	Per cent	£1 Level Stake
Bangor	18-62	5-15	2-2	7-24	4-16	0-5	29.0	+38.71
Sedgefield	13-64	3-14	0-0	9-37	1-11	0-2	20.3	+2.08
Haydock	9-24	1-6	3-3	2-8	3-7	0-0	37.5	+17.28
Perth	7-24	2-5	0-1	2-10	2-5	1-3	29.2	+10.10
Musselbgh	7-27	1-6	0-1	2-10	4-9	0-1	25.9	+11.25
Kelso	7-31	0-8	0-0	3-12	3-10	1-1	22.6	-7.18
Ayr	6-16	2-3	0-0	0-4	4-8	0-1	37.5	+5.57
Catterick	5-28	1-7	0-0	1-11	2-9	1-1	17.9	-6.88
Stratford	4-8	1-1	0-0	1-4	1-1	1-2	50.0	+11.25
Wetherby	3-13	1-4	0-1	1-4	1-3	0-1	23.1	+5.00
Cartmel	3-29	2-4	0-5	1-11	0-9	0-0	10.3	-7.76
Carlisle	3-48	0-9	0-2	1-21	1-12	1-4	6.3	-1.13
Worcester	2-10	0-3	0-0	0-3	2-3	0-1	20.0	+12.00
Fontwell	1-2	0-0	0-0	1-1	0-1	0-0	50.0	+0.38
Fakenham	1-4	0-0	0-0	0-2	1-2	0-0	25.0	-1.50
Leicester	1-4	0-0	0-1	0-1	1-2	0-0	25.0	-1.00
Cheltenham	1-9	0-0	0-2	0-2	1-4	0-1	11.1	0.00
Newcastle	1-10	1-5	0-0	0-2	0-3	0-0	10.0	0.00
Doncaster	1-13	0-1	0-1	1-7	0-4	0-1	7.7	-7.00
Uttoxeter	1-17	1-8	0-1	0-4	0-3	0-1	5.9	-11.00
Hexham	1-18	1-6	0-0	0-9	0-1	0-2	5.6	-16.33

WINNING HORSES

Horse	Races Run	1st	2nd	3rd	£
William Of Orange	7	2	1	0	37448
Testify	5	3	0	0	34166
Dear Sire	13	5	3	0	51724
Henry's Joy	6	1	2	0	18768
Desert Cry	1	1	0	0	15640
Tawseef	7	3	3	1	27336
Same Circus	7	2	1	1	17660
Ubaltique	8	2	0	2	19494
The Clock Leary	8	3	1	0	21754
Lastbutnotleast	4	1	0	1	8497
Chti Balko	7	1	1	2	8123
Derintoher Yank	13	2	5	2	11047
What Happens Now	11	4	2	3	17508
Whiskey Chaser	6	1	1	1	6498
Federici	7	1	0	1	6498

Lough Derg Jewel	3	2	0	0	11047
Valleyofmilan	5	1	1	2	6279
Welsh Bard	6	1	0	2	5658
Hills Of Dubai	4	2	1	1	10725
Lofgren	9	2	3	0	9708
Middlebrow	7	2	1	0	8447
Princess Mononoke	9	3	1	1	11177
Waterlord	6	2	0	0	8123
Mahler Lad	4	1	1	0	4614
Nefyn Bay	7	3	1	0	13321
Pinch Of Ginger	7	1	0	1	4614
Whitsundays	7	1	2	1	4614
Kilronan Castle	5	1	0	0	4549
Court Dismissed	6	2	0	0	8707
Clondaw Draft	1	1	0	0	4472
Uppertown Prince	5	2	2	0	7509
Dark Sunset	8	3	0	0	11351
Craig Star	12	2	3	3	4118
Fin And Game	3	2	0	0	7993
Birch Vale	5	1	3	0	4094
Tailor Tom	7	1	1	0	4094
Knockrobin	6	1	2	1	4094
Danceintothelight	10	1	2	0	3899
Secret Escape	5	2	0	0	6431
Golden Investment	9	1	2	0	3899
Prince Khurram	11	3	1	3	9097
Rockalzaro	5	2	0	2	3899
Midnight Walk	9	2	2	1	7097
Derrynane	5	1	1	0	3509
Snougar	5	1	0	1	3379
The Great Getaway	2	1	0	0	3249
Man Look	9	3	3	2	9747
Viserion	8	1	1	0	3249
*Toboggan's Fire	2	1	0	0	3249
Wazowski	6	1	1	2	3119
The Some Dance Kid	2	1	1	0	2924
Thyne For Gold	4	1	0	1	2859
Hit And Run	8	1	3	2	2599
Irish Hawke	6	1	1	0	2599
Cowslip	7	1	0	2	2274
Shantaluze	2	1	0	0	2274
Total winning prize-money					**£540821**
Favourites	31-65		47.7%		21.31

GRAEME MCPHERSON

UPPER ODDINGTON, GLOUCS

	No. of Hrs	Races Run	1st	2nd	3rd	Unpl	Per cent	£1 Level Stake
NH Flat	11	19	2	2	1	14	10.5	-5.50
Hurdles	34	111	9	17	10	75	8.1	-61.60
Chases	14	47	9	11	5	22	19.1	+4.28
Totals	**45**	**177**	**20**	**30**	**16**	**111**	**11.3**	**-62.82**
16-17	40	174	28	24	27	94	16.1	+71.07
15-16	46	158	17	16	19	106	10.8	-27.75

BY MONTH

NH Flat	W-R	Per cent	£1 Level Stake	Hurdles	W-R	Per cent	£1 Level Stake
May	0-2	0.0	-2.00	May	2-10	20.0	+2.00
June	0-0	0.0	0.00	June	2-7	28.6	-1.60
July	0-0	0.0	0.00	July	0-6	0.0	-6.00
August	0-0	0.0	0.00	August	0-4	0.0	-4.00
September	0-1	0.0	-1.00	September	0-5	0.0	-5.00
October	0-2	0.0	-2.00	October	1-12	8.3	-7.00
November	0-4	0.0	-4.00	November	1-15	6.7	-10.50
December	0-3	0.0	-3.00	December	0-16	0.0	-16.00
January	0-1	0.0	-1.00	January	1-9	11.1	0.00
February	1-3	33.3	+6.00	February	1-9	11.1	-1.00
March	0-0	0.0	0.00	March	0-5	0.0	-5.00
April	1-3	33.3	+1.50	April	1-13	7.7	-7.50

Chases	W-R	Per cent	£1 Level Stake	Totals	W-R	Per cent	£1 Level Stake
May	1-5	20.0	+2.00	May	3-17	17.6	+2.00
June	1-7	14.3	-3.00	June	3-14	21.4	-4.60
July	1-3	33.3	+1.00	July	1-9	11.1	-5.00
August	0-2	0.0	-2.00	August	0-6	0.0	-6.00
September	0-2	0.0	-2.00	September	0-8	0.0	-8.00
October	0-2	0.0	-2.00	October	1-16	6.3	-11.00
November	3-6	50.0	+8.60	November	4-25	16.0	-5.90
December	1-5	20.0	-3.82	December	1-24	4.2	-22.82
January	1-5	20.0	+10.00	January	2-15	13.3	+9.00
February	0-4	0.0	-4.00	February	2-16	12.5	+1.00
March	0-2	0.0	-2.00	March	0-7	0.0	-7.00
April	1-4	25.0	+1.50	April	3-20	15.0	-4.50

DISTANCE

Hurdles	W-R	Per cent	£1 Level Stake	Chases	W-R	Per cent	£1 Level Stake
2m-2m3f	4-40	10.0	-22.60	2m-2m3f	4-15	26.7	-0.72
2m4f-2m7f	3-46	6.5	-24.00	2m4f-2m7f	3-21	14.3	+5.50
3m+	2-25	8.0	-15.00	3m+	2-11	18.2	-0.50

TYPE OF RACE

Non-Handicaps	W-R	Per cent	£1 Level Stake	Handicaps	W-R	Per cent	£1 Level Stake
Nov Hrdls	2-17	11.8	-11.60	Nov Hrdls	0-4	0.0	-4.00
Hrdls	0-7	0.0	-7.00	Hrdls	7-80	8.8	-36.00
Nov Chs	2-7	28.6	-3.72	Nov Chs	1-5	20.0	+2.00
Chases	0-0	0.0	0.00	Chases	5-29	17.2	-3.00
Sell/Claim	0-0	0.0	0.00	Sell/Claim	0-2	0.0	-2.00

RACE CLASS

	W-R	Per cent	£1 Level Stake
Class 1	0-4	0.0	-4.00
Class 2	0-6	0.0	-6.00
Class 3	5-38	13.2	-16.82
Class 4	10-86	11.6	-26.00
Class 5	5-33	15.2	0.00
Class 6	0-10	0.0	-10.00

FIRST TIME OUT

	W-R	Per cent	£1 Level Stake
Bumpers	0-11	0.0	-11.00
Hurdles	1-26	3.8	-19.00
Chases	2-8	25.0	+1.10
Totals	3-45	6.7	-28.90

JOCKEYS

	W-R	Per cent	£1 Level Stake
Kielan Woods	12-99	12.1	-21.72
Charlie Deutsch	3-14	21.4	+2.00
Paddy Brennan	3-19	15.8	-9.60
Bryony Frost	1-1	100.0	+3.50
Richard Johnson	1-8	12.5	-1.00

COURSE RECORD

	Total W-R	Non-Hndcps Hurdles	Non-Hndcps Chases	Hndcps Hurdles	Hndcps Chases	NH Flat	Per cent	£1 Level Stake
Ludlow	4-9	0-2	0-0	2-3	2-2	0-2	44.4	+26.00
Southwell	2-8	1-1	0-0	0-5	1-1	0-1	25.0	0.00
Wetherby	2-9	0-1	2-3	0-2	0-2	0-1	22.2	-5.72
Mrket Rsn	2-17	0-2	0-0	0-7	2-6	0-2	11.8	-8.00
Ayr	1-2	0-0	0-0	0-1	1-1	0-0	50.0	+5.50
Hexham	1-2	1-1	0-0	0-1	0-0	0-0	50.0	-0.60
Bangor	1-3	0-0	0-0	0-0	0-2	1-1	33.3	+1.50
Fontwell	1-4	0-0	0-0	1-3	0-1	0-0	25.0	+1.00
Towcester	1-4	0-0	0-1	1-3	0-0	0-0	25.0	+3.00
Doncaster	1-7	0-1	0-0	0-2	0-1	1-3	14.3	+2.00
Taunton	1-7	0-3	0-0	1-2	0-2	0-0	14.3	-2.50
Uttoxeter	1-8	0-1	0-0	1-4	0-2	0-1	12.5	-3.00
Huntingdon	1-13	0-2	0-1	1-8	0-2	0-0	7.7	-5.00
Worcester	1-16	0-3	0-0	0-5	1-5	0-3	6.3	-9.00

WINNING HORSES

Horse	Races Run	1st	2nd	3rd	£
Hey Bill	7	2	1	0	18974
Shady Glen	10	2	3	2	14296
Skipthecuddles	6	1	0	0	7538
Ami Desbois	4	2	0	0	10250
Harry Hunt	4	1	1	0	5848
Dahills Hill	5	1	1	0	5588
Beneficial Joe	9	1	2	1	5317
Stynes	4	2	1	0	7960
Red Admirable	5	2	1	0	7798
Symphony Of Angels	5	2	1	1	7148
Londonia	6	2	1	1	6888
Daydream Aulmes	3	1	1	0	2599
Norman Stanley	3	1	0	1	2274
Total winning prize-money					**£102478**
Favourites	4-17		23.5%		-8.32

REBECCA MENZIES

MORDON, DURHAM

	No. of Hrs	Races Run	1st	2nd	3rd	Unpl	Per cent	£1 Level Stake
NH Flat	4	6	0	0	0	6	0.0	-6.00
Hurdles	24	62	3	8	8	43	4.8	-2.88
Chases	16	63	6	14	8	35	9.5	-37.54
Totals	**37**	**131**	**9**	**22**	**16**	**84**	**6.9**	**-46.42**

16-17	31	122	17	14	17	74	13.9	-13.64
15-16	22	85	7	10	9	59	8.2	-7.50

JOCKEYS

	W-R	Per cent	£1 Level Stake
Brian Hughes	3-32	9.4	-11.25
Tony Kelly	2-54	3.7	-45.00
Grant Cockburn	1-3	33.3	+2.50
Colm McCormack	1-7	14.3	+34.00
Jamie Hamilton	1-10	10.0	-8.17
Conor O'Farrell	1-13	7.7	-6.50

COURSE RECORD

	Total W-R	Non-Hndcps Hurdles	Non-Hndcps Chases	Hndcps Hurdles	Hndcps Chases	NH Flat	Per cent	£1 Level Stake
Newcastle	2-7	0-0	0-0	0-1	2-5	0-1	28.6	+3.00
Hexham	2-10	0-2	0-0	0-1	2-7	0-0	20.0	-5.54
Mrket Rsn	1-4	0-1	0-0	1-2	0-1	0-0	25.0	+11.00
Southwell	1-5	0-0	0-0	1-2	0-3	0-0	20.0	-1.88
Wetherby	1-9	0-2	0-0	0-1	1-6	0-0	11.1	-3.50
Musselbgh	1-11	0-1	0-0	0-5	1-5	0-0	9.1	-5.50
Sedgefield	1-20	0-6	0-0	1-6	0-7	0-1	5.0	+21.00

WINNING HORSES

Horse	Races Run	1st	2nd	3rd	£
Pain Au Chocolat	8	1	3	0	8151
Smiling Jessica	8	1	2	0	5198
Tomkevi	9	2	0	1	9292
Vodka Wells	4	1	1	2	4224
Captain Mowbray	10	1	1	3	3899
Black Kettle	5	1	1	1	3314
Prairie Impulse	4	1	1	0	3249
*Running In Heels	4	1	1	1	3249
Total winning prize-money					**£40576**
Favourites	3-11		27.3%		-3.42

PHIL MIDDLETON

DORTON, BUCKS

	No. of Hrs	Races Run	1st	2nd	3rd	Unpl	Per cent	£1 Level Stake
NH Flat	1	1	0	0	0	1	0.0	-1.00
Hurdles	6	38	7	6	7	18	18.4	+18.63
Chases	2	16	4	3	1	8	25.0	+11.00
Totals	**7**	**55**	**11**	**9**	**8**	**27**	**20.0**	**+28.63**
16-17	6	30	3	5	3	19	10.0	-9.50
15-16	7	35	5	2	5	23	14.3	-2.00

BY MONTH

NH Flat	W-R	Per cent	£1 Level Stake	Hurdles	W-R	Per cent	£1 Level Stake
May	0-0	0.0	0.00	May	0-0	0.0	0.00
June	0-0	0.0	0.00	June	0-1	0.0	-1.00
July	0-0	0.0	0.00	July	0-3	0.0	-3.00
August	0-0	0.0	0.00	August	0-2	0.0	-2.00

	W-R	Per cent	£1 Level Stake
September	0-0	0.0	0.00
October	0-0	0.0	0.00
November	0-1	0.0	-1.00
December	0-0	0.0	0.00
January	0-0	0.0	0.00
February	0-0	0.0	0.00
March	0-0	0.0	0.00
April	0-0	0.0	0.00

	W-R	Per cent	£1 Level Stake
September	3-7	42.9	+24.13
October	0-4	0.0	-4.00
November	1-7	14.3	+1.00
December	3-6	50.0	+11.50
January	0-2	0.0	-2.00
February	0-4	0.0	-4.00
March	0-1	0.0	-1.00
April	0-1	0.0	-1.00

Chases	W-R	Per cent	£1 Level Stake
May	0-0	0.0	0.00
June	0-0	0.0	0.00
July	0-1	0.0	-1.00
August	0-2	0.0	-2.00
September	1-3	33.3	+3.00
October	1-1	100.0	+10.00
November	1-2	50.0	+4.50
December	0-2	0.0	-2.00
January	1-2	50.0	+1.50
February	0-2	0.0	-2.00
March	0-0	0.0	0.00
April	0-1	0.0	-1.00

Totals	W-R	Per cent	£1 Level Stake
May	0-0	0.0	0.00
June	0-1	0.0	-1.00
July	0-4	0.0	-4.00
August	0-4	0.0	-4.00
September	4-10	40.0	+27.13
October	1-5	20.0	+6.00
November	2-10	20.0	+4.50
December	3-8	37.5	+9.50
January	1-4	25.0	-0.50
February	0-6	0.0	-6.00
March	0-1	0.0	-1.00
April	0-2	0.0	-2.00

DISTANCE

Hurdles	W-R	Per cent	£1 Level Stake
2m-2m3f	1-15	6.7	-12.13
2m4f-2m7f	5-18	27.8	+33.50
3m+	1-4	25.0	-1.75

Chases	W-R	Per cent	£1 Level Stake
2m-2m3f	3-8	37.5	+15.50
2m4f-2m7f	0-3	0.0	-3.00
3m+	1-5	20.0	-1.50

TYPE OF RACE

Non-Handicaps	W-R	Per cent	£1 Level Stake
Nov Hrdls	0-6	0.0	-6.00
Hrdls	0-2	0.0	-2.00
Nov Chs	0-0	0.0	0.00
Chases	0-0	0.0	0.00
Sell/Claim	0-1	0.0	-1.00

Handicaps	W-R	Per cent	£1 Level Stake
Nov Hrdls	0-1	0.0	-1.00
Hrdls	6-27	22.2	+26.75
Nov Chs	0-3	0.0	-3.00
Chases	3-11	27.3	+5.00
Sell/Claim	1-1	100.0	+1.88

RACE CLASS

	W-R	Per cent	£1 Level Stake
Class 1	1-7	14.3	-0.50
Class 2	1-6	16.7	0.00
Class 3	6-15	40.0	+36.25
Class 4	2-19	10.5	-2.00
Class 5	1-8	12.5	-5.13
Class 6	0-0	0.0	0.00

FIRST TIME OUT

	W-R	Per cent	£1 Level Stake
Bumpers	0-1	0.0	-1.00
Hurdles	0-5	0.0	-5.00
Chases	0-1	0.0	-1.00
Totals	0-7	0.0	-7.00

JOCKEYS

	W-R	Per cent	£1 Level Stake
James Bowen	3-7	42.9	+5.25
Daniel Sansom	2-8	25.0	+5.00
Conor Shoemark	2-12	16.7	+5.00
Jamie Moore	1-2	50.0	+24.00

	W-R	Per cent	£1 Level Stake
Mr Tommie M O'Brien	1-2	50.0	+2.50
Fergus Gregory	1-4	25.0	+4.00
Harry Stock	1-8	12.5	-5.13

COURSE RECORD

	Total W-R	Non-Hndcps Hurdles	Chases	Hndcps Hurdles	Chases	NH Flat	Per cent	£1 Level Stake
Kempton	2-3	0-0	0-0	1-1	1-2	0-0	66.7	+12.50
Ascot	2-4	0-0	0-0	1-1	1-3	0-0	50.0	+9.50
Sandown	2-6	0-0	0-0	2-5	0-1	0-0	33.3	+8.00
Stratford	2-6	0-0	0-0	1-4	1-2	0-0	33.3	+2.88
Fakenham	1-3	0-0	0-0	0-2	1-1	0-0	33.3	+0.50
Plumpton	1-4	0-2	0-0	1-2	0-0	0-0	25.0	-1.75
Worcester	1-5	0-0	0-0	1-4	0-1	0-0	20.0	+21.00

WINNING HORSES

Horse	Races Run	1st	2nd	3rd	£
Exitas	12	3	2	1	43267
Golan Fortune	10	3	1	3	25508
*Holly Bush Henry	13	4	1	0	33990
Astrum	12	1	3	2	2599
Total winning prize-money					**£105364**
Favourites	3-5	60.0%			3.63

ROD MILLMAN

KENTISBEARE, DEVON

	No. of Hrs	Races Run	1st	2nd	3rd	Unpl	Per cent	£1 Level Stake
NH Flat	2	3	1	0	2	0	33.3	+9.00
Hurdles	3	6	2	1	1	2	33.3	+1.10
Chases	0	0	0	0	0	0	0.0	0.00
Totals	5	9	3	1	3	2	33.3	+10.10
16-17	3	9	4	0	0	5	44.4	+14.25
15-16	3	11	1	1	1	8	9.1	-8.00

JOCKEYS

	W-R	Per cent	£1 Level Stake
Daryl Jacob	1-1	100.0	+1.10
Harry Cobden	1-2	50.0	+10.00
Nick Scholfield	1-2	50.0	+3.00

COURSE RECORD

	Total W-R	Non-Hndcps Hurdles	Chases	Hndcps Hurdles	Chases	NH Flat	Per cent	£1 Level Stake
Chepstow	1-1	1-1	0-0	0-0	0-0	0-0	100.0	+4.00
Worcester	1-1	1-1	0-0	0-0	0-0	0-0	100.0	+1.10
Nton Abbot	1-2	0-0	0-0	0-0	0-0	1-2	50.0	+10.00

WINNING HORSES

Horse	Races Run	1st	2nd	3rd	£
Champagne Champ	3	1	1	1	4094
Taws	1	1	0	0	3379
*Bubbles Arcade	2	1	0	1	1711

Total winning prize-money			£9184
Favourites	1-1	100.0%	1.10

NICK MITCHELL

PIDDLETRENTHIDE, DORSET

	No. of Hrs	Races Run	1st	2nd	3rd	Unpl	Per cent	£1 Level Stake
NH Flat	1	1	0	0	0	1	0.0	-1.00
Hurdles	9	31	3	3	2	23	9.7	+14.00
Chases	2	7	0	0	1	6	0.0	-7.00
Totals	12	39	3	3	3	30	7.7	+6.00
16-17	17	67	6	7	9	45	9.0	-7.50
15-16	10	32	3	3	2	24	9.4	+11.38

JOCKEYS

	W-R	Per cent	£1 Level Stake
Sean Bowen	1-1	100.0	+12.00
Daryl Jacob	1-9	11.1	-3.00
Nick Scholfield	1-9	11.1	+17.00

COURSE RECORD

	Total W-R	Non-Hndcps Hurdles	Chases	Hndcps Hurdles	Chases	NH Flat	Per cent	£1 Level Stake
Exeter	1-3	0-1	0-0	1-1	0-1	0-0	33.3	+3.00
Towcester	1-3	0-1	0-0	1-2	0-0	0-0	33.3	+10.00
Plumpton	1-4	0-2	0-0	1-2	0-0	0-0	25.0	+22.00

WINNING HORSES

Horse	Races Run	1st	2nd	3rd	£
Drumlee City	5	1	1	0	5588
This Is It	6	1	2	0	3899
Jully Les Buxy	4	1	0	1	3119
Total winning prize-money					£12606
Favourites	0-2		0.0%		-2.00

RICHARD MITFORD-SLADE

NORTON FITZWARREN, SOMERSET

	No. of Hrs	Races Run	1st	2nd	3rd	Unpl	Per cent	£1 Level Stake
NH Flat	0	0	0	0	0	0	0.0	0.00
Hurdles	5	15	3	4	2	6	20.0	+110.75
Chases	2	2	0	0	0	2	0.0	-2.00
Totals	6	17	3	4	2	8	17.6	+108.75
16-17	1	1	0	0	0	1	0.0	-1.00

JOCKEYS

	W-R	Per cent	£1 Level Stake
Micheal Nolan	3-12	25.0	+113.75

COURSE RECORD

	Total W-R	Non-Hndcps Hurdles	Chases	Hndcps Hurdles	Chases	NH Flat	Per cent	£1 Level Stake
Taunton	2-4	2-3	0-1	0-0	0-0	0-0	50.0	+118.00
Bangor	1-4	1-4	0-0	0-0	0-0	0-0	25.0	-0.25

WINNING HORSES

Horse	Races Run	1st	2nd	3rd	£
*Applesolutely	3	1	2	0	5458
Samuel Jackson	4	2	0	1	5198
Total winning prize-money					£10656
Favourites	0-1		0.0%		-1.00

JAMES MOFFATT

CARTMEL, CUMBRIA

	No. of Hrs	Races Run	1st	2nd	3rd	Unpl	Per cent	£1 Level Stake
NH Flat	0	0	0	0	0	0	0.0	0.00
Hurdles	23	69	9	8	8	44	13.0	+17.75
Chases	12	36	2	3	8	23	5.6	-20.50
Totals	27	105	11	11	16	67	10.5	-2.75
16-17	20	97	12	16	19	50	12.4	+3.00
15-16	17	83	11	11	14	47	13.3	-10.75

BY MONTH

NH Flat	W-R	Per cent	£1 Level Stake	Hurdles	W-R	Per cent	£1 Level Stake
May	0-0	0.0	0.00	May	4-16	25.0	+3.00
June	0-0	0.0	0.00	June	2-10	20.0	+3.75
July	0-0	0.0	0.00	July	2-11	18.2	+9.00
August	0-0	0.0	0.00	August	0-6	0.0	-6.00
September	0-0	0.0	0.00	September	0-2	0.0	-2.00
October	0-0	0.0	0.00	October	1-5	20.0	+29.00
November	0-0	0.0	0.00	November	0-7	0.0	-7.00
December	0-0	0.0	0.00	December	0-1	0.0	-1.00
January	0-0	0.0	0.00	January	0-1	0.0	-1.00
February	0-0	0.0	0.00	February	0-1	0.0	-1.00
March	0-0	0.0	0.00	March	0-2	0.0	-2.00
April	0-0	0.0	0.00	April	0-7	0.0	-7.00

Chases	W-R	Per cent	£1 Level Stake	Totals	W-R	Per cent	£1 Level Stake
May	1-4	25.0	+2.50	May	5-20	25.0	+5.50
June	0-1	0.0	-1.00	June	2-11	18.2	+2.75
July	0-7	0.0	-7.00	July	2-18	11.1	+2.00
August	0-7	0.0	-7.00	August	0-13	0.0	-13.00
September	0-2	0.0	-2.00	September	0-4	0.0	-4.00
October	1-5	20.0	+4.00	October	2-10	20.0	+33.00
November	0-0	0.0	0.00	November	0-7	0.0	-7.00
December	0-5	0.0	-5.00	December	0-6	0.0	-6.00
January	0-1	0.0	-1.00	January	0-2	0.0	-2.00
February	0-1	0.0	-1.00	February	0-2	0.0	-2.00
March	0-0	0.0	0.00	March	0-2	0.0	-2.00
April	0-3	0.0	-3.00	April	0-10	0.0	-10.00

DISTANCE

Hurdles	W-R	Per cent	£1 Level Stake	Chases	W-R	Per cent	£1 Level Stake
2m-2m3f	4-42	9.5	-11.63	2m-2m3f	1-12	8.3	-3.00
2m4f-2m7f	3-20	15.0	-2.63	2m4f-2m7f	0-14	0.0	-14.00
3m+	2-7	28.6	+32.00	3m+	1-10	10.0	-3.50

TYPE OF RACE

Non-Handicaps	W-R	Per cent	£1 Level Stake	Handicaps	W-R	Per cent	£1 Level Stake
Nov Hrdls	0-10	0.0	-10.00	Nov Hrdls	0-2	0.0	-2.00
Hrdls	1-5	20.0	+3.00	Hrdls	8-51	15.7	+27.75
Nov Chs	0-4	0.0	-4.00	Nov Chs	0-0	0.0	0.00
Chases	0-0	0.0	0.00	Chases	2-31	6.5	-15.50
Sell/Claim	0-1	0.0	-1.00	Sell/Claim	0-0	0.0	0.00

RACE CLASS

	W-R	Per cent	£1 Level Stake
Class 1	0-3	0.0	-3.00
Class 2	2-23	8.7	-7.00
Class 3	4-38	10.5	+19.38
Class 4	4-32	12.5	-11.13
Class 5	1-9	11.1	-1.00
Class 6	0-0	0.0	0.00

FIRST TIME OUT

	W-R	Per cent	£1 Level Stake
Bumpers	0-0	0.0	0.00
Hurdles	4-20	20.0	+4.38
Chases	1-7	14.3	-0.50
Totals	5-27	18.5	+3.88

JOCKEYS

	W-R	Per cent	£1 Level Stake
Charlotte Jones	4-20	20.0	+46.00
Brian Hughes	4-30	13.3	-17.25
Henry Brooke	2-27	7.4	-12.50
Richard Johnson	1-6	16.7	+3.00

COURSE RECORD

	Total W-R	Non-Hndcps Hurdles	Chases	Hndcps Hurdles	Chases	NH Flat	Per cent	£1 Level Stake
Cartmel	8-56	1-8	0-4	6-30	1-14	0-0	14.3	+0.88
Aintree	1-4	0-0	0-0	1-3	0-1	0-0	25.0	+30.00
Wetherby	1-6	0-0	0-0	0-5	1-1	0-0	16.7	+3.00
Carlisle	1-7	0-0	0-0	1-5	0-2	0-0	14.3	-4.63

WINNING HORSES

Horse	Races Run	1st	2nd	3rd	£
Altruism	3	1	0	0	16891
Morning Royalty	6	1	1	2	12512
Lough Kent	6	2	1	0	12512
Bon Chic	8	1	1	1	7820
*Nicolas Chauvin	7	1	1	1	6498
Idder	5	1	0	1	5393
Munsaab	6	1	0	1	4549
Boruma	7	2	0	0	7473
Think Ahead	3	1	1	0	2599
Total winning prize-money					**£76247**
Favourites	2-6		**33.3%**		**-0.63**

LAURA MONGAN

EPSOM, SURREY

	No. of Hrs	Races Run	1st	2nd	3rd	Unpl	Per cent	£1 Level Stake
NH Flat	2	5	1	0	0	4	20.0	+29.00
Hurdles	7	14	0	0	3	11	0.0	-14.00
Chases	2	4	0	0	0	4	0.0	-4.00
Totals	10	23	1	0	3	19	4.3	+11.00
16-17	12	33	1	4	3	25	3.0	-20.00
15-16	15	36	1	3	2	30	2.8	-25.00

JOCKEYS

	W-R	Per cent	£1 Level Stake
Joshua Moore	1-3	33.3	+31.00

COURSE RECORD

	Total W-R	Non-Hndcps Hurdles	Chases	Hndcps Hurdles	Chases	NH Flat	Per cent	£1 Level Stake
Fontwell	1-9	0-1	0-0	0-4	0-3	1-1	11.1	+25.00

WINNING HORSES

Horse	Races Run	1st	2nd	3rd	£
Liz's Dream	2	1	0	0	1560
Total winning prize-money					**£1560**
Favourites	0-0		0.0%		0.00

GARY MOORE

LOWER BEEDING, W SUSSEX

	No. of Hrs	Races Run	1st	2nd	3rd	Unpl	Per cent	£1 Level Stake
NH Flat	19	30	1	2	5	22	3.3	-27.38
Hurdles	74	234	34	25	28	147	14.5	-19.33
Chases	35	137	16	19	20	82	11.7	-57.31
Totals	110	401	51	46	53	251	12.7	-104.02
16-17	95	331	39	45	42	204	11.8	-109.09
15-16	85	292	54	38	40	159	18.5	+82.84

BY MONTH

NH Flat	W-R	Per cent	£1 Level Stake	Hurdles	W-R	Per cent	£1 Level Stake
May	0-4	0.0	-4.00	May	2-17	11.8	-3.00
June	0-0	0.0	0.00	June	0-7	0.0	-7.00
July	0-0	0.0	0.00	July	0-1	0.0	-1.00
August	0-0	0.0	0.00	August	0-5	0.0	-5.00
September	0-0	0.0	0.00	September	2-8	25.0	+10.75
October	0-2	0.0	-2.00	October	5-16	31.3	+14.90
November	0-5	0.0	-5.00	November	1-27	3.7	-21.00
December	0-5	0.0	-5.00	December	7-40	17.5	-7.50
January	0-2	0.0	-2.00	January	6-30	20.0	+9.50
February	1-4	25.0	-1.38	February	3-27	11.1	-15.50
March	0-4	0.0	-4.00	March	5-22	22.7	+32.20
April	0-4	0.0	-4.00	April	3-34	8.8	-26.68

Chases	W-R	Per cent	£1 Level Stake
May	0-8	0.0	-8.00
June	0-7	0.0	-7.00
July	0-1	0.0	-1.00
August	0-1	0.0	-1.00
September	0-1	0.0	-1.00
October	3-10	30.0	+8.25
November	3-25	12.0	-15.31
December	2-24	8.3	-11.25
January	3-14	21.4	-0.50
February	2-16	12.5	-3.50
March	1-14	7.1	-11.00
April	2-16	12.5	-6.00

Totals	W-R	Per cent	£1 Level Stake
May	2-29	6.9	-15.00
June	0-14	0.0	-14.00
July	0-2	0.0	-2.00
August	0-6	0.0	-6.00
September	2-9	22.2	+9.75
October	8-28	28.6	+21.15
November	4-57	7.0	-41.31
December	9-69	13.0	-23.75
January	9-46	19.6	+7.00
February	6-47	12.8	-20.38
March	6-40	15.0	+17.20
April	5-54	9.3	-36.68

Course	W-R						Per cent	£1 Level
Sandown	3-29	1-8	0-3	1-8	1-10	0-0	10.3	-16.17
Worcester	2-4	1-2	0-0	0-0	1-2	0-0	50.0	+28.00
Warwick	2-5	1-1	0-2	0-1	1-1	0-0	40.0	+6.00
Newbury	2-15	1-6	0-0	1-5	0-2	0-2	13.3	+9.50
Lingfield	2-21	1-6	0-1	1-6	0-8	0-0	9.5	-13.25
Nton Abbot	1-1	0-0	0-0	1-1	0-0	0-0	100.0	+2.25
Leicester	1-2	0-1	0-0	0-0	1-1	0-0	50.0	+0.25
Ffos Las	1-2	1-1	0-0	0-1	0-0	0-0	50.0	-0.60
Doncaster	1-3	0-0	0-0	1-1	0-1	0-0	33.3	0.00
Ludlow	1-4	0-0	0-0	0-0	1-3	0-1	25.0	0.00
Mrket Rsn	1-4	0-1	0-0	0-1	1-2	0-0	25.0	+1.50
Taunton	1-8	0-1	0-0	1-5	0-2	0-0	12.5	-5.25
Wincanton	1-10	1-1	0-0	0-6	0-1	0-2	10.0	-7.13
Cheltenham	1-14	0-4	0-2	0-2	1-5	0-1	7.1	-6.50
Kempton	1-34	1-10	0-1	0-14	0-8	0-1	2.9	-27.00

DISTANCE

Hurdles	W-R	Per cent	£1 Level Stake
2m-2m3f	28-162	17.3	+20.98
2m4f-2m7f	4-54	7.4	-28.07
3m+	2-12	16.7	-6.25

Chases	W-R	Per cent	£1 Level Stake
2m-2m3f	7-57	12.3	-26.00
2m4f-2m7f	8-49	16.3	-3.56
3m+	1-31	3.2	-27.75

TYPE OF RACE

Non-Handicaps	W-R	Per cent	£1 Level Stake
Nov Hrdls	7-52	13.5	+4.44
Hrdls	12-44	27.3	+7.15
Nov Chs	4-16	25.0	+6.19
Chases	0-7	0.0	-7.00
Sell/Claim	0-2	0.0	-2.00

Handicaps	W-R	Per cent	£1 Level Stake
Nov Hrdls	1-7	14.3	-3.75
Hrdls	14-125	11.2	-21.17
Nov Chs	1-16	6.3	-13.75
Chases	8-77	10.4	-42.25
Sell/Claim	0-2	0.0	-2.00

RACE CLASS

	W-R	Per cent	£1 Level Stake
Class 1	2-39	5.1	-28.75
Class 2	3-32	9.4	-12.00
Class 3	15-82	18.3	+20.53
Class 4	21-170	12.4	-54.42
Class 5	10-69	14.5	-20.38
Class 6	0-9	0.0	-9.00

FIRST TIME OUT

	W-R	Per cent	£1 Level Stake
Bumpers	0-19	0.0	-19.00
Hurdles	9-60	15.0	+2.38
Chases	3-31	9.7	-12.25
Totals	12-110	10.9	-28.87

JOCKEYS

	W-R	Per cent	£1 Level Stake
Jamie Moore	35-175	20.0	-14.21
Joshua Moore	12-156	7.7	-51.68
William Clarke	3-33	9.1	-13.13
Jason Nuttall	1-10	10.0	+2.00

COURSE RECORD

	Total W-R	Non-Hndcps Hurdles	Chases	Hndcps Hurdles	Chases	NH Flat	Per cent	£1 Level Stake
Plumpton	15-72	4-20	3-7	6-20	2-20	0-5	20.8	-4.62
Fontwell	9-90	5-21	0-2	1-36	2-22	1-9	10.0	-51.25
Ascot	3-26	1-4	1-3	0-4	1-10	0-5	11.5	-11.75
Huntingdon	3-27	1-5	0-0	2-13	0-8	0-1	11.1	+22.00

WINNING HORSES

Horse	Races Run	1st	2nd	3rd	£
Traffic Fluide	7	2	0	0	39173
Mister Chow	4	2	1	0	31190
Casse Tete	5	1	0	0	25024
Benatar	4	3	0	1	36655
Sussex Ranger	4	2	1	0	16411
Darebin	9	2	2	2	18190
Antony	5	1	0	1	7946
San Pedro De Senam	8	1	1	2	7882
Dell Oro	5	1	2	1	7798
Remind Me Later	7	1	4	1	6882
Not Another Muddle	2	2	0	0	13099
Maquisard	4	1	0	0	6498
Eragon De Chanay	7	2	1	2	11372
Clayton	5	1	1	0	6330
Not Never	3	2	1	0	11527
Knocknanuss	6	2	2	0	5393
East Indies	4	1	0	0	5393
Thounder	3	2	0	0	9097
Leo Luna	6	1	1	1	4874
All Currencies	5	2	0	1	8577
Stoical Patient	5	3	0	0	11112
Graasten	2	1	0	0	4354
Distingo	4	2	1	0	8317
Ar Mest	6	1	0	1	4159
*Goldslinger	4	1	0	0	4159
Larry	7	2	1	1	8187
*Cheque En Blanc	7	2	1	3	7018
Argyle	5	1	2	0	3379
Aiguille Rouge	4	2	0	2	6498
Le Capricieux	6	1	0	1	3249
Lord E	2	1	0	0	3249
Osgood	7	1	0	0	2599
The Flying Sofa	4	1	0	2	2274
Total winning prize-money					**£347865**
Favourites		18-37		48.6%	12.40

LAURA MORGAN

GRANTHAM, LINCOLNSHIRE

	No. of Hrs	Races Run	1st	2nd	3rd	Unpl	Per cent	£1 Level Stake
NH Flat	3	6	1	1	0	4	16.7	+3.00
Hurdles	12	29	2	0	4	23	6.9	-11.50
Chases	3	20	7	2	1	10	35.0	+18.88
Totals	15	55	10	3	5	37	18.2	+10.38
16-17	15	49	1	1	3	44	2.0	-39.00

BY MONTH

NH Flat	W-R	Per cent	£1 Level Stake	Hurdles	W-R	Per cent	£1 Level Stake
May	0-1	0.0	-1.00	May	0-3	0.0	-3.00
June	0-1	0.0	-1.00	June	1-2	50.0	+6.50
July	0-0	0.0	0.00	July	0-2	0.0	-2.00
August	0-0	0.0	0.00	August	0-0	0.0	0.00
September	0-0	0.0	0.00	September	0-0	0.0	0.00
October	0-0	0.0	0.00	October	0-2	0.0	-2.00
November	0-0	0.0	0.00	November	0-0	0.0	0.00
December	0-1	0.0	-1.00	December	0-5	0.0	-5.00
January	0-1	0.0	-1.00	January	1-5	20.0	+4.00
February	1-1	100.0	+8.00	February	0-1	0.0	-1.00
March	0-0	0.0	0.00	March	0-3	0.0	-3.00
April	0-1	0.0	-1.00	April	0-6	0.0	-6.00

Chases	W-R	Per cent	£1 Level Stake	Totals	W-R	Per cent	£1 Level Stake
May	0-1	0.0	-1.00	May	0-5	0.0	-5.00
June	0-0	0.0	0.00	June	1-3	33.3	+5.50
July	0-0	0.0	0.00	July	0-2	0.0	-2.00
August	0-0	0.0	0.00	August	0-0	0.0	0.00
September	0-0	0.0	0.00	September	0-0	0.0	0.00
October	0-0	0.0	0.00	October	0-2	0.0	-2.00
November	0-2	0.0	-2.00	November	0-2	0.0	-2.00
December	0-2	0.0	-2.00	December	0-8	0.0	-8.00
January	0-1	0.0	-1.00	January	1-7	14.3	+2.00
February	3-6	50.0	+17.75	February	4-8	50.0	+24.75
March	2-3	66.7	+3.63	March	2-6	33.3	+0.63
April	2-5	40.0	+3.50	April	2-12	16.7	-3.50

DISTANCE

Hurdles	W-R	Per cent	£1 Level Stake	Chases	W-R	Per cent	£1 Level Stake
2m-2m3f	1-21	4.8	-12.00	2m-2m3f	4-13	30.8	+13.63
2m4f-2m7f	1-6	16.7	+2.50	2m4f-2m7f	3-7	42.9	+5.25
3m+	0-2	0.0	-2.00	3m+	0-0	0.0	0.00

TYPE OF RACE

Non-Handicaps	W-R	Per cent	£1 Level Stake	Handicaps	W-R	Per cent	£1 Level Stake
Nov Hrdls	1-7	14.3	+2.00	Nov Hrdls	0-0	0.0	0.00
Hrdls	0-8	0.0	-8.00	Hrdls	1-10	10.0	-1.50
Nov Chs	0-0	0.0	0.00	Nov Chs	1-4	25.0	-0.50
Chases	0-0	0.0	0.00	Chases	5-14	35.7	+18.50
Sell/Claim	0-1	0.0	-1.00	Sell/Claim	0-1	0.0	-1.00

RACE CLASS

	W-R	Per cent	£1 Level Stake
Class 1	0-2	0.0	-2.00
Class 2	0-1	0.0	-1.00
Class 3	1-3	33.3	-0.13
Class 4	5-21	23.8	+5.25
Class 5	4-25	16.0	+11.25
Class 6	0-3	0.0	-3.00

FIRST TIME OUT

	W-R	Per cent	£1 Level Stake
Bumpers	1-3	33.3	+6.00
Hurdles	0-11	0.0	-11.00
Chases	0-1	0.0	-1.00
Totals	1-15	6.7	-6.00

JOCKEYS

	W-R	Per cent	£1 Level Stake
Patrick Cowley	8-24	33.3	+23.88
Miss Antonia Peck	1-2	50.0	+6.50
Jonjo O'Neill	1-4	25.0	+5.00

COURSE RECORD

	Total W-R	Non-Hndcps Hurdles	Chases	Hndcps Hurdles	Chases	NH Flat	Per cent	£1 Level Stake
Southwell	4-10	0-3	0-0	0-2	4-4	0-1	40.0	+7.50
Towcester	2-4	0-1	0-0	0-0	2-3	0-0	50.0	+13.88
Musselbgh	1-2	0-0	0-0	0-1	0-0	1-1	50.0	+7.00
Fakenham	1-2	0-0	0-0	1-1	0-1	0-0	50.0	+6.50
Carlisle	1-3	0-0	0-0	0-0	1-3	0-0	33.3	+0.50
Leicester	1-3	1-1	0-0	0-0	0-2	0-0	33.3	+6.00

WINNING HORSES

Horse	Races Run	1st	2nd	3rd	£
Skipping On	9	4	1	0	21849
*The New Pharaoh	4	1	0	1	5458
Ulis De Vassy	10	3	1	1	13841
Beaumont's Party	4	1	0	0	3743
Zakharova	2	1	0	0	2599
Total winning prize-money					£47490
Favourites	2-2		100.0%		5.88

HUGHIE MORRISON

EAST ILSLEY, BERKS

	No. of Hrs	Races Run	1st	2nd	3rd	Unpl	Per cent	£1 Level Stake
NH Flat	4	6	1	1	1	3	16.7	+2.00
Hurdles	4	10	0	2	2	6	0.0	-10.00
Chases	2	7	1	2	2	2	14.3	-4.25
Totals	10	23	2	5	5	11	8.7	-12.25
16-17	7	29	5	4	1	19	17.2	-14.75
15-16	8	22	5	1	3	13	22.7	+6.54

JOCKEYS

	W-R	Per cent	£1 Level Stake
Andrew Tinkler	1-1	100.0	+7.00
Tom O'Brien	1-10	10.0	-7.25

COURSE RECORD

	Total W-R	Non-Hndcps Hurdles	Chases	Hndcps Hurdles	Chases	NH Flat	Per cent	£1 Level Stake
Hereford	1-1	0-0	0-0	0-0	0-0	1-1	100.0	+7.00
Cheltenham	1-2	0-0	0-0	0-0	1-1	0-1	50.0	+0.75

WINNING HORSES

Horse	Races Run	1st	2nd	3rd	£
Sister Sibyl	6	1	2	1	15640
Apres Le Deluge	1	1	0	0	2599
Total winning prize-money					£18239
Favourites	1-6	16.7%			-3.25

MRS BRIDGET LEWIS

CLYNDERWEN, CARMARTHEN

	No. of Hrs	Races Run	1st	2nd	3rd	Unpl	Per cent	£1 Level Stake
NH Flat	0	0	0	0	0	0	0.0	0.00
Hurdles	0	0	0	0	0	0	0.0	0.00
Chases	1	4	1	2	1	0	25.0	-1.90
Totals	1	4	1	2	1	0	25.0	-1.90
16-17	1	1	0	1	0	0	0.0	-1.00

JOCKEYS

	W-R	Per cent	£1 Level Stake
Mr Peter Bryan	1-1	100.0	+1.10

COURSE RECORD

	Total W-R	Non-Hndcps Hurdles	Chases	Hndcps Hurdles	Chases	NH Flat	Per cent	£1 Level Stake
Chepstow	1-2	0-0	1-2	0-0	0-0	0-0	50.0	+0.10

WINNING HORSES

Horse	Races Run	1st	2nd	3rd	£
*Tinkers Hill Tommy	4	1	2	1	3120
Total winning prize-money					£3120
Favourites	1-2	50.0%			0.10

WILLIAM MUIR

LAMBOURN, BERKS

	No. of Hrs	Races Run	1st	2nd	3rd	Unpl	Per cent	£1 Level Stake
NH Flat	1	3	0	0	0	3	0.0	-3.00
Hurdles	1	1	1	0	0	0	100.0	+4.50
Chases	0	0	0	0	0	0	0.0	0.00
Totals	2	4	1	0	0	3	25.0	+1.50

JOCKEYS

	W-R	Per cent	£1 Level Stake
James Bowen	1-1	100.0	+4.50

COURSE RECORD

	Total W-R	Non-Hndcps Hurdles	Chases	Hndcps Hurdles	Chases	NH Flat	Per cent	£1 Level Stake
Warwick	1-1	0-0	0-0	1-1	0-0	0-0	100.0	+4.50

WINNING HORSES

Horse	Races Run	1st	2nd	3rd	£
Chief Brody	1	1	0	0	4549
Total winning prize-money					£4549
Favourites	0-0	0.0%			0.00

NEIL MULHOLLAND

LIMPLEY STOKE, WILTS

	No. of Hrs	Races Run	1st	2nd	3rd	Unpl	Per cent	£1 Level Stake
NH Flat	23	37	4	7	5	21	10.8	-20.80
Hurdles	104	332	40	46	35	211	12.0	-144.13
Chases	42	133	15	17	18	83	11.3	-69.82
Totals	137	502	59	70	58	315	11.8	-234.75
16-17	129	550	106	76	59	309	19.3	+11.68
15-16	109	426	60	58	43	265	14.1	-144.57

BY MONTH

NH Flat	W-R	Per cent	£1 Level Stake	Hurdles	W-R	Per cent	£1 Level Stake
May	1-3	33.3	0.00	May	5-17	29.4	+13.91
June	0-3	0.0	-3.00	June	3-23	13.0	-11.00
July	0-2	0.0	-2.00	July	4-32	12.5	-15.26
August	0-0	0.0	0.00	August	5-23	21.7	-0.57
September	0-1	0.0	-1.00	September	3-24	12.5	-4.76
October	0-3	0.0	-3.00	October	2-29	6.9	-14.00
November	0-7	0.0	-7.00	November	5-48	10.4	-33.26
December	0-2	0.0	-2.00	December	1-30	3.3	-26.00
January	0-3	0.0	-3.00	January	5-29	17.2	-13.27
February	1-4	25.0	+5.00	February	2-29	6.9	-22.43
March	1-2	50.0	-0.43	March	1-25	4.0	-17.50
April	1-7	14.3	-4.38	April	4-23	17.4	0.00

Chases	W-R	Per cent	£1 Level Stake	Totals	W-R	Per cent	£1 Level Stake
May	1-4	25.0	-1.63	May	7-24	29.2	+12.28
June	1-9	11.1	-1.00	June	4-35	11.4	-15.00
July	0-9	0.0	-9.00	July	4-43	9.3	-26.26
August	2-7	28.6	-0.13	August	7-30	23.3	-0.70
September	0-9	0.0	-9.00	September	3-34	8.8	-14.76
October	2-15	13.3	-8.70	October	4-47	8.5	-25.70
November	3-22	13.6	-9.90	November	8-77	10.4	-50.16
December	3-20	15.0	-4.67	December	4-52	7.7	-32.67
January	1-9	11.1	-2.50	January	6-41	14.6	-18.77

February	1-10	10.0	-8.80		February	4-43	9.3	-26.23
March	1-10	10.0	-5.50		March	3-37	8.1	-23.43
April	0-9	0.0	-9.00		April	5-39	12.8	-13.38

DISTANCE

Hurdles	W-R	Per cent	£1 Level Stake	Chases	W-R	Per cent	£1 Level Stake
2m-2m3f	19-165	11.5	-70.51	2m-2m3f	7-32	21.9	-13.39
2m4f-2m7f	16-135	11.9	-74.12	2m4f-2m7f	4-60	6.7	-33.63
3m+	5-27	18.5	+5.50	3m+	4-41	9.8	-22.80

TYPE OF RACE

Non-Handicaps	W-R	Per cent	£1 Level Stake	Handicaps	W-R	Per cent	£1 Level Stake
Nov Hrdls	11-81	13.6	-51.95	Nov Hrdls	2-26	7.7	-18.50
Hrdls	3-32	9.4	-21.76	Hrdls	23-187	12.3	-47.65
Nov Chs	7-21	33.3	+5.93	Nov Chs	0-17	0.0	-17.00
Chases	0-0	0.0	0.00	Chases	8-82	9.8	-45.75
Sell/Claim	0-2	0.0	-2.00	Sell/Claim	0-0	0.0	0.00

RACE CLASS

	W-R	Per cent	£1 Level Stake
Class 1	1-27	3.7	-23.00
Class 2	2-27	7.4	-12.00
Class 3	10-87	11.5	-33.30
Class 4	31-239	13.0	-116.15
Class 5	14-102	13.7	-33.30
Class 6	1-20	5.0	-17.00

FIRST TIME OUT

	W-R	Per cent	£1 Level Stake
Bumpers	3-23	13.0	-9.43
Hurdles	10-81	12.3	-22.10
Chases	4-33	12.1	-21.73
Totals	17-137	12.4	-53.26

JOCKEYS

	W-R	Per cent	£1 Level Stake
Noel Fehily	32-219	14.6	-67.99
Tom Scudamore	10-82	12.2	-36.60
Philip Donovan	4-27	14.8	-4.00
Richard Johnson	2-7	28.6	-0.80
Robert Dunne	2-18	11.1	-9.80
James Best	2-21	9.5	-8.50
Harry Reed	2-41	4.9	-37.29
A P Heskin	1-1	100.0	+0.33
Tom O'Brien	1-2	50.0	+1.50
Sam Twiston-Davies	1-2	50.0	+6.00
Niall P Madden	1-5	20.0	-3.60
Mr James King	1-34	2.9	-31.00

COURSE RECORD

	Total W-R	Non-Hndcps Hurdles	Chases	Hndcps Hurdles	Chases	NH Flat	Per cent	£1 Level Stake
Fontwell	10-47	1-10	0-0	4-21	3-10	2-6	21.3	-5.49
Plumpton	6-25	1-7	0-0	2-9	2-5	1-4	24.0	+0.15
Sedgefield	5-13	2-5	1-1	1-5	1-2	0-0	38.5	+2.38
Worcester	4-53	2-11	0-4	2-26	0-9	0-3	7.5	-27.27
Chepstow	3-19	0-8	1-2	2-5	0-2	0-2	15.8	-2.00
Uttoxeter	3-21	0-6	0-0	3-13	0-2	0-0	14.3	-1.50
Southwell	3-25	2-5	1-2	0-11	0-4	0-3	12.0	-18.26
Catterick	2-7	2-2	0-2	0-1	0-1	0-1	28.6	-3.93

Warwick	2-10	0-3	1-1	1-5	0-1	0-0	20.0	-2.80
Ffos Las	2-11	0-4	1-1	1-2	0-3	0-1	18.2	+2.00
Taunton	2-13	0-2	0-0	2-10	0-1	0-0	15.4	-0.50
Cheltenham	2-14	1-3	1-2	0-4	0-4	0-1	14.3	+1.00
Nton Abbot	2-20	1-6	0-0	0-10	1-3	0-1	10.0	-5.00
Wincanton	2-28	0-8	0-1	1-9	1-8	0-2	7.1	-21.50
Perth	1-1	1-1	0-0	0-0	0-0	0-0	100.0	+1.10
Wetherby	1-3	0-0	0-0	1-2	0-0	0-1	33.3	+1.00
Hereford	1-4	1-1	0-0	0-1	0-2	0-0	25.0	-2.67
Hexham	1-4	0-1	0-0	0-2	0-0	1-1	25.0	-1.00
Fakenham	1-5	0-1	0-0	1-2	0-2	0-0	20.0	+3.00
Aintree	1-6	0-0	0-0	1-2	0-3	0-1	16.7	+1.00
Cartmel	1-10	1-5	0-0	0-3	0-2	0-0	10.0	-7.80
Doncaster	1-11	0-3	0-0	1-5	0-3	0-0	9.1	-5.50
Stratford	1-15	0-4	0-1	1-7	0-3	0-0	6.7	-11.00
Bangor	1-16	0-4	1-1	0-6	0-1	0-4	6.3	-14.67
Exeter	1-18	0-6	0-0	1-9	0-2	0-1	5.6	-12.50

WINNING HORSES

Horse	Races Run	1st	2nd	3rd	£
Kalondra	5	2	1	1	19539
Tikkanbar	4	2	0	0	17487
Rossetti	6	2	0	0	19508
Bishops Court	6	1	1	1	9495
Solighoster	6	2	0	1	15882
Solomn Grundy	7	1	3	0	8058
*Charlie Rascal	3	1	1	0	7115
Knight Of Noir	6	3	2	0	18676
Perfect Timing	3	1	0	0	6498
Rainy Day Dylan	7	2	1	0	10267
Vancouver	5	2	0	2	9153
The Way You Dance	4	1	0	0	5198
Prettylittlething	9	1	0	0	4874
Dieg Man	4	2	0	0	8058
Master Burbidge	5	2	0	1	8512
Moving In Style	5	2	0	0	7278
Minellatillmorning	6	2	1	0	8252
Inaminna	4	1	0	2	4094
Kansas City Chief	6	1	2	0	4094
Chirico Vallis	5	2	1	0	7893
Deja Bougg	1	1	0	0	3899
Espoir De Teillee	1	1	0	0	3899
The Wicket Chicken	5	3	1	0	9097
Runasimi River	4	1	0	0	3899
Highbury High	6	1	1	0	3899
Cesar Et Rosalie	4	1	1	0	3798
Mrs Burbidge	3	1	1	1	3798
Novis Adventus	4	2	1	0	7278
Carole's Vigilante	3	1	0	1	3639
Dalaman	4	3	1	0	10072
Mount Oliver	4	1	0	2	3314
*Boy In A Bentley	6	2	1	0	6498
Poetic Lady	6	2	2	0	5848
Code Of Law	7	1	0	2	2599
Magical Thomas	7	1	1	0	2599
Willyegolassiego	4	1	1	0	2599

Irish Odyssey	2	1	0	0	2274
Dandolo Du Gite	2	1	0	1	2274
Queen's Magic	2	1	0	1	2274
Total winning prize-money					£283488
Favourites	22-68		32.4%		-21.68

SEAMUS MULLINS

WILSFORD-CUM-LAKE, WILTS

	No. of Hrs	Races Run	1st	2nd	3rd	Unpl	Per cent	£1 Level Stake
NH Flat	16	27	2	2	4	19	7.4	-16.00
Hurdles	55	192	20	23	24	125	10.4	-67.13
Chases	15	69	8	5	9	47	11.6	+24.50
Totals	70	288	30	30	37	191	10.4	-58.63
16-17	57	232	17	26	34	155	7.3	-33.38
15-16	52	203	19	24	21	139	9.4	+20.30

BY MONTH

NH Flat	W-R	Per cent	£1 Level Stake	Hurdles	W-R	Per cent	£1 Level Stake
May	1-5	20.0	-1.50	May	3-21	14.3	+15.83
June	0-3	0.0	-3.00	June	1-9	11.1	-6.63
July	0-1	0.0	-1.00	July	2-11	18.2	-0.50
August	0-1	0.0	-1.00	August	2-2	100.0	+8.00
September	0-2	0.0	-2.00	September	1-5	20.0	+4.00
October	0-4	0.0	-4.00	October	4-16	25.0	-1.09
November	0-1	0.0	-1.00	November	0-19	0.0	-19.00
December	0-5	0.0	-5.00	December	1-21	4.8	-17.00
January	1-1	100.0	+6.50	January	1-22	4.5	-16.50
February	0-2	0.0	-2.00	February	2-16	12.5	-2.00
March	0-0	0.0	0.00	March	2-24	8.3	-17.25
April	0-2	0.0	-2.00	April	1-26	3.8	-15.00

Chases	W-R	Per cent	£1 Level Stake	Totals	W-R	Per cent	£1 Level Stake
May	1-7	14.3	+2.00	May	5-33	15.2	+16.33
June	0-1	0.0	-1.00	June	1-13	7.7	-10.63
July	0-4	0.0	-4.00	July	2-16	12.5	-5.50
August	1-2	50.0	+8.00	August	3-5	60.0	+15.00
September	0-4	0.0	-4.00	September	1-11	9.1	-2.00
October	0-4	0.0	-4.00	October	4-24	16.7	-9.09
November	1-13	7.7	-8.50	November	1-33	3.0	-28.50
December	2-6	33.3	+41.00	December	3-32	9.4	+19.00
January	0-12	0.0	-12.00	January	2-35	5.7	-22.00
February	0-6	0.0	-6.00	February	2-24	8.3	-10.00
March	3-6	50.0	+17.00	March	5-30	16.7	-0.25
April	0-4	0.0	-4.00	April	1-32	3.1	-21.00

DISTANCE

Hurdles	W-R	Per cent	£1 Level Stake	Chases	W-R	Per cent	£1 Level Stake
2m-2m3f	7-102	6.9	-41.13	2m-2m3f	1-31	3.2	-10.00
2m4f-2m7f	9-65	13.8	-19.59	2m4f-2m7f	5-19	26.3	+34.50
3m+	3-23	13.0	-8.17	3m+	2-19	10.5	0.00

TYPE OF RACE

Non-Handicaps	W-R	Per cent	£1 Level Stake	Handicaps	W-R	Per cent	£1 Level Stake
Nov Hrdls	5-47	10.6	+3.50	Nov Hrdls	2-12	16.7	-0.50
Hrdls	3-32	9.4	-24.63	Hrdls	10-99	10.1	-43.51
Nov Chs	0-5	0.0	-5.00	Nov Chs	2-14	14.3	+22.00
Chases	0-0	0.0	0.00	Chases	6-45	13.3	+12.50
Sell/Claim	0-0	0.0	0.00	Sell/Claim	0-1	0.0	-1.00

RACE CLASS / FIRST TIME OUT

	W-R	Per cent	£1 Level Stake		W-R	Per cent	£1 Level Stake
Class 1	0-18	0.0	-18.00	Bumpers	1-16	6.3	-12.50
Class 2	1-7	14.3	-3.25	Hurdles	5-46	10.9	-1.17
Class 3	7-38	18.4	+8.00	Chases	1-8	12.5	+1.00
Class 4	12-118	10.2	-9.29				
Class 5	10-93	10.8	-22.09	Totals	7-70	10.0	-12.67
Class 6	0-14	0.0	-14.00				

JOCKEYS

	W-R	Per cent	£1 Level Stake
Daniel Sansom	10-103	9.7	-50.72
Kevin Jones	9-82	11.0	-7.17
Jeremiah McGrath	5-50	10.0	-20.75
Michael Heard	2-16	12.5	0.00
Andrew Thornton	2-17	11.8	+16.00
Liam Treadwell	1-3	33.3	+18.00
Nick Scholfield	1-3	33.3	0.00

COURSE RECORD

	Total W-R	Non-Hndcps Hurdles	Chases	Hndcps Hurdles	Chases	NH Flat	Per cent	£1 Level Stake
Fontwell	4-47	0-11	0-0	1-18	3-15	0-3	8.5	-2.67
Lingfield	3-11	1-3	0-0	1-3	1-5	0-0	27.3	+24.25
Worcester	3-22	1-5	0-1	2-8	0-4	0-4	13.6	-14.09
Leicester	2-2	1-1	0-0	0-0	1-1	0-0	100.0	+8.00
Stratford	2-5	1-1	0-0	1-2	0-1	0-1	40.0	+26.00
Towcester	2-11	0-2	0-0	1-5	0-2	1-2	18.2	-4.00
Warwick	2-12	0-2	0-0	1-6	1-3	0-1	16.7	+3.50
Taunton	2-13	1-7	0-0	0-4	1-2	0-0	15.4	0.00
Nton Abbot	2-18	0-3	0-2	2-9	0-2	0-2	11.1	-5.00
Wincanton	2-22	1-8	0-0	0-7	1-5	0-2	9.1	-9.00
Plumpton	2-24	1-5	0-0	1-12	0-7	0-0	8.3	-8.50
Wetherby	1-2	0-0	0-0	0-0	0-0	1-2	50.0	+5.50
Bangor	1-3	0-1	0-0	1-1	0-1	0-0	33.3	+3.00
Sandown	1-7	0-1	0-0	1-5	0-1	0-0	14.3	+1.00
Uttoxeter	1-8	1-4	0-0	0-0	0-1	0-3	12.5	-5.63

WINNING HORSES

Horse	Races Run	1st	2nd	3rd	£
Landin	7	3	1	0	21869
Cap Horner	11	2	1	3	14556
Somchine	6	1	0	1	8944

Lillian	6	3	1	1	17881
Arthington	8	3	3	1	13646
I See You Well	9	1	0	3	6498
*Nelson's Touch	4	1	0	1	5458
Jarlath	5	1	2	1	5198
Bonds Conquest	4	1	0	0	4809
Jubilympics	7	2	0	2	4549
Plantagenet	10	4	1	1	12671
Kentford Heiress	7	1	3	1	4549
Burst Ya Bubble	6	2	1	1	7733
She's Gina	6	1	1	0	4159
Hardtorock	7	1	0	1	2859
Maebh	4	1	0	2	2599
Flugzeug	8	1	0	1	2599
Norphin	6	1	0	0	2530
Total winning prize-money					£143107
Favourites	8-16		50.0%		9.03

AMY MURPHY

NEWMARKET, SUFFOLK

	No. of Hrs	Races Run	1st	2nd	3rd	Unpl	Per cent	£1 Level Stake
NH Flat	6	11	1	1	3	6	9.1	+15.00
Hurdles	8	25	3	3	0	19	12.0	-9.43
Chases	3	16	4	1	3	8	25.0	+1.35
Totals	13	52	8	5	6	33	15.4	+6.92
16-17	8	31	7	3	7	14	22.6	+31.67

JOCKEYS

	W-R	Per cent	£1 Level Stake
Jack Quinlan	7-43	16.3	-10.08
Lucy K Barry	1-8	12.5	+18.00

COURSE RECORD

	Total W-R	Non-Hndcps Hurdles	Chases	Hndcps Hurdles	Chases	NH Flat	Per cent	£1 Level Stake
Wetherby	2-4	1-1	0-0	0-0	1-1	0-2	50.0	+5.50
Newbury	1-1	0-0	0-0	1-1	0-0	0-0	100.0	+8.00
Doncaster	1-2	1-1	0-0	0-1	0-0	0-0	50.0	-0.43
Fontwell	1-2	0-1	0-0	0-0	1-1	0-0	50.0	+0.10
Kempton	1-2	0-0	0-1	0-0	1-1	0-0	50.0	+1.75
Worcester	1-2	0-1	0-0	0-0	1-1	0-0	50.0	+5.00
Cheltenham	1-4	0-1	0-0	0-0	0-2	1-1	25.0	+22.00

WINNING HORSES

Horse	Races Run	1st	2nd	3rd	£
Kalashnikov	5	3	2	0	97695
Mercian Prince	6	2	0	1	21006
Hawthorn Cottage	3	1	1	1	9747
Mercian King	6	2	1	1	8447
Total winning prize-money					£136895
Favourites	3-4		75.0%		3.42

OLLY MURPHY

WILMCOTE, WARKS

	No. of Hrs	Races Run	1st	2nd	3rd	Unpl	Per cent	£1 Level Stake
NH Flat	18	26	4	8	3	11	15.4	-13.86
Hurdles	54	182	35	33	23	91	19.2	-30.35
Chases	10	36	8	4	6	18	22.2	-11.18
Totals	68	244	47	45	32	120	19.3	-55.39

BY MONTH

NH Flat	W-R	Per cent	£1 Level Stake	Hurdles	W-R	Per cent	£1 Level Stake
May	0-0	0.0	0.00	May	0-0	0.0	0.00
June	0-0	0.0	0.00	June	0-0	0.0	0.00
July	0-0	0.0	0.00	July	7-13	53.8	+27.15
August	0-0	0.0	0.00	August	2-15	13.3	-8.63
September	0-0	0.0	0.00	September	1-6	16.7	-3.50
October	0-2	0.0	-2.00	October	2-22	9.1	-17.27
November	0-4	0.0	-4.00	November	4-25	16.0	-10.65
December	1-4	25.0	-2.09	December	5-26	19.2	-1.39
January	1-2	50.0	+0.50	January	6-23	26.1	+14.75
February	0-4	0.0	-4.00	February	5-23	21.7	-6.39
March	0-1	0.0	-1.00	March	3-20	15.0	-15.42
April	2-9	22.2	-1.27	April	0-9	0.0	-9.00

Chases	W-R	Per cent	£1 Level Stake	Totals	W-R	Per cent	£1 Level Stake
May	0-0	0.0	0.00	May	0-0	0.0	0.00
June	0-0	0.0	0.00	June	0-0	0.0	0.00
July	1-2	50.0	+0.38	July	8-15	53.3	+27.53
August	2-4	50.0	+1.08	August	4-19	21.1	-7.55
September	0-1	0.0	-1.00	September	1-7	14.3	-4.50
October	1-3	33.3	+1.00	October	3-27	11.1	-18.27
November	1-4	25.0	-1.13	November	5-33	15.2	-15.78
December	0-7	0.0	-7.00	December	6-37	16.2	-10.65
January	3-5	60.0	+5.50	January	10-30	33.3	+20.75
February	0-6	0.0	-6.00	February	5-33	15.2	-16.39
March	0-2	0.0	-2.00	March	3-23	13.0	-18.42
April	0-2	0.0	-2.00	April	2-20	10.0	-12.27

DISTANCE

Hurdles	W-R	Per cent	£1 Level Stake	Chases	W-R	Per cent	£1 Level Stake
2m-2m3f	19-104	18.3	-20.33	2m-2m3f	1-8	12.5	-5.63
2m4f-2m7f	15-63	23.8	+2.89	2m4f-2m7f	7-23	30.4	-0.55
3m+	1-15	6.7	-12.90	3m+	0-5	0.0	-5.00

TYPE OF RACE

Non-Handicaps	W-R	Per cent	£1 Level Stake	Handicaps	W-R	Per cent	£1 Level Stake
Nov Hrdls	6-40	15.0	-6.09	Nov Hrdls	6-11	54.5	+15.97
Hrdls	4-27	14.8	-13.00	Hrdls	16-82	19.5	-11.70
Nov Chs	0-1	0.0	-1.00	Nov Chs	2-12	16.7	-6.88
Chases	0-0	0.0	0.00	Chases	6-22	27.3	-2.30
Sell/Claim	3-14	21.4	-6.63	Sell/Claim	1-6	16.7	-3.90

RACE CLASS

	W-R	Per cent	£1 Level Stake
Class 1	1-7	14.3	+3.00
Class 2	1-9	11.1	-4.50
Class 3	2-20	10.0	+2.91
Class 4	21-117	17.9	-39.22
Class 5	21-84	25.0	-12.48
Class 6	1-7	14.3	-5.09

FIRST TIME OUT

	W-R	Per cent	£1 Level Stake
Bumpers	3-18	16.7	-7.59
Hurdles	11-45	24.4	+38.63
Chases	2-5	40.0	+0.08
Totals	16-68	23.5	+31.12

JOCKEYS

	W-R	Per cent	£1 Level Stake
Fergus Gregory	15-58	25.9	-0.03
Richard Johnson	15-64	23.4	-18.11
Charlie Poste	3-24	12.5	-7.88
David England	3-26	11.5	-15.38
Jonjo O'Neill	2-3	66.7	+1.10
James Nixon	1-1	100.0	+0.25
Jack Kennedy	1-1	100.0	+9.00
Graham Watters	1-1	100.0	+1.88
Mr J J Codd	1-3	33.3	-1.09
Lewis Stones	1-3	33.3	+4.00
Brian Hughes	1-4	25.0	+0.50
Bryony Frost	1-4	25.0	+13.00
Aidan Coleman	1-11	9.1	-4.00
Ian Popham	1-20	5.0	-17.63

COURSE RECORD

	Total W-R	Non-Hndcps Hurdles	Chases	Hndcps Hurdles	Chases	NH Flat	Per cent	£1 Level Stake
Fakenham	15-48	5-21	0-0	8-17	2-7	0-3	31.3	+19.94
Stratford	5-17	1-7	0-0	2-7	2-3	0-0	29.4	+5.63
Mrket Rsn	5-20	2-7	0-0	3-11	0-1	0-1	25.0	+8.04
Uttoxeter	3-10	1-4	0-0	2-5	0-1	0-0	30.0	-3.10
Southwell	3-18	1-5	0-1	1-9	1-2	0-1	16.7	-9.50
Nton Abbot	2-4	0-0	0-0	1-3	1-1	0-0	50.0	+0.70
Sedgefield	2-8	0-1	0-0	1-1	0-2	1-4	25.0	-3.77
Musselbgh	1-1	0-0	0-0	0-0	1-1	0-0	100.0	+3.50
Ascot	1-2	0-1	0-0	1-1	0-0	0-0	50.0	+8.00
Carlisle	1-2	1-1	0-0	0-0	0-0	0-1	50.0	+0.63
Chepstow	1-2	0-1	0-0	0-0	0-0	1-1	50.0	+4.00
Leicester	1-2	1-1	0-0	0-0	0-1	0-0	50.0	0.00
Lingfield	1-2	0-0	0-0	1-2	0-0	0-0	50.0	+5.00
Haydock	1-3	0-2	0-0	1-1	0-0	0-0	33.3	-1.33
Doncaster	1-4	0-0	0-0	0-2	0-0	1-2	25.0	-2.09
Hereford	1-4	0-1	0-0	0-1	0-1	1-1	25.0	-1.50
Taunton	1-5	0-1	0-0	0-2	1-2	0-0	20.0	-2.13
Worcester	1-5	0-1	0-0	1-2	0-2	0-0	20.0	-2.50
Ludlow	1-8	0-2	0-0	1-4	0-1	0-1	12.5	-5.90

WINNING HORSES

Horse	Races Run	1st	2nd	3rd	£
Hunters Call	1	1	0	0	85425
*Knockgraffon	5	1	0	0	19494
Whiskey In The Jar	5	2	2	0	10852

Calipso Collonges	5	4	0	0	22223
Piri Massini	4	1	1	1	6498
*Skilled	5	2	1	0	10397
Mullaghboy	6	2	0	2	9852
Weebill	6	1	2	2	5458
*More Than Luck	7	2	0	1	10007
Rio Quinto	6	1	3	0	5198
Mizen Master	7	2	2	1	8447
Wood Pigeon	9	1	2	0	4926
Ballinslea Bridge	6	2	4	0	9097
*The Geegeez Geegee	4	2	0	1	8285
Hurricane Rita	5	1	2	1	4159
After Aspen	3	1	0	1	4159
Bisoubisou	7	1	0	0	4159
*Oxford Blu	6	1	1	1	3899
Saucysioux	9	3	3	0	11220
Knight Commander	6	2	1	1	6498
Pershing	1	1	0	0	3899
Undefined Beauty	6	2	3	1	7148
Cliffside Park	7	3	1	2	3249
Sky Of Stars	7	2	1	1	6498
Gold Class	4	1	0	1	2808
Tunnel Creek	4	1	0	0	2599
Brewin'Upastorm	2	1	0	0	2599
It's O Kay	3	1	1	0	2274
Garrettstown	1	1	0	0	2274
Sangha River	1	1	0	0	1949
Total winning prize-money					**£285550**
Favourites	26-76		34.2%		-18.39

BARRY MURTAGH

LOW BRAITHWAITE, CUMBRIA

	No. of Hrs	Races Run	1st	2nd	3rd	Unpl	Per cent	£1 Level Stake
NH Flat	2	2	0	0	0	2	0.0	-2.00
Hurdles	10	36	1	3	3	29	2.8	-15.00
Chases	3	13	0	0	0	13	0.0	-13.00
Totals	13	51	1	3	3	44	2.0	-30.00
16-17	15	75	3	3	5	64	4.0	-38.50
15-16	21	98	3	11	10	74	3.1	-84.50

JOCKEYS

	W-R	Per cent	£1 Level Stake
Robert Hogg	1-2	50.0	+19.00

COURSE RECORD

	Total W-R	Non-Hndcps Hurdles	Chases	Hndcps Hurdles	Chases	NH Flat	Per cent	£1 Level Stake
Cartmel	1-6	0-0	0-1	1-3	0-2	0-0	16.7	+15.00

WINNING HORSES

Horse	Races Run	1st	2nd	3rd	£
Baraboy	9	1	1	1	2599
Total winning prize-money					**£2599**

Favourites	0-0	0.0%	0.00

HELEN NELMES

WARMWELL, DORSET

	No. of Hrs	Races Run	1st	2nd	3rd	Unpl	Per cent	£1 Level Stake
NH Flat	0	0	0	0	0	0	0.0	0.00
Hurdles	6	15	1	3	0	11	6.7	0.00
Chases	0	0	0	0	0	0	0.0	0.00
Totals	6	15	1	3	0	11	6.7	0.00
16-17	12	35	0	1	2	32	0.0	-35.00
15-16	8	21	0	0	3	18	0.0	-21.00

JOCKEYS

	W-R	Per cent	£1 Level Stake
Paul O'Brien	1-10	10.0	+5.00

COURSE RECORD

	Total W-R	Non-Hndcps Hurdles	Hndcps Chases	Hndcps Hurdles	Chases	NH Flat	Per cent	£1 Level Stake
Nton Abbot	1-5	0-0	0-0	1-5	0-0	0-0	20.0	+10.00

WINNING HORSES

Horse	Races Run	1st	2nd	3rd	£
Kalmbeforethestorm	2	1	1	0	5003
Total winning prize-money					£5003
Favourites	0-0		0.0%		0.00

DR RICHARD NEWLAND

CLAINES, WORCS

	No. of Hrs	Races Run	1st	2nd	3rd	Unpl	Per cent	£1 Level Stake
NH Flat	1	1	0	0	0	1	0.0	-1.00
Hurdles	34	115	25	24	12	54	21.7	-37.69
Chases	21	70	18	14	13	25	25.7	-10.65
Totals	42	186	43	38	25	80	23.1	-49.34
16-17	37	165	35	23	20	87	21.2	-36.85
15-16	36	147	28	29	18	72	19.0	-10.76

BY MONTH

NH Flat	W-R	Per cent	£1 Level Stake	Hurdles	W-R	Per cent	£1 Level Stake
May	0-0	0.0	0.00	May	2-10	20.0	-4.00
June	0-0	0.0	0.00	June	2-12	16.7	-6.13
July	0-0	0.0	0.00	July	9-20	45.0	+7.25
August	0-0	0.0	0.00	August	4-10	40.0	-1.97
September	0-0	0.0	0.00	September	2-8	25.0	-0.75
October	0-0	0.0	0.00	October	2-12	16.7	-5.50
November	0-1	0.0	-1.00	November	0-7	0.0	-7.00
December	0-0	0.0	0.00	December	0-7	0.0	-7.00
January	0-0	0.0	0.00	January	1-10	10.0	-7.50
February	0-0	0.0	0.00	February	2-7	28.6	-0.60
March	0-0	0.0	0.00	March	1-5	20.0	+2.50
April	0-0	0.0	0.00	April	0-7	0.0	-7.00

Chases	W-R	Per cent	£1 Level Stake	Totals	W-R	Per cent	£1 Level Stake
May	0-3	0.0	-3.00	May	2-13	15.4	-7.00
June	1-6	16.7	-3.25	June	3-18	16.7	-9.38
July	1-3	33.3	-1.71	July	10-23	43.5	+5.54
August	2-5	40.0	+0.91	August	6-15	40.0	-1.06
September	2-8	25.0	-1.25	September	4-16	25.0	-2.00
October	0-5	0.0	-5.00	October	2-17	11.8	-10.50
November	2-9	22.2	-3.50	November	2-17	11.8	-11.50
December	2-7	28.6	-0.63	December	2-14	14.3	-7.63
January	2-5	40.0	-0.80	January	3-15	20.0	-8.30
February	4-7	57.1	+8.08	February	6-14	42.9	+7.48
March	1-6	16.7	-2.50	March	2-11	18.2	0.00
April	1-6	16.7	+2.00	April	1-13	7.7	-5.00

DISTANCE

Hurdles	W-R	Per cent	£1 Level Stake	Chases	W-R	Per cent	£1 Level Stake
2m-2m3f	13-63	20.6	-24.41	2m-2m3f	9-27	33.3	+3.05
2m4f-2m7f	11-41	26.8	-4.78	2m4f-2m7f	1-15	6.7	-11.00
3m+	1-11	9.1	-8.50	3m+	8-28	28.6	-2.69

TYPE OF RACE

Non-Handicaps	W-R	Per cent	£1 Level Stake	Handicaps	W-R	Per cent	£1 Level Stake
Nov Hrdls	5-20	25.0	-6.17	Nov Hrdls	0-1	0.0	-1.00
Hrdls	2-10	20.0	-6.64	Hrdls	16-81	19.8	-24.05
Nov Chs	2-8	25.0	-3.96	Nov Chs	3-9	33.3	-0.22
Chases	0-0	0.0	0.00	Chases	12-46	26.1	-7.47
Sell/Claim	2-2	100.0	+1.17	Sell/Claim	0-0	0.0	0.00

RACE CLASS

	W-R	Per cent	£1 Level Stake
Class 1	0-18	0.0	-18.00
Class 2	5-36	13.9	-15.00
Class 3	11-43	25.6	+1.10
Class 4	22-75	29.3	-13.47
Class 5	5-13	38.5	-2.97
Class 6	0-1	0.0	-1.00

FIRST TIME OUT

	W-R	Per cent	£1 Level Stake
Bumpers	0-1	0.0	-1.00
Hurdles	4-32	12.5	-21.13
Chases	1-9	11.1	-2.50
Totals	5-42	11.9	-24.63

JOCKEYS

	W-R	Per cent	£1 Level Stake
Sam Twiston-Davies	22-83	26.5	-20.17
Brian Hughes	7-14	50.0	+11.00
Charlie Hammond	6-34	17.6	-12.38
Richard Johnson	3-9	33.3	-1.38
Henry Brooke	1-2	50.0	+6.00
Mr James King	1-2	50.0	-0.17
Tom O'Brien	1-4	25.0	-0.25
Harry Cobden	1-4	25.0	-1.50
Sean Bowen	1-10	10.0	-6.50

COURSE RECORD

	Total W-R	Non-Hndcps Hurdles	Chases	Hndcps Hurdles	Chases	NH Flat	Per cent	£1 Level Stake
Worcester	7-16	2-2	0-3	4-8	1-3	0-0	43.8	+9.63
Uttoxeter	6-24	1-6	0-0	4-9	1-9	0-0	25.0	-3.85
Stratford	4-11	1-3	1-2	1-5	1-1	0-0	36.4	-3.14
Fontwell	3-7	0-1	0-0	1-3	2-3	0-0	42.9	+1.97
Nton Abbot	3-10	1-3	0-1	1-4	1-2	0-0	30.0	-3.15
Hexham	2-4	2-3	0-0	0-0	0-1	0-0	50.0	-1.25
Huntingdon	2-4	0-0	0-0	1-3	1-1	0-0	50.0	+6.50
Perth	2-5	0-0	1-1	0-1	1-3	0-0	40.0	+1.75
Sedgefield	2-7	0-3	0-0	1-2	1-2	0-0	28.6	-3.10
Mrket Rsn	2-10	1-2	0-0	1-6	0-2	0-0	20.0	-1.14
Ayr	1-1	0-0	0-0	0-0	1-1	0-0	100.0	+2.00
Hereford	1-1	0-0	0-0	0-0	1-1	0-0	100.0	+2.50
Plumpton	1-1	0-0	0-0	0-0	1-1	0-0	100.0	+0.83
Wetherby	1-1	0-0	0-0	0-0	1-1	0-0	100.0	+1.10
Exeter	1-2	0-0	0-0	0-1	1-1	0-0	50.0	+4.50
Wincanton	1-2	1-1	0-0	0-0	0-1	0-0	50.0	+0.50
Ludlow	1-3	0-1	0-0	0-1	1-1	0-0	33.3	+0.50
Doncaster	1-4	0-1	0-0	0-0	1-3	0-0	25.0	-1.00
Ascot	1-8	0-0	0-0	1-4	0-4	0-0	12.5	-3.00
Southwell	1-8	0-1	0-1	1-5	0-1	0-0	12.5	-4.50

WINNING HORSES

Horse	Races Run	1st	2nd	3rd	£
Le Patriote	4	1	0	0	28152
Band Of Blood	5	2	0	0	40136
Audacious Plan	4	3	1	0	33736
*Beau Bay	14	3	5	4	27461
Theo	8	5	0	1	29376
Vosne Romanee	9	3	1	2	25345
Catamaran Du Seuil	6	2	2	0	15205
Aaron Lad	8	2	2	1	11891
Ebony Express	2	1	0	0	6330
Destiny's Gold	10	2	1	2	10229
Caid du Lin	9	1	4	1	5848
Slim Pickens	7	2	3	2	8241
Greyed A	7	3	1	0	13155
Gettysburg Address	4	2	1	0	8509
Capitoul	7	1	0	0	4614
Dashing Perk	5	1	0	0	4159
Trafalgar Rock	5	1	2	1	3899
Lovato	5	2	2	0	6888
Mcgroarty	5	2	1	0	6303
Supreme Steel	5	1	2	0	3379
Milrow	3	1	0	1	3249
*Mr Caffrey	2	2	0	0	5848
Total winning prize-money					**£301953**
Favourites	**25-58**		**43.1%**		**-0.55**

ANNA NEWTON-SMITH

JEVINGTON, E SUSSEX

	No. of Hrs	Races Run	1st	2nd	3rd	Unpl	Per cent	£1 Level Stake
NH Flat	1	1	0	0	0	1	0.0	-1.00
Hurdles	3	13	0	0	2	11	0.0	-13.00
Chases	3	15	3	0	4	8	20.0	+1.50
Totals	5	29	3	0	6	20	10.3	-12.50
16-17	8	39	3	3	3	30	7.7	-20.00
15-16	9	38	3	6	5	24	7.9	-7.00

JOCKEYS

	W-R	Per cent	£1 Level Stake
Andrew Thornton	2-10	20.0	+4.50
Paddy Brennan	1-10	10.0	-8.00

COURSE RECORD

	Total W-R	Non-Hndcps Hurdles	Chases	Hndcps Hurdles	Chases	NH Flat	Per cent	£1 Level Stake
Fontwell	2-8	0-0	0-0	0-3	2-5	0-0	25.0	-2.50
Wincanton	1-3	0-0	0-0	0-0	1-3	0-0	33.3	+8.00

WINNING HORSES

Horse	Races Run	1st	2nd	3rd	£
Burgess Dream	9	1	0	3	3314
Goring One	8	2	0	3	5523
Total winning prize-money					**£8837**
Favourites	**1-1**		**100.0%**		**1.00**

PAUL NICHOLLS

DITCHEAT, SOMERSET

	No. of Hrs	Races Run	1st	2nd	3rd	Unpl	Per cent	£1 Level Stake
NH Flat	20	32	4	2	4	22	12.5	-21.46
Hurdles	81	238	45	37	27	129	18.9	-84.31
Chases	79	300	77	52	43	128	25.7	-27.57
Totals	150	570	126	91	74	279	22.1	-133.34
16-17	161	661	171	90	79	321	25.9	-66.39
15-16	162	568	122	104	74	268	21.5	-73.23

BY MONTH

NH Flat	W-R	Per cent	£1 Level Stake	**Hurdles**	W-R	Per cent	£1 Level Stake
May	0-0	0.0	0.00	May	1-11	9.1	-9.56
June	0-0	0.0	0.00	June	3-5	60.0	+9.00
July	0-0	0.0	0.00	July	0-2	0.0	-2.00
August	0-0	0.0	0.00	August	0-0	0.0	0.00
September	0-1	0.0	-1.00	September	1-3	33.3	-1.43
October	2-5	40.0	-0.33	October	6-33	18.2	-17.41
November	1-5	20.0	-1.75	November	5-39	12.8	-26.26
December	0-4	0.0	-4.00	December	7-37	18.9	-10.97
January	0-1	0.0	-1.00	January	1-10	10.0	-8.17

February	1-6	16.7	-3.38
March	0-3	0.0	-3.00
April	0-7	0.0	-7.00

Chases	W-R	Per cent	£1 Level Stake
May	9-19	47.4	+0.11
June	4-12	33.3	-0.70
July	5-10	50.0	+8.32
August	3-9	33.3	-5.19
September	1-2	50.0	-0.60
October	13-34	38.2	+9.63
November	11-46	23.9	-10.95
December	6-46	13.0	-24.97
January	2-18	11.1	-8.59
February	12-34	35.3	-2.70
March	4-28	14.3	+13.57
April	7-42	16.7	-5.50

February	6-36	16.7	-3.92
March	5-21	23.8	-2.26
April	10-41	24.4	-10.81

Totals	W-R	Per cent	£1 Level Stake
May	10-30	33.3	-9.45
June	7-17	41.2	+8.30
July	5-12	41.7	+6.32
August	3-9	33.3	-5.19
September	2-6	33.3	-3.03
October	21-72	29.2	-8.11
November	17-90	18.9	-39.49
December	13-87	14.9	-39.94
January	3-29	10.3	-17.76
February	19-76	25.0	-10.00
March	9-52	17.3	+8.31
April	17-90	18.9	-23.31

Mr Sam Waley-Cohen	1-4	25.0	-2.70
Henry Morshead	1-5	20.0	+3.50
Alexander Thorne	1-6	16.7	0.00
Stan Sheppard	1-17	5.9	-7.00

COURSE RECORD

	Total W-R	Non-Hndcps Hurdles	Chases	Hndcps Hurdles	Chases	NH Flat	Per cent	£1 Level Stake
Nton Abbot	16-36	3-7	8-13	1-6	4-9	0-1	44.4	+4.34
Wincanton	16-60	6-19	3-4	3-15	4-15	0-7	26.7	-5.63
Kempton	14-44	4-13	8-11	0-5	1-11	1-4	31.8	-8.04
Fontwell	9-23	1-4	6-7	1-3	1-7	0-2	39.1	+2.14
Taunton	8-38	6-18	1-3	1-7	0-7	0-3	21.1	-17.64
Chepstow	6-27	3-9	0-3	1-7	1-5	1-3	22.2	+2.67
Exeter	6-27	4-14	1-5	0-4	1-2	0-2	22.2	-4.60
Cheltenham	6-58	0-4	3-16	0-15	2-22	1-1	10.3	-4.25
Musselbgh	4-11	1-4	1-2	0-2	2-3	0-0	36.4	-0.39
Aintree	4-30	1-5	2-10	0-3	0-9	1-3	13.3	-6.75
Stratford	3-8	1-1	0-3	0-1	2-3	0-0	37.5	-0.33
Mrket Rsn	3-10	1-2	1-4	0-1	1-2	0-1	30.0	+3.17
Warwick	3-10	0-2	3-4	0-2	0-2	0-0	30.0	-5.29
Ascot	3-25	0-2	2-8	1-4	0-9	0-2	12.0	-14.84
Sandown	3-37	0-6	1-12	1-9	1-8	0-2	8.1	-22.50
Bangor	2-7	0-2	1-3	0-0	1-2	0-0	28.6	+1.22
Ludlow	2-10	0-3	1-2	0-0	1-5	0-0	20.0	-1.09
Worcester	2-10	0-3	2-6	0-0	0-1	0-0	20.0	-5.27
Haydock	2-13	0-2	2-2	0-6	0-3	0-0	15.4	-6.75
Newbury	2-25	0-2	1-6	1-9	0-8	0-0	8.0	-15.00
Carlisle	1-1	0-0	1-1	0-0	0-0	0-0	100.0	+0.40
Plumpton	1-1	0-0	0-0	0-0	1-1	0-0	100.0	+3.50
Southwell	1-1	0-0	1-1	0-0	0-0	0-0	100.0	+1.00
Leicester	1-2	0-0	1-2	0-0	0-0	0-0	50.0	-0.60
Newcastle	1-2	1-2	0-0	0-0	0-0	0-0	50.0	+0.38
Perth	1-2	0-0	0-1	0-0	1-1	0-0	50.0	+2.50
Kelso	1-3	0-0	0-2	0-0	1-1	0-0	33.3	-1.09
Wetherby	1-3	1-2	0-0	0-0	0-1	0-0	33.3	-1.09
Huntingdon	1-4	0-0	0-2	0-1	1-1	0-0	25.0	-1.13
Fakenham	1-7	1-3	0-3	0-0	0-1	0-0	14.3	-4.00
Ayr	1-10	1-1	0-1	0-1	0-7	0-0	10.0	-7.13
Doncaster	1-15	0-4	1-5	0-2	0-4	0-0	6.7	-11.25

DISTANCE

Hurdles	W-R	Per cent	£1 Level Stake
2m-2m3f	33-134	24.6	-26.03
2m4f-2m7f	11-77	14.3	-41.28
3m+	1-27	3.7	-17.00

Chases	W-R	Per cent	£1 Level Stake
2m-2m3f	21-73	28.8	-13.22
2m4f-2m7f	35-126	27.8	+0.75
3m+	21-101	20.8	-15.10

TYPE OF RACE

Non-Handicaps	W-R	Per cent	£1 Level Stake
Nov Hrdls	27-86	31.4	-2.08
Hrdls	8-48	16.7	-30.71
Nov Chs	34-87	39.1	-10.94
Chases	17-56	30.4	+16.79
Sell/Claim	0-0	0.0	0.00

Handicaps	W-R	Per cent	£1 Level Stake
Nov Hrdls	1-6	16.7	-1.50
Hrdls	9-95	9.5	-47.02
Nov Chs	3-16	18.8	-8.63
Chases	17-116	14.7	-23.17
Sell/Claim	0-0	0.0	0.00

RACE CLASS

	W-R	Per cent	£1 Level Stake
Class 1	20-155	12.9	-60.67
Class 2	15-104	14.4	-34.23
Class 3	34-132	25.8	-29.33
Class 4	48-138	34.8	+13.57
Class 5	3-26	11.5	-19.82
Class 6	6-15	40.0	-1.86

FIRST TIME OUT

	W-R	Per cent	£1 Level Stake
Bumpers	3-20	15.0	-12.71
Hurdles	8-69	11.6	-30.86
Chases	19-61	31.1	-17.88
Totals	30-150	20.0	-61.45

JOCKEYS

	W-R	Per cent	£1 Level Stake
Sam Twiston-Davies	47-214	22.0	-65.24
Bryony Frost	26-87	29.9	+15.47
Harry Cobden	24-132	18.2	-58.66
Sean Bowen	8-39	20.5	-20.79
Mr Lorcan Williams	6-20	30.0	-7.70
Mr David Maxwell	4-9	44.4	+1.68
Nick Scholfield	3-7	42.9	+0.85
Barry Geraghty	3-18	16.7	-6.74
Miss Harriet Tucker	1-2	50.0	+24.00

WINNING HORSES

Horse	Races Run	1st	2nd	3rd	£
Politologue	6	4	1	0	316858
Le Prezien	5	1	1	1	62645
Topofthegame	4	1	1	0	56270
Diego Du Charmil	6	2	1	1	63251
Old Guard	9	3	0	1	88717
Black Corton	12	8	2	0	128506
Frodon	8	1	2	3	42713
Present Man	5	2	0	1	38069
Clan Des Obeaux	4	1	2	1	32490
Alcala	8	5	0	0	62774
Pacha Du Polder	2	1	0	1	26982
Malaya	6	2	3	0	36414
Cyrname	7	1	2	0	49512

Romain De Senam	6	2	0	0	37980
Modus	6	3	0	0	36997
Copain De Classe	4	1	0	1	16400
As De Mee	5	1	1	0	14076
El Bandit	1	1	0	0	13436
Marracudja	5	1	1	1	13256
Act Of Valour	6	2	1	0	17545
Braqueur D'Or	12	3	4	3	24064
Posh Trish	5	2	0	1	15144
Amour De Nuit	8	2	2	2	15289
Brahms De Clermont	7	4	1	1	23518
Dolos	7	1	3	1	9986
Mr Mix	6	2	0	2	9495
Southfield Vic	4	1	0	0	9199
Captain Cattistock	6	3	0	0	17261
Bagad Bihoue	8	4	1	0	26872
Favorito Buck's	6	2	0	1	13061
Give Me A Copper	2	1	0	0	8133
Risk And Roll	5	2	0	1	13697
Virak	4	2	0	1	11542
Orbasa	10	1	0	1	7798
Capitaine	4	2	0	0	15453
Ridgeway Flyer	3	2	0	0	14094
Tommy Silver	6	1	2	2	7596
Touch Kick	3	1	0	1	7507
Mont Des Avaloirs	7	3	0	1	15416
Moabit	6	2	1	2	12996
Secret Investor	5	1	3	0	6758
Brio Conti	1	1	0	0	6498
Lou Vert	1	1	0	0	6256
The Last But One	7	3	1	0	16440
Trevisani	4	2	0	1	10808
Dynamite Dollars	6	2	0	1	9422
Blu Cavalier	6	3	1	0	14945
Dan McGrue	4	2	0	0	10657
Coastal Tiep	4	1	2	0	4874
Choix Des Armes	5	1	0	2	4809
Diamond Guy	2	1	0	0	4809
Kapcorse	4	1	0	0	4614
Peter The Mayo Man	4	2	0	0	8412
Challico	4	1	0	2	4549
Adrien Du Pont	6	1	2	2	4549
Master Tommytucker	2	2	0	0	8772
Bistouri D'Honore	2	1	0	1	4523
If You Say Run	6	2	3	0	8123
Coup De Pinceau	5	1	2	0	4159
Magoo	1	1	0	0	4094
Port Melon	1	1	0	0	3120
Danny Kirwan	2	1	0	0	3119
Wonderful Charm	4	1	0	1	2998
Unioniste	6	3	1	0	6631
Rebel Rebellion	6	2	1	2	3501
Vivaldi Collonges	2	1	0	0	2184
Bill And Barn	5	1	1	0	0
Total winning prize-money					**£1602636**
Favourites	78-164		47.6%		**-1.71**

ANDREW NICHOLLS

YORK, N YORKS

	No. of Hrs	Races Run	1st	2nd	3rd	Unpl	Per cent	£1 Level Stake
NH Flat	1	1	0	0	0	1	0.0	-1.00
Hurdles	0	0	0	0	0	0	0.0	0.00
Chases	2	5	1	1	0	3	20.0	+3.00
Totals	3	6	1	1	0	4	16.7	+2.00
16-17	1	3	0	0	1	2	0.0	-3.00
15-16	1	1	0	0	0	1	0.0	-1.00

JOCKEYS

	W-R	Per cent	£1 Level Stake
Mr William Milburn	1-5	20.0	+3.00

COURSE RECORD

	Total W-R	Non-Hndcps Hurdles	Chases	Hndcps Hurdles	Chases	NH Flat	Per cent	£1 Level Stake
Cartmel	1-2	0-0	1-2	0-0	0-0	0-0	50.0	+6.00

WINNING HORSES

Horse	Races Run	1st	2nd	3rd	£
Martha's Benefit	3	1	0	0	2398
Total winning prize-money					**£2398**
Favourites	0-0		0.0%		0.00

FRANCESCA NIMMO

DAVENTRY, NORTHANTS

	No. of Hrs	Races Run	1st	2nd	3rd	Unpl	Per cent	£1 Level Stake
NH Flat	2	2	0	0	1	1	0.0	-2.00
Hurdles	0	0	0	0	0	0	0.0	0.00
Chases	4	6	1	0	0	5	16.7	-0.50
Totals	6	8	1	0	1	6	12.5	-2.50
16-17	5	10	3	1	0	6	30.0	+2.00
15-16	2	2	0	0	1	1	0.0	-2.00

JOCKEYS

	W-R	Per cent	£1 Level Stake
Mr James Jackson-Stops	1-3	33.3	+2.50

COURSE RECORD

	Total W-R	Non-Hndcps Hurdles	Chases	Hndcps Hurdles	Chases	NH Flat	Per cent	£1 Level Stake
Carlisle	1-1	0-0	1-1	0-0	0-0	0-0	100.0	+4.50

WINNING HORSES

Horse	Races Run	1st	2nd	3rd	£
*Jimmy The Jetplane	2	1	0	0	2496
Total winning prize-money					**£2496**
Favourites	0-0		0.0%		0.00

PETER NIVEN
BARTON-LE-STREET, N YORKS

	No. of Hrs	Races Run	1st	2nd	3rd	Unpl	Per cent	£1 Level Stake
NH Flat	5	6	0	0	1	5	0.0	-6.00
Hurdles	8	18	2	6	1	9	11.1	-7.75
Chases	3	10	1	3	0	6	10.0	-7.63
Totals	11	34	3	9	2	20	8.8	-21.38
16-17	13	38	1	6	5	26	2.6	-34.25
15-16	15	42	5	7	5	25	11.9	-21.52

JOCKEYS

	W-R	Per cent	£1 Level Stake
Brian Hughes	2-8	25.0	-2.38
Tom O'Brien	1-2	50.0	+5.00

COURSE RECORD

	Total W-R	Non-Hndcps Hurdles	Chases	Hndcps Hurdles	Chases	NH Flat	Per cent	£1 Level Stake
Hexham	2-6	0-0	0-0	1-1	1-4	0-1	33.3	+3.38
Carlisle	1-1	0-0	0-0	1-1	0-0	0-0	100.0	+2.25

WINNING HORSES

Horse	Races Run	1st	2nd	3rd	£
Atomix	2	1	0	0	5523
Brian Boranha	6	1	4	0	4748
Pixiepot	5	1	2	1	4549
Total winning prize-money					£14820
Favourites	2-2		100.0%		3.63

LUCY NORMILE
DUNCRIEVIE, PERTH & KINROSS

	No. of Hrs	Races Run	1st	2nd	3rd	Unpl	Per cent	£1 Level Stake
NH Flat	3	4	0	1	0	3	0.0	-4.00
Hurdles	11	39	2	2	2	33	5.1	-13.00
Chases	2	4	0	1	1	2	0.0	-4.00
Totals	12	47	2	4	3	38	4.3	-21.00
16-17	11	47	1	2	4	40	2.1	-39.00
15-16	15	56	1	5	7	43	1.8	-35.00

JOCKEYS

	W-R	Per cent	£1 Level Stake
Grant Cockburn	2-37	5.4	-11.00

COURSE RECORD

	Total W-R	Non-Hndcps Hurdles	Chases	Hndcps Hurdles	Chases	NH Flat	Per cent	£1 Level Stake
Perth	2-20	0-5	0-0	2-15	0-0	0-0	10.0	+6.00

WINNING HORSES

Horse	Races Run	1st	2nd	3rd	£
Cruachan	4	1	0	0	3833
Karingo	7	1	1	0	3249
Total winning prize-money					£7082
Favourites	0-0		0.0%		0.00

DAVID O'BRIEN
TARPORLEY, CHESHIRE

	No. of Hrs	Races Run	1st	2nd	3rd	Unpl	Per cent	£1 Level Stake
NH Flat	0	0	0	0	0	0	0.0	0.00
Hurdles	0	0	0	0	0	0	0.0	0.00
Chases	1	4	1	1	0	2	25.0	+11.00
Totals	1	4	1	1	0	2	25.0	+11.00

JOCKEYS

	W-R	Per cent	£1 Level Stake
Mr David O'Brien	1-4	25.0	+11.00

COURSE RECORD

	Total W-R	Non-Hndcps Hurdles	Chases	Hndcps Hurdles	Chases	NH Flat	Per cent	£1 Level Stake
Stratford	1-1	0-0	1-1	0-0	0-0	0-0	100.0	+14.00

WINNING HORSES

Horse	Races Run	1st	2nd	3rd	£
*Numbercruncher	4	1	1	0	2496
Total winning prize-money					£2496
Favourites	0-0		0.0%		0.00

FERGAL O'BRIEN
NAUNTON, GLOUCS

	No. of Hrs	Races Run	1st	2nd	3rd	Unpl	Per cent	£1 Level Stake
NH Flat	31	54	10	4	6	34	18.5	-7.90
Hurdles	56	177	25	23	30	99	14.1	-46.77
Chases	36	107	25	15	11	56	23.4	+29.31
Totals	106	338	60	42	47	189	17.8	-25.36
16-17	81	325	60	36	48	181	18.5	+58.59
15-16	56	236	33	35	33	135	14.0	-4.50

BY MONTH

NH Flat	W-R	Per cent	£1 Level Stake	Hurdles	W-R	Per cent	£1 Level Stake
May	0-0	0.0	0.00	May	2-16	12.5	-3.50
June	0-0	0.0	0.00	June	1-11	9.1	-8.38
July	1-4	25.0	-0.75	July	1-13	7.7	-11.27
August	0-1	0.0	-1.00	August	2-7	28.6	+5.50
September	0-2	0.0	-2.00	September	2-8	25.0	+11.00

	W-R	Per cent	£1 Level Stake		W-R	Per cent	£1 Level Stake		W-R	Per cent	£1 Level Stake
October	2-7	28.6	+5.50	October	6-23	26.1	-8.10	Richard Patrick	2-7	28.6	-0.88
November	4-10	40.0	+11.80	November	4-25	16.0	-2.00	LBdr Sally Randell	1-1	100.0	+4.50
December	1-8	12.5	-4.00	December	3-23	13.0	-10.03	Brian Hughes	1-2	50.0	-0.09
January	0-5	0.0	-5.00	January	1-11	9.1	-8.50	Mr Zac Baker	1-3	33.3	-0.13
February	1-3	33.3	-1.70	February	0-9	0.0	-9.00	David Bass	1-5	20.0	-3.00
March	0-6	0.0	-6.00	March	2-16	12.5	+1.50	Noel Fehily	1-6	16.7	-3.75
April	1-8	12.5	-4.75	April	1-15	6.7	-4.00	Jonathan Burke	1-6	16.7	-4.20
								Conor Shoemark	1-19	5.3	-2.00

Chases	W-R	Per cent	£1 Level Stake	Totals	W-R	Per cent	£1 Level Stake
May	3-6	50.0	+15.75	May	5-22	22.7	+12.25
June	2-7	28.6	-1.77	June	3-18	16.7	-10.15
July	2-10	20.0	-0.50	July	4-27	14.8	-12.52
August	2-7	28.6	+0.67	August	4-15	26.7	+5.17
September	1-6	16.7	-1.50	September	3-16	18.8	+7.50
October	1-10	10.0	-5.00	October	9-40	22.5	-7.60
November	4-8	50.0	+21.25	November	12-43	27.9	+31.05
December	2-12	16.7	-5.20	December	6-43	14.0	-19.23
January	0-5	0.0	-5.00	January	1-21	4.8	-18.50
February	6-11	54.5	+22.28	February	7-23	30.4	+11.58
March	0-8	0.0	-8.00	March	2-30	6.7	-12.50
April	2-17	11.8	-3.67	April	4-40	10.0	-12.42

DISTANCE

Hurdles	W-R	Per cent	£1 Level Stake	Chases	W-R	Per cent	£1 Level Stake
2m-2m3f	8-58	13.8	-25.27	2m-2m3f	1-21	4.8	-18.25
2m4f-2m7f	12-88	13.6	-40.00	2m4f-2m7f	11-33	33.3	+26.87
3m+	5-31	16.1	+18.50	3m+	13-53	24.5	+20.69

TYPE OF RACE

Non-Handicaps	W-R	Per cent	£1 Level Stake	Handicaps	W-R	Per cent	£1 Level Stake
Nov Hrdls	6-52	11.5	-31.30	Nov Hrdls	2-15	13.3	0.00
Hrdls	3-26	11.5	-1.60	Hrdls	11-76	14.5	-13.00
Nov Chs	2-3	66.7	+0.71	Nov Chs	2-16	12.5	-10.83
Chases	3-9	33.3	-1.38	Chases	15-63	23.8	+40.56
Sell/Claim	3-5	60.0	+2.13	Sell/Claim	0-1	0.0	-1.00

RACE CLASS

	W-R	Per cent	£1 Level Stake
Class 1	6-47	12.8	-10.02
Class 2	3-33	9.1	-9.00
Class 3	11-58	19.0	+13.83
Class 4	20-115	17.4	-22.66
Class 5	13-66	19.7	-4.67
Class 6	7-19	36.8	+7.18

FIRST TIME OUT

	W-R	Per cent	£1 Level Stake
Bumpers	9-31	29.0	+13.80
Hurdles	9-47	19.1	+5.90
Chases	9-28	32.1	+29.13
Totals	27-106	25.5	+48.83

JOCKEYS

	W-R	Per cent	£1 Level Stake
Paddy Brennan	36-196	18.4	-25.70
Barry Geraghty	4-5	80.0	+20.30
Alain Cawley	4-37	10.8	-2.00
Miss Lilly Pinchin	3-19	15.8	-6.00
Robert Dunne	2-2	100.0	+9.83
Miss Brodie Hampson	2-5	40.0	+12.75

COURSE RECORD

	Total W-R	Non-Hndcps Hurdles	Non-Hndcps Chases	Hndcps Hurdles	Hndcps Chases	NH Flat	Per cent	£1 Level Stake
Perth	6-18	0-2	1-2	0-2	3-10	2-2	33.3	+6.00
Mrket Rsn	6-27	1-6	1-1	3-9	0-7	1-4	22.2	-3.87
Uttoxeter	5-18	1-3	0-0	1-9	3-5	0-1	27.8	+21.13
Huntingdon	4-15	1-2	0-0	1-8	2-4	0-1	26.7	+12.83
Cheltenham	4-37	0-14	1-3	0-7	2-8	1-5	10.8	-8.25
Ayr	3-4	1-1	0-0	1-1	1-2	0-0	75.0	+13.40
Wetherby	3-8	1-1	0-0	1-3	0-1	1-3	37.5	+10.80
Bangor	2-4	0-1	1-1	0-1	1-1	0-0	50.0	+0.60
Towcester	2-4	1-1	0-0	0-0	1-2	0-1	50.0	+8.00
Haydock	2-7	1-2	0-0	0-2	1-3	0-0	28.6	+2.10
Sandown	2-7	0-0	0-1	1-3	0-1	1-2	28.6	+6.50
Fontwell	2-8	0-1	0-0	1-2	1-3	0-2	25.0	+0.50
Exeter	2-9	0-3	0-1	0-1	0-2	2-2	22.2	-3.70
Southwell	2-11	0-1	0-0	1-6	0-0	1-4	18.2	-1.00
Newbury	2-12	2-5	0-0	0-2	0-2	0-3	16.7	-7.13
Chepstow	2-13	1-5	0-0	0-0	0-4	1-4	15.4	-5.50
Stratford	2-16	1-5	0-0	1-4	0-5	0-2	12.5	-4.50
Hexham	1-2	0-0	0-0	0-0	1-2	0-0	50.0	-0.33
Leicester	1-2	1-2	0-0	0-0	0-0	0-0	50.0	+0.50
Musselbgh	1-3	0-1	1-1	0-0	0-1	0-0	33.3	-1.09
Taunton	1-5	0-1	0-0	0-1	1-2	0-1	20.0	-2.75
Wincanton	1-5	0-1	0-0	0-2	1-2	0-0	20.0	+0.60
Kempton	1-7	0-3	0-0	0-1	1-1	0-2	14.3	+2.00
Nton Abbot	1-7	0-1	0-0	1-4	0-0	0-2	14.3	+8.00
Ffos Las	1-7	0-0	0-0	0-1	1-4	0-2	14.3	+1.00
Worcester	1-16	0-3	0-0	1-7	0-5	0-1	6.3	-14.60

WINNING HORSES

Horse	Races Run	1st	2nd	3rd	£
Master Dee	4	1	1	2	56950
Chase The Spud	4	1	0	0	31714
Perfect Candidate	5	1	0	0	28475
Poetic Rhythm	5	2	0	1	42820
Colin's Sister	5	1	0	2	22887
Mighty Leader	7	3	0	0	25277
Tangolan	7	2	0	0	20704
Cap Soleil	4	2	2	0	24386
*Winter Lion	2	1	0	0	11372
Lovely Job	6	3	2	0	20988
Jennys Surprise	6	2	2	0	16263
Ocean Cove	5	1	3	1	10007
Creevytennant	5	2	1	1	10883
Barney Dwan	5	2	0	1	13453
Blue Comet	5	3	0	2	14621
Herecomestheboom	3	1	0	1	6256

Socksy	5	1	1	1	5848
Diamond Fort	3	1	0	0	5523
Iora Glas	3	1	0	1	5198
*Ratify	5	4	0	0	13594
Rockchasebullett	6	1	2	0	4289
Indian Reel	10	1	1	2	4159
Pauls Hill	4	1	0	1	3899
*Lungarno Palace	2	1	0	1	3574
Grand Introduction	4	1	0	0	3509
Sissinghurst	2	2	0	0	6628
Mercy Mercy Me	3	1	0	0	3249
Aristocracy	3	1	1	1	3249
Iniesta	6	1	2	1	3249
Jarveys Plate	1	1	0	0	3165
Icanmotor	4	1	0	1	2924
Lord Landen	1	1	0	0	2859
Global Stage	3	1	0	0	2729
King Muro	3	1	0	1	2599
Wells Gold	7	1	0	0	2599
Grageelagh Girl	4	1	2	0	2599
Are They Your Own	3	1	1	0	2496
Time To Move On	2	2	0	0	4224
Belle Amis	3	1	0	1	2209
Strong Glance	2	1	0	0	1949
Coolanly	4	1	1	0	1949
Benny's Bridge	2	1	0	1	1625
Barrakilla	3	1	1	0	1317
Total winning prize-money					**£458267**
Favourites	**51-96**		**53.1%**		**49.01**

DANIEL O'BRIEN

CAPEL, KENT

	No. of Hrs	Races Run	1st	2nd	3rd	Unpl	Per cent	£1 Level Stake
NH Flat	0	0	0	0	0	0	0.0	0.00
Hurdles	5	14	1	1	1	11	7.1	-10.00
Chases	1	2	0	0	0	2	0.0	-2.00
Totals	**6**	**16**	**1**	**1**	**1**	**13**	**6.3**	**-12.00**
16-17	8	28	1	1	1	25	3.6	-19.00
15-16	8	27	0	3	1	23	0.0	-27.00

JOCKEYS

	W-R	Per cent	£1 Level Stake
Thomas Garner	1-6	16.7	-2.00

COURSE RECORD

	Total W-R	Non-Hndcps Hurdles	Chases	Hndcps Hurdles	Chases	NH Flat	Per cent	£1 Level Stake
Plumpton	1-8	0-5	0-0	1-3	0-0	0-0	12.5	-4.00

WINNING HORSES

Horse	Races Run	1st	2nd	3rd	£
Bostin	4	1	1	1	3249
Total winning prize-money					**£3249**
Favourites	**0-0**		**0.0%**		**0.00**

JEDD O'KEEFFE

MIDDLEHAM MOOR, N YORKS

	No. of Hrs	Races Run	1st	2nd	3rd	Unpl	Per cent	£1 Level Stake
NH Flat	2	3	0	0	2	1	0.0	-3.00
Hurdles	9	21	4	1	3	13	19.0	+11.75
Chases	2	2	0	0	0	2	0.0	-2.00
Totals	**11**	**26**	**4**	**1**	**5**	**16**	**15.4**	**+6.75**
16-17	7	19	3	6	1	9	15.8	-11.77
15-16	4	8	2	2	0	4	25.0	+1.00

JOCKEYS

	W-R	Per cent	£1 Level Stake
Joe Colliver	4-16	25.0	+16.75

COURSE RECORD

	Total W-R	Non-Hndcps Hurdles	Chases	Hndcps Hurdles	Chases	NH Flat	Per cent	£1 Level Stake
Ascot	1-1	1-1	0-0	0-0	0-0	0-0	100.0	+4.50
Haydock	1-1	0-0	0-0	1-1	0-0	0-0	100.0	+6.00
Hexham	1-1	1-1	0-0	0-0	0-0	0-0	100.0	+2.25
Wetherby	1-4	1-3	0-0	0-1	0-0	0-0	25.0	+13.00

WINNING HORSES

Horse	Races Run	1st	2nd	3rd	£
Sam Spinner	5	2	1	1	113900
*American Craftsman	4	1	0	1	3249
Silva Eclipse	1	1	0	0	3165
Total winning prize-money					**£120314**
Favourites	**0-2**		**0.0%**		**-2.00**

JONJO O'NEILL

CHELTENHAM, GLOUCS

	No. of Hrs	Races Run	1st	2nd	3rd	Unpl	Per cent	£1 Level Stake
NH Flat	12	14	1	0	3	10	7.1	-12.50
Hurdles	102	323	34	31	29	229	10.5	-170.60
Chases	60	216	29	21	22	144	13.4	-15.16
Totals	**146**	**553**	**64**	**52**	**54**	**383**	**11.6**	**-198.26**
16-17	156	686	78	84	75	449	11.4	-211.33
15-16	152	559	80	71	44	363	14.3	-118.05

BY MONTH

NH Flat	W-R	Per cent	£1 Level Stake	Hurdles	W-R	Per cent	£1 Level Stake
May	0-1	0.0	-1.00	May	5-29	17.2	-7.13
June	0-0	0.0	0.00	June	4-18	22.2	-7.23
July	0-0	0.0	0.00	July	4-22	18.2	-8.53
August	0-0	0.0	0.00	August	1-14	7.1	-12.09
September	0-0	0.0	0.00	September	2-17	11.8	+3.00
October	1-7	14.3	-5.50	October	8-48	16.7	-9.57
November	0-2	0.0	-2.00	November	2-48	4.2	-35.50

December	0-0	0.0	0.00	December	4-36	11.1	-15.50
January	0-0	0.0	0.00	January	3-36	8.3	-24.63
February	0-3	0.0	-3.00	February	1-15	6.7	-13.43
March	0-0	0.0	0.00	March	0-21	0.0	-21.00
April	0-1	0.0	-1.00	April	0-19	0.0	-19.00

Chases	W-R	Per cent	£1 Level Stake	Totals	W-R	Per cent	£1 Level Stake
May	7-38	18.4	+4.91	May	12-68	17.6	-3.22
June	3-21	14.3	-4.50	June	7-39	17.9	-11.73
July	2-14	14.3	+1.00	July	6-36	16.7	-7.53
August	1-10	10.0	-6.25	August	2-24	8.3	-18.34
September	2-17	11.8	-1.90	September	4-34	11.8	+1.10
October	4-28	14.3	-3.17	October	13-83	15.7	-18.24
November	3-25	12.0	-9.25	November	5-75	6.7	-46.75
December	4-20	20.0	+29.00	December	8-56	14.3	+13.50
January	0-12	0.0	-12.00	January	3-48	6.3	-36.63
February	0-12	0.0	-12.00	February	1-30	3.3	-28.43
March	1-7	14.3	-2.50	March	1-28	3.6	-23.50
April	2-12	16.7	+1.50	April	2-32	6.3	-18.50

DISTANCE

Hurdles	W-R	Per cent	£1 Level Stake	Chases	W-R	Per cent	£1 Level Stake
2m-2m3f	10-127	7.9	-80.08	2m-2m3f	6-27	22.2	+8.60
2m4f-2m7f	21-144	14.6	-51.10	2m4f-2m7f	9-72	12.5	-13.92
3m+	2-50	4.0	-39.00	3m+	14-117	12.0	-9.84

TYPE OF RACE

Non-Handicaps	W-R	Per cent	£1 Level Stake	Handicaps	W-R	Per cent	£1 Level Stake
Nov Hrdls	9-80	11.3	-56.31	Nov Hrdls	3-12	25.0	-2.09
Hrdls	5-55	9.1	-36.95	Hrdls	16-168	9.5	-82.25
Nov Chs	3-11	27.3	-4.07	Nov Chs	2-17	11.8	-7.00
Chases	0-2	0.0	-2.00	Chases	21-167	12.6	-10.59
Sell/Claim	0-0	0.0	0.00	Sell/Claim	0-0	0.0	0.00

RACE CLASS

	W-R	Per cent	£1 Level Stake
Class 1	1-21	4.8	-13.00
Class 2	6-54	11.1	-6.50
Class 3	11-136	8.1	-75.17
Class 4	43-274	15.7	-47.09
Class 5	2-62	3.2	-52.00
Class 6	1-6	16.7	-4.50

FIRST TIME OUT

	W-R	Per cent	£1 Level Stake
Bumpers	1-12	8.3	-10.50
Hurdles	11-87	12.6	-23.08
Chases	10-47	21.3	+7.74
Totals	22-146	15.1	-25.84

JOCKEYS

	W-R	Per cent	£1 Level Stake
Aidan Coleman	41-273	15.0	-75.04
Killian Moore	6-74	8.1	-22.75
Richie McLernon	6-100	6.0	-43.09
Jonjo O'Neill	5-42	11.9	-21.13
Richard Johnson	2-3	66.7	+5.00
Barry Geraghty	2-16	12.5	-5.67
Noel Fehily	1-7	14.3	-5.09
Jack Savage	1-11	9.1	-3.50

COURSE RECORD

	Total W-R	Non-Hndcps Hurdles	Non-Hndcps Chases	Hndcps Hurdles	Chases	NH Flat	Per cent	£1 Level Stake
Worcester	12-59	3-14	3-8	3-22	2-14	1-1	20.3	-2.56
Uttoxeter	11-57	2-15	0-1	5-20	4-21	0-0	19.3	+0.63
Warwick	6-36	0-7	0-1	2-11	4-15	0-2	16.7	+4.41
Huntingdon	5-32	1-12	0-0	3-13	1-6	0-1	15.6	-4.00
Doncaster	4-35	0-11	0-0	1-13	3-10	0-1	11.4	+2.00
Mrket Rsn	4-44	2-11	0-2	0-12	2-18	0-1	9.1	-32.35
Southwell	3-29	0-9	0-0	1-10	2-9	0-1	10.3	-10.50
Cartmel	2-8	1-2	0-0	0-4	1-2	0-0	25.0	+4.50
Wetherby	2-8	1-3	0-0	1-4	0-1	0-0	25.0	-1.50
Aintree	2-12	1-2	0-0	1-4	0-6	0-0	16.7	-5.83
Bangor	2-19	1-7	0-0	1-4	0-8	0-0	10.5	-7.13
Lingfield	1-2	1-1	0-0	0-1	0-0	0-0	50.0	-0.43
Hereford	1-5	1-1	0-0	0-2	0-2	0-0	20.0	+0.50
Haydock	1-7	0-0	0-0	1-3	0-4	0-0	14.3	-3.50
Fontwell	1-8	0-1	0-0	0-0	1-6	0-1	12.5	-3.00
Taunton	1-10	0-3	0-0	0-4	1-3	0-0	10.0	+5.00
Exeter	1-11	0-3	0-0	0-3	1-5	0-0	9.1	-6.50
Ascot	1-12	0-4	0-1	0-3	1-4	0-0	8.3	-4.00
Ffos Las	1-12	1-2	0-0	0-5	0-5	0-0	8.3	-7.50
Ludlow	1-18	0-4	0-0	0-3	1-11	0-0	5.6	-10.00
Kempton	1-21	0-6	0-0	0-6	1-8	0-1	4.8	-17.50
Cheltenham	1-23	0-1	0-0	0-10	1-12	0-0	4.3	-14.00

WINNING HORSES

Horse	Races Run	1st	2nd	3rd	£
Go Conquer	5	2	0	0	68661
I'dliketheoption	3	1	0	0	19461
Another Hero	1	1	0	0	15640
Mustmeetalady	5	1	0	0	15640
A Little Magic	2	1	0	0	14522
Festive Affair	7	2	1	0	23884
Spookydooky	4	1	0	0	9846
Timeforwest	7	1	0	0	9615
Beggars Cross	4	1	0	0	7798
Mont Royale	10	1	1	0	7507
For Instance	3	2	0	1	10342
Fort Worth	4	1	1	1	6963
Compadre	6	1	2	1	6498
Quarenta	7	1	2	1	6498
Kelvingrove	8	1	1	0	6389
Above Board	2	1	0	0	6389
Mad Jack Mytton	5	2	0	1	10814
In The Rough	2	1	0	1	6256
Bronco Billy	4	1	0	0	5580
As You Like	7	1	0	0	5198
Strongly Suggested	9	1	1	2	5198
Cloth Cap	6	1	0	0	5198
Powerful Symbol	3	2	0	0	8963
Pop Rockstar	6	2	1	0	8772
Django Django	8	1	1	0	4549
Walter Oneeightone	5	1	0	1	4549
Noble Robin	3	2	0	0	8447
Washed Ashore	7	1	2	0	4549

Clubs Are Trumps	8	1	1	1	4549
Sky Pirate	3	1	1	1	4431
Minotaur	3	2	0	1	8278
Fleminport	5	2	0	1	8317
Counter Shy	3	1	1	0	4029
The Tailgater	5	2	0	1	7697
Demon D'Aunou	4	1	0	1	3899
Lost Legend	5	1	1	2	3899
Sebastian Beach	5	1	0	0	3899
Walkami	2	1	0	0	3899
Manny Owens	5	1	1	1	3899
Dreamsoftheatre	6	1	1	0	3899
Utility	6	2	0	0	7278
Terry The Fish	7	3	1	0	9617
State The Obvious	6	1	3	1	3379
Knight Destroyer	6	1	2	1	3379
Lithic	7	1	1	2	3249
Pongo Twistleton	4	1	0	0	3249
Palmers Hill	3	1	0	1	3249
Cobolobo	4	1	0	0	3249
Big Penny	6	1	3	0	3249
Borderlinedecision	5	1	0	0	2339
Global Citizen	3	1	1	0	1689
Total winning prize-money					**£418347**
Favourites		22-55		40.0%	-3.14

JOHN O'SHEA

ELTON, GLOUCS

	No. of Hrs	Races Run	1st	2nd	3rd	Unpl	Per cent	£1 Level Stake
NH Flat	4	9	0	0	0	9	0.0	-9.00
Hurdles	8	35	4	2	5	24	11.4	-3.13
Chases	2	5	0	0	0	5	0.0	-5.00
Totals	**11**	**49**	**4**	**2**	**5**	**38**	**8.2**	**-17.13**
16-17	16	48	2	3	4	39	4.2	-31.25
15-16	14	54	3	3	2	46	5.6	-14.00

JOCKEYS

	W-R	Per cent	£1 Level Stake
Miss Brodie Hampson	3-30	10.0	-5.63
Mitchell Bastyan	1-1	100.0	+6.50

COURSE RECORD

	Total W-R	Non-Hndcps Hurdles	Chases	Hndcps Hurdles	Chases	NH Flat	Per cent	£1 Level Stake
Hereford	2-8	0-2	0-0	2-6	0-0	0-0	25.0	+13.50
Leicester	1-1	0-0	0-0	1-1	0-0	0-0	100.0	+1.88
Uttoxeter	1-4	0-0	0-0	1-4	0-0	0-0	25.0	+3.50

WINNING HORSES

Horse	Races Run	1st	2nd	3rd	£
Cougar Kid	14	3	0	3	14771
Outrageous Romana	4	1	0	2	2859
Total winning prize-money					**£17630**

Favourites		1-4	25.0%	-1.13

HENRY OLIVER

ABBERLEY, WORCS

	No. of Hrs	Races Run	1st	2nd	3rd	Unpl	Per cent	£1 Level Stake
NH Flat	5	7	0	0	1	6	0.0	-7.00
Hurdles	21	74	10	11	11	42	13.5	-4.75
Chases	18	74	17	11	7	39	23.0	+37.75
Totals	**36**	**155**	**27**	**22**	**19**	**87**	**17.4**	**+26.00**
16-17	35	145	13	21	10	101	9.0	-72.04
15-16	28	119	15	17	10	77	12.6	-13.53

BY MONTH

NH Flat	W-R	Per cent	£1 Level Stake	Hurdles	W-R	Per cent	£1 Level Stake
May	0-2	0.0	-2.00	May	0-4	0.0	-4.00
June	0-0	0.0	0.00	June	0-1	0.0	-1.00
July	0-1	0.0	-1.00	July	0-0	0.0	0.00
August	0-1	0.0	-1.00	August	0-0	0.0	0.00
September	0-0	0.0	0.00	September	0-0	0.0	0.00
October	0-0	0.0	0.00	October	2-12	16.7	+18.00
November	0-1	0.0	-1.00	November	2-11	18.2	-2.50
December	0-0	0.0	0.00	December	1-8	12.5	-3.00
January	0-0	0.0	0.00	January	0-9	0.0	-9.00
February	0-0	0.0	0.00	February	2-14	14.3	-1.43
March	0-0	0.0	0.00	March	3-6	50.0	+7.18
April	0-2	0.0	-2.00	April	0-9	0.0	-9.00

Chases	W-R	Per cent	£1 Level Stake	Totals	W-R	Per cent	£1 Level Stake
May	3-6	50.0	+10.75	May	3-12	25.0	+4.75
June	1-3	33.3	+7.00	June	1-4	25.0	+6.00
July	0-4	0.0	-4.00	July	0-5	0.0	-5.00
August	0-0	0.0	0.00	August	0-1	0.0	-1.00
September	1-2	50.0	+1.00	September	1-2	50.0	+1.00
October	1-11	9.1	-4.50	October	3-23	13.0	+13.50
November	2-9	22.2	+21.00	November	4-21	19.0	+17.50
December	1-8	12.5	-4.75	December	2-16	12.5	-7.75
January	4-10	40.0	+12.00	January	4-19	21.1	+3.00
February	2-7	28.6	+1.25	February	4-21	19.0	-0.18
March	0-7	0.0	-7.00	March	3-13	23.1	+0.18
April	2-7	28.6	+5.00	April	2-18	11.1	-6.00

DISTANCE

Hurdles	W-R	Per cent	£1 Level Stake	Chases	W-R	Per cent	£1 Level Stake
2m-2m3f	10-61	16.4	+8.25	2m-2m3f	8-36	22.2	+10.50
2m4f-2m7f	0-12	0.0	-12.00	2m4f-2m7f	6-25	24.0	+27.50
3m+	0-0	0.0	0.00	3m+	3-13	23.1	-0.25

TYPE OF RACE

Non-Handicaps		Per cent	£1 Level Stake	Handicaps		Per cent	£1 Level Stake
	W-R				W-R		
Nov Hrdls	3-23	13.0	-8.63	Nov Hrdls	0-4	0.0	-4.00

Hrdls	2-11	18.2	+19.00	Hrdls	6-36	16.7	-4.63
Nov Chs	1-2	50.0	+1.00	Nov Chs	3-8	37.5	+24.75
Chases	0-0	0.0	0.00	Chases	12-52	23.1	+19.50
Sell/Claim	0-1	0.0	-1.00	Sell/Claim	0-0	0.0	0.00

RACE CLASS

	W-R	Per cent	£1 Level Stake
Class 1	0-4	0.0	-4.00
Class 2	0-2	0.0	-2.00
Class 3	4-36	11.1	-20.25
Class 4	17-83	20.5	+36.00
Class 5	6-26	23.1	+20.25
Class 6	0-4	0.0	-4.00

FIRST TIME OUT

	W-R	Per cent	£1 Level Stake
Bumpers	0-5	0.0	-5.00
Hurdles	1-16	6.3	-1.00
Chases	3-15	20.0	-1.00
Totals	4-36	11.1	-7.00

JOCKEYS

	W-R	Per cent	£1 Level Stake
James Davies	8-43	18.6	+17.37
Dave Crosse	6-23	26.1	+24.75
Harry Bannister	2-7	28.6	+9.00
Mr Robert Hawker	2-8	25.0	+2.38
Richard Johnson	2-9	22.2	-3.25
Jason Dixon	2-10	20.0	+4.00
Brian Hughes	1-1	100.0	+2.50
Sam Twiston-Davies	1-1	100.0	+2.25
Tommy Dowling	1-7	14.3	-2.00
Tom O'Brien	1-8	12.5	+3.00
Jack Sherwood	1-15	6.7	-11.00

COURSE RECORD

	Total W-R	Non-Hndcps Hurdles	Chases	Hndcps Hurdles	Chases	NH Flat	Per cent	£1 Level Stake
Towcester	5-16	3-6	0-0	0-6	2-4	0-0	31.3	+15.37
Southwell	4-9	0-1	1-1	1-1	2-5	0-1	44.4	+11.50
Exeter	2-6	1-3	0-0	0-1	1-2	0-0	33.3	+10.00
Hereford	2-6	0-0	0-0	0-1	2-4	0-1	33.3	+14.00
Bangor	2-11	0-3	0-0	1-1	1-6	0-1	18.2	+4.50
Hexham	1-1	0-0	0-0	1-1	0-0	0-0	100.0	+1.38
Taunton	1-2	0-0	0-0	0-1	1-1	0-0	50.0	+1.25
Sedgefield	1-3	0-0	0-0	0-0	1-3	0-0	33.3	+0.50
Catterick	1-5	0-1	0-0	0-3	1-1	0-0	20.0	-1.50
Stratford	1-5	1-2	0-0	0-0	0-3	0-0	20.0	+10.00
Wetherby	1-6	0-2	0-0	0-1	1-3	0-0	16.7	-1.00
Mrket Rsn	1-7	0-0	0-1	1-5	0-1	0-0	14.3	-2.00
Chepstow	1-8	0-1	0-0	1-2	0-5	0-0	12.5	-4.00
Uttoxeter	1-9	0-1	0-0	0-3	1-5	0-0	11.1	-4.50
Warwick	1-10	0-3	0-0	0-3	1-2	0-2	10.0	+9.00
Ludlow	1-11	0-5	0-0	0-1	1-5	0-0	9.1	-8.25
Worcester	1-13	0-2	0-0	0-1	1-9	0-1	7.7	-3.00

WINNING HORSES

Horse	Races Run	1st	2nd	3rd	£
Dresden	6	2	0	1	15465
Ozzy Thomas	6	2	1	1	11660
Major Hindrance	7	1	1	2	7473
Sparkling River	6	2	0	1	12330
Generous Day	6	2	1	2	10397
Burrenbridge Hotel	8	2	1	1	12586
Dr Des	6	3	2	0	15587
Yorgonnahearmeroar	4	1	0	0	4938
Nickname Exit	2	1	0	0	4726
Steps And Stairs	3	2	0	1	7928
Diamond Rock	4	1	1	0	4549
Love Lane	3	1	0	0	4549
Samarayia	6	1	1	2	4484
*Hijran	5	1	1	1	4094
Bertie Lugg	3	1	1	0	3249
Murray Mount	7	2	1	0	6498
Fairy Pol	6	1	0	1	3249
Shroughmore Lass	8	1	2	1	2599
Total winning prize-money					**£136361**
Favourites	6-18		33.3%		-1.25

MARK PATTINSON

EPSOM, SURREY

	No. of Hrs	Races Run	1st	2nd	3rd	Unpl	Per cent	£1 Level Stake
NH Flat	0	0	0	0	0	0	0.0	0.00
Hurdles	2	6	1	0	1	4	16.7	+20.00
Chases	0	0	0	0	0	0	0.0	0.00
Totals	**2**	**6**	**1**	**0**	**1**	**4**	**16.7**	**+20.00**

JOCKEYS

	W-R	Per cent	£1 Level Stake
Sean Houlihan	1-4	25.0	+22.00

COURSE RECORD

	Total W-R	Non-Hndcps Hurdles	Chases	Hndcps Hurdles	Chases	NH Flat	Per cent	£1 Level Stake
Sandown	1-2	0-0	0-0	1-2	0-0	0-0	50.0	+24.00

WINNING HORSES

Horse	Races Run	1st	2nd	3rd	£
Briac	5	1	0	1	4549
Total winning prize-money					**£4549**
Favourites	0-39		0.0%		-39.00

BEN PAULING

BOURTON-ON-THE-WATER, GLOUCS

	No. of Hrs	Races Run	1st	2nd	3rd	Unpl	Per cent	£1 Level Stake
NH Flat	19	36	3	6	2	25	8.3	-3.50
Hurdles	47	157	23	18	16	100	14.6	-31.68
Chases	19	48	10	5	4	29	20.8	-12.62
Totals	**75**	**241**	**36**	**29**	**22**	**154**	**14.9**	**-47.80**
16-17	54	201	32	20	23	126	15.9	-10.42
15-16	44	155	26	23	7	99	16.8	+58.12

BY MONTH

NH Flat	W-R	Per cent	£1 Level Stake	Hurdles	W-R	Per cent	£1 Level Stake
May	0-1	0.0	-1.00	May	0-4	0.0	-4.00
June	0-1	0.0	-1.00	June	1-4	25.0	-0.25
July	0-0	0.0	0.00	July	0-1	0.0	-1.00
August	0-0	0.0	0.00	August	0-2	0.0	-2.00
September	0-0	0.0	0.00	September	0-0	0.0	0.00
October	2-5	40.0	+20.50	October	0-6	0.0	-6.00
November	1-7	14.3	0.00	November	9-28	32.1	+16.44
December	0-5	0.0	-5.00	December	2-28	7.1	-15.75
January	0-1	0.0	-1.00	January	0-12	0.0	-12.00
February	0-7	0.0	-7.00	February	6-21	28.6	-4.11
March	0-4	0.0	-4.00	March	1-23	4.3	-17.00
April	0-5	0.0	-5.00	April	4-28	14.3	+14.00

Chases	W-R	Per cent	£1 Level Stake	Totals	W-R	Per cent	£1 Level Stake
May	3-3	100.0	+8.00	May	3-8	37.5	+3.00
June	0-1	0.0	-1.00	June	1-6	16.7	-2.25
July	0-1	0.0	-1.00	July	0-2	0.0	-2.00
August	0-2	0.0	-2.00	August	0-4	0.0	-4.00
September	0-0	0.0	0.00	September	0-0	0.0	0.00
October	0-5	0.0	-5.00	October	2-16	12.5	+9.50
November	3-10	30.0	+4.40	November	13-45	28.9	+20.84
December	3-11	27.3	-2.92	December	5-44	11.4	-23.67
January	0-3	0.0	-3.00	January	0-16	0.0	-16.00
February	1-7	14.3	-5.09	February	7-35	20.0	-16.20
March	0-3	0.0	-3.00	March	1-30	3.3	-24.00
April	0-2	0.0	-2.00	April	4-35	11.4	+7.00

DISTANCE

Hurdles	W-R	Per cent	£1 Level Stake	Chases	W-R	Per cent	£1 Level Stake
2m-2m3f	10-51	19.6	+1.26	2m-2m3f	2-10	20.0	-5.75
2m4f-2m7f	9-89	10.1	-56.06	2m4f-2m7f	6-25	24.0	-3.62
3m+	4-16	25.0	+24.13	3m+	2-13	15.4	-3.25

TYPE OF RACE

Non-Handicaps	W-R	Per cent	£1 Level Stake	Handicaps	W-R	Per cent	£1 Level Stake
Nov Hrdls	10-62	16.1	-20.08	Nov Hrdls	0-4	0.0	-4.00
Hrdls	4-15	26.7	-2.60	Hrdls	9-74	12.2	-3.00
Nov Chs	5-10	50.0	+1.43	Nov Chs	0-6	0.0	-6.00
Chases	1-2	50.0	+5.00	Chases	2-21	9.5	-15.80
Sell/Claim	0-0	0.0	0.00	Sell/Claim	0-0	0.0	0.00

RACE CLASS

	W-R	Per cent	£1 Level Stake
Class 1	5-32	15.6	+2.13
Class 2	1-21	4.8	-15.00
Class 3	8-50	16.0	-16.90
Class 4	19-101	18.8	-9.39
Class 5	1-26	3.8	-23.13
Class 6	2-11	18.2	+14.50

FIRST TIME OUT

	W-R	Per cent	£1 Level Stake
Bumpers	2-19	10.5	+6.50
Hurdles	6-41	14.6	-13.97
Chases	6-15	40.0	+10.40
Totals	14-75	18.7	+2.93

JOCKEYS

	W-R	Per cent	£1 Level Stake
Daryl Jacob	19-119	16.0	-11.48
Nico de Boinville	11-50	22.0	-18.57
Mr Douglas Gittins	1-1	100.0	+6.00
James Banks	1-4	25.0	+3.00
Richie McLernon	1-8	12.5	+13.00
Tom Bellamy	1-9	11.1	0.00
David Bass	1-13	7.7	-6.00
Mr Alex Ferguson	1-21	4.8	-17.75

COURSE RECORD

	Total W-R	Non-Hndcps Hurdles	Chases	Hndcps Hurdles	Chases	NH Flat	Per cent	£1 Level Stake
Southwell	8-18	4-5	1-1	2-7	0-1	1-4	44.4	+5.10
Towcester	3-10	1-5	2-2	0-2	0-1	0-0	30.0	-2.38
Kempton	3-15	2-5	0-0	1-8	0-0	0-2	20.0	+2.50
Huntingdon	3-20	1-9	1-1	1-5	0-4	0-1	15.0	-2.10
Fakenham	2-3	0-1	0-0	1-1	1-1	0-0	66.7	+2.20
Stratford	2-3	1-1	0-0	1-1	0-1	0-0	66.7	+22.33
Fontwell	2-6	0-2	0-1	1-1	1-2	0-0	33.3	+10.00
Mrket Rsn	2-6	1-1	0-1	0-1	1-2	0-1	33.3	-1.81
Ascot	2-9	1-4	0-0	0-2	0-1	1-2	22.2	+1.75
Doncaster	2-13	1-5	0-0	0-4	1-2	0-2	15.4	-7.25
Newbury	2-20	0-8	1-2	1-6	0-1	0-3	10.0	-13.88
Haydock	1-3	1-1	0-0	0-0	0-2	0-0	33.3	+10.00
Wetherby	1-4	1-1	0-1	0-2	0-0	0-0	25.0	-2.27
Worcester	1-9	0-2	0-1	0-4	0-1	1-1	11.1	+14.00
Sandown	1-11	0-0	0-0	1-6	0-5	0-0	9.1	-2.00
Cheltenham	1-19	0-3	1-2	0-9	0-1	0-4	5.3	-12.00

WINNING HORSES

Horse	Races Run	1st	2nd	3rd	£
A Hare Breath	3	1	0	0	33762
High Bridge	3	1	0	1	28475
Willoughby Court	3	2	0	1	30846
Kildisart	6	2	2	0	28394
*Global Citizen	3	2	0	0	21179
Delire D'Estruval	6	2	0	1	18786
Creep Desbois	5	1	1	0	9747
Markov	5	2	0	0	13875
Le Breuil	5	1	1	0	7213
Raven's Tower	6	1	2	0	6963
Boss Mans Ladder	6	1	0	0	6758
Coeur Pensif	6	1	0	1	5848
Paddy's Field	4	1	1	1	5848
Always Lion	1	1	0	0	5523
Perfect Pirate	4	1	0	0	5111
Two Swallows	3	1	1	1	4614
Newton Geronimo	5	1	0	1	4549
Oistrakh Le Noir	5	1	2	1	4549
Nestor Park	4	1	1	0	4549
Gowiththeflow	4	1	2	0	4159
*Oskar Denarius	2	1	0	0	4094

Equus Secretus	4	2	0	1	7473
Way Back Then	2	1	0	0	3899
Dolatulo	1	1	0	0	3743
Marten	3	1	0	0	3574
Carlos Du Fruitier	6	1	1	0	3249
Linenhall	4	1	1	0	3249
Boreham Bill	5	1	1	0	3119
Hidden Glen	3	1	0	0	1949
Skidoosh	4	1	1	0	1949
Total winning prize-money					**£287046**
Favourites	**14-47**		**29.8%**		**-13.63**

LYDIA PEARCE
NEWMARKET, SUFFOLK

	No. of Hrs	Races Run	1st	2nd	3rd	Unpl	Per cent	£1 Level Stake
NH Flat	1	3	1	0	0	2	33.3	+12.00
Hurdles	1	1	0	0	0	1	0.0	-1.00
Chases	0	0	0	0	0	0	0.0	0.00
Totals	**2**	**4**	**1**	**0**	**0**	**3**	**25.0**	**+11.00**
16-17	2	3	0	0	0	3	0.0	-3.00
15-16	1	4	1	0	0	3	25.0	+30.00

JOCKEYS

	W-R	Per cent	£1 Level Stake
Jack Quinlan	1-4	25.0	+11.00

COURSE RECORD

	Total W-R	Non-Hndcps Hurdles Chases		Hndcps Hurdles Chases		NH Flat	Per cent	£1 Level Stake
Southwell	1-1	0-0	0-0	0-0	0-0	1-1	100.0	+14.00

WINNING HORSES

Horse	Races Run	1st	2nd	3rd	£
Katahdin	3	1	0	0	2395
Total winning prize-money					**£2395**
Favourites	**0-0**		**0.0%**		**0.00**

AMANDA PERRETT
PULBOROUGH, W SUSSEX

	No. of Hrs	Races Run	1st	2nd	3rd	Unpl	Per cent	£1 Level Stake
NH Flat	1	2	0	1	1	0	0.0	-2.00
Hurdles	5	9	1	0	0	8	11.1	0.00
Chases	0	0	0	0	0	0	0.0	0.00
Totals	**5**	**11**	**1**	**1**	**1**	**8**	**9.1**	**-2.00**
16-17	5	15	2	2	3	8	13.3	+22.25

JOCKEYS

	W-R	Per cent	£1 Level Stake
Leighton Aspell	1-8	12.5	+1.00

COURSE RECORD

	Total W-R	Non-Hndcps Hurdles Chases		Hndcps Hurdles Chases		NH Flat	Per cent	£1 Level Stake
Fontwell	1-4	1-3	0-0	0-0	0-0	0-1	25.0	+5.00

WINNING HORSES

Horse	Races Run	1st	2nd	3rd	£
Balancing Time	1	1	0	0	3249
Total winning prize-money					**£3249**
Favourites	**0-2**		**0.0%**		**-2.00**

PAT PHELAN
EPSOM, SURREY

	No. of Hrs	Races Run	1st	2nd	3rd	Unpl	Per cent	£1 Level Stake
NH Flat	3	3	0	0	0	3	0.0	-3.00
Hurdles	6	26	1	0	1	24	3.8	-20.00
Chases	0	0	0	0	0	0	0.0	0.00
Totals	**7**	**29**	**1**	**0**	**1**	**27**	**3.4**	**-23.00**
16-17	10	24	0	0	0	24	0.0	-24.00
15-16	10	24	1	2	3	18	4.2	-20.25

JOCKEYS

	W-R	Per cent	£1 Level Stake
Niall P Madden	1-5	20.0	+1.00

COURSE RECORD

	Total W-R	Non-Hndcps Hurdles Chases		Hndcps Hurdles Chases		NH Flat	Per cent	£1 Level Stake
Plumpton	1-7	1-4	0-0	0-3	0-0	0-0	14.3	-1.00

WINNING HORSES

Horse	Races Run	1st	2nd	3rd	£
The Premier Celtic	6	1	0	0	4094
Total winning prize-money					**£4094**
Favourites	**0-0**		**0.0%**		**0.00**

ALAN PHILLIPS
CALLOW END, WORCS

	No. of Hrs	Races Run	1st	2nd	3rd	Unpl	Per cent	£1 Level Stake
NH Flat	1	2	0	0	0	2	0.0	-2.00
Hurdles	8	25	1	0	0	24	4.0	-19.00
Chases	5	13	1	1	2	9	7.7	-4.00
Totals	**13**	**40**	**2**	**1**	**2**	**35**	**5.0**	**-25.00**
16-17	10	43	6	10	2	25	14.0	-1.25
15-16	10	24	0	1	4	19	0.0	-24.00

JOCKEYS

	W-R	Per cent	£1 Level Stake
Mattie Batchelor	1-2	50.0	+7.00
Sean Bowen	1-15	6.7	-9.00

COURSE RECORD

	Total W-R	Non-Hndcps Hurdles	Chases	Hndcps Hurdles	Chases	NH Flat	Per cent	£1 Level Stake
Southwell	1-3	0-0	0-0	1-2	0-0	0-1	33.3	+3.00
Worcester	1-7	0-2	0-1	0-2	1-2	0-0	14.3	+2.00

WINNING HORSES

Horse	Races Run	1st	2nd	3rd	£
The Model County	6	1	0	0	3119
Lined With Silver	6	1	1	1	2663
Total winning prize-money					£5782
Favourites	0-2	0.0%			-2.00

RICHARD PHILLIPS

ADLESTROP, GLOUCS

	No. of Hrs	Races Run	1st	2nd	3rd	Unpl	Per cent	£1 Level Stake
NH Flat	4	7	0	1	0	6	0.0	-7.00
Hurdles	17	60	6	4	6	44	10.0	-25.67
Chases	3	4	0	2	0	2	0.0	-4.00
Totals	18	71	6	7	6	52	8.5	-36.67
16-17	30	117	5	8	12	92	4.3	-78.25
15-16	29	90	6	9	7	68	6.7	-58.02

JOCKEYS

	W-R	Per cent	£1 Level Stake
Daniel Hiskett	4-43	9.3	-20.00
Tom Bellamy	2-2	100.0	+9.33

COURSE RECORD

	Total W-R	Non-Hndcps Hurdles	Chases	Hndcps Hurdles	Chases	NH Flat	Per cent	£1 Level Stake
Towcester	2-5	0-1	0-0	2-4	0-0	0-0	40.0	+6.83
Kempton	2-7	0-0	0-0	2-7	0-0	0-0	28.6	+6.00
Hereford	1-3	1-1	0-0	0-0	0-1	0-1	33.3	+2.00
Huntingdon	1-8	0-2	0-0	1-5	0-0	0-1	12.5	-3.50

WINNING HORSES

Horse	Races Run	1st	2nd	3rd	£
Bertie Barnes	4	2	0	0	7278
Muthabir	7	1	0	1	3899
Sheelbewhatsheelbe	7	1	1	0	3899
Minella Whisper	6	1	0	2	3249
Totterdown	7	1	1	0	3119
Total winning prize-money					£21444
Favourites	1-4	25.0%			0.50

C C PIMLOTT

SCRAYINGHAM, NORTH YORKS

	No. of Hrs	Races Run	1st	2nd	3rd	Unpl	Per cent	£1 Level Stake
NH Flat	0	0	0	0	0	0	0.0	0.00
Hurdles	0	0	0	0	0	0	0.0	0.00
Chases	1	2	2	0	0	0	100.0	+4.00
Totals	1	2	2	0	0	0	100.0	+4.00

JOCKEYS

	W-R	Per cent	£1 Level Stake
Mr Tom Strawson	2-2	100.0	+4.00

COURSE RECORD

	Total W-R	Non-Hndcps Hurdles	Chases	Hndcps Hurdles	Chases	NH Flat	Per cent	£1 Level Stake
Catterick	1-1	0-0	1-1	0-0	0-0	0-0	100.0	+2.75
Kelso	1-1	0-0	1-1	0-0	0-0	0-0	100.0	+1.25

WINNING HORSES

Horse	Races Run	1st	2nd	3rd	£
*Duhallow Tornado	2	2	0	0	5303
Total winning prize-money					£5303
Favourites	1-1	100.0%			1.25

DAVID PIPE

NICHOLASHAYNE, DEVON

	No. of Hrs	Races Run	1st	2nd	3rd	Unpl	Per cent	£1 Level Stake
NH Flat	19	28	3	2	5	18	10.7	-22.79
Hurdles	59	226	13	24	26	163	5.8	-105.38
Chases	31	107	17	11	13	66	15.9	+14.66
Totals	93	361	33	37	44	247	9.1	-113.51
16-17	116	485	59	47	42	337	12.2	-192.09
15-16	126	571	80	77	68	346	14.0	-111.92

BY MONTH

NH Flat	W-R	Per cent	£1 Level Stake	Hurdles	W-R	Per cent	£1 Level Stake
May	0-2	0.0	-2.00	May	1-19	5.3	-16.50
June	0-1	0.0	-1.00	June	1-14	7.1	-11.38
July	0-0	0.0	0.00	July	0-10	0.0	-10.00
August	0-1	0.0	-1.00	August	1-15	6.7	-9.50
September	0-0	0.0	0.00	September	0-10	0.0	-10.00
October	0-3	0.0	-3.00	October	1-17	5.9	-6.00
November	0-6	0.0	-6.00	November	2-31	6.5	-10.00
December	1-4	25.0	-2.20	December	0-30	0.0	-10.00
January	0-1	0.0	-1.00	January	2-16	12.5	+1.00
February	2-3	66.7	+0.41	February	0-24	0.0	-24.00
March	0-5	0.0	-5.00	March	0-18	0.0	-18.00
April	0-2	0.0	-2.00	April	5-22	22.7	+39.00

Chases

Chases	W-R	Per cent	£1 Level Stake
May	0-12	0.0	-12.00
June	1-4	25.0	+2.00
July	0-3	0.0	-3.00
August	0-5	0.0	-5.00
September	0-3	0.0	-3.00
October	1-6	16.7	+20.00
November	6-19	31.6	+17.63
December	4-19	21.1	+17.50
January	1-9	11.1	-6.63
February	2-8	25.0	-2.84
March	2-9	22.2	0.00
April	0-10	0.0	-10.00

Totals

Totals	W-R	Per cent	£1 Level Stake
May	1-33	3.0	-30.50
June	2-19	10.5	-10.38
July	0-13	0.0	-13.00
August	1-21	4.8	-15.50
September	0-13	0.0	-13.00
October	2-26	7.7	+11.00
November	8-56	14.3	+1.63
December	5-53	9.4	-14.70
January	3-26	11.5	-6.63
February	4-35	11.4	-26.43
March	2-32	6.3	-23.00
April	5-34	14.7	+27.00

DISTANCE

Hurdles	W-R	Per cent	£1 Level Stake
2m-2m3f	6-109	5.5	-49.00
2m4f-2m7f	3-74	4.1	-52.38
3m+	4-41	9.8	-2.00

Chases	W-R	Per cent	£1 Level Stake
2m-2m3f	2-23	8.7	-14.13
2m4f-2m7f	4-31	12.9	+2.41
3m+	11-53	20.8	+26.38

TYPE OF RACE

Non-Handicaps

	W-R	Per cent	£1 Level Stake
Nov Hrdls	1-49	2.0	-46.50
Hrdls	2-20	10.0	+6.50
Nov Chs	2-8	25.0	+13.38
Chases	1-8	12.5	-4.75
Sell/Claim	0-2	0.0	-2.00

Handicaps

	W-R	Per cent	£1 Level Stake
Nov Hrdls	0-4	0.0	-4.00
Hrdls	9-148	6.1	-59.00
Nov Chs	1-8	12.5	-2.00
Chases	10-77	13.0	-19.88
Sell/Claim	0-2	0.0	-2.00

RACE CLASS

	W-R	Per cent	£1 Level Stake
Class 1	1-33	3.0	-25.00
Class 2	5-39	12.8	+8.50
Class 3	8-78	10.3	-40.84
Class 4	12-148	8.1	-24.00
Class 5	6-52	11.5	-22.97
Class 6	1-11	9.1	-9.20

FIRST TIME OUT

	W-R	Per cent	£1 Level Stake
Bumpers	3-19	15.8	-13.79
Hurdles	3-48	6.3	-11.50
Chases	3-26	11.5	+14.88
Totals	9-93	9.7	-10.41

JOCKEYS

	W-R	Per cent	£1 Level Stake
Tom Scudamore	24-221	10.9	-49.26
David Noonan	5-75	6.7	-38.50
Daryl Jacob	1-1	100.0	+12.00
Mr R O Harding	1-1	100.0	+11.00
Capt Guy Disney	1-2	50.0	+1.25
Michael Heard	1-44	2.3	-33.00

COURSE RECORD

	Total W-R	Non-Hndcps Hurdles	Chases	Hndcps Hurdles	Chases	NH Flat	Per cent	£1 Level Stake
Chepstow	4-17	0-3	1-1	0-6	2-5	1-2	23.5	+19.28

	W-R						Per cent	£1 Level Stake
Newbury	3-11	0-4	0-0	2-3	1-3	0-1	27.3	+11.00
Exeter	3-36	1-11	0-2	1-12	1-6	0-5	8.3	-0.75
Plumpton	2-5	0-1	0-1	0-0	2-2	0-1	40.0	+3.41
Kempton	2-7	0-0	0-2	1-4	1-1	0-0	28.6	+10.50
Ludlow	2-14	0-4	0-1	1-4	1-5	0-0	14.3	+5.00
Ayr	1-3	0-0	0-0	1-2	0-1	0-0	33.3	+3.00
Huntingdon	1-4	0-0	0-0	1-4	0-0	0-0	25.0	+6.00
Towcester	1-4	0-1	0-0	0-1	0-0	1-2	25.0	-2.50
Ascot	1-6	0-1	0-0	0-2	1-3	0-0	16.7	-1.50
Haydock	1-6	0-0	1-1	0-1	0-4	0-0	16.7	+13.00
Wetherby	1-6	0-1	0-2	0-2	1-1	0-0	16.7	0.00
Bangor	1-7	1-4	0-0	0-3	0-0	0-0	14.3	-1.50
Stratford	1-8	0-1	0-0	0-2	1-4	0-1	12.5	-5.13
Sandown	1-9	0-0	1-2	0-5	0-1	0-1	11.1	-5.75
Aintree	1-11	0-1	0-0	1-4	0-6	0-0	9.1	-3.00
Fontwell	1-12	0-0	0-0	0-7	1-5	0-0	8.3	-6.00
Wincanton	1-12	0-3	0-0	0-4	1-4	0-1	8.3	-7.50
Ffos Las	1-13	1-5	0-0	0-3	0-3	0-2	7.7	-10.50
Uttoxeter	1-21	0-4	0-0	0-10	0-5	1-2	4.8	-19.20
Cheltenham	1-25	0-1	0-1	0-10	1-11	0-2	4.0	-13.00
Worcester	1-28	1-6	0-1	0-16	0-4	0-1	3.6	-25.38
Taunton	1-39	0-10	0-1	1-23	0-3	0-2	2.6	-26.00

WINNING HORSES

Horse	Races Run	1st	2nd	3rd	£
Mr Big Shot	2	1	0	0	42203
Rathlin Rose	9	2	1	1	18768
Eamon An Cnoic	6	2	0	1	21475
What A Moment	1	1	0	0	13191
Moon Racer	3	1	0	0	12996
Taj Badalandabad	6	1	0	0	12512
Daklondike	5	3	0	0	25178
Dell' Arca	10	1	1	1	9747
You Say What	5	1	0	0	9495
Abracadabra Sivola	9	1	0	1	7408
Ramses De Teillee	9	2	4	1	11242
Miss Tynte	7	1	1	1	6563
Starchitect	3	1	1	0	6498
Red Square Revival	6	2	0	2	9747
Saint John Henry	7	1	0	1	5198
Tobacco Road	4	1	0	0	4549
Friday Night Light	7	1	3	1	4549
Timeforacurfew	6	1	0	2	4094
Whitley Neill	1	1	0	0	4094
Purple 'n Gold	11	1	0	0	3899
Delface	10	1	2	1	3899
Three Star General	8	1	3	1	3119
Bambi Du Noyer	8	1	1	0	2924
Know The Score	2	1	0	0	2599
Aldrin	3	1	0	1	2599
Remastered	1	1	0	0	2274
Queens Cave	2	1	1	0	1949
Total winning prize-money					**£252769**
Favourites	9-30		30.0%		-3.88

MARK PITMAN

UPPER LAMBOURN, BERKS

	No. of Hrs	Races Run	1st	2nd	3rd	Unpl	Per cent	£1 Level Stake
NH Flat	1	1	0	1	0	0	0.0	-1.00
Hurdles	3	7	2	0	0	5	28.6	+1.17
Chases	1	4	0	1	2	1	0.0	-4.00
Totals	**5**	**12**	**2**	**2**	**2**	**6**	**16.7**	**-3.83**
16-17	8	24	0	2	1	21	0.0	-24.00
15-16	8	29	4	4	2	19	13.8	-8.75

JOCKEYS

	W-R	Per cent	£1 Level Stake
Noel Fehily	1-3	33.3	-1.33
A P Heskin	1-5	20.0	+1.50

COURSE RECORD

	Total W-R	Non-Hndcps Hurdles	Chases	Hndcps Hurdles	Chases	NH Flat	Per cent	£1 Level Stake
Towcester	1-1	0-0	0-0	1-1	0-0	0-0	100.0	+5.50
Huntingdon	1-5	0-2	0-0	1-2	0-1	0-0	20.0	-3.33

WINNING HORSES

Horse	Races Run	1st	2nd	3rd	£
Captainofindustry	4	2	0	0	7798
Total winning prize-money					**£7798**
Favourites	1-2	50.0%			-0.33

JACKIE DU PLESSIS

TREHAN, CORNWALL

	No. of Hrs	Races Run	1st	2nd	3rd	Unpl	Per cent	£1 Level Stake
NH Flat	4	6	0	0	0	6	0.0	-6.00
Hurdles	10	20	0	2	2	16	0.0	-20.00
Chases	6	22	1	0	5	16	4.5	-18.50
Totals	**16**	**48**	**1**	**2**	**7**	**38**	**2.1**	**-44.50**
16-17	14	63	5	6	10	42	7.9	-22.75
15-16	13	42	5	4	7	26	11.9	+18.00

JOCKEYS

	W-R	Per cent	£1 Level Stake
David Noonan	1-9	11.1	-5.50

COURSE RECORD

	Total W-R	Non-Hndcps Hurdles	Chases	Hndcps Hurdles	Chases	NH Flat	Per cent	£1 Level Stake
Uttoxeter	1-1	0-0	0-0	0-0	1-1	0-0	100.0	+2.50

WINNING HORSES

Horse	Races Run	1st	2nd	3rd	£
Cailleach Annie	4	1	0	1	3899
Total winning prize-money					**£3899**

MARK PITMAN Favourites	1-1	100.0%	2.50

CHARLES POGSON

FARNSFIELD, NOTTS

	No. of Hrs	Races Run	1st	2nd	3rd	Unpl	Per cent	£1 Level Stake
NH Flat	0	0	0	0	0	0	0.0	0.00
Hurdles	6	27	1	2	2	22	3.7	-22.00
Chases	5	23	1	5	8	9	4.3	-19.25
Totals	**10**	**50**	**2**	**7**	**10**	**31**	**4.0**	**-41.25**
16-17	17	71	3	6	11	51	4.2	-34.67
15-16	16	68	8	11	6	43	11.8	-6.30

JOCKEYS

	W-R	Per cent	£1 Level Stake
Adam Pogson	2-50	4.0	-41.25

COURSE RECORD

	Total W-R	Non-Hndcps Hurdles	Chases	Hndcps Hurdles	Chases	NH Flat	Per cent	£1 Level Stake
Mrket Rsn	2-14	0-1	0-0	1-9	1-4	0-0	14.3	-5.25

WINNING HORSES

Horse	Races Run	1st	2nd	3rd	£
Minella Forfitness	6	1	1	2	4874
Overtoujay	6	1	1	0	3249
Total winning prize-money					**£8123**
Favourites	0-0	0.0%			0.00

R D POTTER

WINCHCOMBE, GLOUCESTERSHIRE

	No. of Hrs	Races Run	1st	2nd	3rd	Unpl	Per cent	£1 Level Stake
NH Flat	0	0	0	0	0	0	0.0	0.00
Hurdles	0	0	0	0	0	0	0.0	0.00
Chases	3	4	1	0	0	3	25.0	-0.25
Totals	**3**	**4**	**1**	**0**	**0**	**3**	**25.0**	**-0.25**
15-16	1	1	0	0	1	0	0.0	-1.00

JOCKEYS

	W-R	Per cent	£1 Level Stake
Miss Emma Yardley	1-3	33.3	+0.75

COURSE RECORD

	Total W-R	Non-Hndcps Hurdles	Chases	Hndcps Hurdles	Chases	NH Flat	Per cent	£1 Level Stake
Fakenham	1-1	0-0	1-1	0-0	0-0	0-0	100.0	+2.75

WINNING HORSES

Horse	Races Run	1st	2nd	3rd	£
*Foxcub	2	1	0	0	2431

Total winning prize-money		**£2431**	
Favourites	**0-0**	**0.0%**	**0.00**

	Total W-R	Non-Hndcps Hurdles	Chases	Hndcps Hurdles	Chases	NH Flat	Per cent	£1 Level Stake
Hereford	1-4	0-2	0-0	0-0	1-2	0-0	25.0	+4.00
Stratford	1-4	0-0	0-0	0-3	0-0	1-1	25.0	+7.00

WINNING HORSES

Horse	Races Run	1st	2nd	3rd	£
Minellacelebration	6	1	1	0	15640
Clondaw Rigger	9	1	3	0	4938
Schindler's Prince	3	1	0	0	4431
Hollow Park	7	1	0	1	4159
Lucca Lady	4	1	3	0	2599
Total winning prize-money					**£31767**
Favourites	**0-1**		**0.0%**		**-1.00**

BRENDAN POWELL

UPPER LAMBOURN, BERKS

	No. of Hrs	Races Run	1st	2nd	3rd	Unpl	Per cent	£1 Level Stake
NH Flat	3	4	0	0	0	4	0.0	-4.00
Hurdles	13	41	2	5	3	31	4.9	-31.25
Chases	4	14	0	2	1	11	0.0	-14.00
Totals	18	59	2	7	4	46	3.4	-49.25
16-17	22	59	5	2	6	46	8.5	+27.00
15-16	22	80	4	12	11	53	5.0	-11.25

JOCKEYS

	W-R	Per cent	£1 Level Stake
Richie McLernon	1-4	25.0	-0.75
Brendan Powell	1-49	2.0	-42.50

COURSE RECORD

	Total W-R	Non-Hndcps Hurdles	Chases	Hndcps Hurdles	Chases	NH Flat	Per cent	£1 Level Stake
Ludlow	1-2	1-2	0-0	0-0	0-0	0-0	50.0	+1.25
Fakenham	1-4	1-1	0-0	0-1	0-2	0-0	25.0	+2.50

WINNING HORSES

Horse	Races Run	1st	2nd	3rd	£
Gannicus	4	1	0	0	4549
Phoenix Dawn	7	1	3	2	4549
Total winning prize-money					**£9098**
Favourites	**0-2**		**0.0%**		**-2.00**

KATY PRICE

HAY-ON-WYE, POWYS

	No. of Hrs	Races Run	1st	2nd	3rd	Unpl	Per cent	£1 Level Stake
NH Flat	5	5	1	0	1	3	20.0	+6.00
Hurdles	13	41	1	5	1	34	2.4	-31.00
Chases	7	25	3	5	0	17	12.0	+4.00
Totals	19	71	5	10	2	54	7.0	-21.00
16-17	17	88	6	11	4	67	6.8	-55.25
15-16	3	12	3	1	3	5	25.0	0.00

JOCKEYS

	W-R	Per cent	£1 Level Stake
Ben Poste	5-68	7.4	-18.00

COURSE RECORD

	Total W-R	Non-Hndcps Hurdles	Chases	Hndcps Hurdles	Chases	NH Flat	Per cent	£1 Level Stake
Uttoxeter	2-8	0-1	0-0	0-2	2-5	0-0	25.0	+13.00
Taunton	1-1	0-0	0-0	1-1	0-0	0-0	100.0	+9.00

RICHARD PRICE

ULLINGSWICK, H'FORDS

	No. of Hrs	Races Run	1st	2nd	3rd	Unpl	Per cent	£1 Level Stake
NH Flat	1	1	0	0	0	1	0.0	-1.00
Hurdles	9	45	3	0	4	38	6.7	-15.00
Chases	3	8	0	1	2	5	0.0	-8.00
Totals	12	54	3	1	6	44	5.6	-24.00
16-17	9	36	2	2	2	30	5.6	+68.25
15-16	5	14	1	1	2	10	7.1	-4.00

JOCKEYS

	W-R	Per cent	£1 Level Stake
James Bowen	1-1	100.0	+8.00
Daryl Jacob	1-2	50.0	+7.00
Liam Heard	1-26	3.8	-14.00

COURSE RECORD

	Total W-R	Non-Hndcps Hurdles	Chases	Hndcps Hurdles	Chases	NH Flat	Per cent	£1 Level Stake
Ludlow	1-4	0-1	0-0	1-3	0-0	0-0	25.0	+5.00
Warwick	1-6	0-3	0-0	1-3	0-0	0-0	16.7	+3.00
Chepstow	1-8	0-5	0-0	1-1	0-2	0-0	12.5	+4.00

WINNING HORSES

Horse	Races Run	1st	2nd	3rd	£
Samson's Reach	8	2	0	1	8187
Flight To Nowhere	8	1	0	0	3119
Total winning prize-money					**£11306**
Favourites	**0-0**		**0.0%**		**0.00**

JOHN QUINN

SETTRINGTON, N YORKS

	No. of Hrs	Races Run	1st	2nd	3rd	Unpl	Per cent	£1 Level Stake
NH Flat	3	5	0	1	0	4	0.0	-5.00
Hurdles	11	33	5	7	4	17	15.2	-10.17
Chases	2	4	1	0	0	3	25.0	+22.00
Totals	16	42	6	8	4	24	14.3	+6.83

16-17	11	27	5	6	3	13	18.5	-7.75
15-16	25	53	8	7	5	33	15.1	-11.13

JOCKEYS

	W-R	Per cent	£1 Level Stake
Richard Johnson	2-3	66.7	+7.67
Tom O'Brien	2-11	18.2	+22.00
Ross Chapman	1-1	100.0	+0.91
Danny Cook	1-4	25.0	-0.75

COURSE RECORD

	Total W-R	Non-Hndcps Hurdles	Chases	Hndcps Hurdles	Chases	NH Flat	Per cent	£1 Level Stake
Catterick	1-1	1-1	0-0	0-0	0-0	0-0	100.0	+2.25
Ludlow	1-1	1-1	0-0	0-0	0-0	0-0	100.0	+0.17
Southwell	1-1	0-0	0-0	1-1	0-0	0-0	100.0	+6.00
Wetherby	1-1	0-0	0-0	1-1	0-0	0-0	100.0	+8.50
Newcastle	1-2	1-2	0-0	0-0	0-0	0-0	50.0	-0.09
Mrket Rsn	1-8	0-4	0-0	0-1	1-1	0-2	12.5	+18.00

WINNING HORSES

Horse	Races Run	1st	2nd	3rd	£
Chebsey Beau	1	1	0	0	6498
Master Of Irony	5	1	0	1	5523
*Look My Way	4	1	2	0	4938
Raised On Grazeon	7	2	4	1	8902
Cosmic Tigress	3	1	0	0	3899
Total winning prize-money					£29760
Favourites	2-8		25.0%		-4.92

DENIS QUINN

NEWMARKET, SUFFOLK

	No. of Hrs	Races Run	1st	2nd	3rd	Unpl	Per cent	£1 Level Stake
NH Flat	1	2	0	0	0	2	0.0	-2.00
Hurdles	5	29	4	2	3	20	13.8	+6.25
Chases	0	0	0	0	0	0	0.0	0.00
Totals	6	31	4	2	3	22	12.9	+4.25
16-17	6	11	1	0	0	10	9.1	+10.00
15-16	6	18	2	5	2	9	11.1	-8.38

JOCKEYS

	W-R	Per cent	£1 Level Stake
Aidan Coleman	4-10	40.0	+25.25

COURSE RECORD

	Total W-R	Non-Hndcps Hurdles	Chases	Hndcps Hurdles	Chases	NH Flat	Per cent	£1 Level Stake
Huntingdon	2-12	0-6	0-0	2-5	0-0	0-1	16.7	+8.50
Worcester	1-1	0-0	0-0	1-1	0-0	0-0	100.0	+10.00
Uttoxeter	1-2	0-1	0-0	1-1	0-0	0-0	50.0	+1.75

WINNING HORSES

Horse	Races Run	1st	2nd	3rd	£
Shining Romeo	11	1	2	2	5198
Stonecoldsoba	12	3	0	1	9162
Total winning prize-money					£14360
Favourites	0-1		0.0%		-1.00

ALASTAIR RALPH

LUDLOW, SHROPSHIRE

	No. of Hrs	Races Run	1st	2nd	3rd	Unpl	Per cent	£1 Level Stake
NH Flat	2	2	0	0	1	1	0.0	-2.00
Hurdles	11	39	11	2	3	23	28.2	+15.60
Chases	6	17	3	2	8	4	17.6	-2.13
Totals	15	58	14	4	12	28	24.1	+11.47
16-17	9	33	4	1	5	23	12.1	+5.75
15-16	5	7	1	1	2	3	14.3	-4.80

BY MONTH

NH Flat	W-R	Per cent	£1 Level Stake	Hurdles	W-R	Per cent	£1 Level Stake
May	0-1	0.0	-1.00	May	2-4	50.0	+11.38
June	0-0	0.0	0.00	June	1-5	20.0	-3.27
July	0-0	0.0	0.00	July	0-0	0.0	0.00
August	0-0	0.0	0.00	August	1-2	50.0	+0.25
September	0-0	0.0	0.00	September	0-3	0.0	-3.00
October	0-0	0.0	0.00	October	0-3	0.0	-3.00
November	0-1	0.0	-1.00	November	1-6	16.7	-0.50
December	0-0	0.0	0.00	December	1-1	100.0	+7.00
January	0-0	0.0	0.00	January	1-6	16.7	-3.75
February	0-0	0.0	0.00	February	2-3	66.7	+11.00
March	0-0	0.0	0.00	March	1-3	33.3	+0.25
April	0-0	0.0	0.00	April	1-3	33.3	-0.75

Chases	W-R	Per cent	£1 Level Stake	Totals	W-R	Per cent	£1 Level Stake
May	0-0	0.0	0.00	May	2-5	40.0	+10.38
June	0-2	0.0	-2.00	June	1-7	14.3	-5.27
July	2-4	50.0	+4.88	July	2-4	50.0	+4.88
August	0-1	0.0	-1.00	August	1-3	33.3	-0.75
September	0-1	0.0	-1.00	September	0-4	0.0	-4.00
October	1-2	50.0	+4.00	October	1-5	20.0	+1.00
November	0-2	0.0	-2.00	November	1-9	11.1	-3.50
December	0-0	0.0	0.00	December	1-1	100.0	+7.00
January	0-1	0.0	-1.00	January	1-7	14.3	-4.75
February	0-1	0.0	-1.00	February	2-4	50.0	+10.00
March	0-1	0.0	-1.00	March	1-4	25.0	-0.75
April	0-2	0.0	-2.00	April	1-5	20.0	-2.75

DISTANCE

Hurdles	W-R	Per cent	£1 Level Stake	Chases	W-R	Per cent	£1 Level Stake
2m-2m3f	9-23	39.1	+13.10	2m-2m3f	1-5	20.0	-2.63
2m4f-2m7f	2-16	12.5	+2.50	2m4f-2m7f	1-7	14.3	-0.50
3m+	0-0	0.0	0.00	3m+	1-5	20.0	+1.00

TYPE OF RACE

Non-Handicaps	W-R	Per cent	£1 Level Stake	Handicaps	W-R	Per cent	£1 Level Stake
Nov Hrdls	5-12	41.7	+5.60	Nov Hrdls	0-3	0.0	-3.00
Hrdls	1-5	20.0	-1.75	Hrdls	5-19	26.3	+14.75
Nov Chs	0-4	0.0	-4.00	Nov Chs	0-0	0.0	0.00
Chases	0-1	0.0	-1.00	Chases	3-12	25.0	+2.88
Sell/Claim	0-0	0.0	0.00	Sell/Claim	0-0	0.0	0.00

RACE CLASS

	W-R	Per cent	£1 Level Stake
Class 1	0-2	0.0	-2.00
Class 2	1-3	33.3	+3.00
Class 3	1-14	7.1	-9.00
Class 4	10-28	35.7	+9.48
Class 5	2-10	20.0	+11.00
Class 6	0-1	0.0	-1.00

FIRST TIME OUT

	W-R	Per cent	£1 Level Stake
Bumpers	0-2	0.0	-2.00
Hurdles	1-9	11.1	-6.63
Chases	1-4	25.0	+2.00
Totals	2-15	13.3	-6.63

JOCKEYS

	W-R	Per cent	£1 Level Stake
Richard Johnson	3-5	60.0	+1.35
Andrew Tinkler	3-10	30.0	+5.25
Lee Edwards	2-8	25.0	+3.25
Mr Alex Edwards	2-15	13.3	-6.13
Sam Twiston-Davies	1-2	50.0	+1.25
Sean Bowen	1-3	33.3	+3.00
Charlie Hammond	1-5	20.0	+0.50
Tom O'Brien	1-6	16.7	+7.00

COURSE RECORD

	Total W-R	Non-Hndcps Hurdles	Chases	Hndcps Hurdles	Chases	NH Flat	Per cent	£1 Level Stake
Uttoxeter	4-6	0-0	0-0	2-3	2-3	0-0	66.7	+13.13
Chepstow	3-4	2-3	0-0	0-0	1-1	0-0	75.0	+13.25
Worcester	2-9	1-3	0-0	1-3	0-3	0-0	22.2	+6.38
Ludlow	2-12	0-4	0-1	2-4	0-3	0-0	16.7	-1.50
Nton Abbot	1-2	1-1	0-0	0-1	0-0	0-0	50.0	+0.25
Southwell	1-2	1-1	0-0	0-0	0-0	0-1	50.0	-0.27
Hereford	1-4	1-2	0-0	0-2	0-0	0-0	25.0	-0.75

WINNING HORSES

Horse	Races Run	1st	2nd	3rd	£
Bob Ford	1	1	0	0	18768
Comber Mill	9	3	0	0	14426
Gustave Mahler	6	3	1	1	12411
*Tempuran	4	1	1	0	4549
*Broughtons Admiral	4	1	0	0	4159
Billingsley	3	2	0	0	8187
*Cut The Corner	10	2	2	3	7798
It's Oscar	5	1	0	2	2599
Total winning prize-money					**£72897**
Favourites	6-8	75.0%			9.48

TIM REED

HAYDON BRIDGE, NORTHUMBERLAND

	No. of Hrs	Races Run	1st	2nd	3rd	Unpl	Per cent	£1 Level Stake
NH Flat	3	3	0	1	0	2	0.0	-3.00
Hurdles	6	13	0	0	2	11	0.0	-13.00
Chases	3	10	2	2	2	4	20.0	+12.50
Totals	9	26	2	3	4	17	7.7	-3.50
16-17	5	11	2	0	3	6	18.2	+7.00
15-16	4	15	1	3	1	10	6.7	-5.50

JOCKEYS

	W-R	Per cent	£1 Level Stake
Harry Reed	2-18	11.1	+4.50

COURSE RECORD

	Total W-R	Non-Hndcps Hurdles	Chases	Hndcps Hurdles	Chases	NH Flat	Per cent	£1 Level Stake
Worcester	1-1	0-0	1-1	0-0	0-0	0-0	100.0	+16.00
Perth	1-5	0-0	0-0	0-3	1-2	0-0	20.0	+0.50

WINNING HORSES

Horse	Races Run	1st	2nd	3rd	£
Indian Temple	6	1	0	2	9384
Work Du Breteau	6	1	1	2	4159
Total winning prize-money					**£13543**
Favourites	0-1	0.0%			-1.00

DAVID REES

CLARBESTON, PEMBROKES

	No. of Hrs	Races Run	1st	2nd	3rd	Unpl	Per cent	£1 Level Stake
NH Flat	3	4	0	0	0	4	0.0	-4.00
Hurdles	7	19	1	0	0	18	5.3	-14.00
Chases	8	42	7	5	4	26	16.7	+8.00
Totals	13	65	8	5	4	48	12.3	-10.00
16-17	12	48	6	5	3	34	12.5	+7.98
15-16	12	52	5	1	7	39	9.6	-26.50

JOCKEYS

	W-R	Per cent	£1 Level Stake
Sean Bowen	5-19	26.3	+11.00
Jonjo O'Neill	1-1	100.0	+4.00
Trevor Whelan	1-8	12.5	+5.00
James Bowen	1-10	10.0	-3.00

COURSE RECORD

	Total W-R	Non-Hndcps Hurdles	Chases	Hndcps Hurdles	Chases	NH Flat	Per cent	£1 Level Stake
Ffos Las	4-25	0-6	0-0	1-3	3-15	0-1	16.0	+2.50
Taunton	1-1	0-0	0-0	0-0	1-1	0-0	100.0	+6.00

Stratford	1-2	0-0	0-1	0-0	1-1	0-0	50.0	+5.00
Hereford	1-4	0-0	0-0	0-0	1-2	0-2	25.0	+4.00
Nton Abbot	1-7	0-0	0-0	0-2	1-5	0-0	14.3	-1.50

WINNING HORSES

Horse	Races Run	1st	2nd	3rd	£
Dream Bolt	9	3	1	1	25416
Misty Mai	8	2	1	0	11956
Steel Native	11	2	0	0	10397
Cawdor House Bert	3	1	1	0	5458
Total winning prize-money					**£53227**
Favourites	1-5		**20.0%**		**-2.00**

NICKY RICHARDS

GREYSTOKE, CUMBRIA

	No. of Hrs	Races Run	1st	2nd	3rd	Unpl	Per cent	£1 Level Stake
NH Flat	10	18	3	5	2	8	16.7	-7.00
Hurdles	36	111	18	17	15	61	16.2	-21.50
Chases	19	67	8	17	10	32	11.9	-24.33
Totals	54	196	29	39	27	101	14.8	-52.83
16-17	66	238	45	34	12	147	18.9	+5.85
15-16	54	188	40	29	20	99	21.3	-13.53

BY MONTH

NH Flat	W-R	Per cent	£1 Level Stake	Hurdles	W-R	Per cent	£1 Level Stake
May	0-1	0.0	-1.00	May	2-9	22.2	-3.38
June	0-2	0.0	-2.00	June	0-2	0.0	-2.00
July	0-0	0.0	0.00	July	1-3	33.3	+18.00
August	0-2	0.0	-2.00	August	0-6	0.0	-6.00
September	0-0	0.0	0.00	September	0-4	0.0	-4.00
October	1-2	50.0	+3.50	October	1-9	11.1	-7.38
November	0-3	0.0	-3.00	November	2-13	15.4	-6.59
December	0-2	0.0	-2.00	December	5-17	29.4	+3.25
January	1-2	50.0	+1.00	January	2-15	13.3	-12.15
February	0-0	0.0	0.00	February	0-9	0.0	-9.00
March	1-3	33.3	-0.50	March	3-10	30.0	+5.75
April	0-1	0.0	-1.00	April	2-14	14.3	+2.00

Chases	W-R	Per cent	£1 Level Stake	Totals	W-R	Per cent	£1 Level Stake
May	0-2	0.0	-2.00	May	2-12	16.7	-6.38
June	0-5	0.0	-5.00	June	0-9	0.0	-9.00
July	0-0	0.0	0.00	July	1-3	33.3	+18.00
August	0-0	0.0	0.00	August	0-8	0.0	-8.00
September	0-2	0.0	-2.00	September	0-6	0.0	-6.00
October	0-1	0.0	-1.00	October	2-12	16.7	-4.88
November	1-11	9.1	-8.00	November	3-27	11.1	-17.59
December	1-9	11.1	+1.00	December	6-28	21.4	+2.25
January	1-9	11.1	-2.00	January	4-26	15.4	-13.15
February	2-9	22.2	+2.00	February	2-18	11.1	-7.00
March	2-9	22.2	+1.00	March	6-22	27.3	+6.25
April	1-10	10.0	-8.33	April	3-25	12.0	-7.33

DISTANCE

Hurdles	W-R	Per cent	£1 Level Stake	Chases	W-R	Per cent	£1 Level Stake
2m-2m3f	7-46	15.2	-6.41	2m-2m3f	2-15	13.3	-5.00
2m4f-2m7f	6-39	15.4	-14.84	2m4f-2m7f	2-28	7.1	-12.00
3m+	5-26	19.2	-0.25	3m+	4-24	16.7	-7.33

TYPE OF RACE

Non-Handicaps	W-R	Per cent	£1 Level Stake	Handicaps	W-R	Per cent	£1 Level Stake
Nov Hrdls	5-26	19.2	-16.29	Nov Hrdls	2-9	22.2	+16.50
Hrdls	0-11	0.0	-11.00	Hrdls	11-65	16.9	-10.72
Nov Chs	0-2	0.0	-2.00	Nov Chs	0-4	0.0	-4.00
Chases	1-7	14.3	-5.33	Chases	6-46	13.0	-7.00
Sell/Claim	0-0	0.0	0.00	Sell/Claim	0-0	0.0	0.00

RACE CLASS

	W-R	Per cent	£1 Level Stake
Class 1	2-15	13.3	-2.00
Class 2	2-27	7.4	-11.00
Class 3	8-45	17.8	-1.38
Class 4	11-65	16.9	-12.04
Class 5	6-38	15.8	-20.42
Class 6	0-6	0.0	-6.00

FIRST TIME OUT

	W-R	Per cent	£1 Level Stake
Bumpers	2-10	20.0	-1.50
Hurdles	4-30	13.3	-18.26
Chases	0-14	0.0	-14.00
Totals	6-54	11.1	-33.76

JOCKEYS

	W-R	Per cent	£1 Level Stake
Ryan Day	17-97	17.5	-9.70
Craig Nichol	9-61	14.8	-12.05
Mr Danny McMenamin	1-1	100.0	+2.25
Mr John Dawson	1-4	25.0	-2.33
Brian Hughes	1-5	20.0	-3.00

COURSE RECORD

	Total W-R	Non-Hndcps Hurdles	Chases	Hndcps Hurdles	Chases	NH Flat	Per cent	£1 Level Stake
Ayr	10-40	4-10	0-3	2-13	3-13	1-4	25.0	-4.29
Carlisle	4-18	1-3	0-3	1-5	0-4	2-3	22.2	-1.75
Perth	3-28	0-3	1-1	2-14	0-7	0-3	10.7	-2.71
Wetherby	2-10	0-1	0-1	1-4	1-4	0-0	20.0	-2.50
Doncaster	2-14	0-2	0-0	1-8	1-3	0-1	14.3	-3.50
Huntingdon	1-3	0-0	0-0	1-3	0-0	0-0	33.3	0.00
Musselbgh	1-4	0-0	0-0	1-2	0-1	0-1	25.0	+1.50
Cheltenham	1-5	0-1	0-1	0-0	1-3	0-0	20.0	+5.00
Mrket Rsn	1-6	0-0	0-0	1-4	0-1	0-1	16.7	-0.50
Bangor	1-7	0-1	0-0	1-4	0-2	0-1	14.3	0.00
Haydock	1-7	0-0	0-0	1-6	0-1	0-0	14.3	-1.00
Hexham	1-9	0-3	0-0	1-1	0-4	0-1	11.1	-7.09
Newcastle	1-10	0-3	0-0	0-1	1-5	0-1	10.0	-1.00

WINNING HORSES

Horse	Races Run	1st	2nd	3rd	£
Guitar Pete	10	2	3	0	84001

Baywing	6	1	1	2	50048
Duke Of Navan	5	1	1	2	31280
Bernardelli	4	1	0	0	10917
Chapel Stile	5	3	1	1	20144
Takingrisks	6	1	2	1	9586
One For Harry	5	1	1	1	8123
My Old Gold	5	1	3	1	7798
Caius Marcius	5	1	1	0	7535
Progress Drive	5	1	2	0	7343
Uncle Alastair	6	3	0	2	13906
On A Promise	4	3	1	0	4874
Western Rules	5	1	0	1	4804
Better Getalong	5	2	1	1	8382
Wot A Shot	9	2	2	0	7372
Cultram Abbey	6	1	3	1	3272
Derriana Spirit	4	1	2	0	2599
Shotofwine	1	1	0	0	2599
Idee De Garde	1	1	0	0	2274
Peters Cousin	3	1	1	0	2274
Total winning prize-money					**£289131**
Favourites	18-46		39.1%		-8.00

Hurdles	6	14	1	0	1	12	7.1	-3.00
Chases	0	0	0	0	0	0	0.0	0.00
Totals	7	15	1	0	1	13	6.7	-4.00
16-17	7	22	1	5	0	16	4.5	-17.00
15-16	6	22	2	1	0	19	9.1	+29.00

JOCKEYS

	W-R	Per cent	£1 Level Stake
Tom O'Brien	1-8	12.5	+3.00

COURSE RECORD

	Total W-R	Non-Hndcps Hurdles Chases	Hndcps Hurdles Chases	NH Flat	Per cent	£1 Level Stake
Plumpton	1-7	0-2 0-0	1-4 0-0	0-1	14.3	+4.00

WINNING HORSES

Horse	Races Run	1st	2nd	3rd	£
Snippetydoodah	3	1	0	0	5588
Total winning prize-money					**£5588**
Favourites	0-0		0.0%		0.00

DAVE ROBERTS

KENLEY, SHROPSHIRE

	No. of Hrs	Races Run	1st	2nd	3rd	Unpl	Per cent	£1 Level Stake
NH Flat	0	0	0	0	0	0	0.0	0.00
Hurdles	3	12	2	3	4	3	16.7	+8.00
Chases	0	0	0	0	0	0	0.0	0.00
Totals	3	12	2	3	4	3	16.7	+8.00
16-17	3	8	0	0	1	7	0.0	-8.00
15-16	6	17	0	2	3	12	0.0	-17.00

JOCKEYS

	W-R	Per cent	£1 Level Stake
Lee Edwards	2-12	16.7	+8.00

COURSE RECORD

	Total W-R	Non-Hndcps Hurdles Chases	Hndcps Hurdles Chases	NH Flat	Per cent	£1 Level Stake
Warwick	1-2	0-0 0-0	1-2 0-0	0-0	50.0	+9.00
Worcester	1-5	0-1 0-0	1-4 0-0	0-0	20.0	+4.00

WINNING HORSES

Horse	Races Run	1st	2nd	3rd	£
Milan Of Crystal	6	2	1	2	10229
Total winning prize-money					**£10229**
Favourites	0-0		0.0%		0.00

MICHAEL ROBERTS

BODLE STREET GREEN, E SUSSEX

	No. of Hrs	Races Run	1st	2nd	3rd	Unpl	Per cent	£1 Level Stake
NH Flat	1	1	0	0	0	1	0.0	-1.00

PAULINE ROBSON

KIRKHARLE, NORTHUMBERLAND

	No. of Hrs	Races Run	1st	2nd	3rd	Unpl	Per cent	£1 Level Stake
NH Flat	1	1	0	0	1	0	0.0	-1.00
Hurdles	7	24	3	5	4	12	12.5	-9.50
Chases	7	23	1	8	2	12	4.3	-20.00
Totals	11	48	4	13	7	24	8.3	-30.50
16-17	13	48	9	6	6	27	18.8	+5.00
15-16	11	49	9	5	2	33	18.4	-14.75

JOCKEYS

	W-R	Per cent	£1 Level Stake
Mitchell Bastyan	1-1	100.0	+2.25
Ross Turner	1-2	50.0	+1.25
Craig Nichol	1-16	6.3	-8.00
Brian Hughes	1-22	4.5	-19.00

COURSE RECORD

	Total W-R	Non-Hndcps Hurdles Chases	Hndcps Hurdles Chases	NH Flat	Per cent	£1 Level Stake
Perth	2-8	0-3 0-0	1-2 1-2	0-1	25.0	-1.75
Southwell	1-2	0-0 0-0	1-1 0-1	0-0	50.0	+1.25
Ayr	1-7	0-0 0-0	1-3 0-4	0-0	14.3	+1.00

WINNING HORSES

Horse	Races Run	1st	2nd	3rd	£
Martila	3	1	1	0	19494
Martiloo	9	1	4	2	4431
Castletown	7	1	3	2	4266
Special Prep	5	1	0	2	3574
Total winning prize-money					**£31765**
Favourites	7-12		58.3%		10.50

MISS CHLOE RODDICK

SHOSCOMBE, SOMERSET

	No. of Hrs	Races Run	1st	2nd	3rd	Unpl	Per cent	£1 Level Stake
NH Flat	0	0	0	0	0	0	0.0	0.00
Hurdles	0	0	0	0	0	0	0.0	0.00
Chases	1	1	1	0	0	0	100.0	+4.00
Totals	1	1	1	0	0	0	100.0	+4.00
16-17	1	1	0	0	1	0	0.0	-1.00
15-16	1	2	0	0	0	2	0.0	-2.00

JOCKEYS

	W-R	Per cent	£1 Level Stake
Mr Lorcan Williams	1-1	100.0	+4.00

COURSE RECORD

	Total W-R	Non-Hndcps Hurdles	Chases	Hndcps Hurdles	Chases	NH Flat	Per cent	£1 Level Stake
Exeter	1-1	0-0	1-1	0-0	0-0	0-0	100.0	+4.00

WINNING HORSES

Horse	Races Run	1st	2nd	3rd	£
Salubrious	1	1	0	0	1920
Total winning prize-money					£1920
Favourites	0-0	0.0%			0.00

RICHARD ROWE

SULLINGTON, W SUSSEX

	No. of Hrs	Races Run	1st	2nd	3rd	Unpl	Per cent	£1 Level Stake
NH Flat	2	2	0	0	0	2	0.0	-2.00
Hurdles	8	22	1	1	2	18	4.5	-9.00
Chases	7	20	1	1	5	13	5.0	-14.00
Totals	14	44	2	2	7	33	4.5	-25.00
16-17	12	59	5	5	8	41	8.5	-32.25
15-16	11	42	4	3	4	31	9.5	-15.25

JOCKEYS

	W-R	Per cent	£1 Level Stake
Andrew Glassonbury	2-39	5.1	-20.00

COURSE RECORD

	Total W-R	Non-Hndcps Hurdles	Chases	Hndcps Hurdles	Chases	NH Flat	Per cent	£1 Level Stake
Sandown	1-1	0-0	0-0	1-1	0-0	0-0	100.0	+12.00
Plumpton	1-13	0-2	0-0	0-3	1-7	0-1	7.7	-7.00

WINNING HORSES

Horse	Races Run	1st	2nd	3rd	£
Sir Hubert	5	1	0	2	4874

Tzar De L'Elfe	7	1	0	2	4549
Total winning prize-money					£9423
Favourites	0-1	0.0%			-1.00

PHILIP ROWLEY

BRIDGNORTH, SHORPSHIRE

	No. of Hrs	Races Run	1st	2nd	3rd	Unpl	Per cent	£1 Level Stake
NH Flat	0	0	0	0	0	0	0.0	0.00
Hurdles	0	0	0	0	0	0	0.0	0.00
Chases	7	14	6	2	3	2	42.9	+5.08
Totals	7	14	6	2	3	2	42.9	+5.08
16-17	8	13	3	1	3	6	23.1	-1.17
15-16	6	9	0	2	0	7	0.0	-9.00

JOCKEYS

	W-R	Per cent	£1 Level Stake
Mr Alex Edwards	6-14	42.9	+5.08

COURSE RECORD

	Total W-R	Non-Hndcps Hurdles	Chases	Hndcps Hurdles	Chases	NH Flat	Per cent	£1 Level Stake
Chepstow	1-1	0-0	1-1	0-0	0-0	0-0	100.0	+3.00
Leicester	1-1	0-0	1-1	0-0	0-0	0-0	100.0	+0.18
Warwick	1-1	0-0	1-1	0-0	0-0	0-0	100.0	+1.10
Cheltenham	1-2	0-0	1-2	0-0	0-0	0-0	50.0	-0.39
Towcester	1-2	0-0	1-2	0-0	0-0	0-0	50.0	-0.82
Stratford	1-3	0-0	1-3	0-0	0-0	0-0	33.3	+6.00

WINNING HORSES

Horse	Races Run	1st	2nd	3rd	£
Barel Of Laughs	2	1	0	0	14990
*Now Ben	1	1	0	0	12039
*Hazel Hill	2	2	0	0	5056
*Grandturgeon	2	1	0	1	1872
*Battle Dust	2	1	1	0	1248
Total winning prize-money					£35205
Favourites	4-6	66.7%			0.08

LUCINDA RUSSELL

ARLARY, PERTH & KINROSS

	No. of Hrs	Races Run	1st	2nd	3rd	Unpl	Per cent	£1 Level Stake
NH Flat	19	38	5	5	4	24	13.2	-5.67
Hurdles	56	214	26	26	29	133	12.1	-52.71
Chases	35	116	15	17	12	71	12.9	-45.23
Totals	92	368	46	48	45	228	12.5	-103.61
16-17	89	411	43	41	53	274	10.5	-73.29
15-16	93	376	48	47	64	217	12.8	-44.21

BY MONTH

NH Flat	W-R	Per cent	£1 Level Stake	Hurdles	W-R	Per cent	£1 Level Stake
May	0-1	0.0	-1.00	May	1-16	6.3	+3.00

134 TRAINERS JUMPS STATISTICS

	W-R	Per cent	£1 Level Stake		W-R	Per cent	£1 Level Stake
June	1-2	50.0	+9.00	June	1-7	14.3	+5.00
July	0-1	0.0	-1.00	July	1-9	11.1	-5.50
August	0-1	0.0	-1.00	August	1-7	14.3	-2.67
September	0-1	0.0	-1.00	September	0-17	0.0	-17.00
October	0-3	0.0	-3.00	October	1-23	4.3	-15.00
November	2-5	40.0	+6.50	November	2-24	8.3	-6.00
December	0-3	0.0	-3.00	December	0-18	0.0	-18.00
January	2-6	33.3	+3.83	January	5-28	17.9	+9.70
February	0-7	0.0	-7.00	February	2-18	11.1	-8.70
March	0-3	0.0	-3.00	March	2-19	10.5	-14.25
April	0-5	0.0	-5.00	April	10-28	35.7	+16.71

Chases	W-R	Per cent	£1 Level Stake	Totals	W-R	Per cent	£1 Level Stake
May	0-8	0.0	-8.00	May	1-25	4.0	-6.00
June	1-4	25.0	+11.00	June	3-13	23.1	+25.00
July	0-3	0.0	-3.00	July	1-13	7.7	-9.50
August	0-1	0.0	-1.00	August	1-9	11.1	-4.67
September	1-7	14.3	-5.38	September	1-25	4.0	-23.38
October	3-10	30.0	+0.33	October	4-36	11.1	-17.67
November	1-14	7.1	-10.50	November	5-43	11.6	-10.00
December	2-12	16.7	-7.92	December	2-33	6.1	-28.92
January	1-18	5.6	-11.50	January	8-52	15.4	+2.03
February	2-11	18.2	0.00	February	4-36	11.1	-15.70
March	3-14	21.4	+1.75	March	5-36	13.9	-15.50
April	1-14	7.1	-11.00	April	11-47	23.4	+0.71

DISTANCE

Hurdles	W-R	Per cent	£1 Level Stake	Chases	W-R	Per cent	£1 Level Stake
2m-2m3f	12-106	11.3	-15.87	2m-2m3f	4-32	12.5	-17.75
2m4f-2m7f	7-67	10.4	-42.67	2m4f-2m7f	6-43	14.0	-27.31
3m+	7-41	17.1	+5.83	3m+	5-41	12.2	-0.17

TYPE OF RACE

Non-Handicaps	W-R	Per cent	£1 Level Stake	Handicaps	W-R	Per cent	£1 Level Stake
Nov Hrdls	3-45	6.7	-35.58	Nov Hrdls	4-12	33.3	+19.25
Hrdls	3-25	12.0	-2.00	Hrdls	16-132	12.1	-34.38
Nov Chs	1-3	33.3	+0.20	Nov Chs	1-14	7.1	-10.50
Chases	1-4	25.0	-1.50	Chases	10-81	12.3	-31.43
Sell/Claim	0-0	0.0	0.00	Sell/Claim	0-0	0.0	0.00

RACE CLASS / FIRST TIME OUT

	W-R	Per cent	£1 Level Stake		W-R	Per cent	£1 Level Stake
Class 1	0-4	0.0	-4.00	Bumpers	5-19	26.3	+13.33
Class 2	3-16	18.8	-8.00	Hurdles	2-45	4.4	-17.00
Class 3	3-39	7.7	-28.42	Chases	3-28	10.7	-20.06
Class 4	23-202	11.4	-85.02				
Class 5	15-98	15.3	+19.33	Totals	10-92	10.9	-23.73
Class 6	2-9	22.2	+2.50				

JOCKEYS

	W-R	Per cent	£1 Level Stake
Derek Fox	26-187	13.9	-49.72
Blair Campbell	14-98	14.3	-5.08
Thomas Willmott	4-21	19.0	-1.80
Alexander Thorne	1-7	14.3	+5.00
Stephen Mulqueen	1-43	2.3	-40.00

COURSE RECORD

	Total W-R	Non-Hndcps Hurdles	Chases	Hndcps Hurdles	Chases	NH Flat	Per cent	£1 Level Stake
Ayr	10-55	3-15	0-0	2-17	2-15	3-8	18.2	-3.20
Musselbgh	8-55	1-12	0-0	5-23	2-12	0-8	14.5	+3.70
Perth	7-65	0-11	0-0	5-38	1-10	1-6	10.8	-14.55
Newcastle	5-22	1-5	0-0	3-8	1-8	0-1	22.7	-4.13
Kelso	5-42	0-11	2-3	2-14	0-9	1-5	11.9	-24.13
Hexham	5-45	0-9	0-0	2-15	3-19	0-2	11.1	-9.88
Carlisle	3-26	1-2	0-1	0-10	2-11	0-2	11.5	-9.75
Bangor	2-9	0-2	0-0	0-1	2-6	0-0	22.2	+1.33
Sedgefield	1-1	0-0	0-0	1-1	0-0	0-0	100.0	+5.00

WINNING HORSES

Horse	Races Run	1st	2nd	3rd	£
Big River	5	2	1	1	20574
Forest des Aigles	4	3	0	0	26522
Grand Morning	4	3	0	1	20161
Imjoeking	4	1	1	0	9357
Thorpe	9	4	1	0	23564
Vengeur De Guye	8	1	2	1	5848
Behindthelines	4	1	2	1	5338
Kelpies Myth	6	2	0	1	10072
Superior Command	2	1	0	0	5198
Haul Us In	9	3	3	0	13256
Mumgos Debut	6	1	0	1	4920
Chasseur De Tete	7	1	1	1	4809
Itstimeforapint	5	1	0	0	4614
Shanroe Street	4	1	1	1	4614
Celtic Flames	9	2	0	0	8382
Make It Happen	4	1	1	0	4289
The Compeller	4	1	1	0	4265
Orioninverness	5	1	0	1	4260
Jump For Dough	5	2	0	0	8187
Misfits	7	1	2	1	3899
The Road Home	6	1	0	0	3509
Miss Joeking	5	1	0	0	3249
Spoils Of War	8	2	1	0	6368
Rivabodiva	8	2	2	1	5848
Morning Time	5	1	0	0	2924
Mighty Thunder	7	1	0	2	2599
Miss Tiggy	3	1	0	1	2599
Highland Hunter	2	1	0	0	2274
Precious Cargo	3	1	1	0	2274
Ask The Tycoon	4	1	0	1	2053
Emissaire	3	1	0	0	1625
Total winning prize-money					**£227451**
Favourites	11-27		40.7%		-0.43

JOHN RYAN

NEWMARKET, SUFFOLK

	No. of Hrs	Races Run	1st	2nd	3rd	Unpl	Per cent	£1 Level Stake
NH Flat	1	4	1	1	0	2	25.0	+0.50
Hurdles	4	6	0	0	1	5	0.0	-6.00
Chases	0	0	0	0	0	0	0.0	0.00
Totals	5	10	1	1	1	7	10.0	-5.50
16-17	3	9	0	2	3	4	0.0	-9.00
15-16	3	8	1	2	0	5	12.5	+13.00

JOCKEYS

	W-R	Per cent	£1 Level Stake
Paddy Brennan	1-3	33.3	+1.50

COURSE RECORD

	Total W-R	Non-Hndcps Hurdles	Chases	Hndcps Hurdles	Chases	NH Flat	Per cent	£1 Level Stake
Mrket Rsn	1-1	0-0	0-0	0-0	0-0	1-1	100.0	+3.50

WINNING HORSES

Horse	Races Run	1st	2nd	3rd	£
Normal Norman	4	1	1	0	1560
Total winning prize-money					£1560
Favourites	0-0	0.0%			0.00

KEVIN RYAN

HAMBLETON, N YORKS

	No. of Hrs	Races Run	1st	2nd	3rd	Unpl	Per cent	£1 Level Stake
NH Flat	2	2	1	0	1	0	50.0	-0.09
Hurdles	4	10	4	1	3	2	40.0	+2.98
Chases	0	0	0	0	0	0	0.0	0.00
Totals	5	12	5	1	4	2	41.7	+2.89
16-17	2	3	1	1	0	1	33.3	+2.00
15-16	7	17	4	2	1	10	23.5	+10.00

JOCKEYS

	W-R	Per cent	£1 Level Stake
Brian Hughes	5-12	41.7	+2.88

COURSE RECORD

	Total W-R	Non-Hndcps Hurdles	Chases	Hndcps Hurdles	Chases	NH Flat	Per cent	£1 Level Stake
Musselbgh	3-4	3-3	0-0	0-1	0-0	0-0	75.0	+7.31
Kelso	1-1	1-1	0-0	0-0	0-0	0-0	100.0	+0.67
Worcester	1-1	0-0	0-0	0-0	0-0	1-1	100.0	+0.91

WINNING HORSES

Horse	Races Run	1st	2nd	3rd	£
Beyond The Clouds	5	4	0	0	22093

Canny Style	4	1	1	2	3249
Total winning prize-money					£25342
Favourites	4-7		57.1%		-0.12

DIANNE SAYER

HACKTHORPE, CUMBRIA

	No. of Hrs	Races Run	1st	2nd	3rd	Unpl	Per cent	£1 Level Stake
NH Flat	1	1	0	0	0	1	0.0	-1.00
Hurdles	22	70	7	3	5	55	10.0	+18.75
Chases	9	33	2	4	3	24	6.1	-10.50
Totals	24	104	9	7	8	80	8.7	+7.25
16-17	27	134	10	12	11	101	7.5	-57.75
15-16	30	156	8	17	22	109	5.1	-92.00

JOCKEYS

	W-R	Per cent	£1 Level Stake
Brian Hughes	4-40	10.0	-8.50
Colm McCormack	3-27	11.1	+45.00
Harry Challoner	1-1	100.0	+4.00
Lorcan Murtagh	1-9	11.1	-6.25

COURSE RECORD

	Total W-R	Non-Hndcps Hurdles	Chases	Hndcps Hurdles	Chases	NH Flat	Per cent	£1 Level Stake
Perth	4-23	0-3	0-0	3-13	1-7	0-0	17.4	+6.25
Sedgefield	2-13	0-2	0-0	2-9	0-2	0-0	15.4	+22.50
Kelso	1-7	0-1	0-0	1-4	0-2	0-0	14.3	+8.00
Wetherby	1-7	0-0	0-1	1-3	0-3	0-0	14.3	+19.00
Cartmel	1-18	0-1	0-0	0-11	1-6	0-0	5.6	-12.50

WINNING HORSES

Horse	Races Run	1st	2nd	3rd	£
Gold Chain	8	2	0	2	8996
Endeavor	10	2	0	0	3899
Weapon Of Choice	5	1	1	0	3798
Sergeant Pink	3	1	0	0	3798
Main Fact	7	2	0	0	6758
Sendiym	9	1	2	1	3249
Total winning prize-money					£30498
Favourites	1-4	25.0%			-1.25

KATIE SCOTT

GALASHEILS, SCOTTISH BORDERS

	No. of Hrs	Races Run	1st	2nd	3rd	Unpl	Per cent	£1 Level Stake
NH Flat	4	8	0	0	0	8	0.0	-8.00
Hurdles	8	19	0	0	2	17	0.0	-19.00
Chases	5	14	1	1	3	9	7.1	-8.50
Totals	13	41	1	1	5	34	2.4	-35.50
16-17	13	53	3	4	5	41	5.7	-31.00
15-16	17	61	1	4	4	52	1.6	-57.25

JOCKEYS

	W-R	Per cent	£1 Level Stake
Callum Bewley	1-9	11.1	-3.50

COURSE RECORD

	Total W-R	Non-Hndcps Hurdles	Chases	Hndcps Hurdles	Chases	NH Flat	Per cent	£1 Level Stake
Kelso	1-13	0-1	0-0	0-6	1-4	0-2	7.7	-7.50

WINNING HORSES

Horse	Races Run	1st	2nd	3rd	£
Chain Of Beacons	4	1	1	2	6498
Total winning prize-money					**£6498**
Favourites	**0-1**		**0.0%**		**-1.00**

JEREMY SCOTT

BROMPTON REGIS, SOMERSET

	No. of Hrs	Races Run	1st	2nd	3rd	Unpl	Per cent	£1 Level Stake
NH Flat	9	17	1	3	0	13	5.9	-2.00
Hurdles	32	101	12	4	10	75	11.9	+3.25
Chases	19	72	11	4	8	49	15.3	+10.07
Totals	**46**	**190**	**24**	**11**	**18**	**137**	**12.6**	**+11.32**
16-17	37	193	24	24	18	127	12.4	-62.00
15-16	43	192	27	23	28	114	14.1	-19.51

BY MONTH

NH Flat	W-R	Per cent	£1 Level Stake	Hurdles	W-R	Per cent	£1 Level Stake
May	0-1	0.0	-1.00	May	0-11	0.0	-11.00
June	0-0	0.0	0.00	June	0-3	0.0	-3.00
July	0-0	0.0	0.00	July	0-7	0.0	-7.00
August	0-0	0.0	0.00	August	0-2	0.0	-2.00
September	0-0	0.0	0.00	September	1-2	50.0	+9.00
October	0-1	0.0	-1.00	October	0-10	0.0	-10.00
November	0-2	0.0	-2.00	November	2-15	13.3	+26.50
December	0-1	0.0	-1.00	December	1-13	7.7	-8.50
January	0-3	0.0	-3.00	January	2-9	22.2	0.00
February	1-3	33.3	+12.00	February	3-8	37.5	+6.50
March	0-2	0.0	-2.00	March	2-9	22.2	-2.25
April	0-4	0.0	-4.00	April	1-12	8.3	+5.00

Chases	W-R	Per cent	£1 Level Stake	Totals	W-R	Per cent	£1 Level Stake
May	1-3	33.3	+3.00	May	1-15	6.7	-9.00
June	1-4	25.0	-2.43	June	1-7	14.3	-5.43
July	2-8	25.0	+6.75	July	2-15	13.3	-0.25
August	0-4	0.0	-4.00	August	0-6	0.0	-6.00
September	1-5	20.0	+2.00	September	2-7	28.6	+11.00
October	1-4	25.0	-0.25	October	1-15	6.7	-11.25
November	1-9	11.1	-2.00	November	3-26	11.5	+22.50
December	1-7	14.3	+5.00	December	2-21	9.5	-4.50
January	2-7	28.6	+6.00	January	4-19	21.1	+3.00

				February	0-5	0.0	-5.00	February	4-16	25.0	+13.50
				March	0-5	0.0	-5.00	March	2-16	12.5	-9.25
				April	1-11	9.1	+6.00	April	2-27	7.4	+7.00

DISTANCE

Hurdles	W-R	Per cent	£1 Level Stake	Chases	W-R	Per cent	£1 Level Stake
2m-2m3f	4-43	9.3	+9.00	2m-2m3f	2-12	16.7	+8.00
2m4f-2m7f	3-43	7.0	-14.00	2m4f-2m7f	5-26	19.2	+21.00
3m+	5-14	35.7	+9.25	3m+	4-34	11.8	-18.93

TYPE OF RACE

Non-Handicaps	W-R	Per cent	£1 Level Stake	Handicaps	W-R	Per cent	£1 Level Stake
Nov Hrdls	0-12	0.0	-12.00	Nov Hrdls	0-9	0.0	-9.00
Hrdls	0-9	0.0	-9.00	Hrdls	12-71	16.9	+33.25
Nov Chs	0-0	0.0	0.00	Nov Chs	3-20	15.0	+2.32
Chases	0-0	0.0	0.00	Chases	7-50	14.0	-0.25
Sell/Claim	0-1	0.0	-1.00	Sell/Claim	0-0	0.0	0.00

RACE CLASS

	W-R	Per cent	£1 Level Stake
Class 1	0-6	0.0	-6.00
Class 2	2-9	22.2	+31.00
Class 3	3-20	15.0	-6.00
Class 4	10-86	11.6	-12.43
Class 5	9-65	13.8	+8.75
Class 6	0-4	0.0	-4.00

FIRST TIME OUT

	W-R	Per cent	£1 Level Stake
Bumpers	1-9	11.1	+6.00
Hurdles	1-26	3.8	+8.00
Chases	1-11	9.1	-5.00
Totals	**3-46**	**6.5**	**+9.00**

JOCKEYS

	W-R	Per cent	£1 Level Stake
Nick Scholfield	11-65	16.9	+3.07
Matt Griffiths	10-77	13.0	+24.50
Mr Robert Hawker	3-25	12.0	+6.75

COURSE RECORD

	Total W-R	Non-Hndcps Hurdles	Chases	Hndcps Hurdles	Chases	NH Flat	Per cent	£1 Level Stake
Taunton	5-11	0-0	0-0	3-3	2-7	0-1	45.5	+28.50
Fontwell	5-18	0-1	0-0	2-7	3-9	0-1	27.8	+4.07
Wincanton	3-27	0-4	0-0	0-9	2-8	1-6	11.1	+1.75
Warwick	2-13	0-0	0-0	1-6	1-5	0-2	15.4	+10.00
Nton Abbot	2-14	0-2	0-0	0-8	2-4	0-0	14.3	-3.25
Exeter	2-29	0-7	0-0	2-17	0-4	0-1	6.9	-4.50
Huntingdon	1-2	0-0	0-0	1-1	0-1	0-0	50.0	+32.00
Towcester	1-2	0-0	0-0	1-1	0-1	0-0	50.0	+1.50
Chepstow	1-8	0-2	0-0	1-3	0-2	0-1	12.5	-5.75
Worcester	1-8	0-0	0-0	0-2	1-6	0-0	12.5	+3.00
Ludlow	1-10	0-2	0-0	1-3	0-4	0-1	10.0	-8.00

WINNING HORSES

Horse	Races Run	1st	2nd	3rd	£
Unison	7	3	0	1	35149
Notarfbad	7	1	1	2	7596

Moorlands Jack	6	1	0	0	7408		April	1-7	14.3	-3.25	April	1-16	6.3	-12.25
Tikkinthebox	6	1	0	1	6583
Ellens Way	4	2	0	0	9812
Speedalong	5	1	1	0	6563
*Guerrilla Tactics	8	2	0	3	9097
Native Robin	7	2	0	0	9812
Jack Snipe	8	2	1	0	7473
Garrane	9	2	0	1	7278
Shoofly Milly	7	1	0	1	3899
Day Of Roses	2	2	0	0	6888
Gonnabegood	7	2	1	0	6108
Blue April	6	1	1	0	3119
Dashel Drasher	3	1	0	0	2274
Total winning prize-money					**£129059**
Favourites		**7-14**		**50.0%**	**6.57**

DISTANCE

Hurdles	W-R	Per cent	£1 Level Stake	Chases	W-R	Per cent	£1 Level Stake
2m-2m3f	0-28	0.0	-28.00	2m-2m3f	1-3	33.3	+0.75
2m4f-2m7f	2-18	11.1	-10.42	2m4f-2m7f	3-38	7.9	-17.00
3m+	0-11	0.0	-11.00	3m+	6-43	14.0	+31.50

TYPE OF RACE

Non-Handicaps	W-R	Per cent	£1 Level Stake	Handicaps	W-R	Per cent	£1 Level Stake
Nov Hrdls	2-19	10.5	-11.42	Nov Hrdls	0-3	0.0	-3.00
Hrdls	0-8	0.0	-8.00	Hrdls	0-27	0.0	-27.00
Nov Chs	0-2	0.0	-2.00	Nov Chs	1-5	20.0	+8.00
Chases	0-2	0.0	-2.00	Chases	9-73	12.3	+13.25
Sell/Claim	0-0	0.0	0.00	Sell/Claim	0-0	0.0	0.00

MICHAEL SCUDAMORE

BROMSASH, H'FORDS

	No. of Hrs	Races Run	1st	2nd	3rd	Unpl	Per cent	£1 Level Stake
NH Flat	12	23	1	5	0	17	4.3	-19.50
Hurdles	21	57	2	6	6	43	3.5	-49.42
Chases	20	84	10	10	11	53	11.9	+15.25
Totals	**42**	**164**	**13**	**21**	**17**	**113**	**7.9**	**-53.67**
16-17	35	131	26	12	14	79	19.8	+19.42
15-16	22	86	8	16	7	55	9.3	-47.88

RACE CLASS

	W-R	Per cent	£1 Level Stake
Class 1	0-6	0.0	-6.00
Class 2	1-9	11.1	+6.00
Class 3	4-30	13.3	-0.67
Class 4	3-62	4.8	-26.75
Class 5	5-50	10.0	-19.25
Class 6	0-7	0.0	-7.00

FIRST TIME OUT

	W-R	Per cent	£1 Level Stake
Bumpers	1-12	8.3	-8.50
Hurdles	0-16	0.0	-16.00
Chases	1-14	7.1	+1.00
Totals	2-42	4.8	-23.50

BY MONTH

NH Flat	W-R	Per cent	£1 Level Stake	Hurdles	W-R	Per cent	£1 Level Stake
May	0-1	0.0	-1.00	May	0-8	0.0	-8.00
June	0-0	0.0	0.00	June	0-5	0.0	-5.00
July	0-0	0.0	0.00	July	0-4	0.0	-4.00
August	0-0	0.0	0.00	August	0-5	0.0	-5.00
September	0-0	0.0	0.00	September	0-0	0.0	0.00
October	0-3	0.0	-3.00	October	0-3	0.0	-3.00
November	0-4	0.0	-4.00	November	0-9	0.0	-9.00
December	0-6	0.0	-6.00	December	0-1	0.0	-1.00
January	0-2	0.0	-2.00	January	1-6	16.7	-2.75
February	0-1	0.0	-1.00	February	0-8	0.0	-8.00
March	1-3	33.3	+0.50	March	1-2	50.0	+2.33
April	0-3	0.0	-3.00	April	0-6	0.0	-6.00

Chases	W-R	Per cent	£1 Level Stake	Totals	W-R	Per cent	£1 Level Stake
May	0-6	0.0	-6.00	May	0-15	0.0	-15.00
June	1-2	50.0	+11.00	June	1-7	14.3	+6.00
July	0-3	0.0	-3.00	July	0-7	0.0	-7.00
August	0-5	0.0	-5.00	August	0-10	0.0	-10.00
September	0-3	0.0	-3.00	September	0-3	0.0	-3.00
October	0-6	0.0	-6.00	October	0-12	0.0	-12.00
November	1-11	9.1	+4.00	November	1-24	4.2	-9.00
December	2-13	15.4	+13.50	December	2-20	10.0	+6.50
January	1-8	12.5	+3.00	January	2-16	12.5	-1.75
February	2-8	25.0	+12.00	February	2-17	11.8	+3.00
March	2-12	16.7	-2.00	March	4-17	23.5	+0.83

JOCKEYS

	W-R	Per cent	£1 Level Stake
Tom Scudamore	7-49	14.3	-1.92
John Kington	2-6	33.3	+30.00
Robert Dunne	2-29	6.9	-19.75
Ben Poste	1-27	3.7	-22.00
Liam Treadwell	1-31	3.2	-18.00

COURSE RECORD

	Total W-R	Non-Hndcps Hurdles Chases		Hndcps Hurdles Chases		NH Flat	Per cent	£1 Level Stake
Uttoxeter	2-10	1-2	0-0	0-2	0-4	1-2	20.0	-2.17
Leicester	1-2	0-0	0-0	0-0	1-2	0-0	50.0	+9.00
Newcastle	1-2	1-2	0-0	0-0	0-0	0-0	50.0	+1.25
Fakenham	1-3	0-0	0-0	0-1	1-2	0-0	33.3	+2.00
Fontwell	1-3	0-0	0-1	0-0	1-2	0-0	33.3	+0.75
Huntingdon	1-4	0-0	0-0	0-0	1-3	0-1	25.0	+1.00
Nton Abbot	1-4	0-0	0-0	0-0	1-3	0-1	25.0	+9.00
Cheltenham	1-5	0-0	0-0	0-1	1-3	0-1	20.0	+10.00
Wincanton	1-5	0-1	0-0	0-0	1-4	0-0	20.0	0.00
Warwick	1-6	0-0	0-0	0-0	1-5	0-1	16.7	+9.00
Wetherby	1-7	0-1	0-0	0-1	1-4	0-1	14.3	+14.00
Southwell	1-15	0-1	0-0	0-5	1-8	0-1	6.7	-9.50

WINNING HORSES

Horse	Races Run	1st	2nd	3rd	£
Kingswell Theatre	2	1	0	0	15640

Sheneededtherun	8	2	1	1	14945
Two Smokin Barrels	8	1	2	1	9357
Twenty Eight Guns	7	1	0	0	9032
Cadeyrn	5	2	1	0	10600
Zayfire Aramis	7	1	0	2	5200
Oriental Fixer	5	1	3	0	4386
Skint	8	2	1	0	7213
Corner Creek	6	1	0	1	3899
Smiths Cross	2	1	1	0	2599
Total winning prize-money					**£82871**
Favourites	0-7		0.0%		-7.00

FIONA SHAW

BRADFORD PEVERELL, DORSET

	No. of Hrs	Races Run	1st	2nd	3rd	Unpl	Per cent	£1 Level Stake
NH Flat	3	6	0	0	1	5	0.0	-6.00
Hurdles	6	19	2	1	4	12	10.5	+5.75
Chases	1	1	0	0	1	0	0.0	-1.00
Totals	7	26	2	1	6	17	7.7	-1.25
16-17	4	16	2	2	2	10	12.5	-8.80
15-16	4	13	1	0	1	11	7.7	+21.00

JOCKEYS

	W-R	Per cent	£1 Level Stake
Bryony Frost	1-1	100.0	+2.75
Mr Michael Legg	1-20	5.0	+1.00

COURSE RECORD

	Total W-R	Non-Hndcps Hurdles	Chases	Hndcps Hurdles	Chases	NH Flat	Per cent	£1 Level Stake
Chepstow	1-2	0-0	0-0	1-1	0-0	0-1	50.0	+1.75
Fontwell	1-4	0-1	0-0	1-2	0-1	0-0	25.0	+17.00

WINNING HORSES

Horse	Races Run	1st	2nd	3rd	£
*Hollywood Ken	2	2	0	0	4094
Total winning prize-money					**£4094**
Favourites	1-1	100.0%			2.75

DEREK SHAW

SPROXTON, LEICS

	No. of Hrs	Races Run	1st	2nd	3rd	Unpl	Per cent	£1 Level Stake
NH Flat	1	1	0	0	0	1	0.0	-1.00
Hurdles	5	20	2	1	4	13	10.0	-12.00
Chases	1	2	0	0	0	2	0.0	-2.00
Totals	7	23	2	1	4	16	8.7	-15.00
16-17	5	16	0	0	0	16	0.0	-16.00
15-16	4	16	1	2	1	12	6.3	-3.00

JOCKEYS

	W-R	Per cent	£1 Level Stake
Brian Hughes	2-10	20.0	-2.00

COURSE RECORD

	Total W-R	Non-Hndcps Hurdles	Chases	Hndcps Hurdles	Chases	NH Flat	Per cent	£1 Level Stake
Stratford	1-2	0-1	0-0	1-1	0-0	0-0	50.0	+2.50
Southwell	1-9	0-1	0-2	1-6	0-0	0-0	11.1	-5.50

WINNING HORSES

Horse	Races Run	1st	2nd	3rd	£
Polarbrook	10	2	1	2	6498
Total winning prize-money					**£6498**
Favourites	2-2	100.0%			6.00

MATT SHEPPARD

EASTNOR, H'FORDS

	No. of Hrs	Races Run	1st	2nd	3rd	Unpl	Per cent	£1 Level Stake
NH Flat	3	4	0	0	0	4	0.0	-4.00
Hurdles	18	57	1	5	10	41	1.8	-51.50
Chases	12	54	11	8	5	30	20.4	+30.41
Totals	24	115	12	13	15	75	10.4	-25.09
16-17	26	151	14	10	17	110	9.3	-46.75
15-16	26	108	15	10	18	65	13.9	+8.63

BY MONTH

NH Flat	W-R	Per cent	£1 Level Stake	Hurdles	W-R	Per cent	£1 Level Stake
May	0-0	0.0	0.00	May	1-8	12.5	-2.50
June	0-0	0.0	0.00	June	0-4	0.0	-4.00
July	0-0	0.0	0.00	July	0-3	0.0	-3.00
August	0-0	0.0	0.00	August	0-3	0.0	-3.00
September	0-1	0.0	-1.00	September	0-5	0.0	-5.00
October	0-0	0.0	0.00	October	0-9	0.0	-9.00
November	0-0	0.0	0.00	November	0-5	0.0	-5.00
December	0-1	0.0	-1.00	December	0-4	0.0	-4.00
January	0-1	0.0	-1.00	January	0-4	0.0	-4.00
February	0-0	0.0	0.00	February	0-3	0.0	-3.00
March	0-0	0.0	0.00	March	0-5	0.0	-5.00
April	0-1	0.0	-1.00	April	0-4	0.0	-4.00

Chases	W-R	Per cent	£1 Level Stake	Totals	W-R	Per cent	£1 Level Stake
May	0-3	0.0	-3.00	May	1-11	9.1	-5.50
June	0-4	0.0	-4.00	June	0-8	0.0	-8.00
July	0-3	0.0	-3.00	July	0-6	0.0	-6.00
August	0-5	0.0	-5.00	August	0-8	0.0	-8.00
September	0-0	0.0	0.00	September	0-6	0.0	-6.00
October	2-6	33.3	+36.00	October	2-15	13.3	+27.00
November	0-6	0.0	-6.00	November	0-11	0.0	-11.00
December	1-7	14.3	-0.50	December	1-12	8.3	-5.50

January	1-5	20.0	0.00	January	1-10	10.0	-5.00
February	1-4	25.0	-0.50	February	1-7	14.3	-3.50
March	2-5	40.0	+4.41	March	2-10	20.0	-0.59
April	4-6	66.7	+12.00	April	4-11	36.4	+7.00

DISTANCE

Hurdles	W-R	Per cent	£1 Level Stake	Chases	W-R	Per cent	£1 Level Stake
2m-2m3f	1-39	2.6	-33.50	2m-2m3f	4-30	13.3	-10.00
2m4f-2m7f	0-12	0.0	-12.00	2m4f-2m7f	4-16	25.0	+31.41
3m+	0-6	0.0	-6.00	3m+	3-8	37.5	+9.00

TYPE OF RACE

Non-Handicaps	W-R	Per cent	£1 Level Stake	Handicaps	W-R	Per cent	£1 Level Stake
Nov Hrdls	0-3	0.0	-3.00	Nov Hrdls	0-0	0.0	0.00
Hrdls	0-2	0.0	-2.00	Hrdls	1-43	2.3	-37.50
Nov Chs	0-0	0.0	0.00	Nov Chs	1-10	10.0	-6.50
Chases	0-1	0.0	-1.00	Chases	9-42	21.4	+34.91
Sell/Claim	0-6	0.0	-6.00	Sell/Claim	0-1	0.0	-1.00

RACE CLASS / FIRST TIME OUT

Class	W-R	Per cent	£1 Level Stake	First Time Out	W-R	Per cent	£1 Level Stake
Class 1	0-2	0.0	-2.00	Bumpers	0-3	0.0	-3.00
Class 2	0-7	0.0	-7.00	Hurdles	0-13	0.0	-13.00
Class 3	3-6	50.0	+10.50	Chases	0-8	0.0	-8.00
Class 4	7-56	12.5	+3.91				
Class 5	2-43	4.7	-29.50	Totals	0-24	0.0	-24.00
Class 6	0-1	0.0	-1.00				

JOCKEYS

	W-R	Per cent	£1 Level Stake
Stan Sheppard	9-73	12.3	-30.59
Mr Ed Bailey	2-20	10.0	+22.00
Sam Twiston-Davies	1-2	50.0	+3.50

COURSE RECORD

	Total W-R	Non-Hndcps Hurdles	Chases	Hndcps Hurdles	Chases	NH Flat	Per cent	£1 Level Stake
Ludlow	3-16	0-2	0-0	0-6	3-7	0-1	18.8	+2.00
Towcester	2-3	0-0	0-0	0-1	2-2	0-0	66.7	+2.41
Ffos Las	1-1	0-0	0-0	0-0	1-1	0-0	100.0	+33.00
Newbury	1-2	0-0	0-0	0-0	1-2	0-0	50.0	+5.50
Uttoxeter	1-4	0-0	0-0	1-4	0-0	0-0	25.0	+1.50
Exeter	1-5	0-1	0-0	0-3	1-1	0-0	20.0	-1.00
Warwick	1-6	0-0	0-0	0-4	1-2	0-0	16.7	-0.50
Hereford	1-7	0-0	0-0	0-2	1-4	0-1	14.3	-0.50
Chepstow	1-19	0-3	0-0	0-4	1-11	0-1	5.3	-15.50

WINNING HORSES

Horse	Races Run	1st	2nd	3rd	£
Rock On Rocky	11	2	2	1	20729
The Bay Birch	6	3	3	0	21374
Tb Broke Her	3	2	0	1	13218

Patricks Park	2	1	0	0	6498
Phangio	11	1	1	3	5198
Modeligo	9	1	1	1	4614
Go On Henry	8	1	0	1	3743
Orion's Might	8	1	1	1	2599

Total winning prize-money			£77973
Favourites	4-8	50.0%	5.91

OLIVER SHERWOOD
UPPER LAMBOURN, BERKS

	No. of Hrs	Races Run	1st	2nd	3rd	Unpl	Per cent	£1 Level Stake
NH Flat	16	23	2	6	2	13	8.7	-3.13
Hurdles	42	125	11	11	16	87	8.8	-65.01
Chases	22	72	8	8	9	47	11.1	-22.10
Totals	63	220	21	25	27	147	9.5	-90.24
16-17	60	196	22	28	27	119	11.2	-71.77
15-16	59	207	32	34	25	116	15.5	-50.61

BY MONTH

NH Flat	W-R	Per cent	£1 Level Stake	Hurdles	W-R	Per cent	£1 Level Stake
May	0-5	0.0	-5.00	May	1-11	9.1	-7.25
June	0-3	0.0	-3.00	June	0-0	0.0	0.00
July	0-0	0.0	0.00	July	0-1	0.0	-1.00
August	0-0	0.0	0.00	August	0-1	0.0	-1.00
September	0-0	0.0	0.00	September	0-1	0.0	-1.00
October	0-3	0.0	-3.00	October	0-6	0.0	-6.00
November	1-3	33.3	-0.13	November	1-20	5.0	-3.00
December	0-2	0.0	-2.00	December	1-23	4.3	-10.00
January	0-0	0.0	0.00	January	2-15	13.3	-9.63
February	1-5	20.0	+12.00	February	2-18	11.1	-8.25
March	0-0	0.0	0.00	March	3-14	21.4	-6.89
April	0-2	0.0	-2.00	April	1-15	6.7	-11.00

Chases	W-R	Per cent	£1 Level Stake	Totals	W-R	Per cent	£1 Level Stake
May	0-2	0.0	-2.00	May	1-18	5.6	-14.25
June	1-2	50.0	+7.00	June	1-5	20.0	+4.00
July	0-1	0.0	-1.00	July	0-2	0.0	-2.00
August	0-0	0.0	0.00	August	0-1	0.0	-1.00
September	0-0	0.0	0.00	September	0-1	0.0	-1.00
October	0-3	0.0	-3.00	October	0-12	0.0	-12.00
November	2-10	20.0	+10.00	November	4-33	12.1	+6.87
December	0-9	0.0	-9.00	December	1-34	2.9	-21.00
January	1-9	11.1	-4.00	January	3-24	12.5	-13.63
February	2-11	18.2	+3.75	February	5-34	14.7	+3.75
March	1-11	9.1	-7.50	March	4-25	16.0	-14.39
April	1-14	7.1	-12.60	April	2-31	6.5	-25.60

DISTANCE

Hurdles	W-R	Per cent	£1 Level Stake	Chases	W-R	Per cent	£1 Level Stake
2m-2m3f	8-61	13.1	-20.76	2m-2m3f	0-12	0.0	-12.00
2m4f-2m7f	2-50	4.0	-43.25	2m4f-2m7f	7-38	18.4	-1.10
3m+	1-14	7.1	-1.00	3m+	1-22	4.5	-9.00

TYPE OF RACE

Non-Handicaps

	W-R	Per cent	£1 Level Stake
Nov Hrdls	5-42	11.9	-24.51
Hrdls	4-28	14.3	-2.25
Nov Chs	2-10	20.0	-2.60
Chases	2-7	28.6	+3.00
Sell/Claim	0-1	0.0	-1.00

Handicaps

	W-R	Per cent	£1 Level Stake
Nov Hrdls	1-5	20.0	-1.25
Hrdls	1-48	2.1	-35.00
Nov Chs	1-7	14.3	+2.00
Chases	2-39	5.1	-28.50
Sell/Claim	0-0	0.0	0.00

RACE CLASS

	W-R	Per cent	£1 Level Stake
Class 1	1-15	6.7	-10.00
Class 2	1-20	5.0	-7.00
Class 3	3-42	7.1	-22.50
Class 4	11-107	10.3	-45.49
Class 5	4-22	18.2	+3.75
Class 6	1-14	7.1	-9.00

FIRST TIME OUT

	W-R	Per cent	£1 Level Stake
Bumpers	1-16	6.3	+1.00
Hurdles	1-31	3.2	-27.25
Chases	2-16	12.5	0.00
Totals	4-63	6.3	-26.25

JOCKEYS

	W-R	Per cent	£1 Level Stake
Leighton Aspell	11-118	9.3	-57.39
Harrison Beswick	3-24	12.5	+3.50
Thomas Garner	3-28	10.7	-11.60
Conor Shoemark	2-26	7.7	-18.75
Barry Geraghty	1-2	50.0	+11.00
Miss Pippa Glanville	1-4	25.0	+1.00

COURSE RECORD

	Total W-R	Non-Hndcps Hurdles	Chases	Hndcps Hurdles	Chases	NH Flat	Per cent	£1 Level Stake
Fontwell	3-20	3-4	0-3	0-8	0-1	0-4	15.0	-8.00
Ascot	2-7	0-1	0-0	0-1	1-3	1-2	28.6	+8.88
Fakenham	2-7	0-2	0-0	0-1	2-4	0-0	28.6	+3.50
Towcester	2-8	2-4	0-0	0-2	0-2	0-0	25.0	-0.75
Wincanton	2-9	1-2	1-1	0-3	0-3	0-0	22.2	-4.97
Newbury	2-13	1-5	0-1	1-3	0-3	0-1	15.4	+3.00
Kempton	2-14	0-4	0-0	1-5	0-3	1-2	14.3	+6.75
Lingfield	1-1	0-0	1-1	0-0	0-0	0-0	100.0	+4.00
Ffos Las	1-2	0-0	0-0	0-1	1-1	0-0	50.0	+7.00
Bangor	1-6	1-1	0-0	0-0	0-3	0-2	16.7	+11.00
Leicester	1-7	0-1	1-3	0-1	0-2	0-0	14.3	-2.00
Ludlow	1-9	0-5	1-1	0-1	0-2	0-0	11.1	-3.00
Warwick	1-9	1-4	0-0	0-2	0-2	0-1	11.1	-7.64

WINNING HORSES

Horse	Races Run	1st	2nd	3rd	£
The Organist	5	1	0	0	21896
Got Away	3	1	0	0	17085
Enjoy Responsibly	6	2	0	1	13256
Toviere	5	2	1	0	11047
Euxton Lane	7	2	1	1	9357
Rayvin Black	10	2	3	1	11183

Jurby	6	2	2	0	9032
Piton Pete	7	2	2	2	7733
Jersey Bean	6	2	1	1	8642
Danvinnie	2	1	0	0	3899
*Born Legend	10	1	0	1	3249
Seaston Spirit	5	1	2	1	3119
Sevarano	2	1	0	0	2859
*Rouge Et Blanc	4	1	1	0	1248
Total winning prize-money					£123605
Favourites	3-13		23.1%		-7.61

RAYMOND SHIELS

JEDBURGH, ROXBURGH

	No. of Hrs	Races Run	1st	2nd	3rd	Unpl	Per cent	£1 Level Stake
NH Flat	0	0	0	0	0	0	0.0	0.00
Hurdles	1	5	1	1	0	3	20.0	+4.50
Chases	1	5	0	0	1	4	0.0	-5.00
Totals	2	10	1	1	1	7	10.0	-0.50
16-17	2	11	1	1	1	8	9.1	-4.00
15-16	2	13	2	1	3	7	15.4	-4.25

JOCKEYS

	W-R	Per cent	£1 Level Stake
Callum Bewley	1-9	11.1	+0.50

COURSE RECORD

	Total W-R	Non-Hndcps Hurdles	Chases	Hndcps Hurdles	Chases	NH Flat	Per cent	£1 Level Stake
Hexham	1-3	0-1	0-0	1-1	0-1	0-0	33.3	+6.50

WINNING HORSES

Horse	Races Run	1st	2nd	3rd	£
Lucarno Dancer	5	1	1	0	3574
Total winning prize-money					£3574
Favourites	0-1		0.0%		-1.00

DAN SKELTON

ALCESTER, WARWICKS

	No. of Hrs	Races Run	1st	2nd	3rd	Unpl	Per cent	£1 Level Stake
NH Flat	32	42	5	7	4	26	11.9	-16.89
Hurdles	163	548	97	86	78	287	17.7	-150.82
Chases	71	210	53	28	41	87	25.2	+13.85
Totals	215	800	155	121	123	400	19.4	-153.86
16-17	200	694	117	134	99	344	16.9	-261.07
15-16	148	530	104	88	71	267	19.6	-157.34

BY MONTH

NH Flat	W-R	Per cent	£1 Level Stake	Hurdles	W-R	Per cent	£1 Level Stake
May	1-2	50.0	+2.00	May	19-56	33.9	-11.04

	W-R	Per cent	£1 Level Stake
June	0-3	0.0	-3.00
July	0-0	0.0	0.00
August	0-0	0.0	0.00
September	1-3	33.3	-1.39
October	0-6	0.0	-6.00
November	1-6	16.7	+1.00
December	0-3	0.0	-3.00
January	0-3	0.0	-3.00
February	1-6	16.7	+2.00
March	0-2	0.0	-2.00
April	1-8	12.5	-3.50

	W-R	Per cent	£1 Level Stake
June	5-29	17.2	-16.20
July	10-30	33.3	+5.82
August	8-24	33.3	-3.56
September	4-36	11.1	-5.55
October	7-58	12.1	-37.17
November	12-66	18.2	-5.51
December	11-62	17.7	-24.42
January	7-49	14.3	-13.37
February	7-49	14.3	-14.06
March	4-50	8.0	-2.75
April	3-39	7.7	-23.00

	W-R	Per cent	£1 Level Stake
Noel Fehily	3-6	50.0	-0.55
David England	2-17	11.8	-10.00
Fergus Gregory	1-3	33.3	+2.50
Mr Lorcan Williams	1-3	33.3	-0.13
Henry Brooke	1-6	16.7	-1.67
Mr Samuel Davies-Thomas	1-11	9.1	-9.17
Ian Popham	1-22	4.5	-1.00

Chases

	W-R	Per cent	£1 Level Stake
May	5-16	31.3	-2.50
June	3-9	33.3	-0.67
July	4-13	30.8	+0.43
August	6-13	46.2	+12.56
September	3-14	21.4	-0.75
October	7-30	23.3	+25.96
November	8-26	30.8	-3.70
December	6-16	37.5	+9.27
January	2-17	11.8	-12.78
February	4-19	21.1	-2.47
March	2-16	12.5	-3.50
April	3-21	14.3	-8.00

Totals

	W-R	Per cent	£1 Level Stake
May	25-74	33.8	-11.54
June	8-41	19.5	-19.87
July	14-43	32.6	+6.25
August	14-37	37.8	+9.00
September	8-53	15.1	-7.69
October	14-94	14.9	-17.21
November	21-98	21.4	-8.21
December	17-81	21.0	-18.15
January	9-69	13.0	-29.15
February	12-74	16.2	-14.53
March	6-68	8.8	-8.25
April	7-68	10.3	-34.50

DISTANCE

Hurdles

	W-R	Per cent	£1 Level Stake
2m-2m3f	64-341	18.8	-64.30
2m4f-2m7f	29-165	17.6	-55.30
3m+	3-38	7.9	-30.47

Chases

	W-R	Per cent	£1 Level Stake
2m-2m3f	30-94	31.9	+24.61
2m4f-2m7f	13-71	18.3	-0.47
3m+	10-45	22.2	-10.29

TYPE OF RACE

Non-Handicaps

	W-R	Per cent	£1 Level Stake
Nov Hrdls	39-159	24.5	-43.50
Hrdls	14-86	16.3	-30.06
Nov Chs	24-53	45.3	+38.88
Chases	2-10	20.0	-2.00
Sell/Claim	2-5	40.0	-0.13

Handicaps

	W-R	Per cent	£1 Level Stake
Nov Hrdls	2-12	16.7	-1.43
Hrdls	37-272	13.6	-69.79
Nov Chs	7-23	30.4	+16.83
Chases	19-104	18.3	-22.86
Sell/Claim	0-3	0.0	-3.00

RACE CLASS

	W-R	Per cent	£1 Level Stake
Class 1	8-97	8.2	-12.17
Class 2	12-81	14.8	-22.42
Class 3	27-146	18.5	-46.53
Class 4	79-340	23.2	-37.53
Class 5	27-116	23.3	-26.20
Class 6	2-20	10.0	-9.00

FIRST TIME OUT

	W-R	Per cent	£1 Level Stake
Bumpers	5-32	15.6	-6.89
Hurdles	34-144	23.6	-36.22
Chases	10-39	25.6	-11.27
Totals	49-215	22.8	-54.38

JOCKEYS

	W-R	Per cent	£1 Level Stake
Harry Skelton	127-555	22.9	-66.23
Bridget Andrews	18-151	11.9	-41.61

COURSE RECORD

	Total W-R	Non-Hndcps Hurdles	Chases	Hndcps Hurdles	Chases	NH Flat	Per cent	£1 Level Stake
Mrket Rsn	20-61	7-18	3-6	7-24	3-9	0-4	32.8	+28.21
Uttoxeter	14-47	3-13	2-3	6-18	2-10	1-3	29.8	-0.03
Bangor	10-27	5-11	0-2	2-8	3-5	0-1	37.0	+9.12
Wetherby	10-29	5-12	3-5	1-7	1-4	0-1	34.5	-3.51
Worcester	10-47	4-18	2-4	1-14	2-9	1-2	21.3	+1.91
Stratford	9-41	2-12	1-2	2-15	4-12	0-0	22.0	-7.88
Warwick	9-46	4-18	0-3	1-15	4-8	0-2	19.6	-10.42
Sedgefield	7-18	3-5	1-1	2-8	1-2	0-2	38.9	+13.18
Plumpton	5-17	3-8	1-1	1-7	0-1	0-0	29.4	-5.96
Southwell	5-38	0-14	2-5	3-12	0-4	0-3	13.2	-22.54
Cheltenham	5-41	0-10	2-3	3-19	0-8	0-1	12.2	+9.83
Fakenham	4-17	2-5	1-2	1-7	0-3	0-0	23.5	-0.63
Doncaster	4-21	2-9	1-3	1-6	0-2	0-1	19.0	-8.79
Fontwell	4-25	1-7	0-0	2-9	1-7	0-2	16.0	-9.79
Nton Abbot	4-25	2-7	1-2	1-8	0-8	0-0	16.0	-10.06
Ludlow	4-29	3-11	0-0	1-12	0-3	0-3	13.8	-10.40
Aintree	4-30	1-7	1-4	1-10	1-7	0-2	13.3	-16.95
Huntingdon	4-33	1-9	2-2	0-8	0-9	1-5	12.1	-1.00
Towcester	3-16	3-8	0-2	0-5	0-1	0-0	18.8	-8.17
Hexham	2-3	1-2	1-1	0-0	0-0	0-0	66.7	+2.00
Leicester	2-7	1-1	1-1	0-2	0-3	0-0	28.6	-1.28
Catterick	2-10	2-5	0-0	0-3	0-2	0-0	20.0	-5.83
Newbury	2-10	0-5	0-0	1-3	1-2	0-0	20.0	+6.00
Ayr	2-13	0-0	0-1	0-5	2-7	0-0	15.4	-4.00
Chepstow	2-21	1-5	0-2	0-6	0-5	1-3	9.5	-9.00
Wincanton	1-4	1-3	0-0	0-1	0-0	0-0	25.0	-0.50
Lingfield	1-6	0-2	0-0	1-4	0-0	0-0	16.7	-2.75
Ascot	1-8	0-3	0-0	0-2	1-2	0-1	12.5	+2.00
Hereford	1-9	0-1	1-2	0-3	0-2	0-1	11.1	-6.13
Sandown	1-13	0-3	0-1	0-5	1-3	0-1	7.7	-8.00
Taunton	1-19	0-3	0-0	0-14	0-1	1-1	5.3	-14.50
Haydock	1-22	0-5	0-2	1-13	0-2	0-0	4.5	-16.00
Kempton	1-34	1-15	0-3	0-9	0-5	0-2	2.9	-29.00

WINNING HORSES

Horse	Races Run	1st	2nd	3rd	£
Mohaayed	5	2	1	1	61824
Rene's Girl	7	3	2	1	64982
Oldgrangewood	5	1	0	2	31280
Value At Risk	6	2	1	0	34105
Ashoka	9	2	0	2	29016
*Stylish Dancer	4	1	0	0	25024
Get On The Yager	7	2	1	0	29217
Roksana	5	3	1	1	29278
Listen To The Man	4	3	1	1	27033
North Hill Harvey	5	2	1	1	35573

Cobra De Mai	10	5	2	0	35128
Momella	5	3	1	1	30314
Abidjan	5	2	0	3	25024
Sir Mangan	9	1	2	0	16266
Virgilio	4	1	0	0	13928
Tommy Rapper	6	3	1	0	20274
Solomon Grey	5	2	2	1	17545
Honkytonktennessee	10	1	3	1	12660
Whatzdjazz	8	3	1	1	17239
Azzuri	9	4	1	2	21703
Optimus Prime	5	3	1	0	24987
Workbench	8	2	0	1	15714
No Hassle Hoff	6	1	0	1	9384
Captain Chaos	6	3	0	0	19803
Sam Red	10	2	2	1	11887
Work In Progress	8	5	0	0	28970
Spiritofthegames	5	1	1	1	7596
Must Havea Flutter	7	2	1	0	13971
Shantou Rock	5	1	3	1	7280
Red Rising	5	2	1	1	13144
Zamparelli	4	1	0	0	6758
Born Survivor	5	1	0	2	6657
*The Raven Master	4	1	1	1	6647
Destrier	4	2	1	0	11139
Debdebdeb	3	2	0	0	10083
Excellent Team	12	1	0	0	5848
Free Stone Hill	11	1	3	4	5523
Hear No Evil	3	2	0	1	10463
Itsnonofurbusiness	7	1	0	2	5198
Too Many Diamonds	8	4	1	1	13321
Solo Saxophone	4	2	0	1	8058
*Comrade Conrad	5	1	0	1	4809
*Premier Rose	3	2	0	1	7960
Speed Demon	4	1	1	1	4660
*Shrubland	5	3	1	1	9747
Starcrossed	2	1	0	0	4549
Molly The Dolly	4	1	2	0	4549
*Firmount Gent	6	1	0	2	4549
Focaccia	6	1	2	1	4549
One For Billy	6	2	0	1	7798
*Robin Waters	4	1	0	2	4327
Some Invitation	3	1	0	0	4185
*Ashkoul	5	2	2	0	7408
Embole	5	1	0	2	4159
Or De Vassy	5	2	1	1	7343
Rebel Royal	3	1	0	0	4094
Nube Negra	5	2	1	1	4094
Petrou	9	4	2	0	15691
Ravens Hill	6	2	0	2	6498
Knight In Dubai	5	1	0	1	3899
*Get Ready Freddy	6	2	2	0	6758
Blairs Cove	9	2	1	2	7798
Mister Showman	4	1	1	2	3899
*Daulys Anthem	3	2	0	0	7148
Cabaret Queen	3	1	1	1	3899
Bedrock	4	2	0	1	7148
Royal Beekeeper	5	2	0	0	3899
Free Range	7	1	2	1	3899

I'll Be Your Clown	3	1	0	1	3639
*Cosy Club	2	1	0	0	3509
Lieutenant Gruber	4	2	1	0	6628
Ckalco Des Loges	8	1	0	3	3329
Mister Universum	7	2	2	1	6498
Parthenius	3	1	0	1	3249
Miss Spent	6	1	1	1	3249
Marley Firth	6	1	0	1	3249
Pretty Reckless	8	2	0	3	6498
*Wynford	4	2	2	0	5848
Al Shahir	5	1	3	0	3249
Hestina	3	1	1	0	3249
Gibson Park	6	1	4	1	3249
*Anytime Will Do	1	1	0	0	2924
Shannon Bridge	5	1	2	0	2738
Defining Year	6	2	0	1	5328
Horseshoe Bay	2	1	0	0	2599
Hatcher	5	1	2	0	2404
Supremely Lucky	1	1	0	0	2274
Holryale	5	1	3	0	1949
Mabela	2	1	0	0	1949
Total winning prize-money					**£1056768**
Favourites	77-221		34.8%		-46.89

KENNETH SLACK

HILTON, CUMBRIA

	No. of Hrs	Races Run	1st	2nd	3rd	Unpl	Per cent	£1 Level Stake
NH Flat	2	3	1	0	0	2	33.3	+6.00
Hurdles	11	40	6	4	6	24	15.0	-11.75
Chases	3	6	0	1	0	5	0.0	-6.00
Totals	**12**	**49**	**7**	**5**	**6**	**31**	**14.3**	**-11.75**
16-17	15	58	11	10	5	32	19.0	+21.11
15-16	15	73	24	13	6	30	32.9	+49.05

JOCKEYS

	W-R	Per cent	£1 Level Stake
Robert Hogg	3-26	11.5	-8.50
Brian Hughes	2-3	66.7	+4.25
Miss Emma Sayer	1-1	100.0	+2.50
Colm McCormack	1-14	7.1	-5.00

COURSE RECORD

	Total W-R	Non-Hndcps Hurdles	Chases	Hndcps Hurdles	Chases	NH Flat	Per cent	£1 Level Stake
Cartmel	4-10	0-0	0-0	4-10	0-0	0-0	40.0	+8.00
Wetherby	1-3	0-0	0-0	0-2	0-0	1-1	33.3	+6.00
Catterick	1-7	0-1	0-0	1-4	0-2	0-0	14.3	-4.75
Sedgefield	1-16	0-3	0-0	1-9	0-3	0-1	6.3	-8.00

WINNING HORSES

Horse	Races Run	1st	2nd	3rd	£
Beeno	9	4	1	1	25490
Discoverie	9	1	1	1	3509

Oh So Gigolo	6	1	0	0	2599
Kuragina	2	1	0	0	2053
Total winning prize-money					£33651
Favourites	2-9		22.2%		-3.25

PAM SLY

THORNEY, CAMBS

	No. of Hrs	Races Run	1st	2nd	3rd	Unpl	Per cent	£1 Level Stake
NH Flat	3	3	0	0	1	2	0.0	-3.00
Hurdles	11	32	1	4	8	19	3.1	-26.50
Chases	3	15	4	4	1	6	26.7	+23.05
Totals	14	50	5	8	10	27	10.0	-6.45
16-17	13	57	8	15	4	30	14.0	+43.83
15-16	11	38	8	4	4	22	21.1	+15.73

JOCKEYS

	W-R	Per cent	£1 Level Stake
Kielan Woods	3-25	12.0	+11.30
Miss Gina Andrews	2-11	18.2	-3.75

COURSE RECORD

	Total W-R	Non-Hndcps Hurdles	Chases	Hndcps Hurdles	Chases	NH Flat	Per cent	£1 Level Stake
Fakenham	2-11	0-1	0-0	0-4	2-6	0-0	18.2	-5.95
Bangor	1-2	0-0	0-0	1-1	0-1	0-0	50.0	+3.50
Ludlow	1-3	0-0	0-0	0-1	1-2	0-0	33.3	+1.00
Wetherby	1-6	0-1	1-3	0-1	0-1	0-0	16.7	+23.00

WINNING HORSES

Horse	Races Run	1st	2nd	3rd	£
Actinpieces	6	2	1	0	17920
Mortens Leam	6	1	2	1	6498
Walsingham Grange	7	1	1	2	4094
Popelys Gull	7	1	1	1	3899
Total winning prize-money					£32411
Favourites	2-7		28.6%		-1.20

SUE SMITH

HIGH ELDWICK, W YORKS

	No. of Hrs	Races Run	1st	2nd	3rd	Unpl	Per cent	£1 Level Stake
NH Flat	8	14	0	3	4	7	0.0	-14.00
Hurdles	39	125	16	19	14	76	12.8	-34.91
Chases	33	159	24	24	30	81	15.1	-21.92
Totals	58	298	40	46	48	164	13.4	-70.83
16-17	59	280	41	33	36	170	14.6	-31.52
15-16	65	312	44	63	41	163	14.1	-66.35

BY MONTH

NH Flat	W-R	Per cent	£1 Level Stake	Hurdles	W-R	Per cent	£1 Level Stake
May	0-0	0.0	0.00	May	0-2	0.0	-2.00
June	0-0	0.0	0.00	June	0-4	0.0	-4.00
July	0-0	0.0	0.00	July	0-5	0.0	-5.00
August	0-1	0.0	-1.00	August	0-2	0.0	-2.00
September	0-0	0.0	0.00	September	0-0	0.0	0.00
October	0-2	0.0	-2.00	October	2-16	12.5	-0.25
November	0-3	0.0	-3.00	November	0-22	0.0	-22.00
December	0-4	0.0	-4.00	December	3-17	17.6	-2.17
January	0-1	0.0	-1.00	January	6-18	33.3	+3.37
February	0-1	0.0	-1.00	February	3-10	30.0	-1.86
March	0-1	0.0	-1.00	March	1-14	7.1	-10.00
April	0-1	0.0	-1.00	April	1-15	6.7	+11.00

Chases	W-R	Per cent	£1 Level Stake	Totals	W-R	Per cent	£1 Level Stake
May	2-6	33.3	-0.38	May	2-8	25.0	-2.38
June	1-6	16.7	+0.50	June	1-10	10.0	-3.50
July	1-4	25.0	+1.50	July	1-9	11.1	-3.50
August	1-4	25.0	+17.00	August	1-7	14.3	+14.00
September	0-1	0.0	-1.00	September	0-1	0.0	-1.00
October	2-18	11.1	-7.00	October	4-36	11.1	-9.25
November	4-25	16.0	-8.25	November	4-50	8.0	-33.25
December	2-20	10.0	-11.75	December	5-41	12.2	-17.92
January	3-20	15.0	-1.67	January	9-39	23.1	+0.70
February	4-18	22.2	-5.13	February	7-29	24.1	-7.99
March	1-17	5.9	-9.50	March	2-32	6.3	-20.50
April	3-20	15.0	+3.75	April	4-36	11.1	+13.75

DISTANCE

Hurdles	W-R	Per cent	£1 Level Stake	Chases	W-R	Per cent	£1 Level Stake
2m-2m3f	13-80	16.3	+2.06	2m-2m3f	5-35	14.3	-15.88
2m4f-2m7f	2-37	5.4	-30.88	2m4f-2m7f	8-55	14.5	-1.17
3m+	1-8	12.5	-6.09	3m+	11-69	15.9	-4.88

TYPE OF RACE

Non-Handicaps	W-R	Per cent	£1 Level Stake	Handicaps	W-R	Per cent	£1 Level Stake
Nov Hrdls	4-52	7.7	-31.85	Nov Hrdls	0-4	0.0	-4.00
Hrdls	2-9	22.2	+1.50	Hrdls	10-56	17.9	+3.44
Nov Chs	1-7	14.3	+0.50	Nov Chs	2-17	11.8	-10.25
Chases	0-2	0.0	-2.00	Chases	17-119	14.3	-8.29
Sell/Claim	0-2	0.0	-2.00	Sell/Claim	0-1	0.0	-1.00

RACE CLASS

	W-R	Per cent	£1 Level Stake
Class 1	2-22	9.1	+13.00
Class 2	2-25	8.0	-3.50
Class 3	12-71	16.9	-22.97
Class 4	18-135	13.3	-54.02
Class 5	6-38	15.8	+3.66
Class 6	0-7	0.0	-7.00

FIRST TIME OUT

	W-R	Per cent	£1 Level Stake
Bumpers	0-8	0.0	-8.00
Hurdles	1-26	3.8	-14.00
Chases	3-24	12.5	-13.38
Totals	4-58	6.9	-35.38

JOCKEYS

	W-R	Per cent	£1 Level Stake
Danny Cook	30-176	17.0	-12.45
Sean Quinlan	6-57	10.5	-30.63

Mr Kane Yeoman	1-3	33.3	+1.00
Henry Brooke	1-15	6.7	-6.00
Nathan Moscrop	1-19	5.3	+2.00

COURSE RECORD

	Total W-R	Non-Hndcps Hurdles	Chases	Hndcps Hurdles	Chases	NH Flat	Per cent	£1 Level Stake
Newcastle	6-20	2-4	0-0	1-3	3-12	0-1	30.0	+0.03
Catterick	6-23	0-7	1-2	1-4	4-9	0-1	26.1	-0.22
Sedgefield	6-37	2-10	0-0	3-10	1-14	0-3	16.2	-14.17
Carlisle	4-29	0-8	0-1	2-4	2-15	0-1	13.8	-14.55
Cartmel	3-8	0-1	0-0	0-2	3-5	0-0	37.5	+25.00
Haydock	3-26	1-5	0-1	1-7	1-12	0-1	11.5	-9.17
Wetherby	3-37	0-10	0-4	0-6	3-15	0-2	8.1	-24.75
Kelso	2-9	0-1	0-0	0-2	2-6	0-0	22.2	+11.00
Mrket Rsn	2-22	0-5	0-0	0-7	2-10	0-0	9.1	-13.00
Doncaster	1-1	0-0	0-0	0-0	1-1	0-0	100.0	+8.00
Musselbgh	1-4	0-0	0-0	1-1	0-2	0-1	25.0	0.00
Aintree	1-9	0-2	0-0	0-0	1-7	0-0	11.1	-4.00
Ayr	1-12	0-0	0-0	1-4	0-8	0-0	8.3	+14.00
Uttoxeter	1-19	1-3	0-1	0-4	0-11	0-0	5.3	-7.00

WINNING HORSES

Horse	Races Run	1st	2nd	3rd	£
Midnight Shadow	7	2	3	0	63696
Wakanda	6	1	2	0	45560
Smooth Stepper	7	2	1	0	38623
Hainan	5	1	0	1	16245
I Just Know	5	1	1	1	15890
Blottos	7	3	1	0	18714
Joke Dancer	7	3	1	0	20867
Vintage Clouds	6	1	2	2	9097
Straidnahanna	5	1	0	0	8707
Cracking Find	8	3	0	3	20794
Delusionofgrandeur	8	1	0	4	7798
Wolf Sword	8	2	1	0	15205
De Vous A Moi	4	1	0	1	7343
Sharp Response	4	1	1	1	6758
Treshnish	6	2	1	1	9747
Charlie Wingnut	5	1	2	0	5523
Never Up	8	1	2	1	4874
Just Georgie	7	1	2	1	4809
Dick Darsie	6	1	1	0	4660
Maxed Out King	5	1	0	1	4549
Red Danaher	10	2	2	1	7668
Absolutely Dylan	6	1	1	1	4094
Black Art	6	2	2	0	8187
Iskabeg Lane	9	1	1	3	3899
Brother Scott	4	2	1	1	7148
Shine Away	5	1	1	0	3249
Mathayus	4	1	1	1	2599
Total winning prize-money					**£366303**
Favourites	13-45		**28.9%**		**-9.20**

SUZY SMITH

LEWES, E SUSSEX

	No. of Hrs	Races Run	1st	2nd	3rd	Unpl	Per cent	£1 Level Stake
NH Flat	6	9	2	2	1	4	22.2	+22.63
Hurdles	10	31	0	1	5	25	0.0	-31.00
Chases	4	21	1	4	5	11	4.8	-19.00
Totals	18	61	3	7	11	40	4.9	-27.37
16-17	18	48	4	7	4	33	8.3	-14.00
15-16	17	61	6	10	4	41	9.8	-30.92

JOCKEYS

	W-R	Per cent	£1 Level Stake
Jack Sherwood	3-40	7.5	-6.38

COURSE RECORD

	Total W-R	Non-Hndcps Hurdles	Chases	Hndcps Hurdles	Chases	NH Flat	Per cent	£1 Level Stake
Uttoxeter	1-1	0-0	0-0	0-0	0-0	1-1	100.0	+1.63
Mrket Rsn	1-2	0-0	0-1	0-0	1-1	0-0	50.0	0.00
Plumpton	1-13	0-2	0-0	0-6	0-4	1-1	7.7	+16.00

WINNING HORSES

Horse	Races Run	1st	2nd	3rd	£
Red Devil Star	7	1	1	3	6498
Rosy World	3	1	1	1	2274
Hook Lane Roobee	1	1	0	0	1625
Total winning prize-money					**£10397**
Favourites	2-6		33.3%		-1.38

R MIKE SMITH

GALSTON, E AYRSHIRE

	No. of Hrs	Races Run	1st	2nd	3rd	Unpl	Per cent	£1 Level Stake
NH Flat	5	7	0	0	1	6	0.0	-7.00
Hurdles	20	79	4	9	7	59	5.1	-59.75
Chases	7	34	2	3	8	21	5.9	-18.50
Totals	26	120	6	12	16	86	5.0	-85.25
16-17	24	89	4	9	8	68	4.5	-48.50
15-16	13	46	3	3	2	38	6.5	+2.58

JOCKEYS

	W-R	Per cent	£1 Level Stake
Dale Irving	3-35	8.6	-14.00
Brian Hughes	2-5	40.0	+3.25
Conor O'Farrell	1-36	2.8	-30.50

COURSE RECORD

	Total W-R	Non-Hndcps Hurdles	Chases	Hndcps Hurdles	Chases	NH Flat	Per cent	£1 Level Stake
Ayr	2-39	0-8	0-0	2-16	0-10	0-5	5.1	-29.00
Cartmel	1-3	0-0	0-0	0-1	1-2	0-0	33.3	+4.00

Carlisle	1-8	0-0	0-0	1-7	0-1	0-0	12.5	-4.25
Hexham	1-9	0-2	0-0	0-1	1-6	0-0	11.1	-0.50
Perth	1-25	0-8	0-1	1-12	0-3	0-1	4.0	-19.50

WINNING HORSES

Horse	Races Run	1st	2nd	3rd	£
Our Lucas	7	2	3	1	8317
Miss Mackie	6	2	0	1	7798
Trongate	8	1	0	2	3899
Firstymini	5	1	0	1	3249
Total winning prize-money					£23263
Favourites	2-8		25.0%		1.25

JULIAN SMITH

TIRLEY, GLOUCS

	No. of Hrs	Races Run	1st	2nd	3rd	Unpl	Per cent	£1 Level Stake
NH Flat	0	0	0	0	0	0	0.0	0.00
Hurdles	2	5	0	0	0	5	0.0	-5.00
Chases	2	9	2	1	6	0	22.2	+11.00
Totals	4	14	2	1	6	5	14.3	+6.00
16-17	5	19	1	1	3	14	5.3	+2.00
15-16	7	26	3	2	3	18	11.5	-0.92

JOCKEYS

	W-R	Per cent	£1 Level Stake
Mark Grant	2-13	15.4	+7.00

COURSE RECORD

	Total W-R	Non-Hndcps Hurdles	Chases	Hndcps Hurdles	Chases	NH Flat	Per cent	£1 Level Stake
Kempton	1-1	0-0	0-0	0-0	1-1	0-0	100.0	+14.00
Mrket Rsn	1-4	0-0	0-0	0-1	1-3	0-0	25.0	+1.00

WINNING HORSES

Horse	Races Run	1st	2nd	3rd	£
Emerald Rose	5	1	0	4	5523
Iona Days	4	1	1	2	5198
Total winning prize-money					£10721
Favourites	0-0		0.0%		0.00

JAMIE SNOWDEN

LAMBOURN, BERKS

	No. of Hrs	Races Run	1st	2nd	3rd	Unpl	Per cent	£1 Level Stake
NH Flat	11	14	3	2	1	8	21.4	-1.09
Hurdles	30	94	18	17	12	47	19.1	+6.26
Chases	17	62	14	13	10	25	22.6	+20.33
Totals	48	170	35	32	23	80	20.6	+25.50
16-17	57	206	25	36	22	123	12.1	-67.47
15-16	51	179	17	21	16	125	9.5	-47.56

BY MONTH

NH Flat	W-R	Per cent	£1 Level Stake	Hurdles	W-R	Per cent	£1 Level Stake
May	0-2	0.0	-2.00	May	2-10	20.0	-5.13
June	0-0	0.0	0.00	June	0-5	0.0	-5.00
July	0-0	0.0	0.00	July	1-2	50.0	+2.50
August	0-0	0.0	0.00	August	0-1	0.0	-1.00
September	0-1	0.0	-1.00	September	0-2	0.0	-2.00
October	1-2	50.0	+4.00	October	0-13	0.0	-13.00
November	0-2	0.0	-2.00	November	3-12	25.0	+0.53
December	0-0	0.0	0.00	December	3-13	23.1	+5.00
January	1-1	100.0	+4.00	January	2-9	22.2	-4.00
February	1-2	50.0	-0.09	February	2-7	28.6	-0.76
March	0-2	0.0	-2.00	March	1-10	10.0	-5.50
April	0-2	0.0	-2.00	April	4-10	40.0	+34.62

Chases	W-R	Per cent	£1 Level Stake	Totals	W-R	Per cent	£1 Level Stake
May	1-5	20.0	-2.00	May	3-17	17.6	-7.13
June	0-2	0.0	-2.00	June	0-7	0.0	-7.00
July	1-4	25.0	+2.00	July	2-6	33.3	+4.50
August	2-8	25.0	-1.25	August	2-9	22.2	-2.25
September	2-5	40.0	+9.00	September	2-8	25.0	+6.00
October	2-5	40.0	+16.00	October	3-20	15.0	+7.00
November	0-9	0.0	-9.00	November	3-23	13.0	-10.47
December	1-4	25.0	+1.50	December	4-17	23.5	+6.50
January	2-5	40.0	+2.25	January	5-15	33.3	+2.25
February	0-5	0.0	-5.00	February	3-14	21.4	-5.85
March	2-4	50.0	+8.50	March	3-16	18.8	+1.00
April	1-6	16.7	-1.67	April	5-18	27.8	+30.95

DISTANCE

Hurdles	W-R	Per cent	£1 Level Stake	Chases	W-R	Per cent	£1 Level Stake
2m-2m3f	13-54	24.1	-2.54	2m-2m3f	3-12	25.0	+1.75
2m4f-2m7f	1-30	3.3	-25.50	2m4f-2m7f	7-23	30.4	+24.00
3m+	3-9	33.3	+33.50	3m+	4-27	14.8	-5.42

TYPE OF RACE

Non-Handicaps	W-R	Per cent	£1 Level Stake	Handicaps	W-R	Per cent	£1 Level Stake
Nov Hrdls	9-41	22.0	+0.63	Nov Hrdls	0-6	0.0	-6.00
Hrdls	1-17	5.9	-15.20	Hrdls	8-30	26.7	+26.83
Nov Chs	4-11	36.4	+11.75	Nov Chs	3-9	33.3	+4.75
Chases	0-2	0.0	-2.00	Chases	6-36	16.7	+5.33
Sell/Claim	0-0	0.0	0.00	Sell/Claim	0-0	0.0	0.00

RACE CLASS

	W-R	Per cent	£1 Level Stake
Class 1	0-17	0.0	-17.00
Class 2	4-8	50.0	+44.00
Class 3	3-11	27.3	+4.08
Class 4	20-86	23.3	+13.51
Class 5	2-22	9.1	-15.09
Class 6	0-4	0.0	-4.00

FIRST TIME OUT

	W-R	Per cent	£1 Level Stake
Bumpers	2-11	18.2	0.00
Hurdles	3-23	13.0	-15.75
Chases	3-14	21.4	+8.00
Totals	8-48	16.7	-7.75

JOCKEYS

	W-R	Per cent	£1 Level Stake
Gavin Sheehan	23-93	24.7	+21.43
Tom O'Brien	3-6	50.0	+7.95
Aidan Coleman	3-10	30.0	+4.75
Page Fuller	3-21	14.3	+7.00
Sean Bowen	1-1	100.0	+16.00
Richard Johnson	1-1	100.0	+4.00
Micheal Nolan	1-5	20.0	-2.63

COURSE RECORD

	Total W-R	Non-Hndcps Hurdles	Chases	Hndcps Hurdles	Chases	NH Flat	Per cent	£1 Level Stake
Ludlow	3-6	1-3	1-1	0-1	0-0	1-1	50.0	+10.50
Uttoxeter	3-9	1-3	0-0	0-2	2-4	0-0	33.3	+15.33
Haydock	2-2	0-0	0-0	0-0	2-2	0-0	100.0	+10.50
Lingfield	2-3	2-3	0-0	0-0	0-0	0-0	66.7	+9.80
Southwell	2-4	1-2	0-0	1-2	0-0	0-0	50.0	+3.00
Stratford	2-5	0-0	0-0	1-2	1-3	0-0	40.0	+2.25
Chepstow	2-7	1-3	0-0	1-1	0-3	0-0	28.6	-2.00
Cheltenham	2-9	0-2	1-1	1-2	0-2	0-2	22.2	+22.00
Worcester	2-12	0-2	0-0	0-3	2-6	0-1	16.7	+2.00
Cartmel	1-1	0-0	0-0	0-0	1-1	0-0	100.0	+3.00
Ayr	1-2	0-0	0-0	1-1	0-1	0-0	50.0	+15.00
Carlisle	1-2	0-0	0-0	1-1	0-1	0-0	50.0	+0.38
Catterick	1-2	0-1	1-1	0-0	0-0	0-0	50.0	+0.25
Perth	1-2	1-2	0-0	0-0	0-0	0-0	50.0	-0.39
Bangor	1-3	0-0	0-1	0-1	0-0	1-1	33.3	-1.09
Ffos Las	1-3	1-1	0-1	0-1	0-0	0-0	33.3	-1.09
Exeter	1-4	0-2	0-0	1-1	0-1	0-0	25.0	+0.33
Kempton	1-4	0-1	0-1	1-2	0-0	0-0	25.0	-1.50
Warwick	1-5	0-0	0-0	0-2	0-2	1-1	20.0	0.00
Wetherby	1-5	0-1	1-2	0-0	0-2	0-0	20.0	0.00
Towcester	1-6	0-3	0-1	0-1	1-1	0-0	16.7	-1.00
Mrket Rsn	1-7	1-4	0-0	0-0	0-3	0-0	14.3	-5.27
Nton Abbot	1-7	0-3	0-0	0-0	1-4	0-0	14.3	-1.00
Huntingdon	1-8	1-5	0-0	0-1	0-0	0-2	12.5	-3.50

WINNING HORSES

Horse	Races Run	1st	2nd	3rd	£
Naranja	6	3	0	2	30204
Double Treasure	5	3	0	0	29886
Monbeg Theatre	6	1	2	1	12512
Fact Of The Matter	6	1	0	2	12512
Hogan's Height	7	3	2	0	25503
Breaking Bits	2	1	0	0	7507
Kalahari Queen	5	2	2	0	11631
Adrrastos	6	2	0	3	10556
Shockingtimes	6	1	2	0	6498
Our Three Sons	5	2	2	0	10073
Three Ways	5	1	2	1	6258
Midnight Silver	2	1	0	0	5697
Floral Bouquet	4	2	0	1	9629
Scorpion Sid	3	2	1	0	8902
Presenting Pearl	4	2	0	0	8447
Lunar Flow	6	2	1	1	8263
Lostnfound	5	1	2	0	3906
Dans Le Vent	7	1	2	2	3899
Fine Jewellery	2	1	0	0	3769
Oscar Star	7	1	1	2	3574
Thebannerkingrebel	3	2	0	0	2599
Total winning prize-money					**£221825**
Favourites	**11-20**		**55.0%**		**5.34**

MIKE SOWERSBY

GOODMANHAM, E YORKS

	No. of Hrs	Races Run	1st	2nd	3rd	Unpl	Per cent	£1 Level Stake
NH Flat	1	1	0	0	0	1	0.0	-1.00
Hurdles	10	43	4	4	5	30	9.3	-2.25
Chases	2	11	0	2	3	6	0.0	-11.00
Totals	13	55	4	6	8	37	7.3	-14.25
16-17	24	92	2	4	9	77	2.2	-70.00
15-16	18	100	10	12	8	70	10.0	-19.25

JOCKEYS

	W-R	Per cent	£1 Level Stake
Ryan Day	2-22	9.1	+3.00
Gavin Sheehan	1-2	50.0	+11.00
Brian Hughes	1-12	8.3	-9.25

COURSE RECORD

	Total W-R	Non-Hndcps Hurdles	Chases	Hndcps Hurdles	Chases	NH Flat	Per cent	£1 Level Stake
Hexham	1-3	0-0	0-0	1-3	0-0	0-0	33.3	+10.00
Mrket Rsn	1-5	0-0	0-0	1-5	0-0	0-0	20.0	-2.25
Uttoxeter	1-8	0-0	0-0	1-8	0-0	0-0	12.5	+4.00
Southwell	1-13	0-1	0-0	1-8	0-4	0-0	7.7	0.00

WINNING HORSES

Horse	Races Run	1st	2nd	3rd	£
Agent Louise	5	1	1	0	4159
Arboretum	4	2	0	2	6173
Turtle Cask	12	1	1	1	2849
Total winning prize-money					**£13181**
Favourites	**1-4**		**25.0%**		**-1.25**

JOHN SPEARING

KINNERSLEY, WORCS

	No. of Hrs	Races Run	1st	2nd	3rd	Unpl	Per cent	£1 Level Stake
NH Flat	0	0	0	0	0	0	0.0	0.00
Hurdles	4	19	1	1	5	12	5.3	-12.00
Chases	3	12	0	2	0	10	0.0	-12.00
Totals	7	31	1	3	5	22	3.2	-24.00
16-17	6	19	3	1	1	14	15.8	+26.00

15-16	8	40	4	3	9	24	10.0	-13.50

JOCKEYS

	W-R	Per cent	£1 Level Stake
Jamie Moore	1-14	7.1	-7.00

COURSE RECORD

	Total W-R	Non-Hndcps Hurdles	Chases	Hndcps Hurdles	Chases	NH Flat	Per cent	£1 Level Stake
Worcester	1-7	0-0	0-0	1-7	0-0	0-0	14.3	0.00

WINNING HORSES

Horse	Races Run	1st	2nd	3rd	£
Sweeping Rock	8	1	1	2	2859
Total winning prize-money					£2859
Favourites	0-1	0.0%			-1.00

RICHARD SPENCER

NEWMARKET, SUFFOLK

	No. of Hrs	Races Run	1st	2nd	3rd	Unpl	Per cent	£1 Level Stake
NH Flat	1	1	0	1	0	0	0.0	-1.00
Hurdles	5	10	1	2	1	6	10.0	+3.00
Chases	1	5	2	0	1	2	40.0	+6.50
Totals	**6**	**16**	**3**	**3**	**2**	**8**	**18.8**	**+8.50**
16-17	3	13	3	2	2	6	23.1	+5.75

JOCKEYS

	W-R	Per cent	£1 Level Stake
Mr James King	2-4	50.0	+7.50
Brendan Powell	1-7	14.3	+6.00

COURSE RECORD

	Total W-R	Non-Hndcps Hurdles	Chases	Hndcps Hurdles	Chases	NH Flat	Per cent	£1 Level Stake
Kelso	1-1	0-0	1-1	0-0	0-0	0-0	100.0	+2.50
Huntingdon	1-2	1-2	0-0	0-0	0-0	0-0	50.0	+11.00
Mrket Rsn	1-4	0-1	1-1	0-2	0-0	0-0	25.0	+4.00

WINNING HORSES

Horse	Races Run	1st	2nd	3rd	£
Movie Set	2	1	0	0	3249
Sir Jack Yeats	5	2	0	1	4367
Total winning prize-money					£7616
Favourites	0-1	0.0%			-1.00

DANIEL STEELE

HENFIELD, W SUSSEX

	No. of Hrs	Races Run	1st	2nd	3rd	Unpl	Per cent	£1 Level Stake
NH Flat	0	0	0	0	0	0	0.0	0.00

Hurdles	6	17	1	1	1	14	5.9	0.00
Chases	0	0	0	0	0	0	0.0	0.00
Totals	**6**	**17**	**1**	**1**	**1**	**14**	**5.9**	**0.00**
16-17	10	30	0	1	2	27	0.0	-30.00
15-16	6	7	0	0	1	6	0.0	-7.00

JOCKEYS

	W-R	Per cent	£1 Level Stake
William Clarke	1-2	50.0	+15.00

COURSE RECORD

	Total W-R	Non-Hndcps Hurdles	Chases	Hndcps Hurdles	Chases	NH Flat	Per cent	£1 Level Stake
Plumpton	1-11	0-1	0-0	1-10	0-0	0-0	9.1	+6.00

WINNING HORSES

Horse	Races Run	1st	2nd	3rd	£
Cassivellaunus	6	1	0	0	3379
Total winning prize-money					£3379
Favourites	0-0	0.0%			0.00

JACKIE STEPHEN

INVERURIE, ABERDEENS

	No. of Hrs	Races Run	1st	2nd	3rd	Unpl	Per cent	£1 Level Stake
NH Flat	3	5	0	0	0	5	0.0	-5.00
Hurdles	8	19	0	2	2	15	0.0	-19.00
Chases	5	16	3	4	0	9	18.8	+1.50
Totals	**11**	**40**	**3**	**6**	**2**	**29**	**7.5**	**-22.50**
16-17	9	49	6	5	6	32	12.2	-6.25
15-16	7	32	2	2	8	20	6.3	-15.00

JOCKEYS

	W-R	Per cent	£1 Level Stake
Craig Nichol	2-9	22.2	-1.50
Ross Chapman	1-5	20.0	+5.00

COURSE RECORD

	Total W-R	Non-Hndcps Hurdles	Chases	Hndcps Hurdles	Chases	NH Flat	Per cent	£1 Level Stake
Perth	2-17	0-5	0-0	0-5	2-6	0-1	11.8	-9.50
Kelso	1-9	0-2	0-0	0-2	1-5	0-0	11.1	+1.00

WINNING HORSES

Horse	Races Run	1st	2nd	3rd	£
Bright Prospect	3	1	1	0	7928
Welcome Ben	5	2	2	0	7790
Total winning prize-money					£15718
Favourites	1-2	50.0%			0.50

ROBERT STEPHENS

PENHOW, NEWPORT

	No. of Hrs	Races Run	1st	2nd	3rd	Unpl	Per cent	£1 Level Stake
NH Flat	5	7	1	0	1	5	14.3	+4.00
Hurdles	24	60	3	8	5	44	5.0	-21.00
Chases	3	4	0	1	1	2	0.0	-4.00
Totals	28	71	4	9	7	51	5.6	-21.00
16-17	32	120	8	9	18	85	6.7	-51.38
15-16	27	85	7	16	11	51	8.2	-55.38

JOCKEYS

	W-R	Per cent	£1 Level Stake
Tom O'Brien	2-18	11.1	+2.00
Mr Craig Dowson	1-3	33.3	+10.00
Ciaran Gethings	1-15	6.7	+2.00

COURSE RECORD

	Total W-R	Non-Hndcps Hurdles	Chases	Hndcps Hurdles	Chases	NH Flat	Per cent	£1 Level Stake
Worcester	3-12	0-1	0-1	3-10	0-0	0-0	25.0	+27.00
Mrket Rsn	1-2	0-0	0-0	0-0	0-0	1-2	50.0	+9.00

WINNING HORSES

Horse	Races Run	1st	2nd	3rd	£
Mile House	2	1	1	0	5697
Three Colours Red	4	1	2	0	2599
*Balkinstown	8	1	0	3	2246
First Destination	1	1	0	0	1949
Total winning prize-money					**£12491**
Favourites	0-1		0.0%		**-1.00**

ALI STRONGE

EASTBURY, BERKS

	No. of Hrs	Races Run	1st	2nd	3rd	Unpl	Per cent	£1 Level Stake
NH Flat	3	7	0	2	1	4	0.0	-7.00
Hurdles	12	40	4	4	6	26	10.0	+5.00
Chases	3	10	2	1	3	4	20.0	-2.00
Totals	15	57	6	7	10	34	10.5	-4.00
16-17	21	62	5	6	7	44	8.1	-45.23
15-16	23	74	3	4	13	54	4.1	-49.00

JOCKEYS

	W-R	Per cent	£1 Level Stake
Andrew Tinkler	2-2	100.0	+25.00
Lorcan Murtagh	1-2	50.0	+3.00
Mr Joshua Newman	1-3	33.3	+2.00
Adam Wedge	1-13	7.7	-10.00
Brendan Powell	1-23	4.3	-10.00

COURSE RECORD

	Total W-R	Non-Hndcps Hurdles	Chases	Hndcps Hurdles	Chases	NH Flat	Per cent	£1 Level Stake
Chepstow	2-5	0-0	0-0	2-4	0-1	0-0	40.0	+22.00
Leicester	2-6	0-1	0-0	2-4	0-1	0-0	33.3	+12.00
Sedgefield	1-3	0-0	0-0	0-1	1-2	0-0	33.3	+2.00
Fakenham	1-4	0-1	0-0	0-1	1-2	0-0	25.0	-1.00

WINNING HORSES

Horse	Races Run	1st	2nd	3rd	£
Balgemmois	5	1	0	0	6330
Ardmayle	6	2	0	1	9682
Heresmynumber	7	2	1	2	8123
Drewmain Legend	5	1	1	1	3119
Total winning prize-money					**£27254**
Favourites	0-3		0.0%		**-3.00**

TOM SYMONDS

HAREWOOD END, H'FORDS

	No. of Hrs	Races Run	1st	2nd	3rd	Unpl	Per cent	£1 Level Stake
NH Flat	6	9	2	0	0	7	22.2	+53.00
Hurdles	24	87	6	6	5	70	6.9	-16.67
Chases	10	23	0	2	0	21	0.0	-23.00
Totals	30	119	8	8	5	98	6.7	+13.33
16-17	27	96	11	9	13	63	11.5	-21.90
15-16	34	99	9	6	14	70	9.1	-23.25

JOCKEYS

	W-R	Per cent	£1 Level Stake
Ben Poste	4-52	7.7	+16.33
James Davies	2-18	11.1	+12.00
Mr Alex Edwards	1-2	50.0	+19.00
Aidan Coleman	1-4	25.0	+9.00

COURSE RECORD

	Total W-R	Non-Hndcps Hurdles	Chases	Hndcps Hurdles	Chases	NH Flat	Per cent	£1 Level Stake
Hereford	3-6	1-1	0-0	2-3	0-1	0-1	50.0	+26.33
Carlisle	1-1	0-0	0-0	1-1	0-0	0-0	100.0	+3.00
Towcester	1-5	0-2	0-0	1-3	0-0	0-0	20.0	+3.00
Chepstow	1-7	0-3	0-0	0-3	0-0	1-1	14.3	+14.00
Warwick	1-7	0-0	0-0	1-6	0-1	0-0	14.3	+19.00
Ludlow	1-14	0-8	0-0	0-3	0-0	1-3	7.1	+27.00

WINNING HORSES

Horse	Races Run	1st	2nd	3rd	£
Royal Claret	5	1	0	1	6758
Bobo Mac	7	1	0	0	6498
Don Bersy	5	1	1	0	6238
Llantara	7	2	2	0	8577
Brushed Up	3	1	0	0	3899

Royale Zanzibar	3	1	0	0	3639
*Dramatic Pause	1	1	0	0	1949
Total winning prize-money					**£37558**
Favourites	**1-2**		**50.0%**		**2.00**

ROGER TEAL

GREAT SHEFFORD, BERKS

	No. of Hrs	Races Run	1st	2nd	3rd	Unpl	Per cent	£1 Level Stake
NH Flat	1	2	0	0	0	2	0.0	-2.00
Hurdles	8	24	3	0	4	17	12.5	+13.50
Chases	1	1	0	0	0	1	0.0	-1.00
Totals	9	27	3	0	4	20	11.1	+10.50
16-17	6	21	3	2	2	14	14.3	+10.00
15-16	7	15	1	0	2	12	6.7	-2.00

JOCKEYS

	W-R	Per cent	£1 Level Stake
Harry Teal	2-25	8.0	+6.50
Leighton Aspell	1-1	100.0	+5.00

COURSE RECORD

	Total W-R	Non-Hndcps Hurdles	Chases	Hndcps Hurdles	Chases	NH Flat	Per cent	£1 Level Stake
Worcester	2-7	0-3	0-0	2-4	0-0	0-0	28.6	+24.50
Wincanton	1-4	0-0	0-0	1-4	0-0	0-0	25.0	+2.00

WINNING HORSES

Horse	Races Run	1st	2nd	3rd	£
Stonemadforspeed	8	2	0	4	7278
Howaboutnever	6	1	0	0	2274
Total winning prize-money					**£9552**
Favourites	0-0		0.0%		0.00

SAM THOMAS

NORTHLEACH, GLOUCS

	No. of Hrs	Races Run	1st	2nd	3rd	Unpl	Per cent	£1 Level Stake
NH Flat	14	25	1	1	5	18	4.0	-15.50
Hurdles	17	42	6	4	2	30	14.3	+67.13
Chases	7	13	0	3	4	6	0.0	-13.00
Totals	28	80	7	8	11	54	8.8	+38.63
16-17	16	58	4	5	4	45	6.9	-33.38
15-16	11	31	0	1	6	24	0.0	-31.00

JOCKEYS

	W-R	Per cent	£1 Level Stake
Adam Nicol	3-12	25.0	-2.88
Charlie Deutsch	2-22	9.1	+11.00
A P Heskin	1-3	33.3	+64.00
James Davies	1-11	9.1	-1.50

COURSE RECORD

	Total W-R	Non-Hndcps Hurdles	Chases	Hndcps Hurdles	Chases	NH Flat	Per cent	£1 Level Stake
Carlisle	1-2	0-0	0-0	0-0	0-0	1-2	50.0	+7.50
Exeter	1-2	1-1	0-0	0-0	0-0	0-1	50.0	+2.00
Towcester	1-2	1-2	0-0	0-0	0-0	0-0	50.0	+65.00
Ffos Las	1-3	0-0	0-0	1-2	0-1	0-0	33.3	-0.38
Fontwell	1-8	0-3	0-0	1-1	0-0	0-4	12.5	-4.25
Southwell	1-8	0-1	0-1	1-5	0-0	0-1	12.5	-5.25
Huntingdon	1-10	1-4	0-0	0-3	0-1	0-2	10.0	+19.00

WINNING HORSES

Horse	Races Run	1st	2nd	3rd	£
Royal Magic	4	1	0	0	3899
The Cannister Man	5	1	1	0	3249
Sparkleandshine	1	1	0	0	3249
Glentrool	4	1	0	2	2599
Powderonthebonnet	3	1	1	0	2599
Lovely Touch	3	2	1	0	5198
Total winning prize-money					**£20793**
Favourites	2-5		40.0%		0.38

MISS L THOMAS

WROUGHTON, OXON

	No. of Hrs	Races Run	1st	2nd	3rd	Unpl	Per cent	£1 Level Stake
NH Flat	0	0	0	0	0	0	0.0	0.00
Hurdles	0	0	0	0	0	0	0.0	0.00
Chases	2	4	2	1	1	0	50.0	+1.88
Totals	2	4	2	1	1	0	50.0	+1.88
16-17	1	1	1	0	0	0	100.0	+7.00
15-16	2	3	1	0	0	2	33.3	+6.00

JOCKEYS

	W-R	Per cent	£1 Level Stake
Mr Zac Baker	1-1	100.0	+1.63
Mr Jonathan Bailey	1-3	33.3	+0.25

COURSE RECORD

	Total W-R	Non-Hndcps Hurdles	Chases	Hndcps Hurdles	Chases	NH Flat	Per cent	£1 Level Stake
Cheltenham	1-1	0-0	1-1	0-0	0-0	0-0	100.0	+2.25
Ludlow	1-1	0-0	1-1	0-0	0-0	0-0	100.0	+1.63

WINNING HORSES

Horse	Races Run	1st	2nd	3rd	£
Full Trottle	3	2	1	0	5459
Total winning prize-money					**£5459**
Favourites	1-1		100.0%		1.63

DAVID THOMPSON

BOLAM, CO DURHAM

	No. of Hrs	Races Run	1st	2nd	3rd	Unpl	Per cent	£1 Level Stake
NH Flat	0	0	0	0	0	0	0.0	0.00
Hurdles	11	28	0	1	2	25	0.0	-28.00
Chases	4	24	1	7	2	14	4.2	-14.00
Totals	12	52	1	8	4	39	1.9	-42.00
16-17	14	74	5	5	4	59	6.8	-35.17
15-16	18	67	5	8	7	47	7.5	+7.75

JOCKEYS

	W-R	Per cent	£1 Level Stake
Joe Colliver	1-5	20.0	+5.00

COURSE RECORD

	Total W-R	Non-Hndcps Hurdles	Chases	Hndcps Hurdles	Chases	NH Flat	Per cent	£1 Level Stake
Southwell	1-13	0-0	0-0	0-7	1-6	0-0	7.7	-3.00

WINNING HORSES

Horse	Races Run	1st	2nd	3rd	£
Roman Numeral	16	1	3	1	3574
Total winning prize-money					£3574
Favourites	0-0		0.0%		0.00

VICTOR THOMPSON

ALNWICK, NORTHUMBRIA

	No. of Hrs	Races Run	1st	2nd	3rd	Unpl	Per cent	£1 Level Stake
NH Flat	0	0	0	0	0	0	0.0	0.00
Hurdles	7	48	2	5	3	38	4.2	-6.50
Chases	12	57	1	1	6	49	1.8	-54.50
Totals	17	105	3	6	9	87	2.9	-61.00
16-17	18	80	7	4	8	61	8.8	-20.50
15-16	17	102	6	6	16	74	5.9	-70.75

JOCKEYS

	W-R	Per cent	£1 Level Stake
Thomas Dowson	3-44	6.8	0.00

COURSE RECORD

	Total W-R	Non-Hndcps Hurdles	Chases	Hndcps Hurdles	Chases	NH Flat	Per cent	£1 Level Stake
Hexham	2-16	1-6	0-1	0-3	1-6	0-0	12.5	+20.50
Sedgefield	1-28	0-4	0-2	1-7	0-15	0-0	3.6	-20.50

WINNING HORSES

Horse	Races Run	1st	2nd	3rd	£
Nelly La Rue	14	1	1	2	6059

*Pc Dixon	13	1	4	2	4809
Dolly's Dot	8	1	1	0	3119
Total winning prize-money					£13987
Favourites	1-1		100.0%		1.50

SANDY THOMSON

LAMBDEN, BERWICKS

	No. of Hrs	Races Run	1st	2nd	3rd	Unpl	Per cent	£1 Level Stake
NH Flat	2	2	0	0	0	2	0.0	-2.00
Hurdles	18	59	8	11	9	31	13.6	-15.02
Chases	11	29	5	1	5	18	17.2	+23.25
Totals	26	90	13	12	14	51	14.4	+6.23
16-17	23	102	19	20	7	56	18.6	+45.63
15-16	28	99	16	13	20	50	16.2	-31.13

BY MONTH

NH Flat	W-R	Per cent	£1 Level Stake	Hurdles	W-R	Per cent	£1 Level Stake
May	0-0	0.0	0.00	May	0-1	0.0	-1.00
June	0-0	0.0	0.00	June	0-0	0.0	0.00
July	0-0	0.0	0.00	July	0-0	0.0	0.00
August	0-0	0.0	0.00	August	0-0	0.0	0.00
September	0-0	0.0	0.00	September	0-3	0.0	-3.00
October	0-0	0.0	0.00	October	2-6	33.3	+1.23
November	0-0	0.0	0.00	November	0-6	0.0	-6.00
December	0-1	0.0	-1.00	December	3-9	33.3	+14.75
January	0-0	0.0	0.00	January	2-14	14.3	-3.75
February	0-0	0.0	0.00	February	1-8	12.5	-5.25
March	0-0	0.0	0.00	March	0-7	0.0	-7.00
April	0-1	0.0	-1.00	April	0-5	0.0	-5.00

Chases	W-R	Per cent	£1 Level Stake	Totals	W-R	Per cent	£1 Level Stake
May	0-2	0.0	-2.00	May	0-3	0.0	-3.00
June	0-0	0.0	0.00	June	0-0	0.0	0.00
July	0-0	0.0	0.00	July	0-0	0.0	0.00
August	0-0	0.0	0.00	August	0-0	0.0	0.00
September	0-0	0.0	0.00	September	0-3	0.0	-3.00
October	1-4	25.0	+6.00	October	3-10	30.0	+7.23
November	3-5	60.0	+26.25	November	3-11	27.3	+20.25
December	0-2	0.0	-2.00	December	3-12	25.0	+11.75
January	0-1	0.0	-1.00	January	2-15	13.3	-4.75
February	1-4	25.0	+7.00	February	2-12	16.7	+1.75
March	0-3	0.0	-3.00	March	0-10	0.0	-10.00
April	0-8	0.0	-8.00	April	0-14	0.0	-14.00

DISTANCE

Hurdles	W-R	Per cent	£1 Level Stake	Chases	W-R	Per cent	£1 Level Stake
2m-2m3f	6-29	20.7	+2.98	2m-2m3f	2-4	50.0	+8.88
2m4f-2m7f	2-19	10.5	-7.00	2m4f-2m7f	0-9	0.0	-9.00
3m+	0-11	0.0	-11.00	3m+	3-16	18.8	+23.38

TYPE OF RACE

Non-Handicaps				Handicaps			
	W-R	Per cent	£1 Level Stake		W-R	Per cent	£1 Level Stake
Nov Hrdls	2-18	11.1	-1.27	Nov Hrdls	1-1	100.0	+1.75
Hrdls	2-8	25.0	+2.25	Hrdls	3-32	9.4	-17.75
Nov Chs	0-3	0.0	-3.00	Nov Chs	0-0	0.0	0.00
Chases	0-2	0.0	-2.00	Chases	5-22	22.7	+30.25
Sell/Claim	0-0	0.0	0.00	Sell/Claim	0-0	0.0	0.00

RACE CLASS

	W-R	Per cent	£1 Level Stake
Class 1	0-4	0.0	-4.00
Class 2	1-12	8.3	-1.00
Class 3	2-16	12.5	+15.00
Class 4	7-48	14.6	-14.02
Class 5	3-9	33.3	+11.25
Class 6	0-1	0.0	-1.00

JOCKEYS

	W-R	Per cent	£1 Level Stake
Rachael McDonald	6-44	13.6	+13.25
Danny Cook	2-8	25.0	+13.50
Jamie Hamilton	2-8	25.0	-1.50
Robert Hogg	1-2	50.0	+3.50
Henry Brooke	1-3	33.3	+0.75
Brian Hughes	1-9	11.1	-7.27

COURSE RECORD

	Total W-R	Non-Hndcps Hurdles	Chases	Hndcps Hurdles	Chases	NH Flat	Per cent	£1 Level Stake
Musselbgh	7-25	1-4	0-0	3-14	3-7	0-0	28.0	+17.75
Carlisle	2-8	1-3	0-0	0-2	1-2	0-1	25.0	+19.73
Ayr	2-15	2-7	0-0	0-4	0-3	0-1	13.3	-4.75
Hexham	1-4	0-1	0-0	0-1	1-2	0-0	25.0	+6.00
Kelso	1-19	0-5	0-2	1-8	0-4	0-0	5.3	-13.50

WINNING HORSES

Horse	Races Run	1st	2nd	3rd	£
*Full Jack	2	1	0	1	25117
Harry The Viking	4	1	0	1	15640
Buckled	5	2	1	1	9747
Nendrum	7	2	1	1	9292
Blue Kascade	3	1	0	0	5198
John Williams	6	2	1	0	7798
Donna's Delight	5	1	2	1	4224
Ballycrystal Court	4	1	0	0	3249
Caventara	2	1	0	1	3119
Mcgowan's Pass	5	1	0	1	2599
Total winning prize-money					**£85983**
Favourites	5-15		**33.3%**		**-1.52**

COLIN TIZZARD

MILBORNE PORT, DORSET

	No. of Hrs	Races Run	1st	2nd	3rd	Unpl	Per cent	£1 Level Stake
NH Flat	26	37	2	2	6	27	5.4	-30.75
Hurdles	65	243	40	38	27	138	16.5	-39.71
Chases	56	256	37	42	48	129	14.5	-88.89
Totals	111	536	79	82	81	294	14.7	-159.35
16-17	86	402	57	64	54	227	14.2	+11.75
15-16	58	323	50	39	52	182	15.5	-46.75

BY MONTH

NH Flat	W-R	Per cent	£1 Level Stake	Hurdles	W-R	Per cent	£1 Level Stake
May	0-1	0.0	-1.00	May	1-2	50.0	+1.00
June	0-0	0.0	0.00	June	1-2	50.0	-0.39
July	0-0	0.0	0.00	July	0-2	0.0	-2.00
August	0-0	0.0	0.00	August	0-0	0.0	0.00
September	0-0	0.0	0.00	September	0-3	0.0	-3.00
October	1-7	14.3	-4.75	October	8-36	22.2	-5.31
November	0-2	0.0	-2.00	November	8-43	18.6	-7.05
December	0-3	0.0	-3.00	December	6-38	15.8	-8.00
January	0-4	0.0	-4.00	January	1-21	4.8	-18.13
February	1-9	11.1	-5.00	February	7-29	24.1	+1.68
March	0-4	0.0	-4.00	March	7-32	21.9	+32.48
April	0-7	0.0	-7.00	April	1-35	2.9	-31.00

Chases	W-R	Per cent	£1 Level Stake	Totals	W-R	Per cent	£1 Level Stake
May	1-3	33.3	-0.25	May	2-6	33.3	-0.25
June	0-3	0.0	-3.00	June	1-5	20.0	-3.39
July	1-6	16.7	+7.00	July	1-8	12.5	+5.00
August	0-5	0.0	-5.00	August	0-5	0.0	-5.00
September	0-3	0.0	-3.00	September	0-6	0.0	-6.00
October	4-38	10.5	-28.92	October	13-81	16.0	-38.98
November	6-46	13.0	-28.17	November	14-91	15.4	-37.22
December	5-33	15.2	-15.13	December	11-74	14.9	-26.13
January	3-25	12.0	-11.75	January	4-50	8.0	-33.88
February	7-24	29.2	+10.82	February	15-62	24.2	+7.50
March	5-36	13.9	-10.50	March	12-72	16.7	+17.98
April	5-34	14.7	-1.00	April	6-76	7.9	-39.00

DISTANCE

Hurdles	W-R	Per cent	£1 Level Stake	Chases	W-R	Per cent	£1 Level Stake
2m-2m3f	26-136	19.1	-25.02	2m-2m3f	10-57	17.5	-23.82
2m4f-2m7f	11-81	13.6	-34.69	2m4f-2m7f	14-94	14.9	-21.24
3m+	3-25	12.0	+21.00	3m+	13-105	12.4	-43.83

TYPE OF RACE

Non-Handicaps				Handicaps			
	W-R	Per cent	£1 Level Stake		W-R	Per cent	£1 Level Stake
Nov Hrdls	20-97	20.6	+3.09	Nov Hrdls	1-12	8.3	-8.00
Hrdls	6-29	20.7	-7.18	Hrdls	13-105	12.4	-27.63
Nov Chs	8-49	16.3	-24.38	Nov Chs	3-13	23.1	+0.50

FIRST TIME OUT

	W-R	Per cent	£1 Level Stake
Bumpers	0-2	0.0	-2.00
Hurdles	1-15	6.7	-13.27
Chases	1-9	11.1	+17.00
Totals	2-26	7.7	+1.73

Chases	4-18	22.2	-6.81	Chases	20-155	12.9	-56.20
Sell/Claim	0-0	0.0	0.00	Sell/Claim	0-0	0.0	0.00

RACE CLASS

	W-R	Per cent	£1 Level Stake
Class 1	14-107	13.1	-4.02
Class 2	6-54	11.1	-31.05
Class 3	20-130	15.4	-35.97
Class 4	34-195	17.4	-59.32
Class 5	4-43	9.3	-24.25
Class 6	1-7	14.3	-4.75

FIRST TIME OUT

	W-R	Per cent	£1 Level Stake
Bumpers	2-26	7.7	-19.75
Hurdles	6-39	15.4	-18.18
Chases	8-46	17.4	-27.39
Totals	16-111	14.4	-65.32

JOCKEYS

	W-R	Per cent	£1 Level Stake
Harry Cobden	40-202	19.8	+29.66
Tom Scudamore	11-67	16.4	-17.89
Robbie Power	10-57	17.5	-24.68
Paddy Brennan	4-30	13.3	-9.25
B J Cooper	4-39	10.3	-30.96
Richard Johnson	3-10	30.0	-0.02
Mitchell Bastyan	3-14	21.4	-4.13
James Bowen	2-14	14.3	-6.75
Tom O'Brien	2-40	5.0	-32.33

COURSE RECORD

	Total W-R	Non-Hndcps Hurdles	Chases	Hndcps Hurdles	Chases	NH Flat	Per cent	£1 Level Stake
Wincanton	14-75	4-14	0-3	3-24	7-24	0-10	18.7	-17.61
Exeter	9-44	4-14	3-6	1-11	1-11	0-2	20.5	-15.71
Cheltenham	9-61	4-15	4-15	0-6	1-21	0-4	14.8	-1.79
Fontwell	8-28	1-3	0-0	3-9	3-14	1-2	28.6	+2.91
Taunton	7-41	3-12	0-1	2-13	2-14	0-1	17.1	-1.10
Newbury	5-19	1-8	2-4	1-1	1-5	0-1	26.3	+5.98
Chepstow	5-46	2-10	1-3	0-10	2-16	0-7	10.9	-29.42
Ludlow	3-14	3-5	0-0	0-2	0-7	0-0	21.4	-7.48
Plumpton	3-22	1-8	0-1	0-7	2-6	0-0	13.6	-10.50
Nton Abbot	3-27	1-7	0-4	1-7	1-9	0-0	11.1	-18.13
Southwell	2-4	0-0	0-0	2-2	0-1	0-1	50.0	+8.00
Kempton	2-20	1-7	0-4	1-4	0-4	0-1	10.0	+4.00
Aintree	2-21	0-5	1-5	0-2	1-9	0-0	9.5	-2.50
Sandown	2-22	1-5	0-3	0-2	1-12	0-0	9.1	-12.75
Lingfield	1-4	0-1	0-0	0-0	1-3	0-0	25.0	-0.75
Ffos Las	1-4	0-1	1-1	0-0	0-1	0-1	25.0	-1.25
Haydock	1-7	0-1	0-1	0-2	1-3	0-0	14.3	+0.50
Uttoxeter	1-7	0-0	0-2	0-0	1-5	0-0	14.3	+6.00
Worcester	1-8	0-0	0-4	0-1	0-1	1-2	12.5	-5.75

WINNING HORSES

Horse	Races Run	1st	2nd	3rd	£
Native River	2	2	0	0	398297
Ultragold	6	1	1	1	78582
Kilbricken Storm	5	3	0	2	77600
Finian's Oscar	7	3	1	1	87742
The Dutchman	5	1	1	0	42914
Tempestatefloresco	7	4	1	0	57658
Fox Norton	3	1	1	0	42713

Robinsfirth	3	1	1	0	25628
Elegant Escape	7	2	3	2	35560
Silverhow	7	2	2	1	31391
Sizing Tennessee	8	1	2	2	17373
Slate House	6	2	0	0	23341
West Approach	7	2	0	2	25122
Grand Vision	5	2	1	0	22931
Vision Des Flos	6	1	2	1	14238
Valhalla	7	2	0	3	20673
Sizing Granite	4	1	0	1	9747
*Padleyourowncanoe	6	2	1	0	11495
Molineaux	9	2	3	2	11566
Bally Longford	5	1	0	1	7153
Muffins For Tea	8	2	2	3	11469
Bears Rails	8	1	2	0	6758
Buckhorn Timothy	3	2	0	0	12346
Cucklington	9	4	2	1	20599
On Demand	8	1	0	3	6498
Lostintranslation	6	1	3	0	6498
Ainchea	4	1	2	0	6498
Kings Walk	3	1	0	1	6498
Sizing Platinum	5	1	1	1	6393
Fourth Act	6	1	0	1	6077
Storm Home	6	2	1	0	9682
Kalarika	7	1	1	0	5458
The Russian Doyen	6	2	1	1	10249
Bramble Brook	9	2	2	3	9902
Drinks Interval	8	2	0	2	9097
Wizards Bridge	7	3	0	1	13126
White Moon	3	2	0	0	7473
Leg Lock Luke	5	1	0	2	4549
New To This Town	2	1	1	0	4549
Golden Sunrise	7	1	2	2	4224
Brynmawr	5	1	2	0	4094
*Dinos Benefit	3	1	0	2	4094
Quiz Master	9	1	4	1	4094
Mister Malarky	7	1	1	2	3899
Battle Of Ideas	7	1	0	2	3899
Shoal Bay	6	2	1	0	5588
Flaming Charmer	6	1	0	0	3899
Ivor's Queen	10	1	1	2	3899
Queen Of The Wind	7	1	0	0	3119
Jaytrack Parkhomes	2	1	0	0	2274
Total winning prize-money					**£1248526**

Favourites	28-72		38.9%		-4.45

MARTIN TODHUNTER

ORTON, CUMBRIA

	No. of Hrs	Races Run	1st	2nd	3rd	Unpl	Per cent	£1 Level Stake
NH Flat	3	4	0	0	0	4	0.0	-4.00
Hurdles	13	42	5	6	3	28	11.9	-18.50
Chases	11	31	7	5	3	16	22.6	-5.63
Totals	23	77	12	11	6	48	15.6	-28.13
16-17	23	122	8	22	19	73	6.6	-59.00
15-16	22	124	9	10	17	88	7.3	-69.38

BY MONTH

NH Flat	W-R	Per cent	£1 Level Stake	Hurdles	W-R	Per cent	£1 Level Stake
May	0-0	0.0	0.00	May	1-4	25.0	+5.00
June	0-0	0.0	0.00	June	0-3	0.0	-3.00
July	0-0	0.0	0.00	July	1-3	33.3	+2.50
August	0-0	0.0	0.00	August	0-3	0.0	-3.00
September	0-0	0.0	0.00	September	1-6	16.7	-2.75
October	0-0	0.0	0.00	October	0-3	0.0	-3.00
November	0-1	0.0	-1.00	November	0-6	0.0	-6.00
December	0-0	0.0	0.00	December	0-1	0.0	-1.00
January	0-0	0.0	0.00	January	0-3	0.0	-3.00
February	0-2	0.0	-2.00	February	2-2	100.0	+3.75
March	0-1	0.0	-1.00	March	0-4	0.0	-4.00
April	0-0	0.0	0.00	April	0-4	0.0	-4.00

Chases	W-R	Per cent	£1 Level Stake	Totals	W-R	Per cent	£1 Level Stake
May	1-6	16.7	-3.13	May	2-10	20.0	+1.87
June	0-5	0.0	-5.00	June	0-8	0.0	-8.00
July	2-2	100.0	+4.50	July	3-5	60.0	+7.00
August	1-2	50.0	+1.50	August	1-5	20.0	-1.50
September	1-3	33.3	+0.25	September	2-9	22.2	-2.50
October	0-3	0.0	-3.00	October	0-6	0.0	-6.00
November	0-0	0.0	0.00	November	0-7	0.0	-7.00
December	1-2	50.0	+1.75	December	1-3	33.3	+0.75
January	0-0	0.0	0.00	January	0-3	0.0	-3.00
February	0-0	0.0	0.00	February	2-4	50.0	+1.75
March	1-2	50.0	+3.50	March	1-7	14.3	-1.50
April	0-6	0.0	-6.00	April	0-10	0.0	-10.00

DISTANCE

Hurdles	W-R	Per cent	£1 Level Stake	Chases	W-R	Per cent	£1 Level Stake
2m-2m3f	2-22	9.1	-15.75	2m-2m3f	4-14	28.6	-1.38
2m4f-2m7f	2-17	11.8	-5.25	2m4f-2m7f	1-13	7.7	-7.50
3m+	1-3	33.3	+2.50	3m+	2-4	50.0	+3.25

TYPE OF RACE

Non-Handicaps

	W-R	Per cent	£1 Level Stake
Nov Hrdls	1-11	9.1	-7.75
Hrdls	1-2	50.0	+7.00
Nov Chs	1-2	50.0	+0.88
Chases	0-0	0.0	0.00
Sell/Claim	0-0	0.0	0.00

Handicaps

	W-R	Per cent	£1 Level Stake
Nov Hrdls	0-0	0.0	0.00
Hrdls	3-29	10.3	-17.75
Nov Chs	1-6	16.7	-0.50
Chases	5-22	22.7	-5.00
Sell/Claim	0-0	0.0	0.00

RACE CLASS

	W-R	Per cent	£1 Level Stake
Class 1	0-2	0.0	-2.00
Class 2	1-3	33.3	+0.50
Class 3	3-12	25.0	-3.00
Class 4	6-38	15.8	-13.63
Class 5	2-21	9.5	-9.00
Class 6	0-1	0.0	-1.00

FIRST TIME OUT

	W-R	Per cent	£1 Level Stake
Bumpers	0-3	0.0	-3.00
Hurdles	3-13	23.1	+2.25
Chases	2-7	28.6	-0.88
Totals	5-23	21.7	-1.63

JOCKEYS

	W-R	Per cent	£1 Level Stake
Henry Brooke	8-42	19.0	-7.63
Ross Chapman	4-20	20.0	-5.50

COURSE RECORD

	Total W-R	Non-Hndcps Hurdles	Non-Hndcps Chases	Hndcps Hurdles	Hndcps Chases	NH Flat	Per cent	£1 Level Stake
Cartmel	5-16	0-0	1-1	1-8	3-7	0-0	31.3	+2.38
Hexham	2-13	2-5	0-1	0-2	0-5	0-0	15.4	-0.75
Doncaster	1-1	0-0	0-0	0-0	1-1	0-0	100.0	+2.75
Mrket Rsn	1-1	0-0	0-0	0-0	1-1	0-0	100.0	+4.50
Ayr	1-4	0-0	0-0	1-2	0-2	0-0	25.0	-1.25
Newcastle	1-4	0-1	0-0	1-3	0-0	0-0	25.0	-1.00
Perth	1-6	0-1	0-0	0-2	1-3	0-0	16.7	-2.75

WINNING HORSES

Horse	Races Run	1st	2nd	3rd	£
Wisty	5	3	0	0	23651
Monbeg River	5	1	2	0	8839
Bulls Head	3	2	1	0	11177
Bocasien Desbois	5	1	1	0	4614
Presenting Junior	4	1	1	0	3899
Landmeafortune	2	1	0	0	3833
Sophie Olivia	3	1	1	0	3482
Pretty Miss Mahler	6	1	1	2	3249
Talkofgold	4	1	1	1	2924
Total winning prize-money					**£65668**
Favourites	2-6	33.3%			-0.50

J W TUDOR

PENCOED, VALE OF GLAMORGAN

	No. of Hrs	Races Run	1st	2nd	3rd	Unpl	Per cent	£1 Level Stake
NH Flat	1	1	1	0	0	0	100.0	+9.00
Hurdles	0	0	0	0	0	0	0.0	0.00
Chases	3	6	0	0	0	6	0.0	-6.00
Totals	4	7	1	0	0	6	14.3	+3.00
16-17	3	5	1	0	3	1	20.0	0.00
15-16	6	6	0	2	0	4	0.0	-6.00

JOCKEYS

	W-R	Per cent	£1 Level Stake
Mr Connor Brace	1-1	100.0	+9.00

COURSE RECORD

	Total W-R	Non-Hndcps Hurdles	Non-Hndcps Chases	Hndcps Hurdles	Hndcps Chases	NH Flat	Per cent	£1 Level Stake
Exeter	1-1	0-0	0-0	0-0	0-0	1-1	100.0	+9.00

WINNING HORSES

Horse	Races Run	1st	2nd	3rd	£
*Billygwyn Too	1	1	0	0	3249
Total winning prize-money					£3249
Favourites	0-0	0.0%			0.00

BILL TURNER

SIGWELLS, SOMERSET

	No. of Hrs	Races Run	1st	2nd	3rd	Unpl	Per cent	£1 Level Stake
NH Flat	3	10	0	2	1	7	0.0	-10.00
Hurdles	6	30	3	5	2	20	10.0	-10.80
Chases	1	1	0	0	0	1	0.0	-1.00
Totals	9	41	3	7	3	28	7.3	-21.80
16-17	8	24	0	2	1	21	0.0	-24.00
15-16	11	31	2	2	3	24	6.5	-21.75

JOCKEYS

	W-R	Per cent	£1 Level Stake
Sean Houlihan	2-10	20.0	-3.80
James Davies	1-13	7.7	0.00

COURSE RECORD

	Total W-R	Non-Hndcps Hurdles	Chases	Hndcps Hurdles	Chases	NH Flat	Per cent	£1 Level Stake
Sandown	1-1	1-1	0-0	0-0	0-0	0-0	100.0	+3.00
Uttoxeter	1-1	1-1	0-0	0-0	0-0	0-0	100.0	+12.00
Mrket Rsn	1-2	1-2	0-0	0-0	0-0	0-0	50.0	+0.20

WINNING HORSES

Horse	Races Run	1st	2nd	3rd	£
Crucial Moment	6	3	1	1	13205
Total winning prize-money					£13205
Favourites	1-1	100.0%			1.20

NIGEL TWISTON-DAVIES

NAUNTON, GLOUCS

	No. of Hrs	Races Run	1st	2nd	3rd	Unpl	Per cent	£1 Level Stake
NH Flat	37	59	10	7	12	30	16.9	-3.40
Hurdles	73	219	31	26	24	138	14.2	-74.68
Chases	51	249	39	38	24	148	15.7	-24.91
Totals	128	527	80	71	60	316	15.2	-102.99
16-17	108	583	95	97	84	306	16.3	-119.54
15-16	110	482	71	62	45	304	14.7	-83.55

BY MONTH

NH Flat	W-R	Per cent	£1 Level Stake	Hurdles	W-R	Per cent	£1 Level Stake
May	0-3	0.0	-3.00	May	1-12	8.3	-3.00
June	0-2	0.0	-2.00	June	0-7	0.0	-7.00
July	0-0	0.0	0.00	July	0-9	0.0	-9.00
August	0-0	0.0	0.00	August	0-1	0.0	-1.00
September	0-1	0.0	-1.00	September	1-8	12.5	-6.60
October	2-6	33.3	+14.50	October	5-27	18.5	-9.68
November	2-9	22.2	+7.00	November	6-30	20.0	-10.13
December	1-10	10.0	-7.00	December	3-26	11.5	-11.63
January	2-7	28.6	-2.40	January	3-25	12.0	-12.75
February	0-8	0.0	-8.00	February	4-23	17.4	-1.14
March	3-5	60.0	+6.50	March	2-21	9.5	+2.38
April	0-8	0.0	-8.00	April	6-30	20.0	-5.15

Chases	W-R	Per cent	£1 Level Stake	Totals	W-R	Per cent	£1 Level Stake
May	2-12	16.7	-3.25	May	3-27	11.1	-9.25
June	1-5	20.0	+1.00	June	1-14	7.1	-8.00
July	2-6	33.3	-0.63	July	2-15	13.3	-9.63
August	1-3	33.3	-0.25	August	1-4	25.0	-1.25
September	5-8	62.5	+14.86	September	6-17	35.3	+7.26
October	4-31	12.9	-5.75	October	11-64	17.2	-0.93
November	8-37	21.6	+15.23	November	16-76	21.1	+12.10
December	5-39	12.8	-7.50	December	9-75	12.0	-26.13
January	2-31	6.5	-16.50	January	7-63	11.1	-31.65
February	4-21	19.0	+13.00	February	8-52	15.4	+3.86
March	1-25	4.0	-21.00	March	6-51	11.8	-12.12
April	4-31	12.9	-14.13	April	10-69	14.5	-27.28

DISTANCE

Hurdles	W-R	Per cent	£1 Level Stake	Chases	W-R	Per cent	£1 Level Stake
2m-2m3f	13-79	16.5	-10.51	2m-2m3f	10-41	24.4	-0.75
2m4f-2m7f	11-98	11.2	-49.00	2m4f-2m7f	12-74	16.2	+12.74
3m+	6-40	15.0	-14.67	3m+	17-134	12.7	-36.90

TYPE OF RACE

Non-Handicaps	W-R	Per cent	£1 Level Stake	Handicaps	W-R	Per cent	£1 Level Stake
Nov Hrdls	13-64	20.3	-23.92	Nov Hrdls	0-6	0.0	-6.00
Hrdls	4-44	9.1	-29.25	Hrdls	12-98	12.2	-17.38
Nov Chs	4-23	17.4	-12.39	Nov Chs	1-9	11.1	-5.50
Chases	2-12	16.7	-2.90	Chases	28-181	15.5	+2.38
Sell/Claim	0-4	0.0	-4.00	Sell/Claim	0-1	0.0	-1.00

RACE CLASS

	W-R	Per cent	£1 Level Stake
Class 1	11-99	11.1	-8.67
Class 2	14-80	17.5	+1.75
Class 3	22-112	19.6	-16.06
Class 4	23-159	14.5	-58.61
Class 5	6-57	10.5	-31.90
Class 6	4-20	20.0	+10.50

FIRST TIME OUT

	W-R	Per cent	£1 Level Stake
Bumpers	6-37	16.2	+5.00
Hurdles	7-48	14.6	-15.48
Chases	10-43	23.3	+8.12
Totals	23-128	18.0	-2.36

JOCKEYS

	W-R	Per cent	£1 Level Stake
Sam Twiston-Davies	26-170	15.3	-49.78
Jamie Bargary	17-151	11.3	-18.13

Daryl Jacob	13-44	29.5	+9.80
Mr Zac Baker	7-32	21.9	+7.63
Tom Bellamy	5-30	16.7	+8.74
Mark Grant	3-20	15.0	-9.13
Tom Humphries	3-28	10.7	-16.38
Jack Savage	2-10	20.0	-4.50
Jonathan Burke	1-1	100.0	+2.50
Gavin Sheehan	1-3	33.3	-0.25
Davy Russell	1-5	20.0	-3.50
Mr Jordan Nailor	1-9	11.1	-6.00

COURSE RECORD

	Total W-R	Non-Hndcps Hurdles	Chases	Hndcps Hurdles	Chases	NH Flat	Per cent	£1 Level Stake
Cheltenham	7-63	2-13	0-10	1-9	4-27	0-4	11.1	+1.45
Perth	6-17	3-5	1-1	1-4	1-6	0-1	35.3	+0.74
Ffos Las	6-31	3-9	0-2	1-8	1-8	1-4	19.4	-1.88
Sandown	5-20	0-3	0-0	2-3	3-14	0-0	25.0	+31.00
Warwick	5-31	0-6	0-1	1-5	2-11	2-8	16.1	-4.25
Bangor	4-13	1-7	0-0	0-0	0-2	3-4	30.8	+12.88
Haydock	4-24	3-5	1-1	0-6	0-11	0-1	16.7	-10.53
Uttoxeter	4-32	1-5	0-1	0-10	3-14	0-2	12.5	-17.89
Leicester	3-6	0-0	0-0	2-2	1-4	0-0	50.0	+18.00
Exeter	3-11	0-0	1-1	0-2	1-6	1-2	27.3	+0.25
Wetherby	3-12	0-4	2-3	0-1	0-3	1-1	25.0	0.00
Mrket Rsn	3-14	0-1	0-0	1-6	2-5	0-2	21.4	+2.38
Kempton	3-16	0-2	0-3	0-2	3-8	0-1	18.8	-4.25
Worcester	3-22	0-4	1-2	1-9	1-5	0-2	13.6	-13.75
Ludlow	3-27	0-8	0-1	0-3	3-12	0-3	11.1	-17.38
Carlisle	2-4	2-2	0-0	0-0	0-2	0-0	50.0	+2.38
Lingfield	2-7	1-2	0-0	0-2	1-3	0-0	28.6	-1.00
Stratford	2-10	0-1	0-0	1-6	1-3	0-0	20.0	-3.88
Southwell	2-14	0-7	0-0	1-3	1-2	0-2	14.3	-0.50
Chepstow	2-19	0-4	0-1	0-2	0-8	2-4	10.5	-9.90
Musselbgh	1-2	0-0	0-0	1-1	0-1	0-0	50.0	+4.00
Taunton	1-2	0-0	0-0	0-0	1-2	0-0	50.0	+2.50
Fakenham	1-7	0-2	0-0	0-1	1-3	0-1	14.3	-4.13
Nton Abbot	1-9	1-2	0-2	0-2	0-2	0-1	11.1	-3.00
Doncaster	1-12	0-4	0-0	0-0	1-6	0-2	8.3	+3.00
Ascot	1-13	1-3	0-1	0-3	0-5	0-1	7.7	-8.50
Huntingdon	1-15	0-5	0-0	0-5	1-4	0-1	6.7	-9.50
Aintree	1-21	0-3	0-2	0-2	1-13	0-1	4.8	-18.25

WINNING HORSES

Horse	Races Run	1st	2nd	3rd	£
Bristol De Mai	5	2	1	1	170290
Splash Of Ginge	6	1	1	0	91120
Blaklion	5	1	2	0	81443
Ballymoy	5	3	0	1	70087
The New One	7	2	2	0	70969
Ballyhill	8	1	1	1	42713
Mr Antolini	4	2	2	0	48640
Foxtail Hill	6	1	0	0	31280
Cogry	7	1	1	1	31280
Benbens	7	1	0	0	30950
Ballybolley	7	1	0	2	28475
Wholestone	8	1	3	2	28475
Tintern Theatre	9	1	1	0	25024
Ballyoptic	7	2	2	0	34490
Colin's Brother	5	2	1	0	26041
Arthur's Gift	9	3	1	0	20144
Yanmare	5	1	0	0	15640
Calett Mad	7	4	0	0	38313
Robinshill	7	2	0	0	19818
Ballycross	6	1	0	1	13256
*Turning Gold	6	1	2	0	12996
Count Meribel	7	3	1	0	21443
Crievehill	8	2	3	1	22079
Red Riverman	7	2	3	1	16411
Ballyarthur	6	2	1	2	17545
El Terremoto	3	1	0	0	9495
Wicked Willy	6	2	0	0	15855
*Bigbadjohn	3	1	0	0	8447
Templehills	3	1	1	0	8187
Belmount	8	1	0	1	7798
Allthegear No Idea	8	1	2	1	7538
Ballyandy	3	1	0	0	7507
Jameson	7	1	2	0	7507
Muckle Roe	5	1	1	0	6498
Jabulani	6	1	1	1	6498
Ravensdale	3	1	1	0	5848
Lagavara	6	1	0	2	5198
Brownville	5	1	0	0	4809
Better Days	4	1	1	0	4549
Little Pop	8	3	1	2	12606
Another Frontier	5	1	1	0	4494
Blue Flight	5	1	1	2	4431
*Luckofthedraw	5	2	1	0	6758
Granard	3	1	0	1	4159
Ballymalin	7	1	0	3	4159
Supakalanistic	7	1	0	1	4094
Bendomingo	6	1	1	0	3899
Angels Antics	8	1	2	1	3899
The Hollow Ginge	5	1	0	2	3899
Milanstorm	2	1	1	0	2599
Good Boy Bobby	4	3	0	1	7148
*Al Dancer	2	1	0	0	2395
Summit Like Herbie	3	1	0	0	2274
Ballygomartin	3	1	0	0	1949
Kingsplace	2	1	1	0	1949
One For Rosie	1	1	0	0	1949
Total winning prize-money					**£1187317**
Favourites		32-82		39.0%	3.63

MARK USHER

UPPER LAMBOURN, BERKS

	No. of Hrs	Races Run	1st	2nd	3rd	Unpl	Per cent	£1 Level Stake
NH Flat	1	2	0	0	0	2	0.0	-2.00
Hurdles	2	5	1	0	0	4	20.0	+0.50
Chases	0	0	0	0	0	0	0.0	0.00

Totals	3	7	1	0	0	6	14.3	-1.50
16-17	3	15	0	1	2	12	0.0	-15.00
15-16	6	16	1	2	5	8	6.3	-8.00

JOCKEYS

	W-R	Per cent	£1 Level Stake
Dave Crosse	1-2	50.0	+3.50

COURSE RECORD

	Total W-R	Non-Hndcps Hurdles	Chases	Hndcps Hurdles	Chases	NH Flat	Per cent	£1 Level Stake
Uttoxeter	1-1	0-0	0-0	1-1	0-0	0-0	100.0	+4.50

WINNING HORSES

Horse	Races Run	1st	2nd	3rd	£
Bay Fortuna	2	1	0	0	2599
Total winning prize-money					£2599
Favourites	0-0	0.0%			0.00

TIM VAUGHAN

ABERTHIN, VALE OF GLAMORGAN

	No. of Hrs	Races Run	1st	2nd	3rd	Unpl	Per cent	£1 Level Stake
NH Flat	11	11	0	1	0	10	0.0	-11.00
Hurdles	83	238	16	20	20	182	6.7	-88.70
Chases	38	94	11	10	13	60	11.7	-5.56
Totals	106	343	27	31	33	252	7.9	-105.26
16-17	132	535	71	49	53	362	13.3	-132.08
15-16	119	449	42	55	50	301	9.4	-225.75

BY MONTH

NH Flat	W-R	Per cent	£1 Level Stake	Hurdles	W-R	Per cent	£1 Level Stake
May	0-1	0.0	-1.00	May	1-16	6.3	-14.83
June	0-0	0.0	0.00	June	2-18	11.1	+2.00
July	0-0	0.0	0.00	July	0-9	0.0	-9.00
August	0-0	0.0	0.00	August	0-6	0.0	-6.00
September	0-2	0.0	-2.00	September	3-21	14.3	+8.83
October	0-4	0.0	-4.00	October	2-37	5.4	-7.00
November	0-0	0.0	0.00	November	2-31	6.5	-11.50
December	0-0	0.0	0.00	December	1-24	4.2	-18.50
January	0-0	0.0	0.00	January	2-21	9.5	-14.70
February	0-1	0.0	-1.00	February	1-21	4.8	-8.00
March	0-1	0.0	-1.00	March	1-14	7.1	-7.00
April	0-2	0.0	-2.00	April	1-20	5.0	-3.00

Chases	W-R	Per cent	£1 Level Stake	Totals	W-R	Per cent	£1 Level Stake
May	0-6	0.0	-6.00	May	1-23	4.3	-21.83
June	0-5	0.0	-5.00	June	2-23	8.7	-3.00
July	0-2	0.0	-2.00	July	0-11	0.0	-11.00
August	0-3	0.0	-3.00	August	0-9	0.0	-9.00
September	0-8	0.0	-8.00	September	3-31	9.7	-1.17
October	2-14	14.3	+14.00	October	4-55	7.3	+3.00
November	1-14	7.1	-5.00	November	3-45	6.7	-16.50
December	2-15	13.3	-4.00	December	3-39	7.7	-22.50
January	1-6	16.7	0.00	January	3-27	11.1	-14.70
February	3-5	60.0	+19.94	February	4-27	14.8	+10.94
March	0-7	0.0	-7.00	March	1-22	4.5	-15.00
April	2-9	22.2	+0.50	April	3-31	9.7	-4.50

DISTANCE

Hurdles	W-R	Per cent	£1 Level Stake	Chases	W-R	Per cent	£1 Level Stake
2m-2m3f	8-129	6.2	-49.20	2m-2m3f	0-15	0.0	-15.00
2m4f-2m7f	6-79	7.6	-16.17	2m4f-2m7f	8-48	16.7	+10.44
3m+	2-29	6.9	-22.33	3m+	3-31	9.7	-1.00

TYPE OF RACE

Non-Handicaps	W-R	Per cent	£1 Level Stake	Handicaps	W-R	Per cent	£1 Level Stake
Nov Hrdls	4-45	8.9	-13.03	Nov Hrdls	1-18	5.6	-13.50
Hrdls	0-27	0.0	-27.00	Hrdls	9-141	6.4	-33.00
Nov Chs	1-4	25.0	-2.56	Nov Chs	1-11	9.1	-4.50
Chases	0-1	0.0	-1.00	Chases	6-64	9.4	-11.50
Sell/Claim	2-4	50.0	+0.83	Sell/Claim	0-0	0.0	0.00

RACE CLASS

	W-R	Per cent	£1 Level Stake
Class 1	0-4	0.0	-4.00
Class 2	1-15	6.7	-2.00
Class 3	4-40	10.0	-1.56
Class 4	14-162	8.6	-57.03
Class 5	8-117	6.8	-34.67
Class 6	0-5	0.0	-5.00

FIRST TIME OUT

	W-R	Per cent	£1 Level Stake
Bumpers	0-11	0.0	-11.00
Hurdles	4-70	5.7	-43.00
Chases	2-25	8.0	+3.00
Totals	6-106	5.7	-51.00

JOCKEYS

	W-R	Per cent	£1 Level Stake
Alan Johns	14-195	7.2	-82.03
Richard Johnson	5-58	8.6	-26.72
George Blackwell	3-22	13.6	+13.00
Charlie Deutsch	1-1	100.0	+5.50
Richard Patrick	1-2	50.0	+5.00
Sam Twiston-Davies	1-2	50.0	+11.00
Harry Reed	1-3	33.3	+14.00
Tom O'Brien	1-4	25.0	+11.00

COURSE RECORD

	Total W-R	Non-Hndcps Hurdles	Chases	Hndcps Hurdles	Chases	NH Flat	Per cent	£1 Level Stake
Musselbgh	3-14	0-3	0-0	2-7	1-4	0-0	21.4	+6.00
Carlisle	2-5	1-2	0-0	1-3	0-0	0-0	40.0	+0.67
Hexham	2-6	1-2	0-0	1-2	0-2	0-0	33.3	+8.00
Ffos Las	2-23	0-5	0-0	1-11	1-7	0-0	8.7	-4.00
Ayr	1-1	0-0	0-1	0-0	0-0	0-0	100.0	+0.44
Ascot	1-2	1-1	0-0	0-1	0-0	0-0	50.0	+11.00
Newcastle	1-2	0-0	0-0	1-2	0-0	0-0	50.0	+15.00
Sandown	1-2	0-0	0-0	0-0	1-2	0-0	50.0	+15.00
Towcester	1-3	0-0	0-0	1-2	0-1	0-0	33.3	+4.00
Catterick	1-5	1-2	0-0	0-2	0-1	0-0	20.0	-4.20

Plumpton	1-6	0-1	0-0	0-2	1-3	0-0	16.7	+0.50
Mrket Rsn	1-7	1-1	0-0	0-4	0-2	0-0	14.3	+10.00
Wetherby	1-7	0-1	0-0	0-2	1-4	0-0	14.3	-1.00
Cheltenham	1-9	0-1	0-1	1-5	0-2	0-0	11.1	+4.00
Huntingdon	1-10	0-2	0-1	0-5	1-2	0-0	10.0	+5.00
Bangor	1-13	0-4	0-0	0-5	1-4	0-0	7.7	-6.00
Nton Abbot	1-15	0-1	0-0	1-9	0-4	0-1	6.7	+2.00
Southwell	1-16	0-2	0-0	0-7	1-6	0-1	6.3	-9.50
Stratford	1-16	0-3	0-1	0-6	1-5	0-1	6.3	-3.00
Worcester	1-18	1-5	0-1	0-7	0-5	0-0	5.6	-16.17
Uttoxeter	1-20	0-2	0-0	1-15	0-3	0-0	5.0	-3.00
Taunton	1-25	0-7	0-0	0-10	1-8	0-0	4.0	-22.00

WINNING HORSES

Horse	Races Run	1st	2nd	3rd	£
Point Of Principle	6	1	2	0	15640
Tanit River	5	1	0	0	9384
Master Dancer	3	1	0	0	7507
Looksnowtlikebrian	4	2	1	0	12541
Nathans Pride	5	1	1	0	6498
Bells Of Ailsworth	4	1	0	2	6279
Bassarabad	4	1	0	0	5338
Chozen	6	1	0	1	4874
Bennachie	7	2	2	1	8123
Officer Hoolihan	3	1	0	1	4549
Monsieur Arkadin	5	1	0	1	4549
Tara Mac	6	2	1	0	7668
Normandy King	4	1	1	1	4458
C'Est Du Gateau	7	1	0	0	4159
Champagne Chaser	7	1	0	2	4115
Spectator	5	1	1	1	4094
Panis Angelicus	5	1	1	0	3899
Timely Gift	3	1	0	0	3899
Fraser Canyon	4	1	0	0	3574
Rasasee	6	1	1	0	3249
Ballyrock	4	1	0	0	3249
Kalimantan	1	1	0	0	2339
Dusky Raider	5	1	0	1	2339
Jaunty Flyer	7	1	1	2	0
Total winning prize-money					£132324
Favourites	4-19		21.1%		-11.56

LUCY WADHAM

NEWMARKET, SUFFOLK

	No. of Hrs	Races Run	1st	2nd	3rd	Unpl	Per cent	£1 Level Stake
NH Flat	9	17	0	1	2	14	0.0	-17.00
Hurdles	19	75	16	11	10	38	21.3	+13.16
Chases	12	50	4	9	5	32	8.0	-34.38
Totals	30	142	20	21	17	84	14.1	-38.22
16-17	26	97	12	16	16	53	12.4	-41.65
15-16	26	118	21	16	13	68	17.8	+29.58

BY MONTH

NH Flat	W-R	Per cent	£1 Level Stake	Hurdles	W-R	Per cent	£1 Level Stake
May	0-1	0.0	-1.00	May	0-3	0.0	-3.00
June	0-1	0.0	-1.00	June	1-4	25.0	-0.25
July	0-0	0.0	0.00	July	0-3	0.0	-3.00
August	0-0	0.0	0.00	August	0-1	0.0	-1.00
September	0-0	0.0	0.00	September	0-0	0.0	0.00
October	0-0	0.0	0.00	October	0-0	0.0	0.00
November	0-3	0.0	-3.00	November	1-11	9.1	-7.25
December	0-2	0.0	-2.00	December	1-8	12.5	-5.00
January	0-2	0.0	-2.00	January	4-13	30.8	+7.25
February	0-1	0.0	-1.00	February	4-10	40.0	+7.53
March	0-2	0.0	-2.00	March	4-11	36.4	+25.13
April	0-5	0.0	-5.00	April	1-11	9.1	-7.25

Chases	W-R	Per cent	£1 Level Stake	Totals	W-R	Per cent	£1 Level Stake
May	0-3	0.0	-3.00	May	0-7	0.0	-7.00
June	0-0	0.0	0.00	June	1-5	20.0	-1.25
July	0-0	0.0	0.00	July	0-3	0.0	-3.00
August	0-0	0.0	0.00	August	0-1	0.0	-1.00
September	0-0	0.0	0.00	September	0-0	0.0	0.00
October	0-4	0.0	-4.00	October	0-4	0.0	-4.00
November	1-5	20.0	-1.50	November	2-19	10.5	-11.75
December	1-11	9.1	-8.38	December	2-21	9.5	-15.38
January	0-7	0.0	-7.00	January	4-22	18.2	-1.75
February	1-9	11.1	-5.00	February	5-20	25.0	+1.53
March	1-9	11.1	-3.50	March	5-22	22.7	+19.63
April	0-2	0.0	-2.00	April	1-18	5.6	-14.25

DISTANCE

Hurdles	W-R	Per cent	£1 Level Stake	Chases	W-R	Per cent	£1 Level Stake
2m-2m3f	11-33	33.3	+37.58	2m-2m3f	2-19	10.5	-12.88
2m4f-2m7f	4-35	11.4	-21.75	2m4f-2m7f	0-7	0.0	-7.00
3m+	1-6	16.7	-1.67	3m+	2-24	8.3	-14.50

TYPE OF RACE

Non-Handicaps	W-R	Per cent	£1 Level Stake	Handicaps	W-R	Per cent	£1 Level Stake
Nov Hrdls	5-20	25.0	-5.05	Nov Hrdls	0-1	0.0	-1.00
Hrdls	2-10	20.0	+2.75	Hrdls	8-43	18.6	+13.71
Nov Chs	0-2	0.0	-2.00	Nov Chs	0-3	0.0	-3.00
Chases	0-0	0.0	0.00	Chases	4-39	10.3	-23.38
Sell/Claim	0-0	0.0	0.00	Sell/Claim	0-0	0.0	0.00

RACE CLASS

	W-R	Per cent	£1 Level Stake
Class 1	0-8	0.0	-8.00
Class 2	1-11	9.1	-5.50
Class 3	8-41	19.5	-8.00
Class 4	10-59	16.9	+2.53
Class 5	1-17	5.9	-13.25
Class 6	0-6	0.0	-6.00

FIRST TIME OUT

	W-R	Per cent	£1 Level Stake
Bumpers	0-9	0.0	-9.00
Hurdles	2-12	16.7	+0.75
Chases	0-9	0.0	-9.00
Totals	2-30	6.7	-17.25

JOCKEYS

	W-R	Per cent	£1 Level Stake
Maxime Tissier	8-27	29.6	+22.16
Leighton Aspell	5-59	8.5	-36.75
Jack Sherwood	2-8	25.0	-0.50
David Noonan	2-12	16.7	-5.63
Jack Quinlan	1-2	50.0	+7.00
Brian Hughes	1-4	25.0	0.00
Aidan Coleman	1-10	10.0	-4.50

COURSE RECORD

	Total W-R	Non-Hndcps Hurdles	Chases	Hndcps Hurdles	Chases	NH Flat	Per cent	£1 Level Stake
Fakenham	5-17	2-4	0-0	2-6	1-5	0-2	29.4	+5.75
Wetherby	2-6	1-2	0-0	0-0	1-3	0-1	33.3	-1.17
Southwell	2-7	1-1	0-0	1-4	0-0	0-2	28.6	+0.50
Towcester	2-8	1-3	0-1	1-1	0-1	0-2	25.0	+16.75
Mrket Rsn	2-15	0-1	0-0	2-7	0-5	0-2	13.3	-2.25
Carlisle	1-2	0-0	0-0	0-0	1-2	0-0	50.0	+2.00
Ludlow	1-2	1-1	0-0	0-0	0-1	0-0	50.0	+7.00
Fontwell	1-3	0-1	0-0	1-2	0-0	0-0	33.3	-0.63
Haydock	1-3	0-1	0-0	0-1	1-1	0-0	33.3	+2.50
Plumpton	1-6	1-1	0-1	0-2	0-2	0-0	16.7	-2.00
Uttoxeter	1-8	1-3	0-0	0-1	0-3	0-1	12.5	-6.00
Huntingdon	1-12	0-4	0-0	1-5	0-0	0-3	8.3	-7.67

WINNING HORSES

Horse	Races Run	1st	2nd	3rd	£
Potters Legend	8	1	0	0	31022
Shanroe Santos	10	1	2	2	11372
Potters Midnight	6	2	0	2	17155
Artifice Sivola	4	1	2	0	8920
Movie Legend	8	2	1	1	11047
Iconic Sky	7	2	1	2	12736
Game On	6	2	2	0	10592
Banjo Girl	7	3	1	1	14849
Gregarious	7	1	1	1	5588
*Shambra	4	2	0	0	9162
Amberjam	7	1	3	0	4224
Mystic Sky	5	1	1	0	3899
Phoeniciana	7	1	1	1	3509
Total winning prize-money					£144075
Favourites	6-13		46.2%		5.41

JOHN WAINWRIGHT

KENNYTHORPE, N YORKS

	No. of Hrs	Races Run	1st	2nd	3rd	Unpl	Per cent	£1 Level Stake
NH Flat	4	9	0	0	0	9	0.0	-9.00
Hurdles	5	19	0	2	0	17	0.0	-19.00
Chases	1	5	1	0	0	4	20.0	+3.00
Totals	10	33	1	2	0	30	3.0	-25.00
16-17	5	18	0	0	3	15	0.0	-18.00

| 15-16 | 4 | 15 | 0 | 0 | 0 | 15 | 0.0 | -15.00 |

JOCKEYS

	W-R	Per cent	£1 Level Stake
Jamie Hamilton	1-9	11.1	-1.00

COURSE RECORD

	Total W-R	Non-Hndcps Hurdles	Chases	Hndcps Hurdles	Chases	NH Flat	Per cent	£1 Level Stake
Mrket Rsn	1-15	0-4	0-0	0-6	1-3	0-2	6.7	-7.00

WINNING HORSES

Horse	Races Run	1st	2nd	3rd	£
*Rough Justice	5	1	0	0	3899
Total winning prize-money					£3899
Favourites	0-0		0.0%		0.00

MARK WALFORD

SHERRIFF HUTTON, N YORKS

	No. of Hrs	Races Run	1st	2nd	3rd	Unpl	Per cent	£1 Level Stake
NH Flat	4	8	0	2	1	5	0.0	-8.00
Hurdles	22	75	3	10	12	50	4.0	-58.00
Chases	7	29	6	5	4	14	20.7	+1.00
Totals	26	112	9	17	17	69	8.0	-65.00
16-17	28	130	23	20	9	78	17.7	+54.60
15-16	18	82	12	12	9	49	14.6	-4.50

JOCKEYS

	W-R	Per cent	£1 Level Stake
Jamie Hamilton	5-65	7.7	-41.00
Miss Emma Todd	2-15	13.3	-1.50
Daryl Jacob	1-3	33.3	+2.00
Henry Brooke	1-12	8.3	-7.50

COURSE RECORD

	Total W-R	Non-Hndcps Hurdles	Chases	Hndcps Hurdles	Chases	NH Flat	Per cent	£1 Level Stake
Hexham	3-20	0-3	0-0	1-8	2-7	0-2	15.0	-8.50
Mrket Rsn	2-29	0-8	0-0	1-15	1-3	0-3	6.9	-20.00
Bangor	1-2	0-0	0-0	0-1	1-1	0-0	50.0	+3.00
Cartmel	1-4	0-0	0-0	0-1	1-3	0-0	25.0	+1.00
Southwell	1-4	0-2	0-0	1-2	0-0	0-0	25.0	+4.50
Kelso	1-6	0-0	0-0	0-2	1-4	0-0	16.7	+2.00

WINNING HORSES

Horse	Races Run	1st	2nd	3rd	£
Oliver's Gold	7	1	1	1	7535
Mr Snoozy	4	1	0	0	5198
Uno Valoroso	7	1	2	2	4327
Cape Hideaway	10	1	3	0	4224
*Bentons Lad	4	1	0	0	4094
Miss Conway	9	3	1	1	7064

Lilly's Legend 3 1 1 0 3249
Total winning prize-money **£35691**
Favourites 0-9 0.0% -9.00

ROBERT WALFORD

BLANDFORD, DORSET

	No. of Hrs	Races Run	1st	2nd	3rd	Unpl	Per cent	£1 Level Stake
NH Flat	5	6	0	1	0	5	0.0	-6.00
Hurdles	18	54	8	6	4	36	14.8	+5.85
Chases	10	32	4	2	7	19	12.5	-5.50
Totals	28	92	12	9	11	60	13.0	-5.65
16-17	32	103	12	9	8	74	11.7	-30.50
15-16	28	92	7	13	7	65	7.6	-56.38

BY MONTH

NH Flat	W-R	Per cent	£1 Level Stake	Hurdles	W-R	Per cent	£1 Level Stake
May	0-0	0.0	0.00	May	0-3	0.0	-3.00
June	0-0	0.0	0.00	June	0-0	0.0	0.00
July	0-0	0.0	0.00	July	0-0	0.0	0.00
August	0-1	0.0	-1.00	August	0-0	0.0	0.00
September	0-0	0.0	0.00	September	0-0	0.0	0.00
October	0-0	0.0	0.00	October	2-5	40.0	+28.00
November	0-0	0.0	0.00	November	0-10	0.0	-10.00
December	0-1	0.0	-1.00	December	5-12	41.7	+6.85
January	0-1	0.0	-1.00	January	1-11	9.1	-3.00
February	0-0	0.0	0.00	February	0-4	0.0	-4.00
March	0-1	0.0	-1.00	March	0-3	0.0	-3.00
April	0-2	0.0	-2.00	April	0-6	0.0	-6.00

Chases	W-R	Per cent	£1 Level Stake	Totals	W-R	Per cent	£1 Level Stake
May	0-1	0.0	-1.00	May	0-4	0.0	-4.00
June	0-0	0.0	0.00	June	0-0	0.0	0.00
July	0-0	0.0	0.00	July	0-0	0.0	0.00
August	0-0	0.0	0.00	August	0-1	0.0	-1.00
September	0-1	0.0	-1.00	September	0-1	0.0	-1.00
October	1-3	33.3	+0.75	October	3-8	37.5	+28.75
November	1-8	12.5	+1.00	November	1-18	5.6	-9.00
December	1-7	14.3	+4.00	December	6-20	30.0	+9.85
January	1-5	20.0	-2.25	January	2-17	11.8	-6.25
February	0-2	0.0	-2.00	February	0-6	0.0	-6.00
March	0-2	0.0	-2.00	March	0-6	0.0	-6.00
April	0-3	0.0	-3.00	April	0-11	0.0	-11.00

DISTANCE

Hurdles	W-R	Per cent	£1 Level Stake	Chases	W-R	Per cent	£1 Level Stake
2m-2m3f	8-35	22.9	+24.85	2m-2m3f	2-7	28.6	+7.75
2m4f-2m7f	0-19	0.0	-19.00	2m4f-2m7f	1-11	9.1	-8.25
3m+	0-0	0.0	0.00	3m+	1-14	7.1	-5.00

TYPE OF RACE

Non-Handicaps	W-R	Per cent	£1 Level Stake	Handicaps	W-R	Per cent	£1 Level Stake
Nov Hrdls	1-14	7.1	-2.00	Nov Hrdls	0-0	0.0	0.00
Hrdls	1-7	14.3	-3.50	Hrdls	6-33	18.2	+11.35
Nov Chs	0-2	0.0	-2.00	Nov Chs	0-2	0.0	-2.00
Chases	0-0	0.0	0.00	Chases	3-25	12.0	-1.25
Sell/Claim	0-0	0.0	0.00	Sell/Claim	0-0	0.0	0.00

RACE CLASS

	W-R	Per cent	£1 Level Stake
Class 1	0-3	0.0	-3.00
Class 2	1-9	11.1	+2.00
Class 3	3-27	11.1	-7.25
Class 4	5-36	13.9	-12.65
Class 5	3-15	20.0	+17.25
Class 6	0-2	0.0	-2.00

FIRST TIME OUT

	W-R	Per cent	£1 Level Stake
Bumpers	0-5	0.0	-5.00
Hurdles	3-15	20.0	+21.50
Chases	0-8	0.0	-8.00
Totals	3-28	10.7	+8.50

JOCKEYS

	W-R	Per cent	£1 Level Stake
James Best	8-55	14.5	+16.00
Harry Cobden	3-14	21.4	-6.65
James Bowen	1-1	100.0	+7.00

COURSE RECORD

	Total W-R	Non-Hndcps Hurdles	Chases	Hndcps Hurdles	Chases	NH Flat	Per cent	£1 Level Stake
Taunton	3-11	1-5	0-0	2-3	0-2	0-1	27.3	+2.60
Ascot	2-3	0-0	0-0	0-0	2-3	0-0	66.7	+17.00
Wincanton	2-12	1-4	0-0	0-3	1-3	0-2	16.7	+2.75
Cheltenham	1-3	0-0	0-0	1-3	0-0	0-0	33.3	+5.00
Plumpton	1-4	0-1	0-0	1-3	0-0	0-0	25.0	-0.75
Chepstow	1-6	0-3	0-0	1-1	0-2	0-0	16.7	+15.00
Fontwell	1-8	0-3	0-0	1-5	0-0	0-0	12.5	-6.00
Exeter	1-20	0-1	0-2	0-8	1-9	0-0	5.0	-16.25

WINNING HORSES

Horse	Races Run	1st	2nd	3rd	£
Mr Medic	4	2	0	1	28394
Walk In The Mill	4	1	0	1	16245
Le Boizelo	5	1	1	1	7798
Smaoineamh Alainn	3	2	0	0	12706
Vaziani	2	1	1	0	5198
Our Merlin	8	3	1	1	12346
Kohuma	3	1	0	0	4159
Sydney De Baune	3	1	0	1	3249
Total winning prize-money					**£90095**
Favourites	4-9	44.4%			1.60

JAMES WALTON
THROPTON, NORTHUMBERLAND

	No. of Hrs	Races Run	1st	2nd	3rd	Unpl	Per cent	£1 Level Stake
NH Flat	1	2	0	0	0	2	0.0	-2.00
Hurdles	5	15	0	0	2	13	0.0	-15.00
Chases	5	12	1	1	3	7	8.3	-8.50
Totals	8	29	1	1	5	22	3.4	-25.50
16-17	8	23	2	3	1	17	8.7	-8.00
15-16	6	31	1	4	9	17	3.2	-5.00

JOCKEYS

	W-R	Per cent	£1 Level Stake
Miss Catherine Walton	1-20	5.0	-16.50

COURSE RECORD

	Total W-R	Non-Hndcps Hurdles	Chases	Hndcps Hurdles	Chases	NH Flat	Per cent	£1 Level Stake
Musselbgh	1-2	0-0	0-0	0-0	1-2	0-0	50.0	+1.50

WINNING HORSES

Horse	Races Run	1st	2nd	3rd	£
Dun Faw Good	3	1	1	0	3314
Total winning prize-money					£3314
Favourites	0-0		0.0%		0.00

SHEENA WALTON
HEXHAM, NORTHUMBERLAND

	No. of Hrs	Races Run	1st	2nd	3rd	Unpl	Per cent	£1 Level Stake
NH Flat	1	1	0	0	0	1	0.0	-1.00
Hurdles	4	23	2	2	1	18	8.7	+18.00
Chases	2	8	0	0	1	7	0.0	-8.00
Totals	6	32	2	2	2	26	6.3	+9.00
16-17	6	28	0	0	3	25	0.0	-28.00
15-16	5	34	5	2	0	26	14.7	+10.75

JOCKEYS

	W-R	Per cent	£1 Level Stake
Finian O'Toole	1-10	10.0	+2.00
Miss Catherine Walton	1-15	6.7	+14.00

COURSE RECORD

	Total W-R	Non-Hndcps Hurdles	Chases	Hndcps Hurdles	Chases	NH Flat	Per cent	£1 Level Stake
Perth	1-8	0-0	0-0	1-6	0-2	0-0	12.5	+21.00
Hexham	1-12	0-2	0-0	1-6	0-4	0-0	8.3	0.00

WINNING HORSES

Horse	Races Run	1st	2nd	3rd	£

Native Optimist		12	2	2	0	10296
Total winning prize-money						£10296
Favourites	0-0			0.0%		0.00

SHARON WATT
BROMPTON-ON-SWALE, N YORKS

	No. of Hrs	Races Run	1st	2nd	3rd	Unpl	Per cent	£1 Level Stake
NH Flat	1	1	0	0	0	1	0.0	-1.00
Hurdles	3	17	4	4	1	8	23.5	+7.00
Chases	0	0	0	0	0	0	0.0	0.00
Totals	3	18	4	4	1	9	22.2	+6.00
16-17	3	18	1	0	1	16	5.6	-5.00
15-16	5	16	1	0	0	15	6.3	-7.00

JOCKEYS

	W-R	Per cent	£1 Level Stake
Finian O'Toole	4-15	26.7	+9.00

COURSE RECORD

	Total W-R	Non-Hndcps Hurdles	Chases	Hndcps Hurdles	Chases	NH Flat	Per cent	£1 Level Stake
Ayr	3-6	0-2	0-0	3-4	0-0	0-0	50.0	+10.00
Hexham	1-2	1-1	0-0	0-1	0-0	0-0	50.0	+6.00

WINNING HORSES

Horse	Races Run	1st	2nd	3rd	£
Too Many Chiefs	7	3	1	0	13191
Arctic Vodka	7	1	3	1	3444
Total winning prize-money					£16635
Favourites	0-1		0.0%		-1.00

PAUL WEBBER
MOLLINGTON, OXON

	No. of Hrs	Races Run	1st	2nd	3rd	Unpl	Per cent	£1 Level Stake
NH Flat	10	12	1	3	0	8	8.3	-9.25
Hurdles	23	55	4	6	5	40	7.3	-31.25
Chases	10	29	3	7	6	13	10.3	+17.88
Totals	37	96	8	16	11	61	8.3	-22.62
16-17	39	108	7	16	10	75	6.5	-53.50
15-16	40	116	7	14	11	84	6.0	-58.75

JOCKEYS

	W-R	Per cent	£1 Level Stake
Gavin Sheehan	3-18	16.7	+3.38
Richard Johnson	2-5	40.0	-0.25
James Bowen	1-1	100.0	+1.75
Tom O'Brien	1-8	12.5	-4.50
Richie McLernon	1-40	2.5	+1.00

COURSE RECORD

	Total W-R	Non-Hndcps Hurdles	Non-Hndcps Chases	Hndcps Hurdles	Hndcps Chases	NH Flat	Per cent	£1 Level Stake
Towcester	3-7	0-2	0-0	1-1	2-3	0-1	42.9	+43.50
Huntingdon	3-14	2-7	0-0	1-4	0-2	0-1	21.4	+3.75
Taunton	1-2	0-0	0-0	0-1	1-1	0-0	50.0	+0.38
Southwell	1-6	0-0	0-0	0-4	0-1	1-1	16.7	-3.25

WINNING HORSES

Horse	Races Run	1st	2nd	3rd	£
Copperfacejack	7	2	2	2	10287
Miss Tongabezi	6	1	0	2	4549
New Agenda	6	2	1	1	6498
Cosmic Diamond	6	2	1	1	6498
Indefatigable	1	1	0	0	0
Total winning prize-money					£27832
Favourites	3-8	37.5%			-0.88

SIMON WEST

MIDDLEHAM MOOR, N YORKS

	No. of Hrs	Races Run	1st	2nd	3rd	Unpl	Per cent	£1 Level Stake
NH Flat	5	5	0	0	0	5	0.0	-5.00
Hurdles	8	16	1	2	2	11	6.3	+3.00
Chases	1	3	0	0	0	3	0.0	-3.00
Totals	9	24	1	2	2	19	4.2	-5.00
16-17	9	21	1	4	3	13	4.8	-16.00
15-16	6	17	2	2	0	13	11.8	-4.00

JOCKEYS

	W-R	Per cent	£1 Level Stake
Henry Brooke	1-5	20.0	+14.00

COURSE RECORD

	Total W-R	Non-Hndcps Hurdles	Non-Hndcps Chases	Hndcps Hurdles	Hndcps Chases	NH Flat	Per cent	£1 Level Stake
Hexham	1-4	1-2	0-0	0-1	0-0	0-1	25.0	+15.00

WINNING HORSES

Horse	Races Run	1st	2nd	3rd	£
Go Go Lucas	3	1	1	0	3249
Total winning prize-money					£3249
Favourites	0-0	0.0%			0.00

SHEENA WEST

FALMER, E SUSSEX

	No. of Hrs	Races Run	1st	2nd	3rd	Unpl	Per cent	£1 Level Stake
NH Flat	0	0	0	0	0	0	0.0	0.00
Hurdles	6	31	3	3	2	23	9.7	-5.00
Chases	0	0	0	0	0	0	0.0	0.00
Totals	6	31	3	3	2	23	9.7	-5.00
16-17	9	30	3	1	4	22	10.0	-5.50
15-16	16	62	5	8	8	41	8.1	-27.00

JOCKEYS

	W-R	Per cent	£1 Level Stake
Marc Goldstein	3-29	10.3	-3.00

COURSE RECORD

	Total W-R	Non-Hndcps Hurdles	Non-Hndcps Chases	Hndcps Hurdles	Hndcps Chases	NH Flat	Per cent	£1 Level Stake
Plumpton	3-12	1-2	0-0	2-10	0-0	0-0	25.0	+14.00

WINNING HORSES

Horse	Races Run	1st	2nd	3rd	£
*Harmonise	5	1	0	0	4354
Sixties Idol	13	1	1	2	4094
Ding Ding	9	1	2	0	3249
Total winning prize-money					£11697
Favourites	0-0	0.0%			0.00

TOM WESTON

HINDLIP, WORCS

	No. of Hrs	Races Run	1st	2nd	3rd	Unpl	Per cent	£1 Level Stake
NH Flat	1	1	0	0	0	1	0.0	-1.00
Hurdles	8	17	2	0	1	14	11.8	+4.00
Chases	7	21	4	0	2	15	19.0	+16.50
Totals	12	39	6	0	3	30	15.4	+19.50
16-17	16	76	8	3	6	59	10.5	-37.00
15-16	8	20	1	2	1	16	5.0	-16.50

JOCKEYS

	W-R	Per cent	£1 Level Stake
Sean Bowen	4-14	28.6	+18.50
Niall P Madden	1-4	25.0	+13.00
Charlie Poste	1-13	7.7	-4.00

COURSE RECORD

	Total W-R	Non-Hndcps Hurdles	Non-Hndcps Chases	Hndcps Hurdles	Hndcps Chases	NH Flat	Per cent	£1 Level Stake
Uttoxeter	2-7	0-0	0-0	2-6	0-1	0-0	28.6	+14.00
Exeter	1-1	0-0	0-0	0-0	1-1	0-0	100.0	+6.00
Southwell	1-1	0-0	0-0	0-0	1-1	0-0	100.0	+12.00
Huntingdon	1-2	0-0	0-0	0-0	1-2	0-0	50.0	+6.50
Ludlow	1-6	0-3	1-1	0-0	0-2	0-0	16.7	+3.00

WINNING HORSES

Horse	Races Run	1st	2nd	3rd	£
Western Climate	8	2	0	1	21576
Silent Man	8	3	0	1	7148

Sunday Central	1	1	0	0	2469
Total winning prize-money					£31193
Favourites	0-2		0.0%		-2.00

DONALD WHILLANS

HAWICK, BORDERS

	No. of Hrs	Races Run	1st	2nd	3rd	Unpl	Per cent	£1 Level Stake
NH Flat	6	14	4	3	2	5	28.6	+9.00
Hurdles	9	28	4	4	3	17	14.3	+28.50
Chases	1	2	0	0	0	2	0.0	-2.00
Totals	15	44	8	7	5	24	18.2	+35.50
16-17	14	53	4	5	5	39	7.5	+31.00
15-16	12	47	5	5	7	30	10.6	-18.75

JOCKEYS

	W-R	Per cent	£1 Level Stake
Callum Whillans	8-40	20.0	+39.50

COURSE RECORD

	Total W-R	Non-Hndcps Hurdles	Chases	Hndcps Hurdles	Chases	NH Flat	Per cent	£1 Level Stake
Kelso	2-5	0-1	0-0	1-1	0-0	1-3	40.0	+31.00
Ayr	2-12	1-3	0-0	1-7	0-0	0-2	16.7	+12.00
Wetherby	1-1	0-0	0-0	0-0	0-0	1-1	100.0	+3.00
Sedgefield	1-2	0-1	0-0	0-0	0-0	1-1	50.0	+5.50
Musselbgh	1-5	0-0	0-0	0-1	0-0	1-4	20.0	-0.50
Newcastle	1-5	1-2	0-0	0-3	0-0	0-0	20.0	-1.50

WINNING HORSES

Horse	Races Run	1st	2nd	3rd	£
Keyboard Gangster	4	2	0	1	29378
Baby Ticker	5	1	2	0	4809
Eternally Yours	4	2	0	0	5653
Paper Promise	4	2	1	0	5198
Dali Mail	3	1	0	1	2274
Total winning prize-money					£47312
Favourites	0-3		0.0%		-3.00

ALISTAIR WHILLANS

NEWMILL-ON-SLITRIG, BORDERS

	No. of Hrs	Races Run	1st	2nd	3rd	Unpl	Per cent	£1 Level Stake
NH Flat	4	9	0	1	1	7	0.0	-9.00
Hurdles	15	63	8	7	6	42	12.7	-11.13
Chases	6	13	0	0	0	13	0.0	-13.00
Totals	21	85	8	8	7	62	9.4	-33.13
16-17	25	106	10	3	13	80	9.4	-11.50
15-16	25	109	11	14	15	69	10.1	-20.25

JOCKEYS

	W-R	Per cent	£1 Level Stake
Ross Chapman	2-4	50.0	+5.38
Steven Fox	2-8	25.0	+3.75
Mr Ryan Nichol	1-3	33.3	+10.00
Kieron Edgar	1-12	8.3	-2.00
Henry Brooke	1-13	7.7	-9.00
Grant Cockburn	1-13	7.7	-9.25

COURSE RECORD

	Total W-R	Non-Hndcps Hurdles	Chases	Hndcps Hurdles	Chases	NH Flat	Per cent	£1 Level Stake
Musselbgh	2-13	0-0	0-0	2-9	0-1	0-3	15.4	-1.00
Hexham	2-13	1-1	0-1	1-9	0-2	0-0	15.4	+3.75
Catterick	1-3	0-0	0-0	1-2	0-0	0-1	33.3	-0.63
Newcastle	1-4	0-1	0-0	1-3	0-0	0-0	25.0	+3.00
Kelso	1-8	0-0	0-0	1-5	0-2	0-1	12.5	+2.00
Perth	1-13	0-1	0-0	1-7	0-4	0-1	7.7	-9.25

WINNING HORSES

Horse	Races Run	1st	2nd	3rd	£
*Fly Vinnie	3	1	0	0	5198
Chu Chu Percy	4	2	1	0	7083
Meadowcroft Boy	6	1	1	1	3899
Kalaharry	2	1	0	1	3369
Court Baloo	9	1	1	2	3249
Apachee Prince	11	1	2	0	3249
Right Of Reply	1	1	0	0	2924
Total winning prize-money					£28971
Favourites	1-4		25.0%		-1.63

CHARLES WHITTAKER

RADSTOCK, SOMERSET

	No. of Hrs	Races Run	1st	2nd	3rd	Unpl	Per cent	£1 Level Stake
NH Flat	0	0	0	0	0	0	0.0	0.00
Hurdles	4	4	1	0	1	2	25.0	+13.00
Chases	1	1	0	0	0	1	0.0	-1.00
Totals	4	5	1	0	1	3	20.0	+12.00
16-17	6	19	0	0	4	15	0.0	-19.00
15-16	3	5	1	1	0	3	20.0	+3.00

JOCKEYS

	W-R	Per cent	£1 Level Stake
Mr Lorcan Williams	1-1	100.0	+16.00

COURSE RECORD

	Total W-R	Non-Hndcps Hurdles	Chases	Hndcps Hurdles	Chases	NH Flat	Per cent	£1 Level Stake
Wincanton	1-1	0-0	0-0	1-1	0-0	0-0	100.0	+16.00

WINNING HORSES

Horse	Races Run	1st	2nd	3rd	£
Garde Forestier	1	1	0	0	3899
Total winning prize-money					£3899
Favourites	0-0		0.0%		0.00

HARRY WHITTINGTON

SPARSHOLT, OXON

	No. of Hrs	Races Run	1st	2nd	3rd	Unpl	Per cent	£1 Level Stake
NH Flat	19	27	5	5	3	14	18.5	+0.75
Hurdles	26	79	12	6	14	47	15.2	-28.02
Chases	13	29	10	4	1	14	34.5	+6.19
Totals	43	135	27	15	18	75	20.0	-21.08
16-17	42	118	13	15	14	76	11.0	-20.29
15-16	24	90	21	12	19	38	23.3	+21.36

BY MONTH

NH Flat	W-R	Per cent	£1 Level Stake	Hurdles	W-R	Per cent	£1 Level Stake
May	0-0	0.0	0.00	May	1-5	20.0	+1.00
June	0-0	0.0	0.00	June	1-8	12.5	-0.50
July	0-1	0.0	-1.00	July	0-2	0.0	-2.00
August	0-1	0.0	-1.00	August	1-3	33.3	+2.50
September	1-3	33.3	-0.25	September	0-4	0.0	-4.00
October	2-6	33.3	+6.50	October	0-3	0.0	-3.00
November	0-4	0.0	-4.00	November	5-13	38.5	+8.02
December	0-2	0.0	-2.00	December	3-12	25.0	-4.54
January	1-1	100.0	+6.00	January	0-6	0.0	-6.00
February	0-2	0.0	-2.00	February	1-8	12.5	-4.50
March	1-2	50.0	+3.50	March	0-10	0.0	-10.00
April	0-5	0.0	-5.00	April	0-5	0.0	-5.00

Chases	W-R	Per cent	£1 Level Stake	Totals	W-R	Per cent	£1 Level Stake
May	0-0	0.0	0.00	May	1-5	20.0	+1.00
June	0-1	0.0	-1.00	June	1-9	11.1	-1.50
July	0-0	0.0	0.00	July	0-3	0.0	-3.00
August	0-0	0.0	0.00	August	1-4	25.0	+1.50
September	0-0	0.0	0.00	September	1-7	14.3	-4.25
October	1-5	20.0	-2.38	October	3-14	21.4	+1.12
November	3-7	42.9	+4.63	November	8-24	33.3	+8.65
December	2-4	50.0	+3.75	December	5-18	27.8	-2.79
January	2-3	66.7	+3.75	January	3-10	30.0	+3.75
February	1-4	25.0	-2.56	February	2-14	14.3	-9.06
March	0-3	0.0	-3.00	March	1-15	6.7	-9.50
April	1-2	50.0	+3.00	April	1-12	8.3	-7.00

DISTANCE

Hurdles	W-R	Per cent	£1 Level Stake	Chases	W-R	Per cent	£1 Level Stake
2m-2m3f	8-61	13.1	-30.75	2m-2m3f	7-13	53.8	+10.32
2m4f-2m7f	4-13	30.8	+7.73	2m4f-2m7f	1-6	16.7	-1.00
3m+	0-5	0.0	-5.00	3m+	2-10	20.0	-3.13

TYPE OF RACE

Non-Handicaps	W-R	Per cent	£1 Level Stake	Handicaps	W-R	Per cent	£1 Level Stake
Nov Hrdls	4-19	21.1	-10.27	Nov Hrdls	0-3	0.0	-3.00
Hrdls	0-15	0.0	-15.00	Hrdls	5-35	14.3	-3.25
Nov Chs	2-4	50.0	+2.44	Nov Chs	2-4	50.0	+1.00
Chases	0-0	0.0	0.00	Chases	3-11	27.3	-0.88
Sell/Claim	2-2	100.0	+1.00	Sell/Claim	0-0	0.0	0.00

RACE CLASS

	W-R	Per cent	£1 Level Stake
Class 1	2-11	18.2	-4.56
Class 2	0-6	0.0	-6.00
Class 3	5-12	41.7	+5.13
Class 4	14-72	19.4	-7.40
Class 5	4-23	17.4	-5.50
Class 6	2-11	18.2	-2.75

FIRST TIME OUT

	W-R	Per cent	£1 Level Stake
Bumpers	5-19	26.3	+8.75
Hurdles	3-17	17.6	-1.83
Chases	2-7	28.6	-1.63
Totals	10-43	23.3	+5.29

JOCKEYS

	W-R	Per cent	£1 Level Stake
Harry Bannister	21-101	20.8	-8.77
Aidan Coleman	4-5	80.0	+8.44
Gavin Sheehan	1-3	33.3	+2.50
B J Cooper	1-6	16.7	-3.25

COURSE RECORD

	Total W-R	Non-Hndcps Hurdles	Non-Hndcps Chases	Hndcps Hurdles	Hndcps Chases	NH Flat	Per cent	£1 Level Stake
Sedgefield	4-5	2-2	0-0	1-1	1-2	0-0	80.0	+5.75
Newbury	3-5	0-1	0-0	0-0	3-4	0-0	60.0	+5.00
Southwell	3-11	2-5	0-0	1-2	0-1	0-3	27.3	+11.17
Warwick	2-4	0-0	1-1	1-1	0-1	0-1	50.0	+0.94
Kempton	2-5	0-2	0-0	1-2	1-1	0-0	40.0	+7.00
Ludlow	2-5	0-2	0-0	0-0	1-1	1-2	40.0	+3.13
Huntingdon	2-10	0-3	0-0	0-4	1-1	1-2	20.0	+0.25
Hexham	1-1	1-1	0-0	0-0	0-0	0-0	100.0	+1.38
Leicester	1-2	1-1	0-0	0-1	0-0	0-0	50.0	-0.67
Plumpton	1-2	0-1	0-0	0-0	1-1	0-0	50.0	+2.50
Ayr	1-3	0-0	1-1	0-0	0-1	0-1	33.3	+2.00
Hereford	1-3	1-2	0-0	0-1	0-0	0-0	33.3	-1.27
Ffos Las	1-3	0-0	0-0	0-1	0-1	1-1	33.3	+4.00
Fontwell	1-4	0-2	0-0	0-0	0-0	1-2	25.0	+1.50
Nton Abbot	1-5	0-0	0-0	1-3	0-0	0-2	20.0	+0.50
Mrket Rsn	1-11	0-3	0-0	0-4	0-1	1-3	9.1	-8.25

WINNING HORSES

Horse	Races Run	1st	2nd	3rd	£
Bigmartre	5	3	1	0	52303
Saint Calvados	4	3	0	0	38779
Vinnie Lewis	5	2	0	1	22033
Salto Chisco	7	3	1	0	14945
Rouge Vif	1	1	0	0	4809
*Eyesopenwideawake	3	2	0	0	4549

The Dubai Way	5	4	0	0	15920
Court Liability	3	3	0	0	4159
Hoke Colburn	4	1	0	0	3899
Octagon	4	3	0	0	10397
Anemoi	2	1	0	0	2274
Simply The Betts	5	1	1	1	1560
Total winning prize-money					£175627
Favourites	12-22		54.5%		5.67

MICHAEL WIGHAM
NEWMARKET, SUFFOLK

	No. of Hrs	Races Run	1st	2nd	3rd	Unpl	Per cent	£1 Level Stake
NH Flat	1	1	0	0	0	1	0.0	-1.00
Hurdles	2	7	1	0	0	6	14.3	-1.50
Chases	1	5	0	0	2	3	0.0	-5.00
Totals	3	13	1	0	2	10	7.7	-7.50
16-17	5	23	1	1	2	19	4.3	-12.00
15-16	3	13	3	2	1	7	23.1	-0.29

JOCKEYS

	W-R	Per cent	£1 Level Stake
Jack Quinlan	1-9	11.1	-3.50

COURSE RECORD

	Total W-R	Non-Hndcps Hurdles	Chases	Hndcps Hurdles	Chases	NH Flat	Per cent	£1 Level Stake
Fakenham	1-5	0-0	0-1	1-3	0-1	0-0	20.0	+0.50

WINNING HORSES

Horse	Races Run	1st	2nd	3rd	£
Gin And Tonic	11	1	0	2	5198
Total winning prize-money					£5198
Favourites	0-0		0.0%		0.00

DAI WILLIAMS
BROAD HINTON, WILTS

	No. of Hrs	Races Run	1st	2nd	3rd	Unpl	Per cent	£1 Level Stake
NH Flat	2	5	0	0	0	5	0.0	-5.00
Hurdles	6	26	2	0	2	22	7.7	-13.00
Chases	10	55	4	6	9	36	7.3	-27.75
Totals	14	86	6	6	11	63	7.0	-45.75
16-17	10	65	1	9	19	36	1.5	-31.00
15-16	9	58	6	3	3	46	10.3	+50.50

JOCKEYS

	W-R	Per cent	£1 Level Stake
Mr Shane Quinlan	3-21	14.3	-4.75
Dave Crosse	2-22	9.1	-4.00
James Bowen	1-3	33.3	+3.00

COURSE RECORD

	Total W-R	Non-Hndcps Hurdles	Chases	Hndcps Hurdles	Chases	NH Flat	Per cent	£1 Level Stake
Towcester	2-11	0-3	0-2	0-0	2-5	0-1	18.2	+5.00
Hereford	1-2	0-0	0-0	0-0	1-2	0-0	50.0	+6.50
Lingfield	1-2	0-0	0-0	1-1	0-1	0-0	50.0	+5.00
Sedgefield	1-2	0-0	0-0	0-0	1-2	0-0	50.0	+0.75
Worcester	1-11	1-3	0-0	0-0	0-8	0-0	9.1	-5.00

WINNING HORSES

Horse	Races Run	1st	2nd	3rd	£
Bennys Girl	11	3	0	1	17798
Rakaia Rosa	10	1	0	3	5064
Stolberg	10	1	0	1	3509
Mister Mister	6	1	0	1	2859
Total winning prize-money					£29230
Favourites	1-2		50.0%		0.75

IAN WILLIAMS
PORTWAY, WORCS

	No. of Hrs	Races Run	1st	2nd	3rd	Unpl	Per cent	£1 Level Stake
NH Flat	3	6	1	1	0	4	16.7	-2.25
Hurdles	46	132	17	13	19	83	12.9	+0.10
Chases	18	64	6	12	8	38	9.4	-31.88
Totals	60	202	24	26	27	125	11.9	-34.03
16-17	61	249	45	28	23	153	18.1	-9.78
15-16	58	226	28	26	22	149	12.4	-78.60

BY MONTH

NH Flat	W-R	Per cent	£1 Level Stake	Hurdles	W-R	Per cent	£1 Level Stake
May	1-1	100.0	+2.75	May	3-12	25.0	+54.75
June	0-0	0.0	0.00	June	1-5	20.0	+0.50
July	0-3	0.0	-3.00	July	1-5	20.0	-1.75
August	0-0	0.0	0.00	August	0-2	0.0	-2.00
September	0-0	0.0	0.00	September	2-6	33.3	+4.25
October	0-1	0.0	-1.00	October	3-15	20.0	-3.23
November	0-0	0.0	0.00	November	2-29	6.9	-22.00
December	0-1	0.0	-1.00	December	0-14	0.0	-14.00
January	0-0	0.0	0.00	January	2-13	15.4	-4.00
February	0-0	0.0	0.00	February	1-9	11.1	+6.00
March	0-0	0.0	0.00	March	1-10	10.0	-8.80
April	0-0	0.0	0.00	April	1-12	8.3	-9.63

Chases	W-R	Per cent	£1 Level Stake	Totals	W-R	Per cent	£1 Level Stake
May	0-7	0.0	-7.00	May	4-20	20.0	+50.50
June	0-1	0.0	-1.00	June	1-6	16.7	-0.50
July	0-1	0.0	-1.00	July	1-9	11.1	-5.75
August	0-1	0.0	-1.00	August	0-3	0.0	-3.00
September	0-2	0.0	-2.00	September	2-8	25.0	+2.25
October	0-5	0.0	-5.00	October	3-21	14.3	-9.23
November	0-9	0.0	-9.00	November	2-38	5.3	-31.00

December	2-9	22.2	-0.88	December	2-24	8.3	-15.88		
January	1-7	14.3	-2.50	January	3-20	15.0	-6.50		
February	0-8	0.0	-8.00	February	1-17	5.9	-2.00		
March	3-5	60.0	+14.50	March	4-15	26.7	+5.70		
April	0-9	0.0	-9.00	April	1-21	4.8	-18.63		

Stratford	1-10	0-3	0-1	1-2	0-2	0-2	10.0	-4.50

DISTANCE

Hurdles	W-R	Per cent	£1 Level Stake	Chases	W-R	Per cent	£1 Level Stake
2m-2m3f	11-74	14.9	+24.72	2m-2m3f	1-15	6.7	-12.38
2m4f-2m7f	6-45	13.3	-11.63	2m4f-2m7f	2-17	11.8	-2.50
3m+	0-12	0.0	-12.00	3m+	3-32	9.4	-17.00

TYPE OF RACE

Non-Handicaps	W-R	Per cent	£1 Level Stake	Handicaps	W-R	Per cent	£1 Level Stake
Nov Hrdls	4-34	11.8	-2.60	Nov Hrdls	1-10	10.0	-2.00
Hrdls	5-17	29.4	+43.95	Hrdls	6-68	8.8	-39.50
Nov Chs	0-1	0.0	-1.00	Nov Chs	0-3	0.0	-3.00
Chases	0-0	0.0	0.00	Chases	4-51	7.8	-28.38
Sell/Claim	0-1	0.0	-1.00	Sell/Claim	0-0	0.0	0.00

RACE CLASS | FIRST TIME OUT

	W-R	Per cent	£1 Level Stake		W-R	Per cent	£1 Level Stake
Class 1	1-15	6.7	-10.00	Bumpers	1-3	33.3	+0.75
Class 2	3-25	12.0	-2.50	Hurdles	8-42	19.0	+52.32
Class 3	3-43	7.0	-32.63	Chases	0-15	0.0	-15.00
Class 4	12-94	12.8	-28.28				
Class 5	5-23	21.7	+41.38	Totals	9-60	15.0	+38.07
Class 6	0-2	0.0	-2.00				

JOCKEYS

	W-R	Per cent	£1 Level Stake
Tom O'Brien	17-106	16.0	-19.78
Robert Dunne	3-27	11.1	-12.00
Jamie Moore	1-5	20.0	+46.00
Tom Scudamore	1-5	20.0	0.00
Richard Johnson	1-8	12.5	-5.25
Edward Austin	1-16	6.3	-8.00

COURSE RECORD

	Total W-R	Non-Hndcps Hurdles	Chases	Hndcps Hurdles	Chases	NH Flat	Per cent	£1 Level Stake
Doncaster	4-21	2-7	0-0	0-5	2-9	0-0	19.0	+5.13
Warwick	3-21	1-7	0-0	1-6	1-8	0-0	14.3	+43.00
Southwell	2-3	2-3	0-0	0-0	0-0	0-0	66.7	+12.20
Haydock	2-7	0-0	0-0	0-4	2-3	0-0	28.6	+7.50
Uttoxeter	2-7	1-4	0-0	1-3	0-0	0-0	28.6	-2.38
Worcester	2-10	1-2	0-0	1-5	0-2	0-1	20.0	+1.25
Ludlow	2-11	2-5	0-0	0-4	0-2	0-0	18.2	-8.23
Huntingdon	2-13	1-4	0-0	1-7	0-2	0-0	15.4	-6.00
Ffos Las	1-1	0-0	0-0	0-0	0-0	1-1	100.0	+2.75
Wincanton	1-3	0-0	0-0	1-1	0-2	0-0	33.3	+2.00
Kempton	1-8	0-2	0-0	1-4	0-2	0-0	12.5	-5.25
Aintree	1-10	0-1	0-0	0-5	1-4	0-0	10.0	-4.50

WINNING HORSES

Horse	Races Run	1st	2nd	3rd	£
Gas Line Boy	4	1	0	1	43330
London Prize	3	1	0	0	34170
Amber Gambler	5	1	0	0	30950
Psychedelic Rock	7	2	3	0	18499
Zerachiel	5	1	2	0	12686
No Ceiling	4	1	0	0	8758
Red Infantry	7	2	1	2	11112
Cool Sky	3	1	0	0	5317
*Michael's Mount	4	2	0	1	9357
The Statesman	1	1	0	0	5198
First Assignment	4	1	1	1	5198
Sailors Warn	4	1	0	2	4549
North Hill	3	1	0	0	3899
Adman Sam	1	1	0	0	3899
Rebel Yeats	8	2	3	0	3899
Speedo Boy	3	1	0	1	3899
Banditry	4	1	2	0	3574
King Of Realms	4	1	2	0	3119
Eat My Dirt	2	1	0	0	2599
Secret Legacy	4	1	0	2	2599
Total winning prize-money					**£216611**
Favourites	10-30		33.3%		-2.53

NICK WILLIAMS

GEORGE NYMPTON, DEVON

	No. of Hrs	Races Run	1st	2nd	3rd	Unpl	Per cent	£1 Level Stake
NH Flat	6	11	3	1	2	5	27.3	+1.25
Hurdles	27	92	16	13	12	51	17.4	+45.91
Chases	12	47	10	6	9	22	21.3	+0.23
Totals	38	150	29	20	23	78	19.3	+47.39
16-17	35	147	19	18	20	90	12.9	-14.60
15-16	36	112	12	23	20	57	10.7	-52.20

BY MONTH

NH Flat	W-R	Per cent	£1 Level Stake	Hurdles	W-R	Per cent	£1 Level Stake
May	0-0	0.0	0.00	May	1-5	20.0	+1.00
June	0-0	0.0	0.00	June	0-4	0.0	-4.00
July	0-0	0.0	0.00	July	0-1	0.0	-1.00
August	0-1	0.0	-1.00	August	0-4	0.0	-4.00
September	0-1	0.0	-1.00	September	3-5	60.0	+24.00
October	0-0	0.0	0.00	October	2-10	20.0	+4.50
November	0-1	0.0	-1.00	November	3-12	25.0	-3.59
December	2-2	100.0	+7.25	December	1-13	7.7	-5.50
January	0-2	0.0	-2.00	January	3-13	23.1	+24.00
February	0-1	0.0	-1.00	February	2-10	20.0	+8.50
March	1-2	50.0	+1.00	March	1-10	10.0	+7.00
April	0-1	0.0	-1.00	April	0-5	0.0	-5.00

Chases	W-R	Per cent	£1 Level Stake	Totals	W-R	Per cent	£1 Level Stake
May	0-1	0.0	-1.00	May	1-6	16.7	0.00
June	0-0	0.0	0.00	June	0-4	0.0	-4.00
July	0-0	0.0	0.00	July	0-1	0.0	-1.00
August	0-0	0.0	0.00	August	0-5	0.0	-5.00
September	0-0	0.0	0.00	September	3-6	50.0	+23.00
October	0-6	0.0	-6.00	October	2-16	12.5	-1.50
November	1-6	16.7	+6.00	November	4-19	21.1	+1.41
December	3-9	33.3	-1.78	December	6-24	25.0	-0.03
January	2-5	40.0	+6.50	January	5-20	25.0	+28.50
February	2-7	28.6	-1.50	February	4-18	22.2	+6.00
March	2-8	25.0	+3.00	March	4-20	20.0	+11.00
April	0-5	0.0	-5.00	April	0-11	0.0	-11.00

DISTANCE

Hurdles	W-R	Per cent	£1 Level Stake	Chases	W-R	Per cent	£1 Level Stake
2m-2m3f	9-53	17.0	+25.91	2m-2m3f	3-7	42.9	+0.22
2m4f-2m7f	1-24	4.2	-7.00	2m4f-2m7f	4-16	25.0	+12.50
3m+	6-15	40.0	+27.00	3m+	3-24	12.5	-12.50

TYPE OF RACE

Non-Handicaps	W-R	Per cent	£1 Level Stake	Handicaps	W-R	Per cent	£1 Level Stake
Nov Hrdls	0-7	0.0	-7.00	Nov Hrdls	1-4	25.0	+3.50
Hrdls	4-20	20.0	+16.16	Hrdls	11-60	18.3	+34.25
Nov Chs	1-10	10.0	-8.90	Nov Chs	1-6	16.7	-1.00
Chases	2-7	28.6	-1.13	Chases	5-22	22.7	+10.75
Sell/Claim	0-0	0.0	0.00	Sell/Claim	0-0	0.0	0.00

RACE CLASS / FIRST TIME OUT

Race Class	W-R	Per cent	£1 Level Stake	First Time Out	W-R	Per cent	£1 Level Stake
Class 1	2-35	5.7	-19.00	Bumpers	2-6	33.3	+0.25
Class 2	4-17	23.5	+26.88	Hurdles	3-26	11.5	-11.09
Class 3	4-33	12.1	-11.50	Chases	0-6	0.0	-6.00
Class 4	15-52	28.8	+42.76				
Class 5	2-9	22.2	+3.00	Totals	5-38	13.2	-16.84
Class 6	2-4	50.0	+5.25				

JOCKEYS

	W-R	Per cent	£1 Level Stake
Lizzie Kelly	15-79	19.0	+29.91
Mr Chester Williams	8-42	19.0	+7.50
Tom Scudamore	3-8	37.5	-1.02
Sam Twiston-Davies	2-4	50.0	+11.00
Harry Cobden	1-4	25.0	+13.00

COURSE RECORD

	Total W-R	Non-Hndcps Hurdles	Non-Hndcps Chases	Hndcps Hurdles	Hndcps Chases	NH Flat	Per cent	£1 Level Stake
Exeter	4-12	1-3	1-3	0-3	2-3	0-0	33.3	-1.47
Taunton	3-12	1-3	0-0	2-7	0-1	0-1	25.0	0.00
Bangor	2-4	0-1	0-0	0-0	1-2	1-1	50.0	+11.25
Mrket Rsn	2-5	0-0	1-1	1-3	0-0	0-1	40.0	+4.50
Chepstow	2-6	0-1	0-1	2-4	0-0	0-0	33.3	+14.00
Newbury	2-6	0-2	0-0	0-1	1-1	1-2	33.3	+8.00
Wincanton	2-6	0-1	0-1	0-1	1-2	1-1	33.3	0.00
Nton Abbot	2-8	0-2	0-0	2-5	0-0	0-1	25.0	+12.00
Ludlow	2-11	0-0	0-0	2-8	0-3	0-0	18.2	+2.50
Cheltenham	2-19	1-3	0-4	0-6	1-5	0-1	10.5	-3.00
Huntingdon	1-1	1-1	0-0	0-0	0-0	0-0	100.0	+20.00
Sedgefield	1-2	0-0	0-0	1-2	0-0	0-0	50.0	+7.00
Ascot	1-4	0-0	0-0	1-4	0-0	0-0	25.0	+3.50
Haydock	1-5	0-1	0-1	1-2	0-1	0-0	20.0	+12.00
Warwick	1-6	0-0	1-1	0-2	0-2	0-1	16.7	-4.90
Sandown	1-8	0-2	0-0	0-2	1-3	0-1	12.5	-3.00

WINNING HORSES

Horse	Races Run	1st	2nd	3rd	£
Coo Star Sivola	7	2	1	1	72491
Agrapart	3	1	2	0	34170
Culture De Sivola	5	3	0	1	40307
Le Rocher	7	3	0	1	34716
Esprit De Somoza	4	1	1	0	15640
Diamant Bleu	3	1	0	0	7692
Peruvien Bleu	7	2	1	1	12794
Horatio Hornblower	7	1	2	2	7343
Siruh Du Lac	4	2	0	1	11047
One Of Us	3	1	0	0	6498
Mercenaire	4	1	1	1	5198
Cabernet D'Alene	7	3	0	0	13646
Gamain	8	2	1	3	8837
Dentley De Mee	7	1	3	2	4549
Daisy De Sivola	4	1	0	0	4094
Zephyr	3	1	0	0	2599
One For The Team	1	1	0	0	2274
Moonlighter	2	1	0	0	2053
Aimee De Sivola	4	1	1	0	1949
Total winning prize-money					**£287897**
Favourites	**9-29**		**31.0%**		**-1.24**

EVAN WILLIAMS

LLANCARFAN, VALE OF GLAMORGAN

	No. of Hrs	Races Run	1st	2nd	3rd	Unpl	Per cent	£1 Level Stake
NH Flat	*17*	*24*	*1*	*9*	*0*	*14*	*4.2*	*-15.00*
Hurdles	*79*	*284*	*35*	*33*	*28*	*188*	*12.3*	*-67.85*
Chases	*40*	*153*	*16*	*21*	*26*	*90*	*10.5*	*-59.64*
Totals	**103**	**461**	**52**	**63**	**54**	**292**	**11.3**	**-142.49**
16-17	*110*	*459*	*51*	*57*	*55*	*296*	*11.1*	*-144.51*
15-16	*101*	*448*	*70*	*52*	*61*	*265*	*15.6*	*+12.95*

BY MONTH

NH Flat	W-R	Per cent	£1 Level Stake	Hurdles	W-R	Per cent	£1 Level Stake
May	0-1	0.0	-1.00	May	5-23	21.7	+5.16
June	0-0	0.0	0.00	June	3-9	33.3	+18.00
July	0-2	0.0	-2.00	July	3-9	33.3	+10.25

	W-R	Per cent	£1 Level Stake		W-R	Per cent	£1 Level Stake
August	0-1	0.0	-1.00	August	0-8	0.0	-8.00
September	0-1	0.0	-1.00	September	1-11	9.1	-7.00
October	0-1	0.0	-1.00	October	4-24	16.7	+11.50
November	0-10	0.0	-10.00	November	6-47	12.8	-8.99
December	0-2	0.0	-2.00	December	5-30	16.7	-16.52
January	0-1	0.0	-1.00	January	1-32	3.1	-27.00
February	0-0	0.0	0.00	February	0-40	0.0	-40.00
March	0-1	0.0	-1.00	March	4-29	13.8	-8.50
April	1-4	25.0	+5.00	April	3-22	13.6	+3.25

Chases	W-R	Per cent	£1 Level Stake	Totals	W-R	Per cent	£1 Level Stake
May	3-10	30.0	+0.63	May	8-34	23.5	+4.79
June	0-11	0.0	-11.00	June	3-20	15.0	+7.00
July	1-17	5.9	-6.00	July	4-28	14.3	+2.25
August	0-6	0.0	-6.00	August	0-15	0.0	-15.00
September	1-7	14.3	-3.00	September	2-19	10.5	-11.00
October	2-12	16.7	-2.50	October	6-37	16.2	+8.00
November	1-19	5.3	-14.00	November	7-76	9.2	-32.99
December	1-18	5.6	-12.50	December	6-50	12.0	-31.02
January	3-21	14.3	+3.36	January	4-54	7.4	-24.64
February	3-14	21.4	+7.00	February	3-54	5.6	-33.00
March	1-10	10.0	-7.63	March	5-40	12.5	-17.13
April	0-8	0.0	-8.00	April	4-34	11.8	+0.25

DISTANCE

Hurdles	W-R	Per cent	£1 Level Stake	Chases	W-R	Per cent	£1 Level Stake
2m-2m3f	19-176	10.8	-65.09	2m-2m3f	7-69	10.1	-35.76
2m4f-2m7f	12-79	15.2	+15.35	2m4f-2m7f	5-39	12.8	-16.88
3m+	4-29	13.8	-18.11	3m+	4-45	8.9	-7.00

TYPE OF RACE

Non-Handicaps	W-R	Per cent	£1 Level Stake	Handicaps	W-R	Per cent	£1 Level Stake
Nov Hrdls	8-69	11.6	-48.38	Nov Hrdls	2-15	13.3	-2.75
Hrdls	3-44	6.8	-29.40	Hrdls	20-151	13.2	+12.14
Nov Chs	2-16	12.5	-8.64	Nov Chs	1-15	6.7	-4.00
Chases	0-2	0.0	-2.00	Chases	13-107	12.1	-32.00
Sell/Claim	2-2	100.0	+3.25	Sell/Claim	0-0	0.0	0.00

RACE CLASS

	W-R	Per cent	£1 Level Stake
Class 1	3-41	7.3	-15.00
Class 2	7-43	16.3	+15.88
Class 3	7-85	8.2	-44.77
Class 4	21-204	10.3	-87.42
Class 5	14-81	17.3	-3.17
Class 6	0-7	0.0	-7.00

FIRST TIME OUT

	W-R	Per cent	£1 Level Stake
Bumpers	1-17	5.9	-8.00
Hurdles	10-62	16.1	+24.41
Chases	6-24	25.0	+16.00
Totals	17-103	16.5	+32.41

JOCKEYS

	W-R	Per cent	£1 Level Stake
Adam Wedge	20-229	8.7	-117.37
Mitchell Bastyan	12-103	11.7	-28.02
Conor Ring	6-68	8.8	-18.83
Miss Isabel Williams	5-16	31.3	+11.50

	W-R	Per cent	£1 Level Stake
Leighton Aspell	4-13	30.8	+13.86
Davy Russell	2-3	66.7	+8.00
Tom Scudamore	1-1	100.0	+4.00
Brian Hughes	1-4	25.0	+6.00
Richard Johnson	1-8	12.5	-5.63

COURSE RECORD

	Total W-R	Non-Hndcps Hurdles	Non-Hndcps Chases	Hndcps Hurdles	Chases	NH Flat	Per cent	£1 Level Stake
Ffos Las	10-52	4-13	0-1	4-20	1-16	1-2	19.2	+1.61
Chepstow	9-43	4-14	0-0	3-14	2-13	0-2	20.9	+15.71
Exeter	7-24	1-4	0-4	5-13	1-3	0-0	29.2	+21.00
Uttoxeter	5-30	0-6	1-1	3-13	1-8	0-2	16.7	+25.00
Ludlow	3-29	0-8	0-2	2-7	1-9	0-3	10.3	-16.13
Nton Abbot	3-30	1-8	0-1	1-7	1-13	0-1	10.0	-19.75
Bangor	2-12	0-5	0-0	1-3	1-3	0-1	16.7	-6.83
Haydock	2-16	1-2	0-2	1-7	0-5	0-0	12.5	-7.50
Warwick	2-20	0-3	0-2	1-10	1-5	0-0	10.0	-4.00
Catterick	1-4	0-1	0-1	0-0	1-2	0-0	25.0	+6.00
Wetherby	1-4	0-1	0-1	0-0	1-2	0-0	25.0	+6.00
Mrket Rsn	1-5	0-0	0-0	1-5	0-0	0-0	20.0	0.00
Carlisle	1-9	1-3	0-1	0-2	0-2	0-1	11.1	-4.50
Aintree	1-10	0-2	0-0	0-2	1-5	0-1	10.0	-5.00
Southwell	1-10	1-6	0-0	0-2	0-2	0-0	10.0	-8.47
Sandown	1-11	0-1	0-0	0-8	1-1	0-1	9.1	+2.00
Hereford	1-12	0-4	1-1	0-4	0-2	0-1	8.3	-10.64
Worcester	1-15	0-4	0-0	0-3	1-8	0-0	6.7	-12.00

WINNING HORSES

Horse	Races Run	1st	2nd	3rd	£
Buywise	5	1	0	0	61900
On Tour	6	1	1	0	46425
John Constable	5	2	1	0	54103
Court Minstrel	8	1	1	1	28475
De Dollar Man	4	1	1	0	15640
Tornado In Milan	7	2	1	1	27852
Silver Streak	4	1	1	0	12996
Positively Dylan	9	3	1	3	22082
Clyne	7	1	2	2	12512
Prime Venture	6	1	1	0	9097
Still Believing	9	2	1	0	14128
Skewiff	6	2	0	1	10397
Aqua Dude	2	1	0	0	6330
*In The Hold	2	1	0	0	5592
Report To Base	5	1	1	0	5317
Sutter's Mill	10	1	3	0	5085
Market Road	10	5	0	2	14868
Aerlite Supreme	4	1	1	0	4549
Abbeygrey	7	1	0	0	4549
Holdalltheriver	7	1	2	1	4549
Present Times	4	1	1	0	4224
Cesar Collonges	5	1	1	0	4224
The Last Day	4	2	0	1	7993
Virginia Chick	7	4	1	0	9617
Bonobo	5	1	1	0	3899
Prussian Eagle	7	1	1	1	3899
Jonagold	9	1	3	0	3899

Apollo Creed	4	1	0	1	3899
*Catcher On The Go	5	1	0	0	3899
Cape Caster	5	1	2	1	3899
Oxwich Bay	7	1	3	0	3899
Chooseyourweapon	4	2	0	1	5848
Mick Manhattan	1	1	0	0	3249
Under The Woods	5	1	1	2	3249
Radical Archie	4	1	0	0	3119
Classic Jewel	4	1	0	3	2989
Bach De Clermont	6	1	2	2	2599
Total winning prize-money					£440850
Favourites	18-59		30.5%		-11.11

NOEL WILLIAMS

BLEWBURY, OXON

	No. of Hrs	Races Run	1st	2nd	3rd	Unpl	Per cent	£1 Level Stake
NH Flat	10	16	2	4	2	8	12.5	+10.00
Hurdles	16	42	3	5	6	28	7.1	-28.75
Chases	4	9	3	1	0	5	33.3	+8.13
Totals	24	67	8	10	8	41	11.9	-10.62
16-17	17	70	5	7	7	51	7.1	-39.13
15-16	19	78	10	11	11	46	12.8	-23.11

JOCKEYS

	W-R	Per cent	£1 Level Stake
Wayne Hutchinson	4-31	12.9	-12.00
Tom Scudamore	1-1	100.0	+1.38
Harry Teal	1-3	33.3	+10.00
Leighton Aspell	1-4	25.0	+5.00
Thomas Garner	1-11	9.1	+2.00

COURSE RECORD

	Total W-R	Non-Hndcps Hurdles	Chases	Hndcps Hurdles	Chases	NH Flat	Per cent	£1 Level Stake
Huntingdon	2-6	0-2	0-0	0-1	1-2	1-1	33.3	+10.13
Warwick	2-6	1-2	0-0	1-1	0-1	0-2	33.3	+4.88
Leicester	1-3	0-0	0-0	0-2	1-1	0-0	33.3	+2.00
Exeter	1-4	0-2	1-1	0-1	0-0	0-0	25.0	+5.00
Fontwell	1-4	0-0	0-0	0-3	0-0	1-1	25.0	+9.00
Nton Abbot	1-4	1-3	0-0	0-1	0-0	0-0	25.0	-1.63

WINNING HORSES

Horse	Races Run	1st	2nd	3rd	£
Briery Queen	1	1	0	0	7656
Kincora Fort	6	2	1	0	14361
Sensulano	7	1	3	2	5198
Undisputed	6	1	1	1	5020
Paloma's Prince	2	1	0	0	3574
Breaking Waves	1	1	0	0	2395
Kalinihta	1	1	0	0	2274
Total winning prize-money					£40478
Favourites	3-9		33.3%		1.50

VENETIA WILLIAMS

KINGS CAPLE, H'FORDS

	No. of Hrs	Races Run	1st	2nd	3rd	Unpl	Per cent	£1 Level Stake
NH Flat	16	19	2	2	1	14	10.5	-5.50
Hurdles	46	135	16	9	13	97	11.9	+1.49
Chases	46	151	16	14	18	102	10.6	-43.50
Totals	87	305	34	25	32	213	11.1	-47.51
16-17	92	308	46	38	33	191	14.9	-79.55
15-16	100	419	56	56	63	244	13.4	-104.92

BY MONTH

NH Flat	W-R	Per cent	£1 Level Stake	Hurdles	W-R	Per cent	£1 Level Stake
May	0-2	0.0	-2.00	May	0-3	0.0	-3.00
June	0-0	0.0	0.00	June	0-0	0.0	0.00
July	0-0	0.0	0.00	July	0-0	0.0	0.00
August	0-0	0.0	0.00	August	0-0	0.0	0.00
September	0-0	0.0	0.00	September	0-0	0.0	0.00
October	0-4	0.0	-4.00	October	0-8	0.0	-8.00
November	0-3	0.0	-3.00	November	3-17	17.6	-3.75
December	0-4	0.0	-4.00	December	3-13	23.1	+5.38
January	0-1	0.0	-1.00	January	2-27	7.4	-20.63
February	0-0	0.0	0.00	February	2-24	8.3	-20.39
March	0-1	0.0	-1.00	March	3-22	13.6	+61.50
April	2-4	50.0	+9.50	April	3-21	14.3	-9.63

Chases	W-R	Per cent	£1 Level Stake	Totals	W-R	Per cent	£1 Level Stake
May	0-2	0.0	-2.00	May	0-7	0.0	-7.00
June	0-1	0.0	-1.00	June	0-1	0.0	-1.00
July	0-0	0.0	0.00	July	0-0	0.0	0.00
August	0-0	0.0	0.00	August	0-0	0.0	0.00
September	0-0	0.0	0.00	September	0-0	0.0	0.00
October	1-9	11.1	-4.00	October	1-21	4.8	-16.00
November	3-29	10.3	-11.00	November	6-49	12.2	-17.75
December	1-15	6.7	-10.50	December	4-32	12.5	-9.12
January	2-23	8.7	-13.00	January	4-51	7.8	-34.63
February	1-22	4.5	-13.00	February	3-46	6.5	-33.39
March	3-24	12.5	-0.25	March	6-47	12.8	+60.25
April	5-26	19.2	+11.25	April	10-51	19.6	+11.12

DISTANCE

Hurdles	W-R	Per cent	£1 Level Stake	Chases	W-R	Per cent	£1 Level Stake
2m-2m3f	8-79	10.1	+14.25	2m-2m3f	3-28	10.7	-14.50
2m4f-2m7f	5-42	11.9	-8.25	2m4f-2m7f	6-43	14.0	+9.25
3m+	3-13	23.1	-3.51	3m+	7-80	8.8	-38.25

TYPE OF RACE

Non-Handicaps	W-R	Per cent	£1 Level Stake	Handicaps	W-R	Per cent	£1 Level Stake
Nov Hrdls	5-39	12.8	+39.36	Nov Hrdls	1-5	20.0	+0.50
Hrdls	1-30	3.3	-25.00	Hrdls	8-59	13.6	-14.25
Nov Chs	0-0	0.0	0.00	Nov Chs	1-8	12.5	-4.75

Chases	0-3	0.0	-3.00
Sell/Claim	0-0	0.0	0.00

Chases	15-128	11.7	-23.75
Sell/Claim	0-0	0.0	0.00

RACE CLASS

	W-R	Per cent	£1 Level Stake
Class 1	1-27	3.7	-18.00
Class 2	6-38	15.8	-0.75
Class 3	9-73	12.3	+57.63
Class 4	12-128	9.4	-87.39
Class 5	6-33	18.2	+7.00
Class 6	0-6	0.0	-6.00

FIRST TIME OUT

	W-R	Per cent	£1 Level Stake
Bumpers	2-16	12.5	-2.50
Hurdles	4-31	12.9	-12.25
Chases	5-40	12.5	-0.50
Totals	11-87	12.6	-15.25

JOCKEYS

	W-R	Per cent	£1 Level Stake
Charlie Deutsch	21-150	14.0	-26.89
Mr Hugh Nugent	5-30	16.7	-0.25
Aidan Coleman	3-28	10.7	+43.88
Liam Treadwell	2-31	6.5	-16.00
Sean Bowen	1-5	20.0	-1.25
Wayne Hutchinson	1-5	20.0	0.00
Alain Cawley	1-10	10.0	-1.00

COURSE RECORD

	Total W-R	Non-Hndcps Hurdles	Chases	Hndcps Hurdles	Chases	NH Flat	Per cent	£1 Level Stake
Hereford	5-20	0-9	0-0	2-4	2-6	1-1	25.0	+19.25
Haydock	4-11	1-2	0-0	1-3	2-6	0-0	36.4	+79.50
Chepstow	3-34	0-11	0-0	1-7	2-14	0-2	8.8	-18.50
Catterick	2-5	2-3	0-0	0-1	0-1	0-0	40.0	-0.51
Carlisle	2-8	0-0	0-1	0-2	2-4	0-1	25.0	+2.50
Mrket Rsn	2-10	1-1	0-0	0-3	1-4	0-2	20.0	-5.50
Uttoxeter	2-16	1-5	0-0	1-6	0-4	0-1	12.5	-8.50
Exeter	2-18	0-6	0-0	1-2	1-9	0-1	11.1	-11.88
Wincanton	2-19	1-4	0-0	0-3	1-12	0-0	10.5	-8.50
Ludlow	2-23	1-9	0-0	0-4	1-8	0-2	8.7	-8.00
Wetherby	1-3	0-0	0-0	1-2	0-1	0-0	33.3	+2.50
Kempton	1-4	0-1	0-0	0-1	1-2	0-0	25.0	+11.00
Southwell	1-4	0-0	0-0	0-1	1-3	0-0	25.0	-0.75
Newbury	1-5	0-0	0-0	0-0	1-5	0-0	20.0	+6.00
Taunton	1-7	0-2	0-0	1-1	0-4	0-0	14.3	-4.63
Sandown	1-9	0-0	0-1	0-2	1-6	0-0	11.1	-5.50
Towcester	1-10	0-4	0-0	0-3	0-2	1-1	10.0	-1.00
Warwick	1-16	0-3	0-0	1-4	0-8	0-1	6.3	-12.00

WINNING HORSES

Horse	Races Run	1st	2nd	3rd	£
Yala Enki	8	1	0	1	60067
Cepage	5	1	1	1	25024
Pressurize	6	1	0	0	19166
Houblon Des Obeaux	8	1	0	2	18838
Emperor's Choice	5	1	0	1	13814
Eminent Poet	8	2	0	1	20144
Un Prophete	4	1	0	0	9495
Yalltari	3	3	0	0	20960
Uhlan Bute	5	1	0	1	8837

Calipto	4	1	0	0	8447
Vic De Touzaine	6	1	0	0	8123
Willie Boy	3	1	0	0	7798
Huff And Puff	2	1	0	1	7343
Kapga De Lily	2	1	0	0	6657
Luckime	7	2	0	1	9942
Shalakar	6	1	0	4	4874
Call Carlo	5	1	1	0	4614
One Style	4	2	0	0	9227
Lady Karina	3	1	0	0	4549
Rouergate	7	1	0	1	4549
Pink Tara	2	1	0	0	4159
Enola Gay	6	1	3	0	3899
Saroque	4	1	0	0	3509
Snuff Box	4	1	1	0	3379
Du Soleil	5	1	1	0	3379
Becauseshesaidso	7	1	1	1	3314
Mixchievous	3	1	0	0	3249
Destinee Royale	1	1	0	0	2599
Geordie B	1	1	0	0	2274
Total winning prize-money					**£302229**
Favourites	11-30		36.7%		5.74

CHRISTIAN WILLIAMS
OGMORE-BY-SEA, GLAMORGAN

	No. of Hrs	Races Run	1st	2nd	3rd	Unpl	Per cent	£1 Level Stake
NH Flat	7	9	1	1	2	5	11.1	-6.38
Hurdles	14	44	4	9	4	27	9.1	-28.63
Chases	5	12	3	1	0	8	25.0	-3.50
Totals	21	65	8	11	6	40	12.3	-38.51
16-17	*6*	*6*	*1*	*2*	*2*	*1*	*16.7*	*+0.50*

JOCKEYS

	W-R	Per cent	£1 Level Stake
James Bowen	4-12	33.3	+0.74
Richard Johnson	2-7	28.6	-1.50
Noel Fehily	1-6	16.7	-3.25
Denis O'Regan	1-12	8.3	-6.50

COURSE RECORD

	Total W-R	Non-Hndcps Hurdles	Chases	Hndcps Hurdles	Chases	NH Flat	Per cent	£1 Level Stake
Haydock	2-3	0-0	0-0	2-3	0-0	0-0	66.7	+4.12
Exeter	1-1	0-0	0-0	0-0	0-0	1-1	100.0	+1.63
Sedgefield	1-1	0-0	0-0	0-0	1-1	0-0	100.0	+2.25
Ludlow	1-2	0-1	0-0	0-0	1-1	0-0	50.0	+0.38
Sandown	1-2	0-0	0-0	1-1	0-1	0-0	50.0	+3.50
Nton Abbot	1-5	0-2	0-0	0-2	1-1	0-0	20.0	-2.13
Warwick	1-7	1-4	0-0	0-1	0-1	0-1	14.3	-4.25

WINNING HORSES

Horse	Races Run	1st	2nd	3rd	£
Limited Reserve	5	2	2	0	43792

Cap Du Nord	7	1	0	1	6498
Hedgeinator	7	3	1	0	14750
The Welsh Paddies	3	1	1	0	3899
Volcano	2	1	0	0	1949
Total winning prize-money					**£70888**
Favourites	**4-16**	**25.0%**			**-6.51**

ANDREW WILSON

ORTON, CUMBRIA

	No. of Hrs	Races Run	1st	2nd	3rd	Unpl	Per cent	£1 Level Stake
NH Flat	0	0	0	0	0	0	0.0	0.00
Hurdles	3	9	0	1	0	8	0.0	-9.00
Chases	1	4	1	2	0	1	25.0	+0.50
Totals	**3**	**13**	**1**	**3**	**0**	**9**	**7.7**	**-8.50**
16-17	*4*	*11*	*0*	*0*	*1*	*10*	*0.0*	*-11.00*
15-16	*4*	*19*	*1*	*1*	*1*	*16*	*5.3*	*-6.00*

JOCKEYS

	W-R	Per cent	£1 Level Stake
Brian Hughes	1-10	10.0	-5.50

COURSE RECORD

	Total W-R	Non-Hndcps Hurdles	Chases	Hndcps Hurdles	Chases	NH Flat	Per cent	£1 Level Stake
Sedgefield	1-4	0-0	0-0	0-1	1-3	0-0	25.0	+0.50

WINNING HORSES

Horse	Races Run	1st	2nd	3rd	£
Kings Eclipse	8	1	3	0	3899
Total winning prize-money					**£3899**
Favourites	**0-2**	**0.0%**			**-2.00**

PETER WINKS

LITTLE HOUGHTON, S YORKS

	No. of Hrs	Races Run	1st	2nd	3rd	Unpl	Per cent	£1 Level Stake
NH Flat	1	2	0	0	0	2	0.0	-2.00
Hurdles	7	53	5	7	7	34	9.4	-24.50
Chases	5	19	1	1	3	14	5.3	-14.50
Totals	**10**	**74**	**6**	**8**	**10**	**50**	**8.1**	**-41.00**
16-17	*9*	*76*	*10*	*9*	*14*	*43*	*13.2*	*-27.42*
15-16	*8*	*45*	*5*	*6*	*9*	*25*	*11.1*	*+3.83*

JOCKEYS

	W-R	Per cent	£1 Level Stake
Ryan Winks	3-57	5.3	-43.00
Mitchell Bastyan	2-4	50.0	+10.00
Ryan Day	1-2	50.0	+3.00

COURSE RECORD

	Total W-R	Non-Hndcps Hurdles	Chases	Hndcps Hurdles	Chases	NH Flat	Per cent	£1 Level Stake
Fakenham	1-1	1-1	0-0	0-0	0-0	0-0	100.0	+3.00
Hexham	1-2	0-1	0-0	1-1	0-0	0-0	50.0	+7.50
Cartmel	1-3	0-0	0-0	0-2	1-1	0-0	33.3	+1.50
Doncaster	1-5	0-0	0-0	1-3	0-2	0-0	20.0	0.00
Carlisle	1-6	0-0	0-0	1-5	0-0	0-1	16.7	-1.50
Wetherby	1-7	0-0	0-0	1-5	0-2	0-0	14.3	-1.50

WINNING HORSES

Horse	Races Run	1st	2nd	3rd	£
Gran Maestro	14	1	3	2	4549
Domtaline	7	2	1	0	7798
Back To Balloo	10	2	2	0	6173
Hartside	12	1	0	2	3119
Total winning prize-money					**£21639**
Favourites	**0-5**	**0.0%**			**-5.00**

ADRIAN WINTLE

WESTBURY-ON-SEVERN, GLOUCS

	No. of Hrs	Races Run	1st	2nd	3rd	Unpl	Per cent	£1 Level Stake
NH Flat	3	3	0	0	0	3	0.0	-3.00
Hurdles	10	28	1	1	5	21	3.6	-21.50
Chases	3	10	0	1	1	8	0.0	-10.00
Totals	**14**	**41**	**1**	**2**	**6**	**32**	**2.4**	**-34.50**
16-17	*17*	*48*	*2*	*2*	*3*	*41*	*4.2*	*+76.00*
15-16	*21*	*66*	*4*	*2*	*5*	*55*	*6.1*	*-42.38*

JOCKEYS

	W-R	Per cent	£1 Level Stake
Mr Lorcan Williams	1-8	12.5	-1.50

COURSE RECORD

	Total W-R	Non-Hndcps Hurdles	Chases	Hndcps Hurdles	Chases	NH Flat	Per cent	£1 Level Stake
Ffos Las	1-4	0-2	0-0	1-2	0-0	0-0	25.0	+2.50

WINNING HORSES

Horse	Races Run	1st	2nd	3rd	£
*De Bene Esse	4	1	0	1	3509
Total winning prize-money					**£3509**
Favourites	**0-1**	**0.0%**			**-1.00**

KAYLEY WOOLLACOTT

SOUTH MOLTON, DEVON

	No. of Hrs	Races Run	1st	2nd	3rd	Unpl	Per cent	£1 Level Stake
NH Flat	1	1	0	0	0	1	0.0	-1.00
Hurdles	7	12	1	1	1	9	8.3	+3.00
Chases	5	11	1	1	4	5	9.1	-7.50

Totals	13	24	2	2	5	15	8.3	-5.50
16-17	3	3	0	1	1	1	0.0	-3.00
15-16	2	4	2	0	1	1	50.0	+2.10

JOCKEYS

	W-R	Per cent	£1 Level Stake
Richard Johnson	1-2	50.0	+13.00
James Best	1-9	11.1	-5.50

COURSE RECORD

	Total W-R	Non-Hndcps Hurdles	Chases	Hndcps Hurdles	Chases	NH Flat	Per cent	£1 Level Stake
Aintree	1-1	1-1	0-0	0-0	0-0	0-0	100.0	+14.00
Exeter	1-3	0-0	0-0	0-0	1-3	0-0	33.3	+0.50

WINNING HORSES

Horse	Races Run	1st	2nd	3rd	£
*Lalor	2	1	0	0	56130
*The Kings Writ	2	1	1	0	7148
Total winning prize-money					£63278
Favourites	1-5	20.0%			-1.50

RICHARD WOOLLACOTT

SOUTH MOLTON, DEVON

	No. of Hrs	Races Run	1st	2nd	3rd	Unpl	Per cent	£1 Level Stake
NH Flat	2	2	0	0	0	2	0.0	-2.00
Hurdles	15	50	2	9	4	35	4.0	+8.00
Chases	10	21	2	2	2	15	9.5	+7.00
Totals	22	73	4	11	6	52	5.5	+13.00
16-17	33	128	13	10	13	91	10.2	+14.63
15-16	31	101	6	6	8	80	5.9	-72.25

JOCKEYS

	W-R	Per cent	£1 Level Stake
Richard Johnson	1-4	25.0	+37.00
Micheal Nolan	1-5	20.0	+2.00
James Best	1-16	6.3	+5.00
Daryl Jacob	1-17	5.9	0.00

COURSE RECORD

	Total W-R	Non-Hndcps Hurdles	Chases	Hndcps Hurdles	Chases	NH Flat	Per cent	£1 Level Stake
Newbury	1-2	1-1	0-0	0-0	0-1	0-0	50.0	+39.00
Chepstow	1-7	0-0	0-0	0-2	1-5	0-0	14.3	0.00
Nton Abbot	1-9	0-0	0-1	1-8	0-0	0-0	11.1	+8.00
Worcester	1-12	0-1	0-0	0-7	1-3	0-1	8.3	+9.00

WINNING HORSES

Horse	Races Run	1st	2nd	3rd	£
Beer Goggles	4	2	1	1	43833
Sheer Poetry	7	1	1	2	12512

Millanisi Boy		3	1	1	0	6498
Total winning prize-money					£62843
Favourites	0-10		0.0%		-10.00

PHIL YORK

MARTYR'S GREEN, SURREY

	No. of Hrs	Races Run	1st	2nd	3rd	Unpl	Per cent	£1 Level Stake
NH Flat	1	2	0	0	0	2	0.0	-2.00
Hurdles	2	2	0	0	0	2	0.0	-2.00
Chases	2	7	3	2	1	1	42.9	+21.00
Totals	5	11	3	2	1	5	27.3	+17.00
16-17	7	28	0	2	8	18	0.0	-28.00

JOCKEYS

	W-R	Per cent	£1 Level Stake
Miss Katy Lyons	2-9	22.2	+12.50
Mr Phillip York	1-2	50.0	+4.50

COURSE RECORD

	Total W-R	Non-Hndcps Hurdles	Chases	Hndcps Hurdles	Chases	NH Flat	Per cent	£1 Level Stake
Fontwell	3-8	0-0	0-0	0-1	3-6	0-1	37.5	+20.00

WINNING HORSES

Horse	Races Run	1st	2nd	3rd	£
*Spiritofchartwell	6	3	2	1	9243
Total winning prize-money					£9243
Favourites	0-1	0.0%			-1.00

LAURA YOUNG

BROOMFIELD, SOMERSET

	No. of Hrs	Races Run	1st	2nd	3rd	Unpl	Per cent	£1 Level Stake
NH Flat	0	0	0	0	0	0	0.0	0.00
Hurdles	14	43	1	2	2	38	2.3	-33.00
Chases	6	25	0	1	6	18	0.0	-25.00
Totals	15	68	1	3	8	56	1.5	-58.00
16-17	20	71	3	2	6	60	4.2	-46.00
15-16	21	69	1	4	6	58	1.4	-63.00

JOCKEYS

	W-R	Per cent	£1 Level Stake
Sam Twiston-Davies	1-4	25.0	+6.00

COURSE RECORD

	Total W-R	Non-Hndcps Hurdles	Chases	Hndcps Hurdles	Chases	NH Flat	Per cent	£1 Level Stake
Worcester	1-8	0-0	0-1	1-6	0-1	0-0	12.5	+2.00

WINNING HORSES

Horse	Races Run	1st	2nd	3rd	£
Jigsaw Financial	5	1	1	0	3899
Total winning prize-money					**£3899**
Favourites	**0-0**		**0.0%**		**0.00**

LEADING JUMP TRAINERS AT AINTREE (SINCE 2013)

	Total W-R	Nov Hdle	H'cap Hdle	Other Hdle	Nov Chase	H'cap Chase	Other Chase	Hunter Chase	N.H. Flat	Per cent	£1 Level stake
Nicky Henderson	30-151	4-21	6-37	10-28	3-12	4-30	1-7	0-0	2-16	19.9	**15.24**
Paul Nicholls	17-161	3-16	1-22	1-18	4-19	3-58	5-14	0-6	0-8	10.6	-53.38
Tom George	13-73	2-6	0-6	0-4	1-3	7-44	1-3	0-2	2-5	17.8	**35.24**
Colin Tizzard	12-56	3-8	0-7	1-4	2-4	4-26	2-6	0-1	0-0	21.4	**92.49**
Jonjo O'Neill	11-97	2-9	2-34	1-7	2-5	3-30	0-5	0-1	1-6	11.3	-35.65
Nigel Twiston-Davies	11-104	2-11	1-22	2-9	2-6	3-44	0-3	0-2	1-7	10.6	-35.81
W P Mullins	10-62	2-12	1-6	3-9	1-2	0-19	2-7	0-2	1-5	16.1	-14.16
Philip Hobbs	10-101	1-5	1-38	3-8	0-2	5-31	0-7	0-3	0-7	9.9	-26.56
Dan Skelton	9-79	2-13	4-24	1-12	1-5	1-19	0-1	0-0	0-5	11.4	-40.83
Peter Bowen	8-75	0-5	2-29	0-2	0-3	4-29	0-0	0-0	2-7	10.7	-34.75
Alan King	7-75	0-12	1-19	2-11	2-3	1-12	0-5	0-0	1-13	9.3	-17.13
Gordon Elliott	5-45	0-1	1-10	0-4	1-3	2-20	1-4	0-1	0-2	11.1	-5.00
Harry Fry	5-35	0-2	2-8	1-9	0-1	2-11	0-0	0-0	0-4	14.3	-9.27
David Pipe	5-77	0-3	2-21	1-5	0-4	2-40	0-4	0-0	0-0	6.5	-22.38
Rebecca Curtis	5-58	2-9	1-10	0-6	0-6	1-20	0-2	0-1	1-4	8.6	-39.13
Donald McCain	5-126	2-12	1-41	1-12	0-8	1-42	0-1	0-1	0-9	4.0	-95.80
Tim Vaughan	4-39	1-5	2-17	0-1	0-1	1-14	0-0	0-0	0-1	10.3	-6.94
Charlie Longsdon	4-60	0-10	2-15	1-4	0-2	1-22	0-0	0-0	0-7	6.7	-39.47
Dr Richard Newland	3-29	0-0	2-11	0-1	0-0	1-16	0-0	0-1	0-0	10.3	**15.25**
Jennie Candlish	3-21	0-2	2-12	0-2	0-0	1-5	0-0	0-0	0-0	14.3	**28.50**
Kevin Frost	3-13	1-1	0-6	0-0	0-0	2-5	0-0	0-0	0-1	23.1	**35.75**
Malcolm Jefferson	3-22	1-3	1-7	0-0	0-1	1-5	0-1	0-0	0-5	13.6	-1.37
Evan Williams	3-30	0-2	1-6	1-3	0-1	1-14	0-0	0-0	0-4	10.0	-3.50
Dianne Sayer	3-28	0-3	2-13	0-3	1-1	0-8	0-0	0-0	0-0	10.7	-3.67
Warren Greatrex	3-39	0-8	1-10	0-2	0-1	0-7	0-1	0-1	2-9	7.7	-5.00
Lucinda Russell	3-34	1-3	0-11	0-1	0-1	2-16	0-0	0-0	0-2	8.8	-6.13
E Bolger	2-6	0-0	0-0	0-0	0-0	0-1	0-0	2-5	0-0	33.3	**0.38**
Nick Williams	2-14	1-2	0-0	0-6	0-1	0-3	1-2	0-0	0-0	14.3	**0.75**
Harry Whittington	2-7	1-1	0-3	0-0	1-1	0-1	0-0	0-0	0-1	28.6	**1.75**
Oliver Sherwood	2-28	0-3	0-3	0-1	0-1	1-13	1-2	0-2	0-3	7.1	**2.00**

LEADING JUMP TRAINERS AT ASCOT (SINCE 2013)

	Total W-R	Nov Hdle	H'cap Hdle	Other Hdle	Nov Chase	H'cap Chase	Other Chase	Hunter Chase	N.H. Flat	Per cent	£1 Level stake
Paul Nicholls	31-158	3-17	5-29	3-25	6-25	5-36	7-22	1-2	1-6	19.6	-22.05
Nicky Henderson	31-162	6-28	6-44	8-40	4-11	1-14	4-17	0-0	3-15	19.1	-43.15
Venetia Williams	14-81	2-8	2-10	0-3	1-9	9-50	0-0	0-0	0-2	17.3	**43.50**
Harry Fry	14-56	3-7	2-12	6-15	0-4	2-11	1-4	0-0	0-6	25.0	-0.45
Philip Hobbs	13-94	3-6	3-24	1-12	0-14	2-25	3-10	0-1	2-5	13.8	-18.38
Alan King	11-80	2-15	2-26	5-21	1-3	0-8	1-3	0-0	1-7	13.8	-26.14
David Pipe	10-64	1-4	5-28	0-7	1-3	1-19	0-1	0-0	2-4	15.6	-4.03
Colin Tizzard	8-67	1-6	0-7	2-8	2-7	2-22	1-11	0-0	0-7	11.9	-7.73
Gary Moore	8-87	1-11	0-19	1-14	2-14	3-17	1-6	0-0	0-10	9.2	-31.25
Charlie Longsdon	7-62	1-11	1-13	0-6	0-5	3-19	0-2	0-0	2-8	11.3	**14.50**
W P Mullins	6-15	0-1	0-5	3-3	0-0	0-0	3-5	0-0	0-1	40.0	-6.12
Dan Skelton	5-53	1-8	1-16	0-8	2-6	1-11	0-2	0-0	0-4	9.4	-8.50
Rebecca Curtis	4-41	2-4	0-3	0-7	2-7	0-8	0-5	0-0	0-7	9.8	-5.50
Oliver Sherwood	4-31	0-3	0-8	0-8	2-5	0-4	1-2	0-0	1-2	12.9	-9.38
Jonjo O'Neill	4-64	1-6	1-16	0-9	1-8	1-24	0-3	0-0	0-0	6.3	-22.50
Tom George	3-26	0-0	0-0	0-1	1-3	2-18	0-2	0-1	0-1	11.5	**3.00**
Robert Walford	3-12	0-1	0-0	1-5	0-0	2-4	0-0	0-0	0-2	25.0	**11.00**
Ian Williams	3-26	0-4	1-4	0-8	0-3	1-4	0-0	0-0	1-3	11.5	**14.00**
Nick Williams	3-23	1-2	0-7	2-9	0-2	0-4	0-0	0-0	0-0	13.0	-4.75
Ben Pauling	3-23	0-2	1-6	1-4	0-3	0-4	0-0	0-0	1-5	13.0	-4.75
Dr Richard Newland	3-24	1-1	1-9	0-2	0-3	1-8	0-1	0-0	0-1	12.5	-6.00
Neil Mulholland	3-22	0-3	1-5	0-4	0-2	2-7	0-0	0-0	0-1	13.6	-7.75
Evan Williams	3-48	0-3	1-16	0-11	1-5	1-11	0-2	0-1	0-2	6.3	-23.00
Kim Bailey	3-35	1-8	0-9	0-5	2-5	0-3	0-0	0-0	0-5	8.6	-26.81
Neil King	2-18	0-3	1-8	1-5	0-1	0-0	0-0	0-0	0-1	11.1	-4.75
Nick Gifford	2-28	1-4	0-7	0-4	0-1	0-11	0-0	0-0	1-2	7.1	-0.00
Kerry Lee	2-8	0-0	1-3	0-2	1-1	0-0	0-2	0-0	0-0	25.0	**3.75**
Phil Middleton	2-6	0-0	1-2	0-1	0-2	1-2	0-0	0-0	0-0	33.3	**7.50**
James Evans	2-9	1-3	0-1	1-1	0-0	0-2	0-0	0-0	0-2	22.2	**8.00**
Ben Case	2-10	0-2	1-1	0-1	0-1	1-3	0-0	0-0	0-2	20.0	**11.00**

LEADING JUMP TRAINERS AT AYR (SINCE 2013)

	Total W-R	Nov Hdle	H'cap Hdle	Other Hdle	Nov Chase	H'cap Chase	Other Chase	Hunter Chase	N.H. Flat	Per cent	£1 Level stake
Nicky Richards	38-158	7-21	7-46	4-24	4-12	7-33	1-1	0-0	8-21	24.1	-25.52
Lucinda Russell	35-294	3-22	9-80	5-52	4-27	11-79	0-1	0-0	3-33	11.9	-130.46
N W Alexander	24-214	0-12	8-80	2-35	6-23	6-46	0-0	0-0	2-18	11.2	-57.73
Donald McCain	18-93	3-6	2-24	4-14	5-18	2-21	0-0	0-0	2-10	19.4	-31.82
S R B Crawford	18-132	3-11	5-40	4-34	1-9	2-16	0-1	0-0	3-21	13.6	-48.88
James Ewart	13-100	0-7	6-26	1-15	0-7	3-17	0-0	0-0	3-28	13.0	-16.20
Paul Nicholls	12-49	4-6	3-15	0-0	2-9	2-17	0-0	0-0	1-2	24.5	28.88
Jim Goldie	12-107	0-3	6-49	2-20	2-4	2-25	0-0	0-0	0-6	11.2	-44.08
Iain Jardine	10-53	0-4	7-20	0-13	1-4	0-4	0-0	0-0	2-8	18.9	2.23
Martin Todhunter	10-58	0-2	4-21	0-3	0-4	6-27	0-0	0-0	0-1	17.2	10.22
Dan Skelton	10-46	1-4	3-20	2-3	1-8	2-9	0-0	0-0	1-2	21.7	-6.01
Ian Duncan	9-82	0-4	4-31	2-17	0-5	3-17	0-0	0-0	0-8	11.0	5.25
Stuart Coltherd	9-60	0-7	6-21	0-6	1-4	2-20	0-0	0-0	0-2	15.0	10.00
Malcolm Jefferson	8-43	2-5	1-5	1-5	1-5	2-15	0-0	0-0	1-8	18.6	-1.70
Sandy Thomson	8-50	0-4	1-9	3-9	0-3	2-14	0-0	0-0	2-11	16.0	-18.03
Donald Whillans	6-31	1-3	5-19	0-1	0-0	0-2	0-0	0-0	0-6	19.4	60.75
Gordon Elliott	6-37	1-5	1-8	1-8	0-4	1-6	0-0	0-0	2-6	16.2	-16.94
R Mike Smith	6-107	1-15	2-30	1-26	0-8	2-12	0-0	0-0	0-16	5.6	-46.50
Lisa Harrison	5-30	0-0	1-13	0-0	0-0	4-13	0-0	0-0	0-4	16.7	5.00
Fergal O'Brien	5-10	1-1	0-0	2-2	1-3	1-3	0-0	0-0	0-1	50.0	20.77
Alistair Whillans	5-51	0-2	3-22	0-11	1-1	1-7	0-0	0-0	0-8	9.8	-11.00
Brian Ellison	5-56	0-2	1-25	0-3	0-3	3-17	0-0	0-0	1-6	8.9	-18.52
Nicky Henderson	5-43	1-7	0-17	0-0	0-3	2-12	0-0	0-0	2-4	11.6	-27.86
Evan Williams	4-9	0-0	0-2	2-2	0-0	2-5	0-0	0-0	0-0	44.4	17.96
Pauline Robson	4-28	0-1	3-16	0-0	0-0	0-9	0-0	0-0	1-2	14.3	-0.25
Rebecca Menzies	4-34	0-0	1-7	0-1	0-0	3-23	0-0	0-0	0-3	11.8	-6.17
Micky Hammond	4-33	0-1	0-13	0-1	2-5	2-12	0-0	0-0	0-1	12.1	-8.50
Alan King	4-35	1-6	1-14	0-0	1-3	0-9	0-1	0-0	1-2	11.4	-11.75
Philip Kirby	4-39	0-1	3-19	0-3	0-3	0-4	0-0	0-0	1-9	10.3	-15.92
Rose Dobbin	4-47	0-3	0-10	2-12	0-1	2-14	0-0	0-0	0-7	8.5	-17.25

LEADING JUMP TRAINERS AT BANGOR-ON-DEE (SINCE 2013)

	Total W-R	Nov Hdle	H'cap Hdle	Other Hdle	Nov Chase	H'cap Chase	Other Chase	Hunter Chase	N.H. Flat	Per cent	£1 Level stake
Donald McCain	64-321	25-75	17-92	4-35	7-30	8-53	0-0	0-0	3-36	19.9	23.76
Dan Skelton	21-76	6-22	4-16	2-9	4-7	4-13	0-0	0-1	1-8	27.6	1.87
Rebecca Curtis	18-77	5-12	1-12	3-9	5-15	1-12	0-0	1-1	2-16	23.4	-8.27
Alan King	17-60	2-9	4-13	4-11	1-6	3-9	0-0	0-0	3-12	28.3	19.19
Jonjo O'Neill	16-119	2-29	3-27	0-7	2-14	6-36	0-0	0-1	3-5	13.4	-27.51
Nigel Twiston-Davies	13-65	4-11	0-11	1-6	1-6	4-20	0-0	0-0	3-11	20.0	5.64
Warren Greatrex	13-46	3-11	2-11	2-5	0-5	2-4	0-0	0-0	4-10	28.3	13.40
Charlie Longsdon	13-65	3-14	2-18	2-7	2-7	2-13	0-0	0-0	2-6	20.0	-18.60
Henry Daly	11-55	2-11	5-14	0-3	0-6	2-11	0-0	0-0	2-10	20.0	27.00
Venetia Williams	11-99	1-21	1-20	1-5	1-9	7-40	0-0	0-0	0-4	11.1	-39.01
Harry Fry	9-27	3-13	1-3	0-3	1-2	0-0	0-0	0-0	4-6	33.3	16.96
Peter Bowen	9-56	2-6	2-15	1-3	1-5	2-20	0-0	0-0	1-7	16.1	-3.93
Fergal O'Brien	9-35	1-6	3-6	0-2	0-1	3-12	0-0	1-1	1-7	25.7	-4.66
Nicky Henderson	8-44	3-12	1-10	1-6	2-6	0-1	0-0	0-0	1-9	18.2	-22.80
Jennie Candlish	8-69	2-14	1-24	2-4	0-7	3-12	0-0	0-0	0-8	11.6	-38.15
Nicky Richards	6-34	0-5	2-17	0-1	0-2	4-8	0-0	0-0	0-1	17.6	1.50
Lucinda Russell	6-22	0-3	0-3	0-1	1-1	5-14	0-0	0-0	0-0	27.3	9.83
Brian Ellison	6-22	1-4	1-7	1-5	0-0	2-4	0-0	0-0	1-2	27.3	15.49
Graeme McPherson	6-38	0-5	2-16	0-0	1-1	2-8	0-0	0-0	1-8	15.8	26.00
David Pipe	6-42	0-9	2-19	1-3	2-5	1-5	0-0	0-0	0-1	14.3	-19.38
Kim Bailey	6-49	0-9	1-13	2-5	1-7	0-9	1-1	0-0	1-5	12.2	-31.08
Jamie Snowden	5-29	1-2	0-7	1-2	0-4	1-10	0-0	0-0	2-4	17.2	0.53
Paul Nicholls	5-13	1-2	0-0	0-1	3-7	0-1	0-0	1-2	0-0	38.5	2.72
Gary Hanmer	5-22	0-1	1-6	0-2	0-0	2-8	0-0	1-3	1-2	22.7	50.00
Kerry Lee	5-26	0-3	2-5	0-1	2-5	0-11	0-0	0-0	1-1	19.2	-2.87
Tom George	5-30	0-3	0-2	2-4	1-4	1-12	0-0	0-1	1-4	16.7	-13.41
Evan Williams	5-72	1-20	1-17	0-5	0-9	3-12	0-0	0-0	0-9	6.9	-53.23
Jeremy Scott	4-9	0-1	2-3	0-0	1-1	1-3	0-0	0-0	0-1	44.4	2.48
Oliver Sherwood	4-27	1-5	1-2	1-3	1-6	0-6	0-0	0-0	0-5	14.8	2.63
John Spearing	4-8	0-0	1-2	0-0	0-0	3-5	0-0	0-0	0-1	50.0	42.00

LEADING JUMP TRAINERS AT CARLISLE (SINCE 2013)

	Total W-R	Nov Hdle	H'cap Hdle	Other Hdle	Nov Chase	H'cap Chase	Other Chase	Hunter Chase	N.H. Flat	Per cent	£1 Level stake
Donald McCain	35-211	8-64	8-55	3-9	10-36	1-26	0-4	0-0	5-17	16.6	-33.63
Nicky Richards	20-90	2-15	7-26	1-3	1-12	4-20	1-5	0-1	4-8	22.2	14.51
Sue Smith	18-121	0-17	2-19	0-1	4-21	9-47	2-7	0-0	1-9	14.9	-28.59
S R B Crawford	11-31	1-1	3-8	1-3	0-5	0-2	0-1	0-0	6-11	35.5	6.88
Alan Swinbank	11-37	4-13	2-8	0-2	3-6	0-1	0-0	0-0	2-7	29.7	10.98
Brian Ellison	11-64	0-12	5-21	0-0	2-9	1-12	1-1	0-0	2-9	17.2	-25.80
Lucinda Russell	11-167	2-26	2-45	0-3	1-24	6-52	0-3	0-0	0-14	6.6	-98.30
Malcolm Jefferson	10-43	1-4	0-0	0-0	1-13	4-14	2-3	0-0	2-9	23.3	-4.68
Rose Dobbin	10-77	2-13	2-22	0-2	3-12	2-17	1-1	0-0	0-10	13.0	-24.75
Jennie Candlish	10-73	0-15	1-19	1-2	0-7	8-21	0-2	0-0	0-7	13.7	-26.11
Micky Hammond	10-108	1-23	5-30	0-2	1-15	3-28	0-3	0-0	0-7	9.3	-53.03
Venetia Williams	9-34	2-8	0-3	0-1	1-3	5-15	0-1	0-0	1-3	26.5	14.91
Jonjo O'Neill	9-37	4-9	3-8	0-1	0-2	0-11	1-3	0-0	1-3	24.3	-10.42
Charlie Longsdon	9-30	4-6	0-4	0-0	3-7	0-7	1-3	0-0	1-3	30.0	-13.33
Nigel Hawke	8-25	2-6	3-8	0-1	0-2	1-4	0-0	0-0	2-4	32.0	4.13
Maurice Barnes	8-65	0-19	0-13	0-2	1-7	7-16	0-2	0-0	0-6	12.3	-0.25
Stuart Coltherd	7-62	1-12	1-21	0-2	4-9	1-13	0-1	0-1	0-3	11.3	4.50
Philip Kirby	7-47	1-10	3-21	0-1	1-7	2-4	0-0	0-0	0-4	14.9	-2.92
Keith Dalgleish	6-13	1-3	1-3	0-0	0-0	2-3	0-0	0-0	2-4	46.2	17.55
James Ewart	6-43	0-12	1-8	0-0	3-10	2-9	0-0	0-0	0-4	14.0	-9.38
Paul Nicholls	5-7	0-0	0-0	1-1	2-4	0-0	2-2	0-0	0-0	71.4	6.35
Dr Richard Newland	5-9	3-3	1-4	0-0	0-1	1-1	0-0	0-0	0-0	55.6	7.92
John Wade	5-32	2-7	1-10	0-0	1-5	1-8	0-0	0-0	0-2	15.6	-0.56
Ian Duncan	5-19	0-4	2-3	0-1	1-3	2-6	0-0	0-1	0-1	26.3	20.50
Sandy Thomson	5-33	1-9	1-6	0-0	0-2	1-10	1-2	0-0	1-4	15.2	24.10
Tim Vaughan	5-13	5-7	0-2	0-0	0-1	0-1	0-0	0-0	0-2	38.5	-1.40
Evan Williams	5-18	3-5	0-3	0-1	2-5	0-0	0-2	0-0	0-2	27.8	-4.03
David Pipe	5-17	2-5	2-5	1-1	0-0	0-3	0-1	0-0	0-2	29.4	-4.17
Alistair Whillans	5-45	1-9	2-16	0-2	1-8	1-4	0-0	0-0	0-6	11.1	-20.38
James Moffatt	5-39	2-7	2-20	0-0	1-8	0-3	0-1	0-0	0-0	12.8	-21.13

LEADING JUMP TRAINERS AT CARTMEL (SINCE 2013)

	Total W-R	Nov Hdle	H'cap Hdle	Other Hdle	Nov Chase	H'cap Chase	Other Chase	Hunter Chase	N.H. Flat	Per cent	£1 Level stake
James Moffatt	22-164	1-17	10-86	4-12	0-2	5-38	2-9	0-0	0-0	13.4	0.12
Donald McCain	22-122	7-19	10-46	1-13	0-2	0-28	4-13	0-1	0-0	18.0	-25.24
Peter Bowen	13-45	0-1	5-19	1-2	1-1	5-20	1-2	0-0	0-0	28.9	12.88
Gordon Elliott	10-39	2-8	3-13	3-5	0-0	2-9	0-4	0-0	0-0	25.6	-5.56
Dianne Sayer	10-104	1-6	1-51	0-4	0-0	8-43	0-0	0-0	0-0	9.6	-46.67
Martin Todhunter	9-52	0-1	4-28	0-1	0-0	4-21	1-1	0-0	0-0	17.3	-6.13
Kenneth Slack	8-23	4-6	4-14	0-1	0-0	0-2	0-0	0-0	0-0	34.8	51.00
Jonjo O'Neill	7-26	2-2	1-10	1-2	0-0	3-12	0-0	0-0	0-0	26.9	2.80
Micky Hammond	6-55	0-5	0-16	1-6	0-0	5-28	0-0	0-0	0-0	10.9	-13.25
Sue Smith	5-37	0-5	1-8	0-1	0-0	4-21	0-2	0-0	0-0	13.5	14.50
Richard Ford	5-28	0-6	1-8	0-0	1-1	3-12	0-1	0-0	0-0	17.9	-2.14
Brian Ellison	5-31	2-10	0-7	1-5	0-1	2-7	0-1	0-0	0-0	16.1	-10.00
Joanne Foster	4-32	0-0	0-7	0-0	0-0	3-21	1-4	0-0	0-0	12.5	0.75
Julia Brooke	4-20	1-4	3-9	0-2	0-0	0-5	0-0	0-0	0-0	20.0	2.33
Maurice Barnes	4-29	0-2	0-8	0-5	0-0	4-13	0-0	0-1	0-0	13.8	3.00
S R B Crawford	4-24	0-1	1-6	0-7	0-0	1-6	2-4	0-0	0-0	16.7	-8.60
Iain Jardine	3-10	1-1	1-5	1-2	0-0	0-1	0-1	0-0	0-0	30.0	-0.00
John Quinn	3-10	2-5	1-3	0-2	0-0	0-0	0-0	0-0	0-0	30.0	0.38
Alistair Whillans	3-23	0-0	1-15	0-0	0-0	2-7	0-1	0-0	0-0	13.0	1.50
Evan Williams	3-19	0-0	1-10	0-0	0-0	2-7	0-2	0-0	0-0	15.8	3.50
Nicky Richards	3-11	0-0	2-8	0-0	0-0	1-3	0-0	0-0	0-0	27.3	4.75
Mrs Gillian Callaghan	3-7	0-0	2-5	1-2	0-0	0-0	0-0	0-0	0-0	42.9	5.41
James Ewart	3-17	0-2	2-9	0-1	0-0	1-5	0-0	0-0	0-0	17.6	8.50
Philip Kirby	3-27	0-6	3-17	0-4	0-0	0-0	0-0	0-0	0-0	11.1	9.00
Tim Easterby	3-10	1-3	2-4	0-1	0-0	0-2	0-0	0-0	0-0	30.0	9.38
Mark Michael McNiff	3-12	2-4	0-2	0-2	0-0	1-3	0-1	0-0	0-0	25.0	11.50
John Wade	3-16	1-3	0-0	0-0	0-0	2-8	0-3	0-2	0-0	18.8	17.50
Graeme McPherson	3-17	1-4	1-4	0-1	0-0	0-7	1-1	0-0	0-0	17.6	19.50
Barry Murtagh	3-42	0-3	3-26	0-0	0-0	0-11	0-2	0-0	0-0	7.1	26.00
Sam England	3-11	0-2	3-9	0-0	0-0	0-0	0-0	0-0	0-0	27.3	32.50

LEADING JUMP TRAINERS AT CATTERICK (SINCE 2013)

	Total W-R	Nov Hdle	H'cap Hdle	Other Hdle	Nov Chase	H'cap Chase	Other Chase	Hunter Chase	N.H. Flat	Per cent	£1 Level stake
Donald McCain	38-175	9-33	11-57	4-23	4-16	7-28	1-4	0-0	2-14	21.7	-16.51
Sue Smith	30-101	4-18	5-28	0-2	6-11	13-29	2-3	0-0	0-10	29.7	78.71
Brian Ellison	19-69	4-14	3-15	5-13	4-6	0-10	0-3	0-0	3-8	27.5	-13.57
Micky Hammond	13-157	1-17	4-63	1-19	1-12	6-35	0-3	0-0	0-8	8.3	-51.00
John Ferguson	9-15	1-1	0-0	6-8	0-1	0-1	0-1	0-0	2-3	60.0	9.23
Kenneth Slack	8-33	0-2	5-18	0-1	1-2	2-10	0-0	0-0	0-0	24.2	7.26
Dan Skelton	8-29	3-9	0-4	2-5	0-2	2-6	0-2	0-0	1-1	27.6	-7.60
Jonjo O'Neill	7-34	2-8	1-5	1-4	0-4	1-9	1-2	0-0	1-2	20.6	-4.84
Malcolm Jefferson	6-40	0-10	0-3	0-2	1-4	2-8	1-3	0-0	2-10	15.0	-4.25
Pam Sly	5-13	2-3	1-4	1-2	0-0	1-4	0-0	0-0	0-0	38.5	11.56
Alan King	4-6	0-1	0-0	3-4	0-0	0-0	1-1	0-0	0-0	66.7	1.73
Sam England	4-14	0-1	1-2	0-1	0-1	2-7	1-2	0-0	0-0	28.6	7.00
Dianne Sayer	4-35	0-1	3-19	1-11	0-1	0-3	0-0	0-0	0-0	11.4	56.00
Jennie Candlish	4-23	0-3	3-7	0-3	0-1	1-9	0-0	0-0	0-0	17.4	-0.45
Rebecca Menzies	4-29	0-2	1-7	0-2	1-5	2-11	0-1	0-0	0-1	13.8	-9.12
Michael Easterby	4-29	1-6	1-4	0-5	1-4	1-6	0-1	0-0	0-3	13.8	-10.88
John Quinn	4-22	3-7	0-1	1-10	0-1	0-1	0-0	0-0	0-2	18.2	-10.97
Keith Reveley	4-27	2-6	1-6	1-4	0-1	0-3	0-0	0-0	0-7	14.8	-11.75
Philip Kirby	4-51	1-11	1-18	1-10	0-0	0-3	0-0	1-1	0-8	7.8	-30.75
Henry Hogarth	3-28	0-2	1-9	0-1	0-1	2-15	0-0	0-0	0-0	10.7	1.00
Jedd O'Keeffe	3-6	2-3	0-0	0-0	0-1	0-1	0-0	0-0	1-1	50.0	3.23
Evan Williams	3-12	1-2	0-3	0-2	0-1	1-2	0-1	0-0	1-1	25.0	5.88
Barbara Butterworth	3-11	0-0	3-10	0-0	0-0	0-1	0-0	0-0	0-0	27.3	6.25
Michael Smith	3-13	0-4	0-3	1-1	0-0	2-4	0-0	0-0	0-1	23.1	7.50
Martin Keighley	3-14	0-2	1-3	0-0	1-1	1-7	0-0	0-0	0-1	21.4	-2.35
James Ewart	3-24	0-2	1-8	1-4	1-3	0-4	0-0	0-0	0-3	12.5	-3.85
Kim Bailey	3-11	0-2	0-2	0-0	1-2	1-3	0-0	0-0	1-2	27.3	-4.86
Peter Niven	3-22	0-4	1-5	1-2	0-2	1-2	0-1	0-0	0-6	13.6	-6.00
Neil Mulholland	3-12	3-4	0-2	0-0	0-1	0-3	0-1	0-0	0-1	25.0	-7.26
Venetia Williams	3-17	1-3	1-3	1-2	0-1	0-8	0-0	0-0	0-0	17.6	-8.17

LEADING JUMP TRAINERS AT CHELTENHAM (SINCE 2013)

	Total W-R	Nov Hdle	H'cap Hdle	Other Hdle	Nov Chase	H'cap Chase	Other Chase	Hunter Chase	N.H. Flat	Per cent	£1 Level stake
Paul Nicholls	44-391	3-37	11-97	4-63	10-50	9-105	1-36	3-9	3-8	11.3	-1.62
Nicky Henderson	43-380	9-65	9-114	15-74	7-33	1-67	4-25	0-0	1-16	11.3	-158.20
Philip Hobbs	34-260	1-16	7-82	7-30	6-26	10-91	2-15	0-2	3-17	13.1	-35.25
W P Mullins	34-283	8-62	5-57	9-53	4-18	0-18	7-49	0-0	1-27	12.0	-55.60
Nigel Twiston-Davies	28-267	5-36	3-46	4-25	2-40	10-96	1-12	1-3	2-15	10.5	-91.63
David Pipe	23-218	6-18	4-69	1-28	2-13	6-78	2-14	0-0	3-11	10.6	-10.46
Gordon Elliott	21-142	2-16	5-50	4-13	1-9	3-29	5-22	0-1	1-5	14.8	72.85
Jonjo O'Neill	21-200	1-15	3-65	2-11	5-19	9-79	1-10	0-1	0-6	10.5	-18.79
Colin Tizzard	21-216	4-36	0-21	3-14	6-28	5-88	3-20	0-2	0-12	9.7	-69.85
Alan King	18-179	3-22	5-52	3-42	2-10	2-29	4-18	0-0	0-14	10.1	-52.17
Fergal O'Brien	15-126	0-23	2-17	1-9	1-6	7-42	0-4	1-4	4-25	11.9	25.63
Dan Skelton	14-144	3-30	7-54	1-21	2-13	1-22	0-3	0-0	0-6	9.7	-41.80
Harry Fry	13-89	3-15	3-27	3-13	0-7	3-19	0-3	0-0	1-8	14.6	-20.99
Martin Keighley	12-104	3-14	4-28	0-3	0-7	4-30	1-9	0-1	0-14	11.5	21.00
Neil Mulholland	10-78	2-8	0-21	0-13	3-7	5-26	0-5	0-0	0-2	12.8	-18.60
Nick Williams	7-62	2-5	1-13	3-20	0-6	1-13	0-4	0-0	0-3	11.3	23.50
Evan Williams	7-93	0-6	1-26	1-14	2-10	3-37	0-2	0-0	0-1	7.5	-9.00
Tom George	7-117	1-18	1-17	0-9	2-13	2-42	0-11	1-2	0-7	6.0	-65.50
Rebecca Curtis	6-78	0-11	0-7	0-9	2-14	1-17	1-10	0-1	2-9	7.7	-3.75
John Ferguson	6-65	3-18	1-28	2-9	0-3	0-1	0-1	0-0	0-7	9.2	-31.48
Alan Hill	5-16	0-0	0-0	0-0	0-0	0-0	0-0	5-16	0-0	31.3	3.87
Mrs John Harrington	5-37	0-3	1-7	1-12	1-4	1-9	1-2	0-0	0-3	13.5	11.00
E Bolger	5-40	0-1	0-0	0-0	0-0	2-18	1-16	2-5	0-0	12.5	-20.25
Warren Greatrex	5-76	2-14	0-18	1-16	0-3	1-10	0-5	0-4	1-11	6.6	-37.00
Mrs Pauline Harkin	4-12	0-0	0-0	0-0	0-0	0-0	0-0	4-12	0-0	33.3	3.70
Jamie Snowden	4-34	0-6	1-9	0-3	3-4	0-7	0-0	0-1	0-5	11.8	11.50
Anthony Honeyball	4-31	0-1	1-5	0-3	1-3	1-7	0-1	0-0	1-13	12.9	-8.50
Ben Pauling	4-56	2-9	1-22	0-2	0-5	0-6	0-1	1-2	0-10	7.1	-19.50
Henry De Bromhead	4-76	0-12	0-4	1-4	1-22	0-12	2-20	0-1	0-1	5.3	-44.75
Robin Dickin	3-35	1-5	2-7	0-1	0-7	0-12	0-1	0-0	0-2	8.6	12.00

LEADING JUMP TRAINERS AT CHEPSTOW (SINCE 2013)

	Total W-R	Nov Hdle	H'cap Hdle	Other Hdle	Nov Chase	H'cap Chase	Other Chase	Hunter Chase	N.H. Flat	Per cent	£1 Level stake
Evan Williams	32-192	6-30	9-56	5-24	4-16	7-57	0-1	0-0	1-8	16.7	38.49
Philip Hobbs	30-152	5-16	6-34	4-21	6-17	7-44	0-1	0-0	2-19	19.7	-33.49
Paul Nicholls	25-143	8-24	3-23	4-26	3-17	3-38	1-2	0-0	3-13	17.5	-52.40
Peter Bowen	21-116	1-15	6-26	1-20	2-12	8-30	0-0	0-0	3-13	18.1	21.53
Nigel Twiston-Davies	18-114	3-11	2-23	3-18	2-13	5-36	0-0	0-0	3-13	15.8	-5.11
Venetia Williams	18-121	2-16	0-20	1-18	2-10	12-51	0-0	0-0	1-6	14.9	-24.98
David Pipe	17-109	1-11	6-41	0-11	3-9	4-25	0-1	0-0	3-11	15.6	-14.16
Rebecca Curtis	16-128	4-19	1-14	4-16	3-25	2-27	0-3	0-0	2-24	12.5	-42.27
Tom George	15-74	2-7	2-11	2-14	2-7	2-26	0-0	0-0	5-9	20.3	-16.19
Jonjo O'Neill	15-120	5-25	3-27	4-20	0-13	1-28	0-0	0-0	2-7	12.5	-40.70
Colin Tizzard	15-164	2-22	1-28	3-18	3-19	5-53	1-2	0-0	0-22	9.1	-80.00
Matt Sheppard	11-72	1-13	5-22	0-6	0-2	5-26	0-0	0-0	0-3	15.3	17.88
Warren Greatrex	10-51	3-15	3-13	3-11	0-3	1-3	0-0	0-0	0-6	19.6	-1.28
Alan King	10-64	3-10	1-21	3-16	2-4	0-6	1-1	0-0	0-6	15.6	-24.48
Neil Mulholland	10-86	1-21	6-17	0-14	1-8	1-18	0-2	0-0	1-6	11.6	-31.80
Dan Skelton	9-65	3-13	2-17	2-8	0-2	0-11	0-2	0-0	2-12	13.8	-14.25
Tim Vaughan	9-138	2-30	4-44	1-27	1-5	1-17	0-1	0-2	0-12	6.5	-75.75
Tom Lacey	8-24	0-7	1-3	2-4	1-1	1-2	0-0	0-0	3-7	33.3	67.50
Nicky Henderson	8-37	2-8	1-12	3-7	1-4	0-1	0-0	0-0	1-5	21.6	-1.94
Emma Lavelle	8-53	1-9	2-8	2-8	1-3	1-15	0-0	0-0	1-10	15.1	-9.09
Kim Bailey	8-50	2-12	1-11	1-5	1-3	3-16	0-0	0-0	0-3	16.0	-10.48
Fergal O'Brien	7-52	2-11	1-8	1-9	0-6	0-8	0-0	0-0	3-10	13.5	13.50
Robert Walford	6-41	1-11	3-9	0-4	0-2	2-14	0-0	0-0	0-1	14.6	0.37
Henry Oliver	6-40	0-4	3-13	1-4	1-5	0-13	0-0	0-0	1-1	15.0	8.83
Jamie Snowden	6-28	1-9	2-6	0-2	0-1	2-6	0-0	0-0	1-4	21.4	17.00
Charlie Longsdon	6-49	2-7	0-11	0-3	0-2	4-24	0-0	0-0	0-2	12.2	-17.77
Nigel Hawke	6-76	0-17	0-14	0-16	2-3	4-18	0-0	0-0	0-8	7.9	-46.50
Debra Hamer	5-25	0-3	3-9	0-3	0-1	2-8	0-0	0-0	0-1	20.0	24.00
Henry Daly	5-27	0-2	2-10	1-4	0-3	2-5	0-0	0-0	0-3	18.5	-9.33
Jeremy Scott	5-50	1-8	2-15	0-9	0-1	2-9	0-0	0-0	0-8	10.0	-28.75

LEADING JUMP TRAINERS AT DONCASTER (SINCE 2013)

	Total W-R	Nov Hdle	H'cap Hdle	Other Hdle	Nov Chase	H'cap Chase	Other Chase	Hunter Chase	N.H. Flat	Per cent	£1 Level stake
Nicky Henderson	36-102	12-22	5-18	10-25	6-17	0-9	2-2	0-0	1-9	35.3	34.35
Alan King	25-106	5-17	3-25	8-21	2-10	5-23	1-1	0-0	1-9	23.6	28.72
Paul Nicholls	15-78	2-13	1-9	3-12	6-21	2-17	0-3	0-1	1-2	19.2	-27.08
Emma Lavelle	14-49	4-7	4-10	0-4	0-1	3-17	0-0	0-0	3-10	28.6	11.59
Jonjo O'Neill	12-106	1-15	3-33	0-18	2-7	6-30	0-0	0-0	0-3	11.3	-32.84
Keith Reveley	11-97	1-9	2-29	0-10	2-10	6-31	0-0	0-0	0-8	11.3	-31.20
Kim Bailey	10-59	3-15	2-14	1-9	1-4	2-10	0-2	0-0	1-5	16.9	2.09
Ben Pauling	10-46	5-14	1-8	0-6	3-8	1-6	0-0	0-0	0-4	21.7	3.15
Ian Williams	10-76	2-19	3-16	1-19	1-5	2-15	0-0	0-0	1-2	13.2	-1.87
Harry Fry	9-25	0-3	0-5	0-2	5-8	1-2	1-1	0-0	2-4	36.0	4.92
Nicky Richards	9-46	1-7	3-18	1-5	0-1	3-11	0-0	0-0	1-4	19.6	13.25
Warren Greatrex	8-40	0-4	1-6	1-12	1-5	1-4	0-1	3-3	1-5	20.0	-11.48
Charlie Longsdon	8-84	0-11	1-15	2-14	0-12	4-25	0-1	0-0	1-6	9.5	-32.03
Graeme McPherson	7-51	1-12	3-15	0-6	0-4	2-10	0-0	0-0	1-4	13.7	4.50
Tom George	7-67	1-6	0-8	2-14	0-7	3-26	0-1	0-0	1-5	10.4	20.16
Brian Ellison	7-36	1-5	0-11	1-2	2-8	1-5	0-0	0-0	2-5	19.4	-10.33
Ben Case	6-31	2-9	3-7	0-10	0-1	0-2	0-0	0-0	1-2	19.4	12.13
Rose Dobbin	6-21	1-7	1-4	0-0	0-3	4-7	0-0	0-0	0-0	28.6	18.75
John Ferguson	6-27	1-5	2-6	2-7	1-5	0-1	0-1	0-0	0-2	22.2	-0.06
Dan Skelton	6-74	1-19	1-12	2-19	0-2	1-15	1-2	0-0	0-5	8.1	-57.54
Malcolm Jefferson	5-34	2-8	0-4	1-4	1-4	1-8	0-0	0-0	0-6	14.7	-16.76
Neil King	5-51	1-6	2-17	1-13	0-1	0-9	0-0	0-0	1-5	9.8	-33.88
David Pipe	4-30	0-4	0-9	1-8	2-3	1-5	0-0	0-0	0-1	13.3	-9.00
Donald McCain	5-73	1-17	2-20	1-10	1-10	0-13	0-1	0-0	0-2	6.8	-41.60
John Quinn	4-19	1-4	2-6	1-7	0-0	0-1	0-0	0-0	0-1	21.1	1.67
Philip Hobbs	4-27	0-3	1-7	1-5	0-5	2-7	0-0	0-0	0-0	14.8	-14.15
Neil Mulholland	4-36	0-9	3-11	0-5	1-3	0-7	0-0	0-0	0-1	11.1	-17.25
Amy Murphy	3-6	0-1	0-1	1-1	0-1	1-1	1-1	0-0	0-0	50.0	0.74
Peter Atkinson	3-6	0-0	2-4	0-1	1-1	0-0	0-0	0-0	0-0	50.0	3.50
Alex Hales	3-10	3-6	0-3	0-0	0-0	0-0	0-0	0-0	0-1	30.0	5.50

178 TRAINERS JUMPS STATISTICS

LEADING JUMP TRAINERS AT EXETER (SINCE 2013)

	Total W-R	Nov Hdle	H'cap Hdle	Other Hdle	Nov Chase	H'cap Chase	Other Chase	Hunter Chase	N.H. Flat	Per cent	£1 Level stake
Philip Hobbs	44-220	15-49	6-46	6-25	4-26	8-52	1-7	0-1	4-14	20.0	-44.14
Paul Nicholls	40-141	13-45	1-11	10-23	5-23	2-18	7-13	0-0	2-8	28.4	-30.25
Harry Fry	27-71	11-21	3-15	5-13	4-9	1-3	1-4	0-0	2-6	38.0	49.80
David Pipe	26-207	7-44	8-73	6-30	0-10	4-35	0-2	0-0	1-13	12.6	-49.12
Colin Tizzard	23-172	6-29	3-43	3-14	4-18	4-46	3-11	0-0	0-11	13.4	-80.86
Alan King	17-91	3-18	4-30	0-5	5-14	2-11	2-4	0-0	1-9	18.7	-21.57
Evan Williams	16-64	2-7	7-23	1-10	2-8	3-10	1-4	0-0	0-2	25.0	25.95
Venetia Williams	15-89	5-15	2-19	0-6	1-6	7-39	0-2	0-0	0-2	16.9	9.96
Sue Gardner	15-124	1-31	9-50	0-11	0-3	5-17	0-1	0-0	0-11	12.1	-34.05
Victor Dartnall	12-104	3-20	5-35	1-12	1-7	2-22	0-2	0-0	0-6	11.5	-50.63
Fergal O'Brien	11-53	1-12	2-12	0-3	2-6	2-14	1-1	0-0	3-5	20.8	26.13
Emma Lavelle	10-59	0-11	2-11	1-8	2-7	5-17	0-1	0-0	0-4	16.9	-10.25
Anthony Honeyball	9-56	2-14	4-19	0-2	0-3	2-14	0-0	0-0	1-4	16.1	16.08
Robert Walford	9-73	0-15	0-15	0-5	0-5	9-33	0-0	0-0	0-0	12.3	-23.50
Chris Down	9-102	1-25	5-47	0-8	0-6	2-5	1-4	0-0	0-7	8.8	-23.75
Nick Williams	8-47	1-10	0-8	1-9	1-7	2-8	2-3	0-0	1-2	17.0	-20.43
Nigel Hawke	8-89	0-17	5-30	0-20	1-5	1-12	1-3	0-0	0-2	9.0	-39.75
Jonjo O'Neill	8-89	1-15	4-24	1-12	0-4	2-31	0-0	0-0	0-3	9.0	-55.71
Jeremy Scott	8-128	0-37	7-52	0-12	0-4	1-20	0-0	0-0	0-3	6.3	-68.63
Tom George	7-47	0-5	1-8	0-5	1-6	3-18	0-0	1-1	1-4	14.9	8.75
Warren Greatrex	7-36	0-12	5-14	1-1	1-4	0-1	0-1	0-0	0-3	19.4	-2.06
Nicky Henderson	6-25	1-7	1-4	2-2	1-3	0-0	0-3	0-0	1-6	24.0	-3.31
Caroline Keevil	6-45	0-9	2-16	0-1	1-4	2-11	0-1	1-1	0-2	13.3	-8.50
Nigel Twiston-Davies	6-53	0-5	1-17	0-1	2-6	2-22	0-0	0-0	1-2	11.3	-10.75
Seamus Mullins	6-75	2-13	2-27	0-9	0-8	2-11	0-2	0-0	0-5	8.0	-42.32
Neil Mulholland	6-71	1-24	2-21	1-14	1-4	1-7	0-0	0-0	0-1	8.5	-47.75
Tom Lacey	5-21	1-7	1-3	1-2	0-1	0-3	0-0	0-0	2-5	23.8	10.00
Johnny Farrelly	5-47	0-8	4-33	0-3	0-0	1-3	0-0	0-0	0-0	10.6	13.00
Neil King	5-11	1-2	2-4	1-2	1-1	0-2	0-0	0-0	0-0	45.5	23.75
Dan Skelton	5-25	2-9	2-8	0-2	0-1	0-4	1-1	0-0	0-0	20.0	-1.96

LEADING JUMP TRAINERS AT FAKENHAM (SINCE 2013)

	Total W-R	Nov Hdle	H'cap Hdle	Other Hdle	Nov Chase	H'cap Chase	Other Chase	Hunter Chase	N.H. Flat	Per cent	£1 Level stake
Lucy Wadham	20-73	4-11	6-26	1-8	0-2	6-19	0-0	0-0	3-7	27.4	20.36
Dan Skelton	17-62	3-13	4-15	2-10	4-8	2-12	1-2	0-0	1-2	27.4	-2.91
Neil Mulholland	15-49	2-7	10-19	1-6	0-3	2-12	0-0	0-0	0-2	30.6	9.26
Olly Murphy	15-48	4-11	6-15	3-12	1-3	1-4	0-0	0-0	0-3	31.3	19.94
Neil King	13-85	2-10	4-24	1-15	0-5	4-25	1-3	0-0	1-3	15.3	24.23
Nicky Henderson	13-36	3-9	1-6	3-8	1-4	0-2	1-2	0-0	4-5	36.1	-10.03
David Pipe	8-16	2-2	1-3	3-6	1-3	0-1	1-1	0-0	0-0	50.0	1.23
Paul Nicholls	7-20	2-5	0-0	1-2	3-5	1-3	0-4	0-1	0-0	35.0	-0.70
Tim Vaughan	7-53	2-15	2-17	1-4	0-2	1-12	1-2	0-0	0-0	13.2	-31.65
Dr Richard Newland	6-15	0-1	0-3	4-7	0-0	1-3	0-0	1-1	0-0	40.0	5.00
Henry Daly	6-11	0-0	2-2	0-0	0-1	3-6	0-0	1-1	0-1	54.5	7.38
Pam Sly	6-28	0-5	1-10	1-1	2-2	1-5	1-1	0-0	0-4	21.4	10.55
Charlie Mann	6-25	0-2	1-6	1-1	0-0	4-15	0-1	0-0	0-0	24.0	11.00
Ali Stronge	6-23	2-4	2-9	0-5	1-1	1-3	0-0	0-0	0-1	26.1	22.00
Alex Hales	6-41	1-5	2-22	0-2	2-3	1-8	0-0	0-0	0-1	14.6	-5.27
Oliver Sherwood	5-21	0-4	0-2	0-4	1-3	4-7	0-1	0-0	0-0	23.8	7.00
Michael Gates	5-21	0-4	0-4	0-1	0-1	5-11	0-0	0-0	0-0	23.8	7.50
David Dennis	5-17	0-4	2-6	1-2	0-1	1-2	1-1	0-0	0-1	29.4	16.45
James Evans	5-18	0-0	2-6	2-2	0-2	1-6	0-2	0-0	0-0	27.8	29.00
David Thompson	5-30	1-3	2-18	1-4	0-0	1-5	0-0	0-0	0-0	16.7	46.50
Paul Henderson	5-33	0-2	2-7	0-1	0-5	3-18	0-0	0-0	0-0	15.2	-2.00
Brian Ellison	5-21	0-1	2-8	1-5	1-1	1-5	0-0	0-0	0-0	23.8	-3.67
Peter Bowen	5-19	1-1	1-5	0-2	1-2	0-6	1-1	0-0	1-2	26.3	-3.80
John Ferguson	5-17	1-4	0-1	3-5	1-1	0-2	0-1	0-2	0-1	29.4	-4.23
Ben Case	5-36	1-2	1-11	1-7	0-0	2-13	0-0	0-0	0-3	13.9	-11.62
Emma-Jane Bishop	4-16	0-1	0-3	0-0	0-1	4-10	0-0	0-0	0-1	25.0	0.50
Chris Bealby	4-20	1-3	0-3	0-2	0-0	3-12	0-0	0-0	0-0	20.0	3.00
David Kemp	4-12	0-0	0-0	0-0	0-0	0-0	0-0	4-12	0-0	33.3	3.00
Richard Hobson	4-8	1-2	1-2	2-3	0-0	0-0	0-0	0-0	0-1	50.0	24.50

LEADING JUMP TRAINERS AT FFOS LAS (SINCE 2013)

	Total W-R	Nov Hdle	H'cap Hdle	Other Hdle	Nov Chase	H'cap Chase	Other Chase	Hunter Chase	N.H. Flat	Per cent	£1 Level stake
Peter Bowen	50-275	5-39	14-76	5-37	3-18	14-66	3-6	0-0	6-33	18.2	-19.47
Evan Williams	39-319	9-53	14-101	4-23	0-27	7-88	0-2	0-0	5-25	12.2	-91.33
Nigel Twiston-Davies	36-174	8-26	6-46	4-18	0-8	12-53	2-5	0-0	4-18	20.7	9.84
Rebecca Curtis	33-143	4-23	7-33	4-26	4-9	8-26	0-1	0-2	6-23	23.1	7.07
Jonjo O'Neill	18-108	2-11	7-41	1-12	1-5	6-35	0-1	0-0	1-3	16.7	-30.98
Debra Hamer	14-82	0-10	3-26	1-7	3-6	7-28	0-2	0-0	0-3	17.1	17.12
Bernard Llewellyn	13-93	1-18	7-49	4-11	0-5	1-5	0-1	0-0	0-4	14.0	5.01
David Pipe	12-95	2-12	4-42	0-5	0-3	3-15	0-0	0-0	3-18	12.6	-34.15
Tim Vaughan	12-157	0-20	3-54	2-15	2-15	5-42	0-1	0-1	0-9	7.6	-88.02
Nicky Henderson	11-30	8-11	0-6	1-4	0-2	0-1	0-1	0-0	2-5	36.7	-7.39
Warren Greatrex	11-48	2-9	2-8	3-10	0-3	1-7	0-1	0-0	3-10	22.9	-13.33
David Rees	10-105	1-9	4-38	0-14	3-6	2-36	0-1	0-0	0-1	9.5	12.50
Kim Bailey	10-35	1-4	5-15	3-7	1-2	0-6	0-0	0-0	0-1	28.6	21.87
Neil Mulholland	9-74	0-9	4-22	1-7	1-6	1-22	0-1	0-0	2-7	12.2	11.37
Sophie Leech	8-35	1-2	3-12	2-3	0-3	2-12	0-0	0-0	0-3	22.9	3.37
Philip Hobbs	7-34	0-1	1-9	3-8	1-3	1-8	0-0	0-0	1-5	20.6	-8.42
Anthony Honeyball	7-55	1-4	2-17	0-7	1-4	0-10	0-1	0-0	3-12	12.7	-22.54
Jamie Snowden	6-27	2-5	2-9	1-5	0-1	0-2	0-1	0-0	1-4	22.2	-8.09
Paul Morgan	5-26	1-6	1-7	0-1	1-2	1-2	0-1	0-0	1-7	19.2	1.92
Martin Keighley	5-14	1-2	2-6	1-1	0-1	0-1	0-0	0-0	1-3	35.7	14.70
Paul Nicholls	5-20	1-2	2-4	0-4	1-2	0-4	1-2	0-0	0-2	25.0	-2.42
Dr Richard Newland	5-20	0-2	4-11	0-1	0-1	1-5	0-0	0-0	0-0	25.0	-2.65
Venetia Williams	5-45	0-5	1-9	0-1	0-2	4-26	0-0	0-0	0-2	11.1	-26.09
John Flint	5-64	1-8	4-30	0-8	0-2	0-13	0-1	0-0	0-2	7.8	-36.00
Paul Henderson	4-17	0-0	1-5	0-0	1-1	1-10	0-0	0-0	1-1	23.5	4.50
Hywel Evans	4-12	0-0	0-3	0-0	0-0	4-9	0-0	0-0	0-0	33.3	13.35
Sue Gardner	4-28	0-2	2-10	0-4	0-1	2-6	0-0	0-0	0-5	14.3	-3.09
Nick Williams	4-21	1-5	1-3	0-2	0-1	2-9	0-0	0-0	0-1	19.0	-3.25
Tom George	4-21	0-1	0-2	0-4	2-5	1-6	0-0	1-1	0-2	19.0	-4.05
Dan Skelton	4-30	0-4	2-13	0-3	0-0	2-7	0-0	0-0	0-3	13.3	-7.00

LEADING JUMP TRAINERS AT FONTWELL (SINCE 2013)

	Total W-R	Nov Hdle	H'cap Hdle	Other Hdle	Nov Chase	H'cap Chase	Other Chase	Hunter Chase	N.H. Flat	Per cent	£1 Level stake
Gary Moore	50-346	3-38	16-140	12-46	3-17	9-72	1-3	0-0	6-30	14.5	-61.23
Chris Gordon	41-284	2-26	23-124	1-30	4-13	10-69	0-0	0-3	1-19	14.4	-46.56
Neil Mulholland	39-153	3-19	14-47	4-20	4-8	9-36	1-6	0-0	4-17	25.5	15.66
Paul Nicholls	33-88	5-9	2-9	3-19	10-19	2-14	8-10	3-5	0-3	37.5	5.40
Anthony Honeyball	28-84	0-7	8-27	4-10	0-2	9-21	1-3	0-0	6-14	33.3	34.67
Colin Tizzard	21-110	1-11	6-29	2-11	3-8	8-35	0-4	0-0	1-12	19.1	-27.41
Charlie Longsdon	19-89	4-9	3-30	3-9	2-6	5-24	0-1	0-0	2-10	21.3	-13.01
Dan Skelton	17-76	1-5	4-23	2-13	0-2	8-18	1-1	0-0	1-14	22.4	-6.53
Alan King	17-62	6-16	0-10	8-18	0-3	1-6	0-1	0-0	2-8	27.4	-9.52
Harry Fry	13-43	3-9	6-14	0-5	1-2	3-3	0-2	0-0	0-8	30.2	2.17
Dr Richard Newland	13-36	2-4	4-18	2-5	1-2	4-7	0-0	0-0	0-0	36.1	6.21
Jamie Snowden	13-78	2-8	2-19	2-15	0-5	2-13	0-0	0-0	5-18	16.7	-1.95
Seamus Mullins	13-149	0-9	5-49	0-22	2-5	5-56	0-0	0-0	1-8	8.7	-18.17
Philip Hobbs	13-65	3-9	4-22	2-11	0-3	3-13	0-1	1-1	0-5	20.0	-26.18
Warren Greatrex	12-45	2-8	6-16	3-12	0-1	1-4	0-0	0-0	0-4	26.7	17.32
Caroline Keevil	12-50	1-8	4-17	1-4	1-3	3-13	1-1	0-0	1-4	24.0	59.28
Jonjo O'Neill	11-46	2-4	2-14	0-5	1-5	6-17	0-0	0-0	0-1	23.9	1.96
Neil King	11-67	0-9	1-21	4-12	1-3	4-16	0-0	0-0	1-6	16.4	21.41
Jeremy Scott	11-61	0-5	4-25	0-3	1-6	6-20	0-0	0-0	0-2	18.0	-14.43
Oliver Sherwood	11-78	2-11	2-19	4-12	0-4	2-16	0-4	0-0	1-12	14.1	-36.86
Lawney Hill	10-55	0-4	2-17	0-0	0-4	8-27	0-0	0-0	0-3	18.2	-7.82
David Pipe	10-57	1-7	4-28	2-4	0-0	2-14	0-0	0-0	1-4	17.5	-14.13
Ben Pauling	9-34	0-3	2-9	1-3	2-5	3-10	0-1	0-0	1-3	26.5	6.68
Emma Lavelle	9-43	1-9	4-10	1-4	0-3	2-14	0-1	0-0	1-2	20.9	7.75
David Bridgwater	9-52	1-2	0-5	0-4	1-4	7-32	0-1	0-0	0-4	17.3	-10.64
Tim Vaughan	9-79	4-11	2-30	1-6	1-5	1-17	0-1	0-0	0-9	11.4	-32.69
Victor Dartnall	8-24	0-2	3-6	0-1	1-2	2-7	0-1	1-1	1-4	33.3	17.41
Nick Gifford	8-80	1-11	3-32	0-10	0-3	3-16	0-1	0-0	1-7	10.0	-30.63
Venetia Williams	7-39	0-2	1-7	1-4	1-5	3-20	0-0	0-0	1-1	17.9	3.75
Nicky Henderson	7-40	1-4	1-8	2-9	1-3	0-3	1-3	0-0	1-10	17.5	-17.92

LEADING JUMP TRAINERS AT HAYDOCK (SINCE 2013)

	Total W-R	Nov Hdle	H'cap Hdle	Other Hdle	Nov Chase	H'cap Chase	Other Chase	Hunter Chase	N.H. Flat	Per cent	£1 Level stake
Donald McCain	19-101	3-13	3-35	0-12	4-12	7-23	0-0	0-0	2-6	18.8	-10.41
Nigel Twiston-Davies	18-100	1-8	3-24	6-9	1-4	5-49	1-2	0-1	1-3	18.0	-18.32
Venetia Williams	17-89	4-8	3-20	1-4	1-9	7-45	0-1	0-1	1-1	19.1	75.25
Paul Nicholls	16-76	0-3	1-25	3-15	5-7	1-12	4-10	2-2	0-2	21.1	-21.87
Sue Smith	13-119	1-11	3-27	1-8	2-10	5-56	1-5	0-0	0-2	10.9	7.53
David Pipe	13-72	0-2	7-36	0-1	0-0	5-27	1-6	0-0	0-0	18.1	63.00
Lucinda Russell	9-72	2-7	3-25	0-2	1-4	3-31	0-1	0-0	0-2	12.5	23.83
Evan Williams	9-70	1-5	7-25	0-6	0-5	1-27	0-1	0-0	0-1	12.9	34.00
Nicky Henderson	9-48	1-5	2-22	3-9	1-3	1-5	0-2	0-0	1-2	18.8	-17.81
Jonjo O'Neill	8-64	0-1	5-31	0-4	1-4	1-20	1-3	0-0	0-1	12.5	-11.77
Philip Hobbs	8-66	0-3	5-31	0-0	1-4	2-22	0-2	0-0	0-4	12.1	-18.25
Tom George	7-44	2-4	2-13	1-1	0-4	1-18	0-0	0-0	1-4	15.9	-12.25
Dan Skelton	7-68	2-11	2-29	2-10	1-4	0-11	0-2	0-0	0-1	10.3	-31.13
Colin Tizzard	5-25	0-2	0-3	0-1	0-2	1-9	4-8	0-0	0-0	20.0	2.45
Alan King	5-44	1-4	1-22	0-3	0-0	1-9	0-2	0-0	2-4	11.4	9.82
Malcolm Jefferson	5-32	1-5	1-9	1-3	1-2	0-9	1-2	0-0	0-2	15.6	-21.10
Ian Williams	4-18	0-1	0-7	0-0	2-2	2-7	0-0	0-0	0-1	22.2	3.00
Nicky Richards	4-29	0-6	3-17	0-0	0-0	1-4	0-1	0-0	0-1	13.8	3.25
Harry Fry	4-16	1-3	3-9	0-0	0-0	0-4	0-0	0-0	0-0	25.0	8.80
Emma Lavelle	4-17	0-1	2-8	1-1	0-2	1-4	0-1	0-0	0-0	23.5	15.50
Nick Williams	4-22	0-1	2-10	2-5	0-1	0-4	0-1	0-0	0-0	18.2	19.50
Peter Bowen	4-23	1-3	0-6	0-1	0-0	2-12	0-0	0-0	1-1	17.4	-3.97
Charlie Longsdon	4-33	0-2	2-13	1-1	0-1	0-12	0-1	0-0	1-3	12.1	-14.00
Henry Daly	4-35	0-5	1-8	1-4	0-3	0-12	0-0	2-3	0-0	11.4	-19.25
Kerry Lee	3-9	0-0	0-1	0-0	1-1	2-7	0-0	0-0	0-0	33.3	7.80
Graeme McPherson	3-16	0-1	1-7	0-0	0-0	2-5	0-0	0-0	0-3	18.8	16.00
Chris Grant	3-13	0-2	1-3	1-2	0-0	1-5	0-0	0-0	0-1	23.1	50.00
Tim Vaughan	3-23	0-2	2-10	0-1	0-1	1-7	0-1	0-0	0-1	13.0	-0.50
Fergal O'Brien	3-16	2-5	0-3	0-1	0-0	1-5	0-0	0-0	0-2	18.8	-5.23
Jennie Candlish	3-41	0-1	2-23	0-5	0-2	1-8	0-0	0-0	0-2	7.3	-27.50

LEADING JUMP TRAINERS AT HEREFORD (SINCE 2016)

	Total W-R	Nov Hdle	H'cap Hdle	Other Hdle	Nov Chase	H'cap Chase	Other Chase	Hunter Chase	N.H. Flat	Per cent	£1 Level stake
Venetia Williams	8-40	1-8	3-8	0-9	2-5	1-9	0-0	0-0	1-1	20.0	8.22
Henry Oliver	5-18	1-4	1-5	0-0	1-3	2-4	0-0	0-0	0-2	27.8	25.50
Warren Greatrex	5-17	1-4	1-1	1-4	0-3	0-0	1-1	0-0	1-4	29.4	-1.17
Dan Skelton	4-20	1-5	0-5	1-2	1-3	0-2	0-0	1-2	0-1	20.0	-4.22
Philip Hobbs	4-20	2-9	0-2	1-3	0-3	0-1	0-0	0-0	1-2	20.0	-7.74
Nigel Twiston-Davies	4-24	0-2	0-5	1-2	0-1	3-6	0-2	0-0	0-6	16.7	-8.75
Nicky Henderson	3-5	2-3	0-0	1-1	0-0	0-0	0-1	0-0	0-0	60.0	2.13
Harry Fry	3-8	1-3	0-0	0-0	1-2	0-1	1-1	0-1	0-0	37.5	4.45
Nikki Evans	3-10	0-2	3-6	0-1	0-0	0-1	0-0	0-0	0-0	30.0	6.75
Alex Hales	3-6	0-0	2-4	1-1	0-0	0-1	0-0	0-0	0-0	50.0	9.75
David Rees	3-9	0-0	0-1	0-0	0-2	3-4	0-0	0-0	0-2	33.3	9.88
Tom Symonds	3-12	0-2	2-4	1-1	0-1	0-1	0-0	0-0	0-3	25.0	20.33
Tom George	3-16	0-6	2-5	0-0	1-1	0-2	0-0	0-1	0-1	18.8	-3.00
Rebecca Curtis	3-14	0-1	0-0	0-5	2-3	0-1	0-1	0-0	1-3	21.4	-5.63
Neil Mulholland	3-17	0-3	0-5	1-1	0-1	0-3	0-0	0-0	2-4	17.6	-5.84
Kerry Lee	3-32	0-2	1-5	0-2	1-7	1-11	0-3	0-1	0-1	9.4	-16.25
Tom Lacey	2-7	1-4	1-1	0-1	0-0	0-0	0-0	0-0	0-1	28.6	6.50
Johnny Farrelly	2-3	1-1	0-1	0-0	1-1	0-0	0-0	0-0	0-0	66.7	8.50
John O'Shea	2-11	0-1	2-7	0-3	0-0	0-0	0-0	0-0	0-0	18.2	10.50
Oliver Greenall	2-8	0-2	1-1	1-4	0-0	0-1	0-0	0-0	0-0	25.0	12.00
Jonjo O'Neill	2-12	1-3	0-4	1-2	0-0	0-3	0-0	0-0	0-0	16.7	19.50
Dai Williams	2-6	0-0	0-0	0-0	1-2	1-3	0-1	0-0	0-0	33.3	36.50
Alastair Ralph	2-8	1-1	0-4	1-2	0-0	0-0	0-0	0-0	0-1	25.0	-1.25
Charlie Mann	2-5	0-0	1-2	1-3	0-0	0-0	0-0	0-0	0-0	40.0	-1.39
Harry Whittington	2-10	1-5	0-2	0-1	0-0	0-1	1-1	0-0	0-0	20.0	-6.27
Tim Vaughan	2-18	0-2	0-6	0-1	1-3	1-6	0-0	0-0	0-0	11.1	-7.50
Evan Williams	2-30	0-9	0-6	0-4	0-3	1-5	1-1	0-0	0-2	6.7	-25.14
Tom Gretton	1-4	0-0	0-0	0-0	0-1	1-3	0-0	0-0	0-0	25.0	0.33
Anthony Honeyball	1-3	0-0	1-2	0-0	0-0	0-1	0-0	0-0	0-0	33.3	0.75

LEADING JUMP TRAINERS AT HEXHAM (SINCE 2013)

	Total W-R	Nov Hdle	H'cap Hdle	Other Hdle	Nov Chase	H'cap Chase	Other Chase	Hunter Chase	N.H. Flat	Per cent	£1 Level stake
Lucinda Russell	41-244	3-34	9-63	4-28	7-26	17-83	0-0	0-0	1-10	16.8	32.34
Maurice Barnes	18-118	1-14	6-22	1-20	2-14	8-44	0-0	0-0	0-4	15.3	-11.38
Micky Hammond	15-127	3-17	6-40	1-5	1-14	4-43	0-0	0-0	0-8	11.8	-56.67
Donald McCain	15-113	10-30	0-28	3-24	0-10	0-11	0-0	0-0	2-10	13.3	-66.88
Stuart Coltherd	14-74	1-6	2-21	1-8	1-11	9-27	0-0	0-1	0-0	18.9	27.50
Sue Smith	14-126	2-20	3-29	1-14	3-17	4-39	0-0	0-0	1-7	11.1	-57.59
Malcolm Jefferson	13-61	2-13	0-12	4-10	0-3	2-8	0-0	0-0	5-15	21.3	-18.99
Nicky Richards	12-46	2-12	3-9	3-9	3-5	1-9	0-0	0-0	0-2	26.1	6.81
James Ewart	11-57	1-4	3-14	0-6	2-7	5-20	0-0	0-0	0-6	19.3	1.13
Brian Ellison	11-60	0-11	5-16	3-17	2-5	0-9	0-0	0-0	1-2	18.3	-2.47
Martin Todhunter	11-90	2-15	2-27	3-8	0-12	4-26	0-0	0-0	0-2	12.2	-19.38
Mark Walford	10-57	2-5	2-19	1-9	1-3	4-19	0-0	0-0	0-2	17.5	4.13
Jonathan Haynes	10-88	0-14	9-42	0-6	0-1	1-18	0-0	0-0	0-7	11.4	-6.72
George Bewley	9-68	0-7	1-27	2-10	0-5	6-15	0-0	0-0	0-4	13.2	5.25
Henry Hogarth	7-39	0-1	1-7	1-4	2-6	3-20	0-0	0-0	0-1	17.9	1.70
Karen McLintock	7-29	1-5	2-3	0-3	2-5	0-5	0-0	0-0	2-8	24.1	2.16
Alistair Whillans	7-68	0-5	4-30	3-8	0-4	0-16	0-0	0-0	0-5	10.3	-15.38
N W Alexander	7-79	1-10	2-21	0-9	2-8	1-19	0-1	0-3	1-8	8.9	-41.75
Sandy Thomson	6-31	1-5	0-3	1-5	2-5	1-10	0-0	0-0	1-3	19.4	62.38
Iain Jardine	6-39	1-6	2-10	2-10	1-6	0-6	0-0	0-0	0-1	15.4	-0.50
Dianne Sayer	6-56	1-6	4-21	0-4	0-6	1-19	0-0	0-0	0-0	10.7	-4.12
Victor Thompson	6-76	1-7	0-6	0-11	1-13	4-31	0-0	0-8	0-0	7.9	-10.75
Rose Dobbin	6-67	0-9	2-13	0-5	0-6	4-31	0-0	0-0	0-3	9.0	-19.92
Philip Kirby	6-70	1-23	1-16	1-13	0-4	2-8	0-0	0-1	1-5	8.6	-44.25
Susan Corbett	6-95	0-17	5-34	0-20	0-4	1-8	0-0	0-0	0-12	6.3	-66.92
Michael Smith	5-31	4-9	0-6	1-7	0-4	0-1	0-0	0-0	0-4	16.1	1.37
Alan Swinbank	5-13	0-2	2-4	1-1	0-2	0-1	0-0	0-0	2-3	38.5	3.25
Paul Stafford	5-32	0-3	0-3	1-3	0-3	4-18	0-0	0-0	0-2	15.6	5.75
Raymond Shiels	5-17	1-5	3-6	0-2	0-1	1-3	0-0	0-0	0-0	29.4	22.50
Michael Scudamore	5-18	0-1	0-4	1-3	0-2	1-4	0-0	0-0	3-4	27.8	-6.43

LEADING JUMP TRAINERS AT HUNTINGDON (SINCE 2013)

	Total W-R	Nov Hdle	H'cap Hdle	Other Hdle	Nov Chase	H'cap Chase	Other Chase	Hunter Chase	N.H. Flat	Per cent	£1 Level stake
Nicky Henderson	31-96	3-17	4-17	11-24	5-8	3-5	3-6	0-0	2-19	32.3	-12.36
Jonjo O'Neill	29-122	3-17	13-44	2-20	3-11	5-21	0-1	0-0	3-8	23.8	11.06
Alan King	23-113	2-22	2-18	8-29	3-10	3-12	0-0	0-0	5-22	20.4	-29.88
Kim Bailey	20-97	4-19	7-23	1-9	3-10	2-18	1-3	0-0	2-15	20.6	29.97
Dan Skelton	20-125	3-24	4-26	4-22	2-18	3-13	2-2	0-0	2-20	16.0	-42.37
John Ferguson	19-49	10-23	0-5	4-11	1-3	0-0	0-0	0-0	4-7	38.8	8.55
Gary Moore	17-107	0-13	10-36	3-24	3-17	1-11	0-1	0-0	0-5	15.9	32.70
Charlie Longsdon	17-100	2-13	5-30	2-19	3-15	4-13	0-0	0-0	1-10	17.0	-12.89
David Dennis	11-42	1-6	5-16	0-5	2-5	3-9	0-0	0-0	0-1	26.2	30.45
Ben Pauling	11-54	3-10	2-12	1-11	3-9	0-4	0-1	0-0	2-7	20.4	86.42
Ian Williams	10-64	1-9	2-24	2-11	1-6	4-10	0-0	0-0	0-4	15.6	-15.25
Neil King	9-82	1-9	3-30	3-14	1-8	1-10	0-0	0-0	0-11	11.0	6.25
Fergal O'Brien	9-54	1-6	1-15	1-8	2-8	3-10	0-0	0-0	1-7	16.7	6.96
Tim Vaughan	9-58	2-8	4-26	0-5	0-2	2-11	0-0	0-2	1-4	15.5	-10.97
Philip Hobbs	9-53	2-8	0-8	2-14	0-8	0-2	1-3	0-0	4-10	17.0	-17.96
Venetia Williams	9-54	2-6	1-11	1-9	1-9	4-15	0-3	0-0	0-1	16.7	-21.59
David Pipe	8-40	0-1	4-20	0-6	3-6	1-2	0-0	0-0	0-5	20.0	6.24
Paul Nicholls	7-23	1-2	1-6	0-1	2-5	0-1	2-7	0-0	1-1	30.4	8.76
Lucy Wadham	7-52	0-8	2-19	3-10	1-5	1-3	0-0	0-0	0-7	13.5	-2.57
Tom George	7-40	1-5	0-3	2-5	2-8	1-11	0-1	0-0	1-7	17.5	-8.80
Neil Mulholland	7-43	0-2	1-14	2-4	2-7	2-11	0-0	0-0	0-5	16.3	-18.30
Nigel Twiston-Davies	7-79	1-9	2-26	1-9	2-11	1-14	0-2	0-0	0-8	8.9	-51.12
Lawney Hill	6-37	0-2	2-17	0-1	1-4	3-11	0-1	0-0	0-1	16.2	17.87
Paul Webber	6-59	2-9	2-8	1-18	0-8	0-7	0-1	0-0	1-8	10.2	-24.25
Warren Greatrex	6-43	2-8	0-7	1-15	0-1	1-2	0-0	0-0	2-10	14.0	-24.47
Stuart Edmunds	5-19	3-6	1-4	0-3	0-1	0-0	0-0	0-0	1-5	26.3	4.08
Harry Whittington	5-20	0-3	2-8	0-2	0-1	1-2	0-0	0-0	2-4	25.0	5.00
Dr Richard Newland	5-20	0-0	1-9	2-4	1-3	1-4	0-0	0-0	0-0	25.0	5.62
Don Cantillon	5-15	1-5	1-2	1-4	0-1	0-0	0-0	0-0	2-3	33.3	8.04
J R Jenkins	5-49	0-5	4-25	0-9	0-0	0-4	0-0	0-0	1-6	10.2	22.00

LEADING JUMP TRAINERS AT KELSO (SINCE 2013)

	Total W-R	Nov Hdle	H'cap Hdle	Other Hdle	Nov Chase	H'cap Chase	Other Chase	Hunter Chase	N.H. Flat	Per cent	£1 Level stake
Donald McCain	36-167	10-31	7-44	5-27	4-19	8-35	0-3	0-0	2-8	21.6	-2.05
Lucinda Russell	36-278	2-53	10-75	1-20	11-34	9-76	1-2	0-4	2-14	12.9	-76.47
N W Alexander	26-197	8-41	8-53	2-15	2-14	5-47	0-1	1-12	0-14	13.2	39.08
Nicky Richards	26-134	9-24	5-33	2-17	1-9	7-27	0-4	0-8	2-12	19.4	-17.83
James Ewart	17-106	5-20	6-28	0-8	2-18	3-22	0-0	0-0	1-10	16.0	34.45
Rose Dobbin	16-142	5-46	1-39	2-12	2-8	5-29	0-0	0-0	1-8	11.3	-11.06
Malcolm Jefferson	15-70	6-18	0-8	2-4	2-7	1-19	0-1	0-0	4-13	21.4	-8.09
Sandy Thomson	11-94	1-14	3-27	1-10	2-11	3-27	1-3	0-0	0-2	11.7	33.58
Chris Grant	10-76	2-23	1-15	1-5	2-7	3-16	0-0	0-0	1-10	13.2	79.60
Iain Jardine	9-50	2-10	0-12	1-9	1-3	2-8	0-0	0-0	3-8	18.0	8.05
George Bewley	8-68	1-10	4-22	0-5	1-5	2-19	0-0	0-1	0-6	11.8	7.00
Keith Dalgleish	8-21	1-3	5-10	1-2	0-0	0-1	0-0	0-0	1-5	38.1	42.23
Harriet Graham	8-60	0-6	3-23	0-1	0-1	5-23	0-1	0-0	0-5	13.3	-11.17
Dianne Sayer	8-92	0-12	4-43	0-6	3-8	1-21	0-1	0-0	0-1	8.7	-38.00
Stuart Coltherd	8-99	0-22	3-17	0-6	2-16	2-28	0-0	1-8	0-2	8.1	-50.63
Paul Nicholls	7-18	1-2	1-1	0-1	1-5	2-3	2-5	0-1	0-0	38.9	-1.54
Micky Hammond	7-58	2-11	1-12	0-4	1-6	2-21	0-1	0-0	1-3	12.1	-23.25
Michael Smith	6-38	3-10	0-7	1-3	0-8	1-5	0-0	0-0	1-5	15.8	-0.37
Tim Vaughan	5-13	0-2	3-5	2-2	0-1	0-2	0-0	0-0	0-1	38.5	2.71
Mark Walford	5-25	0-1	1-6	0-0	2-2	2-15	0-1	0-0	0-0	20.0	12.00
Karen McLintock	5-19	0-4	2-4	0-2	0-0	2-4	0-1	0-0	1-4	26.3	20.50
Brian Ellison	5-34	1-8	2-11	0-4	1-4	1-4	0-0	0-0	0-3	14.7	-17.89
Sue Smith	5-67	0-6	0-8	0-4	3-18	2-27	0-3	0-0	0-1	7.5	-30.67
Jackie Stephen	4-28	1-6	0-7	0-2	0-3	3-10	0-0	0-0	0-0	14.3	5.25
Nicky Henderson	4-7	0-0	0-0	1-1	1-1	0-0	1-1	0-0	1-4	57.1	5.51
Keith Reveley	4-14	0-0	0-4	2-3	0-1	1-4	0-0	0-0	1-2	28.6	5.62
Simon Waugh	4-32	0-5	2-15	0-5	0-2	2-2	0-0	0-0	0-3	12.5	6.00
Donald Whillans	4-35	1-10	2-15	0-3	0-0	0-1	0-0	0-0	1-6	11.4	11.00
Kenneth Slack	4-14	1-2	2-9	0-0	0-2	1-1	0-0	0-0	0-0	28.6	-0.25
John Wade	4-41	0-5	1-7	0-0	0-7	2-16	0-0	1-2	0-4	9.8	-6.00

LEADING JUMP TRAINERS AT KEMPTON (SINCE 2013)

	Total W-R	Nov Hdle	H'cap Hdle	Other Hdle	Nov Chase	H'cap Chase	Other Chase	Hunter Chase	N.H. Flat	Per cent	£1 Level stake
Nicky Henderson	63-238	17-50	11-58	9-39	8-24	4-24	9-21	0-0	6-27	26.5	-17.76
Paul Nicholls	41-183	6-28	4-28	8-30	12-35	4-32	7-23	1-4	1-8	22.4	-19.70
Alan King	27-180	8-43	2-44	10-28	2-15	0-26	2-8	0-0	3-18	15.0	-76.26
Harry Fry	14-65	2-17	6-16	4-8	1-4	1-13	0-1	0-0	0-7	21.5	-18.31
Chris Gordon	12-63	2-5	2-21	0-5	1-3	6-27	0-0	0-0	1-2	19.0	48.43
Nigel Twiston-Davies	12-70	1-5	1-15	3-11	1-9	6-24	0-4	0-0	0-5	17.1	-24.39
Jonjo O'Neill	12-101	2-25	3-27	2-9	0-5	4-29	1-2	0-1	0-4	11.9	-41.89
Colin Tizzard	11-79	3-14	1-12	1-4	1-12	1-16	3-15	0-0	1-6	13.9	16.48
Tom George	10-67	0-3	1-4	0-2	4-9	5-40	0-7	0-0	0-2	14.9	-8.00
Philip Hobbs	10-106	4-21	1-31	1-6	0-8	3-25	1-6	0-1	0-11	9.4	-70.67
Charlie Longsdon	9-67	1-9	0-21	1-7	4-9	3-21	0-0	0-0	0-2	13.4	-4.05
Dan Skelton	9-118	3-28	2-32	2-21	1-14	1-14	0-3	0-0	0-9	7.6	-86.46
Emma Lavelle	8-69	2-21	1-9	1-4	1-8	2-19	0-2	0-0	1-7	11.6	-40.52
Oliver Sherwood	7-48	3-15	0-12	1-5	1-2	1-8	0-0	0-1	1-5	14.6	6.50
Ben Pauling	7-43	4-11	1-20	0-7	1-2	1-4	0-0	0-0	0-2	16.3	-12.56
David Pipe	7-57	1-4	4-29	1-10	0-2	1-12	0-5	0-0	0-0	12.3	-12.88
Ian Williams	6-29	0-6	4-11	0-2	1-3	1-3	0-2	0-0	0-2	20.7	4.75
Jeremy Scott	6-41	2-9	1-15	0-2	0-2	3-10	0-0	0-1	0-2	14.6	6.00
Kim Bailey	6-56	2-12	1-15	0-3	0-10	3-13	0-1	0-0	0-3	10.7	-12.13
Gary Moore	6-111	1-26	2-35	1-16	1-12	0-14	1-7	0-0	0-2	5.4	-68.50
Nick Williams	5-26	3-6	1-8	1-8	1-3	0-1	0-2	0-0	0-1	19.2	0.37
Martin Keighley	5-28	0-2	2-13	0-2	2-3	1-2	0-3	0-0	0-3	17.9	13.50
John Ferguson	5-24	3-9	1-4	0-6	0-3	0-0	0-0	0-0	1-2	20.8	-11.50
Paul Webber	5-59	0-18	0-6	0-7	0-3	5-19	0-2	0-0	0-4	8.5	-18.00
Venetia Williams	5-56	1-8	1-13	1-6	0-1	2-27	1-4	0-0	0-0	8.9	-18.00
Harry Whittington	4-17	1-5	2-8	0-2	1-2	0-0	0-0	0-0	0-0	23.5	10.50
Robin Dickin	4-34	1-5	0-4	0-2	2-6	1-11	0-2	0-0	0-4	11.8	-3.50
Charlie Mann	4-29	1-10	1-4	1-6	0-2	1-6	0-0	0-0	0-1	13.8	-10.60
Lucy Wadham	4-29	0-4	2-9	0-1	1-5	1-9	0-0	0-0	0-1	13.8	-14.86
Peter Bowen	3-14	0-0	1-5	0-2	0-3	1-2	0-0	0-0	1-2	21.4	1.20

LEADING JUMP TRAINERS AT LEICESTER (SINCE 2013)

	Total W-R	Nov Hdle	H'cap Hdle	Other Hdle	Nov Chase	H'cap Chase	Other Chase	Hunter Chase	N.H. Flat	Per cent	£1 Level stake
Nigel Twiston-Davies	18-67	2-11	5-12	1-4	2-11	8-28	0-1	0-0	0-0	26.9	39.46
Tom George	16-50	0-2	2-7	0-0	5-16	8-24	0-0	1-1	0-0	32.0	19.25
Caroline Bailey	11-43	0-5	2-5	2-3	1-6	5-22	0-1	1-1	0-0	25.6	1.49
David Pipe	11-28	3-5	1-7	2-4	4-5	1-6	0-1	0-0	0-0	39.3	11.07
Fergal O'Brien	8-43	1-6	0-1	0-5	4-11	3-20	0-0	0-0	0-0	18.6	23.63
Venetia Williams	8-43	0-5	1-12	1-3	2-8	3-14	1-1	0-0	0-0	18.6	-19.38
Philip Hobbs	7-19	2-4	2-5	0-2	0-4	3-4	0-0	0-0	0-0	36.8	3.58
Robin Dickin	7-28	0-2	1-3	0-0	2-5	4-17	0-1	0-0	0-0	25.0	11.62
Dan Skelton	6-30	2-8	0-4	0-3	3-5	1-8	0-1	0-1	0-0	20.0	-2.27
Ian Williams	6-21	1-5	1-5	1-1	0-2	2-6	1-1	0-1	0-0	28.6	-3.43
Seamus Mullins	5-15	1-3	0-1	0-0	1-3	3-8	0-0	0-0	0-0	33.3	10.50
Paul Nicholls	5-10	1-2	0-0	0-1	2-2	1-1	1-3	0-1	0-0	50.0	-0.49
Emma Lavelle	4-12	3-4	0-0	0-0	1-3	0-5	0-0	0-0	0-0	33.3	0.23
Zoe Davison	4-21	0-0	1-7	0-0	0-4	3-10	0-0	0-0	0-0	19.0	14.00
Henry Daly	4-17	2-8	1-3	0-0	0-2	1-4	0-0	0-0	0-0	23.5	46.75
Matt Sheppard	4-23	0-0	1-6	0-2	0-1	3-14	0-0	0-0	0-0	17.4	-1.75
Charlie Longsdon	4-29	0-6	0-3	0-2	0-7	2-9	2-2	0-0	0-0	13.8	-17.39
Henry Oliver	4-34	0-2	2-15	0-1	0-5	2-11	0-0	0-0	0-0	11.8	-19.50
Jonjo O'Neill	4-42	1-14	0-8	0-1	2-8	1-11	0-0	0-0	0-0	9.5	-30.50
Tony Carroll	4-61	0-7	1-18	1-10	1-8	1-14	0-4	0-0	0-0	6.6	-31.00
Lawney Hill	3-14	0-3	0-1	0-4	2-5	1-1	0-0	0-0	0-0	21.4	-0.00
John Ferguson	3-5	2-2	0-0	0-0	0-1	0-0	1-2	0-0	0-0	60.0	1.15
Gary Moore	3-17	1-1	0-3	0-5	1-6	1-2	0-0	0-0	0-0	17.6	-1.75
Harry Fry	3-7	0-0	0-1	1-3	1-2	0-0	1-1	0-0	0-0	42.9	2.08
Johnny Farrelly	3-6	0-0	1-4	0-0	2-2	0-0	0-0	0-0	0-0	50.0	3.00
Nick Williams	3-13	1-2	0-1	2-3	0-3	0-4	0-0	0-0	0-0	23.1	5.75
John Groucott	3-9	0-2	0-1	0-0	1-4	2-2	0-0	0-0	0-0	33.3	7.00
Ali Stronge	3-14	0-2	2-4	0-2	1-3	0-3	0-0	0-0	0-0	21.4	9.50
Emma-Jane Bishop	3-12	0-0	1-2	0-0	1-3	1-7	0-0	0-0	0-0	25.0	-2.13
Alan King	3-22	0-3	0-4	2-4	1-5	0-5	0-1	0-0	0-0	13.6	-5.50

LEADING JUMP TRAINERS AT LINGFIELD (SINCE 2013)

	Total W-R	Nov Hdle	H'cap Hdle	Other Hdle	Nov Chase	H'cap Chase	Other Chase	Hunter Chase	N.H. Flat	Per cent	£1 Level stake
Gary Moore	11-90	0-17	3-27	1-8	2-13	5-25	0-0	0-0	0-0	12.2	-26.50
Warren Greatrex	9-21	4-9	2-3	1-3	1-3	0-2	1-1	0-0	0-0	42.9	2.48
Nigel Twiston-Davies	8-28	3-7	1-7	1-2	0-2	3-10	0-0	0-0	0-0	28.6	23.58
Chris Gordon	8-39	1-5	2-17	1-1	1-7	3-9	0-0	0-0	0-0	20.5	-9.15
Seamus Mullins	7-43	2-8	1-12	0-3	1-7	3-13	0-0	0-0	0-0	16.3	9.25
Dan Skelton	7-16	1-3	2-7	0-2	1-1	3-3	0-0	0-0	0-0	43.8	17.25
Oliver Sherwood	4-11	2-4	0-2	1-1	0-0	0-3	0-0	1-1	0-0	36.4	0.87
Dr Richard Newland	4-8	1-2	1-2	0-0	1-2	1-2	0-0	0-0	0-0	50.0	1.95
Martin Keighley	4-14	0-2	3-5	0-3	1-2	0-2	0-0	0-0	0-0	28.6	9.17
Nicky Henderson	4-6	1-2	0-0	2-3	1-1	0-0	0-0	0-0	0-0	66.7	-0.25
Tim Vaughan	4-24	0-3	1-6	0-2	0-1	3-12	0-0	0-0	0-0	16.7	-11.40
Zoe Davison	4-31	0-5	2-9	1-5	0-4	1-8	0-0	0-0	0-0	12.9	-14.50
Venetia Williams	4-31	0-3	1-7	0-0	3-5	0-16	0-0	0-0	0-0	12.9	-15.63
Lucy Wadham	3-12	1-3	1-5	0-0	0-0	1-4	0-0	0-0	0-0	25.0	1.00
Emma Lavelle	3-12	1-5	0-0	0-1	0-1	2-5	0-0	0-0	0-0	25.0	3.50
Anthony Honeyball	3-10	0-0	3-5	0-0	0-2	0-3	0-0	0-0	0-0	30.0	3.60
Anabel K Murphy	3-4	0-0	3-4	0-0	0-0	0-0	0-0	0-0	0-0	75.0	12.75
Neil Mulholland	3-31	1-6	1-12	0-1	0-7	1-5	0-0	0-0	0-0	9.7	18.00
Evan Williams	3-16	0-2	0-3	0-4	1-2	2-5	0-0	0-0	0-0	18.8	-3.00
Colin Tizzard	3-14	0-0	1-4	0-1	0-2	2-7	0-0	0-0	0-0	21.4	-3.75
Anna Newton-Smith	3-23	0-2	2-7	0-2	0-3	1-9	0-0	0-0	0-0	13.0	-5.00
Harry Fry	2-4	0-1	0-1	2-2	0-0	0-0	0-0	0-0	0-0	50.0	0.92
Ali Stronge	2-6	0-0	1-3	0-0	1-2	0-1	0-0	0-0	0-0	33.3	3.57
Samuel Drinkwater	2-3	0-1	2-2	0-0	0-0	0-0	0-0	0-0	0-0	66.7	7.00
Richard Lee	2-3	0-0	0-0	0-0	0-0	2-3	0-0	0-0	0-0	66.7	7.00
Alison Batchelor	2-8	0-3	0-0	0-0	0-0	2-5	0-0	0-0	0-0	25.0	8.50
Kate Buckett	2-6	1-2	1-2	0-0	0-0	0-1	0-1	0-0	0-0	33.3	35.00
David Dennis	2-7	1-3	0-2	0-0	0-0	1-2	0-0	0-0	0-0	28.6	-1.27
Jamie Snowden	2-15	1-7	0-0	1-5	0-1	0-2	0-0	0-0	0-0	13.3	-2.20
Fergal O'Brien	2-10	1-2	1-2	0-0	0-1	0-4	0-1	0-0	0-0	20.0	-2.67

LEADING JUMP TRAINERS AT LUDLOW (SINCE 2013)

	Total W-R	Nov Hdle	H'cap Hdle	Other Hdle	Nov Chase	H'cap Chase	Other Chase	Hunter Chase	N.H. Flat	Per cent	£1 Level stake
Evan Williams	37-239	3-26	6-41	5-36	6-39	11-76	2-2	0-1	4-18	15.5	-57.72
Nicky Henderson	29-103	7-18	1-14	11-29	1-8	1-8	0-2	0-0	8-24	28.2	-21.87
Philip Hobbs	25-115	5-18	7-19	3-23	2-13	4-22	1-2	2-7	1-11	21.7	-25.25
Henry Daly	22-112	1-16	4-23	4-13	3-9	3-27	0-0	5-7	2-17	19.6	-18.51
Dan Skelton	22-107	8-20	7-30	3-25	0-6	2-11	0-0	0-0	2-15	20.6	-20.09
Kim Bailey	20-109	8-19	2-27	2-21	1-8	0-20	0-1	0-0	7-13	18.3	-0.02
Nigel Twiston-Davies	18-149	2-14	2-35	4-28	3-17	6-46	0-1	0-0	1-8	12.1	-80.23
Tom George	17-88	1-4	0-8	1-18	3-10	11-43	1-1	0-0	0-4	19.3	-14.01
Venetia Williams	14-139	1-17	2-29	0-21	4-19	6-47	0-2	0-1	1-3	10.1	-70.28
Ian Williams	13-65	2-10	4-19	4-16	2-10	1-10	0-0	0-0	0-0	20.0	-4.41
Alan King	11-55	1-7	2-14	5-22	2-4	0-6	0-0	0-0	1-2	20.0	4.96
Matt Sheppard	10-62	2-6	1-21	0-3	1-10	6-20	0-0	0-0	0-2	16.1	13.00
David Pipe	10-60	0-9	3-17	2-13	2-6	2-13	0-1	0-0	1-1	16.7	15.04
Kerry Lee	9-38	0-3	1-11	1-5	4-6	2-11	1-2	0-0	0-0	23.7	0.95
Jonjo O'Neill	9-90	1-8	0-14	1-15	1-10	4-39	0-0	1-3	1-1	10.0	-50.13
Tim Vaughan	8-74	1-13	1-17	0-14	2-6	4-14	0-0	0-1	0-9	10.8	1.12
Fergal O'Brien	7-58	2-11	2-9	0-10	2-6	1-14	0-1	0-1	0-6	12.1	-4.13
Harry Fry	7-31	0-0	2-5	1-9	1-2	2-8	0-1	0-1	1-5	22.6	-4.70
Paul Nicholls	7-37	0-1	0-1	2-11	1-7	1-12	0-0	2-2	1-3	18.9	-17.58
Rebecca Curtis	7-52	0-2	1-1	2-13	1-11	1-11	0-0	1-3	1-11	13.5	-29.47
Charlie Longsdon	7-72	2-13	0-13	2-11	0-7	3-21	0-1	0-0	0-6	9.7	-40.83
Jeremy Scott	6-40	0-3	4-16	0-4	1-3	0-11	0-0	1-1	0-2	15.0	-1.00
Peter Bowen	6-36	0-2	1-10	2-5	0-1	1-9	1-1	0-0	1-8	16.7	-4.63
Martin Keighley	5-40	2-8	1-10	0-7	0-3	2-8	0-0	0-0	0-4	12.5	-3.12
Harry Whittington	5-19	0-1	0-3	2-9	2-2	0-1	0-0	0-0	1-3	26.3	22.07
Colin Tizzard	5-33	2-5	1-6	1-4	0-5	0-10	0-0	0-0	1-3	15.2	-12.99
Oliver Sherwood	5-41	0-6	1-4	1-12	1-5	1-8	0-0	0-0	1-6	12.2	-15.50
David Dennis	5-50	3-13	1-9	0-13	1-4	0-7	0-0	0-0	0-4	10.0	-20.52
Tom Lacey	4-17	1-4	3-5	0-5	0-0	0-0	0-1	0-0	0-2	23.5	4.13
Gary Moore	4-17	1-4	0-0	1-5	1-4	1-3	0-0	0-0	0-1	23.5	6.50

LEADING JUMP TRAINERS AT MARKET RASEN (SINCE 2013)

	Total W-R	Nov Hdle	H'cap Hdle	Other Hdle	Nov Chase	H'cap Chase	Other Chase	Hunter Chase	N.H. Flat	Per cent	£1 Level stake
Dan Skelton	41-145	9-24	13-50	8-27	3-11	8-25	1-5	0-1	1-11	28.3	26.22
Jonjo O'Neill	35-226	4-32	12-68	4-22	4-24	10-71	0-1	0-0	1-11	15.5	-68.82
Charlie Longsdon	27-143	7-17	7-42	1-15	1-11	8-38	1-3	0-0	2-18	18.9	-47.69
Brian Ellison	25-152	5-16	8-58	5-33	0-11	3-29	1-3	0-0	3-9	16.4	-22.43
Nicky Henderson	24-76	4-11	2-24	8-14	2-5	1-8	1-4	0-0	6-15	31.6	5.07
Fergal O'Brien	20-88	6-16	4-23	0-6	3-11	5-23	0-1	0-1	2-8	22.7	49.13
Dr Richard Newland	19-74	2-7	7-30	6-23	1-6	6-19	0-1	0-0	0-0	25.7	23.38
Peter Bowen	18-88	0-5	6-29	1-6	1-7	7-34	0-0	0-0	3-11	20.5	-17.42
Malcolm Jefferson	16-84	1-14	7-19	0-7	0-3	2-13	2-2	0-0	4-26	19.0	17.88
John Ferguson	14-48	4-15	5-15	6-17	0-3	0-2	0-0	0-0	1-4	29.2	4.55
Nigel Hawke	11-46	2-10	1-5	2-9	0-5	6-16	0-1	0-0	0-1	23.9	21.84
David Pipe	11-57	2-3	2-26	1-9	5-8	0-11	1-2	0-0	0-4	19.3	-19.61
Micky Hammond	10-65	2-9	6-29	0-4	0-3	2-17	0-0	0-0	0-3	15.4	11.80
Venetia Williams	10-41	1-4	2-12	2-5	1-5	3-12	1-1	0-0	0-2	24.4	-5.37
David Dennis	10-54	1-2	3-23	2-9	0-6	3-12	0-0	0-0	1-5	18.5	-6.71
Alan King	10-79	1-9	4-26	1-12	0-5	2-17	1-2	0-0	1-10	12.7	-21.16
Neil King	10-85	1-10	6-37	1-13	0-1	1-15	0-0	0-0	1-11	11.8	-29.34
Sue Smith	10-86	0-11	4-24	1-8	0-14	5-26	0-2	0-0	0-2	11.6	-47.63
Tim Vaughan	10-103	3-16	2-44	0-10	1-6	2-21	0-1	1-1	1-8	9.7	-49.13
Charles Pogson	9-71	0-13	2-18	1-6	2-7	3-19	0-3	0-0	1-6	12.7	-10.47
Nigel Twiston-Davies	8-43	1-5	2-16	3-11	0-2	2-10	0-0	0-0	0-3	18.6	1.80
Chris Bealby	8-48	1-7	3-13	0-3	2-6	2-14	0-2	0-0	0-3	16.7	-1.84
Warren Greatrex	8-36	1-8	2-14	4-10	0-0	0-1	0-0	0-0	1-3	22.2	-8.64
Philip Hobbs	8-43	3-7	1-8	1-7	0-4	0-11	1-1	0-0	2-6	18.6	-15.90
Neil Mulholland	8-42	1-4	2-15	0-3	1-5	3-15	0-0	0-0	1-2	19.0	-16.59
Alex Hales	8-68	1-7	3-22	0-7	1-7	3-23	0-0	0-0	0-4	11.8	-25.77
Tom George	7-25	1-5	2-4	0-1	1-1	2-11	1-2	0-0	0-1	28.0	26.00
Ian Williams	7-54	2-9	3-22	0-5	1-7	1-10	0-1	0-0	0-3	13.0	-13.75
Jennie Candlish	7-49	2-9	3-15	1-7	1-3	0-13	0-1	0-0	0-2	14.3	-18.84
Donald McCain	7-101	1-13	0-30	3-16	2-16	0-16	1-4	0-0	0-7	6.9	-31.22

LEADING JUMP TRAINERS AT MUSSELBURGH (SINCE 2013)

	Total W-R	Nov Hdle	H'cap Hdle	Other Hdle	Nov Chase	H'cap Chase	Other Chase	Hunter Chase	N.H. Flat	Per cent	£1 Level stake
Lucinda Russell	35-263	0-21	16-96	2-32	6-25	9-70	0-0	0-0	2-20	13.3	-25.45
Donald McCain	31-141	5-15	7-49	6-24	3-16	6-31	0-0	0-0	4-7	22.0	37.20
Sandy Thomson	17-72	3-8	7-32	1-3	2-5	4-22	0-0	0-0	0-2	23.6	58.06
Keith Dalgleish	14-48	3-5	3-15	2-14	1-1	3-5	0-0	0-0	2-8	29.2	6.09
James Ewart	13-84	0-7	9-35	2-16	0-1	1-16	0-0	0-0	1-11	15.5	5.05
Paul Nicholls	10-29	0-6	2-8	3-5	2-5	2-4	0-0	2-2	0-0	34.5	3.71
Rose Dobbin	9-74	0-8	2-24	0-8	0-7	6-24	0-0	0-0	1-3	12.2	7.25
Jim Goldie	9-99	0-5	6-73	3-15	0-2	0-2	0-0	0-0	0-3	9.1	-35.09
John Ferguson	8-26	2-4	2-9	4-10	0-1	0-0	0-0	0-2	1-2	30.8	-0.46
Dianne Sayer	8-66	1-2	4-34	0-6	0-2	3-20	0-0	0-0	0-2	12.1	-3.25
Nicky Henderson	8-28	2-8	2-10	3-8	1-3	0-1	0-0	0-0	0-1	28.6	-9.96
Chris Grant	8-73	0-5	2-19	0-6	0-8	4-19	0-0	0-1	2-15	11.0	-17.00
John Quinn	7-25	1-4	1-12	5-7	0-1	0-0	0-0	0-0	0-1	28.0	3.85
Tim Vaughan	7-43	0-3	4-16	0-6	1-4	2-11	0-0	0-1	0-2	16.3	-2.25
S R B Crawford	5-25	0-3	3-11	1-6	0-1	0-1	0-0	0-0	1-3	20.0	3.38
Rebecca Menzies	5-37	0-1	0-10	0-2	1-5	4-16	0-0	0-0	0-3	13.5	18.90
Iain Jardine	5-52	2-6	2-23	2-10	0-5	0-4	0-0	0-0	0-6	9.6	-10.44
Nicky Richards	5-36	0-3	3-21	2-6	0-1	0-2	0-0	0-0	0-4	13.9	-17.97
Brian Ellison	5-113	0-11	3-49	0-30	1-4	0-16	0-0	0-0	1-12	4.4	-83.09
Peter Niven	4-17	0-1	2-5	0-3	0-0	1-2	0-0	0-0	1-6	23.5	1.25
Charlie Longsdon	4-16	2-2	0-4	2-4	0-2	0-4	0-0	0-0	0-0	25.0	5.63
James Moffatt	4-24	1-5	2-13	1-3	0-0	0-2	0-0	0-0	0-1	16.7	9.50
Kevin Ryan	4-6	2-3	0-0	1-1	0-0	0-0	0-0	0-0	1-2	66.7	10.31
Martin Todhunter	4-28	0-5	0-11	2-6	0-0	2-6	0-0	0-0	0-0	14.3	31.00
Tom George	4-21	1-2	0-5	1-3	0-1	0-6	0-0	0-1	2-3	19.0	-8.63
Alistair Whillans	4-48	0-0	4-35	0-1	0-3	0-1	0-0	0-0	0-8	8.3	-15.00
Pauline Robson	4-35	0-1	2-17	1-2	0-3	1-12	0-0	0-0	0-0	11.4	-17.92
Susan Corbett	4-60	1-6	1-31	0-11	1-2	1-2	0-0	0-0	0-8	6.7	-37.00
N W Alexander	4-70	0-6	2-30	0-7	0-2	1-16	0-0	1-6	0-3	5.7	-45.50
Keith Reveley	3-19	0-1	1-10	0-1	2-3	0-3	0-0	0-0	0-1	15.8	4.50

LEADING JUMP TRAINERS AT NEWBURY (SINCE 2013)

	Total W-R	Nov Hdle	H'cap Hdle	Other Hdle	Nov Chase	H'cap Chase	Other Chase	Hunter Chase	N.H. Flat	Per cent	£1 Level stake
Nicky Henderson	50-194	16-53	6-39	16-35	2-19	2-21	3-5	0-0	6-26	25.8	-7.46
Paul Nicholls	26-168	1-19	4-41	5-16	7-34	7-43	1-15	1-1	0-4	15.5	-33.85
Philip Hobbs	24-128	3-13	5-33	3-15	2-17	9-42	2-3	0-0	1-8	18.8	53.96
Alan King	21-166	3-37	3-41	5-26	5-15	1-16	0-5	0-0	5-28	12.7	-55.73
David Pipe	16-101	2-12	6-33	1-16	2-10	5-25	0-1	0-0	0-4	15.8	-0.97
Colin Tizzard	15-86	0-14	2-11	2-7	3-12	5-26	2-5	0-0	1-11	17.4	-9.54
Harry Fry	13-63	5-13	1-11	1-9	1-9	2-9	0-1	0-0	3-11	20.6	-5.82
Warren Greatrex	11-70	2-16	3-13	1-18	1-3	2-9	0-1	1-1	1-10	15.7	-16.01
Venetia Williams	10-87	0-7	0-11	1-8	2-15	6-42	1-3	0-0	0-1	11.5	-21.63
Ben Pauling	9-45	3-16	1-11	2-5	2-3	1-5	0-1	0-0	1-5	20.0	-10.14
Dan Skelton	8-60	3-16	0-14	2-17	2-7	1-6	0-0	0-0	0-1	13.3	-12.62
Nigel Twiston-Davies	8-99	1-14	5-20	0-4	0-9	1-39	0-3	0-0	1-10	8.1	-18.59
Oliver Sherwood	7-49	1-11	1-8	1-7	1-5	3-15	0-0	0-0	0-4	14.3	7.88
Rebecca Curtis	7-67	1-14	0-9	0-7	3-18	1-9	2-3	0-0	0-7	10.4	-15.67
Gary Moore	7-91	1-20	2-19	1-22	2-10	0-10	0-3	0-0	1-9	7.7	-16.63
Jonjo O'Neill	7-90	2-17	1-23	0-13	3-14	0-18	0-1	1-2	0-3	7.8	-47.85
Nick Williams	6-40	1-4	1-6	1-9	0-5	1-9	0-0	0-0	2-7	15.0	7.50
Harry Whittington	6-23	0-3	0-6	1-3	4-4	0-5	0-0	0-0	1-2	26.1	13.25
Fergal O'Brien	6-42	2-10	0-4	0-2	1-6	1-12	0-0	0-0	2-8	14.3	-16.13
Tom George	6-72	0-8	0-9	1-10	3-14	1-29	1-1	0-0	0-2	8.3	-36.88
Kim Bailey	5-41	0-9	1-8	1-3	0-6	2-8	1-2	0-0	0-5	12.2	-19.80
Robin Dickin	4-22	0-6	1-3	0-3	0-1	3-5	0-0	0-0	0-4	18.2	3.50
Anthony Honeyball	4-26	0-6	1-2	0-2	1-3	0-4	0-0	0-0	2-9	15.4	-3.25
Neil Mulholland	4-39	0-5	4-11	0-3	0-6	0-13	0-0	0-0	0-1	10.3	-14.88
Charlie Longsdon	4-64	2-8	0-10	0-6	1-11	1-25	0-2	0-0	0-4	6.3	-32.50
Richard Lee	3-10	0-1	1-2	0-0	1-2	1-5	0-0	0-0	0-0	30.0	3.50
Hughie Morrison	3-15	2-8	0-1	0-2	0-0	0-0	0-0	0-0	1-4	20.0	6.50
Mark Bradstock	3-8	0-1	0-1	0-0	1-1	1-4	1-1	0-0	0-0	37.5	6.88
David Dennis	3-13	0-1	0-2	0-2	2-3	1-3	0-0	0-0	0-2	23.1	18.00
Kerry Lee	2-12	0-2	0-2	0-0	0-2	1-5	1-1	0-0	0-0	16.7	1.10

LEADING JUMP TRAINERS AT NEWCASTLE (SINCE 2013)

	Total W-R	Nov Hdle	H'cap Hdle	Other Hdle	Nov Chase	H'cap Chase	Other Chase	Hunter Chase	N.H. Flat	Per cent	£1 Level stake
Sue Smith	21-120	2-13	2-26	2-6	6-17	8-50	0-0	0-0	1-8	17.5	-28.20
Lucinda Russell	19-157	5-18	3-37	0-8	3-14	6-49	0-1	0-0	2-10	13.9	-46.60
N W Alexander	16-109	4-18	4-27	0-8	1-9	7-39	0-0	0-0	0-8	14.7	-19.93
Nicky Richards	13-63	2-12	2-10	0-3	0-9	4-18	0-0	0-0	5-11	20.6	-7.24
Donald McCain	11-84	5-27	0-12	2-8	1-9	2-18	1-1	0-0	0-9	13.1	-20.48
Keith Dalgleish	10-23	0-3	4-7	0-4	1-1	3-5	0-0	0-0	2-3	43.5	27.88
Malcolm Jefferson	10-38	3-5	1-6	0-4	1-3	2-11	0-0	0-0	3-9	26.3	-7.90
Brian Ellison	10-59	2-10	2-10	0-5	3-11	3-18	0-0	0-0	0-5	16.9	-19.82
Keith Reveley	9-59	1-8	2-20	1-4	1-3	3-15	0-0	0-0	1-9	15.3	-21.88
Sandy Thomson	8-38	1-6	1-5	1-7	2-5	1-11	0-0	0-0	2-4	21.1	3.54
Philip Kirby	8-42	0-8	4-20	1-3	2-4	0-0	0-0	0-0	1-7	19.0	5.67
Micky Hammond	8-70	3-12	2-17	0-1	0-5	3-28	0-0	0-0	0-7	11.4	-13.13
Ann Hamilton	7-27	0-0	3-6	0-0	3-6	1-14	0-0	0-0	0-1	25.9	2.82
Rose Dobbin	6-62	3-22	1-14	0-5	0-6	2-11	0-0	0-0	0-4	9.7	-35.06
Nicky Henderson	5-6	0-0	0-0	4-5	0-0	1-1	0-0	0-0	0-0	83.3	4.18
Susan Corbett	5-39	0-7	3-15	0-2	0-1	1-6	0-0	0-0	1-8	12.8	5.50
Michael Scudamore	5-11	1-2	0-1	0-1	0-1	4-6	0-0	0-0	0-0	45.5	10.61
Rebecca Menzies	5-27	0-1	0-2	0-2	0-0	5-19	0-0	0-0	0-3	18.5	17.00
Henry Hogarth	4-30	0-1	0-4	0-4	1-4	3-16	0-0	0-0	0-1	13.3	0.50
Tom George	4-8	1-2	1-1	0-0	1-1	1-3	0-0	0-0	0-1	50.0	3.04
Jonathan Haynes	4-25	1-4	3-19	0-0	0-0	0-1	0-0	0-0	0-1	16.0	3.75
Tim Vaughan	4-15	0-1	3-9	0-0	0-1	1-4	0-0	0-0	0-0	26.7	10.16
Donald Whillans	4-28	1-4	3-17	0-2	0-1	0-1	0-0	0-0	0-3	14.3	20.00
Mark Walford	4-19	0-3	1-5	0-0	0-1	3-9	0-0	0-0	0-1	21.1	29.75
Colin Tizzard	4-7	1-1	0-0	1-2	0-1	2-3	0-0	0-0	0-0	57.1	30.00
Simon Waugh	4-22	0-1	2-8	0-1	0-0	2-11	0-0	0-0	0-1	18.2	31.50
Tim Easterby	4-26	2-11	1-8	0-2	1-3	0-0	0-0	0-0	0-2	15.4	-4.13
Stuart Coltherd	4-51	0-5	0-19	0-2	1-6	3-18	0-0	0-0	0-1	7.8	-23.50
James Ewart	4-51	1-9	1-15	0-1	0-4	2-15	0-0	0-0	0-7	7.8	-29.25
Tom Lacey	3-8	1-2	1-3	1-1	0-0	0-1	0-0	0-0	0-1	37.5	2.20

LEADING JUMP TRAINERS AT NEWTON ABBOT (SINCE 2013)

	Total W-R	Nov Hdle	H'cap Hdle	Other Hdle	Nov Chase	H'cap Chase	Other Chase	Hunter Chase	N.H. Flat	Per cent	£1 Level stake
Paul Nicholls	48-152	16-28	1-22	5-18	14-34	5-31	5-12	1-3	1-4	31.6	-33.61
Philip Hobbs	33-157	6-26	9-43	6-25	3-9	4-39	0-4	0-0	5-11	21.0	14.38
Martin Hill	19-129	1-17	12-63	1-14	1-6	3-24	0-0	0-0	1-5	14.7	13.98
Evan Williams	18-122	1-11	5-38	2-13	4-11	6-44	0-3	0-0	0-2	14.8	-39.11
Tim Vaughan	15-100	4-16	5-37	3-19	0-4	2-16	0-1	0-0	1-7	15.0	-19.51
Jonjo O'Neill	15-89	3-10	9-33	1-8	0-7	1-28	0-1	0-1	1-1	16.9	-33.88
John Ferguson	14-37	3-8	4-15	3-6	1-2	0-2	1-1	0-0	2-3	37.8	10.17
Jimmy Frost	14-166	2-28	8-72	0-19	1-13	3-30	0-3	0-0	0-1	8.4	-47.37
Jeremy Scott	13-77	2-11	1-31	0-6	1-5	9-24	0-0	0-0	0-0	16.9	16.00
Neil Mulholland	13-107	1-23	3-31	3-11	0-9	6-27	0-0	0-0	0-6	12.1	-32.68
Colin Tizzard	13-125	3-23	2-34	1-10	2-17	4-34	0-2	0-0	1-5	10.4	-55.01
David Pipe	13-145	2-14	6-74	1-17	3-9	1-22	0-1	0-0	0-8	9.0	-91.16
David Bridgwater	12-48	2-7	1-7	1-4	0-2	8-25	0-1	0-0	0-2	25.0	-1.34
Harry Fry	11-41	0-9	3-16	3-4	1-2	2-3	0-1	0-0	2-6	26.8	-2.97
Nigel Twiston-Davies	10-45	3-9	2-9	1-4	1-4	3-13	0-3	0-0	0-3	22.2	-6.83
Peter Bowen	10-65	1-6	3-23	0-1	2-3	4-29	0-0	0-0	0-3	15.4	-14.05
Nicky Henderson	9-28	1-5	2-10	3-5	1-3	1-3	0-0	0-0	1-2	32.1	1.24
Dr Richard Newland	9-30	1-4	2-11	1-4	2-3	3-8	0-0	0-0	0-0	30.0	-3.50
Mark Gillard	9-110	1-19	2-39	1-20	0-9	5-21	0-2	0-0	0-0	8.2	-34.67
Chris Down	9-101	4-17	4-61	0-10	0-3	1-7	0-0	0-0	0-3	8.9	-47.90
Emma Lavelle	8-27	1-3	3-6	1-5	1-1	1-10	0-0	0-0	1-2	29.6	55.75
Richard Woollacott	8-89	1-15	5-34	0-7	0-7	2-25	0-0	0-0	0-1	9.0	-16.38
Johnny Farrelly	8-65	0-11	4-33	1-5	2-5	1-9	0-1	0-0	0-1	12.3	-18.84
Fergal O'Brien	7-45	1-8	1-11	0-4	1-4	2-10	0-3	1-1	1-4	15.6	13.75
Warren Greatrex	7-28	0-1	3-12	0-5	0-1	0-2	0-0	0-0	4-7	25.0	-4.86
Michael Blake	7-33	2-6	1-15	2-3	0-1	2-8	0-0	0-0	0-0	21.2	-5.79
Dan Skelton	7-56	2-10	1-18	1-8	2-3	0-15	1-2	0-0	0-0	12.5	-33.80
Seamus Mullins	7-83	0-12	5-30	1-15	0-7	1-12	0-1	0-0	0-6	8.4	-37.50
Paul Henderson	7-100	0-8	2-33	1-3	0-12	4-37	0-2	0-0	0-5	7.0	-46.75
Sophie Leech	6-52	1-5	5-32	0-1	0-3	0-9	0-0	0-1	0-1	11.5	-0.00

LEADING JUMP TRAINERS AT PERTH (SINCE 2013)

	Total W-R	Nov Hdle	H'cap Hdle	Other Hdle	Nov Chase	H'cap Chase	Other Chase	Hunter Chase	N.H. Flat	Per cent	£1 Level stake
Gordon Elliott	67-249	19-51	15-62	12-32	4-28	13-53	0-0	0-0	4-23	26.9	-3.63
Lucinda Russell	32-381	9-69	12-144	2-34	3-35	5-79	0-0	0-0	1-20	8.4	-126.10
Fergal O'Brien	23-79	2-11	6-17	0-4	2-12	8-24	0-1	2-2	3-8	29.1	35.88
Lisa Harrison	23-167	1-28	13-66	0-7	1-9	8-40	0-0	0-0	0-17	13.8	-6.09
Donald McCain	23-119	6-22	4-33	3-19	3-17	5-16	0-1	0-0	2-11	19.3	-11.99
Nicky Richards	21-130	4-24	7-56	2-8	3-10	1-22	0-0	2-2	2-8	16.2	4.30
Nigel Twiston-Davies	21-94	5-15	4-32	2-4	5-12	3-23	0-0	0-0	2-8	22.3	-14.64
S R B Crawford	17-152	1-24	4-37	4-35	2-13	2-22	0-0	0-0	4-21	11.2	-68.57
Tom George	15-70	2-8	0-9	2-3	2-13	8-33	0-1	0-0	1-3	21.4	-7.93
David Pipe	13-24	2-4	2-6	2-3	2-3	5-8	0-0	0-0	0-0	54.2	23.11
Dianne Sayer	13-110	2-13	8-61	0-4	0-5	3-27	0-0	0-0	0-0	11.8	-22.00
Peter Bowen	12-32	3-4	2-5	0-1	1-3	3-14	1-1	0-0	2-4	37.5	11.28
Jackie Stephen	9-66	1-11	2-16	1-12	4-9	1-12	0-0	0-0	0-6	13.6	-5.50
Lucy Normile	9-130	2-18	3-54	0-23	1-10	3-23	0-0	0-1	0-1	6.9	-45.50
N W Alexander	9-141	0-21	4-52	0-15	1-7	3-26	0-0	1-12	0-8	6.4	-54.25
Philip Hobbs	7-17	0-1	2-3	3-4	0-1	2-8	0-0	0-0	0-0	41.2	3.88
Tim Vaughan	7-25	1-4	2-9	0-1	2-5	2-6	0-0	0-0	0-0	28.0	12.10
John Ferguson	7-17	2-5	1-4	2-3	0-2	0-1	0-0	0-0	2-2	41.2	-4.26
Alistair Whillans	7-82	3-15	1-34	1-6	1-7	1-17	0-0	0-0	0-3	8.5	-30.25
Rose Dobbin	7-62	1-10	1-23	0-4	1-7	3-15	0-0	0-0	1-3	11.3	-34.23
Susan Corbett	6-43	0-7	5-21	1-6	0-0	0-1	0-0	0-0	0-8	14.0	25.50
Pauline Robson	6-28	2-5	1-5	0-8	0-3	3-6	0-0	0-0	0-1	21.4	-0.50
Keith Dalgleish	6-20	2-6	2-5	1-4	0-0	0-1	0-0	0-0	1-4	30.0	-1.61
Brian Ellison	6-26	1-5	0-6	2-5	1-1	1-8	0-0	0-0	1-1	23.1	-8.44
Malcolm Jefferson	6-42	0-7	3-11	0-4	1-4	2-10	0-0	0-0	0-6	14.3	-9.33
Robert Alan Hennessy	5-20	0-1	0-2	0-2	1-3	4-12	0-0	0-0	0-0	25.0	1.75
Micky Hammond	5-29	2-9	2-8	0-2	0-0	1-10	0-0	0-0	0-0	17.2	6.00
Paul Nicholls	5-11	1-1	0-1	0-0	1-2	3-7	0-0	0-0	0-0	45.5	7.66
Maurice Barnes	5-75	1-12	1-20	0-5	2-9	1-22	0-0	0-0	0-7	6.7	13.50

LEADING JUMP TRAINERS AT PLUMPTON (SINCE 2013)

	Total W-R	Nov Hdle	H'cap Hdle	Other Hdle	Nov Chase	H'cap Chase	Other Chase	Hunter Chase	N.H. Flat	Per cent	£1 Level stake
Gary Moore	58-290	8-50	18-91	11-49	11-41	8-47	2-2	0-0	0-10	20.0	-23.14
Chris Gordon	27-167	1-21	12-85	3-15	6-14	4-22	0-0	0-0	1-10	16.2	27.54
Anthony Honeyball	17-60	3-7	5-24	1-5	3-8	2-8	0-0	0-0	3-8	28.3	-12.02
Sheena West	15-94	1-10	9-53	0-10	0-1	5-18	0-0	0-0	0-2	16.0	15.66
Alan King	15-46	5-8	2-13	4-13	4-8	0-1	0-1	0-0	0-2	32.6	-7.08
Suzy Smith	14-56	0-7	10-33	1-5	0-0	0-4	0-0	0-0	3-7	25.0	82.88
Seamus Mullins	14-134	1-10	6-49	0-9	2-16	5-46	0-0	0-0	0-4	10.4	-57.92
Paul Henderson	13-70	0-4	4-21	0-5	1-6	8-34	0-0	0-0	0-0	18.6	5.63
David Pipe	13-51	2-9	4-19	0-2	2-6	2-5	0-1	0-0	3-9	25.5	16.38
Neil Mulholland	13-80	1-16	5-21	1-13	0-9	5-14	0-0	0-0	1-7	16.3	-12.90
Colin Tizzard	12-70	3-15	2-14	2-11	2-9	3-17	0-1	0-0	0-3	17.1	-25.16
David Bridgwater	12-74	0-11	0-8	1-15	5-17	5-20	0-0	0-0	1-3	16.2	-34.34
Warren Greatrex	11-49	3-14	1-13	5-16	0-2	0-0	0-0	0-0	2-4	22.4	9.64
Neil King	11-70	1-3	2-26	0-9	4-6	4-24	0-0	0-0	0-2	15.7	-21.67
Zoe Davison	10-83	0-6	4-37	0-7	0-8	6-22	0-0	0-0	0-3	12.0	10.75
Charlie Mann	10-30	2-3	2-12	0-2	2-4	4-9	0-0	0-0	0-0	33.3	28.50
Linda Jewell	9-97	0-14	4-36	0-8	0-7	4-25	0-0	0-0	1-7	9.3	-8.75
Venetia Williams	9-38	2-6	3-14	2-3	1-6	1-9	0-0	0-0	0-0	23.7	-15.31
Oliver Sherwood	8-34	2-8	1-2	0-8	1-3	3-7	0-0	0-0	1-6	23.5	-8.67
Lawney Hill	7-35	0-0	3-18	0-4	0-3	3-7	0-0	0-0	1-3	20.0	10.75
Daniel Steele	7-51	0-8	5-33	0-0	0-0	2-10	0-0	0-0	0-0	13.7	15.50
Nicky Henderson	7-23	1-3	1-6	2-5	3-5	0-0	0-1	0-0	0-3	30.4	-2.34
Jim Best	7-73	1-18	2-28	2-20	0-1	0-2	0-0	0-0	2-4	9.6	-11.50
Dan Skelton	7-35	2-5	1-12	3-10	1-4	0-4	0-0	0-0	0-0	20.0	-17.82
Charlie Longsdon	7-45	2-13	2-11	1-3	0-7	2-10	0-0	0-0	0-1	15.6	-20.42
Johnny Farrelly	6-29	0-4	4-11	0-0	0-5	2-8	0-0	0-0	0-1	20.7	-2.13
Paul Nicholls	6-24	1-8	2-5	0-3	3-6	0-2	0-0	0-0	0-0	25.0	-5.04
Richard Rowe	6-68	1-10	1-25	0-6	2-8	2-13	0-0	0-0	0-6	8.8	-34.00
Alexandra Dunn	5-29	0-0	2-14	0-3	1-4	2-8	0-0	0-0	0-0	17.2	-0.37
Nick Gifford	5-75	2-19	0-12	0-16	0-10	2-9	0-0	0-0	1-9	6.7	-40.09

LEADING JUMP TRAINERS AT SANDOWN (SINCE 2013)

	Total W-R	Nov Hdle	H'cap Hdle	Other Hdle	Nov Chase	H'cap Chase	Other Chase	Hunter Chase	N.H. Flat	Per cent	£1 Level stake
Nicky Henderson	39-142	10-28	10-50	10-26	5-15	1-11	4-15	0-0	1-4	27.5	15.48
Paul Nicholls	27-184	2-11	4-42	4-21	5-31	7-41	5-40	0-0	0-4	14.7	-25.94
Gary Moore	24-117	3-17	4-31	4-23	4-13	3-23	5-11	0-0	1-1	20.5	74.32
Philip Hobbs	16-80	2-8	4-19	2-5	0-10	3-29	4-5	0-0	1-5	20.0	5.97
Alan King	12-65	4-12	3-24	2-8	1-6	2-10	0-3	0-0	0-4	18.5	5.71
Fergal O'Brien	9-24	0-4	3-4	1-1	0-0	0-4	3-5	0-0	2-6	37.5	32.46
Nigel Twiston-Davies	9-57	0-5	5-18	0-4	2-4	2-24	0-2	0-0	0-0	15.8	39.16
Venetia Williams	9-97	0-11	1-20	0-3	1-6	7-50	0-7	0-0	0-1	9.3	-55.50
Charlie Longsdon	7-60	1-7	0-12	0-2	0-7	5-30	1-3	0-0	0-1	11.7	17.25
David Pipe	7-58	1-5	1-31	1-9	0-0	1-9	3-5	0-0	0-1	12.1	-28.55
Lucy Wadham	6-35	1-3	1-12	0-1	0-0	4-17	0-1	0-0	0-1	17.1	2.83
W P Mullins	6-17	2-2	1-4	0-2	1-1	0-2	1-4	0-0	1-2	35.3	19.19
Neil Mulholland	5-27	0-4	1-7	0-1	2-4	2-11	0-0	0-0	0-0	18.5	4.00
Oliver Sherwood	5-40	0-4	2-14	0-5	0-2	3-13	0-0	0-0	0-2	12.5	-2.75
Harry Fry	4-26	2-5	1-8	1-4	0-1	0-6	0-2	0-0	0-0	15.4	2.00
Nick Gifford	4-22	1-3	0-5	0-1	1-3	2-9	0-0	0-0	0-2	18.2	6.50
Phil Middleton	4-12	0-2	3-6	0-2	0-0	1-3	0-1	0-0	0-0	33.3	14.33
Stuart Edmunds	4-10	0-3	2-3	1-1	0-0	0-0	0-0	0-0	1-3	40.0	19.50
Kerry Lee	4-21	0-0	0-7	0-1	1-1	3-12	0-0	0-0	0-0	19.0	-0.97
Ian Williams	4-27	0-4	3-10	0-4	0-1	1-7	0-2	0-0	0-0	14.8	-2.00
Emma Lavelle	4-30	0-1	0-9	1-1	1-3	1-12	0-2	0-0	1-2	13.3	-7.83
Nick Williams	4-32	0-7	1-10	0-4	2-3	1-7	0-0	0-0	0-2	12.5	-8.00
Seamus Mullins	3-27	1-5	2-18	0-1	0-0	0-3	0-0	0-0	0-0	11.1	2.50
Nigel Hawke	3-9	0-0	0-2	0-1	0-1	3-5	0-0	0-0	0-0	33.3	8.91
Richard Rowe	3-10	1-3	1-2	0-0	1-2	0-2	0-1	0-0	0-0	30.0	17.50
Tom George	3-33	1-2	0-4	0-1	0-2	2-16	0-8	0-0	0-0	9.1	-12.50
Colin Tizzard	3-56	2-7	0-10	0-2	0-7	1-23	0-7	0-0	0-0	5.4	-46.40
John Spearing	2-5	0-0	0-0	0-0	0-0	2-5	0-0	0-0	0-0	40.0	3.75
Neil King	2-8	0-0	2-5	1-3	0-0	0-0	0-0	0-0	0-1	25.0	7.00
Paul Morgan	2-5	1-1	0-1	0-0	0-0	1-3	0-0	0-0	0-0	40.0	8.75

LEADING JUMP TRAINERS AT SEDGEFIELD (SINCE 2013)

	Total W-R	Nov Hdle	H'cap Hdle	Other Hdle	Nov Chase	H'cap Chase	Other Chase	Hunter Chase	N.H. Flat	Per cent	£1 Level stake
Donald McCain	59-290	10-63	15-96	14-34	5-28	8-44	1-2	0-0	6-23	20.3	-30.47
Brian Ellison	35-157	11-40	10-53	4-14	4-14	1-18	1-2	0-0	4-16	22.3	-24.92
Micky Hammond	35-237	8-33	10-96	1-12	2-16	12-67	0-1	0-0	2-12	14.8	-45.00
Malcolm Jefferson	27-106	3-19	6-32	1-5	5-12	6-16	0-0	0-0	6-22	25.5	11.00
Sue Smith	26-203	5-29	8-56	1-12	3-29	9-63	0-0	0-0	0-14	12.8	-66.66
Kenneth Slack	20-71	0-6	12-42	0-4	3-3	5-15	0-0	0-0	0-1	28.2	30.58
Neil Mulholland	19-41	4-10	5-10	1-5	3-6	4-7	1-1	0-0	1-2	46.3	19.59
Dianne Sayer	16-84	2-14	10-43	0-3	1-6	3-16	0-0	0-0	0-2	19.0	24.75
Dan Skelton	16-54	7-14	4-18	1-4	3-10	1-4	0-0	0-0	0-4	29.6	-3.63
Chris Grant	16-154	2-35	4-37	1-21	1-12	4-25	0-0	0-0	4-24	10.4	-32.69
Keith Reveley	11-27	4-5	5-14	0-0	0-2	2-5	0-0	0-0	0-1	40.7	23.67
James Ewart	10-59	3-8	4-22	0-2	0-4	3-21	0-0	0-0	0-2	16.9	0.25
Joanne Foster	10-81	1-6	0-16	0-6	1-12	8-39	0-0	0-0	0-2	12.3	-8.90
Sam England	9-47	0-5	4-17	0-1	2-9	3-15	0-0	0-0	0-0	19.1	5.90
Ben Haslam	9-52	0-0	4-30	1-3	2-6	2-11	0-1	0-0	0-1	17.3	7.50
Maurice Barnes	8-108	1-23	3-29	1-11	0-10	3-22	0-3	0-0	0-10	7.4	1.00
Philip Kirby	8-85	2-19	4-36	1-12	0-1	0-3	0-0	0-1	1-13	9.4	-35.92
Rebecca Menzies	7-65	0-6	4-24	1-5	0-8	2-21	0-0	0-0	0-1	10.8	2.82
Keith Dalgleish	7-34	1-5	3-21	0-2	1-2	1-1	0-0	0-0	1-3	20.6	-0.27
Alan Swinbank	7-31	0-5	2-8	0-2	0-1	2-4	0-0	0-0	3-11	22.6	-3.88
David Pipe	7-24	2-5	1-7	2-4	0-1	0-3	0-0	0-0	2-4	29.2	-4.36
Evan Williams	7-28	2-4	0-8	1-2	1-4	2-9	0-0	0-0	1-1	25.0	-4.67
Barry Murtagh	6-69	1-5	3-42	0-2	1-7	1-9	0-0	0-0	0-4	8.7	3.00
Mike Sowersby	6-50	0-8	4-31	0-1	0-1	2-8	0-0	0-0	0-1	12.0	4.00
Ann Hamilton	6-31	1-6	0-5	0-1	1-2	4-15	0-0	0-0	0-2	19.4	11.75
Donald Whillans	6-22	0-2	4-14	0-0	0-2	1-2	0-0	0-0	1-2	27.3	20.50
Rose Dobbin	6-67	0-7	2-27	0-1	1-8	2-19	0-0	0-1	1-4	9.0	-14.00
Jennie Candlish	6-42	3-8	3-16	0-2	0-5	0-7	0-1	0-0	0-3	14.3	-21.42
Tim Vaughan	6-49	3-7	3-15	0-6	0-6	0-9	0-1	0-0	0-5	12.2	-32.85
Tim Easterby	6-73	5-22	1-28	0-10	0-2	0-3	0-0	0-0	0-8	8.2	-41.75

LEADING JUMP TRAINERS AT SOUTHWELL (SINCE 2013)

	Total W-R	Nov Hdle	H'cap Hdle	Other Hdle	Nov Chase	H'cap Chase	Other Chase	Hunter Chase	N.H. Flat	Per cent	£1 Level stake
Jonjo O'Neill	28-174	1-21	12-71	3-23	7-17	4-28	0-1	0-0	1-13	16.1	-38.21
Dan Skelton	24-128	2-32	9-33	5-17	4-12	3-15	0-0	0-1	1-18	18.8	-35.78
Tom George	23-73	5-17	5-13	6-13	1-3	4-13	0-0	0-0	2-14	31.5	8.08
Caroline Bailey	22-102	1-14	11-31	0-15	3-7	6-30	0-1	1-2	0-2	21.6	45.60
Charlie Longsdon	18-96	6-19	4-30	0-10	4-12	2-12	0-1	0-0	2-12	18.8	-0.90
Nicky Henderson	15-58	3-15	0-11	3-9	0-5	0-1	0-0	0-0	9-17	25.9	-18.65
Tim Vaughan	13-95	3-18	5-31	0-10	2-9	1-14	1-1	0-2	1-10	13.7	-4.10
Kim Bailey	12-61	2-14	3-14	3-13	2-5	1-8	0-0	0-0	1-7	19.7	17.22
Ben Pauling	12-41	3-9	3-14	2-3	1-4	0-1	0-0	0-0	3-10	29.3	-4.66
Neil Mulholland	12-86	1-7	4-37	1-6	2-8	2-18	1-1	0-0	1-9	14.0	-9.21
Nigel Twiston-Davies	12-73	1-14	3-17	0-9	1-7	3-14	1-1	0-0	3-11	16.4	-21.91
David Bridgwater	10-44	1-8	0-5	0-6	5-9	4-14	0-0	0-0	0-2	22.7	-2.48
Peter Bowen	10-59	0-8	5-18	0-5	2-6	3-11	0-0	0-0	0-11	16.9	-3.45
Lucy Wadham	9-37	2-6	2-13	1-6	0-1	3-5	0-0	0-0	1-6	24.3	2.45
Seamus Mullins	9-57	0-9	1-17	1-6	0-1	4-18	0-0	0-0	3-6	15.8	18.13
Henry Oliver	9-31	1-4	3-11	1-5	1-4	3-6	0-0	0-0	0-1	29.0	24.09
Mike Sowersby	9-70	0-7	6-34	0-4	0-0	3-23	0-0	0-0	0-2	12.9	25.50
Sue Smith	9-78	0-8	3-26	0-4	2-11	3-22	0-0	0-0	1-7	11.5	-33.50
Martin Keighley	8-49	3-9	3-23	1-6	0-0	1-6	0-0	0-0	0-5	16.3	2.17
John Ferguson	8-23	3-5	2-6	1-4	1-3	1-1	0-0	0-0	0-4	34.8	4.65
Philip Kirby	8-46	1-8	3-22	0-4	1-1	0-0	0-0	0-0	3-11	17.4	7.00
Caroline Fryer	8-43	0-5	5-21	0-3	0-1	3-12	0-0	0-0	0-1	18.6	13.78
Graeme McPherson	8-39	1-4	5-20	0-2	0-4	2-5	0-0	0-0	0-4	20.5	-10.13
Venetia Williams	7-30	0-2	0-6	2-3	0-5	3-12	1-1	0-0	1-1	23.3	-4.57
Alan King	7-48	5-9	0-13	1-9	1-4	0-5	0-1	0-0	0-7	14.6	-33.74
Charles Pogson	7-91	2-20	3-22	0-11	0-5	2-30	0-0	0-0	0-3	7.7	-38.00
Ian Williams	6-33	3-11	3-12	0-3	0-0	0-5	0-0	0-0	0-2	18.2	0.95
Tom Symonds	6-44	2-9	2-12	1-4	0-0	1-12	0-0	0-0	0-7	13.6	3.30
Tom Lacey	6-32	3-9	0-4	0-4	0-0	0-3	0-0	0-0	3-12	18.8	34.88
Harry Whittington	6-25	0-0	1-5	4-9	0-1	0-3	0-0	0-0	1-7	24.0	42.64

LEADING JUMP TRAINERS AT STRATFORD (SINCE 2013)

	Total W-R	Nov Hdle	H'cap Hdle	Other Hdle	Nov Chase	H'cap Chase	Other Chase	Hunter Chase	N.H. Flat	Per cent	£1 Level stake
Warren Greatrex	25-69	6-14	3-16	4-13	2-5	2-7	0-0	3-4	5-10	36.2	37.94
Dan Skelton	24-124	3-28	7-34	3-15	5-15	4-22	0-0	0-1	2-9	19.4	-24.32
Philip Hobbs	20-76	1-4	2-10	2-12	1-6	14-40	0-0	0-0	0-4	26.3	31.43
John Ferguson	18-42	6-8	3-12	5-13	1-1	0-2	0-0	0-0	3-6	42.9	7.89
Alan King	15-51	4-7	5-17	2-13	1-3	2-6	0-0	0-0	1-5	29.4	13.97
Tom George	15-58	4-12	2-5	0-4	3-8	5-25	0-0	0-1	1-3	25.9	37.84
Jonjo O'Neill	14-109	5-19	3-27	1-11	2-9	1-35	0-0	0-1	2-7	12.8	-18.48
Tim Vaughan	14-108	2-23	1-28	5-24	1-6	2-19	1-1	1-1	1-6	13.0	-29.54
Peter Bowen	12-59	0-6	2-14	0-1	0-4	8-20	0-0	0-0	2-14	20.3	4.66
Neil Mulholland	11-65	0-18	5-15	3-11	1-8	1-9	0-0	0-0	1-4	16.9	8.68
Charlie Longsdon	11-64	1-6	4-20	3-12	1-6	1-14	1-2	0-0	0-4	17.2	-14.07
Nigel Twiston-Davies	11-94	0-13	4-24	4-10	1-13	2-26	0-1	0-1	0-6	11.7	-38.37
David Bridgwater	9-96	2-22	1-9	1-21	1-15	3-22	0-2	0-0	1-5	9.4	-0.00
David Dennis	9-61	0-9	4-23	3-9	0-7	2-13	0-0	0-0	0-0	14.8	24.50
Paul Nicholls	9-34	4-8	1-3	0-3	2-6	1-9	0-0	0-4	1-1	26.5	-11.50
Ian Williams	9-66	1-14	5-21	0-8	2-5	1-13	0-0	0-0	0-5	13.6	-15.80
David Pipe	9-65	2-10	1-19	2-9	1-5	2-18	0-0	0-0	1-4	13.8	-20.33
Donald McCain	8-48	1-7	1-17	2-4	1-7	1-8	0-0	0-0	2-5	16.7	6.25
Neil King	8-40	1-6	4-13	0-9	0-1	2-8	0-0	0-0	1-3	20.0	10.00
Matt Sheppard	8-63	0-3	1-19	0-4	0-8	7-28	0-0	0-0	0-1	12.7	15.50
Dr Richard Newland	8-37	2-4	1-16	2-6	2-4	1-7	0-0	0-0	0-0	21.6	-14.50
Evan Williams	8-62	3-8	1-9	0-7	1-8	3-26	0-0	0-0	0-4	12.9	-22.38
Nicky Henderson	8-51	0-5	4-23	1-3	1-2	1-9	1-1	0-0	0-8	15.7	-22.90
Charlie Mann	7-22	0-0	4-7	0-3	1-2	2-8	0-0	0-0	0-2	31.8	7.10
Phil Middleton	7-34	0-1	3-15	1-5	0-5	3-6	0-0	0-0	0-2	20.6	-1.46
Emma Lavelle	7-45	0-6	1-9	2-6	0-2	3-14	0-0	0-0	1-8	15.6	-5.75
Rebecca Curtis	6-28	3-6	0-2	1-5	1-3	1-9	0-0	0-0	0-3	21.4	9.80
Bernard Llewellyn	6-30	1-2	4-20	0-3	0-1	1-2	0-1	0-0	0-1	20.0	17.50
Henry Daly	6-45	1-2	4-19	0-2	0-5	1-15	0-0	0-1	0-1	13.3	26.00
Graeme McPherson	6-51	2-9	0-22	0-3	2-5	2-12	0-0	0-0	0-0	11.8	-5.67

LEADING JUMP TRAINERS AT TAUNTON (SINCE 2013)

	Total W-R	Nov Hdle	H'cap Hdle	Other Hdle	Nov Chase	H'cap Chase	Other Chase	Hunter Chase	N.H. Flat	Per cent	£1 Level stake
Paul Nicholls	58-191	20-57	9-41	12-28	8-19	5-24	0-1	0-3	4-18	30.4	-9.97
Harry Fry	22-86	10-32	4-24	2-11	1-2	0-2	0-0	0-1	5-14	25.6	-12.31
Philip Hobbs	22-135	6-31	5-39	1-21	2-9	4-19	0-0	0-0	4-16	16.3	-55.56
Colin Tizzard	18-123	3-19	7-38	2-14	2-15	4-28	0-0	0-0	0-9	14.6	-19.85
David Pipe	16-178	3-54	5-65	3-25	1-9	4-15	0-1	0-0	0-9	9.0	-94.63
Evan Williams	13-105	2-16	7-39	0-15	2-15	2-16	0-0	0-0	0-4	12.4	-30.91
Nicky Henderson	12-39	4-12	2-13	3-6	0-1	0-0	1-2	0-0	2-5	30.8	-2.45
Jeremy Scott	11-58	0-10	6-25	0-2	2-8	3-8	0-0	0-0	0-5	19.0	7.25
Anthony Honeyball	11-58	1-18	8-19	0-6	0-2	1-7	0-0	0-0	1-6	19.0	20.08
Dan Skelton	11-62	5-13	1-29	2-7	1-4	0-4	0-0	0-0	2-5	17.7	-20.15
Nick Williams	10-38	2-8	5-18	3-5	0-1	0-4	0-0	0-0	0-2	26.3	6.35
Venetia Williams	10-64	2-9	3-21	1-7	3-12	1-15	0-0	0-0	0-0	15.6	-12.06
Bob Buckler	9-55	0-6	3-13	0-4	0-9	6-19	0-0	0-0	0-4	16.4	-4.13
Alexandra Dunn	9-83	0-15	6-37	0-11	0-1	2-16	0-0	0-0	1-3	10.8	-6.25
Tim Vaughan	9-97	1-21	2-39	1-10	1-9	4-14	0-0	0-0	0-4	9.3	-48.62
Johnny Farrelly	8-70	1-8	7-49	0-3	0-3	0-6	0-0	0-0	0-1	11.4	-13.63
Neil Mulholland	8-85	0-15	7-41	0-6	1-7	0-8	0-0	0-0	0-8	9.4	-40.00
Chris Down	7-78	1-9	6-65	0-2	0-1	0-0	0-0	0-0	0-1	9.0	5.00
Robert Walford	7-39	0-6	2-11	1-6	2-6	2-7	0-0	0-0	0-3	17.9	-11.53
Warren Greatrex	6-24	2-6	3-10	0-1	0-1	0-1	0-0	0-0	1-5	25.0	1.71
Sarah-Jayne Davies	5-24	0-3	0-7	0-2	1-4	4-8	0-0	0-0	0-0	20.8	2.33
Jamie Snowden	5-25	2-6	0-6	1-2	0-2	0-1	0-0	1-1	1-7	20.0	14.57
Stuart Kittow	5-16	0-4	4-9	0-2	0-0	0-0	0-0	0-0	1-1	31.3	31.75
Nigel Twiston-Davies	5-37	0-7	2-13	0-3	1-6	2-7	0-0	0-0	0-1	13.5	-5.00
Alan King	5-56	1-14	1-20	0-7	0-3	1-3	0-0	0-0	2-9	8.9	-40.67
Michael Blake	4-12	0-1	0-5	3-3	0-0	1-2	0-0	0-0	0-1	33.3	5.67
Tom Lacey	4-10	0-2	3-6	0-1	0-0	0-0	0-0	0-0	1-1	40.0	15.00
Robin Dickin	4-14	0-1	0-3	0-0	2-3	2-6	0-0	0-0	0-1	28.6	-0.63
Rebecca Curtis	4-23	0-7	0-2	1-3	2-6	0-4	0-0	0-0	1-1	17.4	-1.50
Emma Lavelle	4-31	1-5	1-7	0-4	2-5	0-6	0-0	0-0	0-4	12.9	-6.75

LEADING JUMP TRAINERS AT TOWCESTER (SINCE 2013)

	Total W-R	Nov Hdle	H'cap Hdle	Other Hdle	Nov Chase	H'cap Chase	Other Chase	Hunter Chase	N.H. Flat	Per cent	£1 Level stake
Kim Bailey	18-78	1-10	5-18	6-18	1-6	2-12	1-3	0-0	2-11	23.1	1.98
Fergal O'Brien	16-68	3-11	3-12	6-12	0-5	2-15	0-1	0-0	2-12	23.5	14.63
Ben Pauling	15-53	2-15	5-17	0-4	1-1	6-13	1-1	0-0	0-2	28.3	45.01
Nicky Henderson	15-42	4-7	2-3	4-11	2-4	0-0	0-1	0-0	3-16	35.7	-1.66
Henry Oliver	12-41	2-4	3-12	1-10	1-5	5-8	0-0	0-0	0-2	29.3	25.29
Henry Daly	12-42	1-4	2-7	2-12	0-5	4-6	0-0	2-2	1-6	28.6	42.60
Charlie Longsdon	11-61	1-8	2-13	0-12	2-6	3-11	2-5	0-0	1-6	18.0	-22.68
Alan King	10-38	2-11	2-4	2-8	0-1	0-2	0-1	0-0	4-11	26.3	2.71
Oliver Sherwood	9-43	3-12	0-4	1-5	1-4	3-9	1-2	0-0	0-7	20.9	-5.47
Martin Keighley	9-61	1-10	1-17	1-9	1-4	3-14	0-0	0-0	2-7	14.8	-18.75
Venetia Williams	9-57	2-10	1-15	0-5	3-11	2-13	0-1	0-0	1-2	15.8	-21.31
Nigel Twiston-Davies	9-81	1-7	2-22	0-10	0-7	3-18	0-2	0-0	3-15	11.1	-27.13
Neil Mulholland	8-25	2-2	2-9	0-1	1-4	2-5	0-0	0-0	1-4	32.0	1.55
Dan Skelton	8-39	5-12	0-7	0-6	0-5	0-0	1-2	1-1	1-6	20.5	-19.14
Caroline Fryer	7-38	0-4	3-16	1-3	0-0	3-14	0-0	0-0	0-1	18.4	41.38
Jonjo O'Neill	7-60	2-13	2-20	0-12	0-1	3-11	0-0	0-0	0-3	11.7	-32.50
Robin Dickin	7-84	0-9	0-12	1-9	3-13	3-25	0-0	0-0	0-16	8.3	-51.50
Tim Vaughan	6-22	1-1	3-10	0-2	0-0	1-6	0-0	0-1	1-2	27.3	8.25
David Pipe	6-45	0-3	1-17	0-6	2-3	0-5	0-0	0-0	3-11	13.3	-22.03
Lucy Wadham	5-34	0-2	1-11	3-12	0-2	0-1	1-1	0-0	0-5	14.7	4.63
Paul Webber	5-45	1-2	2-8	0-10	1-5	1-11	0-3	0-0	0-6	11.1	18.50
Mark Gillard	5-19	0-0	1-4	0-0	1-3	3-12	0-0	0-0	0-0	26.3	21.25
Gary Moore	5-34	0-0	1-16	2-6	2-5	0-2	0-2	0-0	0-3	14.7	-5.25
Tom Symonds	5-38	0-2	3-13	0-6	0-4	2-6	0-1	0-0	0-6	13.2	-9.25
Ben Case	5-57	1-11	2-18	1-9	0-5	0-8	0-0	0-0	1-6	8.8	-19.00
Brendan Powell	4-24	0-3	0-5	1-2	0-1	1-4	0-1	0-0	2-8	16.7	5.00
Kevin Bishop	4-14	0-0	3-9	0-0	1-1	0-4	0-0	0-0	0-0	28.6	26.50
Grant Cann	4-11	0-0	0-4	0-2	0-0	3-4	1-1	0-0	0-0	36.4	32.50
Stuart Edmunds	4-21	0-6	2-5	0-2	0-2	0-2	0-0	0-0	2-4	19.0	-3.00
Warren Greatrex	4-21	0-2	1-6	2-5	0-2	0-2	0-0	0-0	1-4	19.0	-5.45

LEADING JUMP TRAINERS AT UTTOXETER (SINCE 2013)

	Total W-R	Nov Hdle	H'cap Hdle	Other Hdle	Nov Chase	H'cap Chase	Other Chase	Hunter Chase	N.H. Flat	Per cent	£1 Level stake
Jonjo O'Neill	36-280	5-36	9-84	6-43	5-33	8-62	1-6	0-1	2-15	12.9	-88.69
Charlie Longsdon	28-124	5-12	4-26	6-29	3-11	6-34	4-5	0-0	0-7	22.6	10.55
Nigel Twiston-Davies	27-160	1-15	6-44	6-22	3-15	9-46	1-4	0-0	1-14	16.9	-14.44
Dan Skelton	25-109	5-14	8-31	2-19	4-10	5-22	0-3	0-0	1-10	22.9	-13.76
David Pipe	24-144	1-9	6-54	4-18	2-12	5-32	2-3	0-0	4-16	16.7	-5.73
Warren Greatrex	23-64	2-5	4-20	3-11	1-5	3-6	0-0	0-0	10-17	35.9	31.85
Philip Hobbs	21-111	3-11	5-29	6-23	0-10	2-23	2-7	0-0	3-8	18.9	-7.68
Nicky Henderson	21-69	3-6	2-16	10-21	0-6	1-5	3-8	0-0	2-7	30.4	-12.95
Tim Vaughan	19-160	3-23	10-65	2-34	2-14	1-14	0-4	0-0	1-6	11.9	-56.19
Fergal O'Brien	18-101	3-20	3-25	1-14	1-9	6-20	0-1	0-0	4-12	17.8	13.29
Sue Smith	18-115	2-10	7-34	1-7	0-18	6-38	2-8	0-0	0-0	15.7	-12.21
Evan Williams	17-112	2-7	5-30	2-27	2-8	4-29	1-4	0-0	1-7	15.2	24.85
Dr Richard Newland	17-65	3-10	6-25	5-11	2-5	1-13	0-1	0-0	0-0	26.2	-14.94
Peter Bowen	16-99	2-7	4-33	3-15	1-8	4-23	0-2	0-0	2-11	16.2	-28.52
Neil King	15-94	2-16	6-30	4-21	1-9	0-10	0-0	0-0	2-8	16.0	-31.46
Neil Mulholland	13-96	3-23	7-35	1-13	1-8	1-15	0-0	0-0	0-2	13.5	-27.59
Alan King	13-70	2-13	1-13	5-19	2-5	0-9	1-3	0-0	2-8	18.6	-28.80
Martin Keighley	12-92	1-9	3-30	2-18	0-5	3-17	2-5	0-0	1-8	13.0	-12.00
Venetia Williams	12-95	2-9	3-23	2-13	3-17	1-29	1-1	0-0	0-3	12.6	-45.71
Jennie Candlish	11-128	1-26	6-48	1-14	1-13	2-21	0-3	0-0	0-3	8.6	-24.13
Anthony Honeyball	10-66	0-6	5-29	2-7	0-5	0-7	0-1	0-0	3-11	15.2	-9.13
Kim Bailey	10-107	2-21	3-28	2-22	1-9	0-11	2-8	0-0	0-8	9.3	-68.85
Oliver Sherwood	9-51	1-5	1-9	3-11	2-7	1-11	0-1	0-1	1-6	17.6	1.50
Philip Kirby	9-58	3-11	4-31	0-7	1-3	0-3	0-1	0-0	1-2	15.5	3.00
Harry Fry	9-37	1-1	1-6	0-7	4-7	1-7	1-2	0-0	1-7	24.3	3.97
Jeremy Scott	9-60	0-5	2-13	2-9	3-11	2-14	0-2	0-1	0-5	15.0	-6.00
Mark Walford	8-34	0-2	3-16	0-0	0-7	5-7	0-1	0-0	0-1	23.5	26.33
Donald McCain	8-148	1-19	2-39	2-39	0-6	0-17	2-12	0-0	1-16	5.4	-91.25
Kerry Lee	7-35	0-1	0-9	2-6	2-4	3-14	0-1	0-0	0-0	20.0	1.50
Jim Best	7-22	1-2	3-11	2-6	0-0	0-1	0-1	0-0	1-1	31.8	3.25

LEADING JUMP TRAINERS AT WARWICK (SINCE 2013)

	Total W-R	Nov Hdle	H'cap Hdle	Other Hdle	Nov Chase	H'cap Chase	Other Chase	Hunter Chase	N.H. Flat	Per cent	£1 Level stake
Alan King	31-134	3-18	5-35	12-34	7-12	1-12	0-6	0-0	3-23	23.1	-49.11
Dan Skelton	30-154	8-35	3-32	3-28	7-19	3-15	0-0	0-2	6-23	19.5	-42.19
Philip Hobbs	26-109	4-15	2-19	5-15	3-9	3-21	0-1	2-4	7-25	23.9	-12.04
Nigel Twiston-Davies	23-152	2-18	4-32	1-15	2-14	9-48	1-1	0-0	4-24	15.1	-50.00
Jonjo O'Neill	21-147	2-26	9-47	1-19	0-4	8-36	0-1	0-2	1-12	14.3	4.64
Venetia Williams	17-98	5-11	1-19	1-8	4-9	4-44	0-0	1-1	1-6	17.3	-12.07
Nicky Henderson	14-53	3-8	4-10	2-11	2-5	1-2	0-0	0-0	2-17	26.4	-9.46
Paul Nicholls	13-49	0-7	2-6	1-6	6-16	1-6	1-2	1-2	1-4	26.5	-10.18
Henry Daly	12-64	3-9	3-16	1-5	2-9	1-14	0-0	0-2	2-9	18.8	-8.37
Charlie Longsdon	12-107	1-20	2-23	3-19	1-8	4-22	0-1	0-0	1-14	11.2	-49.02
Ben Pauling	10-47	1-9	0-10	2-6	0-2	0-4	0-0	0-1	7-15	21.3	7.25
Warren Greatrex	9-55	0-4	3-16	0-14	0-2	1-5	0-0	0-0	5-14	16.4	7.33
Neil Mulholland	9-44	1-6	2-14	0-4	3-10	2-8	0-0	0-0	1-2	20.5	-9.03
Ian Williams	8-83	0-15	5-25	1-16	0-7	2-15	0-0	0-1	0-4	9.6	23.25
Jeremy Scott	8-42	0-5	3-17	1-5	0-0	3-11	0-0	1-1	0-3	19.0	37.24
Evan Williams	8-60	2-11	2-16	1-5	1-6	2-14	0-0	0-0	0-8	13.3	-26.99
W P Mullins	7-11	2-4	0-0	4-5	1-1	0-1	0-0	0-0	0-0	63.6	6.87
Kim Bailey	7-67	2-12	1-23	0-9	0-6	1-8	0-0	0-0	3-9	10.4	-22.50
Henry Oliver	6-42	1-11	4-13	0-2	1-3	0-8	0-0	0-0	0-5	14.3	10.75
Gary Moore	6-21	0-2	0-5	2-3	1-4	3-5	0-0	0-0	0-2	28.6	20.50
Neil King	6-41	1-4	2-16	2-2	0-0	1-11	0-0	0-0	0-8	14.6	-1.90
David Pipe	6-62	1-6	3-30	0-4	1-2	1-12	0-0	0-0	0-8	9.7	-17.50
Stuart Edmunds	5-18	0-2	3-6	2-5	0-0	0-3	0-0	0-0	0-2	27.8	7.13
Matt Sheppard	5-24	0-0	1-7	0-0	0-3	4-12	0-0	0-0	0-2	20.8	7.62
Ben Case	5-45	1-6	0-8	0-9	2-2	1-10	0-0	0-0	1-10	11.1	22.00
Tim Vaughan	5-47	0-14	2-13	0-6	1-2	0-8	0-0	1-1	1-3	10.6	32.83
Seamus Mullins	5-40	0-5	2-12	1-8	0-6	2-7	0-0	0-0	0-2	12.5	-2.50
Nick Williams	5-32	2-5	0-5	1-7	1-2	0-10	1-1	0-0	0-2	15.6	-13.45
Harry Fry	5-32	1-7	1-4	1-5	1-5	1-2	0-1	0-0	0-8	15.6	-14.56
David Dennis	5-60	2-8	0-18	0-9	0-2	2-14	0-0	0-0	1-9	8.3	-34.00

LEADING JUMP TRAINERS AT WETHERBY (SINCE 2013)

	Total W-R	Nov Hdle	H'cap Hdle	Other Hdle	Nov Chase	H'cap Chase	Other Chase	Hunter Chase	N.H. Flat	Per cent	£1 Level stake
Sue Smith	31-227	2-39	6-53	0-13	4-29	18-83	0-2	0-0	1-8	13.7	-94.66
Dan Skelton	30-89	7-20	3-20	6-12	5-11	6-15	0-1	0-1	3-9	33.7	10.65
Micky Hammond	25-261	3-46	10-102	3-23	0-8	6-66	0-2	0-0	3-14	9.6	-10.42
Warren Greatrex	20-67	6-18	4-16	3-11	3-7	1-4	0-0	0-0	3-11	29.9	11.34
Philip Kirby	20-143	3-38	9-62	2-18	1-3	2-5	0-0	0-1	3-16	14.0	-15.58
Jonjo O'Neill	18-85	5-20	6-25	3-8	1-6	3-20	0-3	0-1	0-2	21.2	-13.52
Brian Ellison	16-114	2-14	3-38	4-22	2-10	3-19	0-1	0-0	2-10	14.0	-13.84
Donald McCain	16-127	5-28	4-39	2-16	2-12	2-25	1-1	0-0	0-6	12.6	-43.42
Kim Bailey	13-36	1-4	1-9	2-6	2-3	3-8	2-2	0-0	2-4	36.1	28.65
Lucinda Russell	11-106	0-9	3-26	0-8	3-13	5-42	0-0	0-0	0-8	10.4	-24.62
Neil Mulholland	10-32	1-4	2-8	2-6	2-4	2-6	0-0	0-0	1-4	31.3	3.33
Mark Walford	10-66	2-13	3-29	2-7	1-5	2-8	0-0	0-0	0-4	15.2	12.00
Rose Dobbin	10-70	1-13	5-26	0-1	0-6	3-20	0-0	0-0	1-4	14.3	-0.29
Philip Hobbs	10-34	3-8	1-3	2-4	1-3	2-11	1-5	0-0	0-0	29.4	-0.37
Nigel Twiston-Davies	10-48	3-10	1-6	0-5	4-6	0-15	1-4	0-0	1-2	20.8	-12.80
Malcolm Jefferson	10-79	2-14	1-13	2-11	1-5	4-29	0-1	0-0	0-6	12.7	-26.42
Michael Easterby	9-56	0-8	4-19	2-4	2-3	1-14	0-0	0-0	0-8	16.1	13.32
Nicky Richards	9-35	0-3	5-13	0-1	1-3	2-9	0-0	0-0	1-6	25.7	55.25
Charlie Longsdon	9-49	2-9	0-10	2-5	1-6	4-16	0-0	0-0	0-3	18.4	-5.67
John Quinn	8-38	1-8	4-14	3-11	0-0	0-0	0-0	0-0	0-5	21.1	3.17
Graeme McPherson	7-32	1-3	3-14	0-0	3-6	0-7	0-0	0-0	0-2	21.9	3.40
Paul Nicholls	6-20	0-3	0-0	4-7	2-3	0-3	0-4	0-0	0-0	30.0	0.32
Dr Richard Newland	6-17	1-3	0-6	1-3	1-1	3-4	0-0	0-0	0-0	35.3	12.30
Michael Scudamore	6-22	0-4	0-3	2-3	1-4	3-6	0-0	0-0	0-2	27.3	13.92
Fergal O'Brien	6-20	1-5	1-3	1-1	0-1	1-2	0-0	0-0	2-8	30.0	27.93
Venetia Williams	6-31	0-3	1-2	0-2	0-1	5-22	0-0	0-0	0-1	19.4	-2.56
Nicky Henderson	6-20	2-2	0-6	2-4	1-3	0-2	0-1	0-0	1-2	30.0	-3.14
James Ewart	6-41	0-5	3-15	1-2	0-2	1-12	0-0	0-0	1-5	14.6	-3.80
Alan King	6-42	3-9	0-7	1-16	1-4	0-1	1-2	0-0	0-3	14.3	-23.71
David Pipe	6-44	2-6	1-12	0-6	1-3	2-10	0-4	0-0	0-3	13.6	-29.69

LEADING JUMP TRAINERS AT WINCANTON (SINCE 2013)

	Total W-R	Nov Hdle	H'cap Hdle	Other Hdle	Nov Chase	H'cap Chase	Other Chase	Hunter Chase	N.H. Flat	Per cent	£1 Level stake
Paul Nicholls	89-271	32-69	16-54	11-34	10-28	9-50	1-2	3-5	7-29	32.8	-13.23
Colin Tizzard	35-257	4-54	7-56	5-22	3-24	15-65	0-1	0-0	1-35	13.6	-69.32
Philip Hobbs	24-175	3-42	7-37	2-16	4-12	4-44	0-1	0-0	4-23	13.7	-31.01
Harry Fry	21-95	4-28	5-26	1-11	1-5	2-7	0-1	0-0	8-17	22.1	-3.14
David Pipe	16-109	1-14	3-43	3-14	1-5	8-26	0-0	0-0	0-7	14.7	-32.32
Venetia Williams	14-94	4-13	1-13	1-7	2-7	6-54	0-0	0-0	0-0	14.9	-27.77
Neil Mulholland	14-150	2-40	4-38	1-15	2-13	4-31	0-0	0-0	1-13	9.3	-57.15
Emma Lavelle	13-74	1-10	6-18	0-4	1-7	2-23	0-0	0-0	3-12	17.6	-0.62
Alan King	12-74	3-17	2-25	2-11	0-7	3-7	0-1	0-0	2-6	16.2	-16.11
Jeremy Scott	11-106	1-20	4-36	1-12	2-8	2-25	0-0	0-1	1-14	9.5	-43.38
Seamus Mullins	10-97	2-22	2-31	0-5	2-8	4-22	0-0	0-0	0-9	10.3	-12.95
Tom George	10-60	0-6	1-4	0-2	3-6	5-36	0-0	1-2	0-4	16.7	-18.80
Dan Skelton	9-39	3-11	1-8	2-7	2-3	0-6	0-0	0-1	1-3	23.1	0.75
Kim Bailey	9-44	3-15	3-14	1-3	0-1	1-9	1-1	0-0	0-1	20.5	9.50
Anthony Honeyball	9-70	2-19	1-13	1-5	1-6	1-15	0-1	0-0	3-11	12.9	-29.69
Tim Vaughan	8-45	3-13	4-19	0-2	0-4	1-6	0-0	0-0	0-1	17.8	21.20
Warren Greatrex	8-46	3-12	3-21	0-4	0-3	1-2	0-0	0-0	1-4	17.4	-6.88
Nicky Henderson	7-28	0-3	2-10	3-5	2-5	0-1	0-0	0-0	0-4	25.0	1.46
Chris Down	6-51	1-12	5-30	0-3	0-4	0-2	0-0	0-0	0-0	11.8	1.00
Chris Gordon	6-46	0-3	4-24	0-1	0-2	2-15	0-0	0-0	0-1	13.0	15.75
Robert Walford	6-62	0-12	0-9	1-9	1-2	4-24	0-0	0-0	0-6	9.7	-17.25
Oliver Sherwood	6-39	2-8	0-9	2-5	1-2	1-11	0-0	0-0	0-4	15.4	-21.78
Richard Woollacott	6-63	0-9	3-26	0-4	2-8	0-9	0-1	0-0	1-6	9.5	-38.01
Nick Williams	5-33	0-1	1-9	2-8	0-3	1-10	0-0	0-0	1-2	15.2	-12.50
Nigel Twiston-Davies	5-37	1-5	0-8	0-3	0-3	4-15	0-0	0-0	0-3	13.5	5.23
Evan Williams	5-38	1-7	1-11	0-2	1-5	1-7	0-0	0-0	1-6	13.2	7.08
Polly Gundry	4-24	0-4	2-7	0-0	0-4	2-8	0-0	0-0	0-1	16.7	2.75
Dr Richard Newland	4-13	2-2	1-4	0-1	1-1	0-3	0-0	0-1	0-1	30.8	-0.50
Ron Hodges	4-28	0-3	2-7	0-1	1-1	1-14	0-0	0-0	0-2	14.3	-6.00
Richard Mitchell	4-29	1-9	3-16	0-1	0-1	0-0	0-0	0-0	0-2	13.8	-9.67

LEADING JUMP TRAINERS AT WORCESTER (SINCE 2013)

	Total W-R	Nov Hdle	H'cap Hdle	Other Hdle	Nov Chase	H'cap Chase	Other Chase	Hunter Chase	N.H. Flat	Per cent	£1 Level stake
Jonjo O'Neill	58-293	9-44	13-95	3-24	5-29	22-80	3-9	0-1	3-11	19.8	-40.39
Philip Hobbs	31-116	7-15	7-26	4-24	2-16	8-26	1-1	0-0	2-8	26.7	34.13
Neil Mulholland	27-161	4-17	11-60	3-18	2-18	5-32	2-3	0-0	0-13	16.8	-19.09
Nicky Henderson	25-78	6-12	3-20	7-14	2-6	1-4	1-2	0-0	5-20	32.1	12.93
David Pipe	24-161	2-18	9-66	4-15	1-12	3-26	0-2	0-0	5-22	14.9	-60.16
Dan Skelton	23-126	7-22	2-29	3-22	4-15	4-23	1-3	0-0	2-12	18.3	-32.23
Dr Richard Newland	22-79	8-12	6-33	4-15	0-4	3-12	1-3	0-0	0-0	27.8	-17.92
Peter Bowen	21-100	0-5	5-33	1-4	1-8	8-32	0-3	0-0	6-15	21.0	11.62
Nigel Twiston-Davies	20-110	0-9	5-32	3-19	4-14	5-22	0-2	0-0	3-12	18.2	2.54
Paul Nicholls	17-54	3-9	1-7	3-6	8-21	1-7	1-4	0-0	0-0	31.5	-4.97
Rebecca Curtis	16-58	3-11	2-10	2-10	3-7	2-7	1-1	0-0	3-12	27.6	39.67
John Ferguson	16-42	3-5	2-12	5-12	1-3	0-3	0-0	0-0	5-7	38.1	-7.19
Donald McCain	16-111	2-14	2-31	5-22	2-10	5-19	0-5	0-0	0-10	14.4	-12.10
Tim Vaughan	16-127	3-18	2-39	3-15	2-9	5-36	1-2	0-0	0-8	12.6	-36.72
Kim Bailey	14-58	3-10	1-13	3-8	2-9	5-12	0-3	0-0	0-3	24.1	1.30
Charlie Longsdon	14-98	1-10	2-25	3-15	1-16	3-17	0-0	0-0	4-15	14.3	-22.34
Evan Williams	13-94	2-11	4-25	3-12	1-9	1-35	1-1	0-0	1-1	13.8	-12.06
Emma Lavelle	10-50	1-7	1-10	2-6	3-5	3-14	0-2	0-0	0-6	20.0	-5.38
Seamus Mullins	10-85	0-7	3-25	2-15	2-8	1-15	0-1	0-0	2-14	11.8	-16.72
Debra Hamer	9-58	3-13	6-23	0-7	0-0	0-13	0-0	0-0	0-2	15.5	-0.30
Jeremy Scott	9-58	0-2	4-16	1-6	1-7	3-22	0-1	0-0	0-4	15.5	-2.54
Johnny Farrelly	8-38	1-5	5-22	1-1	0-1	0-6	0-0	0-0	1-3	21.1	13.58
Alan King	8-42	0-8	3-11	3-5	1-6	0-6	0-0	0-0	1-6	19.0	-7.38
Robert Stephens	8-41	0-2	6-22	2-10	0-0	0-0	0-3	0-0	0-4	19.5	25.88
Brendan Powell	8-53	0-8	0-18	3-6	1-3	2-12	0-1	0-0	2-5	15.1	50.35
Anthony Honeyball	8-45	0-4	3-13	3-15	1-4	1-6	0-0	0-0	0-3	17.8	-20.45
Fergal O'Brien	8-82	1-12	3-24	2-13	0-7	1-17	1-1	0-0	0-8	9.8	-38.85
Martin Keighley	8-109	1-8	3-40	0-18	1-8	1-24	0-0	0-0	2-11	7.3	-41.50
Laura Young	7-47	0-3	7-28	0-4	0-2	0-5	0-0	0-0	0-5	14.9	16.25
Ian Williams	7-49	1-7	4-23	0-4	0-2	2-10	0-0	0-0	0-3	14.3	-0.75

LEADING JUMP TRAINERS AT FAIRYHOUSE (SINCE 2013)

	Total W-R	Nov Hdle	H'cap Hdle	Other Hdle	Nov Chase	H'cap Chase	Other Chase	Hunter Chase	N.H. Flat	Per cent	£1 Level stake
W P Mullins	98-391	0-0	0-14	52-207	0-0	0-3	30-103	0-1	16-63	25.1	-83.78
Gordon Elliott	73-520	0-0	7-75	32-214	0-0	2-22	16-141	0-1	16-67	14.0	-226.23
Noel Meade	27-240	0-0	2-30	9-102	0-0	0-10	7-62	0-0	9-36	11.3	-86.91
Henry De Bromhead	14-124	0-0	2-18	7-50	0-0	0-2	3-41	0-0	2-13	11.3	-22.85
A J Martin	13-161	0-0	3-28	5-70	0-0	1-13	2-42	0-0	2-8	8.1	-86.93
Mrs John Harrington	13-163	0-0	1-21	5-81	0-0	0-4	6-30	0-0	1-27	8.0	-88.41
D T Hughes	12-59	0-0	2-10	6-30	0-0	1-6	3-12	0-0	0-1	20.3	-14.51
Ms Sandra Hughes	10-94	0-0	0-14	5-37	0-0	0-4	5-32	0-0	0-7	10.6	1.57
P A Fahy	10-69	0-0	1-17	2-23	0-0	2-7	2-10	0-0	3-12	14.5	17.25
Paul Nolan	8-89	0-0	2-28	3-36	0-0	1-5	2-16	0-0	0-4	9.0	46.25
Dermot A McLoughlin	8-76	0-0	5-28	0-22	0-0	1-9	1-12	0-0	1-5	10.5	-10.47
Edward Cawley	7-71	0-0	5-28	0-26	0-0	1-7	1-7	0-0	0-3	9.9	1.75
Robert Tyner	7-98	0-0	1-17	1-31	0-0	1-21	4-26	0-0	0-3	7.1	-60.00
C A Murphy	6-33	0-0	2-9	0-12	0-0	1-1	3-10	0-0	0-1	18.2	11.75
Thomas Gibney	6-53	0-0	1-15	3-21	0-0	0-4	2-11	0-0	0-2	11.3	12.00
Ms Margaret Mullins	6-27	0-0	1-5	2-9	0-0	0-0	1-2	0-0	2-11	22.2	16.86
J P Dempsey	6-49	0-0	2-11	1-16	0-0	2-11	1-8	0-0	0-3	12.2	22.40
John Joseph Hanlon	6-60	0-0	4-19	0-13	0-0	2-10	0-9	0-1	0-8	10.0	30.50
J T R Dreaper	6-26	0-0	1-3	0-7	0-0	0-0	2-8	3-7	0-1	23.1	-2.25
Alan Fleming	5-37	0-0	1-5	3-20	0-0	0-0	1-6	0-3	0-3	13.5	3.25
M F Morris	5-59	0-0	2-7	0-15	0-0	0-5	3-31	0-0	0-1	8.5	15.50
C Roche	5-39	0-0	3-14	1-12	0-0	1-5	0-8	0-0	0-0	12.8	-6.00
Denis Gerard Hogan	5-63	0-0	2-21	0-16	0-0	1-8	2-13	0-0	0-5	7.9	-22.38
Gavin Cromwell	5-59	0-0	0-12	4-35	0-0	0-2	0-8	0-1	1-1	8.5	-29.51
Peter Fahey	4-40	0-0	2-10	1-12	0-0	0-2	0-9	0-0	1-7	10.0	11.50
Thomas Foley	4-53	0-0	3-20	0-12	0-0	0-1	0-8	0-0	1-12	7.5	-3.00
Thomas Mullins	4-64	0-0	0-14	2-27	0-0	0-1	0-11	0-0	2-11	6.3	-3.50
E Bolger	4-28	0-0	2-10	0-5	0-0	0-1	2-7	0-5	0-0	14.3	-10.88
Miss Elizabeth Doyle	4-59	0-0	1-17	2-21	0-0	0-5	0-4	0-0	1-12	6.8	-11.80
Mrs Denise Foster	4-46	0-0	3-17	0-18	0-0	1-1	0-4	0-1	0-5	8.7	-21.25

LEADING JUMP TRAINERS AT LEOPARDSTOWN (SINCE 2013)

	Total W-R	Nov Hdle	H'cap Hdle	Other Hdle	Nov Chase	H'cap Chase	Other Chase	Hunter Chase	N.H. Flat	Per cent	£1 Level stake
W P Mullins	78-313	0-0	1-17	40-161	0-0	0-2	23-100	1-2	13-31	24.9	-31.97
Gordon Elliott	20-240	0-0	2-32	8-100	0-0	0-7	7-74	0-1	3-26	8.3	-81.35
Henry De Bromhead	17-122	0-0	2-18	9-37	0-0	2-10	4-52	0-0	0-5	13.9	24.53
Mrs John Harrington	16-138	0-0	2-20	8-73	0-0	0-2	2-23	0-0	4-20	11.6	-27.76
A J Martin	11-157	0-0	3-46	2-60	0-0	3-17	3-26	0-0	0-8	7.0	-66.00
Noel Meade	10-120	0-0	1-18	3-42	0-0	0-7	5-37	0-1	1-15	8.3	-44.26
Thomas Mullins	8-55	0-0	5-18	0-20	0-0	1-3	1-6	0-0	1-8	14.5	13.00
Joseph Patrick O'Brien	8-60	0-0	2-7	1-30	0-0	1-3	1-7	0-0	3-13	13.3	63.50
Paul Nolan	6-54	0-0	2-17	1-9	0-0	2-10	1-12	0-1	0-5	11.1	17.50
John E Kiely	5-24	0-0	0-6	2-6	0-0	0-1	3-8	0-0	0-3	20.8	19.50
Edward P Harty	5-30	0-0	2-10	2-13	0-0	0-0	1-4	0-0	0-3	16.7	-9.75
D K Weld	5-27	0-0	0-3	1-14	0-0	0-0	0-0	0-0	4-10	18.5	-13.42
C Byrnes	4-23	0-0	2-8	1-9	0-0	0-1	1-3	0-0	0-2	17.4	-3.45
D T Hughes	4-39	0-0	1-7	3-16	0-0	0-2	0-13	0-0	0-1	10.3	-16.25
Robert Tyner	4-40	0-0	2-11	1-7	0-0	0-10	0-9	0-0	1-3	10.0	-19.00
A P O'Brien	4-33	0-0	0-2	2-21	0-0	0-0	0-3	0-0	2-7	12.1	-20.76
John Joseph Hanlon	3-26	0-0	2-10	1-8	0-0	0-0	0-3	0-0	0-5	11.5	2.00
Philip Fenton	3-8	0-0	0-1	1-2	0-0	0-0	1-1	0-0	1-4	37.5	7.00
Karl Thornton	3-17	0-0	0-1	0-4	0-0	2-6	1-6	0-0	0-0	17.6	13.50
Liam P Cusack	3-14	0-0	3-8	0-3	0-0	0-1	0-1	0-0	0-1	21.4	25.50
Miss Elizabeth Doyle	3-32	0-0	0-8	1-8	0-0	0-3	2-6	0-0	0-7	9.4	-11.25
Denis W Cullen	2-14	0-0	0-2	1-4	0-0	1-4	0-3	0-1	0-0	14.3	2.00
P A Fahy	2-26	0-0	1-12	1-8	0-0	0-1	0-2	0-0	0-3	7.7	-4.00
Andrew Lynch	2-11	0-0	1-5	0-1	0-0	0-0	1-5	0-0	0-0	18.2	11.00
Sean Thomas Doyle	2-3	0-0	0-0	1-2	0-0	0-0	1-1	0-0	0-0	66.7	23.00
Desmond McDonogh	2-8	0-0	0-3	2-5	0-0	0-0	0-0	0-0	0-0	25.0	31.00
J H Culloty	2-26	0-0	1-4	0-4	0-0	1-3	0-10	0-1	0-4	7.7	-7.00
Gavin Cromwell	2-24	0-0	0-3	1-14	0-0	1-3	0-3	0-0	0-1	8.3	-15.50
T M Walsh	2-24	0-0	0-2	0-4	0-0	0-1	1-14	1-1	0-2	8.3	-15.60
Ms Sandra Hughes	2-38	0-0	0-8	2-14	0-0	0-2	0-10	0-0	0-4	5.3	-26.00

LEADING JUMP TRAINERS AT PUNCHESTOWN (SINCE 2013)

	Total W-R	Nov Hdle	H'cap Hdle	Other Hdle	Nov Chase	H'cap Chase	Other Chase	Hunter Chase	N.H. Flat	Per cent	£1 Level stake
W P Mullins	143-574	0-0	4-32	71-291	0-0	0-6	42-158	0-1	26-86	24.9	18.85
Gordon Elliott	77-497	0-0	8-65	30-199	0-0	4-27	23-140	0-2	12-64	15.5	-51.01
Mrs John Harrington	45-259	0-0	9-33	17-107	0-0	2-8	10-50	0-0	7-61	17.4	75.76
Noel Meade	26-243	0-0	1-30	9-75	0-0	1-26	7-55	0-0	8-57	10.7	-142.49
E Bolger	20-107	0-0	1-6	1-13	0-0	1-9	10-62	7-17	0-0	18.7	-16.44
Henry De Bromhead	19-213	0-0	0-24	2-63	0-0	3-13	14-90	0-2	0-21	8.9	-149.21
D T Hughes	12-79	0-0	1-12	5-29	0-0	2-11	3-18	0-0	1-9	15.2	-18.91
Thomas Mullins	10-105	0-0	3-27	5-34	0-0	0-6	0-13	0-0	2-25	9.5	-42.93
P A Fahy	9-79	0-0	0-13	4-30	0-0	1-8	2-9	0-0	2-19	11.4	0.25
Joseph Patrick O'Brien	9-74	0-0	1-10	4-38	0-0	0-1	1-8	0-0	3-17	12.2	-34.32
Gavin Cromwell	7-39	0-0	2-8	3-18	0-0	1-7	1-5	0-0	0-1	17.9	11.48
A J Martin	7-123	0-0	0-34	3-45	0-0	2-12	2-20	0-0	0-12	5.7	-82.80
Edward P Harty	6-54	0-0	3-10	3-27	0-0	0-2	0-7	0-0	0-8	11.1	41.75
John Joseph Hanlon	6-68	0-0	3-19	1-25	0-0	1-6	1-9	0-0	0-9	8.8	-23.30
Robert Tyner	6-86	0-0	0-18	0-16	0-0	3-24	1-16	0-0	2-12	7.0	-28.50
Peter Maher	6-86	0-0	0-3	0-3	0-0	0-4	4-46	2-26	0-4	7.0	-37.00
M F Morris	6-118	0-0	0-5	2-33	0-0	2-21	2-48	0-0	0-11	5.1	-58.58
Denis W Cullen	5-41	0-0	1-12	2-12	0-0	0-4	0-1	2-7	0-5	12.2	4.25
Dermot A McLoughlin	5-37	0-0	3-18	1-6	0-0	0-11	0-0	0-0	1-2	13.5	19.00
J P Dempsey	5-54	0-0	0-8	1-17	0-0	2-9	1-12	0-4	1-4	9.3	-6.25
Miss Elizabeth Doyle	5-79	0-0	1-29	1-16	0-0	1-7	0-6	0-0	2-21	6.3	-45.43
Alan Fleming	4-28	0-0	2-6	2-11	0-0	0-1	0-7	0-1	0-2	14.3	4.75
Harry Fry	4-10	0-0	0-1	2-5	0-0	1-1	0-1	0-0	1-2	40.0	16.00
Nicky Henderson	4-35	0-0	0-0	4-19	0-0	0-0	0-11	0-0	0-5	11.4	-2.12
John E Kiely	4-49	0-0	2-15	0-14	0-0	0-2	2-10	0-0	0-8	8.2	-2.50
Colin Bowe	4-38	0-0	0-7	1-14	0-0	1-5	2-9	0-1	0-2	10.5	-19.83
C Byrnes	4-40	0-0	2-12	0-12	0-0	1-6	0-7	0-0	1-3	10.0	-25.75
M Phelan	3-15	0-0	0-5	1-2	0-0	1-3	0-4	0-0	1-1	20.0	1.00
Jonathan Sweeney	3-8	0-0	0-1	1-4	0-0	0-0	0-0	0-0	2-3	37.5	5.88
Colin Tizzard	3-16	0-0	0-0	0-5	0-0	0-0	3-11	0-0	0-0	18.8	7.50

LEADING TRAINERS BY MONTH 2013-2018

JANUARY

	Total W-R	Nov Hdle	H'cap Hdle	Other Hdle	Nov Chase	H'cap Chase	Other Chase	Hunter Chase	N.H. Flat	Per cent	£1 Level stake
Nicky Henderson	70-234	23-56	7-37	22-68	9-19	3-25	3-11	0-0	4-23	29.9	**33.32**
Philip Hobbs	62-258	14-48	7-46	13-45	6-29	14-70	1-5	2-3	5-15	24.0	**11.70**
Donald McCain	59-309	11-60	11-88	4-38	15-36	14-63	1-4	0-0	3-20	19.1	-13.39
Venetia Williams	48-350	10-38	8-64	6-35	6-47	18-158	1-4	0-0	0-7	13.7	-121.21
Alan King	40-169	7-31	9-36	11-40	5-15	3-24	3-9	0-0	2-16	23.7	**24.91**
Nigel Twiston-Davies	39-261	4-29	7-60	5-32	4-29	15-94	0-4	0-0	4-16	14.9	-59.38
Sue Smith	38-159	5-19	14-40	0-7	3-15	14-68	1-6	0-0	1-4	23.9	**77.23**
Paul Nicholls	38-223	5-34	6-32	12-45	3-30	8-60	3-18	1-4	2-5	17.0	-37.52
David Pipe	37-263	10-50	9-70	8-60	6-21	2-45	0-5	0-0	2-17	14.1	-97.18
Harry Fry	36-116	7-30	5-19	7-26	5-9	4-12	3-6	0-2	5-13	31.0	**20.64**
Lucinda Russell	29-260	1-19	10-81	4-33	1-20	9-84	0-1	0-1	4-21	11.2	-11.09
Evan Williams	28-228	4-30	5-51	3-34	5-29	7-58	2-5	0-1	2-20	12.3	-24.58
Neil Mulholland	27-156	5-29	8-41	5-38	2-19	7-22	0-2	0-0	0-6	17.3	-15.97
Brian Ellison	27-139	5-21	6-45	2-16	8-16	1-22	1-3	0-0	4-16	19.4	-48.81
Colin Tizzard	25-224	5-33	2-32	4-25	5-29	5-70	1-12	1-2	2-21	11.2	-96.95
Nicky Richards	23-107	3-19	6-27	3-10	1-8	6-26	0-2	0-2	4-13	21.5	**17.19**
Dan Skelton	23-219	6-50	5-53	7-46	1-16	2-38	2-4	0-2	0-13	10.5	-124.48
Tom George	22-165	5-28	3-21	5-26	5-20	4-57	0-4	0-1	0-8	13.3	-61.17
Jonjo O'Neill	20-224	3-41	7-62	3-41	1-17	3-57	2-3	0-3	1-1	8.9	-111.64
Gary Moore	19-169	1-24	4-42	4-34	4-26	3-32	3-5	0-0	0-7	11.2	-65.96
Malcolm Jefferson	18-85	4-21	2-15	1-6	2-10	6-23	1-1	0-0	2-9	21.2	**8.98**
Warren Greatrex	17-137	5-33	3-28	4-46	2-7	1-10	0-1	1-1	1-12	12.4	-69.11
Nick Williams	16-88	3-9	3-20	9-33	0-7	1-16	1-2	0-0	0-4	18.2	**33.38**
Ben Pauling	16-98	7-33	1-21	1-16	4-10	1-15	0-0	0-2	2-4	16.3	-19.45
Micky Hammond	16-171	0-25	4-65	2-14	2-14	5-47	0-0	0-0	3-6	9.4	-33.25
Lucy Wadham	14-87	3-13	4-31	4-14	0-5	1-14	1-3	0-0	1-7	16.1	-8.75
Oliver Sherwood	14-106	2-16	2-17	2-33	3-9	2-20	3-5	0-2	0-4	13.2	-30.74
John Ferguson	13-45	3-13	1-7	7-17	1-5	0-0	0-1	0-0	1-2	28.9	**2.73**
Rebecca Curtis	13-96	2-16	1-9	3-21	4-14	3-25	0-2	0-0	0-9	13.5	**13.16**
Seamus Mullins	13-117	3-21	3-35	1-21	2-15	3-24	0-0	0-0	1-2	11.1	**17.83**
Anthony Honeyball	13-79	1-10	1-15	2-14	2-5	5-23	0-2	0-0	2-11	16.5	-11.86
Henry Daly	13-89	1-13	4-24	2-15	0-12	4-18	0-0	1-3	1-5	14.6	-32.49
Charlie Longsdon	13-145	3-27	1-34	2-27	1-15	5-37	0-1	0-0	1-6	9.0	-72.97
John Quinn	12-44	4-10	2-12	5-14	0-2	0-3	0-0	0-0	1-3	27.3	**9.84**
Kerry Lee	12-64	1-7	2-8	0-4	2-7	6-29	1-5	0-0	0-4	18.8	**37.60**
Sandy Thomson	12-51	2-8	4-18	1-4	2-3	1-14	0-0	0-0	2-4	23.5	**60.32**
Kim Bailey	12-93	3-18	2-18	3-20	1-6	2-21	0-4	0-0	1-7	12.9	-8.05
Tom Symonds	12-85	0-7	3-28	3-18	0-11	4-16	1-1	0-0	1-6	14.1	-24.22
Peter Bowen	12-107	2-13	3-29	2-17	2-8	0-30	1-1	0-0	2-9	11.2	-54.34
Alex Hales	11-64	1-11	2-19	1-6	1-3	6-23	0-0	0-0	0-2	17.2	**5.33**
Chris Gordon	11-97	0-9	7-45	0-8	0-6	4-25	0-0	0-0	0-4	11.3	**8.85**
David Dennis	11-88	1-15	6-24	1-21	1-11	0-12	0-0	0-0	2-7	12.5	-5.00
Emma Lavelle	11-94	2-12	4-16	0-13	0-9	1-24	0-1	0-0	4-20	11.7	-22.51
Jennie Candlish	11-99	2-12	6-40	0-9	0-5	3-32	0-0	0-0	0-2	11.1	-47.31
Henry Oliver	10-59	0-10	4-15	1-6	2-9	3-16	0-0	0-0	0-3	16.9	**5.75**
Robert Walford	10-59	0-7	1-13	2-12	3-4	4-20	0-0	0-0	0-3	16.9	**7.75**
Olly Murphy	10-30	2-6	3-9	1-9	1-1	2-4	0-0	0-0	1-2	33.3	**20.75**
Rose Dobbin	10-83	1-13	4-28	2-7	0-8	2-25	0-0	0-0	1-2	12.0	-10.73
Jamie Snowden	10-70	1-15	1-14	1-16	2-5	2-11	0-3	1-1	2-5	14.3	-16.25
Dr Richard Newland	10-49	2-6	0-16	1-11	2-4	5-14	0-0	0-0	0-0	20.4	-19.44
N W Alexander	10-138	0-20	5-39	2-19	0-10	3-38	0-1	0-2	0-9	7.2	-73.93
Alexandra Dunn	9-49	0-7	6-24	0-7	1-1	2-10	0-0	0-0	0-0	18.4	**19.75**
Keith Dalgleish	9-52	1-9	3-18	0-14	0-0	3-5	0-0	0-0	2-6	17.3	**21.75**
David Bridgwater	9-56	2-12	0-9	1-7	2-7	3-15	1-4	0-0	0-2	16.1	-3.84
James Ewart	9-92	0-8	4-33	0-9	0-2	4-22	0-0	0-0	1-18	9.8	-13.20
Robin Dickin	9-67	1-14	2-12	0-6	3-13	3-14	0-2	0-0	0-6	13.4	-28.87
Ian Williams	9-90	1-19	2-19	2-20	2-6	2-18	0-1	0-0	0-7	10.0	-51.02
Philip Kirby	9-96	0-15	9-51	0-8	0-4	0-3	0-0	0-0	0-16	9.4	-52.17
Fergal O'Brien	9-112	1-18	2-21	1-16	2-10	1-29	0-3	0-1	2-16	8.0	-60.01
Tom Lacey	8-43	2-11	3-13	2-9	0-1	1-4	0-1	0-0	0-4	18.6	**40.50**
Caroline Bailey	8-56	0-6	2-14	1-8	2-6	3-22	0-0	0-0	0-0	14.3	-15.80

196 TRAINERS JUMPS STATISTICS

FEBRUARY

	Total W-R	Nov Hdle	H'cap Hdle	Other Hdle	Nov Chase	H'cap Chase	Other Chase	Hunter Chase	N.H. Flat	Per cent	£1 Level stake
Paul Nicholls	84-332	12-59	17-63	15-57	15-50	7-47	7-28	9-15	3-14	25.3	-57.30
Nicky Henderson	68-261	20-60	5-56	20-55	8-22	2-17	6-15	0-0	7-39	26.1	-84.81
David Pipe	50-252	7-32	17-107	5-24	6-14	8-50	2-7	0-0	5-19	19.8	-6.31
Alan King	48-251	8-58	6-56	10-49	10-19	4-23	1-8	0-0	9-38	19.1	-26.58
Dan Skelton	45-242	17-61	6-59	8-43	3-21	4-25	1-4	1-5	5-25	18.6	-100.50
Donald McCain	42-296	8-54	13-98	9-36	5-36	3-49	0-4	0-0	4-20	14.2	-67.80
Venetia Williams	41-338	7-42	3-69	2-34	7-37	20-143	1-8	0-2	1-3	12.1	-155.77
Colin Tizzard	39-212	6-38	6-50	3-15	2-13	14-59	6-12	0-1	2-24	18.4	-35.59
Jonjo O'Neill	39-248	8-48	12-77	4-33	7-23	4-47	1-6	1-2	2-12	15.7	-81.40
Philip Hobbs	39-222	6-33	7-45	5-26	4-23	6-55	1-7	2-5	8-28	17.6	-94.42
Nigel Twiston-Davies	31-254	4-33	8-64	3-23	5-24	8-80	1-7	1-3	1-20	12.2	-50.58
Sue Smith	30-157	3-18	6-39	0-3	4-20	17-67	0-2	0-0	0-9	19.1	8.90
Gary Moore	28-177	2-30	4-38	7-35	4-23	8-32	1-7	0-0	2-12	15.8	-19.89
Kim Bailey	27-121	10-19	7-37	2-16	1-9	1-22	3-4	0-1	3-13	22.3	14.89
Tom George	27-156	3-13	0-15	1-17	8-27	8-59	1-4	2-6	4-15	17.3	22.41
Warren Greatrex	27-138	7-29	6-32	4-29	1-9	2-14	1-1	3-4	3-20	19.6	-30.29
Neil Mulholland	24-142	1-24	13-57	0-15	1-9	5-28	0-0	0-0	4-9	16.9	-23.96
Lucinda Russell	23-210	2-23	4-58	0-19	5-28	11-63	1-2	0-1	0-17	11.0	-71.08
Evan Williams	23-211	2-32	8-70	1-30	3-22	7-42	0-1	0-0	2-14	10.9	-80.38
Fergal O'Brien	20-96	2-17	1-16	2-10	4-11	6-25	2-3	1-2	2-12	20.8	30.22
Nicky Richards	19-93	2-15	3-25	1-8	5-6	4-23	0-4	1-4	3-9	20.4	5.97
Peter Bowen	19-99	1-11	6-31	2-14	4-9	4-21	0-1	0-0	2-12	19.2	16.02
Charlie Longsdon	19-117	5-23	2-26	4-12	2-11	3-31	0-2	0-0	3-12	16.2	-7.52
Oliver Sherwood	19-125	2-18	1-19	6-28	3-16	5-28	0-3	1-1	1-12	15.2	-24.84
Ben Pauling	18-105	6-27	3-25	5-13	1-7	1-17	0-2	1-1	1-13	17.1	-1.22
Brian Ellison	18-147	6-29	3-53	0-21	3-10	2-26	0-0	0-0	4-17	12.2	-54.56
Micky Hammond	17-139	5-18	6-56	0-6	2-12	4-38	0-1	0-0	0-8	12.2	-0.16
Tim Vaughan	17-159	2-25	4-58	0-17	4-15	5-26	1-1	1-3	0-14	10.7	-62.20
Anthony Honeyball	16-83	1-14	6-26	1-6	1-5	4-23	0-0	0-0	3-9	19.3	-7.56
Harry Fry	16-109	4-18	3-28	3-17	1-12	3-15	0-4	0-0	2-16	14.7	-39.42
Henry Daly	15-75	1-11	4-19	2-10	1-8	3-13	0-0	3-5	1-9	20.0	0.67
Henry Oliver	15-71	5-13	5-32	0-2	0-6	5-18	0-0	0-0	0-0	21.1	-4.85
Chris Gordon	14-99	2-13	6-44	0-9	0-5	4-21	0-1	0-0	2-6	14.1	3.46
N W Alexander	14-122	4-13	2-36	0-12	4-9	3-37	0-1	0-9	1-5	11.5	13.83
Lucy Wadham	14-77	5-12	3-26	0-7	0-8	5-17	0-0	0-0	1-8	18.2	-16.90
Nick Williams	13-85	3-11	4-26	3-19	0-4	2-16	1-3	0-0	0-6	15.3	-8.57
Rebecca Curtis	13-99	1-15	0-15	5-16	2-14	0-14	0-5	2-6	3-14	13.1	-47.37
Philip Kirby	12-80	1-9	6-40	0-7	3-5	1-5	0-0	0-1	1-13	15.0	18.08
Jamie Snowden	12-63	1-8	4-16	0-7	0-9	3-8	0-3	1-1	3-11	19.0	-2.36
Kerry Lee	11-62	0-2	0-12	1-5	3-10	5-28	1-3	0-1	1-1	17.7	2.90
John Ferguson	11-49	3-11	2-8	5-16	0-4	0-1	0-0	0-2	2-9	22.4	-15.51
Emma Lavelle	11-76	3-13	4-20	3-7	0-2	0-19	0-0	0-0	1-15	14.5	-19.75
David Bridgwater	11-80	0-7	1-11	1-11	2-14	6-28	0-2	0-0	1-7	13.8	-21.84
Graeme McPherson	10-61	1-9	4-26	0-3	2-6	2-12	0-0	0-0	1-5	16.4	-6.58
Ian Williams	10-88	1-19	3-22	3-17	1-7	2-20	0-0	0-2	0-3	11.4	-31.18
Johnny Farrelly	9-50	0-4	5-24	0-1	3-8	0-8	0-1	0-0	1-4	18.0	3.25
Nigel Hawke	9-80	0-7	2-30	2-19	3-8	1-9	0-1	0-0	1-6	11.3	-2.00
Neil King	9-76	0-11	2-19	1-7	3-8	0-15	0-1	0-0	3-15	11.8	-3.50
Rose Dobbin	9-89	2-20	1-21	0-13	0-8	6-20	0-0	0-0	0-7	10.1	-42.00
Harry Whittington	8-40	3-10	2-8	1-5	1-3	1-8	0-0	0-0	0-6	20.0	3.44
Matt Sheppard	8-40	0-2	0-14	0-2	2-4	6-15	0-0	0-0	0-3	20.0	7.00
Sandy Thomson	8-50	2-7	2-16	1-4	1-4	1-14	0-2	0-0	1-3	16.0	7.62
Pam Sly	8-28	1-7	2-8	1-1	0-1	1-4	1-1	0-0	2-6	28.6	63.33
Stuart Coltherd	8-66	0-4	1-24	0-1	3-7	3-25	0-0	1-4	0-1	12.1	-3.00
Martin Keighley	8-59	3-6	3-28	0-7	0-0	2-7	0-0	0-0	0-11	13.6	-25.06
Jeremy Scott	8-80	2-17	4-36	1-8	0-6	0-8	0-0	0-0	1-5	10.0	-29.88
David Dennis	8-78	2-14	2-21	1-12	3-10	0-14	0-0	0-0	0-7	10.3	-39.97
Chris Grant	7-74	0-17	1-22	1-5	0-4	4-16	0-0	0-1	1-9	9.5	8.00
Michael Easterby	7-32	2-4	2-5	0-2	0-4	3-13	0-0	0-0	0-4	21.9	14.99
Robin Dickin	7-53	1-5	2-18	0-5	2-5	2-13	0-1	0-0	0-6	13.2	-8.25
Ben Case	7-67	1-12	1-19	1-9	1-3	2-15	0-0	0-0	1-9	10.4	-13.00

MARCH

	Total W-R	Nov Hdle	H'cap Hdle	Other Hdle	Nov Chase	H'cap Chase	Other Chase	Hunter Chase	N.H. Flat	Per cent	£1 Level stake
Nicky Henderson	67-365	20-69	17-109	13-60	5-26	0-37	4-26	0-0	9-44	18.4	-121.88
Paul Nicholls	58-335	11-47	17-87	6-43	7-34	8-70	2-35	6-14	1-11	17.3	26.04
Dan Skelton	52-292	10-45	8-96	13-44	4-22	5-40	2-4	1-3	9-38	17.8	-43.15
Donald McCain	50-332	19-75	8-100	7-35	3-30	8-58	0-8	0-0	5-26	15.1	-107.03
Venetia Williams	46-346	6-44	8-75	2-24	8-34	18-153	1-11	1-1	2-6	13.3	-47.89
Philip Hobbs	45-337	13-49	5-96	10-37	3-28	9-77	0-13	1-6	5-42	13.4	-113.36
David Pipe	42-293	5-43	12-124	1-20	4-13	14-66	3-12	0-0	3-21	14.3	7.16
Nigel Twiston-Davies	42-302	5-30	11-77	5-29	1-25	10-102	1-11	0-1	9-31	13.9	-54.97
Harry Fry	33-137	10-32	5-38	2-18	6-13	1-10	0-4	0-1	9-22	24.1	15.02
Lucinda Russell	31-244	2-33	13-73	2-17	4-24	9-76	0-0	0-0	1-21	12.7	-70.06
Jonjo O'Neill	31-262	4-39	6-81	6-30	1-16	10-74	1-10	1-3	2-13	11.8	-112.77
Warren Greatrex	30-182	7-43	7-53	5-32	1-5	4-18	0-5	1-5	5-23	16.5	-6.66
Ian Williams	29-134	1-26	12-47	1-11	4-12	10-29	1-3	0-2	0-4	21.6	36.60
Colin Tizzard	28-248	6-45	8-55	2-17	4-28	7-74	1-13	0-2	0-15	11.3	-56.52
Neil Mulholland	28-206	3-32	11-70	3-23	4-15	2-46	0-5	0-0	5-16	13.6	-64.77
Tim Vaughan	27-210	3-30	17-83	2-25	0-9	3-45	0-1	1-6	1-12	12.9	-79.56
Alan King	26-284	6-49	4-96	5-45	2-10	1-29	2-13	0-0	6-44	9.2	-152.02
Nigel Hawke	25-98	6-15	7-32	1-10	1-10	7-22	0-1	0-0	3-8	25.5	46.43
Gary Moore	25-205	5-27	6-75	2-25	6-24	3-37	1-5	0-0	2-12	12.2	-7.31
Rebecca Curtis	24-132	4-21	4-20	5-23	5-20	3-20	1-10	0-2	2-16	18.2	-3.09
Tom George	24-170	2-21	3-21	3-15	3-23	10-63	0-8	2-4	1-16	14.1	-65.75
Chris Gordon	23-110	1-7	10-57	1-5	1-5	10-31	0-1	0-1	0-3	20.9	40.77
Kim Bailey	23-194	8-47	4-52	2-16	3-15	3-34	1-5	0-0	2-26	11.9	-79.77
Charlie Longsdon	23-206	10-31	2-68	3-18	1-16	4-54	2-3	0-0	1-19	11.2	-98.48
Nicky Richards	22-106	5-15	8-35	0-2	1-6	3-22	0-5	0-2	5-19	20.8	-15.56
Micky Hammond	22-173	2-24	7-60	1-8	3-14	8-50	0-1	0-0	1-16	12.7	-43.38
Sue Smith	22-203	1-22	6-64	1-4	4-18	10-77	0-4	0-0	0-14	10.8	-117.54
Evan Williams	22-237	6-32	7-67	1-27	1-22	4-67	1-2	0-1	2-21	9.3	-135.06
Jennie Candlish	20-80	0-4	8-41	2-5	1-4	9-20	0-1	0-0	0-6	25.0	32.70
Philip Kirby	19-107	2-23	6-36	4-12	0-5	2-9	0-0	1-3	4-19	17.8	1.46
Malcolm Jefferson	19-83	6-17	3-14	0-7	1-7	5-23	0-1	0-0	4-14	22.9	-5.34
N W Alexander	18-124	1-18	6-42	1-6	5-16	3-26	0-0	1-4	1-12	14.5	-33.88
Peter Bowen	17-96	2-10	4-29	1-10	1-4	7-32	0-0	0-0	2-12	17.7	-8.45
Fergal O'Brien	17-149	2-27	2-30	2-14	1-9	5-40	2-5	0-2	3-23	11.4	-36.58
Stuart Colthard	16-80	2-12	6-33	0-1	2-11	6-21	0-0	0-2	0-0	20.0	52.75
Anthony Honeyball	16-91	3-16	8-33	1-12	1-5	2-11	0-1	0-0	1-14	17.6	-20.31
Brian Ellison	16-143	2-22	5-59	3-16	2-7	1-25	0-2	0-0	3-12	11.2	-85.88
Seamus Mullins	15-131	0-13	4-54	1-16	0-6	10-34	0-1	0-0	0-7	11.5	-23.88
Oliver Sherwood	15-133	4-22	1-26	1-12	1-12	6-38	1-4	0-1	1-18	11.3	-75.75
Keith Reveley	13-60	2-10	3-20	1-4	1-1	4-15	0-0	1-2	1-9	21.7	4.42
Tom Lacey	13-46	1-7	4-15	0-2	0-1	5-7	0-0	0-1	3-13	28.3	12.57
Robin Dickin	13-86	1-13	5-25	0-8	3-12	4-24	0-0	0-0	0-4	15.1	19.00
Henry Oliver	13-82	3-19	9-32	0-3	0-4	1-23	0-1	0-0	0-0	15.9	-10.68
Lucy Wadham	13-90	0-3	5-35	3-14	0-2	4-26	0-2	0-0	1-8	14.4	-19.53
Jamie Snowden	13-100	1-19	3-24	2-13	2-8	2-12	0-6	0-1	3-17	13.0	-24.25
Neil King	13-96	2-9	6-41	1-13	1-7	3-19	0-0	0-0	0-7	13.5	-34.95
Charlie Mann	12-77	1-10	5-23	1-8	0-3	5-28	0-2	0-0	0-3	15.6	2.83
Michael Scudamore	12-57	1-7	1-7	2-4	0-3	7-27	0-1	0-0	1-8	21.1	4.48
Caroline Bailey	12-65	0-5	5-18	0-5	2-5	5-26	0-1	0-1	0-4	18.5	22.49
Kerry Lee	12-59	0-5	3-15	0-6	3-6	4-21	2-4	0-0	0-2	20.3	-5.64
Nick Williams	11-72	2-9	3-27	1-10	1-6	3-14	0-2	0-0	1-6	15.3	17.25
Tim Easterby	11-69	6-12	2-33	0-6	0-4	2-7	1-1	0-0	0-9	15.9	34.15
Jeremy Scott	11-77	1-10	7-36	0-10	1-5	1-12	0-0	1-1	0-5	14.3	-20.38
Kenneth Slack	10-31	0-2	7-20	0-0	2-3	1-6	0-0	0-0	0-0	32.3	13.63
Keith Dalgleish	10-35	0-4	6-15	0-4	0-1	2-4	0-0	0-0	2-7	28.6	18.38
Iain Jardine	10-51	4-10	3-16	2-7	0-2	1-10	0-0	0-0	0-6	19.6	-11.47
James Ewart	10-79	0-10	4-29	2-8	3-7	0-14	0-0	0-0	1-11	12.7	-14.55
Ben Case	10-85	1-9	4-29	2-11	1-4	2-22	0-0	0-0	0-10	11.8	-17.88
Ben Pauling	10-111	2-20	2-45	1-11	0-5	4-15	0-1	0-1	1-13	9.0	-62.86
Emma Lavelle	10-105	1-15	1-20	3-13	2-7	2-27	0-2	0-0	1-22	9.5	-66.46
Sue Gardner	9-51	0-3	6-28	0-6	0-2	3-6	0-0	0-0	0-6	17.6	2.08

198 TRAINERS JUMPS STATISTICS

APRIL

	Total W-R	Nov Hdle	H'cap Hdle	Other Hdle	Nov Chase	H'cap Chase	Other Chase	Hunter Chase	N.H. Flat	Per cent	£1 Level stake
Paul Nicholls	112-497	34-71	13-92	15-62	20-69	11-120	6-34	2-14	11-36	22.5	-81.20
Nicky Henderson	78-406	16-68	11-118	22-72	5-25	7-47	4-20	0-0	14-63	19.2	-69.94
Philip Hobbs	68-360	18-41	17-103	5-34	3-21	12-83	4-13	1-10	8-56	18.9	-38.98
Dan Skelton	62-309	15-63	21-104	5-28	6-23	8-48	1-3	0-1	6-42	20.1	-21.70
Jonjo O'Neill	45-310	7-35	11-101	4-25	4-22	16-90	2-10	0-5	1-22	14.5	-1.81
Donald McCain	42-319	7-55	12-110	7-32	7-38	7-60	0-2	0-0	2-22	13.2	-95.30
Nigel Twiston-Davies	34-313	6-36	8-88	3-24	3-19	9-104	0-3	1-4	4-36	10.9	-140.77
Kim Bailey	33-177	5-33	9-49	2-16	3-12	5-39	2-3	0-1	7-26	18.6	0.21
Tom George	33-196	6-19	2-24	1-10	4-19	13-87	2-10	1-5	4-22	16.8	-25.00
Colin Tizzard	28-235	5-31	5-58	3-19	3-18	6-65	5-20	0-1	1-24	11.9	0.49
Warren Greatrex	28-182	5-34	6-57	3-28	0-4	2-19	0-2	1-3	11-37	15.4	-50.23
Gary Moore	27-187	6-28	11-67	2-16	1-19	5-32	1-7	0-0	1-18	14.4	-49.91
Fergal O'Brien	25-162	2-26	6-34	2-16	1-15	10-43	0-2	2-6	3-23	15.4	7.91
Harry Fry	25-140	3-22	4-33	6-28	1-5	6-25	0-4	0-0	5-25	17.9	-5.42
Neil Mulholland	25-194	2-24	6-72	3-17	5-12	4-42	0-4	0-0	5-25	12.9	-88.66
Peter Bowen	24-131	2-9	7-41	1-6	1-4	7-51	2-2	0-0	4-18	18.3	69.22
Micky Hammond	24-138	6-18	10-46	0-2	1-7	7-54	0-2	0-0	0-9	17.4	-9.71
Tim Vaughan	22-181	3-30	8-79	2-14	2-10	6-35	0-0	1-6	0-9	12.2	-28.50
Lucinda Russell	22-223	5-27	10-78	0-12	0-22	7-66	0-1	0-2	0-15	9.9	-76.85
David Pipe	21-247	5-30	11-95	3-25	0-8	1-69	0-6	0-0	1-15	8.5	-104.79
Alan King	21-239	5-48	4-70	5-30	4-12	2-38	0-6	0-0	2-39	8.8	-110.17
Neil King	19-101	2-8	6-38	3-10	1-1	6-30	0-1	0-0	1-14	18.8	11.81
Oliver Sherwood	19-117	3-22	0-19	3-15	5-15	6-28	1-3	0-4	1-14	16.2	-22.60
Venetia Williams	19-207	3-18	1-37	1-15	4-20	7-99	1-9	0-3	2-6	9.2	-113.55
Malcolm Jefferson	18-96	4-12	4-21	0-5	2-11	3-25	0-0	0-0	5-22	18.8	6.38
Nicky Richards	18-119	3-17	5-47	2-6	1-9	4-27	1-3	1-2	1-9	15.1	-7.38
Jamie Snowden	17-112	5-23	2-21	2-19	1-14	4-22	0-0	0-0	3-14	15.2	21.65
Charlie Longsdon	17-234	1-32	1-67	2-26	5-16	7-75	0-2	0-0	1-17	7.3	-124.48
Dr Richard Newland	16-75	0-1	7-30	2-4	3-3	4-35	0-0	0-2	0-0	21.3	9.77
Chris Gordon	16-98	1-8	6-39	0-4	5-7	3-31	0-1	0-0	1-8	16.3	-21.26
Jeremy Scott	15-101	2-12	4-37	0-9	2-6	6-20	0-1	1-3	0-13	14.9	25.28
Ian Williams	15-115	3-19	5-38	3-8	1-8	3-30	0-0	0-2	0-10	13.0	-27.80
Sue Smith	15-156	0-18	3-34	0-5	3-18	9-73	0-2	0-0	0-6	9.6	-45.92
Matt Sheppard	14-54	2-11	2-21	0-3	1-2	9-16	0-0	0-0	0-1	25.9	52.00
Henry Daly	14-100	1-15	5-32	2-10	0-8	2-24	0-0	3-7	2-9	14.0	-15.04
Nigel Hawke	13-91	1-14	3-27	2-13	4-12	4-15	0-1	0-0	0-10	14.3	-14.17
Emma Lavelle	13-112	0-16	3-17	1-9	1-12	5-43	0-2	0-0	3-15	11.6	-24.69
Seamus Mullins	13-142	0-14	8-54	0-14	2-9	2-32	0-0	0-0	1-21	9.2	-43.25
Anthony Honeyball	12-75	0-4	7-26	1-7	1-5	1-16	0-5	0-0	2-13	16.0	-9.50
Evan Williams	12-179	4-32	4-47	0-23	0-12	3-51	0-2	0-1	1-11	6.7	-80.34
Rebecca Curtis	11-94	3-13	0-16	2-15	1-9	4-22	1-10	0-1	0-8	11.7	15.55
Tom Lacey	11-37	0-4	5-10	0-1	0-1	2-4	0-0	0-0	4-17	29.7	29.13
Brian Ellison	11-126	1-14	6-60	1-12	0-7	3-24	0-1	0-0	0-8	8.7	-62.75
Chris Down	10-70	1-7	9-52	0-8	0-2	0-1	0-0	0-0	0-2	14.3	23.00
Nick Williams	10-65	2-7	2-22	2-13	0-3	0-7	3-9	0-0	1-4	15.4	-22.70
David Dennis	10-100	2-16	3-39	2-8	0-8	1-15	0-0	0-0	2-14	10.0	-45.94
N W Alexander	10-144	3-16	1-57	0-9	0-9	5-34	0-0	1-12	0-7	6.9	-77.31
Charlie Mann	9-59	0-11	5-20	1-3	1-7	2-16	0-0	0-0	0-2	15.3	3.96
Ben Pauling	9-87	0-20	6-38	0-7	0-2	1-7	0-0	0-0	2-14	10.3	25.50
James Ewart	9-60	1-5	5-18	0-4	1-9	2-15	0-3	0-0	0-6	15.0	-6.75
Jennie Candlish	8-70	0-3	3-37	0-3	0-6	5-15	0-0	0-0	0-6	11.4	3.04
Mark Walford	8-50	1-3	3-28	1-2	0-1	3-15	0-0	0-0	0-1	16.0	22.25
Stuart Coltherd	8-59	0-5	0-18	0-1	4-11	4-20	0-0	0-4	0-0	13.6	-10.75
Henry Oliver	8-64	0-10	3-26	1-2	0-6	3-12	0-0	0-0	1-8	12.5	-14.79
Martin Keighley	8-75	2-13	2-29	0-11	1-2	3-17	0-0	0-0	0-5	10.7	-22.00
Philip Kirby	8-77	1-11	5-39	0-5	0-4	1-5	0-0	1-4	0-9	10.4	-24.42
Richard Woollacott	7-51	0-3	3-22	0-3	1-4	2-14	0-1	0-0	1-4	13.7	11.46
Dai Burchell	7-42	0-7	3-16	0-0	1-3	3-15	0-0	0-0	0-1	16.7	21.75
George Bewley	7-50	0-4	2-21	1-4	1-5	3-13	0-0	0-0	0-3	14.0	22.00
Alex Hales	7-59	1-10	2-19	2-6	1-5	1-14	0-0	0-0	0-5	11.9	-7.50
Mick Channon	7-33	1-4	0-5	2-6	3-5	0-7	0-3	0-0	1-3	21.2	-12.78

MAY

	Total W-R	Nov Hdle	H'cap Hdle	Other Hdle	Nov Chase	H'cap Chase	Other Chase	Hunter Chase	N.H. Flat	Per cent	£1 Level stake
Nicky Henderson	62-237	13-39	4-46	12-35	5-17	9-25	3-15	0-0	16-60	26.2	-25.82
Donald McCain	54-307	19-56	6-96	11-40	8-32	3-54	2-11	0-2	5-16	17.6	-115.11
Jonjo O'Neill	52-321	9-37	14-103	3-31	2-25	21-95	1-6	0-4	2-20	16.2	-72.94
Dan Skelton	47-168	14-29	13-62	4-21	8-21	7-26	0-1	0-1	1-7	28.0	-22.24
Paul Nicholls	41-154	12-23	3-30	3-16	12-30	4-35	3-6	3-7	1-7	26.6	-42.96
Alan King	38-159	9-26	5-44	6-25	5-10	3-23	0-7	0-0	10-24	23.9	-11.69
Peter Bowen	37-171	4-19	11-62	6-15	1-6	9-47	0-2	0-0	6-20	21.6	14.33
David Pipe	34-212	2-15	12-80	4-29	6-15	4-44	0-3	0-0	6-26	16.0	-35.64
Philip Hobbs	31-177	1-11	8-57	5-19	3-12	11-58	1-3	0-1	2-16	17.5	-38.91
Evan Williams	29-190	3-20	12-70	4-18	0-11	10-59	0-7	0-0	0-5	15.3	0.41
Neil Mulholland	28-157	1-22	15-66	2-14	2-14	7-30	0-1	0-0	1-10	17.8	43.52
Warren Greatrex	27-100	4-11	7-37	3-10	0-5	1-11	0-3	2-3	10-20	27.0	35.58
Charlie Longsdon	27-165	4-17	3-42	4-15	2-22	10-46	3-4	0-0	1-19	16.4	-32.83
Kim Bailey	24-153	3-22	2-43	9-21	3-11	3-29	1-7	0-0	3-20	15.7	-41.14
Nigel Twiston-Davies	21-175	1-21	5-53	0-10	1-11	12-57	1-1	0-1	1-21	12.0	-51.01
Harry Fry	20-68	2-12	3-13	7-11	0-2	4-14	2-2	0-0	2-14	29.4	1.87
Fergal O'Brien	20-128	3-23	8-36	1-15	0-8	2-24	1-3	2-5	3-14	15.6	46.01
Tim Vaughan	20-213	7-36	6-71	1-22	0-10	4-48	1-3	0-5	1-18	9.4	-92.43
Dr Richard Newland	18-69	1-1	6-40	5-10	0-2	5-14	0-1	1-1	0-0	26.1	3.20
Sue Smith	17-92	1-10	4-14	1-6	2-14	8-39	1-2	0-0	0-7	18.5	1.24
Lucinda Russell	17-151	3-20	3-45	1-12	3-20	7-48	0-0	0-0	0-6	11.3	5.68
Tom George	17-106	2-15	1-10	2-15	3-13	5-38	3-9	0-1	1-5	16.0	16.22
Henry Daly	17-79	3-8	5-29	2-6	0-4	2-14	0-0	1-4	4-14	21.5	22.36
Gary Moore	17-147	2-12	7-66	6-20	1-7	0-29	0-3	0-0	1-10	11.6	-26.75
Dianne Sayer	16-91	2-11	7-38	0-2	2-13	5-27	0-0	0-0	0-0	17.6	17.33
Oliver Sherwood	16-104	4-12	2-23	3-16	1-10	3-20	0-2	0-2	3-19	15.4	-25.09
John Ferguson	15-48	7-12	2-13	3-12	0-3	0-3	0-0	0-1	3-4	31.3	12.02
Charlie Mann	14-54	3-8	3-12	2-7	1-4	4-19	0-2	0-0	1-2	25.9	23.36
Chris Gordon	14-88	0-2	8-45	1-8	1-3	4-23	0-0	0-3	0-4	15.9	32.50
Nicky Richards	14-76	2-14	5-23	2-7	2-11	2-14	0-0	1-2	0-5	18.4	-15.66
Seamus Mullins	14-164	2-17	5-56	2-25	0-8	3-38	0-1	0-0	2-19	8.5	-51.99
David Dennis	13-99	2-13	6-34	1-18	0-8	4-20	0-0	0-0	0-6	13.1	-5.80
Jeremy Scott	13-87	1-7	4-34	2-6	2-4	4-24	0-0	0-2	0-10	14.9	-6.59
Jamie Snowden	12-78	1-10	4-22	3-16	2-11	1-9	0-1	0-0	1-9	15.4	2.12
Ben Case	12-69	2-8	4-24	2-9	0-7	1-10	0-2	0-0	3-9	17.4	21.23
Johnny Farrelly	11-70	1-14	6-33	0-3	2-7	2-8	0-1	0-0	0-4	15.7	-11.55
Malcolm Jefferson	11-76	0-7	1-14	0-5	2-9	2-17	0-0	0-0	6-24	14.5	-29.58
Martin Todhunter	10-66	2-10	3-22	1-3	0-6	3-19	1-1	0-0	0-5	15.2	-5.58
Rebecca Curtis	10-51	0-10	2-8	3-6	3-4	1-9	0-4	0-0	1-10	19.6	-17.62
Micky Hammond	10-87	1-8	6-35	0-3	0-8	3-31	0-0	0-0	0-2	11.5	-28.00
Chris Down	9-65	2-6	7-46	0-4	0-0	0-4	0-0	0-0	0-5	13.8	3.00
Brian Ellison	9-73	0-13	5-32	0-8	0-2	3-14	1-2	0-0	0-2	12.3	-1.50
Ian Williams	9-92	3-20	3-34	2-8	0-5	0-18	0-0	0-0	1-7	9.8	-2.75
Sophie Leech	9-76	2-6	1-29	1-3	2-4	1-26	1-1	1-4	0-3	11.8	-15.50
Graeme McPherson	9-81	1-13	3-34	1-5	2-6	1-14	0-1	0-0	1-8	11.1	-17.83
Paul Webber	9-90	1-15	2-15	1-18	0-7	5-21	0-4	0-0	0-10	10.0	-35.75
Neil King	9-100	0-12	7-45	0-10	0-5	2-26	0-0	0-0	0-2	9.0	-46.63
Martin Keighley	9-96	2-12	3-34	1-11	1-7	2-21	0-1	0-0	0-10	9.4	-55.28
Mark Walford	8-42	1-5	3-18	1-3	0-3	3-10	0-1	0-0	0-2	19.0	4.25
Alan Hill	8-24	0-0	0-0	0-0	0-0	0-0	0-0	8-24	0-0	33.3	11.91
David Bridgwater	8-75	3-18	0-8	1-11	0-11	4-22	0-2	0-0	0-3	10.7	-2.25
Keith Reveley	8-36	0-2	2-8	0-2	0-3	4-17	1-1	0-0	1-3	22.2	-4.73
Rose Dobbin	8-60	0-14	1-15	0-0	3-8	3-20	0-0	0-0	1-3	13.3	-16.50
Anthony Honeyball	8-77	0-7	0-26	3-16	0-2	2-12	0-1	0-0	3-13	10.4	-25.33
James Ewart	8-72	0-6	4-39	0-6	0-3	3-13	1-4	0-0	0-1	11.1	-28.50
Emma Lavelle	8-71	1-11	1-18	1-6	0-2	4-28	0-0	0-0	1-6	11.3	-31.88
Venetia Williams	8-88	2-7	0-20	3-6	1-13	0-37	1-1	0-0	1-4	9.1	-53.58
Iain Jardine	7-32	0-6	0-7	2-5	2-6	2-4	0-1	0-0	1-3	21.9	3.50
Bernard Llewellyn	7-37	0-5	6-22	0-4	0-0	1-4	0-0	0-0	0-2	18.9	23.75
Joanne Foster	7-38	0-2	1-8	0-3	1-3	4-21	1-1	0-0	0-0	18.4	44.25
Richard Woollacott	7-80	0-10	5-38	0-6	1-8	1-16	0-0	0-1	0-1	8.8	-1.00

200 TRAINERS JUMPS STATISTICS

JUNE

	Total W-R	Nov Hdle	H'cap Hdle	Other Hdle	Nov Chase	H'cap Chase	Other Chase	Hunter Chase	N.H. Flat	Per cent	£1 Level stake
Jonjo O'Neill	42-223	4-17	14-86	4-15	8-25	9-72	0-2	0-0	3-6	18.8	6.35
Peter Bowen	40-155	3-15	12-50	0-5	3-11	16-58	1-1	0-0	5-15	25.8	18.68
Nicky Henderson	29-87	8-12	3-21	8-18	4-7	0-9	1-2	0-0	5-18	33.3	11.20
Paul Nicholls	26-77	8-15	2-9	1-10	10-18	5-21	0-2	0-2	0-0	33.8	18.47
Dan Skelton	22-104	6-20	6-31	3-17	3-10	3-18	1-2	0-0	0-6	21.2	-38.97
Neil Mulholland	20-123	1-20	10-49	0-6	3-10	4-29	0-0	0-0	2-9	16.3	-2.22
Charlie Longsdon	19-70	2-6	6-19	1-6	3-10	7-24	0-1	0-0	0-4	27.1	35.01
Dr Richard Newland	19-69	1-8	6-33	8-14	3-7	1-6	0-1	0-0	0-0	27.5	-12.13
David Pipe	19-142	2-10	3-66	3-9	3-12	5-31	0-0	0-0	3-14	13.4	-51.52
John Ferguson	16-65	3-8	7-25	3-16	0-2	0-5	0-1	0-0	3-8	24.6	-9.86
Tim Vaughan	16-142	5-22	1-51	3-19	2-14	4-29	1-2	0-0	0-5	11.3	-55.83
Philip Hobbs	15-78	1-8	2-17	0-10	0-8	8-28	1-1	0-0	3-6	19.2	-1.02
Tom George	14-62	2-9	1-10	3-9	4-8	3-24	1-1	0-0	0-1	22.6	-19.22
Fergal O'Brien	14-92	3-11	2-29	2-7	2-10	4-23	0-1	0-0	1-11	15.2	-22.65
Lucinda Russell	13-84	2-10	2-32	0-5	2-6	5-26	1-1	0-0	1-4	15.5	20.21
Warren Greatrex	13-58	0-11	5-17	2-9	0-3	2-9	0-1	0-0	4-8	22.4	-5.30
Nigel Twiston-Davies	12-86	1-7	4-29	3-8	1-5	2-25	0-0	0-0	1-12	14.0	-22.64
Brian Ellison	11-55	0-5	3-11	4-19	2-5	1-13	0-1	0-0	1-1	20.0	-15.70
Evan Williams	11-125	5-15	3-40	1-7	0-18	2-42	0-2	0-0	0-1	8.8	-39.75
Donald McCain	11-162	3-21	1-52	3-34	1-12	3-28	0-3	0-0	0-12	6.8	-91.08
Maurice Barnes	10-64	1-6	2-13	0-6	2-10	5-26	0-0	0-0	0-3	15.6	3.12
Jennie Candlish	10-53	0-9	2-15	2-6	1-7	5-13	0-1	0-0	0-2	18.9	11.13
Kim Bailey	10-38	4-5	1-11	0-3	2-11	3-5	0-1	0-0	0-2	26.3	-7.84
David Bridgwater	10-71	1-7	1-9	2-15	1-10	5-29	0-0	0-0	0-1	14.1	-12.87
Seamus Mullins	9-68	0-9	3-16	3-11	0-5	2-18	0-1	0-0	1-8	13.2	23.37
Mark Walford	9-34	0-2	4-17	1-2	0-1	4-10	0-0	0-0	0-2	26.5	25.75
David Dennis	9-60	1-9	1-24	2-9	1-1	4-14	0-0	0-0	0-3	15.0	-8.00
Ian Williams	9-63	1-9	6-31	1-6	1-5	0-10	0-0	0-0	0-2	14.3	-15.00
Alan King	9-52	3-10	0-15	4-8	2-4	0-14	0-0	0-0	0-1	17.3	-21.91
Graeme McPherson	8-49	3-10	2-14	0-3	1-6	2-16	0-0	0-0	0-0	16.3	5.65
Anthony Honeyball	8-37	1-5	4-12	0-6	1-2	0-6	0-0	0-0	2-6	21.6	9.82
Dianne Sayer	8-55	0-7	8-30	0-1	0-1	0-16	0-0	0-0	0-0	14.5	12.12
Rebecca Curtis	8-23	1-5	2-7	0-2	0-1	4-7	0-0	0-0	1-1	34.8	42.75
Micky Hammond	8-55	3-9	3-17	0-2	1-4	1-21	0-0	0-0	0-2	14.5	-30.13
Jim Best	7-30	1-6	3-9	3-10	0-1	0-1	0-1	0-0	0-2	23.3	-10.50
Caroline Bailey	6-33	0-7	3-5	0-2	0-3	3-15	0-0	0-0	0-1	18.2	10.50
James Ewart	6-34	0-5	3-16	1-3	0-0	2-10	0-0	0-0	0-0	17.6	11.25
Phil Middleton	6-24	0-0	1-11	0-2	0-2	5-8	0-0	0-0	0-1	25.0	14.66
Dai Burchell	6-44	1-12	0-13	0-1	0-2	5-14	0-1	0-0	0-1	13.6	-4.75
Paul Henderson	6-50	0-4	1-16	0-0	1-6	4-20	0-0	0-0	0-4	12.0	-7.25
Martin Todhunter	6-54	0-6	2-18	1-3	0-3	3-21	0-0	0-0	0-3	11.1	-12.00
Malcolm Jefferson	6-40	0-4	1-6	0-4	0-5	2-6	0-0	0-0	3-15	15.0	-12.38
Jeremy Scott	6-49	0-4	2-13	0-5	2-7	2-20	0-0	0-0	0-0	12.2	-13.18
Sue Smith	6-52	0-6	3-10	1-10	0-5	1-17	0-0	0-0	1-4	11.5	-22.75
Tony Carroll	5-42	0-5	2-14	1-9	1-4	1-7	0-1	0-0	0-2	11.9	3.22
Alistair Whillans	5-41	2-7	1-14	1-2	0-3	1-8	0-1	0-0	0-6	12.2	5.00
James Moffatt	5-38	0-4	3-22	0-2	0-0	1-8	1-2	0-0	0-0	13.2	5.75
John Flint	5-24	0-2	5-16	0-2	0-1	0-2	0-0	0-0	0-1	20.8	17.75
Neil King	5-43	2-12	0-10	1-11	0-1	1-7	1-1	0-0	0-1	11.6	31.25
Oliver Sherwood	5-26	0-3	0-1	0-1	2-3	1-8	1-1	0-0	1-9	19.2	-4.25
Chris Gordon	5-36	0-3	3-15	0-0	0-4	2-12	0-0	0-0	0-2	13.9	-13.75
Nigel Hawke	5-36	2-8	1-7	0-6	1-1	1-13	0-1	0-0	0-0	13.9	-13.97
Johnny Farrelly	5-44	0-3	2-25	2-5	0-3	1-6	0-0	0-0	0-2	11.4	-18.09
Charlie Mann	4-20	0-4	1-6	0-1	1-2	1-5	0-0	0-0	1-2	20.0	0.98
Richard Ford	4-22	1-3	1-8	1-3	0-2	1-6	0-0	0-0	0-0	18.2	1.33
Michael Scudamore	4-30	0-1	1-11	0-3	1-1	1-10	0-0	0-0	1-4	13.3	4.08
Rosemary Gasson	4-13	0-1	2-4	0-3	1-1	1-4	0-0	0-0	0-0	30.8	29.50
Laura Mongan	4-21	0-4	2-11	0-1	0-0	1-3	0-0	0-0	1-2	19.0	53.00
Stuart Coltherd	4-26	0-3	2-8	1-4	0-3	1-7	0-0	0-1	0-0	15.4	-1.00
Seamus Durack	4-13	1-2	0-4	1-3	0-0	0-0	0-0	0-0	2-4	30.8	-1.64
Ben Pauling	4-24	0-2	3-12	0-1	0-4	0-0	0-1	0-0	1-4	16.7	-3.50

JULY

	Total W-R	Nov Hdle	H'cap Hdle	Other Hdle	Nov Chase	H'cap Chase	Other Chase	Hunter Chase	N.H. Flat	Per cent	£1 Level stake
Jonjo O'Neill	43-236	7-24	16-99	3-13	3-17	12-74	1-6	0-0	1-5	18.2	-53.48
Donald McCain	33-178	10-28	6-52	3-28	3-15	6-32	3-11	0-0	2-12	18.5	-28.40
John Ferguson	30-74	5-13	8-26	11-24	1-2	0-4	1-1	0-0	6-8	40.5	15.48
Dr Richard Newland	29-99	11-18	10-37	3-25	3-7	3-16	0-1	0-0	0-0	29.3	3.75
Peter Bowen	26-145	2-7	6-43	1-12	1-6	10-55	1-4	0-0	5-21	17.9	-39.17
Dan Skelton	24-115	5-19	8-39	3-19	4-11	5-27	0-2	0-0	0-2	20.9	-23.94
Evan Williams	23-121	4-8	8-37	4-19	3-11	5-46	0-2	0-0	0-2	19.0	17.23
Tim Vaughan	22-152	5-24	3-50	5-25	2-9	6-35	0-2	0-0	1-7	14.5	-38.00
Neil Mulholland	19-136	5-29	3-33	6-26	0-10	3-34	1-1	0-0	1-4	14.0	-61.54
David Bridgwater	15-92	2-20	0-5	5-20	1-13	7-29	0-3	0-0	0-3	16.3	-17.21
Charlie Longsdon	14-65	0-1	5-20	3-7	3-6	2-28	1-3	0-0	0-1	21.5	3.98
Jeremy Scott	13-58	0-5	3-19	1-3	1-6	8-22	0-2	0-0	0-1	22.4	17.62
Lisa Harrison	13-74	0-5	10-38	0-3	0-5	3-17	0-0	0-0	0-6	17.6	26.25
David Pipe	13-117	2-11	4-60	0-11	2-9	2-23	3-4	0-0	0-4	11.1	-62.76
Alan King	11-51	2-6	6-20	1-11	0-6	1-9	0-0	0-0	1-1	21.6	2.82
Paul Nicholls	11-53	1-2	0-7	2-7	4-14	2-17	1-6	0-0	1-1	20.8	-9.13
Fergal O'Brien	11-98	2-11	1-22	0-16	1-10	5-25	0-3	0-0	2-12	11.2	-24.02
Martin Keighley	10-64	1-8	1-23	2-11	1-2	3-14	0-0	0-0	2-6	15.6	4.75
Warren Greatrex	10-42	3-6	4-14	1-8	0-3	0-4	0-0	0-0	2-7	23.8	-0.78
Nicky Henderson	10-55	2-6	1-21	6-11	1-9	0-7	0-1	0-0	0-2	18.2	-24.85
Philip Hobbs	10-75	0-2	1-20	2-20	2-5	4-23	0-3	0-0	1-2	13.3	-28.27
Nicky Richards	9-40	1-2	5-24	0-2	1-2	2-9	0-0	0-0	0-1	22.5	22.46
Martin Hill	9-45	1-2	5-26	0-4	1-1	1-11	0-0	0-0	1-2	20.0	33.38
Graeme McPherson	9-45	3-9	2-22	0-3	0-4	4-6	0-0	0-0	0-1	20.0	47.08
Neil King	8-41	2-7	1-10	3-15	0-1	1-7	0-0	0-0	1-3	19.5	4.93
Malcolm Jefferson	8-21	0-0	2-4	1-4	1-2	1-5	2-2	0-0	1-4	38.1	22.38
Olly Murphy	8-15	4-5	2-7	1-1	1-2	0-0	0-0	0-0	0-0	53.3	27.53
Robert Stephens	8-53	1-7	3-20	1-14	0-2	0-3	0-1	0-0	3-6	15.1	39.38
Nigel Twiston-Davies	8-59	0-8	2-20	2-10	0-6	4-15	0-1	0-0	0-1	13.6	-11.34
Lucinda Russell	8-103	0-12	5-42	1-11	1-7	1-28	0-0	0-0	0-3	7.8	-52.67
Emma Lavelle	7-23	0-2	1-6	2-3	0-0	4-10	0-1	0-0	0-1	30.4	28.95
Johnny Farrelly	7-55	2-8	1-29	0-1	1-4	2-11	0-0	0-0	1-2	12.7	-9.13
Jim Best	6-30	0-1	1-15	3-8	0-0	0-1	1-2	0-0	1-3	20.0	0.54
James Moffatt	6-47	0-2	1-23	4-7	0-0	1-13	0-2	0-0	0-0	12.8	1.00
Jennie Candlish	6-56	1-11	4-17	1-7	0-5	0-14	0-2	0-0	0-1	10.7	1.41
Nigel Hawke	6-37	1-6	1-13	0-7	0-2	4-9	0-1	0-0	0-0	16.2	7.50
Lawney Hill	6-36	1-5	0-9	1-4	2-4	2-14	0-0	0-0	0-0	16.7	8.23
Michael Blake	6-27	0-2	3-15	2-5	0-0	0-5	0-0	0-0	1-1	22.2	24.44
Sophie Leech	6-58	0-2	4-26	1-8	0-0	1-18	0-2	0-0	0-2	10.3	-7.33
Tom George	6-32	1-6	0-4	2-3	1-3	2-16	0-0	0-0	0-0	18.8	-12.68
Seamus Mullins	6-57	0-7	3-17	0-12	0-4	1-11	0-0	0-0	2-6	10.5	-18.50
Brian Ellison	6-53	0-3	2-22	2-18	0-0	1-11	0-0	0-0	1-1	11.3	-24.31
Jimmy Frost	5-39	2-8	2-15	0-5	0-1	1-7	0-2	0-0	0-1	12.8	2.00
Rebecca Curtis	5-17	1-3	0-3	0-2	4-5	0-4	0-0	0-0	0-0	29.4	-0.93
Philip Kirby	5-48	1-6	3-31	0-6	0-2	0-0	0-0	0-0	1-3	10.4	6.55
Mike Sowersby	5-53	0-9	4-26	0-1	0-3	1-11	0-1	0-0	0-2	9.4	25.00
Alexandra Dunn	5-47	0-6	1-15	0-3	0-3	4-16	0-0	0-0	0-4	10.6	35.20
John Quinn	5-12	1-3	2-5	1-3	1-1	0-0	0-0	0-0	0-0	41.7	47.38
Martin Todhunter	5-24	0-1	2-13	1-3	0-0	2-7	0-0	0-0	0-0	20.8	-2.50
David Dennis	5-56	0-6	1-23	2-9	0-8	1-11	1-1	0-0	0-0	8.9	-16.53
Dianne Sayer	5-63	0-3	2-35	0-2	0-1	3-22	0-0	0-0	0-0	7.9	-33.50
Lucy Normile	4-37	0-3	2-17	0-7	0-3	2-7	0-0	0-0	0-0	10.8	-0.00
Debra Hamer	4-27	1-4	3-10	0-2	0-2	0-5	0-0	0-0	0-4	14.8	0.50
Barry Brennan	4-20	0-1	1-8	1-4	0-1	2-6	0-0	0-0	0-0	20.0	3.75
Bernard Llewellyn	4-28	1-5	2-16	0-1	0-1	0-1	1-2	0-0	0-2	14.3	4.50
George Baker	4-9	0-0	0-3	4-6	0-0	0-0	0-0	0-0	0-0	44.4	4.73
Richard Ford	4-24	0-5	2-7	1-1	0-3	1-7	0-1	0-0	0-0	16.7	6.00
Kim Bailey	4-26	0-2	3-11	0-0	0-3	1-7	0-1	0-0	0-2	15.4	-0.75
Mark Walford	4-21	0-1	1-12	0-3	0-3	3-5	0-0	0-0	0-0	19.0	-2.17
Anthony Honeyball	4-29	0-3	3-14	1-4	0-1	0-4	0-0	0-0	0-3	13.8	-8.75
Rose Dobbin	4-27	1-4	1-10	0-1	0-4	2-8	0-0	0-0	0-0	14.8	-11.88

202 TRAINERS JUMPS STATISTICS

AUGUST

	Total W-R	Nov Hdle	H'cap Hdle	Other Hdle	Nov Chase	H'cap Chase	Other Chase	Hunter Chase	N.H. Flat	Per cent	£1 Level stake
Jonjo O'Neill	40-157	7-18	15-59	1-9	3-12	14-59	0-0	0-0	0-0	25.5	-6.77
Donald McCain	29-144	9-34	9-49	2-14	2-14	4-21	1-4	0-0	2-8	20.1	31.82
Neil Mulholland	26-108	2-12	12-43	2-8	2-11	7-29	1-4	0-0	0-1	24.1	14.48
Dan Skelton	21-81	2-13	5-17	2-11	5-10	7-26	0-0	0-0	0-4	25.9	-12.43
Peter Bowen	20-98	1-7	6-35	0-4	2-5	10-39	0-1	0-0	1-7	20.4	-8.42
David Pipe	20-123	3-13	6-55	3-15	2-9	5-24	0-1	0-0	1-6	16.3	-18.18
John Ferguson	17-49	5-16	4-12	6-14	1-3	0-1	0-0	0-0	1-3	34.7	-5.02
Tim Vaughan	17-137	6-24	5-44	2-25	1-9	2-26	0-2	0-0	1-7	12.4	-56.65
Philip Hobbs	15-65	1-6	5-18	3-8	2-6	4-25	0-0	0-0	0-2	23.1	12.54
Alan King	14-36	3-6	1-6	2-9	1-1	7-12	0-0	0-0	0-2	38.9	27.60
Nigel Twiston-Davies	14-59	0-4	3-13	4-9	1-3	3-21	3-6	0-0	0-3	23.7	-3.42
Fergal O'Brien	14-72	4-17	4-20	0-7	2-7	4-18	0-1	0-0	0-2	19.4	-10.62
Evan Williams	13-115	0-8	4-29	1-18	2-7	5-47	0-3	0-0	1-3	11.3	-32.25
Jim Best	11-26	1-3	6-10	2-7	0-0	2-4	0-0	0-0	0-2	42.3	3.98
Gary Moore	11-39	1-4	7-21	2-6	0-0	0-6	0-0	0-0	1-2	28.2	37.40
Philip Kirby	11-34	5-8	4-17	0-3	0-0	0-1	0-0	0-0	2-5	32.4	44.93
Dr Richard Newland	11-59	5-10	0-20	4-14	2-5	0-9	0-1	0-0	0-0	18.6	-34.49
Brian Ellison	10-46	5-13	2-19	3-7	0-3	0-3	0-1	0-0	0-0	21.7	-6.72
Warren Greatrex	9-33	1-6	2-10	2-4	1-4	0-3	0-1	0-0	3-5	27.3	-5.69
Ian Williams	8-35	1-3	3-17	0-3	1-2	2-7	1-2	0-0	0-1	22.9	3.66
Seamus Mullins	8-27	0-1	4-10	0-6	3-3	0-3	0-0	0-0	1-4	29.6	22.88
Kim Bailey	7-20	0-1	0-4	2-2	1-3	4-9	0-0	0-0	0-1	35.0	3.71
John Quinn	4-19	1-5	2-7	1-5	0-0	0-0	0-0	0-0	0-2	21.1	-3.12
Charlie Mann	7-21	1-4	1-4	1-3	1-3	3-7	0-0	0-0	0-0	33.3	20.35
Jamie Snowden	7-35	2-7	0-8	1-4	2-7	2-8	0-0	0-0	0-1	20.0	25.00
Seamus Durack	7-11	1-1	0-1	2-3	0-0	0-0	0-0	0-0	4-6	63.6	33.86
Lucinda Russell	7-48	2-12	1-16	0-1	1-3	2-13	1-1	0-0	0-2	14.6	-4.67
Anthony Honeyball	7-28	0-2	4-11	1-4	0-3	2-4	0-2	0-0	0-2	25.0	-8.17
Paul Nicholls	7-35	2-3	0-3	1-2	3-12	0-13	1-2	0-0	0-0	20.0	-20.40
Dianne Sayer	6-42	0-4	0-19	0-2	0-0	6-17	0-0	0-0	0-0	14.3	7.00
Charlie Longsdon	6-34	0-2	3-12	1-5	1-4	1-11	0-0	0-0	0-0	17.6	-6.52
Jeremy Scott	6-37	0-1	3-15	0-0	0-3	3-18	0-0	0-0	0-0	16.2	-7.25
Nicky Henderson	6-27	1-3	3-12	0-3	2-5	0-3	0-0	0-0	0-1	22.2	-7.78
David Dennis	6-53	1-6	0-16	4-11	1-6	0-14	0-0	0-0	0-0	11.3	-20.03
David Bridgwater	6-49	2-8	0-5	2-7	2-7	0-16	0-0	0-0	0-6	12.2	-27.00
Don Cantillon	5-13	2-4	3-4	0-3	0-0	0-0	0-0	0-0	0-2	38.5	5.30
Martin Hill	5-21	0-0	2-10	1-3	0-1	2-6	0-0	0-0	0-1	23.8	10.60
Lawney Hill	5-38	0-6	2-9	0-2	0-5	3-14	0-0	0-0	0-2	13.2	13.21
Brendan Powell	5-35	0-5	0-7	1-6	1-5	2-8	1-1	0-0	0-3	14.3	16.25
Nicky Richards	5-31	1-4	1-20	1-1	0-0	1-3	0-0	0-0	1-3	16.1	-1.87
James Moffatt	5-48	2-11	3-21	0-1	0-1	0-12	0-1	0-0	0-1	10.4	-14.25
Joanne Foster	4-17	1-3	1-3	0-0	0-2	2-8	0-1	0-0	0-0	23.5	7.50
Tony Coyle	4-17	1-3	1-4	0-3	0-0	1-5	0-0	0-0	1-2	23.5	8.50
Iain Jardine	4-17	1-4	1-9	1-2	0-1	0-0	0-0	0-0	1-1	23.5	12.50
Ben Case	4-16	0-1	3-7	0-1	0-1	1-5	0-0	0-0	0-1	25.0	13.00
Olly Murphy	4-19	1-4	1-8	0-3	0-1	2-3	0-0	0-0	0-0	21.1	-7.56
Robert Stephens	4-32	1-5	1-11	1-7	0-1	0-2	0-2	0-0	1-4	12.5	13.50
Adrian Wintle	4-15	0-2	3-9	0-0	1-1	0-3	0-0	0-0	0-0	26.7	99.13
Graeme McPherson	4-25	0-3	2-12	1-3	0-1	0-5	1-1	0-0	0-0	16.0	-8.88
Harry Fry	4-22	0-1	1-11	1-3	1-1	1-6	0-0	0-0	0-0	18.2	-11.31
Jimmy Frost	4-30	0-2	2-14	0-4	0-3	2-6	0-0	0-0	0-1	13.3	-11.88
Neil King	4-38	0-5	2-18	0-7	0-0	0-4	1-1	0-0	1-3	10.5	-17.90
Alexandra Dunn	4-38	1-7	0-11	0-6	0-3	3-10	0-0	0-0	0-1	10.5	-19.00
Chris Down	3-20	1-2	1-14	0-1	0-1	1-2	0-0	0-0	0-0	15.0	1.50
J R Jenkins	3-18	0-1	2-12	0-1	0-2	0-0	0-0	0-0	1-2	16.7	6.83
Robin Dickin	3-10	1-3	0-0	0-3	1-1	1-2	0-0	0-0	0-0	30.0	15.50
Lucy Normile	3-16	1-5	0-5	0-0	1-3	1-3	0-0	0-0	0-0	18.8	30.50
Ben Haslam	3-14	0-0	1-7	1-1	1-3	0-3	0-0	0-0	0-0	21.4	-1.00
Debra Hamer	3-28	1-4	1-9	0-3	0-3	1-7	0-0	0-0	0-2	10.7	-1.80
George Baker	3-11	0-0	2-8	1-3	0-0	0-0	0-0	0-0	0-0	27.3	-2.15
Tom George	3-13	1-3	0-1	0-1	1-1	1-7	0-0	0-0	0-0	23.1	-2.70

SEPTEMBER

	Total W-R	Nov Hdle	H'cap Hdle	Other Hdle	Nov Chase	H'cap Chase	Other Chase	Hunter Chase	N.H. Flat	Per cent	£1 Level stake
Charlie Longsdon	33-93	4-15	6-23	5-10	3-9	11-24	1-2	0-0	3-10	35.5	40.98
Nigel Twiston-Davies	29-118	7-24	1-30	3-11	7-15	7-27	1-4	0-0	3-9	24.6	15.39
David Pipe	24-116	1-18	10-51	4-15	3-8	4-17	0-0	0-0	2-8	20.7	-0.25
Tim Vaughan	22-129	7-28	7-54	3-19	0-6	4-19	1-2	0-0	0-5	17.1	-26.99
Jonjo O'Neill	21-142	2-19	8-41	0-14	1-10	9-53	1-3	0-0	0-3	14.8	-17.40
Neil Mulholland	18-109	4-20	8-36	1-13	1-12	2-23	2-2	0-0	0-4	16.5	-18.06
Dr Richard Newland	17-57	3-7	4-23	6-15	0-2	5-15	1-2	0-0	0-0	29.8	12.80
Donald McCain	16-121	5-22	5-33	1-24	1-14	4-20	0-4	0-0	0-5	13.2	-49.36
John Ferguson	14-39	5-14	2-9	4-13	1-3	0-1	0-0	0-0	2-3	35.9	-11.75
Peter Bowen	14-110	0-5	5-35	0-10	2-6	5-40	0-2	0-0	2-13	12.7	-40.30
Fergal O'Brien	13-69	2-13	6-18	0-3	1-8	4-20	0-2	0-0	0-5	18.8	7.88
Philip Hobbs	13-74	4-9	2-25	1-5	1-6	2-21	3-5	0-0	0-4	17.6	-10.88
Dan Skelton	13-95	3-19	3-33	2-15	1-8	4-14	0-0	0-0	1-11	13.7	-35.55
Evan Williams	12-79	2-10	1-18	3-10	2-9	3-29	1-1	0-0	0-2	15.2	-42.61
Nicky Henderson	11-36	2-5	5-20	2-6	0-2	0-0	1-2	0-0	1-4	30.6	0.77
Kim Bailey	11-38	4-6	1-11	0-2	2-5	3-9	1-4	0-0	0-1	28.9	7.04
Brian Ellison	11-61	4-8	2-18	3-19	2-3	0-12	0-1	0-0	0-5	18.0	-24.04
Alan King	10-38	1-5	3-14	4-11	0-0	1-6	0-0	0-0	1-2	26.3	8.58
Dianne Sayer	10-54	2-9	6-20	0-5	0-3	2-15	0-0	0-0	0-2	18.5	11.00
Ian Williams	9-42	3-8	5-19	1-7	0-4	0-4	0-1	0-0	0-1	21.4	7.60
Paul Nicholls	9-23	2-4	0-2	1-3	5-8	0-3	1-1	0-0	0-2	39.1	-6.23
Lucinda Russell	9-127	4-31	3-38	0-9	0-8	2-33	0-1	0-0	0-7	7.1	-43.63
Gary Moore	8-43	1-7	2-18	4-10	0-2	1-5	0-0	0-0	0-1	18.6	4.41
Sophie Leech	7-47	3-14	3-17	1-3	0-3	0-11	0-0	0-0	0-0	14.9	9.60
Keith Dalgleish	7-15	1-2	2-5	1-4	1-1	0-0	0-0	0-0	2-3	46.7	10.04
Mike Sowersby	7-33	0-5	3-13	1-3	0-0	3-12	0-0	0-0	0-0	21.2	20.75
Chris Gordon	7-33	0-3	3-18	0-2	1-2	2-5	0-0	0-0	1-3	21.2	23.25
Sue Smith	7-26	2-2	2-11	0-2	0-3	2-7	0-0	0-0	1-1	26.9	28.08
Jamie Snowden	7-36	1-4	0-12	0-5	1-1	2-7	0-0	0-0	3-7	19.4	-2.00
Martin Keighley	7-57	1-9	2-20	0-8	1-3	2-10	1-2	0-0	0-5	12.3	-13.50
Lisa Harrison	7-53	0-5	2-19	0-0	1-3	4-22	0-0	0-0	0-4	13.2	-17.92
Jeremy Scott	6-40	0-3	2-10	0-5	1-4	3-18	0-0	0-0	0-0	15.0	0.88
Nigel Hawke	6-29	1-7	1-4	3-8	1-5	0-4	0-0	0-0	0-1	20.7	1.25
Ben Haslam	6-26	1-2	1-13	0-3	1-1	3-7	0-0	0-0	0-0	23.1	8.84
David Bridgwater	6-48	0-10	2-5	1-6	2-7	0-15	0-2	0-0	1-3	12.5	10.50
Emma Lavelle	6-42	0-5	3-11	1-1	1-4	1-13	0-4	0-0	0-4	14.3	16.08
Phil Middleton	6-27	0-2	5-20	1-2	0-1	1-3	0-0	0-0	0-0	22.2	22.13
Martin Todhunter	6-32	0-5	2-13	1-5	1-3	2-7	0-0	0-0	0-0	18.8	-0.50
Johnny Farrelly	6-38	0-5	5-25	0-1	0-0	1-6	0-0	0-0	0-1	15.8	-8.33
Malcolm Jefferson	6-52	2-11	1-11	0-3	1-4	2-11	0-0	0-0	0-12	11.5	-31.33
Paul Henderson	5-26	0-1	1-12	0-0	1-3	2-8	0-0	0-0	1-2	19.2	2.75
Anthony Honeyball	5-13	0-0	2-6	1-1	0-0	1-4	0-1	0-0	1-1	38.5	7.38
Tom George	5-16	2-2	0-2	0-0	0-1	3-9	0-1	0-0	0-1	31.3	7.70
Lawney Hill	5-35	0-1	1-13	0-2	0-4	4-14	0-0	0-0	0-1	14.3	-0.63
Rebecca Curtis	5-19	1-4	0-4	0-1	2-2	1-3	1-1	0-0	0-4	26.3	12.50
Rose Dobbin	5-27	0-3	0-9	0-1	2-3	3-11	0-0	0-0	0-0	18.5	-4.35
David Dennis	5-52	0-6	4-21	0-9	0-3	1-13	0-0	0-0	0-1	9.6	-28.00
Nick Williams	4-28	0-1	3-5	0-7	0-2	0-5	1-7	0-0	0-1	14.3	3.60
Alistair Whillans	4-19	0-2	2-10	1-1	0-1	1-4	0-0	0-0	0-1	21.1	6.75
Charlie Mann	4-22	2-6	0-3	0-4	0-1	2-7	0-1	0-0	0-0	18.2	13.33
Neil King	4-49	1-5	1-21	1-9	1-1	0-9	0-0	0-0	0-4	8.2	14.20
N W Alexander	4-18	0-4	3-8	0-2	0-0	1-3	0-0	0-0	0-1	22.2	16.75
Stuart Edmunds	4-19	0-2	1-7	3-8	0-1	0-1	0-0	0-0	1-4	21.1	-2.15
Jennie Candlish	4-20	0-3	0-6	0-4	1-1	3-5	0-0	0-0	0-1	20.0	-7.30
Micky Hammond	4-34	0-4	1-15	0-3	0-1	2-8	0-0	0-0	1-3	11.8	-8.50
Nicky Richards	4-25	0-4	3-13	0-2	0-0	1-6	0-0	0-0	0-1	16.0	-9.38
Sheena West	3-18	0-1	3-14	0-2	0-0	0-0	0-0	0-0	0-1	16.7	0.33
Tony Carroll	3-23	0-4	2-10	0-2	0-1	1-5	0-0	0-0	0-1	13.0	1.50
John Mackie	3-17	0-1	1-4	2-4	0-1	0-6	0-0	0-0	0-1	17.6	1.50
Kerry Lee	3-12	0-0	0-3	0-0	0-1	3-8	0-0	0-0	0-0	25.0	3.00
Jedd O'Keeffe	3-4	1-1	1-1	1-2	0-0	0-0	0-0	0-0	0-0	75.0	5.25

204 TRAINERS JUMPS STATISTICS

OCTOBER

	Total W-R	Nov Hdle	H'cap Hdle	Other Hdle	Nov Chase	H'cap Chase	Other Chase	Hunter Chase	N.H. Flat	Per cent	£1 Level stake
Paul Nicholls	83-282	22-56	4-43	15-45	14-46	12-53	12-25	0-0	4-16	29.4	-19.81
Nigel Twiston-Davies	64-279	9-35	12-54	9-34	10-44	19-79	0-9	0-0	5-24	22.9	69.78
Charlie Longsdon	63-294	13-40	14-67	9-36	6-43	11-64	4-6	0-0	6-39	21.4	-56.70
Philip Hobbs	58-314	12-51	13-70	11-49	4-29	11-79	2-13	0-0	6-24	18.5	-70.28
Jonjo O'Neill	53-355	10-64	12-95	7-38	7-38	12-92	1-5	0-0	4-23	14.9	-118.40
Dan Skelton	51-284	13-52	11-79	7-42	10-28	6-50	2-9	0-0	2-26	18.0	-70.29
Alan King	43-199	6-33	7-51	16-46	6-22	4-26	2-3	0-0	2-18	21.6	-38.05
Neil Mulholland	40-217	4-31	12-57	5-33	6-23	11-49	1-6	0-0	1-18	18.4	-26.85
Tim Vaughan	34-270	5-45	16-97	4-31	3-27	5-44	0-3	0-0	1-23	12.6	-44.90
Evan Williams	33-159	5-26	12-46	3-21	5-24	5-37	1-2	0-0	2-5	20.8	71.07
Brian Ellison	30-142	3-19	13-42	4-20	2-22	2-23	2-4	0-0	4-12	21.1	-24.63
Colin Tizzard	30-235	4-39	5-38	8-23	2-31	7-72	3-12	0-0	1-20	12.8	-95.09
Nicky Henderson	28-136	4-18	10-49	8-24	2-16	0-11	1-5	0-0	3-14	20.6	-22.48
Donald McCain	27-264	5-44	9-71	6-36	4-42	2-47	0-5	0-0	1-19	10.2	-117.86
Emma Lavelle	25-129	2-18	5-28	5-13	6-16	6-42	1-3	0-0	0-9	19.4	4.58
David Pipe	25-189	2-14	5-74	6-25	5-16	6-39	0-5	0-0	1-17	13.2	-79.53
Lucinda Russell	25-224	0-28	4-56	3-25	7-27	10-69	0-1	0-0	1-18	11.2	-92.70
Rebecca Curtis	24-146	3-18	5-21	1-23	4-21	2-24	3-10	0-0	6-29	16.4	1.50
Kim Bailey	24-157	8-34	4-33	5-25	3-20	2-34	1-2	0-0	1-9	15.3	-33.30
Gary Moore	23-150	2-17	4-46	7-25	5-30	5-23	0-3	0-0	0-6	15.3	-16.37
Fergal O'Brien	22-155	2-25	6-30	3-21	3-13	3-39	0-0	0-0	5-27	14.2	7.77
John Ferguson	21-62	11-23	3-17	5-8	2-6	0-1	0-0	0-0	1-8	33.9	-6.03
Harry Fry	21-98	3-19	7-24	2-10	4-8	1-10	1-7	0-0	3-22	21.4	-14.34
Tom George	19-135	1-12	2-16	1-12	5-18	6-59	0-2	0-0	4-16	14.1	14.38
Nicky Richards	18-91	3-13	4-32	3-18	1-6	4-14	1-3	0-0	2-5	19.8	-5.56
Peter Bowen	17-149	2-16	2-41	3-15	0-16	9-38	1-2	0-0	0-21	11.4	-32.61
Martin Keighley	15-101	2-15	5-29	1-11	1-6	3-23	1-3	0-0	2-14	14.9	43.16
Rose Dobbin	14-106	3-15	2-29	2-13	2-7	3-29	1-1	0-0	1-12	13.2	30.75
Dr Richard Newland	14-73	0-5	6-36	2-5	0-4	6-23	0-0	0-0	0-0	19.2	-15.17
Malcolm Jefferson	14-85	2-15	0-12	3-10	3-10	2-19	1-2	0-0	3-17	16.5	-24.41
Warren Greatrex	13-66	1-10	1-16	3-15	1-5	2-3	0-1	0-0	5-16	19.7	-16.38
Neil King	13-80	1-4	8-30	1-15	2-7	1-18	0-0	0-0	0-6	16.3	-21.15
Maurice Barnes	12-94	0-11	3-24	1-15	2-10	6-29	0-2	0-0	0-3	12.8	3.00
James Ewart	12-47	2-7	5-20	0-4	0-6	5-6	0-0	0-0	0-4	25.5	27.75
Anthony Honeyball	12-58	1-7	2-14	0-8	0-3	3-9	0-1	0-0	6-16	20.7	-0.89
Charlie Mann	12-68	0-10	4-14	3-12	3-9	2-20	0-2	0-0	0-1	17.6	-7.14
Jamie Snowden	12-101	1-23	1-18	1-19	2-9	5-19	0-1	0-0	2-12	11.9	-14.88
Harry Whittington	11-46	2-7	1-7	2-10	2-6	1-5	1-1	0-0	2-10	23.9	36.62
Keith Dalgleish	9-20	0-2	1-6	3-6	0-0	2-2	0-0	0-0	3-4	45.0	12.19
Sandy Thomson	9-46	1-8	1-7	1-8	1-8	4-10	1-1	0-0	0-4	19.6	-1.14
David Bridgwater	9-72	0-6	0-6	0-17	5-10	4-27	0-1	0-0	0-5	12.5	-14.40
Seamus Mullins	9-87	1-8	2-27	2-14	0-7	2-17	0-3	0-0	2-12	10.3	-18.09
Nick Williams	9-93	1-13	3-16	1-24	2-10	1-19	1-8	0-0	0-3	9.7	-21.53
Philip Kirby	9-89	2-14	3-38	1-17	0-1	2-5	0-1	0-0	1-13	10.1	-32.02
Sue Smith	9-177	2-29	1-45	0-9	2-27	4-54	0-6	0-0	0-7	5.1	-129.17
Graeme McPherson	8-70	0-6	6-31	1-10	1-8	0-6	0-1	0-0	0-8	11.4	4.63
Michael Scudamore	8-40	0-5	0-5	0-6	1-3	6-16	0-0	0-0	1-5	20.0	7.12
N W Alexander	8-84	0-13	3-26	2-12	0-4	3-19	0-2	0-0	0-8	9.5	7.75
Henry Daly	8-67	3-6	2-22	0-3	0-10	3-18	0-0	0-0	0-8	11.9	9.00
Johnny Farrelly	8-48	1-7	4-26	0-3	1-1	2-11	0-0	0-0	0-0	16.7	21.88
Lucy Wadham	8-29	1-3	0-3	0-2	0-3	5-13	0-1	0-0	2-4	27.6	70.42
Chris Grant	8-66	0-17	2-12	2-8	0-12	2-9	0-0	0-0	2-8	12.1	-0.12
Nigel Hawke	8-79	1-18	4-23	1-12	1-3	0-13	1-5	0-0	0-5	10.1	-27.15
Chris Gordon	8-88	1-10	2-32	2-12	1-6	2-19	0-0	0-0	0-9	9.1	-32.42
Ian Williams	8-85	1-8	3-30	2-21	2-7	0-11	0-1	0-0	0-7	9.4	-50.86
Jeremy Scott	8-102	0-12	2-36	0-13	2-8	4-27	0-0	0-0	0-6	7.8	-63.50
Henry Oliver	7-73	0-10	3-26	3-11	0-10	1-15	0-0	0-0	0-1	9.6	22.00
Tom Symonds	7-49	1-13	4-24	1-4	1-3	0-2	0-0	0-0	0-3	14.3	22.50
Dianne Sayer	7-70	1-7	3-29	0-11	3-9	0-12	0-0	0-0	0-2	10.0	-31.67
Iain Jardine	6-38	1-4	2-13	1-13	1-3	0-1	0-0	0-0	1-4	15.8	8.75
James Moffatt	6-41	1-3	4-19	0-5	0-3	1-8	0-1	0-0	0-2	14.6	17.25

NOVEMBER

	Total W-R	Nov Hdle	H'cap Hdle	Other Hdle	Nov Chase	H'cap Chase	Other Chase	Hunter Chase	N.H. Flat	Per cent	£1 Level stake
Paul Nicholls	111-471	17-68	12-86	16-75	36-90	12-90	14-51	0-0	4-24	23.6	-19.08
Nicky Henderson	89-368	15-63	12-87	31-86	11-35	2-40	11-29	0-0	10-38	24.2	-59.84
Philip Hobbs	79-403	12-69	18-93	15-70	8-41	15-99	7-19	0-0	6-23	19.6	-15.10
Dan Skelton	68-355	17-80	9-75	11-72	15-41	12-49	1-10	0-0	3-31	19.2	-45.28
Alan King	64-387	11-58	10-94	21-94	10-47	3-44	7-14	0-0	4-42	16.5	-135.67
Venetia Williams	57-332	8-46	8-67	2-32	8-28	28-147	1-6	0-0	2-8	17.2	23.34
Harry Fry	53-179	13-43	12-43	8-27	6-19	3-16	2-8	0-0	9-24	29.6	13.32
David Pipe	53-349	9-48	14-123	7-39	3-20	14-84	1-13	0-0	6-29	15.2	-33.18
Colin Tizzard	51-290	7-36	6-46	7-35	11-43	14-95	6-22	0-0	0-17	17.6	-4.12
Nigel Twiston-Davies	47-362	10-57	6-73	7-38	8-43	11-118	2-10	0-0	3-24	13.0	-145.91
Evan Williams	45-295	11-44	8-78	7-43	7-32	9-74	1-6	0-0	2-21	15.3	-56.14
Warren Greatrex	43-178	9-36	7-39	13-38	3-22	3-11	0-0	0-0	8-34	24.2	-23.88
Lucinda Russell	42-302	3-36	9-72	2-41	13-41	13-93	0-3	0-0	2-16	13.9	-84.79
Donald McCain	41-286	10-55	7-67	8-45	1-26	8-57	2-3	0-0	5-33	14.3	-27.06
Neil Mulholland	41-269	7-55	14-72	2-30	6-33	10-55	0-3	0-0	2-22	15.2	-68.67
Fergal O'Brien	40-191	11-43	3-22	4-24	2-17	9-49	0-2	0-0	11-34	20.9	91.44
Jonjo O'Neill	40-416	8-80	12-105	3-55	7-41	6-106	1-10	0-0	3-24	9.6	-196.07
Kim Bailey	33-212	7-50	8-52	4-30	3-28	4-35	4-9	0-0	3-11	15.6	-10.09
Tom George	33-214	3-17	9-35	2-22	3-23	11-84	1-10	0-0	4-25	15.4	-51.81
Gary Moore	32-239	2-33	8-74	5-46	6-27	9-51	1-4	0-0	1-10	13.4	-39.16
Ben Pauling	31-133	10-34	5-25	5-18	5-17	1-12	0-3	0-0	5-25	23.3	59.96
Sue Smith	30-265	2-40	3-47	1-22	7-42	13-98	3-9	0-0	1-7	11.3	-128.07
Emma Lavelle	28-143	5-29	4-19	3-11	5-23	8-46	0-3	0-0	3-12	19.6	-4.40
Charlie Longsdon	26-291	3-48	3-67	3-46	1-32	11-70	0-6	0-0	5-26	8.9	-151.14
Nicky Richards	25-139	5-26	11-39	2-15	0-15	3-23	0-8	0-0	4-13	18.0	-15.11
Oliver Sherwood	25-160	2-30	0-24	5-25	5-19	8-36	3-7	0-0	2-21	15.6	-17.14
Brian Ellison	25-170	4-21	2-55	5-28	5-18	5-27	0-1	0-0	4-21	14.7	-30.70
Malcolm Jefferson	23-126	1-19	6-22	5-20	3-14	4-27	2-5	0-0	2-19	18.3	-32.60
Anthony Honeyball	22-129	2-19	8-33	1-11	3-15	3-22	1-3	0-0	4-26	17.1	-20.29
Henry Daly	21-125	2-15	6-28	1-20	6-21	5-26	0-4	0-0	1-13	16.8	-32.76
Micky Hammond	18-163	2-28	6-51	2-14	0-12	8-46	0-4	0-0	0-8	11.0	6.80
James Ewart	18-115	2-17	5-31	1-10	2-14	7-29	0-0	0-0	1-14	15.7	-1.93
Neil King	18-107	3-12	2-31	5-16	1-9	4-24	1-3	0-0	2-12	16.8	-23.27
Rebecca Curtis	18-163	7-25	0-13	3-29	4-32	2-30	1-5	0-0	1-29	11.0	-90.71
Tim Vaughan	18-229	3-39	7-78	0-37	3-18	4-44	0-2	0-0	1-13	7.9	-105.82
Harry Whittington	17-70	4-10	3-13	4-19	3-5	3-15	0-0	0-0	0-9	24.3	4.00
Ian Williams	17-144	2-14	9-50	3-37	0-14	1-22	0-1	0-0	2-7	11.8	-29.84
Henry Oliver	15-80	1-8	5-19	0-11	4-13	5-25	0-0	0-0	0-4	18.8	46.25
John Ferguson	15-86	8-23	3-26	1-16	0-6	0-2	1-3	0-0	3-11	17.4	-14.45
David Dennis	15-103	4-22	2-22	1-14	1-5	5-26	2-3	0-0	0-11	14.6	-22.41
Kerry Lee	14-73	2-6	3-16	0-8	3-9	6-28	0-4	0-0	0-2	19.2	-2.07
Jamie Snowden	14-102	6-26	3-11	3-21	0-14	2-16	0-1	0-0	0-13	13.7	-56.23
Nick Williams	13-114	1-7	4-25	5-41	0-11	1-19	2-10	0-0	0-4	11.4	-11.79
Jeremy Scott	13-132	0-20	10-50	0-14	0-9	3-30	0-1	0-0	0-8	9.8	-25.37
Martin Keighley	13-117	1-15	3-29	1-16	2-14	4-27	0-4	0-0	2-12	11.1	-34.08
Dr Richard Newland	13-78	1-7	3-32	1-15	1-6	7-19	0-2	0-0	0-1	16.7	-38.21
John Quinn	12-50	0-11	3-15	8-18	1-4	0-0	0-0	0-0	0-3	24.0	0.62
Alan Swinbank	12-42	3-14	2-11	1-3	1-1	3-6	0-0	0-0	2-7	28.6	13.90
Graeme McPherson	12-95	1-11	6-47	0-4	2-9	3-14	0-0	0-0	0-11	12.6	38.85
Peter Bowen	12-145	1-16	3-40	1-17	1-13	5-44	1-2	0-0	1-15	8.3	-68.88
Tom Lacey	11-52	0-12	5-15	3-8	0-4	0-1	0-1	0-0	3-11	21.2	35.63
Tom Symonds	11-101	0-11	8-36	2-21	0-8	1-12	0-3	0-0	0-10	10.9	-38.25
N W Alexander	11-121	1-12	5-37	1-19	1-13	2-28	0-1	0-0	1-11	9.1	-48.92
Keith Reveley	10-54	2-7	1-18	1-7	2-3	2-11	0-0	0-0	2-8	18.5	1.50
Stuart Edmunds	10-41	2-5	3-14	2-5	0-1	1-7	0-0	0-0	2-9	24.4	8.95
Sandy Thomson	10-52	1-7	0-10	2-9	3-7	4-13	0-3	0-0	0-3	19.2	24.30
Lucy Wadham	10-88	1-14	1-26	2-15	3-6	3-16	0-2	0-0	0-9	11.4	-33.32
Chris Grant	10-105	3-25	3-23	0-12	1-13	2-13	0-1	0-0	1-18	9.5	-49.45
Chris Gordon	10-122	0-12	5-48	1-16	1-9	3-26	0-0	0-0	0-11	8.2	-54.40
Philip Kirby	10-127	1-34	7-63	0-14	2-3	0-4	0-0	0-0	0-9	7.9	-59.67
Keith Dalgleish	9-34	2-4	1-8	2-12	0-1	1-2	0-0	0-0	3-7	26.5	-8.87

206 TRAINERS JUMPS STATISTICS

DECEMBER

	Total W-R	Nov Hdle	H'cap Hdle	Other Hdle	Nov Chase	H'cap Chase	Other Chase	Hunter Chase	N.H. Flat	Per cent	£1 Level stake
Nicky Henderson	103-373	19-81	13-68	36-88	17-54	4-36	10-31	0-0	6-23	27.6	-18.78
Paul Nicholls	80-440	11-66	4-59	13-72	24-84	12-99	15-51	0-0	1-16	18.2	-104.84
Philip Hobbs	60-329	11-52	13-70	9-45	3-44	13-77	4-15	0-0	7-28	18.2	0.25
Donald McCain	60-344	12-59	14-90	7-44	9-42	11-70	3-11	0-0	4-28	17.4	-35.12
Nigel Twiston-Davies	55-372	9-57	11-64	7-48	3-43	22-134	0-5	0-0	3-21	14.8	-64.18
Dan Skelton	55-330	12-77	11-75	9-75	9-36	8-44	1-4	0-0	5-22	16.7	-80.59
Alan King	53-295	15-60	6-72	20-69	2-27	5-34	0-8	0-0	5-28	18.0	-63.20
Venetia Williams	47-298	4-36	8-48	4-24	7-39	24-137	0-10	0-0	0-5	15.8	-42.33
David Pipe	42-307	3-38	11-95	9-55	6-25	9-74	1-7	0-0	3-15	13.7	-75.21
Evan Williams	37-260	3-33	9-66	5-25	5-34	10-75	0-3	0-0	5-25	14.2	-17.03
Sue Smith	37-244	2-29	8-50	3-13	10-46	11-88	2-4	0-0	1-14	15.2	-35.60
Gary Moore	35-230	5-44	9-53	5-45	9-31	3-41	4-10	0-0	0-8	15.2	-20.22
Warren Greatrex	34-175	9-36	9-44	4-31	4-16	2-18	1-5	0-0	5-25	19.4	6.83
Jonjo O'Neill	34-366	7-67	8-87	2-62	4-42	8-88	0-10	0-0	5-10	9.3	-134.09
Tom George	32-226	0-23	3-28	5-30	6-29	14-92	0-11	0-0	4-13	14.2	-52.25
Colin Tizzard	32-263	7-54	2-32	3-21	6-40	12-80	2-18	0-0	0-18	12.2	-59.33
Harry Fry	30-139	10-31	6-35	4-20	5-14	1-18	1-6	0-0	3-15	21.6	-25.60
Ben Pauling	27-134	5-28	5-28	4-20	4-9	8-32	0-1	0-0	3-18	20.1	52.23
Charlie Longsdon	26-225	7-39	4-45	2-30	7-37	4-58	2-8	0-0	0-10	11.6	-59.40
Nicky Richards	25-110	3-18	8-38	2-13	1-7	6-19	1-7	0-0	4-8	22.7	-4.95
Henry Daly	24-127	4-26	8-32	6-11	2-15	3-28	0-1	0-0	1-14	18.9	60.61
Lucinda Russell	24-204	3-29	6-60	1-11	5-23	7-70	0-1	0-0	2-10	11.8	-74.00
Nick Mullins	23-106	4-12	2-20	6-31	5-12	1-21	2-7	0-0	3-4	21.7	39.55
Fergal O'Brien	22-146	6-31	2-22	0-11	6-25	4-32	0-2	0-0	4-23	15.1	-33.90
Brian Ellison	21-133	4-20	4-45	5-19	1-15	3-20	1-5	0-0	3-9	15.8	-41.23
Malcolm Jefferson	20-105	5-20	3-26	2-8	2-6	3-26	1-4	0-0	4-16	19.0	-30.06
Ian Williams	20-135	4-31	4-35	1-26	3-16	8-23	0-0	0-0	0-5	14.8	-40.53
Neil Mulholland	20-198	4-49	5-40	1-17	4-28	6-44	0-1	0-0	0-19	10.1	-94.54
Anthony Honeyball	18-98	2-19	6-19	1-8	3-13	2-21	0-2	0-0	4-16	18.4	-0.42
John Ferguson	18-84	3-14	2-23	9-31	2-12	0-2	0-1	0-0	2-4	21.4	-28.42
Micky Hammond	18-197	2-28	4-65	1-16	0-19	10-54	0-3	0-0	1-12	9.1	-96.12
Seamus Mullins	17-145	3-30	4-43	2-14	2-17	6-28	0-1	0-0	0-12	11.7	89.50
Dr Richard Newland	17-78	3-9	4-23	2-11	3-12	5-23	0-0	0-0	0-2	21.8	-1.76
Emma Lavelle	17-122	6-23	4-17	0-14	2-14	4-37	0-2	0-0	1-15	13.9	-42.93
Oliver Sherwood	17-138	6-27	3-29	2-21	2-16	2-36	1-3	0-0	1-6	12.3	-58.19
Kim Bailey	17-195	3-45	3-33	3-31	2-21	5-42	0-6	0-0	1-18	8.7	-122.56
N W Alexander	16-124	5-22	3-32	0-7	3-21	5-33	0-0	0-0	0-9	12.9	-35.87
Rebecca Curtis	16-126	2-21	1-12	0-16	2-23	3-28	1-4	0-0	7-22	12.7	-59.75
David Dennis	15-101	1-13	2-24	2-19	5-13	5-22	0-1	0-0	0-9	14.9	-20.84
Rose Dobbin	14-93	4-24	4-25	0-3	0-11	5-23	0-0	0-0	1-7	15.1	-13.31
Graeme McPherson	13-104	1-21	7-41	0-9	2-11	3-15	0-0	0-0	0-8	12.5	21.43
Tom Lacey	13-49	3-15	6-17	2-9	1-2	1-1	0-0	0-0	0-5	26.5	21.95
Harry Whittington	13-56	3-12	3-13	3-13	2-5	1-7	0-1	0-0	1-5	23.2	46.56
Rebecca Menzies	13-70	1-8	2-19	1-4	3-7	6-28	0-2	0-0	0-2	18.6	64.22
Peter Bowen	13-153	0-20	6-52	0-7	1-18	3-40	0-1	0-0	3-15	8.5	-64.88
Tim Vaughan	13-206	2-37	4-77	0-25	3-21	3-31	0-2	0-0	1-13	6.3	-127.97
Philip Kirby	12-101	4-22	4-50	0-12	2-5	0-2	0-0	0-0	2-10	11.9	-2.79
Martin Keighley	12-102	1-10	4-26	1-15	1-8	4-26	0-5	0-0	1-12	11.8	-19.30
Lucy Wadham	12-83	4-14	4-20	0-8	1-10	2-21	1-1	0-0	0-9	14.5	-22.14
Jeremy Scott	12-109	0-20	5-40	1-10	2-12	3-20	0-0	0-0	1-8	11.0	-28.11
Neil King	12-127	2-15	5-36	4-27	0-7	1-29	0-0	0-0	1-14	9.4	-63.13
Sandy Thomson	11-47	2-8	2-13	1-3	2-7	3-13	0-1	0-0	1-2	23.4	93.24
Chris Gordon	11-133	3-18	4-49	0-13	3-13	1-35	0-5	0-0	0-5	8.3	-45.27
Michael Scudamore	10-65	0-3	1-8	0-8	3-7	5-27	0-0	0-0	1-12	15.4	1.25
Tom Symonds	10-101	1-19	3-26	0-12	1-13	2-18	0-0	0-0	3-13	9.9	24.63
Charlie Mann	10-81	2-12	1-15	1-16	1-14	5-24	0-0	0-0	0-1	12.3	43.25
Victor Dartnall	10-85	0-9	5-25	0-14	0-5	4-25	0-0	0-0	1-7	11.8	-35.42
Henry Oliver	10-82	1-12	3-24	0-5	0-13	6-26	0-0	0-0	0-2	12.2	-35.75
Jennie Candlish	10-128	3-20	3-42	0-15	1-13	3-34	0-0	0-0	0-5	7.8	-83.19
Richard Lee	9-37	0-2	0-6	1-2	3-3	5-23	0-0	0-0	0-1	24.3	44.85
Robert Walford	9-73	1-12	5-17	1-12	0-3	2-26	0-2	0-0	0-1	12.3	-27.15

LEADING JUMPS TRAINERS 2017-18

	NAME	WINS-RUNS	%	2ND	3RD	WNRS-RNRS	WIN PRIZE	TOTAL PRIZE	£1 STAKE
1	N Henderson	141-524	27%	82	49	85-155	£2,612,359	£3,477,474	-76.49
2	P Nicholls	127-576	22%	94	74	68-150	£1,612,108	£2,513,233	-132.84
3	C Tizzard	79-536	15%	82	81	50-111	£1,272,105	£1,975,899	-159.35
4	N Twiston-Davies	80-527	15%	71	60	56-128	£1,201,080	£1,896,193	-102.99
5	D Skelton	156-801	19%	121	124	90-215	£1,065,532	£1,738,235	-153.35
6	W P Mullins	10-74	14%	8	6	9-66	£831,911	£1,553,695	8.96
7	G Elliott	21-106	20%	16	16	19-72	£1,054,952	£1,338,270	35.32
8	T George	47-356	13%	66	44	34-105	£527,124	£964,237	-135.81
9	A King	58-389	15%	68	71	36-125	£553,491	£923,496	-133.86
10	D McCain	98-539	18%	84	77	58-113	£556,818	£838,514	-17.29
11	H Fry	53-245	22%	35	34	34-71	£502,550	£787,617	-40.74
12	E Williams	52-461	11%	63	54	37-103	£446,876	£783,136	-144.49
13	F O'Brien	60-338	18%	42	47	43-106	£462,748	£711,945	-25.36
14	P Hobbs	63-460	14%	70	66	46-143	£363,186	£709,992	-161.95
15	Jonjo O'Neill	64-553	12%	52	54	51-146	£418,344	£608,802	-198.26
16	Mrs S Smith	40-298	13%	46	48	27-58	£366,302	£608,624	-70.82
17	G L Moore	52-405	13%	46	54	34-111	£353,061	£587,244	-104.01
18	W Greatrtex	52-278	19%	47	34	38-75	£365,201	£546,799	16.23
19	H de Bromhead	3-35	9%	2	3	3-23	£323,363	£534,170	-7.75
20	C Longsdon	44-389	11%	45	46	29-95	£317,588	£521,845	-113.32
21	N Mulholland	59-502	12%	70	58	39-137	£283,487	£517,296	-234.75
22	P Bowen	52-293	18%	37	37	30-59	£357,318	£517,224	-18.65
23	D Pipe	33-361	9%	37	44	27-93	£260,504	£497,554	-113.51
24	N Williams	29-150	19%	20	23	19-38	£287,898	£479,405	47.38
25	K Bailey	47-292	16%	47	31	23-84	£265,591	£472,646	-87.8
26	Mrs V Williams	34-305	11%	25	33	29-87	£302,226	£468,431	-47.51
27	Dr R Newland	43-188	23%	38	25	22-42	£301,953	£463,667	-51.34
28	K Lee	28-181	15%	25	18	15-39	£227,450	£449,563	-47.04
29	N Richards	29-197	15%	40	27	20-54	£295,890	£441,590	-53.84
30	A Honeyball	34-162	21%	28	18	24-45	£263,466	£427,333	-20.55
31	B Pauling	36-243	15%	29	22	30-76	£287,044	£396,275	-49.79
32	I Williams	24-202	12%	26	27	20-60	£219,535	£388,164	-34.03
33	B Ellison	34-249	14%	27	37	23-65	£251,332	£388,123	-138.47
34	O Murphy	47-250	19%	46	32	30-70	£292,048	£382,935	-61.39
35	N King	19-183	10%	27	27	15-36	£186,304	£371,695	-51.88
36	T Lacey	39-158	25%	24	18	20-41	£284,089	£359,309	79.8
37	Miss L Russell	46-367	13%	49	45	31-92	£227,452	£355,071	-102.6
38	M D Hammond	46-349	13%	35	42	31-85	£207,254	£323,017	9.13
39	Miss E Lavelle	28-205	14%	24	21	21-62	£214,620	£321,754	-58.71
40	J Snowden	35-170	21%	32	23	21-48	£224,101	£311,854	25.5
41	C Gordon	29-194	15%	40	27	18-39	£159,648	£306,736	-10.42
42	J S Mullins	31-292	11%	30	38	19-70	£150,578	£268,299	-56.63
43	S Edmunds	23-121	19%	21	16	14-33	£164,410	£247,854	-25.26
44	H Whittington	27-135	20%	15	18	12-43	£184,037	£238,663	-21.08
45	Miss R Curtis	9-89	10%	12	9	6-27	£182,194	£234,332	-21
46	H Daly	33-162	20%	21	13	17-37	£163,371	£233,604	29.96
47	D Dennis	25-207	12%	25	26	16-43	£131,332	£232,327	-42.51
48	Mrs L Wadham	20-143	14%	22	17	13-31	£144,074	£230,204	-39.22
49	T Vaughan	27-344	8%	32	33	24-107	£135,432	£229,064	-106.16
50	J M Jefferson	17-116	15%	19	13	12-48	£132,982	£220,042	-46.78
51	O Sherwood	21-222	9%	25	28	14-63	£123,605	£211,170	-92.24
52	P Kirby	24-202	12%	20	24	17-50	£130,758	£204,327	-65.5
53	Mrs R Dobbin	25-173	14%	23	19	15-39	£134,893	£203,226	-45.14
54	H Oliver	27-155	17%	22	19	18-36	£136,248	£202,582	26
55	Amy Murphy	8-53	15%	5	7	4-13	£136,895	£193,629	5.92
56	Ruth Jefferson	3-41	7%	3	10	3-25	£104,346	£186,989	-19.5
57	I Jardine	22-136	16%	17	13	13-36	£134,462	£184,762	-12.65
58	J Scott	24-190	13%	11	18	15-46	£129,059	£181,572	11.32
59	N Hawke	17-189	9%	15	22	13-50	£100,187	£181,528	-69.74
60	R Hobson	10-71	14%	9	7	8-20	£78,086	£171,878	-5.65

RACEFORM JUMPS RECORD TIMES

AINTREE

Distance	Time	Age	Weight	Going	Horse	Date
1m 7f 176y C	3m 45.30	9	10-7	Firm	Nohalmdun	Apr 7 1990
2m 103y H	3m 44.80	6	10-7	Firm	Spinning I	Apr 3 1993
2m 209y H	4m 4.30	5	10-12	Good	Gabrial The Great	May 16 2014
2m 209y H	4m 4.30	4	11-10	Good	Hawk High	Oct 25 2014
2m 3f 200y C	4m 46.60	8	11-6	Good To Firm	Wind Force	Apr 2 1993
2m 4f H	4m 37.10	5	10-11	Good To Firm	Gallateen	Apr 2 1993
2m 5f 19y C	5m 19.30	10	10-4	Good	Always Waining	Apr 8 2011
3m 149y H	5m 50.70	6	10-2	Good To Firm	Andrew's First	Apr 1 1993
3m 210y C	6m 3.40	7	11-3	Good To Firm	Cab On Target	Apr 2 1993
3m 1f 188y C	6m 46.60	10	11-7	Good	Eurotrek	Nov 19 2006
4m 2f 74y C	9m 3.50	8	10-11	Good To Soft	One For Arthur	Apr 8 2017

ASCOT

Distance	Time	Age	Weight	Going	Horse	Date
1m 7f 152y H	3m 33.30	4	10-8	Good	Brampour	Oct 29 2011
2m 192y C	3m 55.90	7	11-1	Good	Quite By Chance	Oct 29 2016
2m 2f 175y C	4m 29.50	7	11-5	Good	Master Dee	Oct 29 2016
2m 3f 58y H	4m 30.80	7	11-0	Good	Overturn	Nov 19 2011
2m 5f 8y C	5m 12.60	9	10-13	Good	Kew Jumper	Apr 11 2008
2m 5f 141y H	5m 10.90	6	10-11	Good	Emmaslegend	Nov 19 2011
2m 7f 118y H	5m 34.10	6	11-2	Good	Heronry	Mar 30 2014
2m 7f 180y C	5m 49.60	9	10-10	Good	Exmoor Ranger	Oct 29 2011
3m 97y H	5m 54.30	8	11-7	Good To Soft	Unowhatimeanharry	Dec 17 2016

AYR

Distance	Time	Age	Weight	Going	Horse	Date
1m 7f 112y C	3m 38.60	6	11-0	Good To Firm	Clay County	Oct 12 1991
2m H	3m 27.40	6	10-7	Firm	Secret Ballot	Apr 19 1980
2m H	3m 41.50	5	10-4	Good	Midnight Shadow	Apr 21 2018
2m 4f 100y H	4m 54.00	6	10-9	Good To Soft	Calivigny	Oct 26 2015
2m 4f 110y C	5m 2.00	7	11-7	Good	Cloudy Dream	Apr 22 2017
2m 5f 91y H	4m 58.40	6	11-9	Good To Soft	Island Heights	Oct 31 2015
2m 5f 110y H	5m 4.70	7	10-13	Good	Cucumber Run	Apr 21 2012
2m 5f 110y C	5m 10.20	6	11-5	Good To Firm	Star To The North	May 9 2001
3m 67y C	5m 57.70	9	11-0	Good To Firm	Top 'N' Tale	May 12 1982
3m 70y H	5m 42.00	13	10-11	Firm	Nautical Lad I	Apr 6 1964
3m 2f 197y C	6m 50.20	5	10-12	Good	Joaaci	Apr 15 2005
3m 7f 176y C	7m 55.10	8	9-9	Good To Firm	Hot Weld	Apr 21 2007

BANGOR-ON-DEE

Distance	Time	Age	Weight	Going	Horse	Date
2m 145y H	3m 44.50	9	10-2	Firm	Andy Rew	Apr 24 1982
2m 1f 77y C	4m 1.80	9	11-4	Good	Daulys Anthem	Aug 4 2017
2m 3f 123y H	4m 34.10	5	11-3	Good To Firm	Smithy's Choice	Apr 25 1987
2m 4f 72y C	4m 49.70	8	10-12	Good	The Disengager	Jly 24 2012
2m 7f 32y H	5m 34.00	5	11-2	Good To Firm	General Pershing	Apr 20 1991
3m 30y C	5m 50.60	8	11-3	Good To Firm	He's The Gaffer	Aug 16 2008
3m 5f 142y C	7m 34.10	6	12-0	Good	Kaki Crazy	May 23 2001

CARLISLE

Distance	Time	Age	Weight	Going	Horse	Date
1m 7f 207y C	3m 53.70	6	11-8	Good	Germany Calling	Oct 15 2015
2m 1f H	4m 6.10	8	11-12	Good	Lyric Street	May 5 2016
2m 1f 16y H	4m 6.00	6	10-11	Good	Idder	May 11 2017
2m 1f 33y H	4m 2.60	9	11-3	Firm	Supertop	Oct 25 1997
2m 3f 61y H	4m 39.50	6	10-9	Good	Officer Hoolihan	May 5 2016
2m 4f C	5m 0.40	6	11-2	Good	New Alco	Nov 12 2007
2m 4f 8y H	4m 50.60	9	11-8	Firm	Gods Law	Sep 29 1990
2m 4f 198y C	5m 20.90	8	10-8	Good To Soft	Amilliontimes	Oct 13 2016
3m 110y C	6m 0.70	8	10-13	Good To Firm	Ripalong Lad	Oct 9 2009
3m 110y H	5m 46.50	8	11-2	Firm	Kinda Groovy	Oct 25 1997
3m 123y H	6m 2.30	7	9-8	Good	Maggie Blue	Oct 15 2015
3m 1f H	6m 17.90	7	11-12	Good	Takingrisks	Mar 26 2016
3m 2f 34y C	6m 38.10	8	10-2	Good	Basford Ben	May 5 2016

CARTMEL

Distance	Time	Age	Weight	Going	Horse	Date
2m 1f 46y H	3m 56.20	5	10-9	Good To Firm	Lisbon	May 25 2013
2m 1f 61y C	4m 5.80	6	11-2	Good	Altruism	May 28 2016
2m 5f 34y C	5m 4.40	7	11-0	Good	Princeton Royale	Jun 24 2016
2m 6f 31y H	5m 10.40	5	10-12	Good	Shantou Tiger	Jly 19 2014
3m 1f 83y H	5m 58.00	10	11-3	Firm	Portonia	May 30 1994
3m 1f 107y C	6m 13.40	13	12-0	Good	Better Times Ahead I	Aug 28 1999
3m 5f 80y C	7m 12.00	10	11-4	Good	Chabrimal Minster	May 26 2007

CATTERICK

Distance	Time	Age	Weight	Going	Horse	Date
1m 7f 145y C	3m 44.60	6	10-0	Firm	Preston Deal	Dec 18 1971
1m 7f 156y H	3m 36.50	7	11-3	Firm	Lunar Wind	Apr 22 1982
2m 3f 51y C	4m 47.70	4	10-8	Good	Laissez Dire	Nov 30 2016
2m 3f 66y H	4m 31.50	5	11-6	Good	Smadynium	Dec 4 2013
3m 1f 54y C	6m 14.00	10	10-1	Good To Firm	Clever General	Nov 7 1981
3m 1f 71y H	6m 3.80	6	10-9	Good To Firm	Seamus O'Flynn	Nov 7 1981
3m 5f 214y C	7m 46.00	8	11-10	Good	Straidnahanna	Jan 12 2017

CHELTENHAM

Distance	Time	Age	Weight	Going	Horse	Date
1m 7f 199y C	3m 44.70	8	12-0	Good	Edredon Bleu	Mar 15 2000
2m 62y C	3m 52.40	7	10-11	Good To Firm	Samakaan	Mar 16 2000
2m 87y H	3m 45.10	8	11-3	Good To Soft	Annie Power	Mar 15 2016
2m 179y H	3m 51.20	4	11-0	Good	Detroit City	Mar 17 2006
2m 179y H	3m 51.20	5	11-2	Good To Firm	Moody Man	Mar 15 1990
2m 3f 166y C	4m 53.30	6	11-8	Good	Shantou Village	Oct 22 2016
2m 3f 198y C	4m 55.20	7	11-4	Good	Black Hercules	Mar 17 2016
2m 3f 200y H	4m 45.00	7	11-5	Good To Soft	Vroum Vroum Mag	Mar 15 2016
2m 4f 56y H	4m 48.80	7	11-4	Good	William Henry	Apr 19 2017
2m 4f 78y C	4m 49.60	9	10-3	Good	Dark Stranger	Mar 15 2000
2m 4f 166y C	5m 5.50	7	11-10	Good	Vautour	Mar 17 2016
2m 5f 26y H	4m 52.00	6	11-7	Good	Monsignor	Mar 15 2000
2m 7f 208y H	5m 46.96	7	11-4	Good	Trackmate	Oct 18 2013
2m 7f 213y H	5m 36.60	6	11-10	Good To Firm	Bacchanal	Mar 16 2000
3m 80y C	5m 59.70	8	10-3	Good	Marlborough	Mar 14 2000
3m 1f C	6m 59.30	10	11-8	Soft	Linden's Lotto	Jan 1 1999
3m 1f C	6m 17.80	7	11-7	Good To Soft	Un Temps Pour Tout	Mar 15 2016
3m 1f 56y C	6m 13.40	9	10-11	Good To Firm	Bigsun	Mar 15 1990
3m 1f 67y H	6m 3.40	9	11-2	Good	Rubhahunish	Mar 14 2000
3m 2f C	6m 40.80	9	11-4	Good	Theatre Guide	Dec 9 2016
3m 2f 70y C	6m 29.70	6	11-10	Good	Long Run	Mar 18 2011
3m 3f 71y C	7m 1.00	6	10-2	Good	Shardam	Nov 15 2003
3m 4f 21y C	7m 14.50	8	11-12	Good	Gentle Ranger	Apr 16 2010
3m 6f 37y C	7m 51.70	8	10-9	Good To Firm	Balthazar King	Mar 13 2012
3m 7f 170y C	8m 0.60	8	12-0	Good	Relaxation	Mar 15 2000
4m 120y C	8m 33.20	7	11-11	Good	Hot Weld	Mar 16 2006

CHEPSTOW

Distance	Time	Age	Weight	Going	Horse	Date
2m 11y H	3m 43.20	4	10-1	Firm	Tingle Bell	Oct 4 1986
2m 11y C	3m 53.70	7	11-5	Good	Valseur Du Granval	Nov 2 2016
2m 3f 98y C	4m 42.50	5	11-4	Good	Balder Succes	Oct 12 2013
2m 3f 100y H	4m 37.20	6	11-0	Good	Ballyoptic	Oct 8 2016
2m 7f 131y H	5m 33.60	10	10-0	Firm	Chucklestone	May 11 1993
2m 7f 131y C	5m 47.90	9	11-10	Firm	Broadheath	Oct 4 1986
3m 2f 54y C	6m 39.40	7	12-0	Firm	Jaunty Jane	May 26 1975

DONCASTER

Distance	Time	Age	Weight	Going	Horse	Date
2m 78y C	3m 57.00	4	10-9	Good To Soft	Clic Work	Dec 29 2016
2m 128y H	3m 53.50	5	11-7	Good	All Set To Go	Dec 10 2016
2m 3f 31y C	4m 40.70	6	11-4	Good To Soft	Gold Present	Nov 26 2016
2m 3f 88y H	4m 32.30	5	10-5	Good	Just Milly	Dec 29 2016
2m 4f 115y C	5m 1.70	7	10-12	Good	Kalane	Dec 29 2016
2m 7f 214y C	5m 55.80	10	10-9	Good	Killala Quay	Feb 22 2017
3m 84y H	5m 47.50	8	11-3	Good	Parish Business	Dec 29 2016
3m 2f 1y C	6m 35.80	7	11-4	Good	Dancing Shadow	Dec 9 2016

EXETER

Distance	Time	Age	Weight	Going	Horse	Date
2m 175y H	3m 49.20	6	11-0	Good To Firm	Remind Me Later	Apr 21 2015
2m 1f 109y C	3m 57.50	7	10-8	Good	Sir Valentino	Nov 1 2016
2m 2f 111y H	4m 14.70	5	10-13	Firm	My Brother Sylvest	Oct 18 2011
2m 3f 48y C	4m 27.90	8	11-11	Good To Firm	West With The Wind	May 7 2013
2m 5f 135y H	5m 5.20	10	11-8	Good To Firm	I'm In Charge	Oct 6 2016
2m 7f 25y H	5m 26.20	8	10-11	Good To Firm	Very Cool	May 4 2010
3m 54y C	5m 42.80	8	10-5	Good To Firm	Dennis The Legend	May 13 2009
3m 6f 153y C	7m 14.70	10	10-13	Good To Firm	Thomas Wild	Apr 14 2015

FAKENHAM

Distance	Time	Age	Weight	Going	Horse	Date
2m 3y H	3m 47.80	5	11-10	Good To Firm	Tom Clapton	May 25 1992
2m 59y C	3m 44.90	11	12-4	Firm	Cheekio Ora	Apr 23 1984
2m 4f 1y H	4m 41.20	4	10-3	Good To Firm	Ayem	May 16 1999
2m 5f 44y C	5m 10.30	13	12-2	Good To Firm	Skipping Tim	May 25 1992
2m 7f 95y H	5m 49.10	12	10-8	Good	Phare Isle	Apr 17 2017
3m 38y C	5m 56.90	7	11-1	Good To Firm	Specialize	May 16 1999
3m 5f 24y C	7m 24.90	13	11-2	Good	Rebeccas Choice	May 3 2016

FFOS LAS

Distance	Time	Age	Weight	Going	Horse	Date
1m 7f 182y H	3m 37.00	5	11-12	Good	Comanche Chieftain	May 9 2017
1m 7f 202y H	3m 33.60	6	10-11	Good	Valain	Aug 28 2009
2m C	3m 45.25	6	11-12	Good To Firm	West With The Wind	Aug 25 2011
2m C	3m 57.60	7	11-9	Good	Get Rhythm	Jun 22 2017
2m 3f 83y C	4m 37.34	7	10-12	Firm	Cold Harbour	May 31 2011
2m 4f H	4m 39.40	6	10-9	Good	Plunkett	Jun 18 2009
2m 4f H	4m 40.80	6	11-2	Good	Positively Dylan	May 9 2017
2m 4f 199y C	5m 9.70	8	11-11	Good To Firm	Putney Bridge	Jun 17 2010
2m 5f 192y H	5m 15.40	6	11-0	Good	Koultas King	Aug 22 2013
2m 7f 177y C	5m 49.60	7	11-7	Good	Sea Wall	Jun 18 2009
2m 7f 191y H	5m 39.00	5	11-8	Good	Chill Factor	Aug 21 2014
3m 1f 60y C	6m 7.10	7	10-1	Good	Backstage	Aug 28 2009
3m 3f 208y C	7m 28.10	8	11-2	Good	The Bay Oak	Apr 16 2017

FONTWELL

Distance	Time	Age	Weight	Going	Horse	Date
2m 1f 96y C	4m 14.50	12	10-1	Good To Firm	A Thousand Dreams	Jun 3 2002
2m 1f 145y H	4m 6.80	7	10-2	Good To Firm	Hyperion Du Moulin II	Jun 3 2002
2m 3f 33y H	4m 30.50	8	10-7	Good To Firm	Hillswick	Aug 27 1999
2m 3f 35y C	4m 38.10	6	11-0	Good To Firm	Chalcedony	Jun 3 2002
2m 5f 31y C	5m 13.90	10	10-0	Good To Firm	Contes	Jun 3 2002
2m 5f 139y H	5m 6.70	7	10-1	Good To Firm	Mister Pickwick	Jun 3 2002
3m 1f 106y C	6m 24.30	5	10-2	Good To Firm	Il Capitano	May 6 2002
3m 1f 142y H	6m 14.00	7	11-2	Good	Sir Mangan	Oct 2 2015
3m 3f 45y C	7m 11.10	8	10-6	Good	Strolling Vagabond	Mar 18 2007

HAYDOCK

Distance	Time	Age	Weight	Going	Horse	Date
1m 7f 144y H	3m 32.30	6	10-0	Good	She's Our Mare	May 1 1999
1m 7f 157y C	3m 52.30	7	11-7	Good	Witness In Court	Apr 19 2014
2m 45y H	4m 1.60	7	11-3	Soft	Irving	Nov 21 2015
2m 67y C	4m 19.80	6	10-10	Soft	Cloudy Dream	Nov 18 2016
2m 2f 191y H	4m 32.10	6	11-12	Good	Horizontal Speed	Apr 19 2014
2m 2f 191y H	4m 33.00	7	10-11	Good	Carlton Jack	Apr 19 2014
2m 2f 211y C	4m 45.70	7	11-12	Good	Purple 'N Gold	May 7 2016
2m 3f 203y C	5m 2.40	8	11-5	Good	Ballybolley	Apr 15 2017
2m 4f 135y C	5m 24.40	7	11-8	Good	Some Buckle	Mar 23 2016
2m 5f 64y C	5m 20.20	7	11-3	Good	Javert	May 7 2016
2m 5f 127y C	5m 50.40	5	11-2	Soft	Politologue	Nov 18 2016
2m 6f 54y C	5m 47.50	9	10-6	Good	Magic Money	Apr 15 2017
2m 6f 177y H	5m 37.60	5	10-13	Good To Soft	Dynaste	Nov 19 2011
2m 6f 177y H	5m 28.90	7	11-0	Good	Whataknight	May 7 2016
2m 6f 204y C	5m 41.50	7	10-6	Good	No Planning	Apr 19 2014
3m 24y C	6m 13.40	10	11-10	Good	Willoughby Hedge	Apr 15 2017
3m 3f 57y C	7m 7.70	9	10-8	Good	Blenheim Brook	Apr 19 2014
3m 4f 97y C	7m 25.10	8	11-6	Good To Soft	Vieux Lion Rouge	Feb 18 2017

HEREFORD

Distance	Time	Age	Weight	Going	Horse	Date
2m 8y C	3m 46.10	6	10-9	Good To Firm	Smolensk I	Mar 21 1998
2m 53y H	3m 42.20	10	10-1	Hard	Tasty Son	Sep 11 1973
2m 2f 208y C	4m 30.00	9	10-11	Good	Kings Wild	Sep 28 1990
2m 3f 147y H	4m 38.90	4	11-4	Good To Firm	Pigeon Island	Sep 5 2007
2m 4f 194y C	5m 6.90	8	11-1	Good To Firm	Fealing Real	Jun 20 2010
2m 5f 163y H	5m 12.30	7	11-1	Good To Firm	Another Kate	Aug 17 2011
3m 1f 44y C	6m 7.50	7	11-2	Good	Belmount	Oct 6 2016
3m 1f 119y H	6m 2.80	6	10-1	Good To Firm	Wee Danny	Sep 10 2003

HEXHAM

Distance	Time	Age	Weight	Going	Horse	Date
1m 7f 133y C	3m 52.80	7	10-12	Good	Imjoeking	Jun 22 2014
2m 48y H	3m 57.80	8	11-7	Good To Firm	Francies Fancy	Jun 19 2005
2m 4f 15y C	4m 55.40	8	9-11	Firm	Mr Laggan	Sep 14 2003
2m 4f 28y H	4m 31.50	6	11-0	Good To Firm	Pappa Charlie	May 27 1997
2m 7f 63y H	5m 45.50	7	9-9	Firm	Fingers Crossed	Apr 29 1991
3m 41y C	6m 7.60	9	9-11	Good To Firm	Silent Snipe	Jun 1 2002
3m 7f 199y C	8m 34.00	10	10-12	Good	Simply Smashing	Mar 18 2010

HUNTINGDON

Distance	Time	Age	Weight	Going	Horse	Date
1m 7f 171y H	3m 32.70	5	11-11	Good To Firm	Weather Front	Aug 31 2009
2m 104y C	3m 53.30	5	10-0	Good To Firm	No Greater Love	May 23 2007
2m 3f 137y H	4m 30.20	6	11-10	Good To Firm	Sabre Hongrois	Oct 4 2009

2m 3f 189y C	4m 46.40	10	10-13	Good To Firm	Peccadillo	Sep 26 2004
2m 4f 145y H	4m 45.80	6	11-5	Firm	Sound of Laughter	Apr 14 1984
2m 7f 129y C	5m 44.40	7	11-2	Good To Firm	Ozzie Jones	Sep 18 1998
3m 1f 10y H	5m 50.20	8	11-12	Good To Firm	Orchard King	Aug 31 2009
3m 6f 162y C	8m 2.70	9	10-4	Good To Soft	Kinnahalla	Nov 24 2001

KELSO

Distance	Time	Age	Weight	Going	Horse	Date
2m 51y H	3m 38.90	6	11-12	Good To Firm	Life And Soul	May 26 2013
2m 1f 14y C	3m 57.80	8	11-12	Good To Firm	Simply Ned	Oct 4 2015
2m 2f 25y H	4m 8.70	6	11-7	Good To Firm	Croco Bay	May 26 2013
2m 4f 189y H	4m 49.50	6	11-0	Good To Firm	Waterclock	Sep 16 2015
2m 5f 133y C	5m 19.80	9	11-12	Good To Firm	Romany Ryme	Sep 16 2015
2m 6f 151y H	5m 12.20	4	11-3	Firm	Hit The Canvas	Sep 30 1995
2m 7f 96y C	5m 50.20	10	10-12	Good To Soft	Gas Line Boy	Dec 4 2016
3m 1f 170y H	6m 10.10	8	10-13	Good To Firm	Dook's Delight	May 19 1999
3m 2f 39y C	6m 33.80	7	11-12	Good To Firm	Looking Well	May 29 2016

KEMPTON

Distance	Time	Age	Weight	Going	Horse	Date
2m H	3m 40.40	7	11-8	Good	Australia Day	Oct 17 2010
2m H	3m 45.20	6	11-7	Good	Yanworth	Dec 26 2016
2m H	3m 38.20	5	11-0	Good	Hargam	Oct 16 2016
2m C	3m 46.25	9	11-0	Good	Special Tiara	Dec 27 2016
2m C	3m 43.60	11	11-3	Good	Australia Day	May 5 2014
2m 2f C	4m 21.60	9	11-1	Good	Miss Tenacious	Oct 16 2016
2m 4f 110y C	5m 1.50	6	11-0	Good	Rum And Butter	May 5 2014
2m 4f 110y C	4m 58.90	8	11-9	Good	Max Ward	Mar 18 2017
2m 5f H	4m 57.80	5	10-12	Good	Work In Progress	Oct 18 2015
2m 5f H	4m 58.20	6	11-0	Good	Chilworth Screamer	May 5 2014
2m 5f H	5m 1.90	6	11-6	Good	Breath Of Blighty	Apr 18 2017
3m C	5m 53.50	8	11-10	Good	Thistlecrack	Dec 26 2016
3m C	5m 54.20	10	11-7	Good	American Spin	May 5 2014
3m 110y H	6m 2.10	5	11-10	Good	Timeforwest	Apr 4 2017
3m 110y H	6m 5.20	5	10-13	Good	Follow The Bear	May 1 2017
3m 110y H	6m 6.50	5	11-9	Good	Dreamsoftheatre	Nov 25 2013

LEICESTER

Distance	Time	Age	Weight	Going	Horse	Date
1m 7f 113y H	3m 43.10	7	11-4	Good	Amantius	Dec 1 2016
1m 7f 201y C	3m 45.30	6	11-7	Firm	Thankyou Very Much	Dec 1 2016
2m 4f 45y C	4m 54.20	7	10-6	Good To Firm	Oliver's Hill	Dec 28 2016
2m 4f 110y H	4m 45.50	4	11-7	Good To Firm	Prince of Rheims	Dec 5 1989
2m 4f 110y H	4m 58.60	6	11-8	Good	Ten Sixty	Dec 7 2016
2m 6f 151y C	5m 37.40	10	11-12	Firm	Forgotten Gold	Nov 27 2016

LINGFIELD

Distance	Time	Age	Weight	Going	Horse	Date
2m C	3m 48.70	9	11-2	Good To Firm	Rapide Plaisir	Sep 28 2007
2m H	3m 46.20	8	11-12	Good	Bobble Emerald	Nov 8 2016
2m C	3m 57.80	5	11-5	Good To Firm	Authorized Too	Nov 8 2016
2m 3f 110y H	4m 36.80	5	11-5	Good	Phobiaphiliac	Nov 8 2016
2m 3f 110y H	4m 37.30	6	10-3	Firm	Bellezza	Mar 20 1993
2m 4f C	4m 55.80	5	11-8	Good To Firm	Mr Medic	Nov 8 2016
2m 7f H	5m 31.90	8	11-6	Good To Firm	Herecomestanley	Sep 28 2007
2m 7f 110y C	6m 7.60	7	10-0	Good To Soft	Onderun	Dec 10 2016

LUDLOW

Distance	Time	Age	Weight	Going	Horse	Date
1m 7f 169y H	3m 35.70	7	11-4	Good	Frozen Over	May 10 2015
1m 7f 212y C	3m 47.30	7	11-0	Good	Bullet Street	May 10 2015
1m 7f 212y C	3m 47.30	5	11-7	Good To Firm	Pearl King	Apr 5 2007
2m 4f 11y C	4m 47.30	10	11-8	Good To Firm	Handy Money	Apr 5 2007
2m 5f 55y H	4m 55.80	5	10-9	Good To Firm	Templehills	Oct 5 2016
2m 7f 171y C	5m 54.70	6	11-4	Good To Firm	Braqueur D'or	Oct 11 2017
2m 7f 174y H	5m 33.30	5	9-11	Good	Dark Spirit	Oct 9 2013
3m 1f 125y C	6m 17.30	12	11-4	Good To Firm	Moving Earth	May 12 2005

MARKET RASEN

Distance	Time	Age	Weight	Going	Horse	Date
2m 148y H	3m 57.40	7	11-5	Good	Australia Day	Jly 17 2010
2m 1f 43y C	4m 13.60	11	10-2	Good To Firm	Mister Wiseman	Jly 7 2013
2m 2f 140y H	4m 26.10	6	11-9	Good To Soft	Attaglance	Feb 19 2012
2m 3f 34y C	4m 41.40	8	11-1	Good	Bocciani	May 10 2013
2m 4f 139y H	5m 3.70	7	11-3	Good To Soft	Fiulin	Feb 19 2012
2m 5f 89y C	5m 17.40	7	10-6	Good	Vintage Vinnie	Sep 24 2016
2m 7f 16y H	5m 38.80	6	12-5	Firm	Trustful	May 21 1977
2m 7f 191y C	6m 1.00	8	11-8	Good To Firm	Allerlea	Jun 1 1985
3m 3f 123y C	7m 26.10	8	11-1	Good To Soft	Carli King	Dec 26 2014

MUSSELBURGH

Distance	Time	Age	Weight	Going	Horse	Date
1m 7f 124y H	3m 35.00	6	11-12	Good	Superb Story	Jan 1 2017
1m 7f 182y C	3m 48.10	8	10-12	Good To Firm	Sonsie Mo	Dec 6 1993
2m 85y H	3m 58.50	11	11-3	Good	Civil Unrest	Mar 24 2017
2m 195y C	4m 13.10	8	11-1	Good To Soft	Celtic Flames	Mar 16 2018
2m 3f 81y H	4m 34.70	9	11-7	Good	Strongpoint	Dec 9 2013
2m 3f 193y C	4m 44.50	7	11-9	Good To Firm	Bohemian Spirit	Dec 18 2005
2m 6f H	5m 27.60	6	10-12	Good	Mondlicht	Nov 14 2016
2m 7f 170y C	5m 47.70	7	11-10	Firm	Snowy	Dec 18 2005
2m 7f 180y H	5m 47.80	6	11-10	Good	Monbeg Charmer	Feb 5 2017
3m 2f 26y H	6m 26.90	6	11-5	Good	El Bandit	Feb 5 2017

3m 2f 139y C	6m 47.10	6	11-5	Good	Present Flight		Nov 6 2015
4m 176y C	8m 28.60	8	10-9	Good	Dancing Shadow		Feb 4 2017

NEWBURY

Distance	Time	Age	Weight	Going	Horse	Date
2m 69y H	3m 45.20	5	10-2	Good To Firm	Dhofar	Oct 25 1985
2m 92y C	3m 57.34	6	11-5	Good	Valdez	Nov 30 2013
2m 2f 183y H	4m 26.70	4	11-0	Good	Songsmith	Mar 24 2012
2m 3f 187y C	4m 47.90	8	11-12	Good To Firm	Espy I	Oct 25 1991
2m 4f 118y H	4m 48.63	6	11-0	Good	Argento Luna	Mar 21 2009
2m 6f 93y C	5m 28.93	5	11-10	Good	Pepite Rose	Mar 24 2012
2m 7f 86y C	5m 42.53	7	11-10	Good To Soft	Long Run	Feb 17 2012
3m 52y H	5m 45.40	8	10-9	Good	Lansdowne	Oct 25 1996
3m 1f 214y C	6m 22.86	9	10-8	Good	Ikorodu Road	Mar 24 2012

NEWCASTLE

Distance	Time	Age	Weight	Going	Horse	Date
2m 75y C	3m 56.70	7	11-12	Firm	Greenheart	May 7 1990
2m 98y H	3m 40.70	7	10-10	Good	Padre Mio	Nov 25 1995
2m 4f 19y C	4m 46.70	7	9-13	Firm	Snow Blessed	May 19 1984
2m 4f 133y H	4m 42.00	4	10-10	Hard	Mils Mij	May 13 1989
2m 6f H	5m 24.90	6	10-12	Good To Soft	Bygones Of Brid	Nov 28 2009
2m 7f 91y C	5m 48.10	-2	10-4	Firm	Even Swell	Oct 30 1975
3m 10y H	5m 40.10	4	10-5	Good	Withy Bank	Nov 29 1986
4m 122y C	8m 30.40	7	10-0	Good	Domaine De Pron	Feb 21 1998

NEWTON ABBOT

Distance	Time	Age	Weight	Going	Horse	Date
2m 75y C	3m 49.70	5	11-0	Good	Shantou Rock	Oct 13 2017
2m 167y H	3m 45.00	5	11-0	Firm	Windbound Lass	Aug 1 1988
2m 2f 110y H	4m 15.20	5	10-8	Good To Firm	Rum And Butter	Aug 22 2013
2m 4f 216y C	5m 2.10	7	11-0	Good	Mhilu	Jly 13 2009
2m 5f 122y H	4m 55.40	7	10-0	Firm	Virbian	Jly 30 1983
3m 1f 170y C	6m 9.50	8	11-7	Good To Firm	No Loose Change	Jly 8 2013
3m 2f 105y H	6m 9.90	7	10-13	Good To Firm	Veneaux Du Cochet	Jly 1 2016

PERTH

Distance	Time	Age	Weight	Going	Horse	Date
2m C	3m 44.50	7	10-4	Good	Robin's Command	Jly 3 2014
2m C	3m 48.00	8	11-5	Good To Firm	Robin's Command	Sep 7 2015
2m 47y H	3m 40.20	8	11-4	Good	Court Minstrel	Aug 22 2015
2m 4f 20y C	4m 48.20	9	10-7	Good To Firm	Strobe	Jly 14 2013
2m 4f 35y H	4m 41.20	8	10-2	Firm	Valiant Dash	May 19 1994
2m 7f 180y C	5m 46.20	7	10-12	Good To Firm	Problema Tic	Jun 9 2013
2m 7f 207y H	5m 41.60	10	11-1	Good To Firm	Imtihan	Jly 2 2009
3m 2f 127y H	6m 37.20	5	10-11	Good To Firm	Noir Et Vert	Apr 28 2006
3m 6f 121y C	7m 43.70	8	11-6	Good	Laertes	Apr 24 2009

PLUMPTON

Distance	Time	Age	Weight	Going	Horse	Date
1m 7f 195y H	3m 31.00	3	11-1	Firm	Royal Derbi	Sep 19 1988
2m 214y C	4m 4.40	10	11-12	Good To Firm	Pearls Legend	Apr 17 2017
2m 1f 164y H	4m 8.50	4	11-0	Good	Arthington	Sep 24 2017
2m 3f 164y C	4m 42.80	6	11-0	Good To Firm	Dead Or Alive	May 10 2009
2m 4f 114y H	4m 46.80	4	11-2	Good To Firm	Urban Warrior	Sep 21 2008
3m 217y H	5m 49.80	8	10-13	Good To Firm	Listen And Learn	Sep 18 2016
3m 1f 152y C	6m 23.50	9	9-7	Good To Firm	Sunday Habits	Apr 19 2003
3m 4f 102y C	7m 19.80	6	11-7	Good To Firm	Ecuyer Du Roi	Apr 15 2002

SANDOWN

Distance	Time	Age	Weight	Going	Horse	Date
1m 7f 119y C	3m 43.40	9	11-6	Good To Firm	Dempsey	Apr 28 2007
1m 7f 216y H	3m 42.00	6	10-0	Firm	Olympian	Mar 13 1993
2m 3f 173y H	4m 35.70	5	11-3	Good To Firm	Oslot	Apr 28 2007
2m 4f 10y C	4m 57.10	8	11-7	Good	Coulton	Apr 29 1995
2m 5f 110y H	5m 20.50	7	11-0	Good	L'Ami Serge	Apr 29 2017
2m 6f 164y C	5m 41.40	12	11-10	Good	Menorah	Apr 29 2017
2m 7f 98y H	5m 39.10	6	11-5	Good To Firm	Rostropovich I	Apr 26 2003
3m 37y C	5m 59.00	8	12-7	Good To Firm	Arkle	Nov 6 1965
3m 4f 166y C	7m 9.10	9	10-1	Good	Cache Fleur	Apr 29 1995

SEDGEFIELD

Distance	Time	Age	Weight	Going	Horse	Date
2m 77y C	3m 49.90	6	11-7	Good	Mixboy	Sep 27 2016
2m 178y H	3m 45.70	6	10-5	Good To Firm	Country Orchid	Sep 5 1997
2m 3f 65y C	4m 38.80	6	11-9	Good To Firm	The Backup Plan	Aug 27 2015
2m 3f 188y H	4m 32.80	8	9-13	Good To Firm	Grams And Ounces	Aug 27 2015
2m 5f 28y C	5m 10.50	7	11-10	Good	Degooch	Sep 1 2016
2m 5f 34y H	4m 46.30	7	10-0	Good To Firm	Palm House	Sep 4 1992
3m 2f 59y C	6m 29.30	6	10-2	Good To Firm	The Gallopin'Major	Sep 14 1996
3m 3f 9y H	6m 19.70	7	9-13	Firm	Pikestaff	Jly 25 2005
3m 5f 48y C	7m 20.40	9	10-11	Good	Buachaill Alainn	Oct 27 2016

SOUTHWELL

Distance	Time	Age	Weight	Going	Horse	Date
1m 7f 153y C	3m 53.70	6	11-5	Good	Unify	Sep 27 2016
1m 7f 153y H	3m 44.30	7	10-8	Good	Dealing River	Jly 22 2014
2m 4f 62y C	5m 6.60	7	10-13	Good	Gentleman Anshan	May 17 2011
2m 4f 62y H	4m 57.30	8	11-3	Good	Red Not Blue	May 17 2011
2m 7f 209y C	6m 10.10	8	11-2	Good	Best Boy Barney	Jly 22 2014
2m 7f 209y H	5m 55.40	10	11-7	Good	Jawaab	Jly 22 2014
3m 1f 129y C	7m 8.50	7	11-2	Good To Soft	Silent Man	Dec 17 2017

STRATFORD

Distance	Time	Age	Weight	Going	Horse	Date
2m 70y H	3m 40.40	6	11-12	Hard	Chusan	May 7 1956
2m 213y C	3m 56.70	6	11-0	Good To Firm	Professeur Emery	Aug 1 2013
2m 2f 148y H	4m 17.30	4	10-13	Good	Lostock Hall	Aug 24 2016
2m 3f 98y C	4m 35.40	9	10-0	Good To Soft	Gentleman Anshan	May 19 2013
2m 4f 205y C	4m 56.50	6	9-10	Good To Firm	Spare Change	Sep 16 2007
2m 6f 7y H	5m 6.80	6	11-0	Firm	Broken Wing	May 31 1986
2m 6f 125y C	5m 22.80	8	11-0	Good	Danandy	Jly 19 2015
3m 2f 83y H	6m 13.10	7	10-8	Good To Firm	Burren Moonshine	Jun 11 2006
3m 3f 119y C	6m 38.30	10	12-0	Good	Mossey Joe	Jun 7 2013

TAUNTON

Distance	Time	Age	Weight	Going	Horse	Date
2m 12y C	3m 49.50	8	10-9	Firm	I Have Him	Apr 28 1995
2m 104y H	3m 39.40	4	12-0	Hard	Indian Jockey	Oct 3 1996
2m 2f 40y C	4m 24.90	7	11-3	Firm	Wait No More	Mar 28 2012
2m 3f 1y H	4m 19.70	5	10-6	Firm	Prairie Spirit	Apr 2 2009
2m 5f 150y C	5m 31.80	6	11-10	Good	Howlongisafoot	Nov 12 2015
2m 7f 3y C	5m 39.80	7	11-10	Firm	Glacial Delight	Apr 24 2006
2m 7f 198y H	5m 30.20	7	10-4	Firm	On My Toes	Oct 15 1998
3m 2f 57y C	6m 51.00	7	11-12	Good To Firm	Copperfacejack	Nov 1 2017
3m 4f 85y C	7m 21.70	9	10-11	Good To Firm	No Buts	Apr 27 2017

TOWCESTER

Distance	Time	Age	Weight	Going	Horse	Date
1m 7f 151y H	3m 42.60	7	11-12	Good To Firm	Moonday Sun	Oct 5 2016
1m 7f 181y H	3m 39.50	4	11-0	Firm	Naskracker	May 22 1987
2m 20y C	3m 51.90	4	10-4	Good To Firm	Pinkie Brown	Oct 5 2016
2m 70y C	3m 52.40	12	10-3	Good	Crack At Dawn	May 21 2013
2m 3f 34y H	4m 31.50	6	11-4	Good	Ballygrooby Bertie	May 19 2014
2m 3f 179y C	4m 53.40	8	11-5	Good To Firm	Rakaia Rosa	May 4 2017
2m 4f 217y H	4m 58.60	5	10-5	Good To Firm	Plantagenet	Oct 11 2017
2m 5f 153y C	5m 14.30	7	11-2	Good To Firm	Midnight Shot	May 4 2017
2m 7f 211y H	5m 44.00	9	9-10	Firm	Dropshot I	May 25 1984
3m 102y C	5m 52.60	10	10-13	Good To Firm	Lucky Luk	May 29 2009

UTTOXETER

Distance	Time	Age	Weight	Going	Horse	Date
1m 7f 168y H	3m 42.20	4	10-5	Good	Mountainside	Jun 26 2016
1m 7f 214y C	3m 45.70	9	11-2	Good	Festive Affair	Jly 2 2017
2m 3f 207y H	4m 39.10	8	10-9	Good To Firm	Chicago's Best	Jun 11 1995
2m 4f C	4m 42.60	7	12-0	Good To Firm	Bertone	Oct 5 1996
2m 4f C	4m 54.70	7	11-9	Good To Soft	Midnight Shot	Sep 24 2017
2m 5f 105y H	5m 6.80	8	11-8	Good To Firm	Fealing Real	Jun 27 2010
2m 6f 108y C	5m 35.60	6	11-0	Good	Brassick	Jly 26 2013

2m 7f 70y H	5m 36.60	6	11-12	Good	Princeton Royale	Oct 4 2015
3m 2y C	6m 0.10	9	10-5	Good	Big Sound	Jun 9 2016
3m 2f 13y C	6m 23.10	8	10-3	Good	Drop Out Joe	Jun 26 2016
4m 1f 92y C	8m 41.30	8	10-3	Good To Soft	Goulanes	Mar 15 2014

WARWICK

Distance	Time	Age	Weight	Going	Horse	Date
2m H	3m 30.80	5	11-7	Firm	High Knowl	Sep 17 1988
2m H	3m 38.60	6	11-9	Good	Satanic Beat	Oct 1 2015
2m C	3m 48.88	6	10-3	Good To Firm	Lake Imperial	Nov 5 2007
2m C	3m 51.00	5	11-8	Good	Wells De Lune	Sep 20 2016
2m 3f H	4m 15.00	6	11-7	Good To Firm	Runaway Pete	Nov 2 1996
2m 3f H	4m 22.60	5	11-4	Good	Rebel Yeats	Sep 26 2017
2m 3f H	4m 32.50	5	10-12	Good	Blairs Cove	May 13 2017
2m 4f C	4m 56.20	8	11-8	Good	Dictum	Nov 2 1999
2m 4f C	4m 55.60	7	11-2	Good	Gone Too Far	Sep 22 2015
2m 5f H	4m 43.60	5	10-10	Firm	Three Eagles	May 11 2002
2m 5f H	4m 57.10	6	11-0	Good	Bendomingo	May 13 2017
2m 5f H	4m 54.10	5	11-0	Good	Atlantic Gold	Oct 1 2015
3m C	5m 52.60	7	11-3	Good	Urcalin	Oct 1 2015
3m 1f H	5m 53.50	7	11-0	Good To Firm	City Poser	Apr 2 2002
3m 1f H	5m 56.40	11	11-2	Good	The Tourard Man	Apr 24 2017
3m 1f 100y C	6m 20.20	8	11-0	Good	Belmount	Sep 26 2017
3m 2f C	6m 16.10	12	10-12	Firm	Castle Warden	May 6 1989
3m 2f H	6m 8.60	6	11-5	Good	Mr Shantu	Sep 22 2015
3m 2f H	6m 18.50	5	10-5	Good	Braventara	Nov 4 2016
3m 5f 54y C	7m 37.10	11	11-0	Good	Big Casino	Apr 24 2017

WETHERBY

Distance	Time	Age	Weight	Going	Horse	Date
1m 7f 36y C	3m 41.60	7	11-2	Good	Oliver's Gold	Oct 14 2015
2m H	3m 43.20	9	11-5	Good	Lightening Rod	Oct 31 2014
2m 3f 85y C	4m 44.80	8	11-3	Good	Village Vic	Oct 14 2015
2m 3f 154y H	4m 40.90	5	10-12	Good	Mustmeetalady	Oct 14 2015
2m 5f 56y H	5m 2.10	7	11-9	Good	Kaysersberg	Oct 15 2014
2m 5f 75y C	5m 17.60	11	10-5	Good	Rosquero	May 4 2016
3m 26y H	5m 46.30	5	9-7	Good	Lilly's Legend	May 21 2015
3m 26y H	5m 46.30	7	11-3	Good	Minella Hero	May 21 2015
3m 45y C	5m 59.70	7	11-6	Good	Irish Cavalier	Oct 29 2016

WINCANTON

Distance	Time	Age	Weight	Going	Horse	Date
1m 7f 65y H	3m 22.60	3	9-11	Good To Firm	Cliffs Of Dover	Oct 14 2016
1m 7f 149y C	3m 37.90	6	11-11	Good	Kie	Apr 13 2014
2m 3f 166y H	4m 28.30	5	11-9	Good To Firm	Deserter	Oct 14 2016
2m 4f 35y C	4m 54.20	8	11-1	Good To Firm	Meldrum Lad	Apr 23 2017
2m 5f 82y H	4m 53.10	6	11-6	Good To Firm	San Satiro	Apr 23 2017
3m 1f 30y C	6m 9.70	7	11-6	Good To Firm	Swansea Bay	Nov 8 2003
3m 2f 162y C	6m 37.20	7	11-8	Good	Gullible Gordon	Oct 24 2010

WORCESTER

Distance	Time	Age	Weight	Going	Horse	Date
2m H	3m 33.40	10	11-5	Good	Chilbury Hill	Aug 28 2013
2m H	3m 37.30	7	11-11	Good	Moonday Sun	Aug 30 2016
2m C	3m 41.46	7	10-10	Good	Fit to Drive	Sep 25 2009
2m 110y C	3m 51.40	6	11-1	Good To Firm	Sedgemoor Express	Jly 29 2014
2m 110y C	3m 50.90	6	12-0	Good To Firm	Mercian King	Oct 12 2017
2m 4f H	4m 38.50	5	11-12	Good	Mont Choisy	Oct 14 2015
2m 4f C	4m 38.20	8	10-5	Good	Moorlands Jack	Sep 10 2013
2m 4f C	4m 39.90	7	10-12	Good	Rene's Girl	Oct 12 2017
2m 4f H	4m 28.70	7	10-4	Good To Firm	Jigsaw Financial	Jly 17 2013
2m 7f C	5m 29.70	6	10-2	Good	Whistling Senator	Aug 28 2013
2m 7f H	5m 23.50	7	11-5	Good	Saticon	Jun 27 2012
2m 7f C	5m 31.10	6	11-1	Good	Pawn Star	Aug 30 2016
2m 7f H	5m 28.12	6	10-11	Good	Net Work Rouge	Oct 14 2015

NOTES

NOTES

NOTES

NOTES

NOTES